POVERTY AND
THE WTO

POVERTY AND THE WTO

Impacts of the Doha Development Agenda

*Edited by Thomas W. Hertel
and L. Alan Winters*

**A copublication of Palgrave Macmillan
and the World Bank**

A copublication of The World Bank and Palgrave Macmillan.

Palgrave Macmillan
Houndmills, Basingstoke, Hampshire RG21 6XS and
175 Fifth Avenue, New York, NY 10010
Companies and representatives throughout the world

Palgrave Macmillan is the global academic imprint of the Palgrave Macmillan division of St. Martin's Press, LLC and of Palgrave Macmillan Ltd.

Macmillan® is a registered trademark in the United States, United Kingdom and other countries. Palgrave is a registered trademark in the European Union and other countries.

ISBN-10: 0-8213-6314-X (softcover)
ISBN-10: 0-8213-6370-0 (hardcover)
ISBN-13: 978-0-8213-6314-0
eISBN-10: 0-8213-6315-8
eISBN-13: 978-0-8213-6315-7
DOI: 10.1596/978-0-8213-6314-0

Library of Congress Cataloging-in-Publications Data

Poverty and the WTO : Impacts of the Doha Development Agenda / edited by Thomas W. Hertel, L. Alan Winters.
        p. cm. – (Trade and development series)
    Includes bibliographical references and index.
    ISBN-13: 978-0-8213-6314-0
    ISBN-10: 0-8213-6314-X
    1. World Trade Organization—Developing countries. 2. International trade. 3. Poverty—Developing countries. 4. Developing countries—Economic conditions. 5. Developing countries—Economic policy. I. Hertel, Thomas W. (Thomas Warren), 1953- II. Winters, L. Alan. III. Series.

HF1385.P68 2005
339.4'6091724—dc22

2005044583

CONTENTS

Tables

ACKNOWLEDGMENTS

The editors are grateful to all the authors in this volume for their valuable contributions and for the high priority that they gave this project over the past year. We also thank the discussants who provided valuable input at the conference held in The Hague, December 2–4, 2004, where these papers were first presented. In addition to authors listed elsewhere in this volume, these discussants included: Rashad Cassim, Alexander Keck, Hernan Lacunza, Sam Laird, Patrick Osakwe, and George Rapsomanikis. This research also benefited greatly from the input of Carlos Primo Braga, who participated in the conference and helped to guide subsequent dissemination activities. Finally, William Cline provided a comprehensive and incisive set of referee comments on the entire manuscript.

This entire project would not have been possible without the generous support of the Bank-Netherlands Partnership Program, which had the foresight both to commission this research work, as well as to ensure that sufficient funds were available for its widespread dissemination. We also express our thanks for the excellent logistical support provided by Rebecca Martin of the World Bank, and by the Dutch Agricultural Economics Research Institute (LEI), which hosted the December 2004 conference. Maria Lourdes Kasilag of the World Bank did an outstanding job formatting the manuscripts. These acknowledgments would not be complete without thanking our spouses, Adriela Fernandez and Zhen Kun Wang. Their understanding and encouragement is greatly appreciated.

CONTRIBUTORS

Kym Anderson, World Bank

Nabil Annabi, Université Laval, Québec City, Québec, Canada

Channing Arndt, Ministry of Planning and Development, Maputo, Mozambique, and Purdue University, West Lafayette, Indiana

Jorge Balat, World Bank

Maurizio Bussolo, World Bank

John Cockburn, Université Laval, Québec City, Québec, Canada

Erwin Corong, De La Salle University, Manila, Philippines

Caesar B. Cororaton, International Food Policy Research Institute, Washington, DC

Bernard Decaluwé, Université Laval, Québec City, Québec, Canada

Christian Arnault Emini, Centre d'Etudes et Recherches en Economie et Gestion (CEREG), University of Yaoundé II, Yaoundé, Cameroon, and Université Laval, Québec City, Québec, Canada

Joaquim Bento de Souza Ferreira Filho, Universidade de São Paulo, Brazil

Thomas W. Hertel, Purdue University, West Lafayette, Indiana, and World Bank

J. Mark Horridge, Monash University, Centre of Policy Studies, Melbourne, Australia

Maros Ivanic, World Bank

Bazlul Khondker, University of Dhaka, Dhaka, Bangladesh

Marijke Kuiper, Agricultural Economics Research Institute, Wageningen University and Research Centre, Wageningen, the Netherlands

Jann Lay, Kiel Institute for World Economics, Kiel, Germany

Will Martin, World Bank

Dominique van der Mensbrugghe, World Bank

Alessandro Nicita, World Bank

Guido Porto, World Bank

Selim Raihan, University of Dhaka, Dhaka, Bangladesh, and University of Manchester, Manchester, United Kingdom

Anne-Sophie Robilliard, Institut de Recherche pour le Développement (IRD), Paris

Sherman Robinson, University of Sussex, Brighton, United Kingdom

Thomas Rutherford, University of Colorado, Boulder, Colorado

Oleksandr Shepotylo, University of Maryland, College Park, Maryland

David Tarr, World Bank

Frank van Tongeren, Agricultural Economics Research Institute, Wageningen University and Research Centre, Wageningen, the Netherlands

L. Alan Winters, World Bank

Fan Zhai, Asian Development Bank, Manila, Philippines

ABBREVIATIONS
AND ACRONYMS

ACP	African, Caribbean and Pacific Group of States
AGE	applied general equilibrium
AMS	aggregate measure of support
ASEAN	Association of Southeast Asian Nations
ATC	Agreement on Textiles and Clothing
BaU	business as usual
BOP	balance of payments
CEPAL	Comisión Económica par América Latina y el Caribe
CEPII	Centre d'Etudes et Prospectives d'Informations Internationales
CES	constant elasticity of substitution
CET	constant elasticity of transformation
CGE	computable general equilibrium
CHNS	China Health and Nutrition Survey
CIF	cost, insurance, and freight
CNIS	Cameroon National Institute of Statistics
CPI	consumer price index
CRS	constant returns to scale
CV	coefficient of variation
DDA	Doha Development Agenda
DWP	Doha Work Program
EFTA	European Free Trade Association
ENIGH	Encuesta de Ingresos y Gastos de los Hogares (Survey of Household Income and Expenditures)

EPA	Economic Partnership Agreement
EPR	effective protection rate
EU	European Union
EV	equivalent variation
FAO	UN Food and Agriculture Organization
FDI	foreign direct investment
FGT	Foster-Greer-Thorbecke
FIES	Family Income and Expenditure Survey
FOB	free on board
FTAA	Free Trade Area of the Americas
GATT	General Agreement on Tariffs and Trade
GDP	gross domestic product
GEP	*Global Economic Prospects*
GTAP	Global Trade Analysis Project
haz	height-for-age
HBS	household budget survey
HES	household expenditure survey
HIPC	heavily indebted poor country
IBGE	Instituto Brasileiro de Geografia e Estatística (Brazilian Institute of Geography and Statistics)
INE	Instituto Nacional de Estatística (National Institute of Statistics)
ITC	International Trade Centre
LCMS	Living Conditions Monitoring Surveys
LDC	least developed country
LES	linear expenditure system
Mercosur	Mercado Común del Sur
MFN	most favored nation
MH	multiple households
MPS	market price support
MS	microsimulation
NAFTA	North American Free Trade Agreement
OECD	Organisation for Economic Co-operation and Development
PNAD	Pesquisa Nacional por Amostragem de Domicílios (National Household Survey)
POF	Pesquisa de Orçamentos Familiares (Household Expenditure Survey)
QR	quantitative restrictions
RH	representative household
ROW	rest of the world

SAM	social accounting matrix
SDT	special and differential treatment
SITC	Standard International Trade Classification
SKTIR	Special Survey on Saving and Household Investment
TOT	terms of trade
TRP	trade reform program
TRQ	tariff rate quota
UN	United Nations
VAT	value added tax
waz	weight for age
whz	weight for height
WTO	World Trade Organization

PART I

EVALUATION OF THE DOHA DEVELOPMENT AGENDA

1

POVERTY IMPACTS OF A WTO AGREEMENT: SYNTHESIS AND OVERVIEW

Thomas W. Hertel and L. Alan Winters

Summary

This chapter reports on the findings from a major international research project investigating the poverty impacts of a potential Doha Development Agenda (DDA). It combines in a novel way the results from several strands of research. First, it draws on an intensive analysis of the DDA Framework Agreement, with particularly close attention paid to potential reforms in agriculture. The scenarios are built up using newly available tariff line data, and their implications for world markets are established using a global modeling framework. These world trade impacts form the basis for 12 country case studies of the national poverty impacts of these DDA scenarios. The focus countries are Bangladesh, Brazil (2 studies), Cameroon, China (2 studies), Indonesia, Mexico, Mozambique, the Philippines, the Russian Federation, and Zambia. Although the diversity of approaches taken in these studies limits the ability to draw broader conclusions, an additional study that provides a 15-country cross-section analysis is aimed at this objective. Finally, a global analysis provides estimates for the world as a whole.

Some of the main findings are:

- The liberalization targets under the DDA have to be quite ambitious if the round is to have a measurable impact on world markets and hence poverty.
- Assuming an ambitious DDA, the near-term poverty impacts are found to be mixed; some countries experience small poverty rises and others more

substantial poverty declines. On balance, poverty is reduced under this DDA, and this reduction is more pronounced in the longer run.

- Allowing minimal tariff cuts for just a small percentage of special and sensitive products virtually eliminates the global poverty reduction due to the DDA.
- Deeper cuts in developing country tariffs would make the DDA more poverty-friendly.
- Key determinants of the national poverty impacts include the incomplete transmission of world prices to rural households, barriers to the mobility of workers between sectors of the economy, and the incidence of national tax instruments used to replace lost tariff revenue.
- To generate significant poverty reductions in the near term, complementary domestic reforms are required to enable households to take advantage of new market opportunities made available through the DDA.
- Sustained long-term poverty reductions depend on stimulating economic growth. Here, the impact of the DDA (and trade policy more generally) on productivity is critical. To fully realize their growth potential, trade reforms need to be far reaching, addressing barriers to services trade and investment in addition to merchandise tariffs.

Introduction and Motivation

International trade is arguably the most direct economic means by which rich countries influence poor countries. Exports of manufactures by developing countries have increased rapidly over the last 30 years, due in part to falling tariffs in the Organisation for Economic Co-operation and Development (OECD) countries as well as in developing countries, declining transport costs, increased specialization, and sustained economic growth. Manufactures accounted for just 25 percent of developing country exports in 1965, and this share tripled to nearly 75 percent over the next three decades, while agriculture's share of developing country exports has fallen from 50 percent to under 10 percent (Hertel and Martin 2000). Increased manufactures trade has benefited many developing countries, helping them make the transition out of agriculture and lifting many out of poverty.

Some of the poorest developing countries, however, have gained relatively little from increased manufactures trade. Market access for their most competitive manufactured export (apparel) remains highly restricted, as it does for their key source of employment and exports, farming, and the problem with agricultural exports is exacerbated by the massive government subsidies provided to farmers in OECD countries. When poverty within the poorest countries is considered, developed countries' agricultural policies become even more central. A majority of the poor are concentrated in rural areas, where agriculture is usually the main source of economic activity (World Bank 2004), and in the poorest developing countries, large shares of households (including most of the very poorest) depend on self-employment in agriculture for virtually all of their income (Hertel and others 2004). Together, these facts highlight the potential influence that multilateral trade policies can have on poverty in developing countries.

The DDA negotiations, sponsored by the World Trade Organization (WTO), experienced a blow in Cancún, Mexico, because of the question of rich countries' agricultural support and its potential impacts on poverty in developing countries. The Doha negotiations are now emphasizing the need to better understand the linkages between trade policies—particularly in rich countries—and poverty in the developing world. Moreover, poverty reduction is now widely accepted as a central focus for development efforts and has become the main mission of the World Bank and other development institutions. For example, the Millennium Development Goals commit the international community to halve poverty in developing countries by 2015 and identify several key means to achieving this goal with international trade.

With this high level of policy interest, it is hardly surprising that the issue of trade and developing-country poverty has become a focus of much research activity over the last several years. This book contributes to this literature by offering the first comprehensive analysis of the national poverty impacts of specific policy reforms proposed under the auspices of the WTO. To do so, it combines the results from several strands of research in a novel way. First, it draws on an intensive analysis of the July 2004 DDA Framework Agreement, particularly of potential reforms in agriculture, which, as will be shown, have special significance to the poor. The scenarios analyzed below are built up from newly available tariff line data on bound and applied tariff rates. Similarly detailed analysis is undertaken in the case of domestic support for agriculture and export subsidies, as well as for nonagricultural market access.

Second, the research assesses the implications of these alternative Doha scenarios for world markets. These are established using a state-of-the-art, global modeling framework that incorporates the most recent econometric evidence on supply and demand elasticities, with particularly close attention paid to food and agriculture markets that prove crucial in assessing the poverty impacts of the DDA. The outputs of this part of the project include export and import price changes for each region of the world, along with changes in export volumes.

Third, these world trade impacts form the basis for analyzing the poverty impacts of the DDA on 10 individual countries by way of a dozen case studies.

These case studies use a variety of innovative techniques to establish the potential impacts of the DDA on different household groups and, in some cases, different regions within the country. The focus countries are Bangladesh, Brazil (two studies), Cameroon, China (two studies), Indonesia, Mexico, Mozambique, the Philippines, Russia, and Zambia.

Some case studies also examine other poverty policies in addition to trade reforms—for example, education reform or agricultural extension services. Sometimes these are complementary to the Doha Round in the sense of enhancing its effect, but more often they are independent. They are explored here as yardsticks against which trade reform can be measured and as suggestions concerning how governments can seek to overcome any adverse poverty effects from the Doha Round. However, the authors do not subscribe to the view that such "complementary policies" are necessary for the Doha Round to be beneficial.

Choice of Methodologies

Organization of the research underpinning this volume had two contrasting objectives. On the one hand, the studies had to be consistent with one another to ensure an accurate global assessment of the DDA, as well as comparability across studies. On the other hand, research into the poverty impacts of trade reform is new, and almost the only consensus it has reached is that countries differ. From this perspective, it was important to both encourage a variety of approaches at the country level and exploit the specific skills and knowledge of the case studies' authors to gear their country models most closely to local characteristics and issues.[1]

The project, therefore, is a composite in which the global analysis—the methodology for deriving the global findings and passing them over to the national case studies—is unique and consistent with current standards in the field of quantitative trade policy analysis, the country case studies display a wide range of methodological innovations and topical design features. This variety has been fruitful, with different country studies emphasizing alternative links between trade and poverty and providing a diversity of insights. Nevertheless, as a check and to draw some broader conclusions, two more uniform exercises are included: a 15-country cross-section analysis, in which a common, fully integrated trade-poverty analysis is provided for a range of developing countries, and, a global analysis of aggregate poverty impacts derived by applying simple poverty elasticities to the predicted outcomes for developing countries in a global simulation of a prospective Doha agreement.

In most of this book, the methodology known as computable general equilibrium (CGE) analysis is used. This is the dominant methodology for the ex ante analysis of the economic consequences of comprehensive trade agreements whether multilateral or bilateral in nature (Francois and Shiells, 1994). This is the dominant methodology because no other approach offers the same flexibility for looking at prospective changes in trade policy while respecting the fundamental economy-wide consistency requirements such as balance of payments equilibrium and labor and capital market constraints that are so important in determining the consequences of comprehensive trade reforms. The CGE approach has come under substantial criticism (for example, from Jorgenson [1984], McKitrick [1998], and Kehoe [2005]) for having insufficient econometric underpinnings and for not being adequately validated. Accordingly, this volume offers a number of econometric-based analyses that focus on key dimensions of the trade and poverty question, including price transmission from the border to households, cropping choices made by farm households, labor market participation decisions, and the intersectoral movement of labor. In addition, when the global market impacts are assessed, a CGE model is used that is based on the most recent econometric evidence on supply and demand elasticities and for which some (modest) validation has been undertaken.

The majority of the studies reported in this volume are based on *comparative static* analysis. The authors abstract from the impact of trade reform on investment and productivity and therefore economic growth. There are two reasons for this emphasis. First, most of the issues that arise in the popular debate over the poverty impacts of trade policy are fundamentally comparative static in nature. Concerns about the urban poor being adversely affected by higher food prices, the potential loss of jobs by women in the apparel sector, or the poverty impacts on low-income farmers in developing countries are all questions about the redistributive impact of trade policy reform. Answering them requires a disaggregated, comparative static framework. Of course, there is also a keen interest in the potential for economic growth to alleviate poverty, and five of the studies use a dynamic framework that accounts for the growth effects of changes in investment deriving from trade policy reform. However, quantifying the impact of trade reform on growth and poverty through channels such as the effect on productivity or the benefits of increasing the range of available goods remains a lively topic for current research on which consensus has yet to emerge. Hence, the second reason for using the comparative static approach is to avoid any appearance of overstating the poverty-alleviating benefits of liberalization.

In the end, it must be said that this project has proven to be a very ambitious undertaking—attempting to bridge micro-based research focusing on the choices and opportunities facing individual households in developing countries with macro-based research on the global impacts of multilateral trade policy reform. The payoff to this exercise must be judged by the insights offered.

The Global Impact of the Doha Development Agenda

Chapter 2 of this book, by Kym Anderson and Will Martin, takes as its starting point the July, 2004, WTO Framework Agreement for the Doha Agenda. It explores the issues emerging from of this document—in particular, the annexes dealing with export subsidies, domestic support and market access in agriculture, and market access for nonagricultural goods. Chapter 2 examines seven different Doha scenarios, one of which is adopted as the core scenario for this book. In constructing this scenario, the authors have taken considerable care to distinguish those trade reforms that are actually being negotiated under the DDA from those that have been agreed to previously. This distinction is complicated because nearly all of the policy databases used predate completion of the Uruguay Round Agreement. In fact, the starting point for all of the analysis in this book is 2001, the most recent year for which comprehensive data are available for tariffs, domestic support, and export interventions. Therefore, before constructing the Doha scenario, a "pre-experiment" is undertaken to account for the major developments in trade policy since 2001. These include tariff reforms undertaken by newly acceding WTO members (most notably China), the phase-in of remaining Uruguay Round commitments by developing countries, European Union (EU) enlargement to 25 countries, and the abolition of export quotas on textiles and apparel under the Agreement on Textiles and Clothing. Thus, even though the full impact of some of these reforms is yet to be felt, the analysis in this book looks beyond these reforms, envisioning a global economy in which they have been fully implemented and focusing on the further impacts of trade liberalization undertaken in the context of the Doha negotiations.

The most important finding from chapter 2 is that, unless the DDA is considerably more ambitious than the Uruguay Round in terms of depth of cuts in bound tariffs and domestic support, it will achieve little development stimulus. The main problem on the market access side is binding overhang. For example, in agriculture—one of the key areas of the DDA with respect to trade and poverty— bound tariffs in developing countries average 48 percent, but applied tariffs average only 21 percent. In the case of the least developed countries (LDCs), the respective figures are 78 percent and 13 percent. Even in the EU (21 percent binding versus 12 percent applied) and the United States (6 percent binding versus 3 percent applied), there is substantial binding overhang in agriculture. So, for many countries and products, bound tariffs can be cut deeply with no impact on applied protection and hence international trade.

In the central Doha scenario featured in this book, agricultural tariffs are cut using a tiered formula, with marginal cuts changing at 15 and 90 percent bound tariff rates. The marginal cuts are 45 percent for the lowest agricultural tariffs, 70 percent for tariffs in the middle range, and 75 percent marginal cuts for the highest tariffs.[2] For developing countries, the inflection points are placed at 20, 60, and 120 percent bound tariff levels in agriculture, with marginal cuts of 35, 40, 50, and 60 percent, respectively. The LDCs are not required to cut tariffs under this central scenario. Because of a lack of specificity in the July Framework Agreement, nonagricultural tariffs are simply cut by 50 percent across the board (33 percent in developing countries and 0 percent in LDCs). Box 1.1 summarizes the central Doha scenario.

There is much more to the DDA than just agriculture and nonagricultural market access—for example, trade facilitation, services liberalization, and rules on antidumping and regionalism. This book focuses on the former issues partly because they are quantifiable and provide a large agenda in themselves. Mainly, however, they are likely to be the major issues in terms of both effects and negotiators' need for detailed quantitative advice. Moreover, the other issues are basically additive to the analysis of market access for goods, so that as their outcomes and consequences become clear, they may be added to these results to get an overall picture.

As a consequence of the relatively ambitious tariff cuts analyzed here, average worldwide tariffs for all merchandise trade drop from 4.7 percent in the baseline to 3.2 percent. This masks rather different cuts for countries at different income levels. High-income countries' tariffs fall from 2.9 percent to 1.6 percent, middle-income countries' tariffs from 7.2 percent to 6.3 percent, and low-income countries' tariffs (including LDCs, which do not cut tariffs at all) fall from 15.6 percent to 14.6 percent. (Anderson and Martin report these cuts in detail in chapter 2.)

In the case of domestic support, there is also a problem of bound versus applied protection, with bindings generally much higher than applied aggregate measure of support (AMS). But even more severe is the definition of the AMS itself—particularly its reliance on administered prices as a benchmark. This feature makes it possible for administrators in some countries to bring programs into WTO compliance with the stroke of a pen, simply by abolishing the administered price. The core Doha scenario assumes that industrial countries with domestic support in excess of 20 percent of production cut their bound AMS commitments by 75 percent, and others cut by 60 percent. Developing countries are assumed to cut their AMS by 40 percent. Even with these ambitious reductions, only six WTO members would be required to reduce actual support, based on 2001 notifications: Australia, the EU, Iceland, Norway, Thailand, and the United States.

Export subsidies are the one area where bold cuts (full elimination) are on the table, but these have diminished in importance over time. At present, they remain a significant factor only in the case of the EU (and in the United States for

---

Box 1.1. Elements of the DDA Scenario Based on the July Framework Agreement

- **Agriculture:**
  - Market access—use nonlinear (tiered) formula (as with progressive income tax):
    - For developed countries, marginal rates (45, 70, and 75 percent) change at 10 and 90 percent tariffs
    - For developing countries, marginal rates (35, 40, 50, and 60 percent) change at 20, 60, and 120 percent tariffs
    - For LDCs, no cuts to tariffs
  - AMS: apply tiered formula:
    - For developed countries, marginal rates of 60 percent (AMS less than 20 percent) and 75 percent
    - For developing countries, marginal rate of 40 percent
    - For LDCs, no cuts to domestic subsidies
  - Export subsidies abolished
- Nonagriculture market access: 50 percent cuts in tariffs (33 percent developing countries, 0 percent LDCs).

---

dairy products), and the abolition of export subsidies has been made conditional on equivalent treatment of food aid and state trading. Preliminary estimates suggest that reform of the latter two items will have little impact, but the linking of these features to the WTO negotiations makes the whole process much more complex. The central Doha scenario in this book assumes that export subsidies are abolished.

In addition to this central Doha scenario, this book also considers an important variant in which developing countries fully reciprocate the tariff cuts made by developed countries, thereby eliminating one of the historical pillars of special and differential treatment. The rationale for considering this alternative, labeled Doha-all, becomes clear with the discussion of the results of the global poverty analyses later in this chapter. Under Doha-all, average merchandise tariffs in the middle- and low-income countries drop further, to 5.6 and 13.4 percent, respectively. In the case of the low-income countries, this represents a larger incremental cut in average tariffs than was achieved in the central Doha scenario itself.

Assuming that negotiators honor their initial vision as set forth in the DDA and make significant cuts in agricultural and nonagricultural protection, what impact might this have on poverty? Will they really put development squarely into the DDA? Answering these questions is the primary goal of this book.

The impact of the Doha reforms on world market prices is the subject of chapter 3. Here, Thomas Hertel and Maros Ivanic use a global CGE model to assess the potential impact on world market prices and trade volumes. As established in chapter 2, agricultural protection is central to any assessment of global trade reform, and the analysis in chapter 3 bears this out. The trade reform scenarios invariably have the biggest impact on prices and trade volumes for farm and food products, followed by textiles and apparel. Given the predominance of the poor in rural areas and their heavy reliance on unskilled wages elsewhere, these are the key industries in any poverty assessment. The strongest world price increases are for the heavily subsidized farm products: rice and other grains, cotton, dairy products, and beef. The ranking of the price increases arises from the composition of cuts, both across the three sets of agricultural distortions and across countries. The other important point made in chapter 3 is that, given the increasingly differentiated nature of traded products, there is no one "world price," and careful attention must be paid to bilateral patterns of trade and country-specific price changes.

Finally, chapter 3 outlines the methodology for transmitting the price and volume changes to the national case studies. This represents an important innovation in the linking of global economic outcomes with national impacts.

Price Transmission

The analysis of the country case studies is structured around the conceptual framework laid out by Winters (2000) and Winters, McCulloch, and McKay (2004). This begins with the question of price transmission: How much of the world price shock is transmitted to producers and consumers?

With a majority of the poor in most countries located in rural areas—often poorly served by transportation and communication infrastructure—it is important to ask whether developments in global markets will really have an impact on these households. Of course, this is an empirical question, subject to econometric investigation, and this is precisely what Alessandro Nicita does in chapter 4 for the case of Mexico. He shows that, indeed, world prices are differentially transmitted to the regions of the country, depending on their distance from the border and the nature of the commodity in question. He begins his analysis by examining the extent of "pass-through" from international prices to domestic prices at the border. Here, he finds that for manufactured goods, about two-thirds of the international price change passes through to the domestic market, whereas the comparable figure for agriculture is just one-quarter.

Nicita's econometric estimates also show that the transmission of world market price changes diminishes with distance from the border. In addition, urban areas are more sensitive to border prices changes, when compared to rural areas. Therefore, he concludes that in the more remote, rural regions of Mexico, very little of the international price changes will be felt, particularly in the case of agricultural products. As a consequence, the impact of the Doha scenarios—which have only modest impacts on world prices, anyway—are negligible in rural Mexico, except in the north, near the U.S. border, where rural households see some small gains. Urban consumers face higher food prices and a small decline in unskilled wages as the privileged Mexican position in the U.S. market is eroded by most-favored-nation tariff cuts. Thus, the urban poor experience small losses.

Nicita also explores the impact of complementary domestic reforms that might permit rural producers to respond to improved world market conditions without incurring additional costs (for example, a productivity gain or the employment of surplus labor). This enhances the welfare outcome for rural households in all regions except the south. Rural households in the south benefit from Doha only when the reforms are accompanied by enhanced price transmission—for example, through improved transport and market infrastructure. Thus, there is an important interaction between price transmission and the distribution of gains from global trade reforms.

One of the poorest countries in the world, which also has very poor infrastructure and is plagued by high domestic marketing costs, is Mozambique. In fact, work by Arndt and others (2000) estimates producer-consumer margins as high as 300 percent (for cassava). The biggest margins reported in their study are for food products, which tend to dominate both the consumption and production bundles of the poor. So the existence and behavior of these margins is critically important for any poverty study. Chapter 5, by Channing Arndt, explores this issue in the context of the Doha Round scenarios for Mozambique. As with the Mexico study, the combination of these marketing margins with modest world price changes means that the impact on household welfare in Mozambique is quite small. Indeed, about one-third of rural households are unaffected by the Doha scenario. The largest rural losses are about 1 percent of income, with some households experiencing modest gains. The dispersion among urban households is larger because of the presence of smaller marketing margins. Overall, the impact of multilateral trade reform on Mozambique is adverse as preferences are eroded and prices of imports rise.

The Disaggregated Impact on Households

Moving beyond the question of price transmission, the studies in this book move on to the issue of household-level impacts of—and household responses to—the price changes ensuing from trade reforms. The simplest way of exploring this link is to focus on a single commodity. This is the approach taken by Jorge Balat and Guido Porto in chapter 6 on the impact of trade reform on cotton producers in Zambia. They note that the critical factor in this case is the share of household income generated by cotton production. To a first-order approximation, the real income impact of a change in the price of cotton may be obtained by multiplying this income share by the percentage change in cotton price. This leads Balat and Porto to focus on the evolution of cotton income shares among the poor in Zambia. Because cotton is grown in significant quantities in only three provinces, this is where they focus attention.

One of the striking things about world cotton markets in the late 1990s was the collapse in world prices. Between 1996 and 1998, cotton prices in Zambia fell by 20 percent. Therefore, it is surprising that cotton's share in income among the poor rose sharply in the eastern and southern provinces over this same period. Among the poorest households in the eastern province, the increase was nearly fivefold, even as the income share fell for wealthier households. Although there are many factors that may bear on this change, the authors argue that the most likely reason was the reform of the cotton marketing board system and the implementation of an out-grower scheme that proved effective in getting seed and fertilizer into the hands of credit-constrained, small-scale producers. This increase in the cotton share boosts the potential benefits from multilateral agricultural reforms, because one of the main consequences of such reform would be to raise cotton prices.

Despite the increase in cotton income shares over this period, the income impact on the poor of higher cotton prices—the authors assume a 12 percent price rise, based on several independent studies of world cotton markets—is still relatively modest (on the order of 1 percent of real income, on average) because the average income share is about 8 percent. This brings the authors to a discussion of complementary domestic reforms. In particular, they cite evidence from other research they have conducted in Zambia, which finds that access to extension services can boost productivity by more than 8 percent, resulting in an aggregate gain of more than 9 percent when combined with higher cotton prices.

But the largest poverty reduction benefits appear to arise when subsistence households switch to cotton production in the wake of increased demand for exports. Here, a careful matching of subsistence and cotton-producing households shows that, all else constant, subsistence producers could boost their incomes by nearly 20 percent if they switched to cotton production. Such a switch would be greatly facilitated by continued improvement of the out-grower schemes and strong demand for cotton exports. When combined with improved extension services and higher cotton prices, the switch from subsistence production to cotton could boost incomes of some of the poorest households in Zambia by nearly one-third. In sum, Balat and Porto conclude that trade reform alone is not sufficient to raise a large number of poor out of poverty in Zambia, but when the market opportunities presented by trade reforms are combined with complementary domestic reforms, significant headway in the fight against poverty is possible.

Of course, global trade reforms do not simply alter one single commodity price: rather they potentially affect *all* prices in the economy, including the prices of nontradeable commodities and services as well as wages and returns to land and capital. So, the next study seeks to account for the full range of price impacts at a highly disaggregated level. The unusual thing about Joaquim Ferriera-Filho and Mark Horridge's chapter 7 in this volume is the very large number of individuals considered in their analysis—264,000 adults who are members of 112,000 households spread across the 27 regions of Brazil. The authors argue that the regional dimension of their study is critical, given the tremendous disparities in income and poverty incidence across regions. The proportion of poor households ranges from about 14 percent in parts of the southeast, to nearly 60 percent in the north (Amapá). When combined with large variations in industrial composition across regions, there is a recipe for great differences in poverty impacts due to trade reform.

Ferriera-Filho and Horridge find that the Doha scenarios benefit agriculture at the expense of industry. This is no surprise, because virtually all previous studies of global agricultural trade reform have concluded that Brazil would be a substantial beneficiary from such a development. However, the real question is, which households within Brazil will benefit? Many believe that all of the benefits will go to large farmers, thereby worsening the income distribution in Brazil. The research reported in chapter 7 argues that, when one takes account of the additional employment generated by the expansion of agriculture and related industries in many of the poorer states of Brazil, the largest gainers are actually the households that are most heavily reliant on low-skill labor. As a consequence, the income distribution in Brazil *improves* under the Doha scenario. This is a very important finding. It is a point that has been previously emphasized in more highly aggregate research on trade and poverty reported by Harrison and others (2003).

As a percentage of initial poverty, the estimated national decline in chapter 7 is modest (less than 1 percent), but it still amounts to a large number of persons: Under the Doha scenario, poverty falls by about 236,000, and it declines by about twice that amount in the case of the full-liberalization scenario. The declines in poverty are fueled by the growth in agricultural activity—Brazilian farm and food exports expand strongly in the wake of trade reform—and the subsequent increase in demand for the lowest skill workers, 41 percent of whom still work in the farm sector.

Of course, these wage gains hinge on the existence of an operational labor market. Such a market may not exist in some cases, and the potential consequences of factor market failure are explored in considerable depth in chapter 8 by Marijke Kuiper and Frank van Tongeren. These authors approach this problem by employing a village-level model of a community in Jiangxi province in China. They capture the heterogeneity of household types by grouping them according to their factor endowments. In particular, they distinguish whether or not households have access to draft power and whether or not they have family members involved in temporary migration outside the province. After a detailed analysis of circumstances in this village, they conclude that the markets for labor, land, and capital are imperfect, thereby preventing households from simply taking wages and rental payments as given when making decisions about consumption and production. This "nonseparability" complicates the household's decision-making process and can result in some striking results in the wake of trade reforms.

In the case of Doha reforms, the real income gains for the village are quite modest—about 1.2 percent of income—and relatively evenly spread across the different household groups. However, in the case of full liberalization, the aggregate gains are four times as large and much more unevenly spread across households, with the gains to households with draft power nearly twice as large as those for the other household groups. This reflects the intensification of production in agriculture engendered by higher prices for rice and other farm products.

Labor Markets

The main resource with which the poor are endowed is their own labor. Whether they are self-employed farmers, providers of services, or wage earners, their income is closely tied to conditions in the labor market. This point surfaces clearly in the Brazil and China studies discussed above, both of which emphasize the importance of labor markets as a mechanism for transmitting favorable developments in the world marketplace, as well as elsewhere in the domestic economy, to impoverished households. The next set of studies focuses primarily on the labor markets in Brazil and China, as well as on a third country, Indonesia. The first of these is chapter 9, by Maurizio Bussolo, Jann Lay, and Dominique van der Mensbrugghe, on Brazil. Their focus is specifically on the link between the farm and nonfarm labor forces. They model the decision to move out of agriculture based on an econometric model that predicts the likelihood of a given individual changing sectors, based on the historical evidence in Brazil. The other important feature of this chapter is the authors' analysis in the context of a 2001–15 baseline for the Brazilian economy. This permits viewing the impacts of trade reform in the context of ongoing changes in the economy, labor markets, and poverty.

In their baseline projection, Bussolo, Lay, and van der Mensbrugghe find that the poverty headcount falls by almost 14 percent. The majority of this decline is due to poverty reduction in agriculture, a sector that grows considerably faster than the nonfarm economy under their business-as-usual forecast. The majority of this poverty reduction is due to factor price changes (for example, higher wages), but a significant portion is attributable to the exit of labor from the relatively low-wage agricultural sector to higher-wage, nonfarm jobs. This intersectoral movement is particularly important to the poorest farm households.

Having established this baseline scenario, Bussolo, Lay, and van der Mensbrugghe analyze the implications of alternative trade reforms for poverty—in particular for the different labor force groups: the "movers" who move from agriculture to nonagriculture over the course of the baseline, the "stayers" who remain in agriculture, and the "stayers" in nonagriculture. The largest percentage point reduction in poverty over the baseline is for the "movers," who experience a 22.4 percentage point reduction in their headcount (down from 53.4 percent to 31 percent). This is the poorest of the three groups, and it is also the group that experiences the greatest incremental poverty reduction, above and beyond the baseline, as a result of the Doha trade reforms. Overall, the authors find quite modest poverty gains from the Doha scenarios (just 3 percent of the baseline change over the 2001–15 period). Full liberalization generates estimates of national poverty reduction that are three times as large as the Doha reductions, but still modest in the context of projected baseline changes. This underscores the fact that trade reforms taken alone are a relatively small piece of the overall poverty reduction puzzle.

Chapter 10 by Fan Zhai and Thomas Hertel takes a deeper look at the Doha reforms through the lens of a labor-focused CGE model of China and the scope for enhancing these outcomes through complementary education reforms. Like chapter 9, this chapter emphasizes the farm-nonfarm labor market linkage, which Zhai and Hertel argue is partly a function of educational attainment and therefore susceptible to change through educational policy. They also emphasize the link between rural and urban labor markets in China through the temporary migration of workers. (Permanent migration is still restricted in that country.) In their analysis of multilateral trade reforms, the authors find that poverty falls across all of their household categories: by 1.3 percent in the case of Doha and 2.7 percent in the case of full liberalization. Inequality also declines slightly under these scenarios.

Zhai and Hertel cite econometric evidence that suggests that an additional year of education boosts an individual's chances of obtaining an off-farm job in China by 14 percent. Educational attainment is also important for workers seeking to meet the needs of an increasingly integrated global marketplace, yet education expenditures per pupil in the rural areas lag significantly behind their urban counterparts in China. The authors explore the implications of accompanying trade reform with additional educational investments in rural areas to enhance rural labor mobility, productivity, and income. In particular, they boost expenditures per pupil enrolled in mandatory education by 16 percent to reach the comparable urban level. This increment is assumed to be financed in part by public funds, raised through additional taxation, and in part through increased private contributions taken out of rural households' disposable income. This combination of educational and trade reforms has a much stronger impact on poverty alleviation, with the number of poor (living on less than US$2 per day) falling by 13.4 percent. This scenario also has a favorable impact on rural-urban income inequality.

The final chapter focusing on labor markets, chapter 11, is a case study of Indonesia by Anne-Sophie Robilliard and Sherman Robinson. Instead of focusing on the farm-nonfarm or rural-urban movement of labor, these authors draw a sharp distinction between the formal and informal labor markets. The formal sector offers high wages, but few opportunities for employment. The informal sector, by contrast, has a flexible wage that is assumed to clear the market. Robilliard and Robinson explicitly model each individual's decision to participate in one or the other of these labor markets. In this way, they are able to predict which types of individuals will lose their job when formal sector employment contracts and which will be hired when employment expands. These changes in employment represent an important determinant of the welfare impacts on households of any change in a country's pattern of trade, production, and employment.

Robilliard and Robinson explore the poverty impacts of multilateral trade reform under three alternative labor market closures: fixed aggregate employment and flexible wages; fixed, sector-specific labor (no change in employment by sector); and fixed real wages and variable aggregate employment (that is, changes in unemployment are permitted). They focus on the full-liberalization scenario for this sensitivity analysis and find that the largest reduction in poverty comes from the fixed employment scenario: about 1.4 million people are lifted out of poverty. The proportional reduction is slightly higher in the rural areas and more favorable to the poorest of the poor as well, so that the national Gini index falls in this closure. When labor is not permitted to move across sectors, the poverty reduction is much smaller—only 900,000—because the economy is not permitted to fully adjust to the new world prices, efficiency gains are blunted, and the national rise in per capita income is muted.

The third case, in which wages are fixed and the unemployment rate is permitted to fall in the wake of increasing labor demand, presents a particularly interesting contrast in chapter 11. With increasing aggregate employment, national per capita income rises more than in the first case with fixed employment and flexible wages. The authors point out that the poverty outcome depends critically on who gets the new jobs. If the new jobs go to individuals from nonpoor households (that is, families with other wage earners or other sources of income), the unemployment specification could worsen income inequality because the pool of unemployed workers prevents unskilled wages from rising and, without the benefit of higher wages, the poverty reduction would be muted. To quantify this outcome, the authors have estimated the likelihood that each type of unemployed individual will obtain one of the newly available jobs. There is a considerable uncertainty associated with these estimates, and Robilliard and Robinson reflect this by reporting their results in terms of the mean and standard deviation of a Monte Carlo simulation for each closure or scenario. Although the mean poverty reduction under the unemployment closure is larger than that under the standard labor market specification, the standard deviations suggest that the two are not significantly different in a statistical sense.

Interactions with Tax Policies

An important theme in many of the chapters in this volume is the potential for interactions between the Doha scenarios and domestic policies to alter the poverty outcomes obtained from multilateral trade reform. Does multilateral trade liberalization lessen the distortions introduced by domestic commodity and factor market policies, or does it exacerbate them? To what extent can complementary reforms of domestic policies enhance the degree of poverty reduction? When trade liberalization results in reduced tax revenues, how will this shortfall be made up? Two of the chapters in this volume focus squarely on the question of tax replacement.[3]

Chapter 12, by Christian Arnault Emini, John Cockburn, and Bernard Decaluwé, focuses on the case of Cameroon. They examine the poverty impacts of the central Doha scenario, paying particular attention to the structure of the domestic tax system and the different options available for replacement of the lost tariff revenue. They view the value added tax (VAT) as the most likely tax replacement tool in Cameroon. This tax has a very heterogeneous impact on sectors, with effective rates ranging from 0 percent in the case of agriculture to 13 percent in the case of petroleum refining. When the authors combine this tax replacement tool with the Doha scenario, they find that poverty falls slightly, by about 22,000 people, in Cameroon, as does inequality. Of course, with relatively small tariff cuts under the Doha scenario, tax replacement is not all that central in this scenario.

In the case of full liberalization, tax replacement becomes much more important, and the authors consider three alternative tax scenarios with these tariff cuts. In every case, poverty rises, but the size of the poverty increase, as well as its causes, vary with the choice of replacement tax. When Arnault Emini, Cockburn, and Decaluwé use a nondistorting production tax, 106,000 people are estimated to be lifted out of poverty, but 193,000 formerly nonpoor fall into poverty, resulting in a net poverty increase of 87,000 people. This occurs despite an increase in aggregate welfare in Cameroon, so it is clearly a consequence of the pattern of imports and exports in that country. When trade reform is coupled with an increase in consumption taxes, the poverty rise is much larger—nearly half a million people. This impact is lessened somewhat (a 300,000-person increase) by the use of the VAT to replace the forgone tariff revenue. Clearly, in the case of Cameroon, the choice of tax instrument used to replace the lost tariff revenue can be as important as the type of trade liberalization (full liberalization versus Doha reforms only).

Chapter 13, by Caesar Cororaton, John Cockburn, and Erwin Corong, is a study focusing on the issue of tax replacement in the Philippines. This is an interesting case because the agriculture sector has evolved from net exporter to net importer over the past three decades. Because the country is a relatively recent net food importer, there is widespread concern in the Philippines that trade reforms will jeopardize food security. However, in their analysis of the Doha scenarios, the authors find that the national poverty headcount is barely affected. There is a small rise in poverty among the self-employed households, particularly those in rural areas, but poverty among salaried urban workers falls. In contrast to many of the focus economies studied in this volume, the Doha reforms are not favorable to Philippine agriculture, and this effect is more pronounced under full liberalization. Because Philippine agriculture currently receives relatively high protection, full liberalization results in a contraction of the agricultural sector and an increase in rural poverty. This is offset by a reduction in poverty among the urban population, where wages rise. As a consequence, there is a small decline in the national poverty headcount. However, when the authors switch from the VAT to a uniform income tax for purposes of tariff replacement, poverty rises in the full-liberalization case. Once again, the pattern of exemptions in the indirect tax system favors the poor, and its use for purposes of tax replacement is a critical piece of the poverty puzzle.

Cross-Country Comparisons

With their differences in factor market closures, elasticities of substitution, methodologies for grouping households and modeling labor markets, and so forth, the country case studies discussed up to this point have not been comparable. This makes it difficult to generalize on the basis of cross-country comparisons. Therefore, chapter 14, by Maros Ivanic, features a cross-country comparison for 15 countries, each of which has been treated symmetrically. Although this approach is somewhat stylized, and therefore less definitive for any given country, each of the focus country databases has been built up from the same types of individual household surveys as the single-country case studies. Another virtue of this chapter is that is offers a fully integrated, global-national-micro modeling approach. In particular, Ivanic has augmented the Global Trade Analysis Project (GTAP) global CGE model with reconciled data on 140 disaggregated household groups for each of the 15 focus countries. His grouping is based on income specialization—for example, agriculture-specialized households rely almost entirely on agricultural self-employment for their income, and similarly for a wage-specialized stratum, and so forth. Because Ivanic uses a global framework, he can simulate all of the trade reform scenarios directly in his model, which also facilitates further decomposition of the elements of trade reform and their poverty impacts.

Ivanic's findings with respect to the poverty impacts of the DDA are particularly interesting. Specifically, he finds that the Doha trade reform scenarios are not as poverty friendly as the global liberalization scenario. If Doha represented the same mix of policy reforms as full liberalization, both simulations would be expected to have the same pattern of poverty reduction, but with larger cuts under full liberalization because of its deeper cuts in protection (for example, 100 percent versus 33 percent). However, this is not the case, and, in a decomposition analysis, Ivanic shows why.

The DDA as outlined in chapter 2 has a variety of different elements, and these have conflicting impacts on poverty. The removal of export subsidies in the EU and the United States tends to raise poverty in most of the developing countries in Ivanic's sample, even while reducing poverty among the agricultural households in these poorer countries. This is hardly surprising in light of earlier studies highlighting the vulnerability of low-income, net-food-importing countries to higher world prices for these products (see, for example, Valdes and McCalla [2004]).[4] Because these export subsidies are fully removed under the Doha scenario, this impact is fully realized under that partial reform. However, Ivanic finds that cuts in developing-country tariffs as a group have a very favorable impact on national poverty in the focus countries.[5] Yet there is very little reform of developing-country tariffs under Doha—first as a result of limited reciprocity (part of special and differential treatment), and second as a result of the extensive binding overhang in developing countries. Thus, although developing-country tariff cuts are among the most poverty-friendly elements of global trade reform, very little of the beneficial impact of these reforms is felt under the Doha scenario. When combined, these facts explain why Doha is less poverty friendly than the comprehensive reform scenario. It accentuates those aspects of reform that adversely affect poverty (export subsidies), while largely omitting those aspects that benefit the poor.

This suggests that deeper cuts in developing-country tariffs under the Doha scenario might have a beneficial impact on the poverty outcome. This is explored

under the alternative scenario, Doha-all, in which developing countries fully reciprocate the developed-country reductions in tariff bindings. Ivanic shows that Doha-
all does have a more favorable poverty outcome than the base Doha scenario.

An additional finding from Ivanic's cross-section analysis pertains to the common assumption that "a rising tide lifts all boats," that is, that poverty rises and
falls in concert with changes in national per capita income. Ivanic shows that this
is not always the case in the near term because trade reform generates uneven
gains in the economy. One sector gains and another loses, so it matters greatly
where the poverty is concentrated. If most of the poor work in agriculture, and
agriculture is hurt by trade reform, poverty may rise even if real national income
rises. This is the case in Malawi, where 40 percent of the population is specialized
in agricultural self-employment.

Effects on Productivity and Economic Growth

Sustained reductions in poverty require economic growth, which leads naturally
to the question of how a prospective DDA might affect the growth rates of countries currently experiencing the highest levels of poverty. This is a challenging area
of research—worthy of an entire volume in its own right—but the final section of
this book offers two country case studies and a global synthesis chapter oriented
toward this theme.

Chapter 15 on Bangladesh focuses on the growth question by emphasizing the
impact of trade reform on capital accumulation. Nabil Annabi, Bazlul Khandker,
Selim Raiham, John Cockburn, and Bernard Decaluwé begin with a short-run
analysis in which they find that Bangladesh experiences an aggregate loss, as well
as a small rise in poverty, under the Doha scenario. There are two reasons to
expect such short run losses. First, Bangladesh is a net agricultural importer and,
as such, will suffer from higher world prices of agricultural products. Second, as
an LDC, Bangladesh currently enjoys tariff-free access to many of the rich countries' markets. When tariffs in these markets fall, Bangladesh is expected to suffer
from preference erosion—that is, the value of these tariff preferences diminishes.
The analysis in this book suggests that the first explanation is the relevant one,
with the main losses associated with imports of cotton, wheat, and oilseeds. There
is no evidence of *net* preference erosion adversely affecting the terms of trade for
Bangladesh. Because the apparel exports displaced by erosion from the EU are
absorbed in the North American market, where, de facto, most apparel exports
from Bangladesh do not enjoy preferential market access, Bangladesh benefits
from the tariff cuts. The terms of trade losses facing Bangladesh under Doha are
magnified under full liberalization. In addition to the above, to pay for additional
imports, Bangladesh must expand the volume of its textile and apparel exports,

which account for nearly 80 percent of export revenues. This tends to depress their prices.

However, these short-run losses are transitory and the authors of chapter 15 estimate that after two to three years, the economy will be better off under full liberalization than under the business-as-usual scenario. The reason is that the cost of investment goods will fall, and increased investment will flow to the more competitive sectors, thereby stimulating additional growth. The authors estimate that in the long run (15 years), gross domestic product (GDP) will be 1.44 percent higher and poverty 6.1 percent lower under the full-liberalization scenario. A closer look at these results reveals that most of the stimulus for the increased investment and economic growth comes from the reduction in Bangladesh's own tariffs, which would be missing under the Doha scenario.

These authors also explore an issue that has been the subject of much discussion recently in the context of the WTO: remittances from overseas workers. They formally explore the implications of a 50 percent increase in the flow of remittances to Bangladesh—and specifically to those households currently receiving these transfers. As a result, the domestic labor supply is reduced. This development has a favorable impact on poverty, reducing it by 0.8 percent in the short run and 4.0 percent in the long run. To the extent that rich countries are concerned about the impact on Bangladesh of higher food prices and preference erosion, a policy that permits increased temporary migration appears to be a good way to offset some of these negative effects, because the benefits of increased remittances dominate the short-run costs of trade liberalization.

Chapter 16, by Thomas Rutherford, David Tarr, and Oleksandr Shepotylo, explores one of the key trade-growth linkages in the case of Russia. They focus particularly on the potential for international trade and foreign direct investment (FDI) in the services sector to bring new varieties of goods and new technologies to Russia, thereby enhancing productivity, generating economic growth, and lifting households out of poverty. The role of services sector reforms—an important aspect of future WTO agreements—is often neglected in analyses of trade and poverty. Yet, as Mattoo, Rathindran, and Subramamian (2001) demonstrate, such reforms, particularly in telecommunications and financial services, can boost long-run growth rates. The chapter on Russia begins by analyzing the Doha scenario explored by other authors. The impact of this scenario is mixed, but most of the households experience a small welfare loss. The full-liberalization scenario shifts the distribution of welfare impacts in the positive direction, so that most Russian households now gain and poverty falls, but again the changes are quite modest.

The authors then turn to domestic reforms in the services sectors—a part of the economy that the DDA is not expected to affect to any great degree, but an area that is currently receiving a great deal of attention in the context of Russia's WTO accession negotiations. The authors show that the liberalization of barriers to FDI greatly enhances the potential welfare gains. The main vehicle for this enhancement is the provision of new varieties of services, which improve productivity, not only in the services sector, but also in services-using sectors as well. Indeed, the added productivity boost from the elimination of services FDI barriers alone is sufficient to generate a per capita income increase of 5.3 percent, ensuring that virtually all Russian households benefit from the reform. There are two lessons to be drawn from this work. First, productivity growth is essential for generating widespread gains from trade reforms, and second, one way of obtaining such growth is through ambitious services sector reforms, such as those that have been a part of recent WTO accession negotiations, most notably in China, but also now in Russia.[6]

The final chapter in the book provides an integrated, global analysis of the potential for multilateral trade reforms to reduce poverty in the long run (by 2015). In this chapter, Kym Anderson, Will Martin, and Dominique van der Mensbrugghe use the latest version of the World Bank's LINKAGE model, along with the same GTAP dataset used in chapters 3 and 14, to project the growth path of the global economy from 2001 to 2015. They find that trade reforms have a modest impact on capital accumulation and thereby boost the projected global gains from multilateral trade reform by about one-quarter. However, they devote most of their attention to the potential impacts of increased trade on productivity growth. (It should be noted, however, that the authors focus entirely on productivity growth associated with increased manufactures exports, not services trade or investment as in the Russia study).

There is now a rapidly growing literature on the impacts of trade and trade policy reforms on productivity, and Anderson, Martin, and van der Mensbrugghe draw on this in their chapter. When they incorporate the additional impact of openness on labor productivity, they find a substantial boost to the global gains (40 percent larger gains in 2015) with a disproportionate share accruing to the South and East Asia developing economies. The poverty impacts of these alternative scenarios are elicited by first estimating the income gains to the poorest households and then applying to this an estimated elasticity of poverty reduction with respect to income growth at the poverty line. Instead of using real per capita income for the region as a whole, the authors use the unskilled wage rate, deflated by an index of food and clothing prices, reflecting the dual facts that the main endowment of the poor is their own labor and they spend the bulk of their income on nondurable goods. Another critical assumption is that the poor do not pay taxes, so that any increase in tax rates required to offset forgone tariff revenues does not affect them.

Applying these estimates of earnings at the poverty line to the poverty elasticity of income in each region, which varies depending on the regional distribution of income, the authors predict the extent of poverty reduction in developing countries. Of course, this depends on the poverty line. It also depends on the baseline poverty projections, which decline considerably between 2001 and 2015. For US$1 per day poverty, the estimated reduction in 2015, in the absence of additional productivity gains, is 2.5 million people for the Doha scenario and 31.9 million people for full liberalization. When applied to current (2001) poverty levels, the authors' calculations result in poverty reductions of 9.7 million and 80.5 million people under the Doha and full-liberalization scenarios, respectively. The 2015 poverty reductions are increased to 4.3 million and 43.5 million, for Doha and full liberalization, respectively, when productivity gains are factored in. For US$2 per day poverty, the reduction in the number of the poor is larger, but the percentage reduction is smaller (see table 1.1).[7]

Based on the Doha–full liberalization comparison, it is clear that the (rather ambitious) Doha scenarios capture only a relatively small portion of the total poverty reduction possible under trade reforms. When the authors consider the Doha-all scenario, they find that implementing deeper cuts in the developing countries enhances the poverty outcome, nearly doubling the poverty reduction obtained under the central Doha scenario. This finding reinforces Ivanic's conclusions, in chapter 14, with respect to the beneficial poverty impacts of developing-country tariff cuts under the DDA. It is also hardly surprising in light of the increasing importance of south-south trade and the relatively high level of developing country tariffs, as reported in chapter 3.

Another important finding from the Anderson, Martin, and van der Mensbrugghe chapter relates to sensitive agricultural products, as well as special products, in developing countries. Industrial countries have proposed that certain sensitive products be exempt from steep tariff reductions, instead being liberalized through a combination of quota expansion and tariff reduction. In chapter 2, Anderson and Martin suggest that a cut in bound tariffs might be most effective, and they consider the case in which these commodities, limited to 2 percent of industrial-country tariff lines in agriculture, face a modest 15 percent cut in bound tariffs. In the case of developing countries, an additional category of exemptions is provided for in the Framework Agreement. These special products, identified "based on criteria of food security, livelihood security and rural development needs," will be eligible for more flexible treatment as well (WTO 2004). Allowing for this additional category, the scenario outlined by Anderson and Martin permits developing countries to exempt 4 percent of agricultural tariff lines from the tiered cuts, facing instead just a 15 percent cut in bound tariffs.

Of course, both special and sensitive products invariably have the highest tariffs, so that exempting them can make a big difference in the results. The authors find that merely introducing these modest exemptions for a maximum of 2 percent of the industrial tariff lines in agriculture (4 percent for developing countries) virtually eliminates the poverty impacts of a Doha agreement. Therefore, to have a significant poverty impact, the DDA must not only have ambitious numerical targets, it must also seek to limit—indeed, eliminate—the use of sensitive and special product exemptions.[8]

Summary and Conclusions

Assessing the impact of multilateral trade liberalization on poverty is a challenging assignment. As Winters (2000, p. 43) notes, "Tracing the links between trade and poverty is going to be a detailed and frustrating task, for much of what one wishes to know is just unknown. It will also become obvious that most of the links are very case specific." This book represents an attempt to make known a few more of these unknown linkages. As such, the approach has been heterogeneous and opportunistic, calling on experts in this field to undertake in-depth studies in countries for which appropriate data and analytical infrastructure are available. All of this research capacity has been directed toward the analysis of the trade policy question that is central in many policy makers' minds today: What are the likely poverty impacts of a successful DDA? And what elements could be added to enhance this outcome?

As noted previously, the approach taken in this book ensures consistency of methods in the global analysis of the multilateral trade reform scenarios, as well as in the methodology for incorporating these results into the national analyses. However, at the country level, different authors have had the liberty to take a variety of approaches depending on the particular circumstances facing their countries and their own analytical interests. This is why there are two studies of the Brazilian economy—one of which focuses on near-term impacts across heterogeneous individuals, households, and regions in Brazil, and one of which focuses on longer-term impacts, particularly in light of the barriers to intersectoral labor mobility. In the case of China, one study focuses on market failure at the village level, and another focuses on labor mobility at the national level. Similarly, there are differences in methodology taken across country case studies, with a mix of partial and general equilibrium approaches, and static and dynamic frameworks. The base years differ across studies, and even the poverty lines chosen are not uniform across all studies. Their findings, therefore, are not strictly comparable. Finally, because the choice of countries to include in this volume was made on the basis of preexisting work that laid a foundation for the current research project, this is not a random sample of developing countries. With these qualifications in mind, let us take an overview of the findings.

Table 1.1 summarizes the poverty results from each of the national studies (subnational studies are not reported here) for both the Doha and full-liberalization scenarios, distinguished by length of run for the analysis. The long-term studies factor in the impact of trade policy on investment and capital accumulation—and in the case of the global analysis, productivity as well—whereas the short-term studies do not. The national poverty changes are reported in two different ways: first, as the change in number of persons in poverty, and second, as the percentage change in the poverty headcount. Thus, a negative number in table 1.1 means that the number of poor has fallen as a result of multilateral trade reform, and a positive number indicates that the number of poor has risen.

Table 1.1 suggests several tentative conclusions. First, the near-term analyses are mixed in terms of their outcomes, with poverty rising in some cases and falling in others. We view this diversity as correct and as a strength of the country-based approach. Even setting aside the methodological differences between studies, the case specificity alluded to above leads us to expect differences between countries' interests in the DDA, and the chapters explain exactly why this is so.

The largest poverty reductions in table 1.1, in both absolute and relative terms, are in countries with agricultural export potential to the markets that liberalize most (that is, East Asia and Europe). The strong poverty reduction in Brazil is driven by increased agricultural production, which tends to be concentrated in regions with relatively higher poverty incidence. In China, the poverty reduction is fueled by increased agricultural exports to the highly protected agricultural markets of East Asia. However, the poverty increases tend to be in countries that are net importers of agricultural products (for example, Bangladesh) and that may eventually benefit from preferential market access (for example, Mozambique). Thus, the strongest difference between countries concerns their exposure to the shocks generated by the DDA. Even holding this constant, however, poverty impacts can vary with, for example, the degree of transmission of world prices to rural households, the barriers to the mobility of workers between sectors of the economy, and the incidence of national tax instruments used to replace lost tariff revenue. Taken as a whole, the number of countries where poverty declines under the Doha scenario is about the same as the number of countries where it falls, although looking at the absolute number of poor, it can be seen that poverty declines in several of the most populous countries (Brazil, China, and Indonesia) and therefore declines overall in this nonrandom sample of countries.

As for the long-run results, all of the studies that consider the impact of trade on capital accumulation, productivity, or both predict a reduction in poverty

Table 1.1. Poverty Impacts of a Prospective DDA

Country (chapter number)	Change in poverty headcount							
	Near term: fixed capital				Long term: investment impacts			
	Doha		Full liberalization		Doha		Full liberalization	
	1,000 people	%	1,000 people	%	1,000 people	%	1,000 people	%
Bangladesh (15)	38	0.3	1,354	1.1	0	0	-5,758	-4.6
Brazil (7)	-236	-0.4	-482	-0.8				
Brazil (9)					-380	-1.1	-1,030	-2.9
Cameroon (12)	-22	-0.4	303	4.8				
China (10)	-4,590	-1.1	-8,271	-2.0	-5,378	-1.3	-11,170	-2.7
Indonesia (11)	-48	-0.1	-1,384	-3.5				
Mexico (4)	4	0.0	127	1.0				
Mozambique (5)	27	0.3	60	0.6				
Philippines (13)	12	0.0	-7	0.0				
Russia (16)	209	0.9	-122	-0.5				
All developing countries (17)								
US$1 per day:								
2001[a]	-7,000		-66,300		-9,700		-80,500	
2015[b]	-1,700	-0.3	-23,800	-3.8	-2,500	-0.4	-31,900	-5.1
US$2 per day:								
2001	-8,700		-103,900		-12,600		-123,200	
2015	-4,100	-0.2	-52,300	-2.7	-6,200	-0.3	-65,600	-3.3
Productivity effects added[c]								
US$1 per day:								
2001					-20,400		-126,500	
2015					-4,300	-0.6	-43,500	-6.5
US$2 per day:								
2001					-29,600		-193,200	
2015					-12,100	-0.6	-94,700	-4.9

Source: Studies reported in this book.

a. Based on percentage changes in 2015, but applied to 2001 poverty headcount.

b. Computed for the year 2015 when the total number of poor is projected to be significantly lower.

c. Productivity gains from increased openness to trade apply to both manufactures and agriculture. (Earlier versions assumed only productivity gains in manufactures. See chapter 17 for details.)

(with the exception of Doha-Bangladesh, where there is no long-run measurable impact). Trade stimulates investment, investment stimulates growth, and growth reduces poverty. When productivity impacts are also considered (bottom group of rows in table 1.1), this effect is even stronger. This distinction between the short run and the long run is particularly striking in the case of the full-liberalization scenarios for Bangladesh, where the short-run impacts of trade reform translate into a rise in headcount poverty, and the long-run impacts of trade reform suggest a substantial decline.

In addition to the quantitative summary reported in table 1.1, the research documented in this book has generated some additional insights. First, the liberalization targets under the DDA have to be ambitious if the round is to have a measurable impact on world markets and hence poverty. Second, assuming an ambitious DDA, the near-term poverty impacts are likely to be mixed.

The analysis suggests, however, that countries can enhance the impact on poverty by pursuing complementary domestic reforms to enable households to take advantage of market opportunities created by the DDA.[9] These include improved infrastructure and the reform of domestic marketing institutions to improve price transmission to rural areas, rural education reform to enhance labor mobility between the farm and nonfarm sectors, and extension outreach to permit farmers to take advantage of new export opportunities opened up by the DDA.

Of course, sustained poverty reduction depends on stimulating economic growth. Here, the impact of the DDA on productivity is critical. Empirical evidence suggests that increased merchandise trade will likely bring with it productivity gains through disciplinary effects of import competition on domestic firms as well as, possibly, learning by doing on the export side. To fully realize potential productivity gains, however, trade reforms need to be far reaching and should include reducing barriers to services trade and investment in addition to merchandise tariffs, which lie mainly or wholly outside the DDA. Thus, even if the DDA is very successful, a major agenda of unilateral reform and further rounds of multilateral talks remains. Only through such comprehensive reforms can long-term growth and poverty reduction be ensured.

Notes

1. The forthcoming book, *Globalization and Poverty*, edited by Ann Harrison, adopts the same strategy, combining a set of cross-country econometric studies with several individual country case studies.

2. For example, a tariff of, say, 100 percent is cut by 66–95 percent: [15%*0.45 + (90-15)%*0.70 + (100-90)%*0.75]. Applying the cuts at the margin avoids the discontinuities implied by the July Framework.

3. Of course, some assumption about tax replacement is required in each of the studies in this volume. The standard assumption used is one of replacement of lost tariff revenue with an equiproportional (distribution-neutral) income tax. Although not a realistic assumption in most cases, it facilitates the comparability of results across regions. In those cases where country case study authors have emphasized the treatment of the domestic tax system, they have been encouraged to explore the impacts of replacing the lost tariff revenue with the most likely instrument (usually the value added tax).

4. Dimaranan, Hertel, and Keeney (2004) demonstrate that many developing countries have become much more dependent on imports of subsidized crops from OECD countries over the past 40 years. Removing these subsidies will obviously have an adverse effect in the near term.

5. In Ivanic's analysis, most of these gains come from improved market access to other developing countries. This is due to the relatively high optimal tariff in the underlying GTAP model, which makes unilateral reform relatively unattractive (see also chapter 3). This implies that to reap the benefits, developing countries must liberalize together—the multilateral aspect of reform is important.

6. Similarly dominant welfare effects from services reforms have been found in the case of China's WTO accession agreement (Walmsley, Hertel, and Ianchovichina Forthcoming).

7. These estimates of poverty reduction are considerably smaller than earlier predictions using the World Bank's LINKAGE model. The difference is due to the fact that these estimates are based on the most recent (Version 6) GTAP database, which is further updated to account for EU enlargement as well as the WTO accession of China and others. These recent trade reforms have reduced the overall level of protection worldwide, thereby lessening the gains from reform. In addition, the Version 6 database has a complete treatment of preferential tariffs, including the EU's 2001 Everything but Arms initiative, which means that gains to the LDCs from trade reform are considerably reduced.

8. It is not argued that individual developing countries couldn't improve their poverty outcomes by exempting a few special products from liberalization. But given the multitude of products and countries, such cases cannot be identified here. Besides, it is implausible that developing countries could leave the exemptions door open in any significant fashion without industrialized countries also squeezing their sensitive products through the same opening.

9. The volume edited by Harrison (Forthcoming) reaches a similar conclusion, based on a set of ex post analyses of trade reform and poverty.

References

Arndt, Channing, Henning Tarp Jensen, Sherman Robinson, and Finn Tarp. 2000. "Marketing Margins and Agricultural Technology in Mozambique." *Journal of Development Studies* 37 (1): 121–37.

Francois, J. F., and C. R. Shiells. 1994. "Applied General Equilibrium Models of North American Free Trade: An Introduction." In *Modelling Trade Policy: Applied General Equilibrium Assessments of North American Free Trade*, 3–46. Cambridge: Cambridge University Press.

Harrison, G. W., T. F. Rutherford, D. G. Tarr, and A. Gurgel. 2003. "Regional, Multilateral, and Unilateral Trade Policies of Mercosur for Growth and Poverty Reduction in Brazil." Policy Research Working Paper 3051, World Bank, Washington, DC.

Hertel, Thomas W., Maros Ivanic, Paul V. Preckel, and John Cranfield. 2004. "The Earnings Effects of Multilateral Trade Liberalization: Implications for Poverty." *World Bank Economic Review* 18 (2): 205–36.

Hertel, Thomas W., and Will Martin. 2000. "Liberalizing Agriculture and Manufactures in a Millennium Round: Implications for Developing Countries." *World Economy* 23: 455–70.

Jorgenson, D. W. 1984. "Economic Methods for Applied General Equilibrium Analysis." In *Applied General Equilibrium Analysis*, ed. H. E. Scharf and J. B. Shoven, 139–203. Cambridge: Cambridge University Press.

Kehoe, Timothy J. 2005. "An Evaluation of the Performance of Applied General Equilibrium Models of the Impact of NAFTA." In *Frontiers in Applied General Equilibrium Modeling: Essays in Honor of*

Herbert Scarf, ed. Timothy J. Kehoe, T. N. Srinivasan, and John Whalley, 341–77. Cambridge: Cambridge University Press.

Mattoo, A., R. Rathindran, and A. Subramamian. 2001. "Measuring Services Trade Liberalization and Its Impact on Economic Growth." Policy Research Working Paper 2655, World Bank, Washington, DC.

McKitrick, R. R. 1998. "The Econometric Critique of Computable General Equilibrium Modeling: The Role of Functional Forms." *Economic Modeling* 15 (4): 543–73.

Valdes, A., and A. McCalla. 2004. "Where the Interests of Developing Countries Converge and Diverge." In *Agriculture in the New Trade Agenda*, ed. M. Ingco and L. A. Winters, 136–150. Cambridge: Cambridge University Press.

Walmsley, T., T. W. Hertel, and E. I. Ianchovichina. Forthcoming. "Assessing the Impact of China's WTO Accession on Investment." *Pacific Economic Review*.

Winters, L. A. 2000. "Trade and Poverty: Is There a Connection?" In *Trade, Income Disparity and Poverty*, ed. D. Ben David, H. Nordstrom and L. A. Winters, Special Study No. 5. Geneva: WTO.

Winters, L. A., N. McCulloch, and A. McKay. 2004. "Trade Liberalisation and Poverty: The Evidence So Far." *Journal of Economic Literature* 42: 72–115.

World Bank. 2004. *Global Economic Prospects 2004—Realizing the Development Promise of the Doha Agenda*. Washington, DC: World Bank.

WTO. 2004. *Doha Work Programme: Decision Adopted by the General Council on 1 August, 2004*. Geneva: WTO.

2

SCENARIOS FOR GLOBAL TRADE REFORM

Kym Anderson and Will Martin

Introduction

Since the failure of the Trade Ministerial meeting in Seattle in late 1999, the WTO membership has stressed continually that the organization's first multilateral trade negotiation round will have development at its heart (WTO 2001, 2004b). Simultaneously, the United Nations has emphasized that trade reform is crucial for achieving its first Millennium Development Goal of halving, between 1990 and 2015, the proportion of people earning less than US$1 a day (Zedillo, Messerlin, and Nielson 2005).

This chapter examines the decisions that have been made since the launch of the WTO's DDA in late 2001, and it draws out their implications for genuine trade reform. A set of numerical scenarios is developed to provide the basis for exploring the DDA's potential impacts on the economy and on poverty in the various developing countries considered in subsequent chapters.

The chapter begins by examining what is at stake. It shows where the major potential gains from complete trade liberalization would come from in terms of sectors and, within agriculture, in terms of the three key classes of policy measures (import restrictions, export subsidies, and domestic support). How far the DDA will go toward reaching that potential is then explored. A sensible starting point is to begin with what the Doha Declaration and the Doha Work Program (DWP) Framework promise in terms of generalities and then examine the specifics of the annexes to that decision of August 1, 2004, beginning with agriculture and then turning to nonagricultural trade reforms and the special provisions for developing countries. These are then brought together to provide a series of overall Doha scenarios, the world market effects of which can be estimated using global trade models. These world market effects, outlined in chapter 3, will then form the basis for the individual country case studies of potential poverty impacts of the DDA.

What Is at Stake?

Merchandise trade barriers have come down a long way in developed countries since the signing of the General Agreement on Tariffs and Trade (GATT) in 1947, with the notable exceptions of agriculture and textiles. Services trade barriers remain high, though, and many merchandise trade barriers in developing countries have only recently begun to be lowered. What would happen if all those barriers and agricultural subsidies were to be removed? In particular, how important are the various types of barriers currently in place?

Those questions are addressed by Hertel and Keeney (2006), using a medium-run closure of the GTAP–AGR model[1] in comparative static, perfectly competitive mode. That is, they assume full employment and partially mobile factors (with some segmentation between agriculture and nonagriculture), no imperfect competition or economies of scale, and no dynamic gains from trade (drawing on Hertel 1997). The model uses Version 6.05 of the GTAP database (see www.gtap.org), which in turn owes much to the protection estimates in the MAcMap database assembled by the Centre d'Etudes Prospectives et d'Informations Internationales (CEPII) in Paris (Bouët and others 2004). That database is far superior for present purposes to earlier versions in that it includes agricultural tariff rate quotas (TRQs), ad valorem equivalents of specific tariffs, all preferential tariffs (reciprocal, as in free-trade areas, as well as nonreciprocal, as in various developing country preference schemes), and is compatible with measures of bound tariffs which we obtain from Behir, Jean, and Laborde.

Shifting to zero agricultural subsidies and complete free trade in goods and services from that post–Uruguay Round base is conservatively estimated by Hertel and Keeney to boost comparative static, global welfare by US$151 billion per year.[2] Developing countries would enjoy a disproportionately large share of those gains (more than one-quarter, well above their one-sixth share of global GDP).[3] The reason is twofold: they have relatively high tariffs themselves and, more important (as discussed see below), their exporters face much higher tariffs than do exporters from the high-income countries themselves. These full-liberalization numbers provide a benchmark against which to compare the gains likely from any partial reform to emerge from the Doha Round.

What are the policy measures contributing most to those potential gains from full trade liberalization? Table 2.1 focuses just on merchandise trade policies. It decomposes them into measures affecting markets for agriculture and food, for textiles and clothing, and for other goods.

Table 2.1. Sectoral Contributions to Comparative Static Estimates of Economic Welfare Gains from Completely Removing Merchandise Trade Barriers Globally, Post-Uruguay Round (percent of total global gains)

Benefiting region	Agriculture and food	Textiles and clothing	Other merchandise	All merchandise
High-income countries[a]	52	1	21	74
Low- and middle-income countries	14	10	2	26
All countries	66	11	23	100

Source: Drawn from several tables in Hertel and Keeney (2006).

a. "High-income" here refers to developed countries, the four East Asian "tiger" economies, and all European transition economies.

The results in table 2.1 are striking. Although agriculture contributes only 4 percent to global GDP, policies for that sector are responsible for an enormous two-thirds of the global cost of merchandise trade protection. More than three-quarters of that contribution is due to high-income countries' policies, so not surprisingly, high-income countries would gain most from the removal of farm programs—but developing countries also gain a sizable portion. Indeed, agriculture would contribute more than half the total gains to developing countries from removing all merchandise trade restrictions globally (14 of its total 26 percentage points).

Second in importance is textiles and clothing liberalization. Although it would contribute only one-fifth as much to global welfare as agricultural reform, its contribution to welfare in developing countries would be considerably greater, equal to more than two-thirds of that from farm trade reform and accounting for most of developing countries' gains from nonfarm merchandise reform (middle row of table 2.1).

What would this freeing up of merchandise trade do to developing country exports? It turns out that every region in the Hertel-Keeney study would expand its exports of both farm and textile products by more than 10 percent, with the exception of Argentina's and Brazil's textile exports, which fall slightly in the wake of those countries' large increase in farm exports. Global annual exports of those two product groups each expand by about one-fifth in real terms. For developing countries, the increase is US$48 billion in agricultural goods and US$69 billion in textiles and clothing, valued at 2001 base prices. Other merchandise exports grow by only 5 percent globally, but that still represents an additional US$50 billion per year for developing countries, with only Brazil and Indonesia not enjoying an increase. Unsurprisingly, exports of textiles and clothing grow more for developing than for high-income countries, but in the case of farm products, they each expand by a similar amount (almost US$50 billion per year). The changes for individual developing countries and regions are summarized in table 2.2.

What happens when services trade reform also is included? Estimates are very much more difficult to obtain for this category, especially when it potentially involves FDI (commercial presence) and temporary labor migration (movement of natural persons). Hertel and Keeney (2006) do not attempt to include the latter services,[4] but they do provide an estimate (based on distortion measures from Francois, van Meijl, and Tongeren [2005]) for direct trade in a few services,

Table 2.2. Change in Exports Valued at 2001 Base Prices from Completely Removing Merchandise Trade Barriers Globally, Post-Uruguay Round (2001 US$ billions)

Country/region	Agriculture and food	Textiles and clothing	Other merchandise
China	7.7	36.7	7.8
Indonesia	1.1	3.2	-0.3
Other Southeast Asia	6.7	8.8	6.5
India	6.0	4.8	14.6
Other South Asia	1.3	4.2	1.3
Argentina	1.5	-0.2	1.4
Brazil	8.3	-0.6	-0.7
Other Latin America	5.6	3.9	4.9
North Africa and Middle East	2.2	7.4	10.4
South African Customs Union	1.8	0.1	0.2
Other Southeastern Africa[a]	1.3	-0.0	0.4
Other Sub-Saharan Africa	1.8	0.5	3.3
All low- and middle-income countries	48.3	68.7	49.9
All high-income countries[b]	47.7	18.3	178.7
All countries	96.0	87.0	228.6

Source: Summarized from Hertel and Keeney (2006, table 6).

a. Botswana, Madagascar, Malawi, Mozambique, Tanzania, Uganda, Zambia, and Zimbabwe.

b. "High-income" here refers to developed countries, the four East Asian "tiger" economies, and all European transition economies.

Table 2.3. Sectoral and Regional Contributions to Comparative Static Estimates of Economic Welfare Gains from Completely Removing Merchandise and Services Trade Barriers Globally, Post-Uruguay Round (percent of total global gains)

Liberalizing region	Agriculture and food				Textiles and other services			sectors
	Market access	Domestic support	Export subsidies	Total agriculture	Clothing	Merchandise	Services	
High-income countries[a]	30	2	1	33	3	6		
Low- and middle-income countries	4	0	0	4	4	6		
All countries	34	2	1	37	7	12	44	100

Source: Drawn from several tables in Hertel and Keeney (2005).

a. "High-income" here refers to developed countries, the four East Asian "tiger" economies, and all European transition economies.

including transportation, trade, and business services.[5] Table 2.3 shows the huge potential importance of liberalizing services trade. Even with just this small subset of services included, they enhance considerably the potential gains from trade reform, accounting for 44 percent of those total gains from goods and services reforms. That exceeds agriculture's share of that total, namely 37 percent (with other merchandise accounting for just 19 percent).

Table 2.3 also exposes the relative importance of the three separate pillars of agricultural support programs: import market access inhibited by tariffs and TRQs, domestic support measures, and export subsidies. According to these results, import market access measures deliver by far the greatest prospects for gains from agricultural reform—12 times the combined contribution of domestic support and export subsidies. Farm export subsidies are now of relatively minor importance globally, thanks to their cuts following the Uruguay Round. But developing countries would lose slightly from their removal because as a group they are net importers of the subsidized program commodities.[6] The loss is equal to -0.7 percent of the global gains included in table 2.3 (or -0.8 percent if implicit export subsidies in the form of food aid and export credits are also included). All developing countries would gain from the removal of developed-country domestic subsidies. Four West African countries made headlines by stressing the plight of their cotton producers—that cotton has been explicitly targeted for domestic subsidy cuts in the Doha Round, even though the potential contribution to global welfare is only a small fraction of the gains from liberalizing all farm subsidies and tariffs. This again underlies the importance of making each of these reforms part of a comprehensive liberalization package so that there is scope for all countries to gain.

Because of the differing signs of the welfare effects of the various policy measures, it is necessary to look more closely to see if there are some countries that could lose from a move to free trade. Hertel and Keeney (2006, table 2.11) show that all the big developing countries would gain from complete global farm trade reform. But in North Africa and the Middle East, as well as in Sub-Saharan Africa (other than the southeastern African countries separately identified in the tables), there are more losses than gains. For some of those countries, this is because the prices of their imports would rise (for example, importers of temperate foods no longer to be dumped on international markets), but more commonly it is because the prices of their agricultural exports fall (for example, because their tariff preference margin disappears as developed countries move to zero tariffs; another reason for the losses under free trade is that they and their neighbors expand exports so much as to depress their price in international markets enough to offset efficiency gains from their own reform). Likewise, Hertel and Keeney show some farm-exporting developing countries (Argentina, Brazil and Sub-Saharan Africa other than South Africa) losing from textiles and clothing reform for terms of trade reasons. The terms of trade also explain the loss to smaller Latin American countries from other merchandise trade reform. But for services, each of the regions shown would gain. When all sectors are considered together, the only region not shown to benefit from a move to free trade is Sub-Saharan Africa other than the identified countries of southeastern Africa. But even that latter group loses less than US$1 billion per year, which could be easily offset by extra foreign aid. And the Hertel-Keeney study shows that their loss becomes a gain as soon as some trade facilitation is provided. Whether poor people *within* those or other developing countries would gain or lose is not answered directly in that study, but is instead the subject of chapters 4–17 of this volume.

Given these results, a key question is: how close can the Doha Round come to realizing this potential for the global economy and especially for developing countries? In addressing that question, it needs to be kept in mind from the outset that WTO trade negotiators are focusing on reductions not to the applied tariffs used in the Hertel-Keeney analysis but rather to members' legally bound tariffs, export subsidies, and domestic support commitments. These are higher than applied rates in nearly all countries, but especially so in most developing countries. Hence, if cuts to bound rates are sufficiently small, or the gap between bound and applied rates sufficiently large, no actual reform need take place from an agreed set of bound rate reductions. Before turning to empirical modeling results that bear on this issue, it is necessary to first consider what the agreed framework and modalities for the negotiations are likely to deliver, particularly in the key policy areas identified in table 2.3.

What the Doha Declaration and July 2004 Framework Decision Promise

The DDA, as outlined in the Doha Ministerial Declaration of November 2001, is unequivocal in its aim to ensure that developing countries benefit from this first multilateral trade negotiation since the formation of the WTO. On its first page, the declaration states:

> "International trade can play a major role in the promotion of economic development and the alleviation of poverty. We recognize the need for all our peoples to benefit from the increased opportunities and welfare gains that the multilateral trading system generates. The majority of WTO Members are developing countries. We seek to place their needs and interests at the heart of the Work Programme adopted in this Declaration. Recalling the Preamble to the Marrakesh Agreement, we shall continue to make positive efforts designed to ensure that developing countries, and especially the least-developed among them, secure a share in the growth of world trade commensurate with the needs of their economic development. In this context, enhanced market access, balanced

rules, and well targeted, sustainably financed technical assistance and capacity-building programmes have important roles to play.

We recognize the particular vulnerability of the least-developed countries and the special structural difficulties they face in the global economy. We are committed to addressing the marginalization of least-developed countries in international trade and to improving their effective participation in the multilateral trading system. We recall the commitments made by Ministers at our meetings in Marrakesh, Singapore and Geneva, and by the international community at the Third UN Conference on Least-Developed Countries in Brussels, to help least-developed countries secure beneficial and meaningful integration into the multilateral trading system and the global economy. We are determined that the WTO will play its part in building effectively on these commitments under the Work Programme we are establishing." (WTO 2001)

Since that meeting in late 2001, WTO members have sought to implement those commitments. However, the following Trade Ministerial meeting, in Cancún in September 2003, ended with acrimony and without an agreement on how to proceed. At Cancún, developing countries made it abundantly clear that further progress would not be possible without a commitment by developed countries to significantly lower their import barriers and agricultural subsidies (including importantly for cotton, despite its relatively minor role in developed country agriculture, see Sumner [2006]). An intense period of consultations in July 2004 ended with a decision on how the DWP should proceed (WTO 2004b). The decision again stresses the importance of keeping development at the heart of the DDA and particularly stresses agricultural reform as key to that. In its annexes, the decision provides guidance as to how a Doha agreement might be structured, with frameworks for establishing modalities for agriculture and nonagricultural market access, and for negotiations on trade facilitation, as well as providing recommendations for trade in services. The analysis in this chapter begins with the three agricultural pillars.

Agricultural Market Access

The impacts of agricultural trade reforms cannot be understood without a detailed analysis of the structure of the protection to which they are being applied. For this analysis, the MAcMap database developed by the International Trade Centre (ITC), Geneva, and Paris-based CEPII. The latest version of the database covers tariffs for 2001 and takes into account ad valorem tariffs, specific tariffs, and tariff preferences (Bouët and others 2004). Bound tariffs have also been prepared on a comparable basis and documented in Bchir, Jean, and Laborde (forthcoming). Some important presimulation changes were required before the Doha analysis, including modification of China's tariffs to take account of its WTO accession commitments, the phase-in of remaining commitments from the Uruguay Round (especially the elimination of quotas on textiles and clothing trade), and changes due to the accession in April 2004 of 10 new members to the EU. Fortunately, the MAcMap database permitted isolation of these changes so that the model-based analysis could implement these "pre-experiment" shocks before proceeding with the simulation of the DDA.

Overview of Agricultural Tariffs

A critical issue in analyzing tariff protection in agriculture has to do with the treatment of TRQs. Here, the effective tariff assumed to be applied on any given TRQ commodity depends on whether the quota is filled or not. If the quota is less than 90 percent filled, the in-quota tariff is assumed to apply on these commodities. If the quota is between 90 and 99 percent filled, the effective tariff is assumed to be the average of the in- and the out-of-quota tariff. If the quota is more than 99 percent filled, then the out-of-quota tariff is applied.[7]

Another critical issue has to do with the role of specific tariffs (for example, US $10 per ton), which cannot be aggregated and used in global modeling exercises without first being converted to ad valorem equivalent form. To do so requires an assumption about the price of the product being traded. In the MAcMap database, the associated prices for a given commodity are allowed to vary between developed, developing, and LDCs. And because poor countries tend to export low-value products, the specific tariffs affect a larger share of their export value.

Using the MAcMap database, table 2.4 shows that specific tariffs are indeed quite important. The global average tariff of 17 percent is made up of 11 percentage points from ad valorem tariffs and an additional 6 percentage points from the ad valorem equivalents of non–ad valorem measures. However, there are large variations between countries and country groups around these levels. For developed countries as a group, the average tariff of 14 percent is made up of only 4 percent contributed by ad valorem tariffs and 10 percent from the ad valorem equivalents of specific, mixed, or compound duties. As noted previously, this is a particular concern to developing countries, because specific tariffs tend to impose greater burdens on low-income country exports. Within the developed country group, there is considerable variation in average tariffs, with Japan having an average agricultural tariff of 36 percent, mostly derived from non–ad valorem tariffs, and the European Free Trade Association (EFTA) having a tariff of 29 percent. The average agricultural tariff in the EU is considerably lower, at 12 percent; in the United States and Australia, they are lower again at 3 percent.

Developing countries, at 20 percent, have a higher average tariff than developed countries, but only 2 percentage points of this protection is provided by specific tariffs. Average tariffs are extremely high in the Republic of Korea,[8] at 94 percent, and also high in China, India, Pakistan, and Sub-Saharan Africa. The net agricultural exporting Mercado Común del Sur (Mercosur) region has quite low tariffs, at an average of 5 percent. Interestingly, both LDCs as a group, and Sub-Saharan African LDCs in particular, have relatively low tariffs, consistent with the tendency noted in the political economy literature for poor countries to have low agricultural protection (see, for example, Anderson and Hayami [1986]).

Another feature of agricultural protection evident in table 2.4 is the height of the barriers by countries protecting with TRQs. The analysis by de Gorter and Kliauga (2006) indicates that these products cover 20 percent of agricultural tariff lines in the countries using TRQs and 52 percent of the value of production.[9] The fact that average applied tariffs on these commodities are so high, although some imports are permitted at lower in-quota tariffs, is striking testimony to the importance of protection on these commodities. Given their large import shares in countries such as the Republic of Korea, and their extremely high tariff levels, it is clear that protection on these commodities constitutes a very important part of total agricultural protection in developed countries and in those developing countries using these measures. Had these commodities been automatically treated as sensitive products, as was proposed in WTO (2004a), it is clear that a very large share of total protection would have been shielded from liberalization.

Another key element of the geography of market access is the relationship between applied and bound tariffs. The higher are bindings relative to applied rates, the larger the reductions in bound rates that must be made before applied rates change to improve market access. The gap between applied and bound duties has two origins: the binding overhang, which is the gap between bound and most-favored-nation (MFN) tariffs, and preferential arrangements, which cause a difference between the MFN and applied rate.[10]

It is widely known that there was substantial binding overhang in many developing countries after the Uruguay Round. Developing countries had the right to set their tariff bindings without reference to previous levels of protection, under the so-called ceiling binding option. Many developing countries used this right to set their bindings at high—and frequently uniform—levels, such as 150 or 250 percent. The effects are evident in table 2.5, where the bound tariff in developing countries is 2.4 times the average applied rate.

While developed countries did not have the right to use ceiling bindings, negotiators used a highly protected base period (1986–88) and many members used so-called "dirty tariffication" to set their tariff rates well above the previously prevailing

Table 2.4. Key Features of Applied Agricultural Tariffs, by Country and Region, 2001 (trade weighted averages, percent)

Country/ region	Overall average	Ad valorem tariffs	Specific tariffs	Tariff for TRQs	TRQ share
Australia	3	2	1	1	6
Bangladesh	14	14	0	0	0
Cameroon	17	17	0	0	0
Canada	10	8	1	31	21
China	39	39	0	6	22
Indonesia	32	5	1	14	12
Japan	36	10	26	103	9
Korea, Rep. of	94	94	0	226	39
Mexico	11	11	0	34	24
Pakistan	30	10	21	0	0
India	55	54	1	0	0
Turkey	14	14	0	0	0
United States	3	1	2	11	17
Mercosur	13	13	0	7	3
EFTA	29	2	27	58	34
Association of Southeast Asian Nations (ASEAN)	11	8	4	32	8
Philippines	47	10	0	30	7
Sub-Saharan LDCs	13	13	0	0	0
Other Sub-Saharan Africa	26	26	0	0	0
Maghreb	18	16	2	39	14
South African Customs Union	13	4	9	16	56
EU15	12	3	9	36	22
Russia	13	12	1	0	0
Developed countries	14	4	10	37	17
Low- and middle-income countries	21	19	2	64	12
LDCs	13	13	0	0	0
All countries	17	11	6	47	14

Source: Jean, Laborde, and Martin (2006).

**Table 2.5. Bound and Applied Agricultural Tariff Rates,
by Country and Region, 2001 (trade weighted
averages, percent)**

Country/region	Bound tariff	MFN tariff	Applied tariff	CV[a] bound	CV MFN applied[a]
Australia	6	4	3	2	2
Bangladesh	157	14	14	9	3
Cameroon	80	17	17	0	0
Canada	20	19	10	24	24
China[b]	16	51	39	11	19
Indonesia	58	7	32	14	0
Japan	62	52	36	81	90
Korea, Rep. of	104	120	94	43	58
Mexico	49	32	11	18	25
Pakistan	108	30	30	3	5
India	153	55	55	23	13
Turkey	50	16	14	13	7
United States	6	6	3	14	14
Mercosur	34	13	13	2	1
EFTA	71	48	29	22	24
ASEAN	60	12	11	25	10
Philippines	35	10	47	6	0
Sub-Saharan LDCs	63	15	13	2	1
Other Sub-Saharan Africa	104	27	26	1	7
Maghreb	38	19	18	11	5
South African Customs Union	52	14	13	12	5
EU15	21	17	12	41	36
Russia	16	13	13	6	0
Developed countries	27	22	14	37	38
All low- and middle-income countries	48	27	21	14	15
LDCs	78	14	13	4	2
All countries	37	24	17	26	27

Source: Jean, Laborde, and Martin (2006).

a. CV is the weighted coefficient of variation for the power of this tariff.

b. The bound average duty reported for China takes into account commitments not in effect in 2001, hence its lower level compared to the MFN rate.

average applied tariffs (Hathaway and Ingco 1996). Table 2.5 indicates that binding overhang is substantial in developing countries, and smaller, but by no means nonexistent, in developed countries.[11] These results are broadly consistent with the findings of Martin and Wang (2004), which are based on an entirely different dataset.

For developed countries, the average bound rate was almost twice as high as the applied rate. But this difference mainly comes from the large gap between MFN and applied rates, reflecting the importance of preferential agreements and TRQs in reducing average applied rates below their MFN levels. The difference is large in relative terms for all developed countries. A key feature of table 2.5 is the sharp difference between countries in the extent of the binding overhang. Low-income countries, such as the LDC group, tend to have a very large degree of binding overhang, with bindings for the LDC group six times applied rates. For Bangladesh, the difference is more than 150 percentage points. In Japan, the United States, and the EU, average bound rates are more than 50 percent above the applied rates, suggesting that relatively large cuts in bound rates would be needed before there would be any reductions in applied rates.

Tiered Formulas

The DWP Framework proposes the use of a tiered formula with deeper cuts in higher tariffs. Attempts to apply higher rates of tariff reduction to higher tariffs confront a problem of discontinuities. This is evident in figure 2.1, which maps tariffs before application of the formula to postformula tariffs using the transition points of 15 and 90 percent, and cut rates of 40, 50, and 60 percent as suggested in the Harbinson proposal (WTO 2003). The discontinuity problem is most evident around the 90 percent transition point, where a tariff of 90 percent becomes a tariff of 45 percent, and a tariff of just over 90 percent becomes a tariff of 36 percent. This discontinuity would not only result in a change in the ordering of tariffs, but could potentially raise the costly variability of tariffs. Most important from a political economy perspective, such discontinuities would likely create major political resistance from firms just above each of the transition points.

One way to deal with the discontinuity problem is to follow the approach of the progressive income tax, where the higher proportional rate is applied to the part of the tariff that lies above the limit of the lower band. Although it has the disadvantage of cutting high tariffs by less in absolute terms than a proportional cut (because the lower portion of the tariff is cut at a lower rate), it does impose the higher cut on higher tariffs required by the DWP Framework. Further, it provides a continuous mapping from the old tariffs to the new, as depicted in figure 2.2.

With this approach, Jean, Laborde, and Martin (2006) examine a range of tariff-cutting scenarios. Before these scenarios were developed, a priori adjustments were performed to introduce the developments already agreed to before any tariff reductions arising from the DDA. These pre-experiment changes include the expansion to the EU25, the phase-in of remaining agricultural commitments by developing countries,[12] the abolition of the quotas on exports of textiles and clothing originally imposed under the Multifibre Arrangement, and the tariff reforms agreed to by countries that recently acceded to the WTO, particularly China.

The Doha scenario of central interest in this book is performed by cutting the bound tariffs but reducing applied rates only when and to the extent that the new bound rate is below the initial applied rate. This Doha scenario uses a tiered formula with inflexion points at 15 and 90 percent and marginal tariff cuts[13] of 45, 70, and 75 percent in developed countries. For developing countries, the inflexion points were placed at 20, 60, and 120 percent and the marginal cuts at 35, 40, 50, and 60 percent. Also consistent with the special and differential treatment provisions in the DWP Framework, LDCs are not required to undertake any reduction commitments.

Jean, Laborde, and Martin (2006) perform several alternative experiments exploring the consequences of different specifications of possible variants of the tiered formula. In particular, they examine the consequences of including flexibility in the form of so-called sensitive products and, for developing countries additionally, so-called special products. They allow countries to classify 2 percent (or 5 percent) of tariff lines as sensitive products. They also allow just developing countries to classify a similar proportion of tariff lines as special products. Jean, Laborde, and Martin found that allowing sensitive and special products in these ways greatly diminished the extent of trade liberalization. They also compared the tiered formula with a proportional cut approach and examined the effects of a tariff cap of 200 percent, finding that it was quite effective in restoring the discipline lost by allowing sensitive and special products. Another policy experiment compared the Swiss formula, which reduces higher tariffs more sharply, with the tiered formulas.[14] Finally, they examined whether the loss of market access resulting from flexibility is due to the inclusion of alcoholic beverages and tobacco—where revenue rather than protection might be the reason for high tariffs—and found that this was not the case. The implications of this full range of scenarios for poverty are explored in chapter 17 of this volume.

Agricultural Domestic Support

Reductions in domestic support are, like reductions in tariffs, to be undertaken using tiered formulas with deeper cuts in higher rates of protection. The DWP Framework sets out in some detail a number of constraints to be satisfied, including restrictions on the AMS and on this trade-distorting support plus blue box

Figure 2.1. Converting the Harbinson Formula into a Tiered Formula

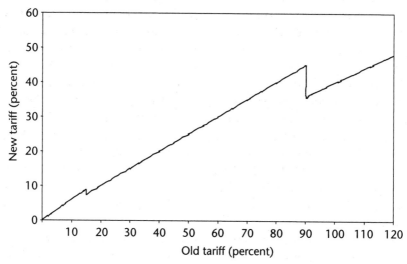

Figure 2.2. Tiered Tariff-Cutting Formula without Discontinuities

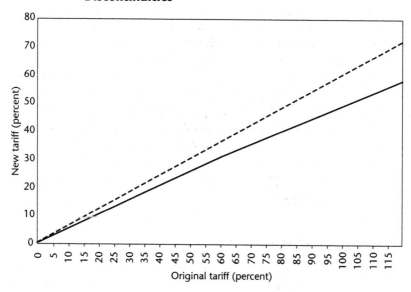

Note: Upper line shows the 40 percent reduction. Lower line shows the 40:50:60 percent progressive tiered formula.

and de minimis support in developed countries. In addition, product-specific support is to be capped at historic levels. As in the case of market access, special and differential treatment provisions allow for smaller cuts and longer implementation periods in developing countries.

Analyses of this aspect of the agreement by Jensen and Zobbe (2006) and by Hart and Beghin (2006) lead to the conclusion that there are two key features determining the impact of these disciplines. One is the ability of WTO members to "abolish" the market price support (MPS) component of their domestic support without making any substantive changes in policy; the other is the gap between actual support and WTO commitments. For members such as the EU, Japan, and the Republic of Korea, where a very large fraction of domestic support is provided through administered market prices, the current AMS can be sharply reduced by abolishing (as Japan already has in the case of rice) the "administered prices" that are central to calculating the MPS component of AMS (see WTO [1995], annex 3, paragraph 8). Under current rules, this removes MPS from the reported current AMS, while leaving commitment levels unchanged.

Once this feature of the AMS and the gaps between the latest notified levels of support and the binding commitment levels are taken into account, it becomes clear that very large reductions in domestic support commitments would be needed to bring about reductions in distorting support. Jensen and Zobbe (2006) examined the effects of a rule requiring developed countries providing domestic support above 20 percent of production to cut by 75 percent, while others cut by 60 percent, and developing countries cut by 40 percent. As shown in table 2.6, they conclude that this would require reductions in domestic support in only six WTO members: Australia, the EU, Iceland, Norway, Thailand, and the United States. Thus, these reductions in domestic support, as reported in table 2.6, are the only ones used in the Doha simulations underlying the analysis in this book. (Of course, the above full-liberalization scenarios consider the impact of abolishing domestic support for agriculture.) Clearly, unless the loophole provided by the ability to abolish the current AMS without removing it from the binding is addressed, very large reductions in domestic support commitments will be required to bring about reductions in actual domestic support, and most of those reductions will be in lightly protected countries.

Agricultural Export Subsidies

Farm export subsidies are inconsistent with GATT rules and for that reason alone deserve to be eliminated (Hoekman and Messerlin 2006). As noted by Hertel and Keeney (2006) and reported in table 2.3, the overall impact of eliminating export

Table 2.6. Cuts in Domestic Support under a Tiered Formula with 75 Percent Cuts in High-Supporting Countries

Country/region	Required cut in domestic support (%)
United States	28
EU	16
Iceland	1
Australia	10
Norway	18
Thailand	30

Source: Jensen and Zobbe (2006), tables 9.6 and A9.1.

subsidies would be very small relative to the impact of abolishing barriers to market access. Additional analysis showed that to be true even when implicit export subsidies in the form of food aid and export credits are included. These subsidies are heavily concentrated in a few high-income countries, with the EU alone accounting for almost 90 percent of the total (although Switzerland has the highest average export subsidy rate, at three times the EU average). EU export subsidies are heavily concentrated in just a few commodities, with beef, sugar, dairy products, wheat, coarse grains, and processed foods accounting for more than 80 percent of total export subsidies.

However, the DWP Framework does envisage complete abolition of export subsidies, although the outcome for tariffs and domestic support is likely to be considerably less than full abolition. Furthermore, as will be seen in chapter 14, among others, export subsidies have a disproportionate impact on the poor. For these reasons, and because of their historical importance in the policy debate, export subsidies rightly represent a key part of any DDA in agriculture.

Nonagricultural Market Access

Given the importance of food and agriculture to the poor—both as a source of earnings, as well as a large expenditure item—this chapter, and indeed the entire book, focuses heavily on reforms to these sectors. This is also an area where the decision of August 1, 2004, is most explicit. However, developing countries as a group are far more reliant on nonagricultural exports for foreign exchange earnings, thus this area must also be considered in the scenarios. Lacking explicit direction from the 2004 decision, the core Doha scenario simply assumes that developed countries cut bound tariffs on nonagricultural products by 50 percent and developing countries by two-thirds of this amount (and again no cut by the LDCs).

Implications of Doha for Market Access

To obtain some insights into the implications of Doha reform for market access, table 2.7 presents estimates of the average tariffs recently and prospectively facing each country. The first column of this table reports the average tariffs in 2001 for agriculture and food alone (table 2.7a) and for total merchandise trade (table 2.7b). It then reports those averages after the baseline pre-experiment in which significant policy changes to the end of 2004 are implemented (EU expansion, Uruguay Round completion, WTO accession by China and other countries). The tariff averages are based on 2015 trade flows, because this is the end of the baseline period used in the closing chapter (17) of this book. The pre-experiment tariffs are then compared with what they would be following either of two Doha scenarios—the core scenario involving lower reform commitments for developing countries and none for LDCs (Doha), and another scenario in which those countries forgo that element of special and differential treatment and liberalize to the same degree as developed countries (Doha-All).

First, note in table 2.7b that the global average tariff declines about one-tenth (from 5.2 to 4.7 percent) in the pre-experiment, thanks to the above-mentioned actual reforms (especially those of China) during the 2001–04 period. That is also true of average import tariffs applying to food and agriculture alone.

Second, the Doha scenario reduces average tariffs globally by a further one-quarter, from 4.7 to 3.5 percent (table 2.7b). Most of that is concentrated in agriculture and clothing, whose average tariffs fall about one-third. (Average agricultural tariffs fall from 15.2 to 9.9 percent [table 2.7a].) A number of countries, particularly in East Asia and Western Europe show very sharp tariff reductions in agriculture, because the top-down nature of the tiered formula substantially reduces the tariffs on farm products that are subject to particularly high tariff rates.

Third, as a result of those cuts to tariffs, the average rate of protection facing many exporters falls substantially. Table 2.8 reports this information, showing the average tariffs applied to exports from each region for food and agriculture alone (table 2.8a) and for all merchandise trade (table 2.8b). For example, food exporters, such as those that are members of the Cairns Group, experience reductions in the average tariffs applied to their exports that amount to as much as five percentage points or more under the Doha scenario. But even exporters in some net-food-importing economies—such as China, the EU, and even the Republic of Korea—experience large declines in the agricultural tariffs they face. And the same is true even for some low-income food exporters, such as Cambodia, Cameroon, and Zimbabwe, although they have been previously eligible for preferences into the EU.

Table 2.7a. Agricultural and Food Tariffs, Percent

Country/region	Baseline 2001	2015	Doha 2015	Doha- All
Australia and New Zealand	2.6	2.6	1.7	1.7
EU25 plus EFTA	13.9	13.9	7.0	7.0
United States	2.4	2.4	1.7	1.7
Canada	9.0	9.0	4.9	4.9
Japan	29.4	29.3	14.7	14.7
Korea, Rep. of, and Taiwan, China	55.0	53.0	27.9	18.7
Hong Kong, China, and Singapore	0.1	0.1	0.1	0.1
Argentina	7.1	7.1	6.9	6.1
Bangladesh	12.7	12.7	12.7	11.9
Brazil	5.0	5.0	4.9	4.4
China	37.6	10.3	7.9	6.9
India	50.3	49.9	45.5	37.4
Indonesia	5.0	5.0	4.9	4.5
Thailand	29.7	16.7	13.5	11.0
Vietnam	37.1	37.1	37.1	37.1
Russia	13.5	13.5	8.7	6.5
Mexico	11.6	10.3	8.6	6.5
South Africa	8.8	8.6	8.1	6.6
Turkey	16.7	16.6	13.8	10.6
Rest of South Asia	21.3	21.1	20.9	16.5
Rest of East Asia	13.7	13.4	12.7	11.2
Rest of Latin America and the Caribbean	11.0	10.8	9.8	8.9
Rest of Europe and Central Asia	16.0	15.7	14.3	12.9
Middle East and North Africa	14.1	13.1	11.5	10.4
Selected Sub-Saharan African countries	11.9	11.8	11.5	11.0
Rest of Sub-Saharan Africa	21.4	21.2	19.6	16.1
Rest of the world	12.1	11.8	11.5	9.4
High-income countries	16.0	15.9	8.2	7.5
Quad (Canada, EU, Japan, and U.S.) plus Australia and New Zealand	13.6	13.6	7.0	7.0
Other high-income countries	31.3	30.2	15.9	10.7
Low- and middle-income countries	17.7	14.2	12.4	10.6
Developing countries—WTO definition	20.0	16.9	13.0	10.7
Middle-income countries	16.5	12.1	10.3	8.9
Low-income countries	22.2	22.0	20.7	17.5
World total	16.7	15.2	9.9	8.8

Table 2.7b.   Aggregate Merchandise Trade Tariffs, percent

Country/region	Baseline 2001	2015	Doha 2015	Doha-All
Australia and New Zealand	4.8	4.7	4.0	4.0
EU25 plus EFTA	3.2	3.1	1.7	1.7
United States	1.8	1.8	0.9	0.9
Canada	1.4	1.4	0.8	0.8
Japan	5.2	5.1	2.7	2.7
Korea, Rep. of, and Taiwan, China	7.6	7.3	5.0	3.9
Hong Kong, China, and Singapore	0.0	0.0	0.0	0.0
Argentina	10.0	10.0	9.9	9.2
Bangladesh	18.4	18.4	18.4	18.3
Brazil	9.5	9.5	9.2	8.5
China	13.6	6.1	4.3	3.3
India	28.1	26.9	23.1	19.6
Indonesia	4.8	4.7	4.6	4.5
Thailand	10.2	8.6	8.0	7.3
Vietnam	16.7	16.7	16.7	16.7
Russia	9.7	9.7	6.5	4.8
Mexico	5.1	5.0	4.7	4.3
South Africa	6.6	6.6	6.0	4.9
Turkey	2.5	2.4	2.2	2.0
Rest of South Asia	14.6	14.4	14.3	13.3
Rest of East Asia	4.6	4.5	4.1	3.7
Rest of Latin America and the Caribbean	9.1	9.1	8.3	7.7
Rest of Europe and Central Asia	5.0	4.9	4.7	4.4
Middle East and North Africa	9.8	9.4	8.8	8.3
Selected Sub-Saharan African countries	8.7	8.5	8.3	8.2
Rest of Sub-Saharan Africa	16.2	16.3	15.9	15.0
Rest of the world	9.1	9.0	8.8	8.3
High-income countries	2.9	2.9	1.6	1.6
Quad (Canada, EU, Japan, and U.S.) plus Australia and New Zealand	2.7	2.7	1.5	1.5
Other high-income countries	4.1	3.9	2.6	2.1
Low- and middle-income countries	9.9	8.4	7.5	6.8
Developing countries—WTO definition	8.5	7.3	6.3	5.6
Middle-income countries	8.9	7.2	6.3	5.6
Low-income countries	15.9	15.6	14.6	13.4
World total	5.2	4.7	3.5	3.2

Source: GTAP 6.05 and CEPII scenario file; authors' aggregation.

Note: EU tariffs are net of intra-EU trade.

Table 2.8a.   Agricultural and Food Tariffs Faced by Exporters, percent

Country/region	Baseline 2001	2015	Doha 2015	Doha- All
Australia and New Zealand	17.4	16.8	9.5	8.7
EU25 plus EFTA	15.5	14.7	11.2	9.7
United States	23.4	20.5	12.2	10.7
Canada	9.5	9.2	6.0	5.6
Japan	9.6	8.1	6.1	4.9
Korea, Rep. of, and Taiwan, China	11.5	10.2	6.9	6.4
Hong Kong, China, and Singapore	21.4	20.0	18.2	17.0
Argentina	23.0	13.7	9.6	8.1
Bangladesh	3.9	2.9	2.8	2.7
Brazil	24.2	19.5	11.1	9.6
China	26.8	26.2	14.0	11.2
India	10.4	9.5	6.9	6.2
Indonesia	14.1	13.0	11.6	9.9
Thailand	19.6	19.2	11.5	10.4
Vietnam	9.9	9.9	9.9	9.9
Russia	7.0	6.2	4.6	4.3
Mexico	4.9	4.8	3.4	3.3
South Africa	15.0	14.8	10.4	9.5
Turkey	11.1	10.9	8.0	7.3
Rest of South Asia	15.0	14.5	10.9	9.1
Rest of East Asia	17.2	16.6	15.0	12.4
Rest of Latin America and the Caribbean	11.4	11.2	6.3	5.8
Rest of Europe and Central Asia	8.8	8.8	7.5	7.3
Middle East and North Africa	8.8	8.8	7.1	6.9
Selected Sub-Saharan African countries	10.1	9.3	6.0	5.6
Rest of Sub-Saharan Africa	11.1	10.9	6.8	6.5
Rest of the world	23.0	21.7	14.3	13.7
High-income countries	17.8	16.3	10.6	9.4
Quad (Canada, EU, Japan, and U.S.) plus Australia and New Zealand	17.9	16.4	10.5	9.3
Other high-income countries	15.5	14.1	11.4	10.7
Low- and middle-income countries	15.6	14.1	9.2	8.1
Developing countries—WTO definition	15.6	14.1	9.3	8.3
Middle-income countries	16.5	14.7	9.4	8.2
Low-income countries	12.4	11.7	8.7	8.0
World total	16.7	15.2	9.9	8.8

Table 2.8b. Aggregate Merchandise Trade Tariffs Faced by Exporters, percent

Country/region	Baseline 2001	2015	Doha 2015	Doha-All
Australia and New Zealand	8.0	7.6	4.7	4.3
EU25 plus EFTA	6.7	6.1	5.1	4.6
United States	4.7	4.2	2.9	2.7
Canada	1.3	1.2	0.9	0.8
Japan	5.5	4.5	3.5	3.1
Korea, Rep. of, and Taiwan, China	6.1	4.9	3.8	3.4
Hong Kong, China, and Singapore	5.7	4.6	3.5	3.2
Argentina	14.1	9.4	7.2	6.2
Bangladesh	5.1	4.9	2.9	2.8
Brazil	9.8	8.4	5.6	5.0
China	6.1	5.9	4.1	3.7
India	6.6	6.3	4.9	4.6
Indonesia	6.5	5.9	4.8	4.4
Thailand	7.6	7.0	4.8	4.4
Vietnam	7.6	7.6	7.6	7.6
Russia	2.1	1.8	1.5	1.4
Mexico	1.0	0.9	0.8	0.7
South Africa	5.5	5.4	4.3	3.9
Turkey	5.5	5.0	4.1	3.8
Rest of South Asia	9.6	9.3	6.7	6.1
Rest of East Asia	3.7	3.1	2.6	2.3
Rest of Latin America and the Caribbean	5.2	5.1	3.4	3.2
Rest of Europe and Central Asia	3.2	3.0	2.8	2.7
Middle East and North Africa	2.8	2.8	2.6	2.5
Selected Sub-Saharan African countries	4.8	4.4	3.1	2.9
Rest of Sub-Saharan Africa	3.4	3.5	2.4	2.4
Rest of the world	10.4	9.9	6.4	6.2
High-income countries	5.4	4.7	3.6	3.3
Quad (Canada, EU, Japan, and U.S.) plus Australia and New Zealand	5.3	4.7	3.6	3.3
Other high-income countries	6.0	4.8	3.7	3.4
Low- and middle-income countries	4.9	4.5	3.4	3.1
Developing countries—WTO definition	5.1	4.6	3.4	3.2
Middle-income countries	4.7	4.3	3.2	2.9
Low-income countries	6.3	6.0	4.6	4.3
World total	5.2	4.7	3.5	3.2

Source: GTAP 6.05 and CEPII scenario file; authors' aggregation.

Note: EU tariffs are net of intra-EU trade.

The Doha-All scenario reported in the final columns of tables 2.7 and 2.8 shows what would happen to average tariffs if developing countries and LDCs were to fully reciprocate the tariff cuts made by developed countries. This would lower their average applied tariffs by one-tenth (slightly more so for farm products and slightly less so for other merchandise), or by about as much again as under the central Doha scenario. Although that may seem a nontrivial additional reduction, it is still proportionately smaller than for developed countries because of the higher degree of tariff binding overhang in those poorer countries. Yet it would boost substantially the likely economic benefits of Doha to developing countries not only because of more own-country reform but also because it would mean more market access abroad for developing country exporters, in two respects: (a) because a significant share of developing countries' trade is with other developing countries and (b) because such an increased willingness to participate in the Doha Round would provide an opportunity for developing countries to demand greater access to developed-country markets for farm and textile products (and possibly more foreign aid for trade facilitation investments).

Conclusions

The two objectives of this chapter were to examine the potential impacts of removing trade barriers and agricultural subsidies (what's at stake) and specify a core Doha scenario that can be used in subsequent chapters as representative of the July 2004 DWP Framework agreement. In terms of potential reform, the analysis by Hertel and Keeney (2006) shows that increased agricultural market access is the key to successful liberalization of merchandise trade, accounting for well over half the potential economic welfare gains to developing countries and the world as a whole from removing all merchandise trade distortions and farm subsidies. Within agriculture, the potential gains from market access are shown to be far more important than those from abolition of domestic support and export subsidies, accounting for 93 percent of the gains from total agricultural liberalization.

The chapter also lays out the approach used to assess the potential impact of partial liberalization of the type envisaged in the DWP Framework agreement. In the case of market access, it highlights a potentially serious problem with tiered formulas: the problem of discontinuities at the transition point from one depth of cut to another. In the simulations used in this book, that problem is resolved by applying higher cuts at the margin—that is, applying only to the part of each tariff above the transition point from one tariff to another.

Meaningful evaluation of tariff reforms using a tiered formula can only be undertaken using detailed data on WTO tariff bindings, applied tariff data that reflect the importance of specific tariffs, and tariff preferences granted either unilaterally or in the context of bilateral or regional arrangements. In this chapter, the data on applied tariffs are drawn from the CEPII-ITC MAcMap database, and the tariff bindings are based on comparable data prepared by CEPII. Before the policy experiments are performed, the base data from 2001 are modified to take into account commitments reached before 2005, including China's WTO accession commitments, remaining Uruguay Round tariff cuts, the abolition of the export quotas introduced under the Multifibre Arrangement, and the incorporation of 10 additional countries into the EU in May 2004. Finally, the tariff cuts are performed by applying a relatively deep-cutting tiered formula (with maximum tariff cuts of 75 percent) to the bound rates. Impacts of these simulations on prices and other economic variables are presented in chapter 3 of this book. Subsequent chapters of the book will explore the poverty impacts of the core Doha scenario and compare them with the potential impacts of complete global trade reform. Both chapters 14 and 17 will also examine the market and welfare implications of developing countries and LDCs becoming full participants in this round's tariff cuts as in the Doha-All scenario.

Notes

1. The GTAP-AGR is a new variant on the standard GTAP model of the global economy that fine-tunes the specification of the food and agricultural sectors in line with recent econometric work. See Keeney and Hertel (2006) for details.

2. This is considerably below the estimate reported in Anderson and others (2001), based on the GTAP Version 5.4 database for 1997, despite the inclusion of liberalization of commercial services in the results presented here from Version 6.05 for 2001. The reasons for the differences include the reductions in global protection between 1997 and 2001, the inclusion of nonreciprocal tariff preferences for low-income countries in the latest dataset, and structural changes in the global economy. This estimate is also below that reported in Anderson, Martin, and van der Mensbrugghe (2005) for merchandise trade. Those authors reconcile the difference as due (in decreasing order of importance) to their reporting for the year 2015 when the world economy (and especially the economies of more highly protected developing countries) is larger, their inclusion of some of the dynamic gains from trade, and their use of larger (longer-run) trade elasticities.

3. In 2001, based on World Bank (2003), where the term "developing countries" here excludes East Asia's four newly industrialized "tigers" and the transition economies of Eastern Europe and the former Soviet Union.

4. The gain to developing countries from the temporary movement of labor could be enormous, though, swamping the welfare gains from product trade liberalization. See Winters and others (2003) for an early estimate using the GTAP model.

5. The distortion estimates are highly speculative. They have been obtained from an econometric model that aims to predict the volume of services imports into each region in the absence of trade barriers. The tariff equivalent of this barrier is obtained by increasing import prices until import volumes are scaled back to their observed level.

6. See, for example, table 3 in Dimaranan, Hertel, and Keeney (2004).

7. In those cases where there are quota administration reasons for believing this 90 percent rule underestimates TRQ protection, the following discussion will underestimate the gains from Doha.

8. Korea is a self-declared developing country in the WTO, although a member of the OECD and a high-income country by World Bank standards.

9. This percentage corresponds to products that are at least partly protected by a TRQ (see de Gorter and Kliauga [2006] for details). It should therefore be considered as an upper bound.

10. Note, however, that given the methodology used here, TRQs are also a source of difference between MFN and applied rates, because the MFN duty is the out-of-quota tariff rate in this database, but this is not the case for the applied duty as soon as the quota is less than 99 percent filled.

11. Computing perfectly comparable information on MFN and bound ad valorem equivalent tariffs is a complex task. Because treating the information concerning MFN tariffs sometimes involves specific difficulties, such as incomplete raw information, it is possible that the extent of the binding overhang found here for developed countries, although already small, is still overstated (because the level of MFN duties might have been slightly understated in some cases). This is likely to be the case in particular for the EU and for Japan.

12. Developing countries had 10 years from 1994 to implement their Uruguay Round commitments on agriculture.

13. An initial simulation was undertaken with cuts of 35, 60, and 65 percent and is reported in Jean, Laborde, and Martin's agricultural scenario 7 (2006). It was not chosen as the base for further simulations because it created insufficient liberalization to allow evaluation of the effects of liberalization erosion through the addition of sensitive and special products.

14. For details of the results, see Jean, Laborde, and Martin (2006).

References

Anderson, K., B. Dimaranan, J. Francois, T. Hertel, B. Hoekman, and W. Martin. 2001. "The Burden of Rich (and Poor) Country Protectionism on Developing Countries." *Journal of African Economies* 10 (3): 227–57.

Anderson, K., and Y. Hayami. 1986. *The Political Economy of Agricultural Protection: East Asia in International Perspective.* Boston, London, and Sydney: Allen and Unwin.

Anderson, K., and W. Martin, eds. 2006. *Agricultural Trade Reform and the Doha Development Agenda.* Basingstoke, U.K.: Palgrave Macmillan; Washington, DC: World Bank.

Anderson, K., W. Martin, and D. van der Mensbrugghe. 2006. "Market and Welfare Implications of Doha Reform Scenarios." In *Agricultural Trade Reform and the Doha Development Agenda*, ed. K. Anderson and W. Martin. Basingstoke, U.K.: Palgrave Macmillan; Washington, DC: World Bank.

Bchir, M., S. Jean, and D. Laborde. Forthcoming. "Binding Overhang and Tariff-Cutting Formulas: A Systematic, Worldwide Quantitative Assessment." Working Paper, CEPII, Paris. http://www.cepii.fr/anglaisgraph/news/accueilengl.htm

Bouët, A., Y. Decreux, L. Fontagné, S. Jean, and D. Laborde. 2004. "A Consistent, ad valorem Equivalent Measure of Applied Protection across the World: The MAcMap-HS6 Database." Working Paper, CEPII, Paris: http://www.cepii.fr/anglaisgraph/news/accueilengl.htm

de Gorter, H., and E. Kliauga. 2006. "Reducing Tariffs Versus Expanding Tariff Rate Quotas." In *Agricultural Trade Reform and the Doha Development Agenda*, ed. K. Anderson and W. Martin. Basingstoke, U.K.: Palgrave Macmillan; Washington, DC: World Bank.

Dimaranan, B., T. Hertel, and R. Keeney. 2003. "OECD Domestic Support and the Developing Countries." In *The WTO, Developing Countries and the Doha Development Agenda*, ed. B. Kuha-Gasnobis. New York: Palgrave Macmillan.

Francois, J. F., H. van Meijl, and F. van Tongeren. 2005. "Trade Liberalization in the Doha Round." *Economic Policy* 20(42): 349–91.

Hart, C. E., and J. C. Beghin. 2006. "Rethinking Agricultural Domestic Support under the World Trade Organization." In *Agricultural Trade Reform and the Doha Development Agenda*, ed. K. Anderson and W. Martin. Basingstoke, U.K.: Palgrave Macmillan; Washington, DC: World Bank.

Hathaway, D., and M. Ingco. 1996. "Agricultural Liberalization and the Uruguay Round." In *The Uruguay Round and the Developing Countries,* ed. W. Martin and L. A. Winters, pp. 30–58. Cambridge and New York: Cambridge University Press.

Hertel, T. W., ed. 1997. *Global Trade Analysis: Modeling and Applications.* Cambridge and New York: Cambridge University Press.

Hertel, T. W., and R. Keeney. 2006. "What Is at Stake: The Relative Importance of Import Barriers, Export Subsidies, and Domestic Support." In *Agricultural Trade Reform and the Doha Development Agenda,* ed. K. Anderson and W. Martin. Basingstoke, U.K.: Palgrave Macmillan; Washington, DC: World Bank.

Hoekman, B., and P. Messerlin. 2006. "Removing the Exception of Agricultural Export Subsidies." In *Agricultural Trade Reform and the Doha Development Agenda,* ed. K. Anderson and W. Martin. Basingstoke, U.K.: Palgrave Macmillan; Washington, DC: World Bank.

Jean, S., D. Laborde, and W. Martin. 2006. "Consequences of Alternative Formulas for Agricultural Tariff Cuts." In *Agricultural Trade Reform and the Doha Development Agenda,* ed. K. Anderson and W. Martin. Basingstoke, U.K.: Palgrave Macmillan;Washington, DC: World Bank.

Jensen, H., and H. Zobbe. 2006. "Consequences of Reducing Limits on Aggregate Measures of Support." In *Agricultural Trade Reform and the Doha Development Agenda,* ed. K. Anderson and W. Martin. Basingstoke, U.K.: Palgrave Macmillan; Washington, DC: World Bank.

Keeney, R., and T. Hertel. 2005. "GTAP-AGR: A Framework for Assessing the Implications of Multilateral Changes in Agricultural Policies." GTAP Technical Paper 24, Purdue University, West Lafayette, IN. https://www.gtap.agecon.purdue.edu/resources/tech_papers.asp

Martin, W., and Z. Wang. 2004. "Improving Market Access in Agriculture." Unpublished paper,World Bank, Washington, DC.

Sumner, D. A. 2006. "Reducing Cotton Subsidies: The DDA Cotton Initiative." In *Agricultural Trade Reform and the Doha Development Agenda,* ed. K. Anderson and W. Martin. Basingstoke, U.K.: Palgrave Macmillan; Washington, DC: World Bank.

Winters, L. A., T. Walmsley, Z. K. Wang, and R. Grynberg. 2003. "Liberalizing Temporary Movement of Natural Persons: An Agenda for the Development Round." *The World Economy* 26 (8): 1137–61.

World Bank. 2003. *Global Economic Prospects and the Developing Countries.* Washington, DC: The World Bank.

WTO. 1995. "Agreement on Agriculture." In *The Results of the Uruguay Round of Multilateral Trade Negotiations,* 39–68. Geneva: WTO.

———. 2001. "Doha Ministerial Declaration." WT/MIN(01)/DEC/1, WTO Secretariat, Geneva.

———. 2003. "Negotiations on Agriculture: First Draft of Modalities for the Further Commitments." (The Harbinson draft.) TN/AG/W/1/Rev.1, WTO, Geneva.

———. 2004a. "Doha Development Agenda: Draft General Council Decision of July 2004." (The Groser draft.) JOB(04)/96, WTO, Geneva.

———. 2004b. "Decision Adopted by the General Council on 1 August 2004." WT/L/579, WTO Secretariat, Geneva.

Zedillo, E., P. Messerlin, and J. Nielson. 2005. *Trade for Development.* Report of the Task Force on Trade for the UN Millennium Development Goals Project, London: Earthscan.

ASSESSING THE WORLD MARKET IMPACTS OF MULTILATERAL TRADE REFORMS

Thomas W. Hertel and Maros Ivanic

Introduction

To deduce the national poverty impacts of the Doha scenarios outlined in chapter 2, a modeling framework is needed. One approach would be to use a global model with sufficiently disaggregated households at the national level to say something about potential poverty impacts. This is the approach pursued by Ivanic in chapter 14, where he explores the poverty impacts of global trade reform in 15 focus countries. It is a useful way to offer an integrated analysis of the poverty impacts of multilateral trade reforms, but it is also a very demanding exercise that ultimately must abstract from many of the country-specific features that may play an important role in determining the poverty impacts of trade liberalization. Therefore, for most of the studies reported in this volume, a two-step approach is used. The first step uses a global model to estimate, for each of the target countries in turn, the price changes and estimated changes in export volumes, as well as import price changes arising from the liberalization of trade in other countries. In the second stage, the authors who deal with specific countries use these as inputs into their national models, which are tailored to address particularly important features of their focus economy. This chapter describes the first step in the process, the approach to estimating country-specific price and export volume changes and the methodology for passing these on to the country level.

Modeling World Price and Volume Changes

Choice of Model

There is always a tradeoff between the use of detailed, partial equilibrium models of trade reform and less detailed, but more comprehensive, general equilibrium approaches. A good example of the partial equilibrium approach is offered by papers collected in Aksoy and Beghin (2004). They provide a detailed exploration of the impacts of trade reform in nine different agricultural commodity markets. However, the goal of this book is to assess the poverty impacts of comprehensive trade reforms that affect not just a few agricultural commodity markets, but also food processing, textiles and apparel, and other manufacturing trade. Also, because this book assesses the impacts of such reforms on poverty, it must consider not only the impact on traded commodities, but also the resultant changes in the prices of services and primary factors of production. Finally, to the extent that trade reform has adverse impacts on fiscal revenue, the impacts of replacing lost tariff revenue with other tax instruments must be considered. For all of these reasons, a general equilibrium approach is required. Nevertheless, this chapter draws on the commodity-specific studies for insights into the market impacts of farm-specific support policies and also seeks to validate the general equilibrium approach used here against observed behavior in specific commodity markets.

Nearly all the global general equilibrium models today draw on the global production, use, and trade database collected and maintained by Global Trade Analysis Project (GTAP).[1] This database provides a snapshot of the world economy for a single year (Version 6 represents 2001), with complete bilateral trade flows and interindustry sales for a 57-sector disaggregation of each region (of which there are 87 in Version 6). The models built on the GTAP database often differ in their choice of parameters and model closure. Some are comparative static and some are dynamic. The simplest of these models, and therefore one of the most widely used, is the standard GTAP model (Hertel and Tsigas 1997). It has the virtue of being well documented, transparent, and highly flexible in the aggregation of sectors and countries. However, this very flexibility can be a limitation in the analysis of specific commodity markets. As shown in the chapter 2, a disproportionate share of the trade distortions arise in agriculture. Furthermore, as documented in chapter 15, a disproportionate share of the poor is employed in farming, particularly in the lowest-income economies, and the poor spend a disproportionate share of their income on food. Therefore, it is important to "get the story right" in discussing farm and food impacts of trade reform. For this reason, this chapter uses a special-purpose version of the GTAP model, GTAP-AGR, which has been designed to draw on the latest econometric research on the underlying parameters governing supply and demand in the food and agricultural markets (Keeney and Hertel 2005).

Model Description

As documented in Hertel (1997) and on the GTAP Web site,[2] the standard GTAP model includes demand for goods for final consumption, intermediate use, and government consumption; demands for factor inputs; supplies of factors and goods; and international trade in goods and services. The model uses the simplistic but robust assumptions of perfect competition and constant returns to scale in production activities. Bilateral international trade flows are handled using the Armington assumption, by which products are exogenously differentiated by origin. This means that there is not a single "world price" for a given product—for example, rice. Rather, the price varies with the origin of the product. For example, rice exported from Thailand is differentiated from rice produced in and exported from the United States. This is a useful approach for several reasons. First, even at the level of rice (or processed sugar), commodities are heterogeneous. For example, processed sugar trade includes high-fructose corn syrup as well as processed cane sugar and processed beet sugar. The category of rice includes many different varieties, some of which substitute only imperfectly for one another. A second, closely related reason for adopting this product differentiation assumption is that it permits the explanation, within the model, of why an individual country is both an exporter and an importer of a given product. For example, the United States is an exporter of high-quality beef, but it also imports low-quality beef for use in fast food.

Of course, an important and well-known consequence of the Armington assumption is the presence of relatively high optimal tariffs, even for small countries. This is because every country faces a downward-sloping export demand schedule, with the small country elasticity being approximated by the elasticity of substitution among imports in the destination regions. Consequently, the optimal import tariff is roughly equal to the inverse of this Armington elasticity. In the model discussed below, the simple average of these elasticities is about seven, so that the optimal tariff for the countries analyzed in this book is in the neighborhood of 16 percent. Because many developing countries already have average tariffs in this range, further tariff cuts on a unilateral basis will likely generate aggregate welfare losses. This does not mean that poverty will necessarily increase, but it certainly biases the model against showing favorable developments in the wake of own-liberalization. This will be an important point to bear in mind in considering the impacts of developing-country tariff cuts on poverty.

Using this standard modeling framework as a starting point, GTAP-AGR incorporates some alternative representations to bring focus to the intricacies of agricultural production and markets. Several structural features have been highlighted in the agricultural economics literature for their importance in the analysis of agricultural policy changes: intersectoral factor mobility and factor substitution in production, crop-livestock sector interactions, consumer food demand, and trade elasticities. The manner in which these features are introduced into the model is detailed in Keeney and Hertel (2005) and is discussed briefly below.

Work by the OECD (2001) on the cost and world market impacts of agricultural support highlights the role of factor market issues in an empirical partial equilibrium model. This work focuses on the segmentation that occurs in land, labor, and capital markets between the agricultural and nonagricultural economies, and it provides the region-specific factor supply elasticities used in the GTAP-AGR model. Keeney and Hertel (2005) also follow the OECD's factor substitution regime for primary agriculture, focusing on substitution possibilities among farm-owned and purchased inputs, as well as between the two. They calibrate the constant elasticity of substitution cost functions for farm-level sectors to the region-specific Allen elasticities of substitution provided by the OECD.

The interaction between livestock and crop sectors received considerable attention in the literature after European Common Agricultural Policy reform in 1992 and has continued to be an area of concern (Peeters and Surry 1997). The primary concern has to do with the ability of the livestock industry to change the mix of feedstuffs demanded in response to changing relative prices induced by farm support policies. The GTAP-AGR model follows the approach of Rae and Hertel (2000) in modeling the substitution possibilities for feedstuffs in livestock production as an additional part of the firm's cost minimization problem, governed by a constant elasticity of substitution among ingredients. They calibrate this region-generic parameter to an average substitution elasticity calculated from Surry's (1990) three-stage model describing the behavior of European livestock producers, composite feed mixers, and grain producers.

The importance of consumer demand for foodstuffs is prominent in the agricultural economics literature. The unique role of food in the consumer budget has been emphasized in much of this work, especially as it relates to the distribution of incomes (Cranfield and others 2003; Seale, Regmi, and Bernstein 2003). Inelastic demand in many markets, coupled with volatile supplies, translates into volatile prices for staple products, which can have a significant impact on households near or below the poverty line. The GTAP-AGR model uses a recent set of estimates from a cross-country study of demand, keying on own-price and income elasticities of demand for food (Seale, Regmi, and Bernstein 2003). In the GTAP-AGR model, Keeney and Hertel (2005) calibrate the parameters of the GTAP demand system to the elasticities for the eight food aggregates and an additional nonfood aggregate.

International trade elasticities that describe the substitution possibilities between goods differentiated by origin have received considerable attention for the important role they play in simulation models determining the terms of trade (TOT) impacts of liberalization. Hertel and others (2004) provide recent estimates of this substitution relationship at the same level of disaggregation as the sectors in the GTAP model. Those authors also show how the estimated gains from trade liberalization hinge critically on the value of these parameters. The research reported in this chapter makes use of their region-generic estimates of the elasticity of substitution among imported goods from different sources as specified in the model's Armington demand structure.[3]

Model Validation

Although each of these individual model modifications is supported by the current literature, when they are used together in the context of a general equilibrium model, there remains the unanswered question of how well the model as a whole performs relative to the historical record. Valenzuela and others (2005) address this question in a validation exercise aimed at investigating how well the model performs in reproducing historical price volatility in world markets for agricultural products. Their approach makes use of the fact that most of the annual volatility in crop commodity markets is induced by shocks to supply—the majority of which are induced by exogenous natural phenomena (for example, droughts, heat waves, floods, and so on).

The authors' validation experiment focuses specifically on wheat and begins by estimating a time series forecasting model to predict output trends, attributable to either technical advancements or year-to-year market signals, in wheat-producing regions. The remaining year-to-year changes are attributable to nature-induced supply-side shocks. These random shocks are used to build a distribution of annual supply shocks with which to perturb the model. The ensuing distribution of price predictions may then be compared to that observed historically in order to validate the model. Their specific validation criterion is the predicted versus observed standard deviation in wheat prices for each country, where the model prediction is obtained by solving the model repeatedly, each time sampling from the historical distribution of supply-side shocks for each region of the world.

The most recent results from the work of Valenzuela and others (2005) are summarized in figure 3.1. Here, individual countries represented in the model are given by single points. Regions including multiple countries are represented by brackets, because the model predicts only one price per region, but the data from the UN Food and Agriculture Organization (FAO) data show a range of prices—differing for each country in the region. This figure shows that the

Figure 3.1.   Validating the GTAP-AGR Model: Predicted versus Observed Standard Deviations for Wheat

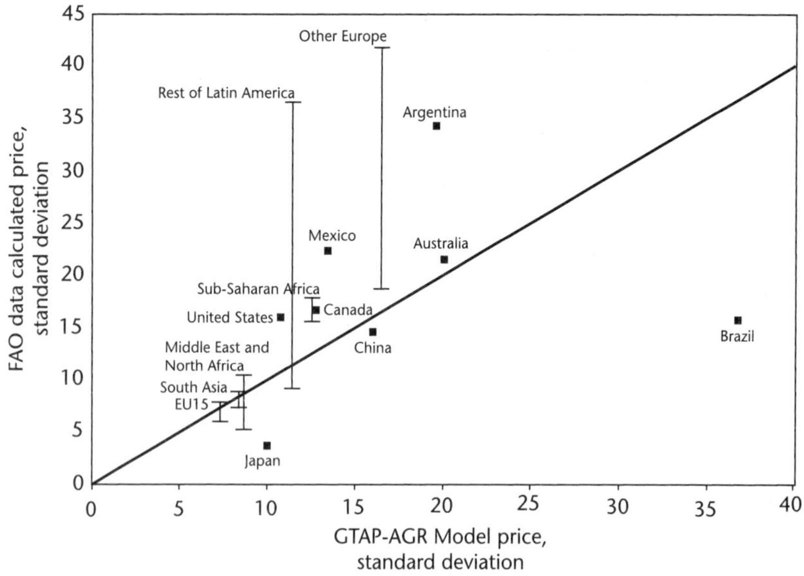

Source: Valenzuela and others (2005).

model-predicted standard deviation of prices is virtually the same as that observed historically for wheat in the cases of Australia, China, the EU, the Middle East and North Africa, and South Asia. For Brazil and Japan, the model over-predicts price volatility. This is hardly surprising, because both of these countries have had domestic policies in place to stabilize prices, and these policies have not been captured in the model simulations. In the remaining individual countries shown in this figure—Argentina, Canada, Mexico, and the United States—the model predicts too little volatility in wheat prices. With the exception of Mexico, which is heavily influenced by the U.S. market, these countries are major wheat exporters. As such, their domestic prices are influenced by other countries' trade policies, which often serve to destabilize markets by dumping excess production on world markets (export subsidies) in times of surplus and restricting sales in times of shortage. Because the model abstracts changes in trade policies from year to year over this period, it appears to understate the variability of prices in the major export markets.

Finally, two regions stand out as having a very large range of price variation. These are the rest of Latin America and Central and Eastern Europe. Hertel,

Keeney, and Valenzuela (2004) attribute some of this price variation to policy volatility (particularly in Eastern Europe), as well as macroeconomic instability and the difficulty of properly deflating year-to-year price changes to obtain estimates of real price variation over this period. Overall, it appears that the GTAP-AGR model shows reasonably valid behavior for many regions. Improving its performance will likely require more attention to how individual commodity policies operate at the margin. This goes well beyond the scope of this book, which focuses instead on the impacts of eliminating or sharply reducing farm and food support policies. Although the authors have thus far conducted this validation analysis only for a single commodity, this evidence is a positive indication that GTAP-AGR is indeed a valid framework for analyzing impacts of global agricultural liberalization on world markets. Therefore, the chapter turns next to an analysis of the price impacts of multilateral agricultural trade reform.

Results

This section considers the global and national impacts of the full-liberalization scenario, as well as the central Doha scenario outlined in chapter 2. The first of these scenarios offers a simple, free-trade benchmark by assessing the impact of removing all merchandise trade barriers as well as domestic support in the OECD countries. The Doha scenario represents an aggressive interpretation of the July 2004 Framework Agreement for the Doha Development Agenda (DDA), including tiered formulae for reductions in tariffs and domestic support and full elimination of agricultural export subsidies. This scenario also embodies special and differential treatment for developing countries whereby cuts in bound commitments are only two-thirds of those in developed countries, and the least developed countries (LDCs) make no cuts whatsoever.

Tariff Landscapes in the Focus Countries

The implications of these two scenarios for average tariffs in the focus countries are reported in table 3.1. Here, average import tariffs on products coming into the country in question[4] are reported in the first column of each block under the heading "original." Thus, in Bangladesh, the average tariff on primary agriculture imports is 6 percent, whereas it is 20 percent on other primary products and processed foodstuffs. Table 3.1 also reports information on the average rate of protection facing a given country's exports. In the case of Bangladesh, this is 8 percent for agriculture, 2 percent for other primary products, and 1 percent for foodstuffs. Comparing tariff entries within a column shows which sectors are more heavily protected and therefore likely to contract under unilateral abolition

Table 3.1. Tariff Rates on Imports to and from the Focus Regions

Sector	Bangladesh						Brazil						China					
	To country			From country			To country			From country			To country			From country		
	Original	Doha	Doha-All	Original	Doha	Doha-All	Original	Doha	Doha-All	Original	Doha	Doha-All	Original	Doha	Doha-All	Original	Doha	Doha-All
Primary agriculture	6	6	6	8	8	8	2	2	2	15	10	10	8	6	6	39	22	22
Other primary	20	20	20	2	2	2	0	0	0	1	1	1	0	0	0	2	1	1
Food	20	20	20	1	1	1	9	9	8	21	11	11	11	9	8	19	12	11
Textile	30	30	30	6	3	3	16	16	14	7	5	5	10	6	5	10	6	6
Other manfactures	16	16	16	3	2	2	10	10	9	4	4	3	6	4	3	3	3	2

Table 3.1. (*Continued*)

Sector	Indonesia To country			Indonesia From country			Mexico To country			Mexico From country			Mozambique To country			Mozambique From country		
	Original	Doha	Doha-All	Original	Doha	Doha-All	Original	Doha	Doha-All	Original	Doha	Doha-All	Original	Doha	Doha-All	Original	Doha	Doha-All
Primary agriculture	2	2	2	6	5	5	11	9	9	2	2	2	7	7	7	9	8	8
Other primary	0	0	0	2	1	1	5	5	5	1	1	1	5	5	5	0	0	0
Food	9	9	9	17	15	15	11	9	9	8	6	6	16	16	16	3	2	2
Textile	9	9	9	11	8	8	7	5	4	1	1	1	22	22	22	15	14	10
Other manfactures	5	4	4	4	3	3	4	4	4	1	1	1	8	8	8	0	0	0

Table 3.1. *(Continued)*

Sector	Philippines						Russia						Vietnam					
	To country			From country			To country			From country			To country			From country		
	Original	Doha	Doha-All	Original	Doha	Doha-All	Original	Doha	Doha-All	Original	Doha	Doha-All	Original	Doha	Doha-All	Original	Doha	Doha-All
Primary agriculture	6	6	6	11	10	10	5	3	3	4	4	4	11	11	11	7	7	7
Other primary	3	3	3	1	1	1	1	1	0	0	0	0	4	4	4	2	2	2
Food	11	10	10	9	7	6	17	11	11	7	5	5	44	44	44	12	12	12
Textile	7	7	7	11	6	6	15	10	7	8	5	5	31	31	31	10	10	10
Other manufactures	2	2	2	1	1	1	8	6	4	3	2	2	12	12	12	7	7	7

Source: GTAP database, Version 6.0.

of trade barriers. Comparing the two "original" columns in a given row shows whether imports are relatively protected when compared to exports and hence whether a given industry is likely to expand or contract global free trade in a given product. Of course, the actual full-liberalization scenario will be a combination of these two forces.

The next column in table 3.1 (labeled "Doha") reports the average tariffs after the Doha reforms. Note that in the case of most of the focus countries, the post-Doha tariffs are the same as the original tariffs. In the cases of Bangladesh and Mozambique, both of which are LDCs, this is due to the fact that the DDA does not require them to make tariff cuts. In the case of many of the other developing countries in this table, there is also no difference. The Doha-negotiated cut in the tariff bindings has no impact because the bound tariffs are far in excess of their applied rates (recall the discussion of binding overhang in chapter 2), thus cutting the bindings still leaves them above the applied rates in many cases. Indeed, the Doha scenario has a measurable impact only in the cases of Brazil, China, Mexico, and Russia,[5] where the binding overhang (the amount by which the bound rate exceeds the applied tariff rate) is less pronounced.

The change in tariffs levied on a given country's exports can also be observed in table 3.1. This is smallest for the LDCs, which already receive preferential access into many markets, as well as for Mexico, which already has nearly free trade with its largest trading partners. For China, the post-Doha tariffs are quite a bit lower—nearly 50 percent in the case of primary agriculture exports.

Full Liberalization

Tables 3.2–3.6 report the results from the full-liberalization experiment. These tables summarize changes in import and export prices, import and export volumes, and commodity trade balances, respectively.[6] Although the model itself contains 29 regions, because of space constraints, and in keeping with the poverty emphasis of this book, these changes are reported only for the world as a whole and for the 10 focus countries for which general equilibrium, national case studies are provided in this book.

Begin with the impact of global trade liberalization on import prices as reported in table 3.2. Price changes in this table are grouped into six broad categories: primary agriculture, other primary products, manufactured food products, textiles and apparel, other manufactures, and services. The first thing to note is the relatively larger price changes for primary agriculture. As shown in chapter 2, this is where the bulk of the commodity market interventions occur, when OECD countries remove domestic support for farm commodities, supply is reduced and world prices tend to rise. When coupled with a reduction in protection for

Table 3.2.   Full Liberalization: Import Prices for All Regions

Sector	World[a]	Bangladesh	Brazil	Cameroon	China	Indonesia	Mexico	Mozambique	Philippines	Russia	Vietnam
Import price index	0.5	1.1	0.3	0.7	0.9	1.0	0.6	0.9	0.8	0.4	0.7
Primary agriculture[a]	6.1	9.5	5.8	5.3	10.8	13.4	17.0	5.1	9.0	1.2	9.2
Paddy rice	22.2	3.0	6.2	4.0	3.0	9.4	52.6	14.4	8.3	3.8	9.2
Wheat	9.0	2.7	8.2	9.1	8.8	7.8	11.4	8.1	8.7	1.3	3.7
Cereal grains	12.2	5.3	7.4	8.0	14.5	8.2	12.6	4.8	8.4	12.7	5.0
Fruits and vegetables	1.6	–0.7	4.1	–1.3	2.3	2.8	1.1	4.0	2.2	0.8	3.0
Oilseeds	15.3	14.8	5.8	7.6	15.4	14.8	19.2	7.8	12.2	5.2	8.5
Raw sugar	3.8	2.2	1.7	–2.1	12.3	2.4	2.7	2.3	2.3	2.4	2.6
Plant fibers	23.1	10.4	4.0	1.2	18.6	15.2	57.4	1.9	16.1	1.9	24.2
Other crops	0.3	–1.3	–1.1	–1.6	1.2	0.1	0.7	2.3	0.1	–0.8	0.4
Cattle	2.5	–1.3	2.3	–2.6	5.0	6.5	4.1	4.7	6.6	–0.1	3.3
Animal products	2.2	0.9	1.9	0.1	2.2	–2.3	2.7	3.5	1.1	0.8	–3.6
Raw milk	0.8	0.1	–0.3	–0.7	–0.5	–0.6	–0.3	–0.6	–0.6	–0.8	–0.8
Wool	6.3	3.1	–2.7	–1.0	6.6	–1.9	4.0	–3.6	1.0	–0.5	3.9
Other primary[a]	0.5	0.5	0.6	0.1	0.5	0.1	0.4	1.7	0.7	0.6	1.2
Forestry	0.3	1.9	–0.2	–0.5	0.1	0.5	–0.1	0.9	1.8	–0.1	1.6
Fishing	1.4	1.1	–0.2	–0.2	1.3	1.3	0.8	1.8	2.1	0.8	1.1
Coal	1.0	–2.4	0.5	0.2	1.3	0.3	0.7	0.6	1.6	2.2	0.6
Crude oil	0.5	0.4	0.6	0.1	0.5	–0.2	0.2	–0.4	0.5	0.1	0.6
Natural gas	0.5	–1.3	–2.7	0.5	0.8	0.4	0.3	1.6	0.4	0.4	0.4
Other minerals	0.7	–0.1	0.1	0.1	0.6	1.0	0.4	2.3	1.1	0.2	1.0
Food[a]	2.8	4.8	2.4	6.0	2.2	4.2	2.5	2.5	3.8	7.4	3.3
Bovine meat products	8.4	1.1	3.5	9.0	4.7	4.8	2.4	4.7	1.5	16.3	6.3
Other meat	3.4	3.8	1.5	3.4	1.3	–2.0	0.6	2.7	–2.2	3.2	–0.6
Vegetable oils and fats	3.4	4.7	3.1	2.1	1.2	–0.1	3.8	3.4	–6.0	0.7	1.6
Milk	11.8	5.7	7.9	17.0	8.4	8.6	5.4	1.9	8.1	7.6	7.6
Processed rice	7.7	5.2	1.7	9.8	15.6	10.6	3.8	7.2	6.8	4.9	5.4
Sugar	4.6	3.3	6.0	4.7	3.5	5.1	0.4	2.6	6.7	4.0	4.4
Food products	0.4	–0.9	0.3	0.6	–1.4	–0.2	0.4	1.0	0.6	–0.1	–0.2
Beverages and tobacco	0.1	0.9	0.2	–0.4	0.4	–0.1	0.1	0.6	2.0	–0.6	2.5
Textile[a]	0.0	0.7	0.5	–0.1	0.8	0.7	–0.1	–0.2	0.9	–0.4	0.8
Textiles	0.2	0.8	0.4	0.0	0.7	0.7	0.3	–0.1	0.8	–0.6	0.8
Wearing apparel	–0.2	0.1	0.1	–0.3	1.2	–0.1	–0.8	–0.8	0.6	–0.2	0.0

Table 3.2.   (Continued)

Sector	World[a]	Bangladesh	Brazil	Cameroon	China	Indonesia	Mexico	Mozambique	Philippines	Russia	Vietnam
Other manufactures[a]	0.1	0.1	0.0	-0.1	0.5	0.5	-0.1	0.5	0.5	-0.1	0.6
Leather products	0.4	-0.7	0.2	0.4	-1.2	-0.8	0.0	0.4	-0.3	0.1	-1.2
Wood products	0.5	1.1	0.2	0.0	1.5	0.6	0.1	0.1	1.2	0.0	1.3
Paper products	0.3	0.9	0.0	0.4	1.0	0.8	0.0	3.0	1.0	0.0	1.6
Petroleum, coal	0.1	0.4	-0.3	0.2	-0.6	0.2	0.0	0.3	-0.2	0.2	0.4
Chemical, plastic	0.0	-0.4	-0.2	-0.6	0.3	0.3	-0.1	0.8	0.4	-0.2	0.3
Mineral products	0.4	1.2	0.3	-0.2	1.1	1.0	0.2	4.0	1.1	0.0	1.8
Iron and steel	0.2	0.1	0.2	-0.5	0.6	0.6	0.2	0.5	0.5	-0.4	0.7
Metals	0.0	-1.4	-0.3	-1.3	0.4	0.7	-0.2	0.5	0.7	-1.1	0.9
Metal products	0.2	-0.3	0.1	-0.6	0.7	0.8	0.0	0.2	0.6	0.0	1.1
Motor vehicles	-0.3	0.1	-0.2	-0.3	0.2	0.1	-0.1	-1.7	0.1	-0.2	-0.2
Transport equipment	0.0	-0.1	-0.2	0.3	-0.5	0.1	-1.2	-0.6	0.0	-0.3	0.6
Electronic equipment	0.4	0.1	0.1	0.1	0.6	0.6	0.2	0.3	0.4	0.1	0.8
Machinery	0.1	-0.4	0.1	-0.1	0.5	0.6	0.0	0.2	0.6	-0.1	0.8
Manufactures	0.0	1.0	0.2	-0.1	0.1	0.6	0.4	0.0	0.5	-0.1	0.7
Electricity	0.1	-1.5	-0.1	-1.2	1.5	0.0	0.0	0.2	0.2	0.0	0.3
Gas	0.1	0.3	0.1	0.1	0.1	0.1	0.0	0.0	0.2	0.0	0.1
Water	0.6	0.5	0.5	0.5	0.4	0.5	0.5	0.5	0.5	0.5	0.5
Construction	0.3	0.2	0.2	0.2	0.2	0.2	0.2	0.2	0.2	0.2	0.2
Services[a]	0.7	0.7	0.5	0.5	1.6	0.6	0.5	0.5	0.8	0.4	0.4
Trade	1.5	2.3	0.9	0.9	2.3	1.0	1.0	0.9	1.9	0.5	0.9
Transport	0.5	0.5	0.4	0.4	0.3	0.3	0.5	0.1	0.4	0.4	0.4
Water transport	0.4	0.2	0.3	0.3	0.3	0.4	0.2	0.2	0.4	0.3	0.4
Air transport	0.4	0.3	0.3	0.3	0.3	0.4	0.3	0.3	0.3	0.3	0.3
Communication	0.6	0.5	0.5	0.5	0.5	0.5	0.5	0.5	0.4	0.5	0.4
Financial services	0.6	0.5	0.5	0.5	0.6	0.6	0.5	0.5	0.5	0.5	0.4
Insurance	0.5	0.4	0.4	0.4	0.4	0.4	0.4	0.4	0.4	0.4	0.4
Business services	0.6	0.6	0.5	0.5	0.5	0.5	0.7	0.5	0.5	0.4	0.4
Recreational services	0.4	0.4	0.3	0.3	0.3	0.3	0.3	0.3	0.3	0.3	0.2
Government services	0.3	0.2	0.1	0.1	0.2	0.2	0.2	0.2	0.2	0.2	0.1
Dwelling	1.5	0.2	6.0	-2.2	2.6	4.3	-0.2	-0.6	2.8	-0.7	22.8

Source: Authors' simulations.

a. Calculated as a weighted average of respective price changes, excluding intra-EU trade

imported products that simultaneously boosts demand, prices rise significantly. The world average price for primary agricultural products rises by 6.1 percent, relative to the numeraire price, which is an index of world primary factor prices. However, there is considerable variation within this broad category of goods, with world average prices rising more than 20 percent for plant-based fibers (primarily cotton) and paddy rice. These are followed by oilseeds and cereals. Wheat and wool also show above-average price rises. Processed food products show the next highest world average price increase, and this category is led by dairy and beef products, as well as processed rice. Most other world average price changes are quite modest.

This variation in commodity-specific price changes also gives rise to regional variation in import price indexes—particularly in food and agriculture. For example, Bangladesh is a heavy importer of cotton and oilseeds, the prices of which rise substantially following global trade reform. Accordingly, Bangladesh's national import price index for primary agriculture rises by 9.5 percent. The largest country-specific average agriculture import price rise is 17 percent in the case of Mexico. As a result of geographic proximity, as well as the success of the North American Free Trade Agreement, the Mexican economy is heavily integrated with that of the United States. And the United States has very large subsidies for cotton, rice, oilseeds, and grains. Mexico sources the vast majority of her imports of these products from the United States and thus feels the full force of this subsidy removal. Indeed, Mexican import prices for paddy rice and plant-based fibers rise by about two-thirds. These import price rises for Mexico are far larger than those for Bangladesh, which sources only a modest share of imports of cotton and oilseeds from the United States—or even the EU, for that matter.

In summary, the commodity-specific import price indexes depend importantly on the source of a given country's imports. This in turn may be traced back to the Armington assumption of product differentiation. Of course, the degree to which prices for a particular commodity are permitted to diverge will depend on the elasticity of substitution among imports within that particular commodity group. As noted above, these elasticities are taken from the recent econometric study by Hertel and others (2004). Their estimates of this key parameter range from 2.6 for other animal products to 34.4 for natural gas.

Table 3.3 reports the export price changes for the same full-liberalization experiment. Although the world price changes are nearly the same as for imports—the difference being due to the presence of international trade and transport margins—the regional price changes are quite different. The difference between the changes in the national export and import price indexes is a measure of the change in each country's TOT, which is also reported at the top of table 3.3.

Bangladesh, Cameroon, Mexico, Mozambique, the Philippines, and Russia all experience negative TOT shocks from full trade liberalization, with Bangladesh's loss standing out in particular.

The strong deterioration in the Bangladeshi TOT is driven by three factors. The first is the fact that Bangladesh is a net importer of food products, and the world price of these products has risen (recall table 3.2). The second stems from the fact that the country already faces very low tariffs in its export markets—particularly the industrial countries, where Bangladesh has tariff-free access as an LDC (recall table 3.1). When the industrial countries liberalize, this preference is croded and export prices fall. The third factor derives from Bangladesh's own-liberalization in the full-liberalization scenario, which involves elimination of the relatively high tariffs imposed on imports into Bangladesh (table 3.1). When these tariffs are eliminated, imports increase. Therefore, exports must also increase to restore external trade balance. The bulk of Bangladeshi exports is in textiles and apparel, and because a substantial increase in these exports is required, the boost in demand following liberalization elsewhere in the world is insufficient to accomplish this, so a large price reduction ensues (-6.4 percent on average for textiles and apparel).

Brazil, China, Indonesia, and Vietnam all experience TOT gains, with the largest gains by far going to Brazil. Global liberalization generates a substantial increase in the demand for Brazilian agricultural exports (recall the large tariffs on Brazilian exports reported in table 3.1). As a result, Brazilian agricultural export prices rise by an average of 13.7 percent—twice the rate of increase worldwide. To restore external trade balance, the prices of all primary factors in Brazil must rise relative to the world average factor price index. This in turn boosts prices for nonagricultural products and services, thus the associated export prices are seen rising across the board in table 3.3. A similar situation, although much more muted, occurs in China, which takes advantage of falling import tariffs in East Asia to increase its farm and food exports (recall the high protection against China's agriculture exports in table 3.1). In Indonesia, the improved TOT are driven by natural resource–based products and light manufactures. Recall also from table 3.1 that Indonesian tariffs are low relative to those imposed against its exports, so full liberalization tends to boost demand for its goods and hence raise the prices for its products.

Tables 3.4 and 3.5 report trade volume changes for the full-liberalization experiment. Worldwide, trade volume (including services trade) rises by 7.2 percent in this scenario. The largest increases come in food products, followed by textiles and apparel, then primary agriculture and other manufactures. Other primary product markets have few trade policy distortions and so experience only a

Table 3.3. Full Liberalization: Export Prices for All Regions

Sector	World[a]	Bangladesh	Brazil	Cameroon	China	Indonesia	Mexico	Mozambique	Philippines	Russia	Vietnam
Terms of trade		-6.1	5.1	-2.8	0.2	1.1	-2.1	-2.2	-0.5	-0.8	0.8
Export price index	0.5	-5.1	5.4	-2.2	1.1	2.2	-1.4	-1.3	0.3	-0.4	1.5
Primary agriculture[a]	6.4	-1.0	13.7	-2.6	4.5	1.1	-1.9	-0.7	-1.0	0.2	2.7
Paddy rice	23.8	-3.6	15.7	-4.2	10.0	2.3	42.5	-1.2	-4.5	1.3	7.0
Wheat	9.4	-3.2	11.7	-3.4	3.2	0.9	18.7	0.0	0.5	0.4	-12.4
Cereal grains	12.8	-3.2	16.2	-4.1	5.1	2.4	12.0	-2.0	-1.6	-0.8	3.9
Fruits and vegetables	1.8	-3.5	13.1	-2.7	4.4	2.9	-2.8	-2.1	-1.9	-2.2	5.3
Oilseeds	16.1	-4.6	13.5	3.0	6.6	10.2	52.2	1.1	4.6	1.6	22.5
Raw sugar	3.6	-4.0	14.1	-4.3	3.8	0.7	-2.2	2.2	-1.4	-2.0	8.7
Plant fibers	24.8	1.8	14.3	0.1	3.5	12.5	2.3	0.3	7.7	11.9	19.7
Other crops	0.3	-4.3	13.2	-3.4	2.8	0.6	-4.2	-1.0	1.4	-3.1	0.5
Cattle	2.9	-3.3	25.1	-3.8	6.3	2.7	-1.0	-2.0	-0.7	-0.3	7.0
Animal products	2.3	-3.1	17.6	-3.9	5.0	4.4	-2.0	-2.7	-1.5	-2.0	6.1
Raw milk	0.8	-3.3	16.4	-3.1	5.3	2.7	-2.5	-1.5	-1.8	-0.4	-1.4
Wool	6.6	-0.2	11.9	-3.7	5.9	2.5	-3.2	-3.0	-3.6	0.1	7.1
Other primary[a]	0.6	-2.6	2.2	-0.2	0.5	1.7	0.2	-0.7	1.1	0.5	3.0
Forestry	0.2	-0.6	6.5	-2.0	1.9	3.6	-0.6	-0.9	2.0	-0.6	12.3
Fishing	1.7	-3.0	3.4	-5.7	3.4	2.5	-1.2	-4.3	1.4	-1.8	4.9
Coal	1.1	2.3	-0.2	-8.0	0.6	2.1	-0.5	-0.9	-2.5	0.7	8.7
Crude oil	0.5	-15.0	1.1	0.1	-0.2	1.0	0.2	-0.4	-1.5	0.7	2.2
Natural gas	0.5	-5.4	-6.6	-3.5	0.7	1.1	-0.8	44.2	2.8	0.4	35.1
Other minerals	0.8	-3.2	2.2	-1.9	0.2	3.2	-0.4	0.3	1.0	0.4	3.4
Food[a]	2.9	-2.4	9.0	-3.7	3.6	3.9	-0.8	-1.3	1.0	-2.0	7.5
Bovine meat products	8.9	-4.8	15.2	-4.0	3.1	3.4	-0.6	-1.8	-0.3	-0.4	2.4
Other meat	3.6	-6.9	14.6	-3.6	4.3	4.0	-1.1	-2.4	-0.4	-2.0	8.1
Vegetable oils and fats	3.6	-3.4	8.6	-2.8	3.6	4.9	11.2	-1.7	2.6	-0.9	6.2
Milk	12.5	-3.9	8.4	-3.9	3.1	3.6	-1.1	-1.5	2.6	-0.8	-0.6
Processed rice	9.1	-2.7	7.9	-4.2	5.4	2.6	0.5	-1.1	-2.1	-0.8	1.0
Sugar	5.1	-4.0	7.1	-3.8	3.0	2.7	-1.0	-1.5	0.3	-13.1	7.2
Food products	0.4	-2.4	5.9	-3.8	3.4	3.5	-0.4	-1.3	0.5	-2.1	7.7
Beverages and tobacco	0.1	-2.7	5.1	-3.6	2.8	2.9	-1.4	-2.4	0.5	-1.7	5.5
Textile[a]	0.0	-6.4	1.9	-7.6	0.9	2.1	-1.0	-2.1	-0.8	-3.0	-7.7
Textiles	0.2	-3.5	1.7	-7.2	1.0	1.9	-1.0	-1.6	-0.3	-2.8	-4.8
Wearing apparel	-0.2	-8.1	2.6	-8.3	0.9	2.3	-1.0	-2.6	-1.0	-3.2	-8.7

Table 3.3. *(Continued)*

Sector	World[a]	Bangladesh	Brazil	Cameroon	China	Indonesia	Mexico	Mozambique	Philippines	Russia	Vietnam
Other manufactures[a]	0.1	–3.5	2.5	–4.7	0.9	2.1	–1.7	–1.4	0.3	–0.7	2.0
Leather products	0.4	–3.8	3.7	–4.7	1.6	3.1	–2.0	–7.4	–0.3	–2.6	–0.2
Wood products	0.5	–3.0	4.1	–3.6	1.4	3.5	–0.6	–1.9	0.9	–0.8	5.7
Paper products	0.3	–4.3	3.1	–4.3	1.6	2.7	–1.1	–2.2	–0.9	–1.3	1.9
Petroleum, coal	0.1	–12.5	1.6	–2.0	0.4	0.9	0.0	–0.4	–2.0	0.5	11.6
Chemical, plastic	0.0	–4.8	2.4	–5.0	0.4	1.2	–1.5	–1.6	–0.6	–1.1	3.7
Mineral products	0.4	–1.7	3.4	–4.7	1.4	2.7	–0.7	–1.8	0.0	–1.0	6.9
Iron and steel	0.2	–5.8	2.9	–7.1	1.1	1.8	–1.6	–1.4	–0.5	–0.5	3.2
Metals	0.0	–4.8	1.5	–4.9	0.8	2.5	–1.3	–1.2	1.3	–0.7	8.2
Metal products	0.2	–4.1	3.0	–6.2	1.1	0.7	–1.8	–3.0	0.6	–0.9	2.9
Motor vehicles	–0.3	–2.4	2.1	–6.9	–0.6	–0.5	–2.3	–5.2	–3.9	–1.8	1.6
Transport equipment	0.0	–2.5	2.8	–5.9	0.7	0.3	–1.9	–3.9	–0.3	–1.5	–9.7
Electronic equipment	0.4	–2.1	–0.3	–4.5	0.3	2.1	–1.8	–4.0	0.5	–1.8	2.6
Machinery	0.1	–2.3	2.5	–5.1	0.7	0.4	–1.5	–3.3	0.1	–1.3	4.2
Manufactures	0.0	–2.5	3.7	–4.8	1.5	2.9	–1.3	–4.1	0.9	–1.7	1.8
Electricity	0.1	–3.7	3.7	–4.0	1.2	2.5	–0.4	–3.3	1.0	0.3	6.4
Gas	0.1	–1.7	2.1	–3.0	1.5	3.1	–0.4	–1.9	0.3	–0.3	20.8
Water	0.6	–0.6	3.7	–3.6	2.0	3.3	–0.5	–2.1	1.6	–0.8	7.9
Construction	0.3	–2.2	4.3	–5.8	1.5	2.5	–0.9	–1.4	1.2	–1.4	8.0
Services[a]	0.7	–0.8	4.5	–3.1	2.0	3.4	–0.4	–1.3	1.4	–0.7	10.8
Trade	1.5	–0.6	4.3	–2.7	2.2	4.2	–0.4	–0.6	2.2	–1.0	12.5
Transport	0.5	–0.8	3.5	–3.6	2.0	3.4	–0.4	–1.5	0.9	–0.6	1.8
Water transport	0.4	–0.8	3.5	–3.7	1.4	2.2	–0.4	–1.3	0.9	–0.8	–3.7
Air transport	0.4	–0.8	3.5	–3.4	1.0	2.6	–0.5	–1.4	0.6	–0.8	1.7
Communication	0.6	0.1	4.7	–3.3	1.8	4.1	–0.3	–2.3	2.3	–0.6	8.8
Financial services	0.6	–0.1	4.6	–2.4	2.2	4.0	–0.3	–0.3	2.5	–0.6	13.6
Insurance	0.5	–0.1	4.5	–2.5	2.1	4.0	–0.3	–0.3	2.2	–0.6	10.8
Business services	0.6	–0.5	5.0	–2.6	2.0	3.5	–0.4	–1.3	1.7	–0.6	16.0
Recreational services	0.4	–0.7	4.5	–2.7	1.4	3.4	–0.4	–1.1	1.0	–0.9	13.8
Government services	0.3	–0.9	4.2	–3.3	1.9	3.8	–0.4	–1.5	1.8	–1.2	12.1
Dwelling	1.5	0.2	6.0	–2.2	2.6	4.3	–0.2	–0.6	2.8	–0.7	22.8

Source: Authors' simulations.

a. Calculated as a weighted average of respective price changes, excluding intra-EU trade

Table 3.4.   Full Liberalization: Import Quantities for All Regions

Sector	World[a]	Bangladesh	Brazil	Cameroon	China	Indonesia	Mexico	Mozambique	Philippines	Russia	Vietnam
Import quantity index	7.2	31.7	22.3	9.3	16.6	8.5	7.7	3.7	4.0	9.0	23.2
Primary agriculture[a]	11.2	1.9	25.2	7.6	6.1	6.5	5.2	2.6	6.6	3.5	21.2
Paddy rice	222.6	–18.6	49.7	8.0	43.8	43.5	8.7	–42.9	53.2	34.3	51.0
Wheat	9.4	–4.0	4.8	–3.9	–12.6	–3.0	17.5	–7.0	2.6	–2.9	–6.0
Cereal grains	5.5	–4.8	19.4	1.8	38.2	–6.1	17.6	–8.7	17.4	–9.7	5.0
Fruits and vegetables	12.4	22.6	19.4	41.3	30.7	9.4	7.9	26.5	7.7	6.8	58.0
Oilseeds	6.3	–30.9	15.6	9.7	–2.7	–1.1	–1.9	–7.5	3.1	–1.1	26.7
Raw sugar	50.4	–18.6	44.7	11.3	2.7	–6.4	–4.0	40.4	–7.2	–4.4	23.0
Plant fibers	5.3	–6.2	17.3	–9.9	–12.6	12.7	–19.7	–30.0	10.1	0.1	8.6
Other crops	9.3	83.5	84.8	17.9	11.8	15.3	19.6	8.1	21.1	4.1	17.5
Cattle	1.6	0.9	194.9	30.0	13.4	–0.9	–4.6	–3.8	–6.1	4.7	–0.8
Animal products	3.7	18.0	80.9	11.2	14.2	17.7	–6.0	–9.8	10.3	–1.7	21.7
Raw milk	–2.0	–9.9	90.5	–9.5	22.9	12.6	–10.5	–4.0	–2.5	3.4	–4.3
Wool	1.9	6.2	131.6	15.5	8.7	45.3	–9.7	–2.0	3.4	2.3	–6.2
Other primary[a]	0.9	–10.3	–1.3	2.4	–3.1	3.2	3.1	2.8	0.7	3.9	12.5
Forestry	2.6	0.5	25.6	14.1	3.2	6.4	5.4	–0.2	–1.5	11.0	20.1
Fishing	3.6	22.8	12.5	4.7	14.8	5.9	16.7	–3.1	5.1	6.8	14.7
Coal	0.9	25.4	–7.4	–2.3	9.3	22.5	–0.3	–4.6	0.6	–3.1	44.4
Crude oil	1.0	–19.2	0.4	0.6	–5.8	3.6	2.2	1.9	1.2	8.3	29.1
Natural gas	0.2	–52.1	–54.9	128.2	77.4	11.7	–8.4	34499.7	57.0	1.2	17424.7
Other minerals	0.2	–1.2	–6.7	13.0	–3.6	0.0	4.8	6.5	–1.7	2.5	8.0
Food[a]	35.9	27.4	37.2	25.3	38.9	21.2	28.3	15.3	24.3	18.1	60.6
Bovine meat products	87.8	31.3	76.9	14.1	18.1	20.8	–0.1	32.5	6.0	–5.2	18.7
Other meat	68.9	94.0	166.0	59.0	86.6	56.2	103.9	46.5	179.5	51.8	139.0
Vegetable oils and fats	61.8	21.0	49.6	39.5	50.2	30.3	39.8	12.4	85.7	23.8	44.7
Milk	41.7	53.4	26.6	–4.6	17.3	1.0	44.1	7.5	1.0	–2.1	14.0
Processed rice	123.0	–6.7	17.0	27.1	–17.6	42.4	5.3	–0.4	115.1	6.8	51.1
Sugar	86.5	44.5	57.4	23.1	23.2	45.7	33.9	1.0	99.0	9.1	61.8
Food products	13.7	31.2	32.2	21.5	34.0	18.5	8.1	24.8	10.3	14.9	62.1
Beverages and tobacco	16.4	35.4	26.6	37.8	20.3	22.8	19.5	13.5	4.1	12.2	87.4
Textile[a]	23.0	113.7	64.2	26.5	40.9	34.7	21.6	19.8	34.5	6.7	99.7
Textiles	23.1	114.5	53.7	21.2	38.6	33.9	9.3	14.4	35.7	7.5	101.5
Wearing apparel	22.9	94.9	114.1	49.8	60.1	47.5	51.8	34.5	23.0	6.1	78.4

Table 3.4. *(Continued)*

Sector	World[a]	Bangladesh	Brazil	Cameroon	China	Indonesia	Mexico	Mozambique	Philippines	Russia	Vietnam
Other manufactures[a]	6.3	17.0	27.6	10.0	16.7	7.8	7.2	2.7	1.4	12.6	19.0
Leather products	17.2	63.0	54.9	66.5	56.6	31.5	57.4	1.0	7.3	32.0	50.6
Wood products	4.2	78.5	61.7	71.6	8.2	20.5	15.4	27.0	7.3	27.4	53.4
Paper products	4.4	29.1	31.9	10.0	9.9	5.9	1.9	0.4	3.4	10.8	27.2
Petroleum, coal	4.9	8.6	1.1	20.7	13.5	4.3	3.7	3.6	2.0	10.0	4.1
Chemical, plastic	8.9	17.4	18.9	12.7	23.2	10.6	4.1	5.6	7.4	11.4	24.9
Mineral products	11.4	35.0	44.5	18.3	38.2	10.1	18.3	3.1	5.2	22.0	74.6
Iron and steel	5.9	-2.5	32.6	-1.0	10.9	6.1	15.5	2.5	0.8	6.4	-2.1
Metals	5.9	13.5	18.1	24.4	12.8	-2.6	10.3	18.8	7.6	18.0	27.2
Metal products	10.9	69.7	80.4	31.4	35.4	19.5	10.1	-0.3	13.1	25.0	6.1
Motor vehicles	9.1	3.5	50.3	0.7	28.1	22.6	6.4	-0.3	10.4	29.0	8.6
Transport equipment	5.5	30.1	11.6	2.3	16.6	4.3	15.7	-0.7	6.3	29.5	20.8
Electronic equipment	1.2	3.2	21.0	2.3	3.5	3.8	6.1	-0.5	-2.2	2.8	18.0
Machinery	6.0	3.2	34.0	1.2	20.8	3.1	5.0	-0.4	2.5	3.8	10.8
Manufactures	10.1	105.1	93.9	62.9	60.9	26.7	29.4	16.4	14.9	40.7	74.2
Electricity	1.2	-4.9	3.4	0.4	-2.1	6.3	-0.8	-0.3	3.3	8.6	26.2
Gas	0.8	-4.4	1.7	-11.1	2.6	8.2	-2.0	9.3	0.6	-0.2	76.0
Water	0.0	8.6	5.6	-11.9	3.7	1.9	-1.9	-7.2	3.3	-2.4	14.6
Construction	0.7	-4.2	17.6	-11.6	2.5	7.9	-0.6	-4.1	3.8	-3.6	22.2
Services[a]	0.1	-0.1	5.7	-5.6	0.6	3.6	-0.9	-2.5	1.7	-1.0	12.6
Trade	-1.2	-4.8	6.9	-5.8	-0.2	5.5	-1.5	-2.2	2.1	-2.5	23.1
Transport	0.7	-2.2	5.5	-7.8	2.7	4.6	-0.6	-1.0	2.4	-0.9	6.4
Water transport	2.5	-2.3	2.0	-5.6	2.1	1.6	-1.1	-3.0	0.7	-0.5	1.0
Air transport	0.2	0.4	3.1	-4.9	0.7	3.4	-0.5	-2.9	1.3	-0.9	12.1
Communication	0.3	5.2	0.7	-7.3	1.8	5.0	-1.3	-5.5	2.1	-1.5	7.0
Financial services	-0.1	15.8	6.2	-6.2	2.5	6.5	-1.0	-1.9	1.5	-0.8	8.1
Insurance	0.2	6.6	6.8	-5.4	2.1	6.2	-0.4	-1.5	2.5	0.4	3.2
Business services	-0.1	0.1	8.1	-4.1	1.8	2.1	-0.6	-3.2	1.3	-0.3	12.6
Recreational services	0.8	-2.4	4.7	-5.3	1.6	6.1	-1.4	-2.0	1.1	-1.3	16.5
Government services	0.3	-3.9	3.3	-8.5	3.0	6.3	-1.7	-2.7	2.4	-1.7	20.2
Dwelling	0.2	-0.5	1.5	-0.8	-0.2	0.6	-0.2	-1.2	-0.4	0.6	0.7

Source: Authors' simulations.

a. Calculated as a weighted average of respective price changes, excluding intra-EU trade

Table 3.5. Full Liberalization: Export Quantities for All Regions

Sector	World[a]	Bangladesh	Brazil	Cameroon	China	Indonesia	Mexico	Mozambique	Philippines	Russia	Vietnam
Export quantity index	7.2	49.5	6.5	17.2	13.4	4.1	8.1	10.4	4.4	6.8	31.2
Primary agriculture[a]	11.2	53.0	-13.3	30.0	76.4	-2.3	9.4	47.4	7.0	28.0	-2.2
Paddy rice	222.6	580.7	428.6	66.4	7,053.0	246.2	129.1	99.5	1,657.8	30.1	113.4
Wheat	9.4	4,409.3	-59.6	106.7	61.6	-3.9	-87.3	45.0	457.1	64.0	372.3
Cereal grains	5.5	151.4	18.2	9.2	81.4	17.9	-4.7	5.2	36.1	28.9	-31.8
Fruits and vegetables	12.4	5.7	-30.2	28.0	52.5	18.0	9.0	33.9	-6.9	24.7	11.4
Oilseeds	6.3	84.3	6.5	202.3	88.6	7.7	-74.7	78.2	48.3	81.0	51.7
Raw sugar	50.4	-4.3	-17.3	-2.0	370.4	755.6	-24.6	-40.8	-33.9	-26.6	16.9
Plant fibers	5.3	83.5	17.5	76.6	81.9	8.0	87.0	46.5	53.7	-7.9	17.0
Other crops	9.3	24.0	-43.0	8.8	-3.8	-4.9	14.1	49.1	48.8	-27.7	-10.5
Cattle	1.6	2.3	-52.1	25.3	-6.7	7.1	22.1	-2.6	40.1	13.7	-31.5
Animal products	3.7	8.2	-28.2	9.9	-4.9	9.3	18.2	5.7	9.8	4.4	-0.5
Raw milk	-2.0	14.6	-69.7	19.3	-35.9	-22.4	13.2	5.1	7.8	-3.3	4.9
Wool	1.9	143.2	-38.0	149.8	13.7	20.5	98.6	37.4	116.2	11.3	20.3
Other primary[a]	0.9	1.9	-2.2	3.8	5.4	-1.9	1.9	5.6	2.1	-0.1	-8.1
Forestry	2.6	8.4	-17.9	12.0	0.8	3.9	9.3	6.3	2.1	3.7	-25.1
Fishing	3.6	0.6	-1.2	10.1	8.8	4.0	6.3	17.4	2.5	11.1	-4.2
Coal	0.9	-14.3	3.1	29.4	6.0	-1.6	3.4	7.7	17.4	0.0	-27.0
Crude oil	1.0	447.5	7.3	3.0	6.0	-1.3	1.8	-0.1	22.7	-0.9	-6.2
Natural gas	0.2	704.5	1,066.3	226.7	5.5	-2.7	63.2	-100.0	-48.2	0.3	-100.0
Other minerals	0.2	7.0	-2.1	4.1	1.8	-3.8	4.2	2.4	1.9	1.5	-4.4
Food[a]	35.9	16.2	107.3	13.1	36.3	23.2	21.8	0.6	21.9	15.8	-2.5
Bovine meat products	87.8	240.3	828.8	64.8	7.9	118.3	89.0	671.9	186.6	587.1	60.9
Other meat	68.9	1,082.8	-2.4	227.0	-0.3	97.2	129.5	-9.5	169.5	70.6	-29.9
Vegetable oils and fats	61.8	55.8	-39.9	-14.1	-12.7	63.8	-34.3	18.0	-5.2	17.1	104.4
Milk	41.7	232.8	49.0	273.4	114.5	60.7	214.6	135.8	82.3	174.4	278.5
Processed rice	123.0	255.3	19.9	63.8	501.6	126.6	73.9	15.9	-25.1	41.9	64.1
Sugar	86.5	-30.3	36.5	2.6	95.1	17.4	-7.9	78.8	177.9	1,15.3	211.9
Food products	13.7	0.1	16.4	7.0	0.2	-11.2	8.5	-7.4	16.7	5.3	-24.8
Beverages and tobacco	16.4	60.3	-6.8	7.5	18.4	26.2	11.3	-0.8	63.5	5.1	21.0
Textile[a]	23.0	67.7	-9.0	77.5	24.5	22.2	-26.6	31.4	49.5	44.3	148.7
Textiles	23.1	32.8	-6.4	73.7	25.0	18.8	-19.4	16.4	48.3	29.6	108.7
Wearing apparel	22.9	89.0	-18.9	85.0	24.2	27.6	-33.0	47.1	50.0	61.7	161.3

Table 3.5.   *(Continued)*

Sector	World[a]	Bangladesh	Brazil	Cameroon	China	Indonesia	Mexico	Mozambique	Philippines	Russia	Vietnam
Other											
manufactures[a]	6.3	25.7	−7.9	38.7	7.9	1.3	10.7	9.3	0.0	10.2	39.6
Leather products	17.2	16.6	−25.3	21.4	21.5	21.0	−30.1	66.8	21.3	3.5	51.9
Wood products	4.2	53.8	−14.8	25.6	0.2	−1.6	4.5	7.0	0.2	10.8	−22.4
Paper products	4.4	28.8	−14.2	23.6	−0.8	−5.9	10.3	47.5	17.8	9.1	15.1
Petroleum, coal	4.9	69.6	4.7	13.2	6.1	2.1	−0.1	17.2	13.5	7.7	−36.0
Chemical, plastic	8.9	36.1	−12.2	49.9	11.8	12.9	13.7	136.4	28.8	8.2	183.9
Mineral products	11.4	26.6	−4.0	−0.7	12.9	9.5	1.5	4.4	6.7	15.4	−19.7
Iron and steel	5.9	64.3	−11.1	18.7	3.0	−2.6	21.0	0.3	8.8	4.9	−4.5
Metals	5.9	77.9	1.6	46.7	6.3	−16.5	8.7	6.8	−6.0	12.4	−50.6
Metal products	10.9	47.5	−8.1	40.2	12.0	5.6	8.3	−1.3	0.0	11.5	−4.8
Motor vehicles	9.1	19.9	16.3	40.7	−6.4	0.2	9.2	35.6	30.7	26.0	−5.2
Transport equipment	5.5	14.5	−21.4	58.3	27.9	30.5	14.8	32.0	20.2	23.2	301.4
Electronic equipment	1.2	23.8	9.8	59.3	5.9	−5.6	16.7	46.6	−3.4	37.9	−11.8
Machinery	6.0	20.9	−13.9	44.0	6.2	6.6	7.9	11.3	6.3	13.0	11.4
Manufactures	10.1	40.4	−22.4	41.1	1.1	−14.0	4.9	40.5	−6.4	0.0	−1.1
Electricity	1.2	23.6	−18.2	18.0	4.0	−11.8	2.5	22.9	−4.6	−4.3	−28.3
Gas	0.8	11.8	−9.7	20.1	−6.7	−14.6	2.2	12.8	1.0	2.8	−64.5
Water	0.0	7.4	−15.7	26.4	−8.2	−14.4	5.8	16.0	−6.1	7.5	−32.8
Construction	0.7	11.6	−13.0	27.0	−4.3	−7.9	5.0	7.0	−3.1	7.0	−24.6
Services[a]	0.1	4.6	−13.5	15.1	−4.8	−10.1	3.8	7.7	−3.0	5.1	−29.2
Trade	−1.2	6.3	−11.5	15.3	−4.7	−11.4	5.0	5.5	−4.8	7.6	−33.8
Transport	0.7	5.9	−10.1	17.5	−5.3	−10.0	4.0	7.6	−1.0	4.6	−4.6
Water transport	2.5	7.1	−8.4	19.8	−1.9	−4.4	5.2	9.3	0.4	7.4	20.1
Air transport	0.2	4.8	−10.8	15.6	−2.4	−8.0	3.6	7.0	−0.6	4.5	−4.9
Communication	0.3	2.0	−14.1	15.9	−4.7	−12.5	3.3	11.6	−6.3	4.5	−26.0
Financial services	−0.1	2.8	−14.0	12.1	−6.0	−12.4	2.9	3.5	−7.1	4.3	−37.4
Insurance	0.2	3.0	−13.8	12.1	−5.8	−12.1	3.2	3.6	−6.3	4.3	−31.1
Business services	−0.1	4.1	−15.2	12.9	−5.1	−10.2	4.1	7.2	−4.2	4.5	−41.9
Recreational services	0.8	5.0	−13.7	13.1	−3.3	−10.2	3.6	6.2	−1.8	5.3	−37.7
Government services	0.3	4.3	−13.9	14.6	−5.7	−12.2	2.8	7.1	−5.3	5.8	−34.6
Dwelling	0.2	−0.5	1.5	−0.8	−0.2	0.6	−0.2	−1.2	−0.4	0.6	0.7

Source: Authors' simulations.

a. Calculated as a weighted average of respective price changes, excluding intra-EU trade

small increase. In the case of services trade, as noted in chapter 2, there are no solid measures of trade barriers, and the DDA does not appear to promise much liberalization, so any liberalization analysis in these markets is ignored.

The country-specific import volume increases range from 3.7 percent, in the case of Mozambique, to 31.7 percent, in the case of Bangladesh. In the case of primary agriculture, Brazil and Vietnam experience import volume changes above the world average, and Vietnam also shows a very strong increase in imports of nonagricultural primary products. In the case of processed food imports, all countries show a strong increase in import volume, with the largest increases arising in nonruminant meat products, beverages, and tobacco. The rise in textiles and apparel imports is even higher for a number of the focus countries. Here, Bangladesh stands out, with more than a doubling of imports as import tariffs fall and apparel exports expand. Other manufactures' import volume changes are quite heterogeneous. In the case of Mozambique, there are declines in import volume for many of these sectors. The change in volume of services imports is small, in keeping with the absence of any liberalization in these markets.

Table 3.5 reports the change in export volumes by country and commodity. Whereas national imports, which reflect a composite of exports from many different sources, showed relatively uniform changes, national export volumes are much more heterogeneous—often showing a mix of positive and negative signs. For example, in the case of Brazil, where processed food exports increase very strongly, primary agriculture exports decline, as do exports of most nonfood manufactures. This is due to the finite primary factor endowments in the country. It is not possible to increase production (and hence exports) of all products simultaneously. As manufactured food production increases, more agricultural products are required as inputs, thereby reducing the amount available for export.

Textiles and apparel exports increase sharply for Bangladesh, Cameroon, and Vietnam. Of course, as shown in table 3.4, imports also increase in these countries. To see the impact on the countries' net trade position, turn to table 3.6, which reports the change in the value of exports less imports (net trade), by commodity, in hundreds of millions of U.S. dollars. Here, the trade balance in textiles and apparel improves markedly for Bangladesh, China, Indonesia, the Philippines, and Vietnam. Because the macroeconomic closure in the analysis fixes the ratio of the aggregate trade balance to national income, a strong increase in net trade in one sector forces some other sectors to experience a deteriorating trade balance. In the economies with a strongly expanding net trade position in textiles and apparel, declines in the net trade balance for nonmanufactures are seen. In the case of Brazil, it is the US$11 billion increase in net exports of food products that drives the net trade story, with compensating reductions in primary agriculture, other manufactures, and services.

Table 3.6. Full Liberalization: Trade Balance (US$ hundreds of millions)

Sector	World[a]	Bangladesh	Brazil	Cameroon	China	Indonesia	Mexico	Mozambique	Philippines	Russia	Vietnam
Trade balance		0.6	-81.3	10.5	48.1	1.9	-15.0	0.2	-2.5	-0.8	-13.1
Primary agriculture[a]	0.0	0.4	-7.8	15.0	43.5	-3.5	-6.8	0.3	-0.8	1.2	-0.7
Paddy rice	-2.2	0.0	-0.4	0.0	33.2	0.0	-0.3	0.0	0.1	0.0	0.1
Wheat	-0.6	0.1	-1.4	-0.2	0.4	-0.2	-1.9	0.0	-0.5	1.1	0.0
Cereal grains	-0.3	0.0	2.3	0.0	4.2	0.0	-4.1	0.0	-0.1	0.3	0.0
Fruits and vegetables	-2.7	-0.3	-1.9	1.6	10.1	0.1	1.2	0.0	-0.6	-0.6	0.0
Oilseeds	-0.8	0.2	6.5	5.1	0.0	-0.3	-2.1	0.0	-0.1	0.8	0.2
Raw sugar	0.0	0.0	0.0	0.0	0.2	0.0	0.0	0.0	0.0	0.0	0.0
Plant fibers	0.2	0.7	0.4	7.2	0.8	-1.8	-0.5	0.1	0.0	0.0	-0.1
Other crops	-2.5	-0.3	-11.9	1.1	-1.7	-1.3	-0.4	0.1	0.5	-0.4	-0.9
Cattle	0.2	0.0	-0.2	0.0	0.0	0.0	0.9	0.0	0.0	0.0	0.0
Animal products	-0.3	0.0	-1.0	0.0	-2.6	0.1	0.2	0.0	0.0	0.1	0.0
Raw milk	0.0	0.0	0.0	0.0	0.0	0.0	0.0	0.0	0.0	0.0	0.0
Wool	0.0	0.0	-0.1	0.2	-1.2	0.0	0.0	0.0	0.0	0.0	0.0
Other primary[a]	0.0	0.2	0.4	6.6	6.1	-0.9	2.0	0.0	-0.3	0.6	-0.8
Forestry	-0.3	0.0	-0.1	1.2	-0.6	0.2	0.0	0.0	0.0	0.5	0.0
Fishing	-0.6	0.0	0.0	0.0	0.4	0.2	0.0	0.0	0.0	0.0	0.0
Coal	-0.5	0.0	0.5	0.1	0.8	0.0	0.0	0.0	0.0	0.1	-0.2
Crude oil	-2.0	0.2	-0.4	5.3	3.8	-0.5	2.1	0.0	-0.4	-1.1	-0.5
Natural gas	-0.1	0.0	0.0	0.0	0.1	-0.6	0.1	0.0	0.0	1.2	0.0
Other minerals	-0.5	0.0	0.4	0.0	1.6	-0.2	-0.1	0.0	0.1	-0.1	0.0
Food[a]	0.0	-1.9	110.8	-14.0	12.7	8.0	-8.6	-0.3	-2.8	-11.3	-6.6
Bovine meat products	-8.8	0.0	100.5	0.0	-0.8	0.2	0.3	0.0	0.0	1.2	0.0
Other meat	-7.0	0.3	1.3	-1.0	-7.8	3.0	-4.1	-0.1	-0.7	-8.6	-0.3
Vegetable oils and fats	-6.2	-0.9	-2.8	-1.7	-2.6	9.4	-1.0	0.0	-0.2	-0.6	-0.2
Milk	-3.1	-0.5	-0.5	0.3	-0.7	0.4	-4.1	0.0	-0.2	1.5	-0.5
Processed rice	-9.3	0.1	-0.1	-4.8	31.0	-0.7	0.0	0.0	-2.4	-0.1	2.7
Sugar	-5.9	-0.3	6.5	-0.6	-0.6	-0.8	-0.3	0.0	-0.1	-1.6	0.1
Food products	-10.6	-0.5	6.4	-3.6	-6.7	-3.7	-0.5	-0.2	0.7	-2.3	-4.8
Beverages and tobacco	-2.8	0.0	0.5	-2.7	0.9	0.2	1.1	0.0	0.1	-0.8	-3.5
Textile[a]	0.0	7.4	-9.1	-4.0	145.8	15.0	-35.9	-0.1	7.6	0.7	10.3
Textiles	-23.2	-13.4	-6.2	-2.7	-9.9	4.5	-12.0	0.0	-1.3	-0.2	-8.9
Wearing apparel	-17.0	20.8	-2.9	-1.2	155.7	10.5	-23.9	0.0	8.9	0.9	19.2

Table 3.6. *(Continued)*

Sector	World[a]	Bangladesh	Brazil	Cameroon	China	Indonesia	Mexico	Mozambique	Philippines	Russia	Vietnam
Other manufactures[a]	0.0	-5.8	-159.6	-6.0	-149.6	-9.8	29.3	0.1	-5.6	0.8	0.6
Leather products	-8.7	0.4	-7.7	-2.3	57.2	6.5	-7.3	0.0	0.9	-4.0	12.6
Wood products	-5.2	-0.1	-3.9	-0.3	-1.4	0.8	-1.4	-0.1	-0.1	-2.0	-1.6
Paper products	-4.2	-0.7	-6.2	-0.9	-8.0	-1.8	0.2	0.0	0.0	-0.3	-1.0
Petroleum, coal	-3.0	-0.2	0.1	-2.7	-5.4	-0.7	-0.8	0.0	0.2	6.2	-0.6
Chemical, plastic	-24.4	-0.8	-25.9	-2.5	-70.1	0.6	1.1	0.0	-0.8	-2.7	2.4
Mineral products	-12.2	-0.8	-5.4	-2.9	-3.5	0.7	-4.0	0.0	-0.2	-2.2	-3.0
Iron and steel	-5.9	0.1	-5.2	0.4	-11.9	-1.1	-1.6	0.0	-0.1	2.5	0.1
Metals	-2.4	-0.1	-1.6	5.7	-8.5	-3.1	-1.4	0.2	-0.7	11.1	-0.9
Metal products	-7.3	-1.0	-7.4	-3.6	2.6	-1.1	-2.6	0.0	-0.9	-1.6	-0.2
Motor vehicles	-9.8	-0.1	-11.6	0.4	-26.2	-3.8	6.6	0.0	0.0	-6.6	-0.4
Transport equipment	-3.4	-1.1	-10.9	3.9	4.1	0.2	-1.2	0.0	0.1	4.2	0.6
Electronic equipment	-3.3	-0.1	-12.6	0.6	21.4	-4.3	36.1	0.0	-3.7	0.1	-2.3
Machinery	-16.3	-0.2	-53.2	0.9	-89.8	0.3	10.7	0.0	0.6	0.6	-2.0
Manufactures	-4.7	-1.1	-7.5	-3.3	-9.4	-2.7	-5.2	0.0	-0.8	-4.1	-1.6
Electricity	0.0	0.0	-0.7	0.1	0.1	0.0	0.0	0.1	0.0	-0.6	0.0
Gas	0.0	0.0	0.0	0.0	0.0	0.0	0.0	0.0	0.0	0.0	0.0
Water	0.0	0.0	0.0	0.0	0.0	0.0	0.0	0.0	0.0	0.0	0.0
Construction	0.0	0.0	-0.1	0.4	-0.6	-0.1	0.2	0.0	-0.1	0.2	-1.3
Services[a]	0.0	0.3	-16.0	12.9	-10.4	-6.9	5.1	0.2	-0.7	7.2	-15.9
Trade	0.0	0.0	-1.5	1.3	-7.0	-1.9	0.5	0.0	-0.4	0.5	-3.0
Transport	45.2	0.0	-0.9	2.1	-2.3	-0.7	1.3	0.0	0.0	1.5	-0.5
Water transport	142.7	0.1	-0.1	1.0	3.2	0.2	0.5	0.0	0.3	1.9	0.3
Air transport	29.7	0.0	-0.6	1.8	0.1	-0.4	0.7	0.0	0.0	1.4	-1.1
Communication	0.0	0.0	-0.3	0.5	-0.3	-0.1	0.3	0.0	-0.2	0.2	-0.6
Financial services	0.0	-0.1	-0.8	0.3	-0.4	-0.3	0.2	0.0	0.0	0.1	-1.1
Insurance	0.0	0.0	-0.7	0.3	-0.5	-0.4	0.5	0.0	-0.1	0.0	-0.5
Business services	0.0	0.0	-9.2	2.9	-1.3	-2.1	0.4	0.1	-0.2	0.6	-5.1
Recreational services	0.0	0.0	-0.6	0.5	-0.5	-0.7	0.4	0.0	-0.1	0.4	-1.7
Government services	0.0	0.3	-1.3	2.2	-1.5	-0.6	0.3	0.0	-0.1	0.7	-2.7
Dwelling	0.0	0.0	0.0	0.0	0.0	0.0	0.0	0.0	0.0	0.0	0.0

Source: Authors' simulations.

a. Calculated as a weighted average of respective price changes, excluding intra-EU trade

A very useful feature of table 3.6 is that it highlights the cases where the extraordinarily large percentage changes in trade volumes are irrelevant as a result of the extremely small size of the initial flow. Brazilian natural gas imports provide a case in point. There is more than a 1,000 percent increase in exports, but the change in net trade is negligible, according to table 3.6.

Doha Scenario

Tables 3.7–3.10 report the price and trade volume results from the core Doha scenario developed in chapter 2 of this book. It represents an aggressive implementation of the framework agreed upon by WTO members on August 1, 2004. The first thing to note is that the impacts on prices and trade volumes are much smaller. Compared with the full trade liberalization, world average agricultural prices rise by only one-third as much under Doha, while world trade volumes for primary agriculture are virtually unchanged. In the latter case, the trade-diminishing effect of export subsidy elimination offsets the trade-enhancing impact of tariff reductions. In the case of food products, the rise in world average prices is more than two thirds of the full-liberalization case, but the rise in import volume is much less—again as a result of the elimination of export subsidies in the United States and the EU.

Because of the nonlinearity in the tariff reduction formulae, as well as the great differences in binding overhang across commodities and regions, the composition of the price differences is quite different between full liberalization and Doha. Under the Doha scenario, Vietnam has a TOT deterioration instead of an improvement: as a nonmember of the WTO, Vietnam does not enjoy the benefits of tariff cuts in other countries. Instead of a dramatic decline in its TOT, Bangladesh now shows a much smaller change. Recall that much of the sharp decline under full liberalization was a result of Bangladesh's own-liberalization and the subsequent increase in export volumes in the face of modest increases or even decreases in export demand. As an LDC, Bangladesh does not reduce its tariffs at all under the Doha scenario (recall table 3.1), so this source of TOT deterioration is not present. In contrast, Brazil still experiences a TOT improvement amounting to about half of the full-liberalization case.

Communicating Global Results to the National Models

As noted at the outset, the goal of these model simulations is to provide country case study authors with a picture of how their external environment is likely to change as a result of multilateral trade reform under the DDA. However, the indi-

Table 3.7.   Doha: Import Prices for All Regions

Sector	World[a]	Bangladesh	Brazil	Cameroon	China	Indonesia	Mexico	Mozambique	Philippines	Russia	Vietnam
Import price index	0.1	0.5	0.1	0.4	0.3	0.4	0.2	0.5	0.3	0.2	0.2
Primary agriculture[a]	1.1	2.4	1.7	1.6	2.9	3.4	4.3	1.3	1.8	0.4	2.2
Paddy rice	7.4	0.1	2.8	0.1	1.3	0.8	17.7	3	3.6	1.4	1.4
Wheat	1.6	1.3	2	2.8	1.3	1.9	1.6	1.7	1.4	0.2	1.4
Cereal grains	3.4	1.3	2.4	4.1	5.8	1.6	2.3	1.8	1.9	8.9	1.2
Fruits and vegetables	−0.1	0.4	1.6	−0.2	0.8	1	1.1	1.1	0.9	0.4	1
Oilseeds	4.1	2.7	2.5	1.7	4.8	4.7	5.2	2.3	4	1.5	2.8
Raw sugar	0.7	1.5	1	0.2	3.8	1.5	1.6	1.5	1.5	1.5	1.5
Plant fibers	5.7	4.4	2.4	1.1	5	6.7	18.2	1.3	6.9	0.1	10
Other crops	−0.2	0	−0.3	−0.4	0.9	0.1	0.6	0.9	0.4	−0.3	−0.1
Cattle	−0.1	0	1	−0.2	1.8	2.3	1.2	1.9	2.3	−1.1	1.1
Animal products	0	0.3	0.4	−0.1	0.7	−0.8	1	1.4	0	0	−1.6
Raw milk	0.3	0.9	0.6	0.2	0.4	0.2	0.4	0.2	0.2	0.1	0
Wool	1.9	1.4	0.4	0.8	2.3	0.5	1.8	0.4	1	0	1.5
Other primary[a]	0.1	0.1	0.1	0.1	0.2	0.1	0.2	1	0.1	0.3	0.3
Forestry	0	0.3	0	−0.2	0	0.1	0	0.1	0.6	−0.2	0.3
Fishing	0.1	0.1	0.2	0.1	0.2	0.1	0.1	0.4	0.5	−0.1	0.1
Coal	0.3	−0.6	0.2	0.2	0.3	0	0.2	0	0.2	1.8	0.2
Crude oil	0.1	0	0.1	0.1	0.1	0	0	0.1	0.1	0	0.2
Natural gas	0	0	−0.2	0	0	0	0	0.3	−0.1	0	−0.1
Other minerals	0.4	0	0.1	0.2	0.4	0.3	0.2	1.7	0.4	−0.1	0.3
Food[a]	0.7	1.7	1.3	3.2	0.8	1.7	1	1.1	1.5	3	1.3
Bovine meat products	2.2	0.9	2.3	7.3	2.3	2.7	0.8	2.2	1.3	14.5	5.5
Other meat	0.8	1	1.8	3	1.2	0.2	0.5	1.1	0	2.1	1.1
Vegetable oils and fats	0.6	2	0.9	0.6	0.5	0.3	1.5	1.3	−0.6	0.3	0.5
Milk	3.9	3.9	4.5	17.5	5.5	5.7	3.9	1.4	4.8	6.5	4.4
Processed rice	1.6	1.1	1.3	1.7	2.6	1.5	1.1	3.2	0.1	0.7	1.6
Sugar	1.9	1.7	5.2	4.3	1.5	2.2	0.7	1.4	4.8	2.2	2
Food products	0	0.3	0.7	1.2	−0.3	0.2	0.3	0.6	0.5	0.5	0.2
Beverages and tobacco	−0.1	0.4	0.3	0.1	0.2	0.3	0.2	0.3	0.5	−0.1	0.6
Textile[a]	0.1	0.4	0.7	0.2	0.3	0.4	0	0.7	0.4	−0.1	0.4
Textiles	0.1	0.4	0.6	0.2	0.3	0.4	0.1	1	0.4	−0.2	0.4
Wearing apparel	0.1	0.1	0.8	0.1	0.4	0.2	−0.2	0	0.8	−0.1	0.2

Table 3.7.   *(Continued)*

Sector	World[a]	Bangladesh	Brazil	Cameroon	China	Indonesia	Mexico	Mozambique	Philippines	Russia	Vietnam
Other manufactures[a]	0	0.1	0	0	0.1	0.2	0	0.4	0.1	-0.2	0.2
Leather products	0	-0.1	0.3	0.1	-0.2	-0.2	-0.2	0.2	-0.1	-0.1	-0.2
Wood products	0	0.3	0.1	-0.1	0.2	0.1	0	0	0.3	-0.2	0.2
Paper products	0	0.3	0	0.3	0.3	0.4	0	2.6	0.3	-0.2	0.4
Petroleum, coal	0	0.1	0.1	0	0.1	0.1	0	0	0.1	0	0.1
Chemical, plastic	-0.1	0.1	0	0	0.1	0.1	-0.1	0.9	0.1	-0.2	0.2
Mineral products	0	0.2	0.1	0.1	0.3	0.3	0	3.6	0.3	-0.1	0.4
Iron and steel	0	0.2	0	-0.1	0.2	0.2	0.1	0.1	0.2	-0.2	0.2
Metals	0	0.1	0	-0.1	0.2	0.4	0	0.1	0.3	-0.2	0.4
Metal products	0	0.1	0	-0.1	0.2	0.3	0	0	0.2	-0.2	0.3
Motor vehicles	-0.1	0.1	0.3	-0.1	0	0.2	-0.1	0	0.2	-0.2	0.1
Transport equipment	-0.1	0.1	-0.2	0	-0.2	0.2	-0.2	-0.2	0.1	-0.2	0.2
Electronic equipment	0.1	0.1	0	-0.1	0.2	0.2	0	-0.1	0.1	-0.1	0.2
Machinery	0	0	0	-0.1	0.1	0.2	-0.1	0	0.2	-0.2	0.2
Manufactures	0	0.3	0	-0.1	0	0.2	0	0	0.1	-0.1	0.2
Electricity	-0.1	-0.1	0	0	0.3	-0.1	-0.1	0	0	-0.2	-0.1
Gas	-0.2	-0.1	-0.2	-0.3	-0.2	-0.2	-0.2	-0.2	-0.2	-0.3	-0.3
Water	0	0	0	0	0	0	0	0	0	0	0
Construction	-0.1	0	0.1	-0.1	-0.1	0	0	-0.1	-0.1	-0.1	-0.1
Services[a]	0	0.1	0	0	0.3	0	0	0	0.1	0	0
Trade	0.2	0.4	0.1	0.1	0.4	0.1	0.1	0.1	0.3	0	0.1
Transport	0	0	0	0	0	0	0	-0.1	0	0	0
Water transport	0	0	0	0	0	0	0	0	0	0	0
Air transport	0	0	0	0	0	0	0	0	0	0	0
Communication	0	0	0	0	0	0	0	0	0	0	0
Financial services	0	0	0	0	0	0.1	0	0	0	0.1	0
Insurance	0	-0.1	-0.1	-0.1	-0.1	-0.1	-0.1	-0.1	-0.1	0	-0.1
Business services	0	0	0	0	0	0	0.1	0	0	0	0
Recreational services	-0.1	0	-0.1	-0.1	0	-0.1	-0.1	0	-0.1	-0.1	-0.1
Government services	0	0	0	0	0	0	0	0	0	0	0
Dwelling	0.1	-0.2	2.4	-0.2	0.8	0.7	0.6	-0.2	0.4	-0.2	-3.3

Source: Authors' simulations.

a. Calculated as a weighted average of respective price changes, excluding intra-EU trade

Table 3.8.   Doha: Export Prices for All Regions

Sector	World[a]	Bangladesh	Brazil	Cameroon	China	Indonesia	Mexico	Mozambique	Philippines	Russia	Vietnam
Terms of trade		-6.1	5.1	-2.8	0.2	1.1	-2.1	-2.2	-0.5	-0.8	0.8
Export price index	0.1	0.2	2.5	-0.1	0.3	0.6	-0.4	-0.1	0.2	-0.2	-1.1
Primary agriculture[a]	1.1	0.6	5.1	-0.1	1.2	0.2	0.1	0.4	-0.1	-0.2	-1.1
Paddy rice	7.9	0.2	5.9	0	1.5	0.9	4.5	0.3	0	0.2	-1
Wheat	1.6	0.4	4.2	0.4	0.9	0.7	-0.2	0.5	0.5	-0.2	0.6
Cereal grains	3.5	0.3	6	-0.1	1.3	0.6	-0.2	0.1	0.2	-0.1	-2
Fruits and vegetables	-0.1	0.1	5	-0.2	1.2	0.8	0.1	0.1	-0.2	-0.4	-1.1
Oilseeds	4.3	0.6	5	0.1	1.9	1.4	1.6	0.8	1.5	0.3	1.4
Raw sugar	0.8	0.3	5.4	-0.2	1.1	0.9	0	1.2	0.7	-0.3	-1.5
Plant fibers	6.1	1	5.6	1	1.2	4.8	1.5	1.1	3.5	0.5	2.8
Other crops	-0.2	0.1	4.8	-0.3	0.6	0.1	0	0.1	0	-0.7	-1.2
Cattle	-0.1	0.2	9.8	-0.2	1.8	1.1	0.2	0.2	0.5	-0.3	-1.6
Animal products	0	0.3	6.7	-0.1	1.3	1.1	0.1	0.1	0.1	-0.5	-1.5
Raw milk	0.3	0.2	6.3	-0.1	1.5	2	-0.1	0.5	0.3	-0.4	-0.6
Wool	2	0.1	3.1	-0.1	1.8	0.9	0.5	0.4	0.3	0	0.4
Other primary[a]	0.1	-0.2	1.2	0	0.1	0.4	0	-0.2	0.6	0.1	-0.6
Forestry	0	-0.2	2.6	-0.3	0.5	0.5	-0.4	-0.3	0.2	-0.3	-1.9
Fishing	0.1	-0.2	1.8	-0.4	0.8	0.6	-0.5	-0.7	0.4	-0.3	-2.5
Coal	0.3	0	0	0.8	0.1	0.4	0.1	0.1	0.4	0.4	-0.2
Crude oil	0.1	0.1	0.4	0.1	-0.1	0.4	0	0	0.2	0.1	-0.5
Natural gas	0	-0.1	-1.9	-0.1	0	0.2	-0.2	1.2	0.5	0	-4.5
Other minerals	0.4	-0.2	1.2	-0.1	0	1	-0.4	0	0.7	0.1	-1.2
Food[a]	0.8	0.2	3.8	-0.1	1	0.8	-0.3	0	0.4	-0.6	-1.4
Bovine meat products	2.3	0.2	6.1	-0.2	1.1	0.9	-0.4	0.3	0.5	0.1	0.6
Other meat	0.8	0.4	5.8	-0.2	1.1	0.9	-0.3	0.1	0.1	-0.5	-1.5
Vegetable oils and fats	0.7	0.9	3.5	-0.1	1.2	0.8	2.6	0.2	0.4	-0.3	-1
Milk	4.1	0.2	3.5	1.9	0.9	0.8	-0.4	0	2.7	-0.3	1.3
Processed rice	1.8	0.1	3.3	0	1.1	0.8	-0.3	0.3	0.1	-0.3	-1
Sugar	2.1	0.1	3.2	-0.2	1	0.8	-0.3	0.1	0.5	-4.4	-1.4
Food products	0	0.2	2.6	-0.1	1	0.7	-0.3	0	0.4	-0.6	-1.5
Beverages and tobacco	-0.1	-0.1	2.4	-0.2	0.8	0.5	-0.4	0	0.3	-0.5	-1.3
Textile[a]	0.1	0.3	1.9	0	0.3	0.9	-0.5	0	0.5	-0.9	-0.5
Textiles	0.1	0.4	1.9	0	0.3	0.9	-0.5	0.1	0.7	-0.9	-0.7
Wearing apparel	0.1	0.3	1.9	-0.1	0.3	0.8	-0.5	-0.1	0.4	-1	-0.4

Table 3.8. *(Continued)*

Sector	World[a]	Bangladesh	Brazil	Cameroon	China	Indonesia	Mexico	Mozambique	Philippines	Russia	Vietnam
Other manufactuers[a]											
Leather products	0	0	2.2	-0.2	0.5	0.7	-0.6	0	0.3	-0.7	-1
Wood products	0	-0.1	2.1	-0.2	0.4	0.6	-0.5	-0.2	0.3	-0.3	-1.2
Paper products	0	-0.1	1.8	-0.2	0.5	0.6	-0.4	0.5	0.3	-0.4	-1
Petroleum, coal	0.1	0	0.6	0	0.1	0.3	-0.1	-0.3	0.1	0.1	-1.7
Chemical, plastic	-0.1	-0.1	1.7	-0.1	0.2	0.4	-0.4	-0.1	0.2	-0.4	-0.9
Mineral products	0	-0.1	1.8	-0.1	0.4	0.5	-0.5	0.1	0.3	-0.3	-1.4
Iron and steel	0	-0.1	1.7	-0.1	0.3	0.4	-0.4	-0.1	0.2	-0.1	-0.3
Metals	0	0	1.4	-0.1	0.3	0.5	-0.4	-0.2	0.3	-0.2	-1.4
Metal products	0	-0.1	1.8	-0.2	0.4	0.5	-0.4	0	0.3	-0.3	-0.7
Motor vehicles	-0.1	-0.1	1.6	-0.2	-0.2	0.5	-0.3	0	0.2	-0.5	-0.9
Transport equipment	-0.1	-0.1	1.8	-0.2	0.2	0.5	-0.5	-0.1	0.3	-0.5	-0.5
Electronic equipment	0.1	-0.1	1.4	-0.2	0.1	0.5	-0.3	-0.1	0.2	-0.6	-0.8
Machinery	-0.1	-0.1	1.8	-0.2	0.2	0.4	-0.4	-0.1	0.2	-0.4	-1
Manufactures	0	-0.1	1.9	0.1	0.5	0.6	-0.4	-0.1	0.4	-0.5	-0.9
Electricity	-0.1	-0.1	1.7	-0.1	0.3	0.4	-0.2	0	0.3	0	-1.3
Gas	-0.2	-0.1	1.2	-0.2	0.5	0.5	-0.5	-0.1	0.2	-0.1	-2.8
Water	0	0	1.7	-0.2	0.6	0.6	-0.5	-0.1	0.3	-0.2	-1.5
Construction	-0.1	-0.1	2.1	-0.2	0.5	0.6	-0.5	0	0.3	-0.4	-1.6
Services[a]	0	-0.1	2.1	-0.2	0.6	0.6	-0.5	-0.1	0.3	-0.2	-1.9
Trade	0.2	-0.1	2	-0.2	0.7	0.7	-0.6	-0.2	0.3	-0.3	-2
Transport	0	-0.1	1.7	-0.2	0.6	0.6	-0.5	-0.1	0.3	-0.2	-1.2
Water transport	0	-0.1	1.7	-0.2	0.4	0.4	-0.5	-0.1	0.3	-0.2	-1.1
Air transport	0	-0.1	1.7	-0.2	0.3	0.5	-0.5	-0.1	0.3	-0.2	-1
Communication	0	-0.2	2.1	-0.2	0.6	0.7	-0.6	-0.1	0.3	-0.2	-1.4
Financial services	0	-0.1	2.1	-0.2	0.7	0.7	-0.6	-0.3	0.3	-0.2	-2
Insurance	0	-0.1	2.1	-0.2	0.6	0.7	-0.6	-0.3	0.3	-0.2	-1.7
Business services	0	-0.1	2.2	-0.2	0.6	0.7	-0.6	-0.1	0.3	-0.2	-2.5
Recreational services	-0.1	-0.1	2.1	-0.2	0.4	0.7	-0.6	-0.1	0.3	-0.3	-2
Government services	0	-0.1	2	-0.2	0.6	0.7	-0.6	-0.1	0.3	-0.4	-1.8
Dwelling	0.1	-0.2	2.4	-0.2	0.8	0.7	-0.6	-0.2	0.4	-0.2	-3.3

Source: Authors' simulations.

a. Calculated as a weighted average of respective price changes, excluding intra-EU trade

Table 3.9. Doha: Import Quantities for All Regions

Sector	World[a]	Bangladesh	Brazil	Cameroon	China	Indonesia	Mexico	Mozambique	Philippines	Russia	Vietnam
Import quantity index	1.3	-0.7	3.4	-0.4	4.6	0.5	-0.3	-0.6	0.0	2.4	-1.9
Primary agriculture[a]	0.0	-3.0	6.3	-1.0	0.5	-0.1	-1.7	-2.1	0.2	1.5	-2.3
Paddy rice	35.7	0.3	14.0	1.1	1.5	0.9	-32.2	-10.7	-11.3	4.8	-11.9
Wheat	0.3	-2.6	1.6	-2.6	-1.1	-0.7	-4.3	-1.4	0.5	-0.5	-1.1
Cereal grains	-0.7	-0.9	6.8	-4.6	6.5	-1.1	1.8	-2.7	1.0	-6.9	-3.2
Fruits and vegetables	1.5	-0.6	4.7	4.4	4.8	-0.4	1.5	-1.9	0.2	2.4	-3.0
Oilseeds	-1.5	-2.5	6.5	-0.1	-1.5	-4.9	-1.3	-0.6	-0.9	-0.6	-0.4
Raw sugar	-1.7	-2.6	9.7	-0.1	-1.7	-1.4	-1.8	9.1	-0.4	-0.8	-5.6
Plant fibers	-1.5	-5.3	2.7	0.5	-3.5	2.3	-11.4	0.9	1.1	1.1	-4.8
Other crops	-2.2	0.5	15.0	0.2	2.0	0.4	2.6	-2.2	-0.4	1.8	-0.3
Cattle	-0.5	-0.2	69.6	1.5	3.5	-0.5	-2.0	-1.8	-2.7	8.6	0.2
Animal products	0.1	-0.1	28.4	1.9	3.1	4.1	-0.6	-1.4	2.7	0.6	-0.3
Raw milk	-6.9	-2.7	27.4	-0.3	4.9	5.1	-1.5	1.9	0.1	0.4	0.5
Wool	-3.8	-0.9	32.5	-4.2	0.4	4.2	-4.2	0.1	-0.3	1.2	2.7
Other primary[a]	0.0	-0.2	-0.2	0.0	-1.1	0.5	-0.2	-0.7	-0.1	0.5	-3.0
Forestry	-0.1	-1.3	6.6	2.8	0.8	0.9	-0.4	-1.3	-1.8	2.3	-3.8
Fishing	0.8	-0.5	1.6	-0.2	4.0	0.3	2.1	-1.9	0.3	3.1	-3.6
Coal	-0.1	1.7	-2.7	-0.4	2.6	0.9	-0.3	1.5	0.0	-3.6	-1.2
Crude oil	0.1	0.1	0.7	0.0	-1.7	0.8	-0.2	0.3	0.1	2.2	-2.2
Natural gas	0.0	-0.6	-27.6	-1.2	14.2	3.1	-2.8	16.3	10.2	0.4	-55.1
Other minerals	-0.3	0.0	-2.9	-0.2	-1.6	-0.4	0.1	-0.8	-0.9	0.8	-2.5
Food[a]	5.9	-2.6	5.1	-2.3	6.6	-0.1	0.3	-1.2	1.2	2.4	-3.5
Bovine meat products	24.9	-0.3	22.5	-16.5	4.5	4.0	-2.4	-5.1	0.5	-12.4	0.5
Other meat	10.8	0.3	15.9	-8.7	11.8	4.1	-2.3	-2.9	30.2	11.7	-9.1
Vegetable oils and fats	7.4	-2.3	8.2	0.1	8.2	1.9	2.7	-2.0	4.0	5.1	-2.6
Milk	-4.4	-7.4	-0.7	-15.1	-1.3	-4.1	5.8	-0.6	-0.5	-9.3	-3.9
Processed rice	22.6	-2.6	5.0	-2.7	-3.6	-1.5	-2.1	-2.0	0.0	2.1	-6.8
Sugar	29.3	-3.6	-1.6	-4.0	0.1	-2.3	-1.6	-0.6	4.9	2.7	-6.6
Food products	1.7	-0.1	4.6	-0.6	7.8	1.3	-0.6	-1.1	0.2	3.7	-3.3
Beverages and tobacco	2.6	-0.5	2.3	8.3	4.0	3.0	1.2	-0.3	-0.2	3.5	-3.1
Textile[a]	6.2	0.1	3.7	-0.2	12.6	3.3	0.7	-0.8	6.8	2.0	-6.0
Textiles	5.5	0.1	3.6	-0.2	12.2	3.2	-1.4	-0.9	7.5	2.2	-6.1
Wearing apparel	7.1	0.4	4.6	-0.1	16.1	3.9	6.0	-0.5	-0.7	1.9	-4.1

Table 3.9.   (Continued)

Sector	World[a]	Bangladesh	Brazil	Cameroon	China	Indonesia	Mexico	Mozambique	Philippines	Russia	Vietnam
Other manufactures[a]	1.1	–0.3	3.7	–0.1	4.6	0.2	–0.2	–0.4	–0.5	3.8	–1.4
Leather products	4.2	–0.6	2.8	–0.2	16.0	9.8	3.9	–0.5	0.1	9.3	–2.8
Wood products	0.1	–1.2	8.1	–0.2	2.9	0.1	–0.6	–0.5	–0.9	8.0	–3.8
Paper products	0.4	–0.5	3.6	–0.9	3.1	–0.4	–0.7	–1.0	–0.2	3.6	–1.8
Petroleum, coal	0.5	–0.1	0.1	0.0	3.1	0.2	–0.2	0.2	0.0	2.9	0.1
Chemical, plastic	1.9	–0.2	2.8	0.1	5.8	1.3	–0.5	–0.5	0.8	3.6	–1.1
Mineral products	2.1	–0.8	5.1	–0.5	10.2	–0.3	–0.6	–4.6	–0.2	6.3	–5.8
Iron and steel	0.5	–0.1	1.6	–0.3	2.9	–0.3	–0.5	–0.2	–0.5	2.0	0.6
Metals	0.8	–0.6	0.9	0.2	3.1	–2.1	–0.3	–0.7	–0.8	4.6	–4.6
Metal products	1.9	–0.5	5.3	–0.2	10.3	0.4	–0.5	0.2	0.0	7.3	0.4
Motor vehicles	2.2	–0.1	7.7	–0.2	8.4	0.6	–0.8	–0.2	0.0	8.5	–1.4
Transport equipment	1.1	–0.7	3.2	–0.2	5.1	0.2	–0.6	–0.2	0.2	7.6	–0.4
Electronic equipment	–0.1	–0.2	2.2	–0.2	0.5	–0.2	0.4	–0.2	–1.0	0.8	–2.2
Machinery	1.4	–0.1	4.7	–0.2	6.5	–0.7	–0.2	–0.1	–0.2	1.2	–1.6
Manufactures	0.5	–1.1	7.4	0.8	14.4	0.9	–0.1	–0.2	0.7	11.8	–3.4
Electricity	0.0	–0.3	1.9	–0.4	–0.3	1.2	–0.1	0.5	1.0	2.9	–4.1
Gas	0.5	0.2	2.6	0.3	1.5	1.9	–0.7	1.2	1.2	0.6	–7.9
Water	–0.2	0.0	3.5	–0.6	1.5	0.3	–1.3	–0.6	0.8	–0.5	–3.0
Construction	–0.1	–0.4	6.2	–0.5	1.2	1.4	–1.5	–0.1	0.8	–0.7	–4.8
Services[a]	–0.1	–0.3	2.9	–0.4	0.5	0.7	–0.7	–0.3	0.4	–0.2	–1.8
Trade	–0.3	–1.0	3.9	–0.5	0.3	0.7	–1.1	–0.5	0.1	–0.5	–2.3
Transport	0.1	–0.3	2.8	–0.5	1.0	0.9	–0.7	0.0	0.8	–0.1	–0.9
Water transport	0.2	–0.4	0.9	–0.4	0.7	0.3	–0.9	–0.2	0.3	–0.1	–0.4
Air transport	0.0	–0.1	1.5	–0.3	0.3	0.8	–0.6	–0.2	0.6	–0.2	–0.8
Communication	0.0	–0.2	0.6	–0.5	0.8	0.9	–1.1	–0.2	0.4	–0.2	–0.1
Financial services	–0.2	0.3	3.5	–0.5	0.9	1.0	–0.7	–0.4	0.2	–0.2	–0.8
Insurance	0.0	0.0	3.6	–0.3	0.9	1.2	–0.5	–0.2	0.5	0.1	–0.5
Business services	–0.1	–0.2	4.1	–0.3	0.8	0.5	–0.9	–0.3	0.3	0.0	–2.2
Recreational services	0.0	–0.2	2.3	–0.5	0.8	1.4	–0.9	–0.2	0.7	–0.1	–3.2
Government services	0.0	–0.2	1.6	–0.5	1.1	1.3	–1.1	–0.4	0.6	–0.4	–3.9
Dwelling	0.0	–0.1	0.6	–0.2	–0.1	0.1	–0.1	–0.4	0.0	0.2	–1.0

Source: Authors' simulations.

a. Calculated as a weighted average of respective price changes, excluding intra-EU trade

Table 3.10. Doha: Export Quantities for All Regions

Sector	World[a]	Bangladesh	Brazil	Cameroon	China	Indonesia	Mexico	Mozambique	Philippines	Russia	Vietnam
Export quantity index	1.3	−0.2	−1.8	0.1	3.7	0.1	0.5	0.0	−0.1	1.8	0.8
Primary agriculture[a]	0.0	6.2	−11.8	−0.7	14.0	−1.6	0.9	1.4	−4.8	6.2	0.6
Paddy rice	35.7	72.4	16.4	1.4	462.5	60.4	36.5	−4.8	203.6	13.4	17.6
Wheat	0.3	328.0	−24.0	7.9	10.7	−0.3	−29.1	−7.4	32.3	8.2	−8.4
Cereal grains	−0.7	31.1	0.5	0.5	20.1	3.7	8.3	1.5	3.7	11.2	−19.6
Fruits and vegetables	1.5	−5.4	−16.2	−3.9	22.7	2.5	1.4	−4.0	−6.4	3.5	0.9
Oilseeds	−1.5	20.5	−4.6	8.2	27.0	9.2	9.1	11.6	7.0	16.2	6.2
Raw sugar	−1.7	−10.5	10.7	−13.0	74.5	95.0	−14.8	−20.7	−22.9	−14.4	7.0
Plant fibers	−1.5	15.0	−1.0	18.1	30.2	2.0	28.7	8.7	12.9	17.0	14.3
Other crops	−2.2	−2.1	−23.1	−5.1	−2.4	−2.1	−3.6	−2.3	−2.0	−6.6	−0.1
Cattle	−0.5	−6.9	−27.9	−0.3	−3.5	−2.8	5.1	−8.5	−7.8	−5.8	−1.7
Animal products	0.1	−1.7	−13.4	−1.2	−1.8	−1.5	2.5	−2.0	0.0	−1.0	3.1
Raw milk	−6.9	−5.8	−38.8	−3.0	−14.5	−17.0	−3.8	−7.4	−5.8	−1.5	0.1
Wool	−3.8	16.6	−26.3	17.5	−4.7	5.4	8.6	4.6	11.1	6.6	13.8
Other primary[a]	0.0	0.9	−1.6	0.2	1.6	−0.3	0.5	1.0	0.1	−0.1	1.3
Forestry	−0.1	0.2	−12.0	0.6	−1.6	−1.0	2.3	1.3	0.4	0.9	8.7
Fishing	0.8	1.0	−1.8	−1.1	2.7	1.7	2.3	0.6	0.3	2.2	5.1
Coal	−0.1	0.3	0.7	−3.6	1.6	−0.2	0.7	0.3	−2.1	−1.0	2.1
Crude oil	0.1	−0.1	−3.2	0.1	2.0	0.0	0.5	0.2	0.8	−0.3	0.8
Natural gas	0.0	3.0	91.9	1.4	1.4	−0.5	8.5	−33.5	−13.7	−0.1	400.2
Other minerals	−0.3	1.1	−1.5	0.5	0.4	−1.0	0.8	0.7	0.0	0.3	1.9
Food[a]	5.9	−3.5	43.4	−1.4	0.3	−0.5	6.1	−2.7	4.1	5.2	0.5
Bovine meat products	24.9	66.9	373.9	15.3	5.6	44.6	3.2	−8.7	86.3	184.4	12.9
Other meat	10.8	11.0	−4.9	21.5	−21.4	16.6	53.1	−13.9	36.0	19.4	11.7
Vegetable oils and fats	7.4	−0.8	0.4	−9.2	−8.0	−5.4	−10.0	4.2	−2.7	1.4	3.0
Milk	−4.4	61.7	30.9	115.0	48.6	51.4	51.0	49.3	22.3	47.8	13.0
Processed rice	22.6	13.0	−0.9	−9.4	49.5	46.5	0.8	−0.9	−35.8	16.7	6.1
Sugar	29.3	−32.0	6.8	−12.7	27.5	−7.2	−5.5	16.7	52.6	30.6	−16.0
Food products	1.7	−4.0	−1.4	−2.9	−0.5	−3.3	2.1	−4.6	3.7	2.6	−1.3
Beverages and tobacco	2.6	3.8	−2.0	2.8	2.1	5.6	1.9	−2.2	3.5	0.3	0.1
Textile[a]	6.2	0.1	−4.4	2.9	10.0	4.1	−13.5	−7.7	13.3	15.8	−9.6
Textiles	5.5	−1.9	−4.5	3.6	8.4	2.4	−10.0	−6.9	12.0	11.4	−2.0
Wearing apparel	7.1	1.3	−3.8	1.6	10.9	6.8	−16.6	−8.6	13.9	21.0	−12.0

Table 3.10. (Continued)

Sector	World[a]	Bangladesh	Brazil	Cameroon	China	Indonesia	Mexico	Mozambique	Philippines	Russia	Vietnam
Other manufactures[a]	1.1	-1.9	-9.3	0.0	1.5	-0.3	1.0	0.2	-1.3	2.7	1.8
Leather products	4.2	-5.6	-14.9	-6.2	8.6	14.7	-20.6	-7.3	-2.4	0.3	-2.7
Wood products	0.1	9.6	-10.0	0.1	-1.5	-0.3	2.6	-0.5	-2.2	1.3	6.8
Paper products	0.4	0.2	-9.0	1.0	-1.7	-1.5	3.3	-3.2	-0.9	2.5	5.5
Petroleum, coal	0.5	0.4	-0.9	0.2	0.0	-0.7	0.4	1.9	0.9	2.0	6.2
Chemical, plastic	1.9	-0.3	-8.4	2.3	2.0	0.5	1.7	23.6	3.4	2.0	2.2
Mineral products	2.1	-0.3	-5.4	1.1	3.4	-0.4	-0.2	-1.1	-1.7	0.4	5.8
Iron and steel	0.5	3.7	-8.2	-0.9	0.0	-1.0	5.2	0.0	-0.8	1.3	2.6
Metals	0.8	-9.9	-5.2	0.7	0.8	-2.9	2.0	-0.1	-2.2	4.2	10.6
Metal products	1.9	1.8	-9.4	0.4	3.0	-2.6	-0.1	-1.4	-2.2	4.3	4.0
Motor vehicles	2.2	-1.6	-5.1	-1.3	-1.7	-1.9	-1.3	1.0	-0.2	2.2	2.5
Transport equipment	1.1	-2.3	-14.3	-1.0	2.1	-2.2	2.3	-1.9	-1.6	7.5	1.8
Electronic equipment	-0.1	1.3	-9.5	1.6	0.3	-2.7	2.7	0.0	-1.3	7.7	7.2
Machinery	1.4	0.9	-11.6	0.1	0.7	-2.4	0.8	-0.1	-1.3	2.6	7.5
Manufactures	0.5	6.7	-12.7	-3.1	-0.5	-5.2	0.6	-0.6	-5.1	1.6	3.3
Electricity	0.0	0.7	-9.4	0.7	0.7	-2.2	0.9	1.4	-1.3	-1.1	7.7
Gas	0.5	-0.1	-7.2	0.2	-3.2	-3.5	1.9	-0.4	-1.5	-0.3	16.5
Water	-0.2	0.5	-8.8	1.1	-3.4	-3.2	3.2	0.7	-1.7	1.5	8.9
Construction	-0.1	1.2	-7.4	0.5	-2.1	-2.4	1.7	-0.1	-1.4	1.5	6.0
Services[a]	-0.1	0.5	-7.5	0.8	-2.1	-2.3	2.2	0.6	-1.0	1.0	7.6
Trade	-0.3	0.8	-7.0	1.1	-2.3	-2.3	2.4	1.2	-1.0	1.5	8.3
Transport	0.1	0.8	-6.0	0.8	-2.2	-2.2	2.3	0.5	-0.9	0.9	5.0
Water transport	0.2	1.0	-5.7	1.1	-1.2	-1.1	2.4	0.9	-0.6	1.4	4.7
Air transport	0.0	0.7	-6.0	0.8	-1.0	-1.9	2.2	0.5	-0.9	1.0	4.2
Communication	0.0	0.7	-7.6	0.8	-2.0	-2.4	2.3	0.3	-1.1	0.7	5.7
Financial services	-0.2	0.6	-7.6	0.9	-2.4	-2.6	2.1	1.2	-1.2	0.7	7.7
Insurance	0.0	0.7	-7.7	0.8	-2.4	-2.6	2.2	1.2	-1.3	0.7	6.6
Business services	-0.1	0.4	-8.1	0.8	-2.3	-2.5	2.2	0.5	-1.2	0.8	10.2
Recreational services	0.0	0.4	-7.6	0.8	-1.7	-2.8	2.0	0.4	-1.3	0.9	7.8
Government services	0.0	0.4	-7.4	0.6	-2.2	-2.6	2.2	0.5	-1.2	1.4	7.3
Dwelling	0.0	-0.1	0.6	-0.2	-0.1	0.1	-0.1	0.4	0.0	0.2	-1.0

Source: Authors' simulations.

a. Calculated as a weighted average of respective price changes, excluding intra-EU trade

vidual country case study authors are the experts in assessing the likely responses of their respective national economies to these external developments and to their own trade policy reforms. Accordingly, there is a need to blend the global and national analysis into a single, coherent story. This section summarizes the approach used for the studies reported in this volume.[7]

The idea of first solving a global model and passing the world price or volume results (or both) on to a national model is rather intuitive, but when faced with implementation, several problems arise. The first problem is that national policy reforms should not want be implemented twice—once in the global model and once in the national model. The global analysis should instead capture only the impact of policy reforms in the rest of the world. Consider, for example, the case of Brazil. It is desirable for the national model to receive results from the two scenarios discussed above, omitting Brazilian reforms in the process. The world price changes passed on to the national model would then reflect the impact on world markets of policy reform in all countries except for Brazil. The national model then takes these world price changes as exogenous and implements the Brazilian portion of the reform package. In the special case where the national model is identical to the Brazilian portion of the global model, this approach should give the same results for Brazil as were obtained under the comprehensive reform simulations reported in the preceding tables.[8] Thus, the first problem is resolved by solving each scenario with the focus economy omitted, thereupon passing the resulting world market effects onto the national studies, to be implemented as exogenous shocks in the country case studies.

A second problem that arises in linking the two models is how specifically to pass the information on world markets to the national model. Because all of the national models take import price as given, and import supply facing the focus economies in the global model is very elastic, it is easy to handle this side of the story. The import price changes generated in the global model are appropriately aggregated and then passed on to the national model, where they are applied as exogenous shocks. Exports, however, are more challenging.

The fundamental problem with exports is that the global model treats products as being differentiated by origin—the Armington assumption discussed earlier in this chapter. Therefore, Brazil's export prices are not exogenous, even for products where their world market share is relatively small. Accordingly, the impact of world market changes on both price and quantity and the models' differences in the connections between these two variables must be considered. Specifically, there are different export supply schedules for commodities in the global and national models due to the differences in the two models' representations of the Brazilian economy. It is often found that the national models of developing countries have less elastic export supply schedules, reflecting domestic constraints on export capacity not captured in the global model. However, the export demand schedule is treated as having the same slope in the two models. Nearly all of the country case study authors have built downward-sloping export demand schedules into their models, and they have taken the elasticity of export demand from the global model.[9]

Figure 3.2 illustrates this point for a specific product—for example, processed sugar. The initial equilibrium for exports of Brazilian sugar is at point A, where the supply schedule (SG in the global model and SN in the national model) intersects the global demand schedule, D. When a Doha scenario is implemented in the

Figure 3.2.   Transmission of Global Results to a National Model

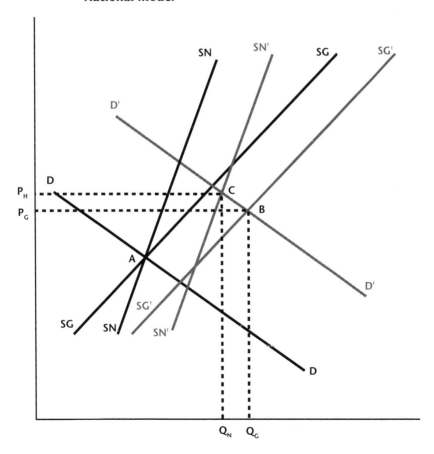

Source: Fan Zhai.

rest of the world, the first thing that happens to Brazilian exports of sugar is that the reduction in protection in the industrialized countries results in an outward shift in export demand to D'D'. But the export supply curve may also be affected—owing, for example, to the limited endowments of land, labor, and capital in Brazil and the simultaneous shifts to import prices and other export demands. Here, it is assumed that there is a reduction in demand in manufacturing, thereby releasing additional resources for use in agriculture and causing export supply to shift to the right. The global model finds a new equilibrium at point B, with price P_G and quantity Q_G. Referring back to the tables of results for Doha shows that point B embodies a small increase in Brazil's sugar price (3.3 percent) and a somewhat larger increase in quantity (6.8 percent).

To communicate these changes in global markets to the national model, it is assumed that the national model will adequately take care of the supply shift due to domestic, general equilibrium changes in response to liberalization in the rest of the world. This makes sense, because both models typically draw on the same underlying social accounting matrix and both embody the same general equilibrium restrictions. Thus, there is only a need to identify the extent to which the demand curve shifts outward in figure 3.2. As shown in the appendix to this chapter, this demand shift can be readily established with three pieces of information: the change in price, the change in quantity, and the slope of the export demand schedule. One can then solve the demand function for the shift necessary to ensure that the new equilibrium still lies on the demand curve.

Of course, this approach is limited by the fact that the two models have different characterizations of supply. For example, in figure 3.2, even assuming the same shifts in demand and supply, the national model generates a different equilibrium at point C, with higher price, P_N, and lower quantity, Q_N, than in the global model as a result of the less elastic nature of supply. In summary, the price and quantity changes generated by the national model in response to these exogenous shocks will not be exactly the same as the global model. A detailed comparison of the price and quantity outcomes in the global and national models has been conducted for Brazil and for China, and they yield correlations of nearly 0.9 for quantities and somewhat less for prices. So, although the two sets of results are different, they are indeed highly correlated.

In summary, there is an inbuilt inconsistency: the global and national models treat exports differently. This cannot be resolved perfectly, but the approach used here to communicating between the global and national models permits use of the strengths of each of the two models while ensuring broad consistency in results. It could be further perfected by modifying the global model to better reflect the national models, but this is well beyond the scope of the present project—and maybe not even desirable, because, for most purposes, a global model needs a degree of consistency in its treatment of individual countries and so cannot reflect all the country details precisely.[10]

In closing, one word of caution to the reader is advisable. In the subsequent chapters, authors report price changes for full liberalization and for the core Doha scenario, obtained from this global exercise. It will seem natural to compare these price changes to those reported in this chapter. However, recall that the price changes provided to the individual country case study authors omit the impacts of that country's own actions. Also, in some cases, the country case study authors have rescaled the price changes by normalizing them on the domestic consumer price index, for example. Although this rescaling doesn't affect the results in their models, which depend only on *relative* price changes, it does make direct comparisons of price changes between chapters more difficult.

Chapter 3 Annex A:
Shocking a Single-Country CGE Model with Export Prices and Quantities from a Global Model

Mark Horridge and Fan Zhai

This annex explores the following problem: suppose a GTAP simulation has produced percent changes in import and export quantities and border prices for a particular country, say Brazil. How are the GTAP results applied to a single-country CGE model of Brazil (assuming it has the same commodity aggregation as the GTAP simulation)? Discussion of this issue distinguishes between the two most common types of single-country CGE models: models where exports and domestically produced goods are perfect substitutes (type A) and those where they substitute only imperfectly (type B).

Type A Single-Country CGE Model

The type A single-country CGE model has capital and labor mobile among sectors, and export goods are identical to those domestically used. In type A models, individual export supply functions tend to be very flat, especially for nonprimary goods. The (small) slope derives from economy-wide factor constraints and, perhaps, sector-specific fixed factors such as land.

Figure 3A.1.   Demand and Supply for Single Export in Type A Model

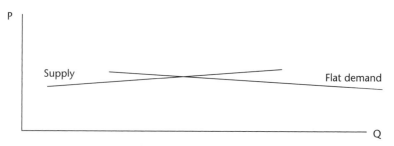

Source: Authors.

Some slope is needed for export demand functions in the type A model. If export prices were fixed (small country assumption), quite small shifts in supply functions could cause export quantities to fluctuate wildly (the overspecialization or flip-flop problem). Indeed, at first order, each commodity price will be a share-weighted average of the prices of factors or imports. Hence, with more goods than factors (and import prices fixed), not all export prices can vary independently. Thus, in a type A model, attempts to exogenously fix all export prices will fail or will simply produce ridiculous results. To prevent this problem, Type A models usually postulate a downward-sloping constant-elasticity demand curve for each export good, as shown in figure 3A.1. This means that export expansion will be accompanied by falling export prices and a TOT loss. Indeed, at modest tariff levels, this TOT loss will dominate the efficiency gains obtained from unilateral tariff reduction and aggregate welfare will fall. This is simply evidence of a nonzero optimal tariff.

Type B Single-Country CGE Model

In a type B single-country CGE model, export prices are *not* identical to prices of domestically used goods. The two are related via a constant elasticity of transformation (CET) transformation frontier. This gives individual export supply functions a marked upward slope. Type B models are therefore compatible with fixed export prices (the small country assumption) and therefore zero optimal tariffs.

Figure 3A.2. Demand and Supply for Single Export in Type B Model

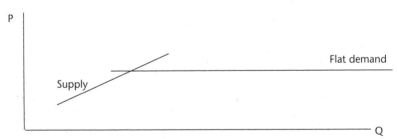

Source: Authors.

For each good, the export price is related to the export and domestic quantity ratio for that good, thus export prices can be shocked independently and export quantities will adjust to suit.

Both types A and B models normally assume that cost, insurance, and freight (CIF) inclusive import prices are fixed, and that users substitute between imports and domestic goods via a constant elasticity of substitution (CES) nest, with the ease of substitution governed by an Armington elasticity. Therefore, there is no difficulty about shocking import prices. Here, the concentration is on the problem of how to shock exports.

Single Country within GTAP

The individual countries (or regions) embedded within the GTAP model are akin to type A models (there is no export and domestic CET). The downward slope on export demand schedules derives from the Armington assumption applied in *other regions*. Indeed, the export demand elasticity for good *i* facing a country with small world market share will be approximately equal to the (interimport) Armington elasticity of substitution. Thus, in the global model, the import and export demand elasticities are inextricably intertwined.

Figure 3A.3.   Demand and Supply for a Single Export in a GTAP Simulation

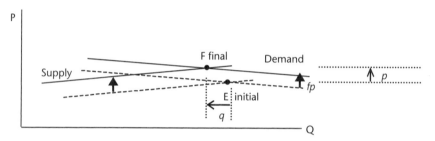

Source: Authors.

Figure 3A.3 shows how shifts in export supply and demand schedules lead to observed changes in price (*p*) and quantity (*q*). Here, the focus is on the vertical shift in the demand schedule, *fp*, because that will prove crucial in the subsequent methodology. Note that *fp* is not equal to the price change, *p*. Depending on the supply shift, *p* and *fp* may even be of opposite sign. Also, note that even if the GTAP simulation shows only the effect of *other* countries' actions, the supply curves would still be expected to shift, because all sectors use the same mobile factors, and an expansion of economic activity in another sector will raise production costs in the focus sector.

What Should the GTAP Model Communicate to the Single-Country Model?

In using the GTAP model to drive a single-country model, should an attempt be made to match the GTAP export prices or quantities or both of these? The aim here is to let the single-country model determine export supply behavior and take world demand changes from the GTAP model. Figure 3A.3 shows that the GTAP export prices and quantities are simultaneously determined by the slopes and shifts of the GTAP export demand and supply curves. The same results would not be expected if the GTAP supply behavior were replaced by a supply curve from another single-country model. Rather, the numbers to take from the GTAP model are the slope and shift (*fp*) of the world demand schedule. Of course, there are alternative methods of communicating the global model results to the national models. The authors experimented with many of these and found them deficient in one way or another.[11]

Calculating the Vertical Shift in the GTAP Model's Export Demand Curve

If export prices and quantities from a GTAP simulation and the slope of the export demand curve are known, *fp*, the vertical shift in the demand curve, can be calculated as follows:

The GTAP export demand curve can be written:

$$(3A.1) \qquad\qquad Q = [FP/P]^{ESUBM}$$

and *ESUBM* is the (positive) slope of the demand curve, approximately equal to the GTAP elasticity of substitution among imports. In proportional (log-change, percent) form this becomes:

$$(3A.2) \qquad\qquad q = - ESUBM^*(p - fp)$$

or

$$(3A.3) \qquad\qquad p = fp - q/ESUBM$$

where lowercase variables denote percentage changes in their uppercase counterparts. Hence

$$(3A.4) \qquad\qquad fp = p + q/ESUBM$$

For example, suppose that the country model for Brazil was type A, based on the same input-output table as used for the GTAP database, used the same factor mobility assumptions as GTAP, and used the same trade elasticities. Further suppose that the export demand elasticities were equal to the GTAP intercountry elasticity of import substitution. In short, suppose that the Brazil model was essentially the same as the Brazil part of the GTAP model. Then it would be expected that appropriate shocks to *FP* would produce very similar price and quantity changes to the GTAP model.

In practice, the similarity criteria just listed will not all be satisfied. Thus, taking the slope and shift (*fp*) of the world demand schedule from the GTAP model will yield export prices and quantities different from the GTAP simulation. That could be desirable if the Brazil single-country model represented Brazil better than the Brazil part of the GTAP model. This is the operating assumption used in this book.

Summary of Recommended Approach

For Type B Models, Add an Export Demand Curve for Each Good

Mimic the GTAP export demand curve by adding equation (3A.1) to the model for each exported good. Type A models already have such an equation: the elasticity, *ESUBM*, should be taken from the GTAP parameter file.

The Shock from the GTAP Model is a Change in FP (Export Demand Curve Shift)

Given *ESUBM*, and percent changes *q* and *p* from the GTAP simulation, the percent change, *fp*, can be computed at first order as using equation (3A.4), or exactly as:

$$(3A.5)\quad fp = 100^*[a - 1] \text{ where } a = [1+0.01^*p]^*([1+0.01^*q]^{1/ESUBM})$$

Tailor the Single-Country Model to Resemble the GTAP Simulation and Model

This includes choosing the trade elasticities, closure, and method of tax redistribution that matches the GTAP treatment. For type B models, the CET should be set to a high value, or eliminated altogether, because the role it has played (to prevent flip-flopping of results) is no longer necessary.

What about the Import Side?

A similar argument could be made about import prices and quantities: The GTAP model presents upward-sloping import supply curves to the single-country model, GTAP changes in import prices and quantities are again simultaneously determined by world import supply curves (which are borrowed from the

GTAP model), and GTAP import demand curves will be replaced with those from the single-country model. Should the GTAP import supply curve indeed mimic and shift? No. It seems that merely shocking import prices is likely to be adequate, because, in the GTAP model, the import supply curves to a small country are really very flat, and in all the models, the import demand curves (which use the import-domestic Armington elasticities) are comparatively steep. Hence, vertical shifts in import supply are well proxied by exogenous price changes (see figure 3A.4).

Figure 3A.4. Demand and Supply for a Single Import

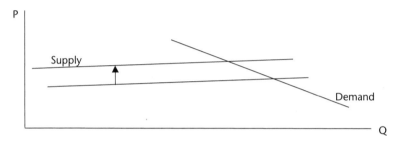

Source: Authors.

Numerical Examples

Tables 3A.1 and 3A.2 illustrate some of the above points using results from a GTAP Doha-all simulation driving single-country models for Brazil and China. The rows, corresponding to commodities, are ordered by the initial value of exports in the GTAP model. The tables show percent price and quantity changes from the GTAP simulation and the implied shift in the GTAP export demand curve, assuming that it has slope dictated by the GTAP model's Armington elasticity of substitution. These tables also report resulting percent price and quantity changes from the single-country models. Import prices were also shocked but are not shown in the table. (The focus country's tariffs were not changed for this simulation.)

Several points are worth making about the tables. First, the GTAP price change is a poor proxy for the GTAP demand shift. Second, the prices and quantities from the single-country model, although highly correlated with those from the GTAP model, are rather different in magnitude (and sometimes sign) because supply behavior is different in the two models. The correlation is higher for the changes in quantities (0.87 for both countries) than for the changes in prices (0.7 for Brazil

Table 3A.1. Interaction of the GTAP Model with the Brazil Model

Sector	Price change (GTAP)	Export change (GTAP)	Demand shift (GTAP)	Price change (model)	Export change (model)	Export values (GTAP)	Elasticity of substitution (GTAP)
Automobiles	1.5	−3.6	0.9	0.7	1.0	5,316.9	5.6
Electric Materials	1.8	−11.9	0.3	0.8	−4.1	5,250.6	8.8
Enterprise services	2.2	−8.3	−2.2	0.9	−6.1	4,475.9	2.0
Chemicals	1.6	−8.9	0.2	0.9	−4.2	4,289.6	6.6
Other food	2.4	−0.6	2.2	0.8	5.9	3,969.1	4.0
Mineral extraction	1.1	−1.4	0.4	0.9	−1.0	3,833.8	1.8
Soybeans	3.8	−9.6	1.7	2.1	−1.7	3,747.7	4.9
Machinery	1.8	−15.2	−0.7	0.8	−10.0	3,656.9	6.7
Iron products	1.7	−8.4	0.2	0.8	−3.3	3,352.2	5.9
Other agriculture	3.8	−19.0	−0.4	−0.1	−1.7	3,250.7	5.0
Slaughtering	5.0	169.7	17.6	7.8	102.5	2,714.7	8.8
Footwear	2.1	−15.6	0.0	1.5	−11.8	2,537.0	8.1
Electronic equipment	1.4	−9.9	0.2	0.7	−4.0	2,513.6	8.8
Paper products	1.8	−9.8	0.0	0.8	−4.6	2,502.6	5.9
Wood furniture	2.0	−10.3	0.4	0.8	−2.7	2,248.6	6.8
Nonferrous metals	1.4	−6.3	0.6	0.8	−1.4	2,185.0	8.4
Transportation	1.6	−6.0	−1.5	0.8	−4.5	1,635.0	2.0
Sugar refining	2.7	4.6	3.6	1.2	13.0	1,435.0	5.4
Nonmetallic minerals	1.8	−5.3	0.8	0.9	−0.7	1,320.3	5.8
Textiles	1.8	−7.2	0.8	0.7	0.3	906.3	7.5
Other metal products	1.8	−10.3	0.2	0.8	−4.3	762.0	7.0
Wholesale-retail trade	2.0	−7.2	−1.8	1.0	−5.5	713.8	2.0
Public administration	2.0	−7.6	−2.0	0.9	−5.8	700.7	2.0
Corn	5.1	10.5	9.2	1.8	19.8	690.9	2.6
Miscellaneous industries	1.9	−14.6	−0.4	1.0	−9.1	671.7	7.0
Financial institutions	2.0	−7.9	−2.1	0.8	−5.7	636.2	2.0
Vegetable oils	2.8	−2.3	2.5	1.5	6.5	521.3	6.6
Petroleum refining	0.5	−1.0	0.3	0.8	−2.0	407.9	4.2
Communications	2.1	−8.0	−2.1	0.9	−5.9	284.5	2.0
Apparel	1.8	−8.1	0.7	0.9	−1.5	243.0	7.4
Farm services	2.0	−7.8	−2.1	1.3	−6.5	173.6	2.0
Cotton	4.0	−13.4	1.1	−1.4	12.9	173.3	5.0
Poultry	5.5	−12.3	0.3	8.6	−19.6	170.0	2.6
Coffee processing	2.2	−2.3	1.2	0.7	1.1	76.0	2.3
Dairy	3.0	35.9	7.4	0.7	55.8	30.6	7.3
Civilian construction	2.1	−7.8	−2.0	1.0	−5.8	30.2	2.0
Petroleum and gas extraction	0.3	−2.8	−0.1	0.9	−7.8	16.7	8.0
Livestock	8.3	−22.8	1.5	13.8	−39.8	5.3	4.0
Paddy rice	4.6	17.6	6.3	1.0	61.2	2.1	10.1
Milk	4.9	−31.9	−13.4	0.4	−26.2	1.1	2.0
Wheat	3.5	−17.1	1.3	1.6	−2.3	0.8	8.9
Sugar cane	4.2	18.0	7.7	1.7	32.2	0.0	5.0
Building rental	2.4	0.3	2.6	1.0	3.1	0.0	2.0

Source: Authors' calculations.

Table 3A.2.   Interaction of the GTAP Model with the China Model

Sector	Price change (GTAP)	Export change (GTAP)	Demand shift (GTAP)	Price change (model)	Export change (model)	Export values (GTAP)	Elasticity of substitution (GTAP)
Electronics	0.6	−2.8	0.2	0.2	0.3	74,798.7	8.8
Apparel	0.9	8.9	2.1	0.9	9.2	69,587.1	7.4
Electrical machinery	0.7	−2.1	0.5	0.3	1.5	53,484.2	8.1
Instruments	0.7	−2.1	0.5	0.3	1.3	53,484.2	8.1
Textiles	1.0	5.5	1.7	0.9	6.4	39,431.7	7.5
Social articles	0.9	−2.2	0.6	0.4	1.6	39,173.8	7.5
Other manufactures	0.9	−2.2	0.6	0.5	0.7	39,173.8	7.5
Leather	1.1	7.2	2.0	0.7	10.5	30,420.6	8.1
Chemical	0.8	−0.1	0.7	0.6	0.8	22,775.9	6.6
Medicine	0.8	−0.1	0.7	0.6	1.0	22,775.9	6.6
Synthetic fibers	0.8	−0.1	0.7	0.3	3.1	22,775.9	6.6
Rubber and plastic	0.8	−0.1	0.7	0.4	2.5	22,775.9	6.6
Transport	0.9	−2.3	0.3	0.3	−0.3	13,476.4	3.8
Furniture	0.8	−2.8	0.4	0.4	0.1	11,505.9	6.8
Metal products	0.8	1.2	0.9	0.6	2.3	10,991.9	7.5
Building materials	0.8	2.6	1.3	0.9	2.3	7,983.8	5.8
Commerce	0.9	−2.5	0.3	0.4	−0.5	7,792.5	3.8
Food processing	1.5	−0.5	1.4	1.0	2.3	7,766.2	5.6
Other transport equipment	0.7	−0.9	0.6	0.3	2.8	5,351.4	8.6
Social services	0.9	−2.4	0.2	0.3	−0.3	5,156.0	3.8
Other crops	1.6	14.7	4.5	2.9	7.5	4,033.6	4.9
Paper and printing	0.9	−2.9	0.4	0.4	−0.1	3,112.6	5.9
Nonferrous mining	0.7	−2.2	0.4	0.6	−1.0	3,041.3	8.4
Nonferrous metals	0.7	−2.2	0.4	0.4	−0.2	3,041.3	8.4
Ferrous mining	0.8	−1.3	0.5	0.5	0.0	2,942.2	5.9
Iron and steel	0.8	−1.3	0.5	0.3	1.0	2,942.2	5.9
Crude oil	0.1	−0.5	0.1	0.1	−0.4	2,739.7	14.9
Machinery	0.7	−6.8	−0.6	0.1	−3.3	2,671.2	5.6
Special equipment	0.7	−6.8	−0.6	0.0	−3.3	2,671.2	5.6
Automobiles	0.7	−6.8	−0.6	0.0	−2.9	2,671.2	5.6
Education, science and health services	0.9	−2.4	0.2	0.4	−0.6	2,249.0	3.8
Public administration	0.9	−2.4	0.2	0.4	−0.6	2,249.0	3.8
Other livestock	1.8	−1.3	1.3	1.1	0.7	1,528.2	3.1
Refined petroleum	0.4	0.2	0.4	0.3	0.4	1,264.3	4.2
Coal mining	0.6	0.8	0.7	0.7	0.3	1,250.8	6.1
Quarrying	0.5	0.1	0.6	0.5	0.3	1,033.9	1.8
Beverages	1.2	2.1	2.1	1.0	2.6	961.9	2.3
Tobacco	1.2	2.1	2.1	1.0	2.6	961.9	2.3
Financial services	0.8	−2.3	0.2	0.3	−0.4	886.0	3.8
Corn	2.0	21.1	9.7	4.5	13.7	721.9	2.6
Construction	0.8	−2.6	0.1	0.3	−0.5	690.5	3.8
Grain milling and forage	1.4	52.9	10.1	4.6	30.1	568.5	5.2
Fishing	1.2	2.9	2.4	1.3	2.6	504.6	2.5

Table 3A.2.   (Continued)

Sector	Price change (GTAP)	Export change (GTAP)	Demand shift (GTAP)	Price change (model)	Export change (model)	Export values (GTAP)	Elasticity of substitution (GTAP)
Telecommunications	0.8	–2.2	0.2	0.2	0.0	482.2	3.8
Utilities	0.7	–1.4	0.5	0.4	0.2	290.7	5.6
Wool	2.2	–7.1	1.6	1.1	6.7	210.5	12.9
Vegetable oils	1.7	–9.2	0.2	0.8	–3.7	190.5	6.6
Forestry	0.7	–1.4	0.4	0.7	–1.3	102.6	5.0
Cotton	1.8	28.6	7.0	4.4	13.2	88.5	5.0
Other agriculture	1.8	28.6	7.0	4.2	14.0	88.5	5.0
Wheat	1.4	6.8	2.1	0.0	0.0	48.3	8.9
Rice	2.1	452.5	20.9	15.3	61.5	42.5	10.1
Sugar	1.4	24.8	5.6	1.5	24.2	27.6	5.4

Source: Authors' calculations.

and 0.61 for China).[12] Nevertheless, if the single-country model best describes the particular country, and world demand changes are well summarized by the demand shift in the global model, then the single-country model price and quantity changes are the best estimates available.

Notes

1. For the details on the database, see Dimaranan and McDougall (2006).

2. http://www.gtap.agecon.purdue.edu/products/models/.

3. Unfortunately, because of a lack of data on domestic purchases and prices, those authors are unable to estimate the elasticity of substitution between domestic goods and imports. As with the standard GTAP model, these parameters are still obtained using the "rule of two" (that is, the import-import elasticities are assumed to be twice as large as the import-domestic elasticities). Liu, Arndt, and Hertel (2004) formally test this hypothesis in a model-based analysis of changing trade shares in East Asia over the 1980s and early 1990s. They fail to reject this hypothesis.

4. Note that two of the focus countries, Cameroon and Zambia, are omitted from table 3.1. Cameroon is omitted because this country is not broken out in the GTAP database. Therefore, price impacts of liberalization in the rest of the world are inferred from the impacts on the "rest of SSA" region. In the case of Zambia, the country study focuses solely on cotton and therefore draws on partial equilibrium studies of trade reform.

5. Because Russia is still in the process of joining the WTO, some assumptions about accession were made to obtain this binding.

6. Price changes for disaggregated products are Divisia indexes. The composite price and quantity indexes reported in these tables represent aggregates of individual bilateral prices or trade flows that have been aggregated using base-period trade weights—free on board in the case of exports and cost, insurance, and freight (CIF) in the case of imports. Intra-EU trade is excluded from the world price and volume changes.

7. This section relies on research conducted by Mark Horridge and Fan Zhai. The authors of this chapter thank those country case study authors for their valuable insights and guidance on this topic. The appendix to this chapter offers a detailed description of the methodology they developed.

8. Of course, if this were the case, then there would be no reason to separate the two analyses. The reason for the two-step approach is that the national models are more complete and accurate in their representation of the focus economies.

9. In the global model, the price elasticity of export demand facing a small country is well approximated by the intercountry elasticity of substitution among imports. These have been econometrically estimated and are reported in table 1 of Hertel and others (2004).

10. A model is, by definition, a simplification of reality—that is the point of models.

11. For instance, the most obvious thing would be to simply perturb the export demand schedule (type A model) or the export price (type B model) by the amount of the GTAP price change. However, as will be seen, this produces perverse results in the type A model case, because fp and p frequently move in opposite directions. In the type B model, this produces reasonable price changes, but it can produce quantity changes that are far too small. Other strategies involve imposing some sort of technical change or export tax or subsidy in the national model, but these have undesirable welfare consequences.

12. The relatively smaller correlation for China's prices is likely due to the fact that this model retained the CET assumption on exports (type B model), whereas the Brazil model dispensed with this assumption as per the preferred approach outlined in this appendix.

References

Aksoy, M. A., and J. C. Beghin, eds. 2004. *Global Agricultural Trade and Developing Countries.* Washington, DC: World Bank.

Cranfield, J. A. L., P. V. Preckel, J. S. Eales, and T. W. Hertel. 2003. "Estimating Consumer Demand Across the Development Spectrum: Maximum Likelihood Estimates of an Implicit Direct Additivity Model," *Journal of Development Economics* (68): 289–307.

Dimaranan, B. V., and R. A. McDougall. 2005. *Global Trade, Assistance, and Production: The GTAP 6 Data Base.* West Lafayette, IN: Center for Global Trade Analysis, Purdue University.

Hertel, T. W., ed. 1997. *Global Trade Analysis: Modeling and Applications.* Cambridge, MA: Cambridge University Press.

Hertel, T. W., D. Hummels, M. Ivanic, and R. Keeney. 2004. "How Confident Can We Be in CGE-Based Assessments of Free Trade Agreements?" GTAP Working Paper 26, Center for Global Trade Analysis, Purdue University, West Lafayette, IN. http://www.gtap.agecon.purdue.edu/resources/working_paper.asp.

Hertel, T. W., and M. E. Tsigas. 1997. "Structure of the GTAP Model." In *Global Trade Analysis: Modeling and Applications*, ed. T. W. Hertel. Cambridge, MA: Cambridge University Press.

Keeney, R., and T. W. Hertel. 2005. "GTAP-AGR: A Framework for Assessing the Impacts of Multilateral Changes in Agricultural Policies." GTAP Technical Paper 24, Center for Global Trade Analysis, Purdue University, West Lafayette, IN. https://www.gtap.agecon.purdue.edu/resources/tech_papers.asp.

Liu, J., T. C. Arndt, and T. W. Hertel. 2004. "Parameter Estimation and Measures of Goodness of Fit in a Global General Equilibrium Model." *Journal of Economic Integration* 19 (3): 626–49.

OECD. 2001. *Market Effects of Crop Support Measures.* Paris: OECD.

Peeters, L., and Y. Surry. 1997. "A Review of the Arts of Estimating Price-Responsiveness of Feed Demand in the European Union." *Journal of Agricultural Economics* 48: 379–92.

Rae, A. R., and T. W. Hertel. 2000. "Future Developments in Global Livestock and Grains Markets: The Impacts of Livestock Productivity Convergence in Asia-Pacific." *Australian Journal of Agricultural and Resource Economics* 44: 393–422.

Seale, James, Anita Regmi, and Jason Bernstein. 2003. *International Evidence on Food Consumption Patterns.* Technical Bulletin 1904, Economic Research Service, U.S. Department of Agriculture, Washington, DC.

Surry, Y. 1990. "Econometric Modeling of the European Compound Feed Sector: An Application to France." *Journal of Agricultural Economics* 41: 404–21.

Valenzuela, E., T. W. Hertel, R. Keeney, and J. J. Reimer. 2005. "Assessing Global CGE Model Validity Using Agricultural Price Volatility." GTAP Working Paper No. 33, Center for Global Trade Analysis, Purdue University, West Lafayette, IN. https://www.gtap.agecon.purdue.edu/resources/working_papers.asp.

PART II

PRICE LINKAGES

4

MULTILATERAL TRADE LIBERALIZATION AND MEXICAN HOUSEHOLDS: THE EFFECT OF THE DOHA DEVELOPMENT AGENDA

Alessandro Nicita[*]

Summary

Empirical evidence suggests that global trade reforms are unlikely to produce analogous results across countries, especially when analyzing their effect on poverty. This implies that the analysis of trade reform on social welfare cannot be generalized and needs to be conducted on a country-by-country basis. Moreover, even within the same country, geographic areas, households, and individuals are likely to be differentially affected, some of them benefiting more than others, while others might lose. With this in mind, this chapter provides a quantitative estimate of the effect on Mexican households from the implementation of the Doha Development Agenda (DDA). The analysis uses a two-step approach for which changes in prices and factors are estimated through a computable general equilibrium (CGE) model (Global Trade Analysis Project—GTAP) and then

[*]The author wishes to thank Thomas Hertel, Marcelo Olarreaga, and George Rapsomanikis and participants of the Conference on the Poverty Impacts of the Doha Development Agenda in The Hague (December 2–4, 2004) for helpful comments and discussions. Also, the author is indebted to Maros Ivanic for estimating and providing the GTAP results.

mapped into the welfare function of the household using household survey data. The empirical approach used in this study measures the impact of Doha implementation by tracing changes in the household prices of goods and factors and their impact on household welfare, taking particular account of the role of domestic price transmission.

The findings suggest that multilateral trade liberalization alone would have a negative effect on Mexican households, even though very small. However, when the implementation of the DDA is complemented by domestic policies intended to increase productivity and improve domestic price transmission, the overall effect becomes positive. The results point to the importance of domestic price transmission in determining the variance of the effects across households. Given the existing structure of markets in Mexico, most of the effects of multilateral trade liberalization would be felt in the northern states, which are more connected to international markets. Conversely, households living in the southern states are isolated from most effects—not because of the composition of their consumption or income bundle, but because of the marginal effect of trade reforms on prices in those areas. An alternative scenario explores the impact of complementary policies (for example, improved extension services) that might enable farm households to respond to increased market opportunities without having to incur additional costs. This enhances the welfare outcome, especially for the poorest rural households in the south of the country, when accompanied by reforms designed to increase price transmission within the Mexican economy.

Introduction

Trade negotiations have recently occupied center stage in multilateral policy discussions. The belief is that international trade, and the reduction of protectionist barriers as a means of increasing it, is a powerful tool to spur economic growth and reduce poverty in developing countries. However, the evidence of the positive effects of international trade reform on poverty in developing countries is fragmentary.[1] In practice, the consensus is that trade policies are only one ingredient in the development recipe, and other policies are generally needed to ensure that trade will enhance welfare for the majority of the poor. Therefore, it is important to investigate the factors that influence the relationship between trade reform and poverty alleviation. This chapter focuses specifically on the role of the marketing system in transmitting price changes from the border to rural and urban households throughout Mexico.

Empirical evidence suggests that similar trade reforms are unlikely to produce analogous results across countries, especially when analyzing their effect on poverty. This implies that the analysis of trade reform on social welfare cannot be generalized and needs to be conducted on a country-by-country basis. Moreover, even within the same country, geographic areas, households, and individuals are likely to be differentially affected, some of them benefiting more than others, while others might lose. Therefore, it is necessary to analyze the impact of trade policies on poverty using a microeconomic framework so as to identify likely winners and possible losers. In particular, the analysis of the distribution of benefits and costs across regions, communities, and individuals is important when thinking about complementary and compensatory policies.

This chapter provides a quantitative estimate of the effect on Mexican households from the implementation of the DDA. The analysis uses a variant of the two-step approach outlined in chapter 3. However, in this case, a national CGE model is not used. Instead, the changes in prices and factors estimated through the GTAP global CGE model (Hertel 1997) are transformed based on the econometrically estimated price transmission relations and then mapped directly into the welfare function of the household.[2] The contribution of this chapter rests in the translation of the national price changes to the local level.

In analyzing the poverty effect of multilateral trade liberalization, this chapter takes into account the changes in factor returns (labor and land) and the cost of the consumption basket and value of income sources of poor households to measure changes in real income and poverty. This study is enriched by the analysis of domestic price transmission to investigate the magnitude of the effect of trade policies at the local level. Simply put, it measures the effect of trade policies on poverty not only on the basis of what the poor produce and consume, but also taking into account the geographic area where this production and consumption take place.

To summarize the main results, the findings suggest that multilateral trade liberalization alone would have a negative effect on Mexican households, albeit a very small one. However, when the implementation of the DDA is complemented by domestic policies intended to increase productivity and improve domestic price transmission, the overall effect become positive. The results point to the importance of domestic price transmission in determining the variation in impacts across households.

Given the existing structure of markets in Mexico, the results indicate that the effects of multilateral trade liberalization would concentrate in the northern states, which are more closely connected to international markets. Conversely, households living in the southern states are largely insulated from these effects—not because of the composition of their consumption or income bundle, but rather because of the very limited effect of trade reforms on prices in those areas.

The remainder of this chapter is organized as follows. Section 1 describes the extent and distribution of poverty in Mexico. First is provided a description of the

extent and distribution of poverty in Mexico, followed by the implication of the
DDA for Mexican households. Next, the empirical framework is presented. Finally,
the last two sections discuss the results and draw some conclusions. More detail on
the household database as well as its reconciliation with, and mapping to, the
macroeconomic data (GTAP) is available in the appendix to Nicita (forthcoming).

Poverty in Mexico

Despite Mexico's status as a middle-income country and a member of the OECD,
poverty in Mexico is widespread. Poverty levels moved substantially during the
1990s, decreasing in periods of economic growth and increasing in economic
downturns. Extreme poverty[3] was estimated to be about 24 percent in the early
1990s. Economic reforms and growth produced a reduction of about 3 percentage
points by 1994. The economic crisis of 1995 and the sharp devaluation of the peso
then led to a sharp increase in poverty (to 37 percent in 1996 and 34 percent in
1998). Finally, economic recovery in the late 1990s produced the largest decline in
poverty, with extreme poverty falling to precrisis levels in 2000 and declining
thereafter to about 20 percent in 2002. The incidence of poverty in Mexico varies
widely by region. Table 4.1 illustrates the incidence of poverty in five Mexican
regions for the year 2000.[4]

Poverty in Mexico is fundamentally a rural phenomenon. More than half of
the households living in rural areas are extremely poor. With the exception of the
Federal District of Mexico City, northern states register the lowest incidence of
poverty. The states in the central regions and especially the southernmost states
register the highest percentage of poor. Although extreme poverty rates are relatively low, especially in urban areas, moderate poverty is more widespread. At the
national level, more than 50 percent of the population is moderately poor, with

Table 4.1. Poverty in Mexico (Headcount)

Region	Extreme poverty			Moderate poverty		
	Total	Urban	Rural	Total	Urban	Rural
Federal district	11.2	11.2		43.3	43.3	
U.S. border	15.9	7.5	32.9	51.2	35.4	67.6
North	23.1	16.1	43.2	52.8	41.4	73.3
Center	27.6	16.5	55.7	59.2	49.4	90.0
South	45.4	25.3	78.6	71.3	56.8	93.8
Total	24.2	13.7	58.5	53.7	43.7	83.8

Source: Author's calculations.

peaks of about 90 percent in rural areas in the central and southern states. Given these premises, it appears that in order to have the greatest effect on poverty, trade policies need to reach the rural poor in the central and southern regions.

Exposure of the Poor to International Price Shocks

The extent to which international trade policies will result in a decrease in poverty in Mexico depends in particular upon the exposure of poor Mexican households to trade shocks. The easiest way to think about how poor rural households are affected by trade policies is in terms of the farm household, which produces goods and services, sells its labor, and consumes goods and services. In this setup, an increase in the price of something of which the household is a net seller increases its real income, and a decrease reduces it. Therefore, this section examines, in turn, the net sales positions of poor Mexican households, as well as the anticipated price shocks in the wake of Doha.

Net Sales Position of the Poor

Figure 4.1 summarizes the income sources of Mexican households. Households are categorized as very poor (those below the extreme poverty line), poor (those below the poverty line but above the extreme poverty line), and nonpoor. This figure points to the importance of labor earnings for Mexican households. Labor earnings represent about 50 percent of income for poor households and slightly less than 40 percent for very poor households. Moreover, the very poor are tied to the performance of the agricultural sector because more than half of their income is related to agriculture (own-consumption plus agricultural sales and agricultural wages).[5]

Figures 4.2a and 4.2b present the composition of the expenditure basket of Mexican households. The consumption basket of very poor households is roughly equally divided among own-consumption, food purchases, and purchases of non-food goods and services. A similar consumption basket is found in the case of poor households, which exchange a lower share in autoconsumption with a higher share of other expenses (especially services). Among food purchases (Figure 4.2b), cereals (mainly maize) take about one-fourth of expenditures. Other vegetables take about 20 percent of purchases, and animal-based products account for about 30 percent. Poor households tend to purchase more animal-based products and fewer cereals and vegetables relative to very poor households.

In summary, the analysis of income sources and expenditure baskets of poor households reveals that (a) Mexican households rely greatly on labor earnings; (b) the income of very poor is strongly related to the agricultural sectors;

Figure 4.1. Household Income

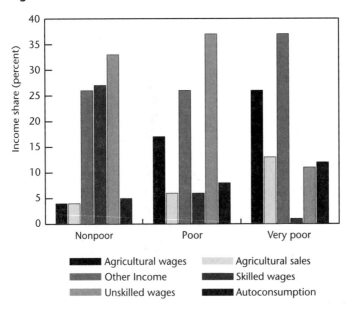

Source: Author's calculations.

(c) there is a net distinction in the labor earnings of different household groups, with the nonpoor relying mostly on skilled labor income and the poor relying mostly on unskilled labor earnings; and (d) on the consumption side, poor households spend most of their income on food purchases, and among those, most is spent on cereal (maize) and animal-based products (meat, dairy). Given these premises, the effect on poverty of the DDA will depend mostly on its effect on the prices of some key products (namely cereals and meats) and on labor earnings. The next section analyzes the impact of a successful Doha implementation on prices and factors important for poor households in Mexico

Doha Implications for Mexico

In this chapter, the implications of the DDA for Mexican households and poverty reduction are estimated analyzing four factors:[6]

1. Impact on prices of goods produced and consumed by Mexican households
2. Impact on the demand for Mexican exports
3. Impact on labor and land earnings in Mexico
4. Extent to which those effects are transmitted to each household

Figure 4.2a and 4.2b.   Household Consumption

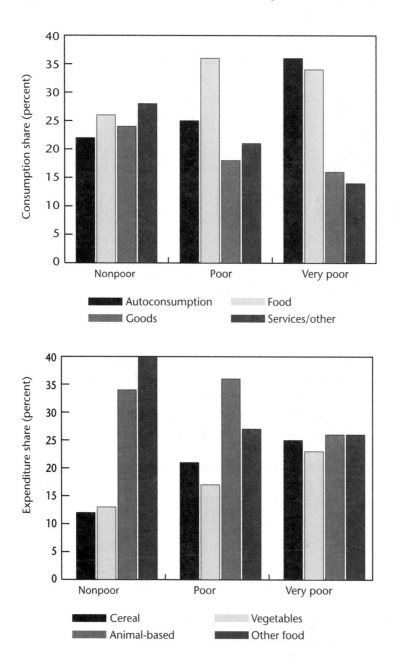

Source: Author's calculations.

The change in average prices, the return to labor, and export supply for the average Mexican household (items 1–3) are estimated through the GTAP model and are discussed below. Price transmission (item 4) is discussed in section 4.4, "Simulation Results."

The change in prices and quantities and returns to labor and land consequent to trade reforms are obtained from the GTAP model, as described in chapter 3. Unlike most of the country studies in this volume, the GTAP results used here are generated by trade reform simulations that include Mexican cuts in tariffs and domestic support. This is because a national CGE model is not introduced in this chapter. Two scenarios are considered, as discussed in chapter 2: the full-liberalization scenario, which assumes full tariff removal, removal of all export subsidies, and domestic support, and the core Doha scenario.

Table 4.2 reports the change in prices and factor returns as estimated for the Mexican economy by the GTAP model for both of these scenarios.[7] From these results, it is clear at the DDA is expected to produce only small changes in the prices of goods and factor returns in Mexico.[8] The largest effect for the Doha scenario is estimated in the return to natural resources, which is expected to increase about by 1.6 percent in real terms. The return to land is expected to increase by 1 percent, and wages (both skilled and unskilled) are expected to decrease minimally. Prices, with the exception of oils and fats, are expected to rise by between 0 and 1 percent. More generally, prices are expected to rise only for agricultural products and not for manufacturing.

Larger effects are estimated for the full-liberalization scenario. In this scenario, return to land is expected to decrease substantially (by about 16 percent) as domestic support for Mexican agriculture is fully removed. Labor earnings are expected to decline by about 0.1 percent (unskilled) and increase by 0.1 percent (skilled). The effects on prices are more interesting. The price of cereals is expected to rise by almost 15 percent, oils and fats by another 15 percent, and the price of dairy products is expected to decline by about 0.6 percent, but little or no effect is found in the price of meat products and sugar. Finally, prices for vegetables and other agricultural products are expected to decline by nearly 2 percent. Smaller changes are estimated for the prices of manufactures, which change between -0.6 percent (household items) and +0.3 percent (food products).

In addition to the change in prices, the trade reforms are estimated to result in a change in production. In the case of the Doha scenario, Mexico's aggregate production is estimated to increase by about US$850 million. Those increases are mostly concentrated in manufacturing and services. In the case of full liberalization, production (and especially exports) is expected to decrease substantially. This is driven by the erosion of Mexico's preferential access to the U.S. market.

Table 4.2.   Scenarios—Doha Implementations and Full Trade Liberalization

	Change in factor returns	
Sector	Doha (%)	Full liberalization (%)
Return to land	1.0	–16.4
Unskilled labor	–0.1	–0.1
Skilled labor	–0.2	0.1
Capital	–0.2	0.0
Natural resources	1.6	1.1

	Doha (%)		Full liberalization (%)	
Product group	Price change (%)	Change in production (US$ million)	Price change (%)	Change in production (US$ million)
Cereals	0.4	18.9	14.6	–351.6
Dairy	0.2	–35.6	–0.6	–418.0
Meat products	0.2	135.6	0.1	–495.8
Oils and fats	3.0	12.3	15.2	–57.9
Sugar	0.2	–2.2	0.0	–27.2
Vegetables	0.6	11.9	–1.8	80.7
Other agricultural	0.5	61.4	–1.9	222.3
Food products	0.0	44.4	0.3	–62.6
Household items	0.0	746.9	–0.6	147.4
Textiles and apparel	0.0	–565.1	0.1	–2,506.0
Other manufacturing	0.0	122.6	–0.3	–1,760.9
Other products	0.3	31.0	0.8	81.4
Services	–0.1	241.4	0.6	361.3

Source: Results based on chapter 3 of this book.

The next section illustrates the empirical strategy used to measure how the changes in the prices and demand for Mexican products, as well as the return to factors for Mexico, translate into household welfare and ultimately affect poverty.

Empirical Framework

The approach used here to estimate the effect of trade liberalization on household welfare can be summarized in three steps. First, the effects of the Doha implementation estimated by the GTAP model are translated into local prices (and quantities) using a pass-through model that allows the transmission from border prices to domestic prices to vary by local markets. Second, the changes in the prices of goods at the local level are used to investigate the movement in earnings and quantities supplied. Last, those changes are mapped to the household survey and fed into the household welfare function using a farm household model to measure the changes in real income.

International Prices and Domestic Prices

As seen in section 2, a successful Doha implementation would have an effect, albeit small, on the prices of various products important in both the consumption baskets and the income sources of Mexican households. However, it is widely recognized that the international prices of products and their retail prices are only loosely linked, because internal factors such as transportation costs and local supply of substitute products act as filters between the two (Frankel, Parsley, and Wei 2005; Winters, McCulloch, and McKay 2004). The isolation of local markets is particularly evident in rural areas, where marketing infrastructure is poorly developed or altogether missing.

Given that domestic price transmission is imperfect, to measure poverty effects of trade reforms, it is necessary first to estimate the magnitude of changes in local retail prices consequent to changes in world prices. In other words, movement in average prices consequential to trade policies (those estimated by the CGE model) need to be translated into changes in retail prices (those faced by the households). The model used here to measure the extent to which local prices vary relative to the international prices follows the approach of Nicita (2004) and is based on the tariff and exchange rate pass-through literature (Goldberg and Knetter 1997; Campa and Goldberg 2002).

In the pass-through estimation, all product groups are aggregated into two main categories: agriculture, and manufacturing. Within these two broad categories, all products are assumed to have the same domestic price pass-through coefficient. This model allows changes in prices to be different across the 32 Mexican states, which are further differentiated by urban and rural areas. To ensure compatibility with the CGE estimates, the changes in regional prices consequent to movement in the international prices are rescaled while keeping the change faced by the average household equal to the one estimated by the GTAP model.[9]

The model used to estimate domestic price pass-through is based on the effect of tariff liberalization on domestic prices as they vary with distance from the U.S. border. In this model, the effect of a change in tariff is perceived in local markets in the same way as a movement in the world price, therefore the extent to which domestic prices move in function of movement of the tariff can be interpreted as the degree of correlation between border prices and retail prices. In summary, the model tracks the effect of a change in price at the U.S. border (produced by the change in tariff) to changes in the price at the regional level so as to capture how much of the movement in the border prices is reflected in each of the retail prices in different geographic areas.[10] To capture differences in pass-through across states, the pass-through coefficient is interacted with the distance variable.[11] This interaction term is further interacted with a rural and an urban dummy to investigate possible differences in pass-through between urban and rural areas.[12] Referring to Nicita (2004) for a detailed explanation of the model, the estimating equation is given by:

$$(4.1) \quad \ln P_{gtr} = \beta_0 + \beta_1 \ln X_{gt} + \beta_2 \ln Z_{gtr} + \beta_3 d_r + $$
$$+ \gamma \ln(1+\tau_{gt}) + \gamma_1 \ln(1+\tau_{gt})d_r U + \gamma_2 \ln(1+\tau_{gt})d_r R + \varepsilon_{gtr}$$

where X_{gt} is the primary control variable (the international price of good g expressed in domestic currency), and Z_{gtr} is a vector of control variables that includes local supply and regional income, R and U denote rural and urban dummies, and ε_{gtr} is an error term. The coefficients of interest are γ, which represents the tariff pass-through elasticity, and γ_1 and γ_2, which are its adjustment for distance from the U.S. border. The pass-through is "full" or "complete" if $\gamma = 1$ and the pass-through is "incomplete" if $\gamma = <1$. Similarly, the effect of the pass-through will be identical in all urban areas if $\gamma_1 = 0$. However, if local prices vary as a consequence of movement in the tariff, then $\gamma \neq 0$. Similar reasoning is applied in the case of rural areas, where the coefficient of interest is γ_2.

The econometric estimation of equation (1) combines a time series of cross-sectional data set into a pseudo panel.[13] The data consist of domestic prices for 63 regions and six time periods. Average prices for each region are arranged into a panel dataset, and the estimation is performed separately for agriculture and for manufacturing. Table 4.3 reports the results of the pass-through model, which indicate a pass-through between the international price and the border price of about 26 percent for agriculture and 67 percent for manufacturing.

The negative sign on the interacted terms indicates that, as the distance from the U.S. border increases, price pass-through coefficients decline, suggesting the possibility of missing markets. Moreover, changes in prices may be internalized by intermediaries or absorbed by trade costs. Therefore, retail prices in the states closer to the U.S. market tend to better "feel" the effect of movement in the tariff. Conversely, southern states seem to be the least connected to the international markets. Another result is the difference between urban and rural areas. Urban areas in all regions "feel" the movement in the tariff to a larger extent, especially in the case of agricultural products. Finally, movement in the tariffs of agricultural products tends to be reflected to a lesser extent in domestic prices relative to manufacturing products (especially in rural areas). This is not surprising and is likely

Table 4.3.   Pass-Through

Variable	Agriculture			Manufacturing		
International price	1.449	***	(0.165)	0.004		(0.007)
Regional consumer price index	0.284	*	(0.149)	1.174	***	(0.247)
Local supply	−0.036	***	(0.011)	−0.016		(0.017)
Urban or rural	0.131	***	(0.043)	0.510	***	(0.064)
Distance	0.002		(0.012)	−0.030	*	(0.016)
Tariff pass–through	0.260	*	(0.155)	0.671	***	(0.101)
Urban transmission	0.003		(0.033)	−0.091	***	(0.034)
Rural transmission	−0.054	**	(0.027)	−0.108	***	(0.027)
Constant	9.498	***	(1.021)	5.201	***	(0.623)
Observations	378			378		
R^2	0.58			0.64		

Source: Author's calculations.

Note: All variables, except distance, are in log. White corrected standard errors are shown in parentheses. Significance level of 1 percent, 5 percent, and 10 percent are indicated by ***, **, and *, respectively.

driven by a greater presence of domestic substitutes and stronger consumer preference for domestically produced varieties.

Production and Export Supply

A successful Doha implementation is estimated to produce an increase in overall production of about US$850 million per year, mostly driven by increases in international demand for Mexican products. It is important to note that an increase in demand for Mexico's exports will not necessarily have a substantial effect on poverty. The reason is twofold. First, poor households may not be directly employed in producing (and marketing) products for which there are increases in export demand. Second, there is a cost associated with the increase in supply, with net gains likely to be much smaller than the change in production volume.

The increase in sales can be decomposed into the quantity effect (the actual value of the increase in production) and the price effect (the increase in value of this quantity due to the higher price). The base case simulation of the Doha scenario assumes that there are real costs associated with the increase in production required to meet increased agricultural demands in the wake of policy reform. Therefore, the net gains to households originate only from the increase in the prices, now applied to the increased production. A second assumption is required to allocate the increase in production to individual households. This is assumed to be proportional to the marketed production of households, and it is also assumed to follow the price pass-through mechanism, with weaker effects in the more remote rural areas. This implies that households producing only for auto-consumption will not be allowed to increase production and households that will not observe any price signals will not adjust their production to fill the increase in demand.

Labor Earnings

The link between trade reforms and labor earnings goes through the price mechanism. International trade reforms operate through changes in prices, and changes in prices will consequentially affect labor earnings. In estimating the impact on wages of Doha implementation, this chapter makes the assumption that movements in wages are directly affected by movements in prices. A more sophisticated approach would require the estimation of price-wage elasticities for different products and different types of labor. However, this would require additional data and would make the analysis more cumbersome while adding little to the overall analysis. Moreover, labor markets in developing countries are seldom integrated, and empirical evidence suggests that returns to labor vary greatly across different geographic areas (Hanson 1997, 2003), calling for a model that allows wage response to vary across geographic areas. The GTAP model estimates an average change in wages (skilled and unskilled) across scenarios that falls between -0.2 and 0.1 percent. Given these small changes, and for the sake of simplicity, wages are assumed to follow the price pass-through mechanism on a regional level. Arguably, this is a reasonable assumption that implies that wages are assumed to move more in regions where price pass-through is greater relative to regions where price pass-through is smaller. As in the case of the prices of goods, the movement of the average wage is kept at the level estimated by the CGE model.

Changes in Household Welfare

Having illustrated the channels used to investigate the effect on households resulting from the implementation of Doha, it is now possible to calculate changes in household welfare.[14] In developing countries, most households are simultaneously consumers and producers of goods and services. Therefore, in analyzing the effect on household welfare from any policy, it is important to recognize this dual role of the household.[15] The farm household model fits this purpose (Singh, Squire, and Strauss 1986). The approach used here to measure the change in real income (dy_h) can be expressed as follows:

$$(4.2) \quad dy_h = \underbrace{\sum_g \theta_h^g dP_h^g \, y_h}_{\text{ag. income (price effect)}} + \underbrace{\sum_g dQ_h^g dP_h^g}_{\text{ag. income (production effect)}} + \underbrace{\theta_h^\ell dw_h \, y_h}_{\text{labor income}} - \underbrace{\sum_g \phi_h^g dP_h^g \, y_h}_{\text{consumption}}$$

where dP_h^g are the changes in prices of good g faced by households h, θ_h^g is the share of income obtained from the sale of good g by household h, θ_h^ℓ is the share of income obtained in the labor market, ϕ_h^g is the share of the consumption basket devoted to good g; y_h is the income of the household[16], and

$$(4.3) \quad dQ_h^g = \Delta \text{Prod}^g \frac{y_h^g}{\sum_h y_h^g}$$

where ΔProd^g is the total change in the production of good g, and y_h^g is the income originating from the sale of good g by household h.[17]

In this setup, equation (2) suggests that a change in the price of good g favors or harms the household based on the net exposure of its budget to that particular good. Moreover, an increase in the international demand for a particular good favors households in proportion to their marketed production of the good, and movement in wages affects households relative to their share of wage income. Finally, the change in welfare is distributed across household members, expenditures are determined by the new level of income, and new welfare indicators are calculated at the new level of consumption.

Simulation Results

The first scenario examined in this section looks at the effects of Doha and revolves around the status quo in which price transmission is kept at the estimated level and increases in farm output are costly. The second scenario builds on the first but mimics an improvement in the Mexican economy, assuming that any increase in agricultural production and exports is achieved at no additional cost to producers.[18] This could be due to an increase in productivity, or it could be a consequence of the household using surplus labor to achieve the increased production. The third scenario builds on the second and adds the assumption that domestic price transmission is improved by half.[19] Finally, a fourth scenario measures the results of full international trade liberalization on Mexican households, while still assuming the status quo in the domestic economy (no complementary reforms).

The change in real income is used as the welfare indicator for each scenario and household group. Results are differentiated by region and presented for three household groupings: all households, all poor (those living below the asset poverty line), and very poor (those living below the food poverty line).

Doha Scenario

The results of the Doha implementation based on the absence of domestic reforms suggest that these trade reforms would have a small negative impact on overall real income in Mexico. Table 4.4 reports the change in real income for the total population, the poor, and the very poor, further differentiated by region and urban and rural areas. The only exceptions to the negative impacts are the positive effects for the very poor in the northern and U.S. border regions. However, the effects, both positive and negative, are in all cases within 0.3 percent of change in real income.

Complementary Reform Scenario 1 ("Doha Plus")

The results of the Doha implementation in the presence of facilitating increases in productivity (or the use of surplus labor) are reported in table 4.5. The results from this scenario, although small, show a positive effect from Doha implementation. On average, Doha is expected to raise real income in Mexico by about 0.4

Table 4.4. Change in Real Income (Doha)
(percentage)

Region	Total	Urban	Rural	All poor	Urban poor	Rural poor	Very poor	Urban very poor	Rural very poor
Federal District	−0.1	−0.1		−0.1	−0.1		0.0	0.0	
Border	−0.3	−0.3	0.1	−0.1	−0.2	0.1	0.2	0.1	0.3
North	−0.1	−0.1	0.1	0.0	−0.1	0.1	0.2	0.3	0.2
Center	−0.1	−0.2	0.0	−0.1	−0.2	0.0	0.0	−0.1	0.0
South	−0.1	−0.2	0.0	−0.1	−0.2	0.0	0.0	−0.2	0.0
National	−0.1	−0.2	0.0	−0.1	−0.2	0.0	0.0	−0.1	0.0

Source: Author's simulations.

Table 4.5. Change in Real Income ("Doha Plus") (percentage)

Region	Total	Urban	Rural	All poor	Urban poor	Rural poor	Very poor	Urban very poor	Rural very poor
Federal District	0.1	0.1		0.3	0.3			1.2	1.4
Border	0.6	0.4	1.5	1.0	0.8	1.6	2.0	1.8	2.4
North	0.9	0.7	1.2	1.1	0.9	1.2	1.8	2.5	1.5
Center	0.3	0.2	0.5	0.4	0.3	0.5	0.6	0.7	0.6
South	0.0	0.0	0.0	0.0	0.0	0.0	0.1	0.2	0.0
National	0.4	0.2	0.6	0.5	0.4	0.5	0.7	0.9	0.6

Source: Author's simulations.

percentage points. However, the poor, and in particular the very poor, gain substantially more, especially in the northern and U.S. border regions. Average gains are about 0.7 percent for the very poor and 0.5 percent for the poor as a whole. Urban areas are expected to gain less relative to rural areas because of the smaller share of agricultural production in total income in the broadly defined urban areas. However, the poor in the remote southern states still gain little from this trade reform.

Complementary Reform Scenario 2 ("Doha Plus-Plus")

The results of the Doha implementation in the presence of both increases in productivity and improved domestic price transmission are reported in table 4.6. The results show the role of domestic price transmission in distributing the effects of Doha implementation across income groups and regions. Improved domestic price transmission is expected to redistribute gains from the northern regions of the country to the south and at the same time from the non-poor to the poor. This scenario estimates a change in the real income of the poor and very poor of 0.6 and 1.1 percent, which when compared to the Doha-plus scenario, translate into an additional increase of 0.1 and 0.4 percent, respectively. This reflects the fact that poor households are generally more remotely located and therefore experience fewer of the gains from increased trade opportunities because of incomplete markets. Overall, the gains from this scenario are more uniformly distributed across regions.

Table 4.6. Change in Real Income ("Doha Plus-Plus")
(percentage)

Region	Total	Urban	Rural	All poor	Urban poor	Rural poor	Very poor	Urban very poor	Rural very poor
Federal District	0.2	0.2		0.4	0.4		1.5	1.4	
Border	0.3	0.2	1.1	0.7	0.5	1.1	1.4	1.1	1.9
North	0.7	0.5	1.1	0.9	0.7	1.1	1.4	1.9	1.3
Center	0.5	0.3	0.9	0.7	0.4	1.0	1.1	0.9	1.2
South	0.4	0.2	0.7	0.5	0.3	0.7	0.8	0.6	0.9
National	0.4	0.2	0.9	0.6	0.4	0.9	1.1	1.0	1.1

Source: Author's simulations.

Based on the results from this Doha-plus-plus scenario, the change in real income at the household level is regressed on household characteristics so as to better investigate the variance of the gains. Clearly, these variables are not purely exogenous to the welfare gains; however, this regression is of descriptive interest in helping to isolate covariates of relevance. This information may prove useful when thinking about compensatory policies. Results of the regression and a summary of descriptive statistics are presented in table 4.7. The share of variance in gains that is accountable to those covariates is about 21 percent. The regression results give a rough indication of how the gains are distributed.[20] As seen in table 4.5, the results suggest that urban areas gain relatively less from the Doha implementation. Moreover, other things being equal, the geographic distribution of gains suggests that northern regions and regions closer to the U.S. border gain substantially more, and southern regions gain the least. The coefficients on household characteristics suggest that larger families gain less than smaller ones. Similarly, lower gains are estimated for female-headed households as well as households where the household head is relatively less educated. Finally, the coefficients on the decile variables suggest that low-income households obtain the largest gains in percentage terms.

Full Liberalization

The results from a hypothetical, multilateral full-liberalization scenario are reported in table 4.8. Full multilateral trade liberalization is expected to produce a

Table 4.7. Improved Scenario: Variance of the Gains

Household characteristic	Regression results (Dependent variable: percentage gains)		Standard error	Household characteristic	Descriptive statistics	Standard deviation
	Coefficient				Mean	
Gender (1 = female)	0.0001	***	(0.0004)	Gender (1 = female)	0.18	0.39
Age	0.0001	***	(0.0000)	Age	46.31	15.38
Share child	0.0006	***	(0.0001)	Share child	1.49	1.50
Share elderly	0.0006	*	(0.0003)	Share elderly	0.30	0.60
Household size	-0.0049	***	(0.0004)	Household size	1.30	0.54
Urban dummy	-0.0050	***	(0.0004)	Urban dummy	0.77	Binary
Region				Mexico City (dropped)	0.23	Binary
U.S. border	0.0015	***	(0.0004)	U.S. border	0.16	Binary
North	0.0031	***	(0.0005)	North	0.10	Binary
Center	0.0010	***	(0.0004)	Center	0.39	Binary
South	-0.0006		(0.0005)	South	0.13	Binary
Education				No education (dropped)	0.15	Binary
Primary	-0.0009	**	(0.0004)	Primary	0.43	Binary
Middle	-0.0013	***	(0.0005)	Middle	0.20	Binary
Secondary	-0.0024	***	(0.0006)	Secondary	0.21	Binary
College	-0.0033	**	(0.0013)	College	0.01	Binary
Income deciles				Income decile 1 (dropped)	0.10	Binary
Income decile 2	-0.0022	***	(0.0006)	Income decile 2	0.10	Binary
Income decile 3	-0.0037	***	(0.0006)	Income decile 3	0.10	Binary
Income decile 4	-0.0032	***	(0.0006)	Income decile 4	0.10	Binary
Income decile 5	-0.0037	***	(0.0007)	Income decile 5	0.10	Binary
Income decile 6	-0.0037	***	(0.0007)	Income decile 6	0.10	Binary
Income decile 7	-0.0034	***	(0.0007)	Income decile 7	0.10	Binary
Income decile 8	-0.0026	***	(0.0007)	Income decile 8	0.10	Binary
Income decile 9	-0.0023	***	(0.0007)	Income decile 9	0.10	Binary
Income decile 10	-0.0042	***	(0.0008)	Income decile 10	0.10	Binary
Constant	0.0125	***	(0.0010)			
Observations	10108					
R^2	0.21					

Source: Author's estimates.

Note: All variables, except distance, are in log. White corrected standard errors are shown in brackets. Significance levels of 1 percent, 5 percent, and 10 percent are indicated by ***, **, and *, respectively.

**Table 4.8.   Change in Real Income ("Doha Plus-Plus")
(percentage)**

Region	Total	Urban	Rural	All poor	Urban poor	Rural poor	Very poor	Urban very poor	Rural very poor
Federal District	–0.8	–0.8	n.a.	–1.1	–1.1	n.a.	–1.0	–2.1	n.a.
Border	–1.4	–1.3	–2.2	–2.1	–2.0	–2.5	–3.3	–3.7	–2.8
North	–1.7	–1.8	–1.5	–2.1	–2.6	–1.5	–2.5	–4.2	–1.7
Center	–0.9	–1.2	–0.2	–1.1	–1.9	–0.2	–0.9	–2.5	–0.2
South	–0.7	–1.2	0.0	–0.8	–1.9	0.0	–0.5	–2.5	0.0
National	–1.0	–1.2	–0.5	–1.3	–1.9	–0.4	–1.0	–2.7	–0.3

Source: Author's simulations.
Note: n.a. = not applicable.

negative impact on Mexican households. Losses are on the order of about 1 percent, with peaks of about 4 percent for the very poor living in urban areas in the northern regions. The negative outcome of this scenario is the result of the increase in the prices of consumption goods for Mexican households and the reduction in exports driven by the sharp erosion of Mexican preferences in the U.S. market.

Summary

The results that emerge from the four scenarios can be summarized as follows: (a) Doha alone, without any complementary reform, is likely to have a negative, albeit very small, impact on Mexican households; (b) Doha implementation with complementary reforms aimed at increasing productivity is expected to produce positive small gains for Mexican households; (c) without improvement of domestic price transmission, the effects of the Doha implementation are expected to be concentrated in the northern regions; and (d) improvement in the domestic price transmission results in a more uniform distribution of the effects and larger benefits for the poorest households.

Most important, the findings suggest that the variance of the gains largely depends on domestic price transmission. When price transmission is assumed to stay at the estimated level, households living in the southern regions (especially rural regions) are largely unaffected by Doha, either positively or negatively. This happens because price signals originating from the Doha-induced movement in world prices subsequent to trade reforms are perceived only marginally in those areas. When domestic price transmission is assumed to improve, the distribution of the gains is more uniform across geographic areas and households.

What emerges from the analysis of the simulation exercise is that without complementary reforms, Mexico is not expected to gain from Doha and is expected to lose in the case of full multilateral trade liberalization. This outcome is not surprising, considering that Mexico has already liberalized trade with its most important trading partner through its membership in NAFTA. Thus, multilateral tariff reductions in the United States result in an erosion of those preferences currently enjoyed by Mexican exports.

Conclusions

This chapter provides a quantitative estimate of the effect on Mexican households from the implementation of the DDA, taking into account the role of domestic price transmission. The findings suggest that multilateral trade liberalization is likely not beneficial for most Mexican households unless it is complemented by domestic reforms aimed at facilitating the response of households to these new market opportunities.

The findings suggest that the poor would likely share in the benefits (and costs) of such trade reforms. The differences in impacts across households are more closely associated with geographic areas of residence than income level. The results point to the importance of domestic price transmission in determining the variance of the effects across households. Given the existing structure of markets in Mexico, most of the effects of multilateral trade policies would be felt in the northern states, which are more connected to international markets. Conversely, households living in the southern states are isolated from most effects, not because of the composition of their consumption or income bundle, but because of the marginal effect of trade reforms on prices in those areas. Measures aimed at enhancing domestic price transmission could ensure that any gains from trade reform (when accompanied by productivity-enhancing policies) would be more evenly spread throughout the country.

Notes

1. A review of the findings of the literature is given by Winters, McCulloch, and McKay (2004); Hertel and Reimer (2004); and Berg and Kruger (2003).

2. The economics involved in this approach is generally well known and has found numerous applications. See Hertel and Reimer (2004) for a review.

3. This corresponds to the food poverty line. The food poverty line is defined as the minimum expenditure necessary to guarantee a 2,200-calorie intake per day.

4. The extreme poverty line corresponds to the food poverty line. The moderate poverty line is the asset poverty line. The difference corresponds to nonfood components in the consumption bundle. Both poverty lines are calculated by CEPAL (2001).

5. Other sources of income include government transfers (about 4 percent of total income) and remittance (about 3 percent of total income). Given their low weight on the overall income source of poor households, income from these categories is assumed to be fixed and therefore not affected by trade policies.

6. The GTAP model was estimated keeping the impact of trade reforms on government revenues neutral (for example, compensated by internal taxation). It is also assumed that transfer payments are indexed such that they do not play a role in the welfare calculation.

7. Within the model, the impact of tariff changes on government revenues and redistribution is kept neutral, adjusting prices by the effect of compensating changes in direct income taxation.

8. The small changes are found because trade is already largely free within the North American Free Trade Agreement (NAFTA) countries.

9. The GTAP Armington specification produces average market prices already adjusted for imperfect price pass-through.

10. Prices are corrected for quality issues following the standard methodology of Prais and Houthakker (1955).

11. The variable used in the model to capture differences in the movement in the retail prices is the driving distance from the U.S. border. Distance is measured in 1,000 kilometers.

12. Higher transport costs and local supply suggest a lower price pass-through in rural areas, especially on agricultural products.

13. From a time series of six cross-section surveys (from 1989 to 2000), synthetic cohorts are defined as groups with fixed membership, whose individuals (or households) can be identified as they show up in the surveys. For this reason, groups are defined according to some time-invariant variables. Means within each cohort are calculated and followed for each temporal unit under examination: this cohort aggregation is defined as a pseudo panel.

14. The change in household welfare is calculated by taking into account only first-order effects.

15. For details and applications, see Deaton (1997).

16. Income is equated to expenditures.

17. Prices are different by region. The subscript r for region is omitted.

18. This implies that the value of the increase in exports is directly transferred to the income of the household through agricultural production.

19. That is, the coefficients in the interaction terms are divided by two.

20. The constant represents low-education households in the Federal District of Mexico City in the first income decile.

References

Berg, A., and A. Kruger. 2003. "Trade, Growth and Poverty: A Selective Survey." IMF Working Paper WP/03/30, International Monetary Fund, Washington, DC.

Campa, J. M., and L. S. Goldberg. 2002 "Exchange Rate Pass-Through into Import Prices: A Macro or Micro Phenomenon?" NBER Working Paper 8934, National Bureau of Economic Research, Cambridge, MA.

CEPAL (Comisión Económica par América Latina y el Caribe). 2001. *Panorama social de América Latina 2000–2001.* Santiago de Chile: United Nations.

Deaton, A. 1997. *The Analysis of Household Surveys. A Microeconometric Approach to Development Policy.* Baltimore and Washington DC: Johns Hopkins University Press for the World Bank.

Frankel, J., D. Parsley, and S. J. Wei. 2005. "Slow Passthrough around the World: A New Import for Developing Countries?" NBER Working Paper 11199, National Bureau of Economic Research, Cambridge, MA.

Goldberg, P., and M. Knetter. 1997. "Good Prices and Exchange Rates: What Have We Learned?" *Journal of Economic Literature* 35: 1243–72.

Hanson, G. 1997. "Increasing Returns, Trade and the Regional Structure of Wages." *The Economic Journal* 440: 113–33.

———. 2003. "What Happened to Wages in Mexico since NAFTA?" NBER Working Paper 9563, National Bureau of Economic Research, Cambridge, MA.

Hertel, T. W. 1997. *Global Trade Analysis: Modeling and Applications.* New York: Cambridge University Press.

Hertel, T. W., and J. J. Reimer. 2004. "Predicting the Poverty Impacts of Trade Reform." Policy Research Working Paper 3444, World Bank, Washington, DC.

Nicita, A. 2004. "Who Benefited from Trade Liberalization in Mexico? Measuring the Effects on Household Welfare." Policy Research Working Paper 3265, World Bank, Washington, DC.

Nicita, A. Forthcoming. "Multilateral Trade Liberalization and Mexican Households: The Effect of the DDA." Policy Research Working Paper, World Bank, Washington, DC.

Singh, I., L. Squire, and J. Strauss. 1986. *Agricultural Household Models, Extensions, Applications and Policy.* Baltimore: World Bank and the Johns Hopkins University Press.

Prais, S. J., and H. S. Houthakker. 1955. *The Analysis of Family Budgets.* Cambridge: Cambridge University Press.

Winters, L. A., N. McCulloch, and A. McKay. 2004. "Trade Liberalization and Poverty: The Evidence So Far." *Journal of Economic Literature.* 42: 72–115.

5

THE DOHA TRADE ROUND AND MOZAMBIQUE

Channing Arndt

Summary

This chapter considers the potential implications of the Doha Development Agenda (DDA), as well as other trade liberalization scenarios, for Mozambique. An applied general equilibrium (AGE) model, which accounts for high marketing margins and home consumption in the Mozambique economy, is linked to results from the Global Trade Analysis Project (GTAP) model of global trade. In addition, a microsimulation module is used to consider the subsequent implications of trade liberalization for poverty. The implications of trade liberalization, particularly the Doha scenarios, are found to be relatively small. Presuming that a more liberal trading regime will positively influence growth in Mozambique, an opportunity exists to put in place such a regime without imposing significant adjustment costs.

Introduction

The Doha Round of trade negotiations seeks explicitly to involve developing countries. In terms of process, developing countries are expected, as a group, to be much more engaged in the actual negotiations. Wealthier nations, on their side, are expected to place greater emphasis on the implications of any agreement for the developing countries, particularly for poverty. The hope is to reach an agreement that enhances opportunities for developing countries to achieve poverty-reducing economic growth through stronger trade linkages with the world economy.

As the region with the highest rate of poverty and relatively weak linkages to the global economy, it seems logical to carefully consider the role of Africa within the DDA. The African continent is both enormous and highly diverse. As a result, implications of any given global trade agreement will differ across economies on the continent. This chapter considers the potential implications of trade liberalization scenarios for the case of Mozambique. Like all African economies, Mozambique has distinguishing features that render it unique. However, as will be discussed, it also shares many structural features with other African countries. The logic of some of the ideas developed here can therefore be applied to a number of other countries across the continent.

Section 1 presents a brief description of Mozambique. Section 2 considers implications of various trade liberalization scenarios derived from an analysis that marries outputs from the GTAP model of global trade with a more detailed country computable general equilibrium (CGE) model of Mozambique. Poverty analysis proceeds using a separate household microsimulation module. Section 3 provides a critique of the main results that come out of the models. Section 4 concludes. The transmission of prices to low-income households is a theme that is developed in particular detail throughout the chapter.

Mozambique

Mozambique is located along the southeastern coast of Africa. In terms of total area, coastline, and shape, it is roughly similar to (a mirror image of) the combined areas of the states of California, Oregon, and Washington that make up the western coast of the United States. Exploitation of natural resources underpins a substantial share of economic activity. Fisheries are a major export industry. The stock of arable land is large, and much arable land remains unexploited. Important agricultural exports include cotton and tobacco. Forestry is also important. With its long coastline and abundance of natural harbors, Mozambique provides port and transport services to neighboring countries. Exploitation of natural gas, uranium, titanium, and other mineral resources has also begun. Finally, Mozambique's natural beauty, particularly its beaches and coral reefs, attracts tourists.

These favorable attributes are spread out over a relatively small population of not quite 19 million people. Nevertheless, more than half of the population is categorized as absolutely poor. This implies that slightly more than one person in two has difficulty in meeting very basic survival needs in terms of calorie consumption and basic nonfood necessities such as housing and clothing.

This pervasive poverty is the result of a complex historical legacy that included weak human capital development over the colonial period even by African standards, failed socialist policies initiated shortly after independence in 1975, and finally, a brutal civil war that endured for more than a decade. The cessation of hostilities in 1992 coincided with one of the worst droughts on record. The cumulative effect of these disasters earned Mozambique the unwanted label of "poorest country in the world" in the early 1990s. Since then, the economic record has been considerably more positive. From a low base, economic growth has averaged in the range of 7-8 percent per year for more than a decade. This growth coincided with the implementation of a fairly standard structural adjustment program. Very considerable flows of external assistance clearly helped to fuel growth and provided major funding for social initiatives, with particularly large investments in basic health and education.[1]

By most objective indicators, living conditions for the Mozambican population have improved considerably. In 1996–97, using real consumption as a metric, about 69 percent of the population was characterized as absolutely poor. By 2002–03, this number had fallen by 15 percentage points to about 54 percent, using the same metric. Indicators such as crop production, asset ownership, income of rural households, school enrollments, infant mortality, and child vaccination coverage rates also showed improvements (Mozambique Ministry of Planning and Finance, International Food Policy Research Institute, and Purdue University 2004).

Because initial development levels were so low, a decade-plus of rapid growth and rapid improvement in many social indicators have placed Mozambique near Sub-Saharan African averages for a range of indicators. In short, the trends are positive, but the absolute levels of such indicators remain dismal. The clear challenge is to maintain the positive momentum developed over the past decade.

Over the coming decade, international trade will likely play a prominent role if growth is to continue. Growth in the past decade has been driven in large measure by internal reconstruction needs (usually donor-funded) and production of basic goods and services that often have been consumed at very local levels, frequently within the household where they are produced.[2] These sources of demand are likely to continue to be important, at least through the medium term, but there is also a clear need to strengthen links to international markets, particularly with respect to exports of labor-intensive products.

This thumbnail sketch illustrates many aspects of Mozambique that are unique on the African continent. However, Mozambique also shares many essential structural features that are quite common. A nonexhaustive list includes:

- A predominantly rural population with economic and social indicators typically at less favorable levels in rural areas—hence, the large majority of the poor reside in rural areas, making improvements in the well-being of current rural dwellers practically a condition sine qua non of any significant reduction in overall poverty levels.

- An overwhelming dependence on agriculture in rural areas.
- Large distances and poor transport infrastructure result in substantial transport costs, particularly between distant regions. These weaken or even sever entirely market linkages across disparate regions of the country. For example, the cost of transporting maize by truck from growing regions in the north to the capital city, located in the far south, is so high as to be effectively prohibitive.

The chapter now turns to an assessment of the implications of the DDA derived from a formal applied general equilibrium (AGE) model of Mozambique that is linked to outputs from the GTAP model of global trade.

Modeling the Implications of Doha

The goal of trade liberalization is to redirect productive resources to areas of comparative advantage. At the global level, this implies that production patterns will shift across countries. Within countries, some industries are likely to contract, thereby freeing productive resources that, at least in principle, might allow other industries to expand. Typically, after trade liberalization, one expects productive patterns within individual countries to concentrate in particular industries that have a comparative advantage. Surplus production is sold on global markets, and the resulting income permits countries to import products that were formerly produced at home.

Because the goal of trade liberalization frequently involves the reallocation of resources across productive sectors, CGE models have come to be the workhorses for analyses of trade agreements. The global CGE model (the GTAP model) used to analyze the implications of various Doha scenarios at the global level has been well-described in other chapters of this book. This chapter focuses on the Mozambique model, including the microsimulation module for poverty analysis. The first subsection below provides a description of the basic features of the Mozambique model. The second subsection discusses structural features of the economy that can be expected to drive model results. The third subsection presents salient model results.

The Mozambique CGE Model

Analysis begins from a standard, trade-focused CGE model, which contains three basic elements: (a) specification of economic behavior for firms and households, (b) operation of markets, and (c) macroeconomic closure.[3] Novel features particularly relevant for this analysis are then discussed.

Behavioral Specification. The model assumes profit maximization by producers under a sectoral constant elasticity of substitution (CES) technology. Consumers are assumed to demand commodities according to a linear expenditure system (LES) utility function formulation. Investment and government expenditures are allocated in a Leontief fashion, with fixed real coefficients rather than fixed expenditure shares.

Foreign trade is specified using the Armington assumption. There are CES functions for sectoral imports. Armington import elasticities are taken from Hertel and others (2004). A constant elasticity of transformation (CET) function is used on the export side. However, to remain consistent with the GTAP model, the sectoral export transformation elasticities were set to a high value (5). Also, a downward-sloping demand function for Mozambican exports was developed, again using elasticities from Hertel and others (2004). The presence of these downward-sloping demand functions permits the Mozambique country model to simulate both the world price changes and the shifts in demand generated by the GTAP model under various global trade liberalization scenarios.[4]

Operation of Markets. A CGE model simulates the operation of product and factor markets, solving for market-clearing prices and wages. It is a closed general equilibrium system, incorporating all elements of the circular flow of income and expenditure and the corresponding real flows. Characteristic features of this type of model include (a) households must respect their budget constraint; (b) the domestic price of imports equals the cost, insurance, and freight (CIF) price multiplied by the exchange rate and the prevailing tariff rate plus any marketing margins or additional domestic sales taxes; (c) the value of imports cannot exceed the availability of foreign exchange; (d) supply of commodities must equal demand for commodities (with inventory accumulation counted as demand); (e) firms collectively cannot use more of any factor than the total availability in the economy; (f) investment must be financed via foreign or domestic savings; and (g) government consumption must be financed through tax revenue, foreign grants (aid), or borrowing on domestic or foreign markets.

Also, in this model, aggregate employment of all factors of production is exogenous, and factor returns adjust to clear factor markets. Finally, the model numeraire is the consumer price index (CPI), so all price changes reported in this chapter are relative to the CPI.

Macro Closure. All CGE models incorporate macro balances. How equilibrium is achieved between savings and investment, the government deficit, and the trade deficit constitutes the macro closure of the model. In the Mozambican model, aggregate investment is determined by savings (private plus government plus foreign), so the model is savings driven. Private savings are endogenous, depending on fixed savings rates by households and enterprises. Government expenditure is set as a fixed share of aggregate absorption in the economy, and the government deficit is exogenous. Direct tax rates across institutions (households and enterprises) vary in order to maintain a constant deficit. Foreign savings and aid are fixed exogenously, and the real exchange rate adjusts to achieve external balance through changes in aggregate exports and imports.

More Novel Features. Importantly for this analysis, the CGE model specifically accounts for the substantial costs required for products to reach commercial markets. This is particularly important in the case of agricultural products. These marketing margins reflect storage and transportation costs, as well as risk associated with trading activities and limited opportunities for diversification. Marketing margins are introduced into the static CGE model by assuming that each unit of a given production good requires a fixed amount of marketing services to reach the market. Because the current model framework treats imported and exported goods as inherently different from domestically consumed production, marketing margins related to exports, imports, and domestic goods are accounted for separately. A single production activity provides the commercial services associated with the marketing of commodities.

Transaction costs vary across sectors. They are zero in the case of service sectors, by definition, and they are nonzero (and sometimes quite large) in other goods sectors—particularly agricultural sectors, where products are bulky and distances between points of production and consumption can be large.

Almost all Mozambican households have some money income, either from goods sales or from factor remunerations. This income is used for purchases of essential goods that cannot be produced by the households themselves. Nevertheless, the possibility of home consumption enables households to bypass the market in so far as they can produce consumption goods themselves. The presence of high marketing margins implies the existence of significant differences between farm gate (and factory gate) sales prices, on the one hand, and prices in the commercial markets, on the other hand. Rather than sell at a low price and purchase at a high price, households—particularly rural agricultural households—often opt to consume at least some of what they produce. In some cases, these marketing margins are so large as to isolate the household from commercial markets altogether. Therefore, explicit modeling of the interaction between marketing costs and home consumption becomes essential for assessing important aspects of the economy. All home-consumed commodities and market consumption of all commodities are captured in the LES formulation mentioned above. Appropriate modeling of home consumption and marketing margins has been shown to be important (Arndt and others 2000).

The Mozambique Microsimulation Model

A microsimulation model in the spirit of Chen and Ravallion (2004) is developed to examine the poverty implications of the trade liberalization scenarios analyzed. The model relies upon data from the 2002–3 Mozambican *National Household Budget Survey* (INE 2004). The survey provides detailed information on consumption patterns for a nationally representative sample of 8,700 households. The survey also provides detail on household members, including sector of economic activity and education level. The analysis examines the first-order implications of the changes in commodity prices and factor prices generated by the Mozambican CGE model for each of the 8,700 households in the sample. Specifically, changes in commodity prices are multiplied by individual household consumption shares, and changes in factor prices are multiplied by the corresponding share of earnings from each factor in total household income. The factor price effect less the commodity price effect yields a money metric indicator of the first-order change in utility due to the trade reforms for each household.

Importantly, in first order analysis, the net effect of price changes for commodities that are home produced and consumed is zero because commodity price changes are exactly offset by gains or losses in factor income. This tends to blunt the impact of trade policy reform on rural households. As mentioned above and detailed in the next section, home consumption is very important in the Mozambican context. In addition, the overwhelming predominance of informal activities implies that wage information is scarce. As a result, earnings by labor category are inferred from educational attainment data combined with econometric estimates of returns to education (Maximiano 2005). Similarly, for the large majority of households, it is practically impossible to separate overall household earnings into labor and capital components. This is less of an issue for poor households because the large majority of earnings can reasonably be assumed to be derived from labor income. In the microsimulation model, 5 percent of total income is assumed to come from capital earnings for households living at less than twice the absolute poverty line.

Structure of the Mozambican Economy

Tables 5.1, 5.2, and 5.3 provide an overview of the structure of the Mozambican economy. Table 5.1 reports the macroeconomic aggregates. For a very poor country, Mozambique allocates fairly substantial resources to government consumption and government investment. The relatively high level of government expenditure is enabled by substantial inflows of external assistance, which are typically used to support government spending and public investment. These same

Table 5.1. Components of GDP

GDP Component	Share (%)
Private consumption	72.4
Private investment	11.2
Government	28.9
Exports	20.6
Imports	-33.0
Total	100.0

Source: Author's calculations.

foreign inflows permit Mozambique to run a trade deficit, with the value of imports substantially exceeding the value of exports.

Table 5.2 indicates the sectoral structure of production and trade. Agriculture, forestry, and fisheries amount to about 25 percent of GDP at factor cost. Trade and transport amount to another 25 percent and construction to nearly 10 percent. More than half of total exports come from two primarily foreign-owned island sectors. Aluminum smelting alone accounted for 48 percent of the value of total exports in 2001. Exports of electricity from the Cahora Bassa dam in northern Mozambique accounted for another nearly 10 percent of total exports. Unfortunately, the large majority of these export revenues are used to pay for imported intermediates, salaries for expatriate personnel, and repatriation of profits. Hence, the links to the Mozambican economy are relatively small.[5] Fisheries provide the next most important source of export revenue. Imports tend to be concentrated in processed food, fuel, and manufactures, particularly transport equipment and other capital goods.

Average tariff rates by commodity are also included in table 5.2. The rates implied by the social accounting matrix (SAM) originally developed for this analysis are presented under the heading "average tariffs," and the rates used in the GTAP model of global trade are presented under the heading "GTAP tariffs." Generally, the tariffs implied by the SAM correlate well with those employed in the GTAP model (the correlation is about 0.58), even though the methodologies for developing these tariff aggregates have been rather different.

Table 5.3 provides a better sense of the degree of competition between imports and domestic production. The results in the table are derived from an analysis of local production and imports comprising all economic activity divided into 144 sectors. Each of the 144 sectors was put into one of three groups. The first group contains sectors where production accounts for at least 90 percent of total availability (production plus imports). The second group contains sectors where imports account for at least 90 percent of total availability. The third group

Table 5.2a. Sectoral Shares in Value Added, Exports, and Imports

Sector	Value added share (%)	Export share (%)	Import share (%)	Average tariff rate	GTAP tariff rate
Paddy rice	1.0	0.0	0.0	0.0	2.3
Wheat	0.0	0.0	1.9	2.4	2.1
Cereal grains nec	2.1	0.2	0.3	2.0	2.3
Vegetables, fruit, nuts	3.8	1.9	0.1	23.0	23.0
Oilseeds	0.8	0.0	0.1	7.8	9.9
Sugar cane, sugar beet	0.2	0.0	0.0	0.0	0.0
Plant-based fibers	1.1	0.1	0.0	23.2	0.0
Crops nec	9.7	2.6	0.4	3.2	5.2
Bovine cattle, sheep, goats, horses	0.6	0.0	0.1	1.9	6.1
Animal products nec	1.1	0.0	0.5	10.4	4.7
Forestry	2.7	1.5	0.0	2.5	2.7
Fishing	2.5	12.6	0.0	22.4	6.8
Minerals nec	0.3	0.3	0.2	5.3	7.1
Bovine meat products	0.4	0.0	0.0	23.2	15.7
Meat products nec	1.2	0.2	1.0	8.9	19.4
Vegetable oils and fats	0.3	1.1	1.1	16.0	13.6
Processed rice	0.1	0.0	4.5	5.8	7.1
Sugar	0.1	0.5	0.6	5.3	7.5
Food products nec	2.5	0.6	3.4	9.2	18.3
Beverages and tobacco products	0.8	0.1	1.6	9.4	24.2
Textiles	0.4	2.6	3.8	11.5	20.7
Wearing apparel	0.6	0.6	0.5	21.7	24.0
Leather products	0.1	0.1	0.3	29.9	22.6
Wood products	0.7	0.4	1.1	14.6	18.0
Paper products, publishing	0.0	0.0	0.8	9.5	6.5
Petroleum, coal products	0.2	2.5	4.4	12.0	4.8
Chemical, rubber, plastic products	0.4	0.3	19.0	6.7	9.4
Mineral products nec	0.5	0.1	2.4	6.4	8.8
Ferrous metals	4.5	49.0	0.2	9.6	6.3
Metal products	0.2	0.4	6.3	5.1	9.9
Motor vehicles and parts	0.0	0.0	6.1	7.9	8.6
Transport equipment nec	0.0	0.2	9.5	7.8	11.5
Electronic equipment	0.0	0.0	6.0	2.4	6.9

continued

Table 5.2b.   Sectoral Shares in Value Added, Exports, and Imports *(Continued)*

Sector	Value added share (%)	Export share (%)	Import share (%)	Average tariff rate	GTAP tariff rate
Manufactures nec	0.0	0.2	1.6	21.6	21.9
Electricity	1.9	7.8	4.2	0.0	0.0
Water	0.3	0.0	0.0	0.0	0.0
Construction	9.4	0.0	0.0	0.0	0.0
Trade	17.3	0.0	0.0	0.0	0.0
Transport nec	7.2	6.5	0.0	0.0	0.0
Water transport	0.2	0.0	0.0	0.0	0.0
Air transport	0.4	0.0	0.0	0.0	0.0
Communication	1.8	0.0	0.0	0.0	0.0
Financial services nec	2.0	0.5	0.2	0.0	0.0
Insurance	0.1	0.0	0.3	0.0	0.0
Business services nec	3.7	4.7	16.3	0.3	0.0
Public administration, defense, education, and health	16.3	2.5	1.1	0.0	0.0
Dwellings	0.4	0.0	0.0	0.0	0.0
Total	100.0	100.0	100.0	n.c.	n.c.

Source: Author's calculations.

Note: nec = not elsewhere classified; n.c. = not calculated.

contains all remaining products. This third group contains sectors where neither domestic supply nor imports dominate the total supply of the commodity. The first two groups are considered to be specialized, and the third group is considered nonspecialized.

Table 5.3 indicates that, in general, sectors tend rather strongly to be either dominated by imports or by domestic production. Overall, about 89 percent of the value of domestic production is specialized, with the large majority of these facing minor to no import competition in their particular product category.[6] The sectors that compete most directly with imports are in primary product processing, which includes processed foods. According to the table, 53 percent of sales in this category come from sectors that are specialized (dominated by either imports or by domestic production). This implies that slightly less than half of sales in these sectors are in sectors where both imports and domestic production account for a significant volume of total domestic supply. These sectors also benefit from fairly substantial tariff protection (see table 5.2). However, these

Table 5.3.   Indications of Import Competition

Sector	Overall production value share (%)	Specialized[a]	
		Share of total supply (%)	Share of production (%)
Total economy	100.0	82.1	88.8
Agriculture, forestry and fisheries	15.1	98.2	98.5
Primary product processing	12.9	46.1	53.4
Other goods	8.1	74.6	74.5
Services	63.9	89.1	95.5

Source: Author's calculations.

a. The figures in this table are drawn from production and import information for 144 sectors representing all commodities. The intent is to discover which productive sectors compete intensively with imports and which are specialized, meaning that either commodity supply comes 90 percent from domestic production or 90 percent from imports.

sectors make up only about 13 percent of the value of total sales and a smaller percentage of value added.

Generally, the volume of resources located in sectors where import competition could be expected to be keen is relatively small. There is little to no possibility for substitution between domestic production and imports in sectors where imports are dominant, such as oil, vehicles, and capital goods. Mozambique quite simply has very little to no productive capacity in these areas. Consequently, imports are expected to dominate under any scenario. Similarly, where production values for tradeables are large, such as in primary agriculture and fisheries, import volumes tend to be minor. Import volumes are also minor in most service sectors.

With respect to households, home consumption of basic food items represents a very important element of total expenditure. The importance of home consumption, from various perspectives, is presented in table 5.4. According to the macroeconomic accounts, home consumption amounts to 22 percent of total consumer expenditure on commodities. Home consumption is much more prevalent in rural than in urban areas. It amounts to about 36 percent of total rural consumer spending and only about 8 percent of total urban consumer expenditure.

Wealthy households whose population weight is small but whose economic weight is large tend to dampen significantly the importance of home consumption in the macroeconomic accounts. Wealthy individuals tend to engage

Table 5.4.   Share of Value of Home Consumption in Total Consumption

Share-weighting scheme	Urban	Rural	Total
Macroeconomic share	7.8	35.7	22.0
Population weight share	15.7	58.2	44.6
Poor population weight share	19.5	59.2	47.1

Source: Author's calculations.

in very little home consumption as a share of total consumption and have large economic weight, thus their presence drives down the share of home consumption in the macroeconomic data. When home consumption shares are derived using population weights (for example, the share of home consumption for the average household), the share of home consumption grows considerably. At the national level, the average household obtains 45 percent of the value of total consumption from home consumption. The average rural household share remains considerably higher than the urban household share, at 58 percent and 16 percent, respectively.

The population categorized as poor tends to home consume proportionately somewhat more than the national average. Nevertheless, in terms of share of goods that are home consumed, households characterized as poor are not all that different from the population average. This is not surprising when one considers that the poor represent more than half the population. In addition, a further large fraction of the population consumes at levels above, but still near, the poverty line. For example, 90 percent of the population consumes at levels less than twice the poverty line. The tendency to home consume apparently remains relatively constant across these basic levels of income.

Inequality

James, Arndt, and Simler (2005) conduct a detailed analysis of inequality based on the 2002–3 *National Household Budget Survey* (INE 2004) for Mozambique. They estimate a national Gini coefficient of 0.42, which represents a fairly high degree of inequality, though not out of line with other Sub-Saharan African countries.[7] Table 5.5 shows an index of real consumption by quintile. Families in the highest quintile consume about eight times the value for the poorest quintile. Inequality varies by region, with consumption tending to be more evenly distributed in rural than in urban zones (a standard result). Regional differences also exist with the south, especially the capital city, Maputo, exhibiting much greater degrees of inequality.

Table 5.5.   Consumption by Quintiles

Population quintile	Real consumption index	As ratio of highest quintile's consumption
0-20%	0.39	7.97
21-40%	0.66	4.63
41-60%	0.94	3.29
61-80%	1.32	2.34
81-100%	3.08	1.00
Mean	1.28	2.41

Source: Author's calculations.

Simulations and Results

Table 5.6 describes the shocks applied in the simulations analyzed, and table 5.7 describes the simulations. Results from the GTAP model of global trade are transmitted to the Mozambique model via changes in import prices and export prices and quantities faced by Mozambique. Import price changes are simply applied to the exogenous import prices in the Mozambique model. Export price and quantity changes derived from the GTAP model are applied in the manner developed by Horridge and Zhai in the appendix to chapter 3 of this volume. Specifically, an export demand function of the form:

$$(5.1) \quad Q = [FP/P]^\wedge ESUBM$$

(where Q is the quantity exported, P is the export price, $ESUBM$ is the elasticity of demand for exports, and FP is a shift parameter) has been added to the Mozambique model to mimic the global GTAP model. In the appendix to Chapter 3, Horridge and Zhai show that export price and quantity changes generated by the GTAP can be mimicked in a country through shocks to the shift parameter FP. Using lowercase to indicate percentage change, the percentage change in FP applied to the Mozambique model can be derived as follows:

$$(5.2) \quad fp = p + q/ESUBM.$$

The four simulations presented are detailed in table 5.7. These are unilateral complete trade liberalization (UniLib), global trade liberalization with Mozambique not participating (Global), complete global trade liberalization

Table 5.6a. Export and Import Price Changes and Tariff Cuts for Simulations

Sector	Global liberalization			Doha		
	Export prices	Import prices	Export quantity	Export prices	Import prices	Export quantity
Paddy rice	n.a.	12.8	n.a.	n.a.	2.9	n.a.
Wheat	n.a.	6.7	n.a.	n.a.	1.5	n.a.
Cereal grains nec	1.6	3.4	-5.2	0.0	1.6	1.8
Vegetables, fruit, nuts	1.4	2.7	14.6	0.0	0.9	-4.3
Oilseeds	3.3	6.4	56.5	0.7	2.2	11.7
Sugar cane, sugar beet	n.a.	n.a.	n.a.	n.a.	n.a.	n.a.
Plant-based fibers	3.5	1.1	26.9	1.0	1.2	9.0
Crops nec	2.0	0.7	20.9	0.0	0.7	-2.4
Bovine cattle, sheep, goats, horses	n.a.	3.3	n.a.	n.a.	1.7	n.a.
Animal products nec	1.6	2.1	-6.3	0.1	1.2	-1.7
Forestry	-0.9	-0.2	3.0	-0.3	0.1	1.8
Fishing	-2.4	0.4	9.5	-0.7	0.4	0.5
Minerals nec	-0.8	1.1	2.2	0.0	1.7	0.7
Bovine meat products	n.a.	3.4	n.a.	n.a.	2.0	n.a.
Meat products nec	1.2	1.4	-37.7	0.1	1.0	-12.6
Vegetable oils and fats	0.5	2.6	-16.2	0.2	1.2	4.0
Processed rice	2.2	5.6	-6.8	0.2	3.0	-2.1
Sugar	0.0	1.3	54.9	0.0	1.3	17.0
Food products nec	0.1	-0.1	-16.1	-0.1	0.6	-4.4
Beverages and tobacco products	-0.7	-0.7	-6.5	-0.1	0.2	-2.1
Textiles	-0.1	-1.3	-2.4	0.1	0.7	-3.8
Wearing apparel	-1.0	-2.0	22.7	-0.2	-0.4	1.7
Leather products	-0.8	-0.9	-8.6	0.0	0.2	-8.8
Wood products	-1.0	-1.1	-5.3	-0.2	-0.2	-1.1
Paper products, publishing	-0.4	1.6	25.2	0.4	2.5	-3.9
Petroleum, coal products	-1.0	-0.8	16.0	-0.3	0.0	1.7
Chemical, rubber, plastic products	-1.0	-0.4	112.5	-0.2	0.8	39.9
Mineral products nec	-0.8	2.8	-8.3	0.0	3.5	-2.9
Ferrous metals	-1.0	-0.7	-7.6	-0.2	0.0	-0.8
Metal products	-0.9	-1.0	-21.9	0.0	-0.1	-3.6

continued

Table 5.6b. Export and Import Price Changes and Tariff Cuts for Simulations (cont.)

Sector	Global liberalization			Doha		
	Export prices	Import prices	Export quantity	Export prices	Import prices	Export quantity
Motor vehicles and parts	n.a.	-2.9	n.a.	n.a.	-0.4	n.a.
Transport equipment nec	-1.0	-0.9	-1.0	-0.1	-0.1	-0.1
Electronic equipment	n.a.	-1.0	n.a.	n.a.	-0.1	n.a.
Manufactures nec	-1.0	-1.1	1.5	-0.1	-0.1	-0.3
Electricity	-0.9	-1.0	2.1	-0.1	-0.1	1.6
Water	n.a.	n.a.	n.a.	n.a.	n.a.	n.a.
Construction	n.a.	n.a.	n.a.	n.a.	n.a.	n.a.
Trade	n.a.	n.a.	n.a.	n.a.	n.a.	n.a.
Transport nec	-1.0	n.a.	1.3	-0.2	n.a.	0.4
Water transport	n.a.	n.a.	n.a.	n.a.	n.a.	n.a.
Air transport	n.a.	n.a.	n.a.	n.a.	n.a.	n.a.
Communication	n.a.	n.a.	n.a.	n.a.	n.a.	n.a.
Financial services nec	-1.2	-0.7	2.4	-0.3	-0.1	1.0
Insurance	n.a.	-0.8	n.a.	n.a.	-0.2	n.a.
Business services nec	-1.0	-0.7	1.2	-0.2	-0.1	0.2
Public administration, defense, education, health	-0.8	-0.8	0.2	-0.2	-0.1	0.4
Dwellings	n.a.	n.a.	n.a.	n.a.	n.a.	n.a.

Source: Based on results from chapter 3 of this book.

Note: nec = not elsewhere classified; n.a. = not applicable (commodity has import or export volume of zero).

including Mozambique (FL), and the Doha scenario (Doha). These scenarios are described in detail in chapter 2. Because of its status as an LDC, Mozambique does not have to reduce its tariffs under the Doha scenario.

Results are presented in tables 5.8, 5.9, and 5.10. Focusing first on the macroeconomic results in table 5.8, one notes that unilateral trade liberalization generates a substantial real exchange rate depreciation. With tariffs removed, imports become more attractively priced and import volumes increase. To obtain the foreign currency to purchase these additional imports, exports must increase more than proportionately because of the large initial trade deficit. As mentioned above, to remain consistent with the GTAP, downward-sloping export demand

Table 5.7. Simulations

Simulation	Description
UniLib	Unilateral complete trade liberalization by Mozambique uniquely
Global	Complete global trade liberation excluding Mozambique
FL	Complete global trade liberalization including Mozambique
Doha	Doha

Source: Scenarios based on chapter 2 of this book.

functions are specified. Therefore, the growth in export volume results in somewhat lower prices for export commodities, leading to a deterioration in the terms of trade (TOT). Devaluation helps to attenuate the import surge and provides additional incentives to exporting sectors. Global trade liberalization with Mozambique not participating operates through shifts in world demand curves for Mozambican export commodities as described above. It turns out that global trade liberalization tends to improve the terms of trade for Mozambique, permitting increased imports even though exports remain flat. The results for the third scenario, FL, are essentially an additive combination of the first two simulations.

In the Doha scenario, the TOT effect is negative for Mozambique as a consequence of the elimination of export subsidies and the erosion of Mozambican tariff preferences in industrial countries. The negative TOT shock is accommodated primarily through compression of imports (recall that initial import values are much larger than export values). A relatively large decline in the export price for the fisheries sector, an important exporter, helps to explain both the direction of the TOT shock and the compression of import values.

Overall household welfare as calculated from the CGE model (table 5.9) is driven largely by the TOT. The presence of downward-sloping export demand functions is a particularly important element in the TOT changes when domestic trade liberalization is considered. By contrast, with the small country assumption (constant world prices) and operatively small export transformation elasticities, unilateral trade liberalization tends to improve household welfare (scenario not shown). In all scenarios, the impacts on welfare are not particularly large.

Microsimulation analysis generally points to similarly small results. Table 5.10 summarizes the implications of trade liberalization on household welfare for the lower four income quintiles. It shows the mean, minimum, and maximum household level welfare impact (in percentage change from the base) for each simulation. The mean effect in the microsimulation model tends to be closer to zero than the equivalent welfare calculation provided in table 5.9. This is due

Table 5.8.   Macroeconomic Indicators (percentage change, relative to base)

Variable	UniLib	Global	FL	Doha
Total absorption	-0.7	0.6	0.0	-0.2
Real exports	4.4	0.0	4.4	0.2
Real imports	0.5	1.9	2.4	-0.4
Real exchange rate	4.3	-3.4	0.8	0.4
TOT	-1.4	0.8	-0.6	-0.7

Source: Author's simulations.

Table 5.9.   Equivalent Variation for Households (percentage change, relative to base)

Variable	Base	UniLib	Global	FL	Doha
Urban	2,538.74	-0.552	0.489	-0.088	-0.219
Rural	2,631.26	-0.75	0.527	-0.192	-0.173
Total	5,170.00	-0.653	0.508	-0.141	-0.195

Source: Author's simulations.

Note: UniLib, Global, FL, and Doha simulations are given as a percentage change from the figures in the "Base" column.

primarily to the insulating effects of the high value of home consumption in the lower 80 percent of the consumption distribution (see table 5.4). Nevertheless, concentration of earnings sources in certain factors and consumption on certain commodities exposes some households to stronger than average effects of trade liberalization. The range of the distribution is captured by the maximum and minimum values. The worst affected household would be one specialized in the factor with least favorable change in factor prices and specialized in consumption of commodities whose prices have tended to rise.

The range of outcomes for the Doha scenario is presented in figure 5.1. Outcomes for both urban and rural households tend to concentrate near the mean. Nevertheless, impacts tend to be much more heterogeneous in urban than in rural areas. This result also holds in all of the other scenarios (histograms not shown). This occurs as a result of more heterogeneous factor endowments across households in urban areas (rural households tend to depend very heavily on unskilled labor), as well as substantially greater reliance on the market for the purchase of commodities (that is, less own-consumption). For rural households, homogeneity in income sources tends to concentrate welfare outcomes near the mean, and the prevalence of home consumption implies that this mean effect is typically quite small.

Table 5.10.   Microsimulation, Percentage Changes in Welfare by Quintile

Quintile	Statistic	UniLib	Global	FL	Doha
Rural					
0–20%	Mean	-0.65	0.14	-0.49	-0.10
21–40%	Mean	-0.62	0.11	-0.48	-0.09
41–60%	Mean	-0.55	0.14	-0.38	-0.09
61–80%	Mean	-0.43	0.15	-0.24	-0.09
0–20%	Maximum	1.99	2.16	2.64	0.17
21–40%	Maximum	2.61	2.56	3.29	0.14
41–60%	Maximum	1.71	2.05	2.87	0.17
61–80%	Maximum	3.19	1.31	4.21	0.16
0–20%	Minimum	-1.37	-0.69	-1.70	-1.06
21–40%	Minimum	-1.90	-0.66	-1.89	-0.96
41–60%	Minimum	-1.43	-0.85	-2.16	-0.90
61–80%	Minimum	-1.72	-0.90	-2.62	-0.93
Urban					
Quintile	Statistic	UniLib	Global	FL	Doha
0–20%	Mean	-0.29	0.08	-0.23	-0.18
21–40%	Mean	-0.27	0.13	-0.16	-0.19
41–60%	Mean	-0.10	0.17	0.05	-0.18
61–80%	Mean	-0.02	0.31	0.27	-0.20
0–20%	Maximum	2.39	1.53	3.38	0.25
21–40%	Maximum	3.05	1.65	4.02	0.29
41–60%	Maximum	2.61	2.27	3.17	0.37
61–80%	Maximum	2.64	2.15	3.48	0.20
0–20%	Minimum	-1.78	-0.89	-1.95	-0.96
21–40%	Minimum	-2.21	-1.09	-2.36	-1.25
41–60%	Minimum	-2.03	-0.99	-2.47	-1.17
61–80%	Minimum	-1.91	-0.91	-1.89	-1.07

Source: Author's simulations.

Note: The top-earning quintile is not presented because of difficulties in separating labor and capital income for this group of households.

Because nearly three of four poor Mozambicans live in rural areas, the overall implications for poverty rates in all of the scenarios tend to be small. In the scenario with the largest effect, unilateral trade liberalization (UniLib), the poverty rate edges up from 54.1 percent nationwide to 54.4 percent. Impacts in the remaining scenarios are much smaller.

Figure 5.1. Distribution of Changes in Household Welfare

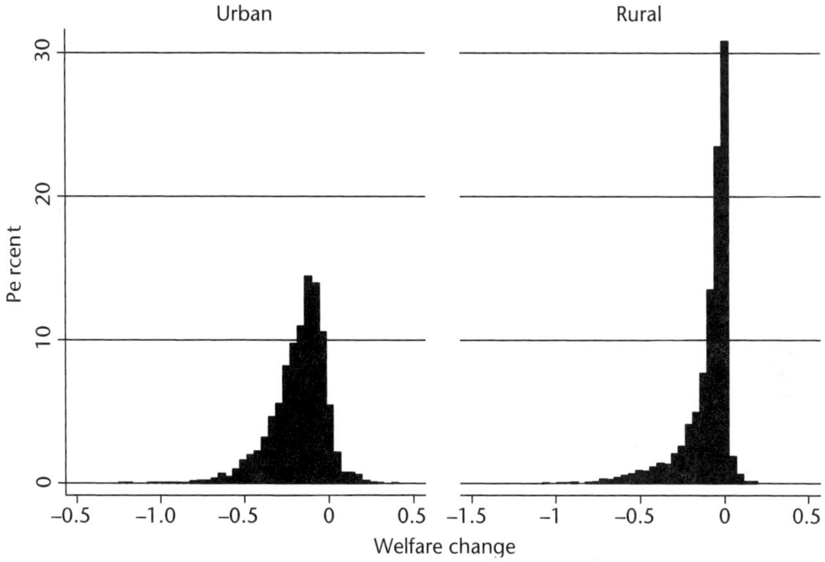

Source: Author's simulations.

Limitations of the Analysis

Price Transmission

As reviewed in Winters, McCulloch, and McKay (2004), marketing costs between the frontier of a country (the port, for example) and the point of production cause the price of an export good at the point of production to be considerably more variable in proportional terms than the free on board (FOB) price. For example, consider a good with an export price at the border of 100 and a marketing wedge between the border and the farm or factory gate of 50. If the FOB price increases by 10 percent to 110 and the marketing wedge remains constant, then the farm or factory gate price also increases by 10, from 50 to 60 for a proportionately double price increment of 20 percent.

The inverse happens with respect to importation. Consider an imported good that is available at the border for a price of 50. Marketing costs of 50 are incurred to get the product to the point of final consumption. If the border price increases by 10 percent and marketing costs remain constant, then the price of the imported good at the point of consumption increases by only 5 percent. Therefore, in terms of proportional price changes, marketing wedges tend to expand the impact of changes in export prices (free on board [FOB] minus export taxes) and dampen the impact of changes in import prices (CIF plus import tariffs). If border price changes are transmitted in the manner described above, it seems likely that past assessments of the implications of past global trade negotiation rounds may have given undue weight to the implications of import price changes and insufficient weight to the implications of export price changes when considering the implications of trade agreements for poverty and well-being for many parts of Africa.

The current model, with its explicit addition of margins for exports, imports, and domestics, partially captures these effects. This represents an important step forward; however, there remains much to do. The impact of trade liberalization on poverty depends crucially upon where the poor are living and the strength of the ensuing links to regional, national, and global markets. Distance and poor transport infrastructure alone may sever links to both import and export markets. Imperfect competition within the marketing system may also sever market linkages (Moser and Minten 2004). Thus, particularly in large countries such as Mozambique, the analysis of trade and poverty forces one to consider building models with finer levels of spatial detail. This is true for both commodity and factor markets.

Unfortunately, attaining enhanced spatial detail is easier said than done. Attempts have been made (see, for example, chapter 7 by Ferreira Filho and Horridge in this volume); however, these attempts tend to be partial and tend not to generate a spatial price map that reflects the appropriate distribution of prices over space.[8] This is crucial because more distant regions often exhibit higher rates of poverty and very high marketing wedges. Although a partial approach to regionalization (for example, regional detail in the production of some agricultural commodities) within an AGE model seems attractive initially, the incompleteness might actually hamper the goal of more faithfully modeling the role of geography in shaping the impact of policy change. Therefore, despite formidable information lacunae on the spatial distribution of economic activity and the complete absence of information on inter-regional trade, it may be better to develop regional SAMs that account for what is known about the regional distribution of economic activity, estimating the remainder under plausible assumptions.[9]

Revenue Replacement

In the case of Mozambique, the GTAP model uses average tariffs obtained by multiplying applied tariff rates by import weights. To remain consistent, the country CGE model also uses these average tariff values. However, as discussed in Arndt and Tarp (2004), published tariff rates are generally larger than the tariff rate implied by the average tariff rate because of official exemptions, smuggling, or both. If the marginal import pays published tariff rates, then the published tariff rate and not the average rate is the operative one for trade policy analysis. In addition, the rents associated with smuggling and official tariff exemptions may be large. Elimination or reduction of these rents through trade liberalization can have substantial distributional effects, often with positive welfare implications for the poor (because the poor typically do not profit from these rents in the initial situation).

Gaps between average and published tariff rates also have implications for revenue. Pritchett and Sethi (1994) find that the gap between these rates tends to fall as published tariff rates decline. Hence, higher collection ratios may substantially attenuate declines in revenues as a result of lower tariff rates. The heavy dependence of Mozambique and many other African countries on VAT applied at the border implies that even complete trade liberalization (tariff rates at zero) may have offsetting revenue implications if a higher share of import volumes pass through official channels and hence pay VAT.

Examination of these revenue issues in the Mozambican context goes beyond the scope of this chapter (though it is an important topic for future research). The use of a neutral income tax for revenue replacement is a poor substitute for realistic modeling of revenue replacement options; however, the complexities of the revenue replacement issue (see Arndt and Tarp [2004]) precluded modeling of options that are effectively more realistic within the time frame available for this analysis.

Downward-Sloping Export Demand Functions

In the analysis undertaken in this chapter, trade liberalization by Mozambique results in increased export volumes. Because the country is presumed to face downward-sloping export demand functions, increases in exports result in lower prices and a deterioration in the nation's TOT. This formulation permits consistency with the GTAP model. Unfortunately, the formulation is the major driver of welfare results in the scenarios where Mozambique undertakes own-liberalization. Although this is perhaps a reasonable specification for some sectors, exports from many sectors are likely to be constrained by supply factors. In this view, more could be exported at a constant price if more could be produced. In fact, for many sectors, low export volumes are often pointed to as a cause of low prices, particularly at the farm or factory gate. Low volumes are viewed as a cause of high marketing costs and diminished confidence of potential importers in the quality and reliability of supply of Mozambican products. As indicated before, changing the modeling assumption to that of supply-constrained exports and constant world prices switches the sign on the welfare result for unilateral trade liberalization, although the implications remain relatively small for the same reasons discussed above.

Despite these limitations of the analytical framework used in this chapter, a few robust conclusions may effectively be drawn. These are discussed in the final section.

Conclusions

To rise out of poverty, Mozambique must achieve rapid growth over a long period. Even with rapid growth, it will take some time, perhaps decades, to lift the bulk of the Mozambican population out of poverty. Seen from this perspective, the static results presented in this chapter are disappointing because they do not contribute to the growth required for such sustained poverty reduction. Nevertheless, as pointed out by Winters, McCulloch, and McKay (2004), most economists believe that more liberal trading regimes tend to be associated with higher rates of economic growth. Difficulties, in their view, come about in making the transition from more restrictive to more open trade regimes. In this respect, the results of this chapter may be viewed in a more positive light. For Mozambique, the short-term poverty impacts of moving to a liberal trade regime appear to be relatively small. Hence, Mozambique has the opportunity to set in place the liberal trade element of a growth strategy at relatively low short-term adjustment cost.

It is well recognized that, especially in the Mozambican context, low or zero barriers to imports are not a sufficient condition for ensuring poverty-reducing economic growth. A key element to sustaining growth over the coming decades very likely involves substantially expanding the volume of exports in sectors where volumes are currently very small—or breaking into new export markets entirely. A liberal import regime helps set the stage for export expansion; however, such expansion will not occur without appropriate complementary policies aimed at improving price transmission to rural areas, as well as facilitating producer supply response. Only after such reforms will the vast majority of the poor in Mozambique be able to take advantage of the improved world market opportunities that are expected to follow from global trade reforms.

Notes

1. For a more complete historical review, see Arndt, Jensen, and Tarp (2000).

2. "Big projects," such as the Mozal aluminum smelter, have contributed considerably to GDP but very little to gross national product.

3. Löfgren, Harris, and Robinson (2001) and Tarp and others (2002) provide detailed explanations of the basic CGE model that was revised for the purposes of this analysis.

4. Downward-sloping export demand functions offer the considerable advantage of consistency with the global modeling framework. Disadvantages are discussed in detail in the penultimate section of this chapter, which presents a critique of the current model.

5. Aluminum smelting is modeled as an island sector. Nearly 100 percent of production is exported. Returns to capital from aluminum smelting are assumed to be repatriated abroad.

6. Substitution across commodities would amplify competition. Thus, for example, maize production faces little direct import competition in the form of imported maize. However, significant volumes of wheat and rice are imported. Because maize meal and bread are substitutes, domestic maize competes indirectly with imports through the potential for consumers to alter dietary choices.

7. For example, the Gini coefficient is 0.43 in Uganda (Uganda Bureau of Statistics 2003).

8. The distribution of prices over time is another important element.

9. Another option is to link the results of a CGE model to a partial equilibrium model(s) to flesh out in more detail implications for important sectors.

References

Arndt, C., H. T. Jensen, S. Robinson, and F. Tarp. 2000. "Agricultural Technology and Marketing Margins in Mozambique." *Journal of Development Studies* 37 (1): 121–37.

Arndt, C., H. T. Jensen, and F. Tarp. 2000. "Stabilization and Structural Adjustment in Mozambique." *Journal of International Development* 12: 299–323.

Arndt, C., and F. Tarp. 2004. "Trade Policy Reform and the Missing Revenue: An Application to Mozambique." National Directorate of Planning and Budget, Mozambique Ministry of Finance, Maputo.

Chen, S., and M. Ravallion. 2004. "Welfare Impacts of China's Accession to the World Trade Organization." *World Bank Economic Review* 18 (1): 29–57.

Ferreira Filho, J. B. S., and M. Horridge. 2005. "The Doha Round, Poverty, and Regional Inequality in Brazil." In *Poverty and the WTO: Impacts of the Doha Development Agenda*, ed. T. W. Hertel and L. A. Winters. Basingstoke, U.K.: Palgrave Macmillan; Washington, DC: World Bank.

Hertel, T., D. Hummels, M. Ivanic, and R. Keeney. 2004. "How Confident Can We Be in CGE-Based Assessments of Free Trade Agreements?" GTAP Technical Paper 26, Purdue University, West Lafayette, IN. http://www.gtap.agecon.purdue.edu/resources/working_paper.asp

INE (Instituto Nacional de Estatística). 2004. *Inquérito Nacional aos Agregados Familiares sobre Orçamento Familiar 2002/3 [National Household Budget Survey]*. Maputo. http://www.ine.gov.mz

James, R. C., C. Arndt, and K. R. Simler. 2005. "Has Economic Growth in Mozambique Been Pro-Poor?" National Directorate of Planning and Budget, Ministry of Planning and Finance, Maputo, Mozambique.

Löfgren, H., R. L. Harris, and S. Robinson. 2001. "A Standard Computable General Equilibrium (CGE) Model in GAMS." Trade and Macroeconomics Discussion Paper 75, International Food Policy Research Institute, Washington, DC.

Maximiano, N. 2005. "A Dinamica dos Determinantes de Pobreza" ["The Dynamics of Poverty Determinants"]. National Directorate of Planning and Budget, Ministry of Planning and Finance, Maputo, Mozambique.

Moser, C., and B. Minten 2004. "Missed Opportunities and Missing Markets: Spatio-Temporal Arbitrage of Rice in Madagascar." Paper presented at the Trade and Industrial Policy Strategies Forum 2004: "African Development and Poverty Reduction: The Macro Micro Linkage," October 13, Somerset West, South Africa.

Mozambique Ministry of Planning and Finance, International Food Policy Research Institute, and Purdue University. 2004. *Poverty and Well-Being in Mozambique: The Second National Assessment (2002–2003)*. Maputo: National Directorate of Planning and Budget, Ministry of Planning and Finance, Mozambique.

Pritchett, L., and G. Sethi. 1994. "Tariff Rates, Tariff Revenue, and Tariff Reform: Some New Facts." *World Bank Economic Review* 8 (1): 1–16.

Tarp, F., C. Arndt, H. T. Jensen, S. Robinson, and R. Heltberg. 2002. "Facing the Development Challenge in Mozambique: An Economy-Wide Perspective." IFPRI Research Report 126, International Food Policy Research Institute, Washington, DC.

Winters, L. A., N. McCulloch, and A. McKay. 2004. "Trade Liberalization and Poverty: The Evidence So Far." *Journal of Economic Literature* 42: 72–115.

PART III

HOUSEHOLD IMPACTS OF PRICE CHANGES

6

THE WTO DOHA ROUND, COTTON SECTOR DYNAMICS, AND POVERTY TRENDS IN ZAMBIA

Jorge F. Balat and Guido G. Porto

Summary

The Zambian cotton sector went through significant reforms during the 1990s. After a long period of parastatal control, a process of liberalization in cotton production and marketing began in 1994. These reforms were expected to benefit farmers. In Zambia, these are rural, often vulnerable, smallholders. This chapter investigates the connection between the dynamics of the cotton sector and the dynamics of poverty and evaluates to what extent cotton can work as a vehicle for poverty alleviation. The findings suggest that cotton can indeed act as an effective mechanism for increased household welfare, and income gains associated with cotton production are likely to have positive impacts on the long-run nutritional status of Zambian children. These impacts, however, are relatively small.

Introduction

The Zambian cotton sector has been profoundly reformed during the last 10 years. Traditionally, cotton production was controlled by the government through public firms and parastatal organizations. Until 1994, Lintco (Lint Company of Zambia) sold inputs on loan and purchased cotton seeds from farmers. The

155

reforms comprised a broad liberalization of the sector that included the privatization of Lintco and the encouragement of market entry. The dynamics of the sector include an initial phase of regional private monopsonies and a later phase of more active competition. At present, the market is relatively unregulated, and several firms seem to freely compete (but may collude) for locally produced cotton seeds.

Poverty in Zambia is a deep phenomenon, particularly in rural areas. In 1998, for example, the head count was 82.1 percent. Moreover, poverty in some regions exceeded 90 percent. Cotton is one of the key agricultural activities in rural Zambia. In cotton-growing provinces, a large share of the cash income of rural farmers comes from the sale of cotton seeds.

This chapter studies the dynamics of cotton production and marketing and the links with rural poverty. It has long been claimed that cash crops can work as an effective vehicle for poverty alleviation in rural areas. Hence, this chapter explores whether cotton can actually achieve significant poverty reduction in Zambia.

The chapter begins with a review of the reforms in the cotton sector. Because cotton can be produced only in selected regions in Zambia, the trends in poverty and cotton income in different provinces are examined. Two different empirical exercises are performed to investigate the role of cotton as a source of household income. First, the evolution of the share of income generated by cotton is examined, and the poverty impacts brought about by an increase in cotton prices and an expansion of the sector are simulated. Second, the potential impact of subsistence households switching to cotton production is evaluated. Income differentials, anthropometric measures, and educational outcomes are also examined.

The findings are mixed. On the one hand, cotton production is associated with higher household income, lower poverty, and higher welfare. This result has two components. First, higher cotton prices would benefit rural farmers directly. Second, cotton farmers enjoy income gains and long-run nutritional gains compared to subsistence farmers. On the other hand, the estimated magnitudes are not as large as expected. Very large price changes of cotton seeds or very large supply responses would be needed to estimate empirically meaningful reductions in poverty rates. Thus, international trade in cotton is indeed a promising activity for farmers, but there is a long way to go to achieve the full benefits from increased market access and higher prices. Reforms in the provision of infrastructure, access to credit, extension services, and social services are essential complementary policies to market access and liberalization of agricultural markets in the developed world.

Section 1 reviews the main reforms in cotton markets, discusses the characteristics of world cotton markets, and provides a poverty profile of Zambian households. Section 2 looks at cotton as a source of cash income and provides a simulation of the impacts of market access and higher international prices. Section 3 provides an estimation of income differential gains in cotton over subsistence agriculture. Nonmonetary outcomes, such as educational and nutritional status, are studied as well. Section 4 reviews the main results and summarizes the conclusions.

Cotton Reforms and Poverty Trends in Zambia

Zambia is a landlocked country located in southern central Africa. Clockwise, its neighbors are Congo, Tanzania, Malawi, Mozambique, Zimbabwe, Botswana, Namibia, and Angola.[1] In 2000, the population was 10.7 million inhabitants. With a per capita GDP of only US$302, Zambia is one of the poorest countries in the world and is considered a least developed country (LDC).

Zambia achieved independence in 1964. A key characteristic of the country is its abundance of natural resources, particularly mineral deposits (for example, copper) and land. As a result of high copper prices, the new republic did quite well in the initial stages of development. Poverty and inequality, however, were widespread, and this raised concerns among the people and the policymakers. Soon, the government began to adopt interventionist policies, with a much larger participation of the state in national development. Interventions included import substitution, price controls on all major agricultural products (such as maize), and nationalization of manufacturing, agricultural marketing, and mining.

In the 1970s and 1980s, the decline in copper prices and negative external conditions led to stagnation and high levels of external debt. A crisis emerged, and a structural adjustment program was implemented between 1983 and 1985. Riots in 1986 forced the government to abandon the reforms in 1987. A second International Monetary Fund program failed in 1989, when the removal of controls in maize led to significant price increases.

In 1991, the Movement for Multiparty Democracy was elected. Faced with a sustained, severe recession and a meager future, the new government began economy-wide reforms including macroeconomic stabilization, exchange rate liberalization, fiscal restructuring, removal of maize subsidies, decontrol of agricultural prices, privatization of agricultural marketing, and new trade and industrial policy. For a more detailed description of the reforms, see World Bank (1994), McCulloch, Baulch, and Cherel-Robson (2001), and Litchfield and McCulloch (2003).

Cotton Reforms

The cotton sector was significantly affected by the agricultural reforms adopted by Zambia during the 1990s.[2] Before 1994, intervention in cotton markets was widespread and involved setting prices for sales of certified cotton seeds, pesticides, and sprayers; providing subsidized inputs to producers, facilitating access to credit, and so forth. From 1977 to 1994, Lintco acted as a nexus between local

Zambian producers and international markets. Lintco had a monopsony in seed cotton markets and a monopoly in inputs sales and credit loans to farmers.

The reforms of the mid-1990s eliminated most of these interventions, and markets were liberalized. After Lintco was sold to Lonrho Cotton in 1994, a domestic monopsony developed soon after liberalization. As market opportunities arose, several firms (private ginners such as Swarp Textiles and Clark Cotton) entered the Zambian cotton market. This initial phase of liberalization, however, did not succeed in introducing much competition in the sector because the three major firms segmented the market geographically. In consequence, liberalization gave rise to geographic monopsonies rather than national oligopsonies.

At that time, Lonrho and Clark Cotton developed an out-grower scheme with the Zambian farmers. This scheme allowed ginners to expand production and take advantage of economies of scale and idle capacity. In these out-grower programs, firms provided seeds and inputs on loans together with extension services to improve productivity. The value of the loan was deducted from the sales of cotton seeds to the ginners at picking time. Prices paid for the harvest supposedly depended on international prices. Initially, repayment rates were high (roughly 86 percent), and cotton production significantly increased.

By 1997, the expansion of the cotton production base attracted new entrants, such as Amaka Holdings and Continental Textiles. Entrants and incumbents started competing in many districts, doing away with localized monopsonies. As a result, the capacity for ginning increased beyond production levels. This caused an excess demand for cotton seeds and tightened the competition among ginners for Zambian cotton. In addition, some entrants that were not using out-grower schemes started offering higher prices for cotton seeds to farmers who had already signed contracts with other firms. This caused repayment problems and increased the rate of loan defaults.

The relationship between ginners and farmers started to deteriorate. On top of all this, world prices began to decline, and farm gate prices declined as a result. After many years of high farm gate prices, and with limited information on world market conditions, farmers started to mistrust the ginners, and suspicions of exploitation arose. In consequence, farmers felt that out-growers' contracts were being breached, and default rates increased. This led firms to increase the price of the loans charged to farmers, who, in the end, received a lower net price for their crops.

Partly as a result of this failure of the out-grower scheme, Lonrho announced its sale in 1999, and Dunavant Zambia Limited entered the market. Today, the major players in Zambian cotton markets are Dunavant Zambia Limited, Clark Cotton Limited, Amaka Holdings Limited, Continental Ginneries Limited, Zambia-China Mulungushi Textiles, and Mukuba Textiles.

At present, most cotton production in Zambia is carried out under the out-grower scheme. Farmers and firms understood the importance of honoring contracts and the benefits of maintaining a good reputation. The out-grower programs were perfected, and there are now two systems used by different firms: the farmer group system and the farmer distributor system. In the latter, firms designate an individual farmer as the distributor and provide inputs. The distributor prepares individual contracts with the farmers. The distributor is also in charge of assessing reasons for loan defaults—being able, in principle, to condone default in special cases—and responsible for renegotiating contracts in incoming seasons. In the farmer group system, small-scale producers deal with the ginneries directly, purchasing inputs on loan and repaying at the time of harvest. Both systems seem to work well.

International Markets and World Prices

The production of cotton and the international trade of cotton products are, and have traditionally been, subject to significant interventions. The distortions include taxes (either directly or indirectly through state marketing monopsonies [parastatals]), border intervention (tariffs, quotas), production and export support, and input subsidies. Aksoy and Beghin (2004) summarize the markets for different commodities, including cotton. They suggest that the combined support in cotton production in the major world producers (Brazil, China, Egypt, Greece, Spain, Turkey, and the United States) between 1997–98 and 2001–2 ranged from US$3.8 billion to US$5.3 billion.

The EU and the United States have historically intervened extensively in cotton markets (Baffes 2004). In the United States, intervention in cotton production is regulated by farm bills, such as those passed in 1996 and 2002. They establish price and income support (usually decoupling payments based on historical areas planted), tariffs, quotas, public agricultural research, provision of infrastructure (irrigation), export subsidies, export credit, subsidized loans and insurance, and so forth. The 2002 farm bill is expected to be in place for the next six years.

The EU intervenes in cotton production to provide support to Spanish and Greek producers. Under the Common Agricultural Policy of the European Union, support is given to cotton growers based on the difference between the market price and a guide (support) price. Advance payments are calculated on the basis of estimated cotton production. Ginners receive these payments and pass them through to producers in the form of higher prices (Baffes 2004).

The effects of the removal of cotton distortions in world markets have been widely researched. Some of the literature is reviewed by Baffes (2004). He reports results from the Food and Agricultural Policy Research Institute (2002), which showed that under global agricultural liberalization, world cotton prices would increase on average by 12.7 percent. Using similar methods, Sumner (2004) reports price increases according to different scenarios of cotton reforms. On average, his findings indicate an expected increase of 11.58 percent in world cotton prices. These numbers are in line with those reported by Baffes (2004). Notice, however, that the latter work focuses mostly on the impact on world prices of the elimination of U.S. domestic support. Comparison of the Baffes and Sumner results indicates that most of the price changes that can be expected from the liberalization of world markets would be generated by U.S. policies. This is confirmed by Hoekman, Nicita, and Olarreaga (2004), who report much lower cotton price changes from a Doha scenario that considers the elimination of trade barriers without changes in domestic support. It is unclear whether the reforms needed to achieve these increases in prices are reasonable or even feasible. Nevertheless, in the subsequent sections of this chapter, these estimates are used to simulate the poverty effects on Zambian farmers. But before doing that, it is useful to review the poverty trends observed in Zambia during the 1990s.

Poverty Trends

In spite of the significant reforms adopted by the Zambian government and of the significant intervention in international agricultural markets, Zambia is one of the poorest countries in the world. Furthermore, poverty rates tended to increase during the 1990s.

The description of the poverty trends in this chapter is based on three household surveys, the 1991 Priority Surveys and the 1996 and 1998 Living Conditions Monitoring Surveys (LCMSs).[3] The Priority Survey of 1991 is a Social Dimension of Adjustment Survey. It was conducted during October and November and covered a total of 9,886 households. Sample sizes were increased to 11,750 and 16,800 households in the 1996 and 1998 LCMSs.

Table 6.1 reports the poverty dynamics. In 1991, the poverty rate at the national level was 69.6 percent. Poverty increased in 1996, when the headcount reached 80 percent, and then declined toward 1998, with a headcount of 71.5 percent. In rural areas, poverty is widespread; the headcount was 88.3 percent in 1991, 90.5 percent in 1996, and 82.1 percent in 1998. Urban areas fared better, with a poverty rate of 47.2 percent in 1991, 62.1 percent in 1996, and 53.4 percent in 1998. In what follows, the focus is on rural areas.

Poverty trends by provinces are reported in table 6.2. Zambia is a large country, and provinces differ substantially in such basic characteristics as land quality, distance to the capital, roads, and so forth. In particular, cotton, the commodity under investigation here, can be produced (because of soil characteristics) in only the Southern, Central, and Eastern provinces. At the national level, poverty increased from 1991 to 1996 and then declined in 1998. Poverty trends in Lusaka, the Copperbelt, and the Northwestern province are similar to those at the national level. In the Central province, poverty first declined in 1996 and then increased in 1998. In the remaining provinces, particularly in the Eastern and Southern provinces, poverty has declined throughout the period.

Table 6.1.   Poverty in Zambia (headcount)

Region	1991	1996	1998
National	69.6	80.0	71.5
Rural	88.3	90.5	82.1
Urban	47.2	62.1	53.4

Source: Authors' calculations based on the 1991 Priority Survey and 1996 and 1998 LCMSs.

Note: The headcount is the percentage of the population below the poverty line.

Table 6.2.   Rural Poverty Trends: 1991, 1996, and 1998 (headcount)

Region	1991	1996	1998
National	88.3	90.5	82.1
Central	83.9	80.3	82.3
Copperbelt	66.2	78.8	82.1
Eastern	92.0	85.5	80.6
Luapula	90.8	86.1	84.6
Lusaka	70.9	78.1	75.7
Northern	94.2	90.6	83.3
Northwestern	86.3	87.3	77.4
Southern	85.4	82.5	73.0
Western	94.1	92.9	90.3

Source: Authors' calculations based on the 1991 Priority Survey and 1996 and 1998 LCMSs.

Note: Rural poverty only. The headcount is the percentage of the population below the poverty line.

Cotton Income and Higher Export Prices

This section investigates the potential effects of higher cotton prices on household income in rural Zambia. As argued by Deaton (1989, 1997), the short-run effects of price changes can be assessed by looking at income shares. Table 6.3 reports the average income shares for different sources of income. At the national level, the main sources of income are income from home consumption (42.5 percent), income from nonfarm businesses (16.8 percent), sales of food crops (9.1 percent), livestock and poultry (8.1 percent), and wages (6.9 percent). Note that the differences in income sources between poor and nonpoor households are not very significant.

Because of regional variation in soil, climate, and infrastructure, the relevant sources of income may be different for households residing in different provinces. To clarify this, table 6.4 reports the main sources of agricultural household income in the rural areas of the nine Zambian provinces. The table shows the average share of total income accounted for by a given activity. In the Central, Eastern, and Southern provinces, the most relevant cash-crop activity is cotton. In the remaining provinces, cotton is not a feasible option, and income shares are negligible or zero. The remainder of this chapter investigates the impacts of cotton reforms only in the relevant provinces.

**Table 6.3. Sources of Income in Rural Areas, 1998
(percentage)**

Income Source	Total	Poor	Nonpoor
Own production	42.5	42.9	42.0
Sales of food crops	9.1	9.5	7.6
Sales of nonfood crops	3.8	4.0	2.9
Livestock and poultry	8.1	8.7	5.9
Wages	6.9	5.9	10.3
Income, nonfarm	16.8	16.3	18.3
Remittances	5.3	5.0	6.1
Other sources	7.5	7.7	6.9
	100.0	100.0	100.0

Source: Authors' calculations based on the 1998 LCMS.

Table 6.4.   Income Shares from Agricultural Activities, Rural Zambia, 1998 (percentage)

	1	2	3	4	5	6	7	8	9	Total
Cotton	8.4	0	9.5	0	0.8	0	0.1	2.8	0.2	3.1
Vegetables	1.1	2.8	0.3	0.2	1.2	0.7	0.5	1.7	0.3	0.8
Tobacco	0.2	0.1	2.3	0	0	0	0.1	0.2	0.1	0.5
Groundnuts	0.9	0.7	2.4	2	0.2	1.4	1.1	0.4	0.2	1.2
Paprika	0	0	0.1	0	0	0	0	0	0	0
Industrial maize	6.1	2	0.7	0.3	1.7	0.6	0.3	1.4	0.5	1.3
Cassava	0.3	0.2	0.1	4.1	0	2.4	2.2	0.1	1.3	1.2
Maize	4.4	3.1	3.2	0.5	1.1	0.9	3.8	0.9	2.6	2.2
Rice	0	0	0.3	0.1	0	0.1	0	0	1.2	0.2
Millet	0.9	0.1	0.2	0.3	0	1.3	0	0	0.2	0.4
Sorghum	0.1	0.2	0	0	0.1	0.2	0.5	0	0.2	0.1
Beans	0.2	0.1	0	0.5	0	2	0.8	0	0	0.5
Soya beans	0.4	0	0.4	0.1	0	0	0	0	0	0.1
Sweet potatoes	0.9	2.8	0.1	1	0	0.3	1.6	0.1	0.5	0.7
Irish potatoes	0	0.1	0	0.1	0	0	0.3	0.1	0	0.1
Sunflowers	0.1	0	0.5	0	0	0.1	0.1	0.2	0	0.1
Livestock	2.9	1.3	4.3	0.6	3.8	2	2.3	8	6.9	3.8
Poultry	6.4	2.2	4.5	2.7	5.9	3.4	2.8	4.6	6.7	4.3

Source: Authors' calculations based on the 1998 LCMS.

Note: Provinces are indexed as follows: 1, Central; 2, Copperbelt; 3, Eastern; 4, Luapala; 5, Lusaka; 6, Northern; 7, Northwestern; 8, Southern; 9, Western.

Figure 6.1 displays the dynamics of cotton shares. The average cotton share is estimated conditionally on household per capita income. These averages are estimated with nonparametric, locally weighted regressions, which are local linear regressions that weigh the data using kernel methods following those of Fan (1992) and Pagan and Ullah (1999). A different nonparametric regression is estimated using data for 1996 and 1998.[4] Figure 6.1 provides details of the evolution of cotton as a cash crop in rural Zambia.

In both 1996 and 1998, the cotton income shares increase at the very bottom of the income distribution and then decline with income. The maximum share is roughly more than 10 percent. At the upper tail, the average share is quite small, about 2 percent. The average share of cotton dynamics is higher in 1998 at the bottom of the distribution (mostly poor households) and at its upper tail. In the middle of the income distribution, the cotton income share is higher in 1996 than in 1998.

Figure 6.1. Dynamics of Cotton Income Shares

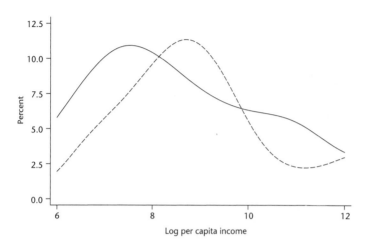

Source: Authors' calculations based on LCMS (1996, 1998).

Note: The graph shows the average cotton income shares in total income. These averages are estimated with nonparametric regressions (Fan 1992; Pagan and Ullah 1999). The solid curve corresponds to cotton shares in 1998, and the broken line to the shares in 1996.

It is instructive to look at the evolution of cotton shares across the different cotton-producing provinces. Figures 6.2–6.4 plot the nonparametric averages for the Central, Eastern, and Southern provinces, respectively. In the Central province, for instance, cotton income shares in 1998 track the shares in 1996 at the bottom of the distribution but become smaller at the middle. The Central province resembles the pattern at the national level, with higher average shares in 1998 at to bottom and at the top of the distribution, and lower shares at the middle. In contrast, cotton shares in the Southern province are higher across the entire income distribution in 1998 than in 1996.

The results in figures 6.2–6.4 indicate a regionally differentiated effect of the reforms on the pattern of income sources in rural Zambia. In particular, the increase in cotton shares in the Southern province is remarkable. This is the region that is perhaps closest to the capital, thus the result indicates that access to markets and infrastructure are key variables in adoption and in the deepening of cotton production.

The link between these dynamics of cotton shares and the timing of the cotton reforms is straightforward. It would seem that this indicates that the increase in cotton shares, particularly among the poorest farmers and in the Southern province, can be attributed to those reforms. This, however, does not necessarily

**Figure 6.2. Dynamics of Cotton Income Shares,
Central Province**

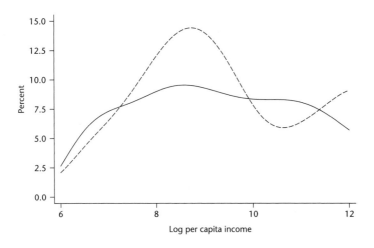

Source: Authors' calculations based on LCMS (1996, 1998).

Note: The graph shows the average cotton income shares in total income. These averages are estimated with nonparametric regressions (Fan 1992; Pagan and Ullah 1999). The solid curve corresponds to cotton shares in 1998, and the broken line to the shares in 1996.

**Figure 6.3. Dynamics of Cotton Income Shares,
Eastern Province**

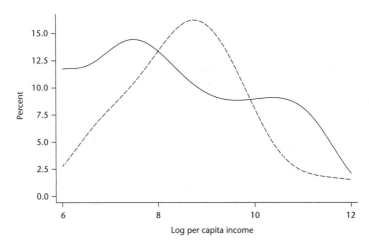

Source: Authors' calculations based on LCMS (1996, 1998).

Note: The graph shows the average cotton income shares in total income. These averages are estimated with nonparametric regressions (Fan 1992; Pagan and Ullah 1999). The solid curve corresponds to cotton shares in 1998, and the broken line to the shares in 1996.

Figure 6.4. Dynamics of Cotton Income Shares, Southern Province

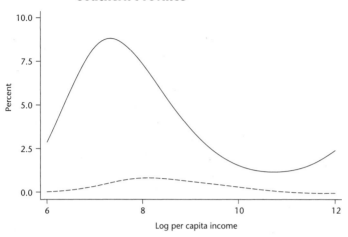

Source: Authors' calculations based on LCMS (1996, 1998).

Note: The graph shows the average cotton income shares in total income. These averages are estimated with nonparametric regressions (Fan 1992; Pagan and Ullah 1999). The solid curve corresponds to cotton shares in 1998, and the broken line to the shares in 1996.

follow. There are other factors simultaneously affecting cotton shares. Key factors include the collapse of the copper sector, the adoption of macroeconomic reforms, and the exogenous changes in international cotton prices. Given the available data, it is impossible to disentangle the contribution of these different factors to the observed trends in cotton shares. However, it is very likely that the marketing reforms are the major determinants.

The collapse of the copper sector (mainly as a result of a declining trend in international copper prices) is perhaps an urban, rather than rural, phenomenon. In addition, copper is mainly associated with the Copperbelt province (where the copper mines and the industrial belt are located) and with Lusaka (the country's administrative center). It seems, therefore, that cotton-producing provinces would be relatively unaffected by changes in the copper sector. Note, however, that the general equilibrium effects of the dramatic changes in a traditionally important sector of the Zambian economy cannot be ignored.

Similar remarks apply to the adoption of other economic policies. There is one important reform that has to be carefully considered, though. Zambia used to have a maize marketing board that set producer prices for maize grain and consumer prices for maize meals. As in cotton, the marketing board was eliminated.

This is a major rural reform, and it should be expected to have significant effects on the allocation of agricultural resources and cotton shares. It is important to note that the maize reforms took place in 1993, well before the 1996–98 period investigated in this chapter. Accordingly, for purposes of the present analysis, it is assumed that the effects of the maize reforms have already taken place in 1996, the baseline period for this chapter.[5] To the extent, however, that these reforms have long-lasting effects on farmers, the observed dynamics in figures 6.1–6.4 will capture them.

There is another element that favors the role of the reform as a major determinant of cotton dynamics. An important observation is that the increase in cotton income shares is larger at the bottom of the distribution of per capita expenditure—that is, among the poorest households. If macroeconomic and aggregate shocks, with magnitudes that affect all households simultaneously, are size neutral, then differences in the impacts at different points along the income distribution shouldn't be expected. This indicates, at least, that the relative changes in cotton dynamics are mostly generated by the marketing reforms. For instance, the larger increase in shares at the bottom of the distribution can be due to expanded access to seeds and fertilizers among the poor.

Finally, it is important to have in mind that cotton prices have continuously declined during this period. From 1996 to 1998, in particular, the real price of cotton in international markets declined by as much as 20 percent.[6] There are two implications for the analysis in this chapter. First, the dynamics in figures 6.1–6.4 show that cotton shares could have been even higher, in the face of the reform, had cotton prices been higher or remained stable. In other words, it would be reasonable to expect larger increases in cotton shares due to the cotton reforms if the change in cotton prices could be controlled for. Second, the decline in the real prices of agricultural products has been similar for other commodities, such as maize, the major alternative crop in rural Zambia. This suggests that the changes in the price of cotton relative to maize have been mild.[7]

In summary, the available information prevents the econometric identification of the effects of the cotton reforms on the dynamics of cotton shares among Zambian farmers. But the observed trends can be mostly linked to those reforms, and the induced increase in cotton shares could have been larger. This is an interesting instance of a domestic policy that had crucial impacts on the farmers and their ability to reap most of the benefits from further trade liberalization.

In what follows, this chapter investigates the effects of the complementarities between domestic reforms and international agricultural liberalization on household welfare. As shown in section 1, international cotton markets are subject to strong intervention, particularly by developed countries. Therefore, the analysis begins by looking at the welfare effects of the increase in world prices that would take place if agricultural markets were liberalized. This involves merging the analysis of cotton shares with the projected increases in world cotton prices.

Define the household income as

(6.1) $$y^h = \pi_c^h + \sum_j \pi_j^h$$

where π_c^h is the income (profit) from cotton sales and π_j^h is income from activity j (wages, vegetables, maize, groundnuts, and so on). The change in income caused by an increase in the price of cotton p_c is

(6.2) $$d\ln y^h = \theta_c^h d\ln p_c.$$

The proportional change in household income is given by the share of cotton income, θ_c^h, multiplied by the proportional change in prices.

Section 1 reviewed some evidence indicating that a full liberalization of agricultural markets along the lines of the Doha Round negotiations would bring about an increase in world cotton prices of around 12.7 percent. Similar results are obtained if the price increase predicted by Sumner (2004) of 11.6 percent is used. Using the data for 1998, it is possible to estimate the average welfare effect given by equation 6.2. These averages, estimated again with a Fan regression, are shown in figure 6.5. It can be observed that the increase in prices would benefit farmers across the income distribution. The effects would range from more than 0.75 percent to nearly 1.5 percent, at the bottom of the distribution, to roughly 0.5 percent at the top. The unconditional average gain would be about 1 percent of the initial household per capita income.

Figure 6.6 explores the regional differences in cotton gains. The solid line corresponds to the nonparametric average in the Central province; the broken line, to the nonparametric average in the Eastern province; and the dotted line, to the nonparametric averages in the Southern province. The figure shows that larger gains would take place in the Eastern province, particularly at the bottom of the distribution. In the Central province, the gains track the average gains in the Southern province at the bottom of the distribution; from the middle to the top, however, the gains in the Central province remain high, whereas the gains in the Southern province sharply decline with income.

These findings show that a 12.7 percent increase in the price of cotton would cause household income to increase by, at most, 1.5 percent (among the poorest households in the Eastern province, for instance). Although these are positive effects associated with welfare gains, it is clear that the magnitudes are quite small. There are several reasons that help explain this fact.

Figure 6.5.   Cotton Prices and Household Income

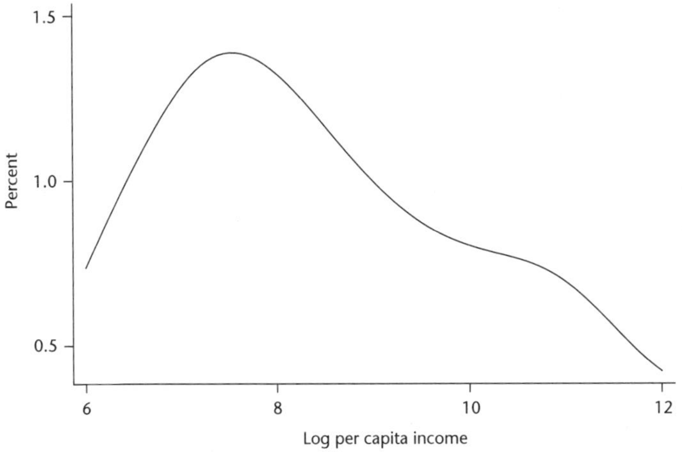

Source: Authors' calculations based on LCMS (1998).

Note: The graph shows the average welfare effects (defined as the cotton shares multiplied by the change in world cotton prices) at different levels of household per capita income. The curves are estimated with nonparametric locally weighted regressions (Fan 1992; Pagan and Ullah 1999).

Figure 6.6.   Cotton Prices and Household Income, Regional Analysis

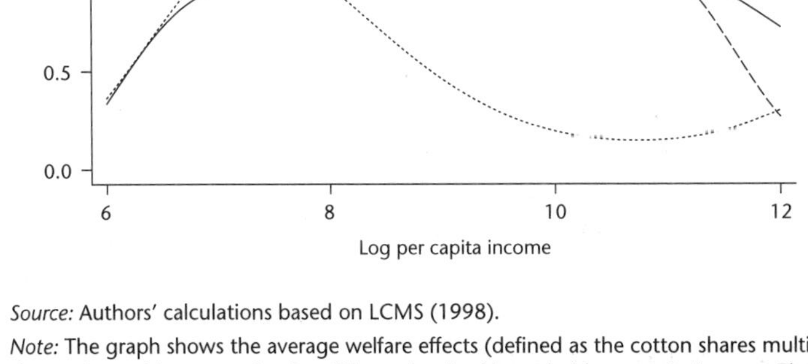

Source: Authors' calculations based on LCMS (1998).

Note: The graph shows the average welfare effects (defined as the cotton shares multiplied by the change in world cotton prices) at different levels of household per capita income. The curves are estimated with nonparametric locally weighted regressions (Fan 1992; Pagan and Ullah 1999). The solid, broken, and dotted lines correspond to the Central, Eastern, and Southern provinces, respectively.

As discussed in section 1, the reforms in cotton markets have been relatively successful but have not been smooth. Initially, the public monopoly was transformed into a private monopoly. Entry was useful in early stages, but the failure of the out-grower scheme limited the expansion of the sector. In fact, the out-grower scheme was still failing in 1998, when the household survey data were collected. This means that the evolution in income shares that can be captured with the available data does not reveal the whole benefits of the reforms.

Using additional farm data, Brambilla and Porto (2005) report that the cotton reforms had two distinctive effects on cotton farming. First, there is a decline of the land area devoted to cotton in 1998–99 (when the out-grower scheme was failing), followed by a significant increase in area planted in 2000–1, when the out-grower scheme was perfected with the entrance of Dunavant. Second, Brambilla and Porto find that farm productivity in cotton showed a similar pattern, declining in 1998–99 and increasing in 2000–1. In addition, their findings indicate that income shares increased, on average, by roughly 10–20 percent. These additional factors could help increase the average gains from a 12 percent price increase to roughly 2 percent of household income, on average. Although these figures are higher, the effects seem still fairly low. The study by Brambilla and Porto (2005) reveals another reason why the increase in cotton prices may not have large impacts. Productivity of smallholder cotton production traditionally has been very low in Zambia. Although there is some evidence that the reforms have caused productivity to increase in recent years, there is still room for improvements in this area.

One additional reason for the small impacts is that cotton activities are not really widespread in Zambia. More important, this chapter has considered only a first-order approximation to the welfare gains. The next section captures some supply responses and second-round effects.

This chapter explores only the poverty alleviation effect of cotton production in rural areas by smallholders. There are vertical linkages in cotton production that suggest that significant additional poverty effects could be secured through the domestic production of textiles and garment products for exports. These important issues, which deserve further consideration and analysis, are not the focus of this investigation.

Cotton Production and Household Outcomes

This section explores the impacts of cotton production on household outcomes. If free trade and cotton liberalization bring about renewed incentives for cotton production in Zambia, farmers could be expected to switch from subsistence to cotton production (and, more generally, to market-oriented agriculture). This section investigates these supply responses with the help of matching methods: by matching households in subsistence agriculture with households in cotton, the average effects of participating in cotton markets on several household outcomes are estimated. The focus here is on income differentials, child anthropometry, and education outcomes.[8]

The Method

The aim here is to estimate the differences in outcomes linked to the production of a cash crop, such as cotton, and explore the poverty alleviation effects of allowing for an expansion of cotton activities among Zambian farmers. Matching methods based on the propensity score are used.[9] This approach begins by estimating a probit model of participation in cotton, which defines the propensity score $p(\mathbf{x})$, for a given vector of observables $\mathbf{x}$. Subsistence farmers are matched with cotton farmers based on this propensity score, and the outcome differential is estimated using kernel methods.

Start with the income gains. Let y_h^m be the income per hectare in cotton of household h. Let y_h^s be the home-produced own-consumption per hectare. The average income differential (per hectare) for those involved in cotton production is defined as

(6.3) $\tau = E[y_h^m - y_h^s | C = 1]$

The task is to estimate the counterfactual quantity $E[y_h^m - y_h^s | C = 1]$, the average return in subsistence agriculture among cotton farmers. This is done by using matching methods.

The main assumption of matching methods is that the participation in market agriculture can be based on observables. This is the ignorability of treatment assignment. Define an indicator variable C, where $C = 1$ if the households derive most of their income from cotton. In practice, most Zambian households in rural areas produce something for own-consumption. As a consequence, $C = 1$ is assigned to households that derive more than 50 percent of their income from cotton. Households that derive most of their income from home production are assigned $C = 0$. The propensity score $p(\mathbf{x})$ is defined as the conditional probability of participating in cotton, $p(\mathbf{x}) = P(C = 1|\mathbf{x})$.

The ignorability of treatment assignment requires that $y_h^m - y_h^s | C |\mathbf{x}$. When the propensity score is balanced, it can be asserted that, conditional on $p(\mathbf{x})$, the participation in cotton C and the observables $\mathbf{x}$ are independent. In other words, observations with a given propensity score have the same distribution of observables $\mathbf{x}$ for households involved in cotton as in subsistence. The importance of the balancing property, which can be tested, is that it implies that, conditionally on $p(\mathbf{x})$, the returns in cotton and in subsistence are independent of market participation, which implies that households in subsistence and cotton are comparable.

The decision to participate in market agriculture depends on three main variables: access to markets, food security and risk, and tradition in subsistence agriculture. These effects are captured by including in the propensity function several key control variables, such as regional (district) dummies, the size of the household, the demographic structure of the family, the age and the education of the household head, and the availability of agricultural tools. These variables $\mathbf{x}$ comprise a comprehensive set of observables to explain the selection mechanism. Once the propensity score is estimated, the balancing condition is tested. This requires partitioning the estimated $p(\mathbf{x})$ and testing that, within each stratum, the mean and variances of the covariates are not statistically different.[10] In the current case of cotton, the balancing property was always satisfied.[11]

Monetary Outcomes

This chapter investigates a constrained model of household agricultural production. This means that households are assumed to face significant constraints in terms of land, family labor supply, or inputs, and expanding cash crop activities would mean forgone income. In this model, if a family were to plant an additional acre of cotton, then an acre of land devoted to own-consumption (and all other relevant resources) should be released.

Table 6.5 reports the results. The first column shows the gains per hectare. In the second column, the constrained household is assumed to expand cotton production by the average size of the plots devoted to cotton in Zambia. The results indicate that there are gains from cotton production: farmers growing cotton are expected to gain 18,232 kwachas (K) on average, more than similar farmers engaged in subsistence agriculture. The gain is equivalent to 19.9 percent of the average expenditure of a representative poor farmer. To get a better sense of what these numbers mean, notice that the food poverty line in 1998 was estimated at K 32,233 per month and the poverty line at K 46,287 per month (per equivalent adult). Further, because the exchange rate in December 1998 was about K 2,200, the gains are equivalent to just over US$8 (in 1998 prices).

The actual gains will depend on the land area allocated to cotton. If farmers are allowed to plant the average size of a typical cotton plot, which is estimated at 1.2 hectares, the estimated gains increase to K 21,878. This is equivalent to 23.9 percent of the income of the poor. Notice that because the average size of the land plots allocated to home production ranges from 1.5 to 5 hectares, with an unconditional average of around 2 hectares, it would be feasible for an average household to switch from own-consumption to cotton-growing activities.

Table 6.5. Income Gains from Cotton Production

	Constrained model (per hectare)		Constrained model	
	Monthly kwachas	% of expenditure	Monthly kwachas	% of expenditure
Cotton	18,232 (7,456)	19.9	21,878 (8,947)	23.9

Source: Authors' simulations.

Note: Results are from propensity score matching of cotton farmers and subsistence farmers using kernel methods. Standard errors in parentheses are estimated with bootstrap methods. The constrained model (per hectare) assumes that the household has to give up 1 hectare of land to produce an additional hectare of cotton. The constrained model assumes that the farmer moves from subsistence to cotton and allocates the average plot size of cotton farmers (1.2 hectares).

The matching results suggest that there might be additional gains from switching to cotton. A natural question is why these opportunities are not exploited by the farmers. Although there are many reasons that can explain this fact, the key role of complementary policies should be emphasized here. Access to international markets is a basic prerequisite. This requires openness and export-oriented incentives on behalf of Zambia and a liberalization of agricultural markets in developed countries. Price and income support, and export and input subsidies, should be eliminated. Other domestic complementary policies should be implemented as well. There are several key policies. Extension services to farmers—including transmission of information and know-how about cropping, crop diversification, fertilizer and pesticide use, and so on—are critical. The provision of infrastructure to reduce transport and transaction costs is also essential. Irrigation may also help. The development of a stronger financial and credit market can also help farmers reduce the costs of the out-grower programs. Finally, education (both formal education and labor discipline) and the provision of better health services will surely help increase farm productivity in cotton.

It is generally difficult to assess the role of complementary policies empirically, but some sense of their importance can be gained by looking at evidence reported in the related literature. For example, Brambilla and Porto (2005) find that farmers that received extension services are 8.4 percent more productive in cotton than farmers that did not receive any technical assistance. Other things being equal, this would imply an 8.4 percent increase in household well-being. This clearly shows that complementary policies can indeed be useful in improving the living conditions of poor farmers in rural Zambia. Of course, a comprehensive assessment of such policies would require an evaluation of the costs of providing these improved services.

In the authors' view, the role of Doha is not only to provide a higher price for cotton, but also to facilitate market access. Complementary policies can help farmers to fully exploit these opportunities. So far, this chapter has explored the effects of increasing prices on household income and provided a quantification of the potential gains of switching from subsistence to cotton. Doha and the complementary policies are considered as vehicles to make these gains feasible. To look at these links more closely, the following experiment is performed. The increase in prices caused by the Doha Round would induce an expansion of quantities produced. If these quantities could be produced and sold by Zambian farmers, then the realization of the gains becomes feasible.

To quantify these effects, the analysis proceeds as follows. First, some quantity changes are induced by Doha. This could be estimated, for instance, by multiplying the price changes reported in above by an export supply elasticity. As an example, if this elasticity were 1, an increase in price of 12.7 percent would cause quantities to react by 12.7 percent, too.[12] Given these quantity changes, the issue is how to allocate them to the different households. To do this, notice that the estimated propensity score indicates the probability of being a cotton producer. One reasonable scenario is thus to allocate the quantity changes on the basis of the relative propensity score. It is important to notice that proceeding in this way allows households in subsistence to switch to some production of cotton. However, this switch can be minor if the relative probability is small for particular farmers. In addition, farmers who are already producing cotton are more likely to have higher estimated probabilities, which can make them better candidates to absorb larger fractions of the export opportunities.

Figure 6.7 plots the average relative probability of being a cotton producer across the income distribution. The curve is estimated with nonparametric methods, as before. The relative probability, and therefore the gains from any expansion in quantities, slightly increases with income at the bottom of the distribution and then remains relatively constant. This finding can be interpreted as indicating that everyone across the entire income distribution would benefit about the same from the Doha market opportunities.

Figure 6.8 plots the relative probabilities for the three provinces. As before, the solid line corresponds to the Central province; the broken line, to the Eastern province; and the dotted line, to Southern province. Although there are differences in the level of the relative probability across provinces (which should resemble the regional differences in the likelihood of cotton production), the distributional effects are the same in all three provinces. No discernible differences across the income distribution can be expected.

It is tempting to use this framework to allocate the potential export opportunities brought about by Doha across Zambian farmers and identify households that would actually switch from subsistence to cotton. In addition, it would be possible

Figure 6.7.   Relative Probability of Cotton Production

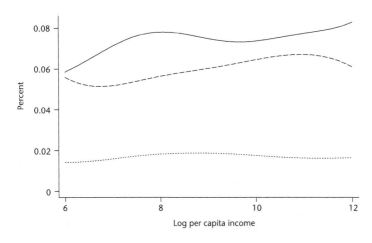

Source: Authors' calculations based on LCMS (1998).

Note: The graph shows the average relative probability of being a cotton producer at different levels of household per capita income. The curves are estimated with nonparametric locally weighted regressions (Fan 1992; Pagan and Ullah 1999).

Figure 6.8.   Relative Probability of Cotton Production, Regional Analysis

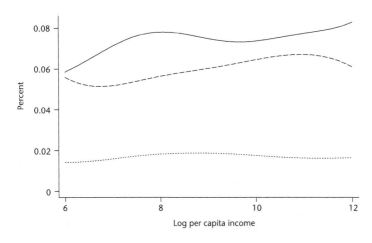

Source: Authors' calculations based on LCMS (1998).

Note: The graph shows the average relative probability of being a cotton producer at different levels of household per capita income. The curves are estimated with nonparametric locally weighted regressions (Fan 1992; Pagan and Ullah 1999). The solid, broken, and dotted lines correspond to the Central, Eastern, and Southern provinces, respectively.

to guess how much substitution would take place for different households. To do this, however, would require recourse to ad hoc rules that would dictate the pattern of agricultural switching. Although some interesting attempts to do this (in the context of labor markets) are being developed, this chapter reports only the estimated relative probabilities of switching. This approach provides estimates of expected gains, which is as far as one can go with the available data and methods. It has the virtue of being based on estimates derived from econometric models rather than from ad hoc rules.

Nevertheless, the estimates can be used to shed additional light on the impacts of Doha and complementary reforms in Zambia. As reported in table 6.5, the estimated gain from switching from subsistence agriculture to cotton would be 19.9 percent. This is a measure of the gains from switching, even in the absence of trade reforms. The price effect (roughly a 12.7 percent increase in cotton prices due to trade reforms) would cause the average income of a cotton producer to increase by approximately 1 percent (figure 6.6). If trade reforms induce a switch from subsistence to cotton, then the gains of a switcher would be of about 20.9 percent (19.9 percent due to higher cotton returns plus 1 percent due to higher prices). An expansion of quantities produced and exported (supply responses) would generate additional gains. An example would be the productivity gains of around 8.4 percent (Brambilla and Porto 2005) induced by successful extension services and made feasible by world markets (through Doha). The average income of a cotton producer would increase by 9.4 percent and that of a subsistence farmer by 29.3 percent. It can thus be concluded that, although the price effect of trade reforms (tariffs plus subsidies in cotton) would be generally small, the combination of new market opportunities and domestic reforms (so that switching and productivity gains become viable) can work as very effective vehicles for poverty alleviation.

Nonmonetary Outcomes

The analysis now turns to the nonmonetary effects of cotton production. The effects on two household outcomes are examined—the nutritional status of infants and young children (from 0 to 60 months old) and education performance of children in primary and secondary school.

Malnutrition remains a widespread problem in developing countries, as it does in Zambia. Nutritional status is assessed on the basis of anthropometric indicators (such as height or weight). The three most commonly used anthropometric indicators for infants and children are used: weight-for-height, height-for-age, and weight-for-age.

Weight-for-height (whz) measures body weight relative to height. It is normally used as an indicator of current nutritional status, and it can be useful for measuring short-term changes in nutritional status. Extreme cases of low whz relative to a child of the same sex and age in a reference population are commonly referred to as "wasting." Wasting may be the consequence of starvation or severe disease (in particular, diarrhea), but it can also be due to chronic conditions. Height-for-age (haz) reflects cumulative linear growth. Deficits in haz indicate past or chronic inadequacies nutrition, chronic or frequent illness, or both, but cannot measure short-term changes in malnutrition. Extreme cases of low haz are referred to as "stunting." Weight-for-age (waz) reflects body mass relative to age. This is, in effect, a composite measure of haz and whz, making interpretation difficult. The term "underweight" is commonly used to refer to severe or pathological deficits in waz.

A problem arises because weight and height depend on both age and gender (and other factors such as genetic variation), but it is possible to use physical measurements by comparing indicators with the distribution of the same indicator for a "healthy" reference group. This chapter uses z-scores (standard deviation scores), the most common way of expressing anthropometric indexes.[13] Table 6.6 presents some summary statistics.

The value of the mean of the haz z-score is -2.21, reflecting long-term cumulative inadequacies of health, nutrition, or both.[14] There seems to be no wasting problem: the mean of the whz is 0.23. Using the summary measure of nutritional status (waz), there is mild underweight, probably caused by long-term nutritional problems.

For the education outcome, an index of school performance for children between ages 7 and 18 was generated—that is, children in primary and secondary

Table 6.6. Child Nutrition in Rural Areas (0–60 months old)

Nutrition indicator	Constrained model (per hectare)		Constrained model	
	Mean	Standard deviation	Moderate	Severe
Stunting (haz)	-2.21	1.77	23	33
Wasting (whz)	0.23	1.40	5	1
Underweight (waz)	-1.21	1.24	20	6

Source: Authors' simulations.

Note: Accumulated undernutrition is measured by haz. Levels of current undernutrition are measured by whz. The summary measure of nutritional status is waz. In medicine, the prevalence rate is the proportion of individuals suffering a disease. "Moderate" refers to those individuals with a z-score between -3 and -2, and "severe" refers to a z-score below-3.

school. The index is the ratio of years of education completed by an individual and the years of education this individual should have for his or her age.[15] The mean of this index for rural areas is 0.49, including children not attending school (approximately 45 percent of the sample).

The analysis now turns to assessing the effects of participation in cotton production in dimensions other than monetary income. This entails using the same matching methods as before. The effects on child nutrition and education of switching from subsistence to cotton are estimated. Table 6.7 reports the results.

Differences in outcomes for the sample of all infants and young children (0 to 60 months old) are estimated for the subsample of males, and for the subsample of females. It is interesting that statistically significant effects are found only in terms of stunting, or long-run nutritional gains. On average, a cotton family would enjoy a higher z-score of 0.64 points. This is equivalent to 30 percent of the average haz z-score for households in subsistence. There are no significant differences in wasting and underweight between cotton and subsistence households. Also, there is no differential effect between females and males, although the magnitudes for males are much larger and marginally significant. Similar results have been found in, for example, von Braun and Kennedy (1994).

These are very interesting results. They indicate that there are no differences in current nutrition among children living in cotton-producing or subsistence households. However, there are statistically significant benefits in terms of long-term nutrition among those children living on cotton farms. One interpretation is that whereas doing cotton or subsistence allows children to be currently well fed, through the consumption of maize or sweet potatoes for instance, cash income derived from cotton allows farmers to purchase milk, fish, or dairy products that have longer-term benefits. Another hypothesis argues that the movement from subsistence to agricultural commercialization implies a change in the use of fertilizers and pesticides that helps prevent health hazards and improve the long-term nutritional status of the children.[16]

In the case of education, our findings indicate that educational outcomes are similar in households involved in cotton and in households involved in subsistence. This result holds for the whole population (all children between 7 and 18 years old), children in primary school, and children in secondary school.

Conclusions

This chapter examines the relationship between cotton reforms and poverty in Zambia. Cotton is one of the main cash crops of smallholders in suitable provinces in rural Zambia. Further, rural poverty is pronounced and widespread. The sector has experienced significant reforms that involved the movement from a publicly controlled parastatal firm to privatization and competition. In this

Table 6.7.   Effects on Child Nutrition and Education from Market Agriculture, Cotton versus Subsistence

	Total			Males			Females		
	Stunting (haz)	Wasting (whz)	Underweight (waz)	Stunting (haz)	Wasting (whz)	Underweight (waz)	Stunting (haz)	Wasting (whz)	Underweight (waz)
	0.64	-0.004	0.34	1.07	-0.25	0.45	0.14	-0.004	0.07
	(0.34)	(0.33)	(0.24)	(0.63)	(0.52)	(0.45)	(0.85)	(0.66)	(0.37)

	Total			Males			Females		
	All	Primary	Secondary	All	Primary	Secondary	All	Primary	Secondary
	-0.02	-0.01	0.01	-0.03	-0.07	-0.02	0.01	-0.01	0.13
	(0.04)	(0.05)	(0.05)	(0.04)	(0.06)	(0.07)	(0.05)	(0.07)	(0.10)

Source: Authors' simulations.

Note: Results are from propensity score matching of cotton farmers and subsistence farmers using kernel methods. Standard errors in parentheses are estimated with bootstrap methods.

context, cotton is claimed to be a major market agricultural activity for vulnerable families in rural areas.

Two angles of the cotton-poverty connection have been explored. On the one hand, the chapter has presented analysis of the welfare effects that would take place if agricultural cotton markets were liberalized and the world price would thereby increase. On the other hand, the differences in several outcomes between households involved in cotton and households involved in subsistence agriculture have been estimated.

The first finding shows that the domestic reforms have caused cotton shares to increase at the bottom of the income distribution. These are poor farmers. Regarding international market access, it is estimated that the increase in world price would benefit cotton producers across the entire income distribution. An estimated 12.7 percent increase in prices would bring about welfare gains reaching roughly 1 percent of household income. In addition, it is found that households involved in cotton enjoy income gains over households involved in subsistence. This implies that a movement from subsistence to market agriculture would benefit rural farmers and would lead to a further decline in poverty rates. After world trade reforms, for instance, the welfare gain of a switcher was estimated at approximately 21 percent. Further, productivity gains induced by extension services (improved during the marketing reforms) and made feasible by expanded international markets (due to Doha) would lead to welfare gains of 9 percent among cotton producers and 30 percent among switchers. In terms of nonmonetary outcomes, higher long-run nutritional status among children residing in cotton producing farms is found, but no significant differences in educational attainments.

These results highlight promising avenues for poverty alleviation through cash agricultural activities such as cotton. It is important to notice that the estimated magnitudes are relatively small. This shows that to take full advantage of the access to international markets (with a liberalization of world agricultural markets), complementary policies are essential. These policies include extension services (information), infrastructure (transport), irrigation, access to credit and finance, education, and health services.

Notes

1. This section relies heavily on Balat and Porto (forthcoming).

2. For more details on cotton reforms in Zambia, see Food Security Research Project (2000) and *Cotton News* (2002).

3. The Zambia Central Statistical Office is in charge of conducting the surveys. The data from the 2001 LCMS were under preparation when this chapter was being written.

4. Unfortunately, the 1991 Priority Survey does not include separate data on cotton income.

5. Similarly, the collapse of Zimbabwe has had significant impacts on the Zambian rural economy. It is observed, for instance, that tobacco has been increasingly adopted in Zambia, mainly as a result of the migration of neighboring peasants from Zimbabwe. However, the Zimbabwean crisis took place in recent years, after 1998, and should not affect this analysis.

6. The decline around the long-term trend seems to be, however, lower. See Food Security Research Project (2000).

7. See Food Security Research Project (2000).

8. The estimation of supply responses has proved very difficult. The survey in Winters, McCulloch, and McKay (2004) highlights these issues and reports some of the available methods and results. For the case of income gains, see Lopez, Nash, and Stanton (1995) and Heltberg and Tarp (2002). For non-monetary outcomes, see Edmonds and Pavcnik (Forthcoming).

9. Seminal papers on matching methods include Rubin (1977); Rosenbaum and Rubin (1983); Heckman, Ichimura, and Todd (1997, 1998); Heckman and others (1996); and Dehejia and Wahba (2002).

10. In general, this involves setting up a series of F-tests for the equality of means, for instance. See Dehejia and Wahba (2002) for more details.

11. The balancing property is a minor requirement that is imposed in this procedure. In many applications, the property is not necessarily satisfied. Balat and Porto (forthcoming), for example, found that the balancing did not hold in cases including cassava or sunflowers. Notice that the ignorability requirement cannot be tested, which is an assumption of the matching method.

12. See Hoekman, Nicita, and Olarreaga (2004) for a nice attempt along these lines.

13. A z-score is defined as the difference between the value for an individual and the median value of the reference population for the same age or height, divided by the standard deviation of the reference population.

14. The World Health Organization uses a z-score cutoff point of -2 to classify low waz, low haz, and low whz as moderate and severe undernutrition, and -3 to define severe undernutrition.

15. Then, for an individual with no education, the index takes a 0, and if she is in the grade that corresponds to her age, the index takes 1.

16. It is also possible that the sample year is one of relatively good subsistence but a relatively bad cotton season. There is actually no evidence that this was so in 1998, however.

References

Aksoy, A., and J. Beghin, eds. 2004. *Global Agricultural Trade and Developing Countries*. Washington, DC: World Bank.

Baffes. J. 2004. "Cotton: Market Setting, Trade Policies, and Issues." In *Global Agricultural Trade and Developing Countries*, ed. A. Aksoy and J. Beghin, 259–274. Washington, DC: World Bank.

Balat, J., and G. Porto. Forthcoming. "Globalization and Complementary Policies. Poverty Impacts in Rural Zambia." In *Globalization and Poverty*, ed. A. Harrison. Chicago: University of Chicago Press.

Brambilla, I., and G. Porto. 2005. "Farm Productivity and Market Structure. Evidence from Cotton Reforms in Zambia." Yale University, New Haven, CT.

Cotton News. 2002. *Cotton Development Trust*. Lusaka.

Deaton, A. 1989. "Rice Prices and Income Distribution in Thailand: A Non-Parametric Analysis." *Economic Journal* 99: 1–37.

———. 1997. *The Analysis of Household Surveys. A Microeconometric Approach to Development Policy.* Baltimore and Washington DC: Johns Hopkins University Press for the World Bank.

Dehejia, R., and S. Wahba. 2002. "Propensity Score Matching Methods for Non-Experimental Causal Studies." *Review of Economic Studies* 84 (1): 151–61.

Edmonds, E., and N. Pavcnik. Forthcoming. "The Effects of Trade Liberalization on Child Labor." *Journal of International Economics.*

Fan, J. 1992. "Design-Adaptive Nonparametric Regression." *Journal of the American Statistical Association* 87 (420): 998–1004.

Food and Agricultural Policy Research Institute. 2002. "The Doha Round of the World Trade Organization: Liberalization of Agricultural Markets and Its Impacts on Developing Economics," University of Missouri, Columbia.

Food Security Research Project. 2000. "Improving Smallholder and Agribusiness Opportunities in Zambia's Cotton Sector: Key Challenges and Options." Working Paper 1. Lusaka.

Heckman, J., H. Ichimura, J. Smith, and P. Todd. 1996. "Sources of Selection Bias in Evaluating Social Programs: An Interpretation of Conventional Measures and Evidence on the Effectiveness of Matching as a Program Evaluation Method." *Proceedings of the National Academy of Sciences* 93 (23): 13416–20.

Heckman, J., H. Ichimura, and P. Todd. 1997. "Matching as an Econometric Evaluation Estimator: Evidence from Evaluating a Job Training Programme." *Review of Economic Studies* 64 (4): 605–654.

———. 1998. "Matching as an Econometric Evaluation Estimator." *Review of Economic Studies* 65 (2): 261–94.

Heltberg, R., and F. Tarp. 2002. "Agricultural Supply Response and Poverty in Mozambique." *Food Policy* 27 (2): 103–24.

Hoekman, B., A. Nicita, and M. Olarreaga. 2004. "Can Doha Deliver the Development Round?" World Bank, Washington, DC.

Litchfield, J., and N. McCulloch. 2003. "Poverty in Zambia: Assessing the Impacts of Trade Liberalization in the 1990s." Poverty Research Unit, Institute for Development Studies, Sussex University, Sussex, U.K.

Lopez, R., J. Nash, and J. Stanton. 1995. "Adjustment and Poverty in Mexican Agriculture. How Farmers' Wealth Affects Supply Response." Policy Research Working Paper 1494, World Bank, Washington, DC.

McCulloch, N., B. Baulch, and M. Cherel-Robson. 2001. "Poverty, Inequality and Growth in Zambia during the 1990s." Presented at the UN World Institute for Development Economics Research Development Conference on Growth and Poverty, Helsinki, May 25–26.

Pagan, A., and A. Ullah. 1999. *Nonparametric Econometrics*. New York: Cambridge University Press.

Rosenbaum, P., and D. Rubin. 1983. "The Central Role of the Propensity Score in Observational Studies of Causal Effects." *Biometrika* 70 (1): 41–55.

Rubin, D. 1977. "Assignment to a Treatment Group on the Basis of a Covariate." *Journal of Educational Statistics* 2 (1): 1–26.

Sumner, D. 2004. "Reducing Cotton Subsidies: The DDA Initiative." In *Agricultural Trade Reform and the Doha Development Agenda*, ed. K. Anderson and W. Martin. Basingstoke, U.K.: Palgrave Macmillan; Washington, DC: World Bank.

von Braun, J., and E. Kennedy. eds. 1994. *Agricultural Commercialization, Economic Development, and Nutrition*. Baltimore and London: John Hopkins University Press for the International Food Policy Research Institute.

Winters, A., N. McCulloch, and A. McKay. 2004. "Trade Liberalization and Poverty: The Evidence So Far." *Journal of Economic Literature* 42: 72–115

World Bank. 1994. *Zambia Poverty Assessment*. Washington, DC: World Bank.

7

THE DOHA ROUND, POVERTY, AND REGIONAL INEQUALITY IN BRAZIL

Joaquim Bento de Souza Ferreira Filho
and Mark Horridge

Summary

This chapter addresses the potential effects of the Doha Round of trade negotiations on poverty and income distribution in Brazil, using an applied general equilibrium (AGE) and microsimulation (MS) model of Brazil tailored for income distribution and poverty analysis. It is particularly important that the representative household hypothesis is replaced by a very detailed representation of households. The model distinguishes 10 different labor types and has 270 different household expenditure patterns. Income can originate from 41 different production activities (which produce 52 commodities) in 27 different regions inside the country. The AGE model communicates to a MS model comprising 112,055 Brazilian households and 263,938 adults.

Economic activity in Brazil, a large country, is spread unevenly across the territory. Manufacturing industries are concentrated in the southeastern region, and agriculture, although more evenly distributed geographically, is the main source of income of the center-west states. Poverty, however, is a pervasive phenomenon in the country, which has one of the worse income distributions in the world. The poorest states in Brazil (defined based on the share of population below the poverty line) are concentrated in the northeastern states.

Poverty and income distribution indexes are computed over the entire sample of households and persons, before and after the policy shocks. Model results show that even important trade policy shocks, such as those applied in this study, do not generate dramatic changes in the structure of poverty and income distribution in the Brazilian economy. The simulated effects on poverty and income distribution are positive but rather small. The benefits are, however, concentrated in the poorest households.

The study also suggests that the poverty reductions would arise from the income-earning changes and not from the fall in the consumption bundle prices. This outcome is highly correlated to the agriculture and related industries, which have their activity levels increased in all simulations. Finally, the bulk of the poverty impacts can be attributed to the liberalization by other countries, rather than to changes in Brazil's tariff structure.

From a methodological point of view, the study emphasizes the need to approach poverty analysis by the household (rather than the personal) dimension, by tracking changes in the labor market from individual workers to households. In the *Pesquisa Nacional por Amostragem de Domicílios* (*National Household Survey* [PNAD]; Instituto Brasileiro de Geografia e Estatística [IBGE] 2001) data used here, the head-of-household income accounts for only 65 percent of aggregated household income in Brazil. As a consequence, using head-of-household income as a proxy for household income may poorly predict the effect of policy changes.

Introduction

One of the most striking aspects of the Brazilian economy is its high degree of income concentration. Despite the changes the economy has faced in the last 20 years—ranging from the country's redemocratization, trade liberalization, hyperinflation, many currency changes, and finally to the macroeconomic stabilization in the mid-1990s—the country still shows one of the worst patterns of income distribution in the world. The resilience of this income distribution problem has attracted the attention of researchers worldwide, and it is the central point of a lively debate in Brazil. The problem is, of course, extremely complex and related to a great number of socioeconomic variables, which makes it a particularly difficult analytical issue, because the effect of many variables upon poverty is uncertain.

At the same time, new changes in the external environment face the Brazilian economy. The Doha Round of international trade negotiations may be one of the most important. A complex phenomenon in itself, the economic integration poses new questions relating to the prospects for the poor. This chapter addresses these questions with a systematic and quantitative approach. For this purpose, an AGE model of Brazil tailored for income distribution and poverty analysis will be used. The model also uses a regional breakdown to examine the associated issue of regional inequality.

The next section shows some figures about the problem of poverty and income distribution in Brazil, with a brief review of the recent literature on the topic. Then, the methodological approach is presented with a discussion of the relevant literature on the many different approaches. Next, the model itself is presented with a discussion of its main aspects and of the database. Finally, results and conclusions are presented.

Poverty and Income Distribution Evolution in Brazil: An Overview

Although Brazil is a country with a large number of poor people, its population is not among the poorest in the world. Drawing on the 1999 *Report on Human Development*, Barros, Henriques, and Mendonça (2001) show that about 64 percent of the countries in the world have per capita income less than that in Brazil, a figure that mounts to 77 percent if the number of persons in the same condition is considered. The same authors show that although 30 percent of the total population in Brazil is poor, only 10 percent on average are poor in other countries with similar per capita income. Indeed, based on the same report, the authors define an international norm that, based on per capita income, would impute only 8 percent of poor for Brazil. That is, if the inequality of income in Brazil were to correspond to the world average inequality for countries in the same per capita income range, just 8 percent (rather than 30 percent) of the Brazilian population would be expected to be poor.

Taking the concept of poverty in its particular dimension of income insufficiency, Barros Henriques, and Mendonça (2001) show that in 1999, about 14 percent of the Brazilian population lived in households with income below the line of extreme poverty (indigence line, about 22 million people), and 34 percent of the population lived in households with income below the poverty line (about 53 million people). Even though the percentage of poor in the population declined from 40 percent in 1977 to 34 percent in 1999, this level is still very high and seemingly stable. The size of poverty in Brazil, measured either as a percentage of the population or in terms of a poverty gap, stabilized in the second half of the 1980s, although at a lower level than was observed in the previous period.

Barros and Mendonça (1997) have analyzed the relations between economic growth and reductions in the level of inequality upon poverty in Brazil. Among their main conclusions, these authors point out that an improvement in the distribution of income would be more effective for poverty reduction than economic growth alone if growth maintained the current pattern of inequality. According to these authors, as a result of the very high level of income inequality in Brazil, it is possible to dramatically reduce poverty in the country, even without economic growth, by turning the level of inequality in Brazil close to what can be observed in a typical Latin American country.

Brazilian poverty also has an important regional dimension. According to calculations by Rocha (1998) in a study of the 1981–95 period, the richer southeastern region of the country, although accounting for 44 percent of total population in 1995, had only 33 percent of the poor. These figures were 15.4 percent for the southern region (8.2 percent of the poor) and 6.8 percent for the center-west region (5.2 percent of the poor). For the poorer regions, on the contrary, the share of population in each region is lower than the share of the poor: 4.6 percent (9.3 percent of the poor) for the northern region and 29.4 percent (44.3 percent of the poor) for the northeastern region, the poorest region in the country.

In terms of evolution of regional inequality, Rocha (1998) concludes that no regular trend could be observed in the period. The author also concludes that the yearly observed variations in concentration are mainly related to what happens in the state of São Paulo (southeastern region) and in the northeastern region. This reinforces the position of these two regions in the extremes of the regional income distribution in Brazil. Rocha also points out that once the effects of income increase that followed the end of the hyperinflationary period in 1995 run out, reduction of national and regional poverty will depend mainly on the macroeconomic determinants related to investment. Also, the author concludes that even keeping unchanged the actual level of poverty, reductions in regional inequality will require reallocation of industrial activity to peripheral regions.

Finally, Rocha (1998) concludes that opening of the economy to the external market (mainly in relation to the formation of Mercosur) would help reduce regional inequality in Brazil. This would happen through reduced consumer prices in the poorest regions, which are lacking in the industries most threatened by new trade flows.

The behavior of wages and the allocation of labor throughout the 1980–99 trade liberalization period in Brazil were analyzed by Green, Dickerson, and Arbache (2001). Among their main findings, the authors point out that wage inequality remained fairly constant for the 1980s and 1990s, with a small peak in the mid-1980s. The main conclusion of the study is that the egalitarian consequences of trade liberalization were not important in Brazil for the period under analysis. As caveats, Green, Dickerson, and Arbache note the low trade exposure of the Brazilian economy (about 13 percent in 1997), as well as the low share of workers that have completed college studies in total (1 in 12 workers at that time).

Gurgel and others (2003) present a computable general equilibrium (CGE) analysis of the effects on Brazil of trade liberalization. They used a Global Trade Analysis Project (GTAP)-derived multicountry model with additional Brazilian detail. For Brazil, 10 urban and 10 rural household income types are recognized. The paper compares the effects of the Free Trade Area of the Americas (FTAA), the EU-Mercosur, and multilateral trade agreements on Brazil. Among the scenarios examined are the effects of the FTAA or the EU-Mercosur if the United States or the EU did *not* offer free access to Brazilian farm products and the interaction *between* trade deals—for example, whether the FTAA makes the EU-Mercosur less attractive. Gurgel and others (2003) conclude that the trade deals are in varying degrees good for Brazil—and especially good for Brazil's poor. The poor benefit more because they tend to work in agriculture, which is export oriented and currently suffers from both foreign trade barriers and indirect taxation through the protection of Brazilian manufacturing.

Methodology

CGE models have long been used for poverty analysis. Many CGE models use a single representative household (RH) to denote consumer behavior in the model. This formulation, although adequate for many purposes, limits the investigation of poverty and income distribution analysis. More recent approaches were developed to deal with these constraints in this study.

Savard (2003) provides a thorough discussion of the topic. He groups CGE models dealing with poverty and income distribution analysis into three main categories: models with a single RH, models with multiple households (MH), and the microsimulation (MS) approach that links a CGE model to an econometric household MS model.

The RH model is the traditional method, and it has been widely used in the literature. The main drawback of this model for income distribution and poverty analysis is that there are no intragroup income distribution changes because the households are all aggregated into a single representative.

The second approach, the MH model, consists of multiplying the number of households. For example, the study by Gurgel and others (2003) distinguished 20 household types. Because they have varying expenditure and income source shares, the households are affected differently by economic changes. However, differences *within* a particular household group are ignored.

Increasing computation capacity allows a large number of households in an MH model. To take an extreme case, the total number of households in a household survey could be used. This approach then allows the model to take into account the full detail in household data and avoids prejudgment about aggregating households into categories. The main disadvantages of this type of approach are that data reconciliation can be difficult and the size of the model can become a constraint.

The third approach, the MS model, draws on microsimulation techniques. Here, a CGE model generates aggregate changes that are later communicated to an MS model based on a large unit-record database. Savard (2003) points out that the drawbacks to the approach are coherence between models, because the causality usually runs from the CGE model to the MS model, with no feedback between them.

Overview of the Modeling Approach

The approach pursued in this chapter takes advantage of the same general idea raised by Savard (2003) to overcome the difficulties posed by the three first options mentioned above: the use of a CGE model linked to an MS model, but with a bidirectional linkage between them that would guarantee a convergence of solution for both models. Savard (2003) links the models by running them in a repeated sequence of CGE-MS model runs, first computing the CGE simulation, then the MS model simulation, in a looping way, until convergence occurs. The main advantages of this approach are avoidance of scaling the microeconomic data to match the aggregated macroeconomic data, accommodation of more households in the MS model, and the ability of the MS model to incorporate discrete choice or integer behavior that might be difficult to incorporate in the CGE model.

The CGE model used here is a static inter-regional model of Brazil based on the well-known ORANI-G model of Australia (Horridge 2000). The model's structure is quite standard: consumption is modeled through the linear expenditure system over composite commodities (domestic and imported), exporters of each commodity face constant-elasticity[1] foreign demand schedules, production for exports or domestic markets is regulated by constant elasticity of transformation[2] (CET) functions for each firm, production is a nested Leontief–constant elasticity of substitution (CES) structure for primary factors and composite inputs, and labor is a CES function of 10 different types of labor. This nonlinear model is solved with GEMPACK software, and it distinguishes among 42 sectors, 52 commodities,[3] and 10 labor occupational categories.

All quantity variables in the model are disaggregated according to 27 regions within Brazil, using an elaboration of the top-down regional modeling method described in chapter 6 of Dixon and others (1982). This methodology recognizes local multiplier effects: many service goods are little traded between regions, so that local service output must follow local demand for services.

The CGE model is calibrated with data from the Brazilian economy for 1996, which was obtained from two main sources: the 1996 Brazilian Input-Output Matrix (IBGE http://ibge.gov.br) and the *Brazilian Agricultural Census* (IBGE 1996a).

On the income generation side of the model, workers are divided into 10 different categories (occupations) according to their wages. These wage classes are then assigned to each regional industry in the model. Together with the revenues from other endowments (capital and land rents), these wages are used to generate household incomes. Each activity uses a particular mix of the 10 different labor occupations (skills). Changes in activity level change employment by sector and region. This drives changes in poverty and income distribution. Using the *Pesquisa de Orçamentos Familiares* (*Household Expenditure Survey* [POF]; IBGE 1996b) data mentioned below, the CGE model is extended to cover 270 different expenditure patterns, composed of 10 different income classes in 27 regions. In this way, all the expenditure-side detail of the MS dataset is incorporated within the main CGE model.

There are two main sources of information for the household MS model: the PNAD (IBGE 2001) and the POF (IBGE 1996b). The PNAD contains information about households and persons, with a total of 331,263 records. The main information extracted from the PNAD was wage by industry and region, as well as other personal characteristics such as years of schooling, sex, age, position in the family, and other socioeconomic characteristics.

The POF is an expenditure survey that covers 11 metropolitan regions in Brazil. It was undertaken during 1996 and covered 16,014 households with the purpose of updating the consumption bundle structure. The main information drawn from this survey was the expenditure patterns of 10 different income classes for the 11 regions. One such pattern was assigned to each individual PNAD household, according to each income class. As for the regional dimension, the 11 POF regions were mapped to the larger set of 27 CGE regions. Here, it must be stressed that the POF contains just information about urban areas (the metropolitan areas of the main state capitals).

Model Running Procedures and Highlights

As noted above, the model consists of two parts, a CGE model and a household model, the MS. The models are run sequentially. There are two strategies to ensure consistency between the two models. First, the CGE model is sufficiently detailed, and its categories and data are close enough to those of the MS model, that the

CGE model very closely predicts MS behavior (which is also included in the CGE model, such as household demands or labor supplies). The role of the MS model is to provide extra information—for example, about the variance of income within income groups or about the incidence of price and wage changes in groups not identified by the CGE model, such as groups identified by ethnic type, educational level, or family status.

A second consistency strategy is that, if the MS model predicts household demands or labor supplies at variance with the CGE model, there is the option of feeding back corrections into the CGE model and running the two models iteratively until they agree. That option was not exercised in the simulations reported here.[4]

The analysis starts with a set of trade shocks generated by a GTAP model simulation that excludes the effect of Brazil's own tariff reductions. These shocks consist of changes in import prices and in export demands. The Brazilian tariff shocks (the trade liberalization in Brazil) are added to these shocks. Import prices and tariffs are naturally exogenous to the Brazil model. The export demand changes are applied via vertical shifts in the export demand curves facing Brazil (table 7.6).

The trade shocks are applied and the results calculated for 52 commodities, 42 industries, 10 households, and 10 labor occupations—all of which vary by 27 regions. Next, the results from the CGE model are used to update the MS model. At first, this update consists basically in updating wages and hours worked for the 263,938 workers in the sample. These changes have a regional (27 regions) as well as sectoral (42 industries) dimension.

The model then relocates jobs according to changes in labor demand.[5] This is done by changing the PNAD weight of each worker to mimic the change in employment—the "quantum weights method."[6] In this approach, then, a true job relocation process occurs. Although the job relocation has very little effect on the distribution of wages among the 270 household groups identified by the CGE model, it may have considerable impact on the variance of income within a group because although the jobs move, the workers do not. Thus, regional adjustment is achieved by workers moving into or out of employment.

One final point about the procedure used in this chapter should be stressed. Although the changes in the labor market are simulated for each adult in the labor force, the changes in expenditures and in poverty are tracked back to the household dimension. This is possible because the PNAD has a key that links persons to households. Each household contains one or more adults, either working in a particular sector and occupation or unemployed, as well as dependents. In the model used here, then, it is possible to recompose changes in the household income from the changes in individual wages. This is a very important aspect of the model, because it is likely that family income variations are cushioned, in general, by this procedure. If, for example, one person in some household loses his job but another in the same household gets a new job, household income may change little. Because households are the expenditure units in the model, household spending variations would be expected to be smoothed by this income-pooling effect. However, the loss of a job will increase poverty more if the displaced worker is the sole earner in a household.

The Base Year Picture

This section extends the above description of poverty and income inequality in Brazil. The reference year for the analysis is 2001. Some general aggregated information about poverty and income inequality in Brazil can be seen in table 7.1.

The rows of table 7.1 correspond to household income classes, grouped according to POF definitions[7] such that POF[1] is the lowest income class and POF[10] the highest. A fair picture of income inequality in Brazil emerges from the table. It can be seen that the first five income classes, although accounting for 52.6 percent of total population in Brazil, get only 17 percent of total income. The highest income class accounts for 11 percent of the population and about 45

Table 7.1.   Poverty and Income Inequality in Brazil, 2001

Income group	PrPop	PrInc	Ave HouInc	Unemp Rate	Pr White	Ave Wage	Pr Child
POF[1]	10.7	0.9	0.1	32.6	35.2	0.2	46.2
POF[2]	8.0	1.8	0.4	17.3	38.3	0.3	37.2
POF[3]	16.0	5.2	0.6	10.4	42.0	0.4	35.1
POF[4]	7.3	3.1	0.8	8.8	45.1	0.4	32.5
POF[5]	11.0	5.8	1.0	7.5	49.2	0.5	28.7
POF[6]	7.9	5.1	1.2	7.4	53.4	0.6	26.4
POF[7]	12.9	11.1	1.7	6.8	60.3	0.8	24.5
POF[8]	7.5	8.7	2.3	6.1	66.3	0.9	21.5
POF[9]	7.7	12.7	3.1	5.9	71.2	1.4	20.5
POF[10]	10.9	45.7	7.9	4.2	81.6	3.2	17.7
Total	100.0	100.0	n.c.	n.c.	n.c.	n.c.	n.c.

Source: IBGE (2001).

Note: n.c. = not computed. PrPop = % in total population; PrInc = % in country total income; AveHouInc = average household income; UnempRate = unemployment rate; PrWhite = % of white population in total; AveWage = average normalized wage; PrChild = share of population under 15 by income class.

percent of total income. The Gini index associated with the income distribution in Brazil in 2001, calculated using an equivalent household[8] basis, is 0.58, placing Brazil's income distribution among the world's worst.

The unemployment rate is also relatively higher among the poorer classes. This is a very important point because of its relevance for modeling. The opportunity to get a new job is probably the most important element lifting people out of poverty: hence the importance for poverty modeling of allowing the model to capture the existence of a switching regime (from unemployment to employment) and not just changes in wages. As can be seen in table 7.1, the unemployment rate reaches 36.5 percent among the lowest-income group (persons older than 15 years) and just 7.7 percent among the richest. The percentage of white people also increases considerably with household income, and the percentage of children decreases markedly. Although the analysis does not specifically focus on gender and ethnic aspects, these are important indicators to take into account when analyzing results.

To further describe the state of income insufficiency in Brazil, a poverty line defined as one-third of the average household income was set.[9] According to that criterion, 30.8 percent of the Brazilian households in 2001 would be poor.[10] This would make up 96.2 percent, 76.6 percent, and 53.5 percent, respectively, of households in the first three income groups,[11] or 34.5 million of 112 million households in 2001.

The first columns in table 7.11 report two overall measures of poverty following Foster, Greer, and Thorbecke ([FGT] 1984)—FGT0, the proportion of poor households (that is, living below the poverty line), and FGT1, the average poverty gap ratio (proportion by which household income falls below the poverty line), and so forth—for each POF group.[12] These figures reveal a large average poverty gap for the two lowest income classes. Together, these two income classes contribute to about half of the general average poverty gap index of the economy. The first income class, for example, falls below the poverty line by about 70 percent. Thus, large income increases for the poor are needed to significantly change the number in poverty.

As stated before, this general poverty and inequality picture also has an important regional dimension in Brazil because economic activity is located mainly in the southeastern region. This is particularly true of manufacturing; agriculture is more dispersed among regions. Figure 7.1 summarizes the regional variation of poverty and income inequality, shading them according to proportions of households in poverty. The states in the northeastern region plus the states of Tocantins and Pará in the north show the highest poverty rates. If, however, regional population is taken into account, the populous regions of

**Figure 7.1.   Brazilian States, Shaded According to Proportion
in Poverty**

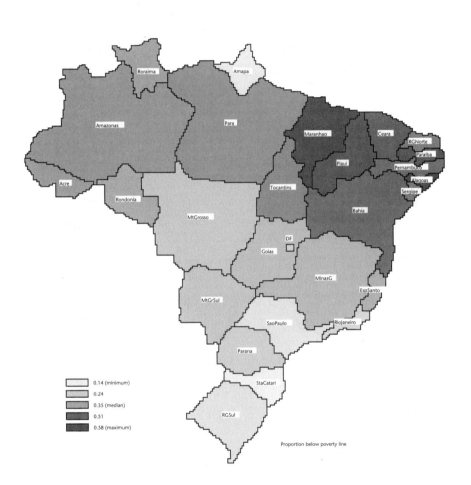

Source: Authors' calculations from PNAD 2001 data (IBGE, 2001).

Ceará, Pernambuco, Bahia, Minas Gerais, and São Paulo play a larger role in the overall poverty picture.[13]

Tables 7.2 and 7.3 report important information about the labor structure of the Brazilian economy. In these tables, sectoral wage bills are split into the model's 10 occupational groups. The occupational groups are defined in terms of a unit wage ranking. More skilled workers, then, would be those in the highest income classes and vice versa. As can be seen in Table 7.2, agriculture is the activity that uses more unskilled labor (40.5 percent of that sector's labor bill), and petroleum and gas extraction and petroleum refinery are the most intensive users of skilled labor (10th labor class) activities, with financial institutions coming next. If labor inputs were measured in hours (rather than in values), the concentration of low-skill labor in agriculture would be even more pronounced.

Agriculture is also the sector that hires the most unskilled labor in Brazil, about 41 percent of total workers in income class 1 (table 7.3). The trade sector is the second largest employer of this type of labor. As for the higher income classes, the

Table 7.2. Share of Occupations in Each Activity's Labor Bill (percentage)

Sector	Occupations (wage class)										
	1	2	3	4	5	6	7	8	9	10	Total
Agriculture	40.5	30.2	5.8	6.0	5.2	3.3	3.7	1.8	1.9	1.6	100
Mineral extraction	12.0	19.4	6.8	6.9	8.4	6.1	12.8	9.9	10.8	6.9	100
Petroleum and gas extraction	0.0	0.0	0.0	0.9	0.9	6.1	16.1	12.1	22.8	41.1	100
Non-metallic minerals	7.1	18.8	7.4	8.9	11.5	11.8	14.1	7.6	7.4	5.3	100
Iron production	1.9	6.8	4.0	6.3	10.2	9.7	22.7	14.0	15.4	9.1	100
Non-ferrous metals	1.9	6.8	4.0	6.3	10.2	9.7	22.7	14.0	15.4	9.1	100
Other metals	1.9	6.8	4.0	6.3	10.2	9.7	22.7	14.0	15.4	9.1	100
Machinery and tractors	0.5	4.6	1.9	4.8	6.8	9.0	19.6	17.2	16.8	18.8	100
Electric materials	0.4	3.8	2.6	3.3	10.3	11.6	20.4	15.5	17.0	15.1	100

Table 7.2. *(Continued)*

Sector	Occupations (wage class)										
	1	2	3	4	5	6	7	8	9	10	Total
Electronic equipment	0.4	3.8	2.6	3.3	10.3	11.6	20.4	15.5	17.0	15.1	100
Automobiles	0.3	2.5	1.0	2.4	7.7	8.6	19.6	15.7	22.4	19.8	100
Other vehicles and spare parts	0.3	2.5	1.0	2.4	7.7	8.6	19.6	15.7	22.4	19.8	100
Wood and furniture	8.2	11.7	6.6	8.8	12.4	11.9	16.6	9.3	9.6	5.0	100
Paper	2.3	7.8	3.7	6.2	8.4	8.1	18.7	13.0	16.7	15.1	100
Rubber manufactures	0.8	4.7	3.2	4.6	14.4	5.5	24.0	13.6	16.6	12.5	100
Chemicals	2.1	7.8	3.0	4.2	9.1	11.8	14.2	15.6	16.4	15.8	100
Petrol refining	0.5	1.5	2.7	0.3	9.0	5.7	13.1	7.2	10.5	49.5	100
Miscellaneous chemicals	0.0	6.8	9.6	13.4	25.3	0.0	14.5	2.8	7.9	19.7	100
Pharmaceutical products	1.7	5.7	3.1	6.8	4.1	7.5	13.5	11.3	18.7	27.4	100
Plastics	1.6	6.3	2.3	8.5	12.8	12.1	24.6	10.3	9.0	12.6	100
Textiles	14.7	9.0	4.9	7.2	12.5	11.0	17.6	11.3	6.2	5.5	100
Apparel	3.2	17.3	7.5	15.1	16.1	9.7	15.7	5.4	4.5	5.5	100
Footwear	4.1	16.2	6.5	13.5	18.2	13.0	14.4	5.7	4.8	3.6	100
Coffee processing	8.6	14.3	6.1	9.6	13.2	11.3	15.1	8.3	7.4	6.0	100
Vegetable processing	8.6	14.3	6.1	9.6	13.2	11.3	15.1	8.3	7.4	6.0	100
Slaughtering	8.6	14.3	6.1	9.6	13.2	11.3	15.1	8.3	7.4	6.0	100
Dairy	8.6	14.3	6.1	9.6	13.2	11.3	15.1	8.3	7.4	6.0	100
Sugar refining	8.6	14.3	6.1	9.6	13.2	11.3	15.1	8.3	7.4	6.0	100
Vegetable oils	8.6	14.3	6.1	9.6	13.2	11.3	15.1	8.3	7.4	6.0	100
Other food	8.6	14.3	6.1	9.6	13.2	11.3	15.1	8.3	7.4	6.0	100

Table 7.2.   Share of Occupations in Each Activity's Labor Bill (percentage) *(Continued)*

Sector	Occupations (wage class)										
	1	2	3	4	5	6	7	8	9	10	Total
Miscellaneous industries	16.8	13.4	6.6	6.2	11.4	7.4	13.1	7.8	10.7	6.5	100
Public utilities	1.7	17.5	5.3	8.6	7.1	6.0	12.9	12.2	14.2	14.5	100
Construction	6.3	13.4	8.6	10.1	12.5	9.0	20.2	9.6	6.9	3.4	100
Trade	10.0	14.2	6.6	8.2	10.7	8.2	15.1	8.3	10.0	8.7	100
Transport	4.6	7.0	4.4	4.7	7.5	7.1	19.0	16.1	18.1	11.6	100
Communications	1.4	4.6	2.4	5.1	7.9	9.4	18.6	13.9	17.2	19.4	100
Financial institutions	0.9	3.5	1.3	3.5	6.6	4.2	10.0	11.8	23.3	34.9	100
Farm services	16.4	20.3	7.4	8.4	9.6	6.8	12.1	6.5	7.2	5.4	100
Enterprise services	2.9	8.1	4.3	5.7	8.1	6.4	13.0	8.6	15.7	27.2	100
Building rentals	2.0	4.3	2.7	4.8	9.9	6.3	17.1	8.8	18.4	25.7	100
Public administration	1.7	13.1	3.6	7.2	7.6	6.8	13.0	12.1	19.3	15.6	100
Other private Services	7.6	16.6	6.0	9.2	9.3	10.9	13.7	8.2	11.6	6.9	100

Source: Authors' computations.

financial institutions and public administration sectors hire the largest numbers of well-paid workers.

Table 7.4 shows the distribution of occupational character class (OCC) wages among the household income classes (POF classes). In this table, the rows show household income classes, and the columns show the wage earnings by occupation. It is evident from this table that the wage earnings of the higher wage occupations (OCC10, for example) are concentrated in the higher income households and vice versa. Most of the wages earned by workers in the first wage class (OCC1) accrue to the three poorest households, POF[1]–[3]. All the workers in the highest wage class are in households from the eighth income class and above. It can be seen, then, that the household income classes are highly positively correlated with the occupational wage-earning classes.

Table 7.3. Share of Each Activity in Total Labor Bill, by Occupation (percentage)

Sector	Occupations (wage class)									
	1	2	3	4	5	6	7	8	9	10
Agriculture	41.0	17.8	9.8	6.9	4.8	3.8	2.2	1.4	1.1	0.9
Mineral extraction	0.5	0.4	0.4	0.3	0.3	0.3	0.3	0.3	0.2	0.1
Petroleum and gas extraction	0.0	0.0	0.0	0.0	0.0	0.1	0.2	0.2	0.3	0.5
Non-metallic minerals	0.5	0.8	0.9	0.8	0.8	1.0	0.6	0.5	0.3	0.2
Iron production	0.1	0.1	0.2	0.2	0.3	0.3	0.4	0.3	0.3	0.2
Non-ferrous metals	0.0	0.1	0.1	0.1	0.2	0.2	0.2	0.2	0.1	0.1
Other metals	0.3	0.7	1.2	1.3	1.7	1.9	2.4	2.0	1.5	0.9
Machinery and tractors	0.1	0.5	0.5	0.9	1.1	1.7	2.0	2.3	1.6	1.8
Electric materials	0.0	0.1	0.2	0.2	0.5	0.7	0.7	0.7	0.5	0.5
Electronic equipment	0.0	0.1	0.2	0.2	0.4	0.6	0.5	0.5	0.4	0.4
Automobiles	0.0	0.1	0.1	0.1	0.3	0.4	0.5	0.5	0.5	0.5
Other vehicles and spare parts	0.0	0.2	0.2	0.3	0.8	1.1	1.3	1.3	1.4	1.2
Wood and furniture	0.9	0.7	1.1	1.0	1.2	1.4	1.0	0.8	0.6	0.3
Paper	0.3	0.6	0.8	0.9	1.0	1.2	1.4	1.3	1.2	1.1
Rubber manufactures	0.0	0.1	0.1	0.1	0.3	0.1	0.3	0.2	0.2	0.1
Chemicals	0.1	0.1	0.2	0.1	0.3	0.4	0.3	0.4	0.3	0.3
Petrol refining	0.0	0.1	0.3	0.0	0.5	0.4	0.5	0.3	0.4	1.7
Miscellaneous chemicals	0.0	0.3	1.1	1.0	1.6	0.0	0.6	0.2	0.3	0.8

Table 7.3.   Share of Each Activity in Total Labor Bill, by Occupation (percentage) (Continued)

Sector	Occupations (wage class)									
	1	2	3	4	5	6	7	8	9	10
Pharmaceutical products	0.1	0.2	0.3	0.4	0.2	0.5	0.5	0.5	0.6	0.9
Plastics	0.1	0.2	0.2	0.5	0.6	0.7	0.8	0.4	0.3	0.4
Textiles	0.7	0.2	0.4	0.4	0.5	0.6	0.5	0.4	0.2	0.1
Apparel	0.3	0.9	1.1	1.5	1.3	1.0	0.8	0.4	0.2	0.3
Footwear	0.2	0.4	0.4	0.6	0.7	0.6	0.3	0.2	0.1	0.1
Coffee processing	0.1	0.1	0.1	0.1	0.1	0.1	0.1	0.1	0.0	0.0
Vegetable processing	0.5	0.4	0.5	0.6	0.6	0.7	0.5	0.3	0.2	0.2
Slaughtering	0.4	0.3	0.4	0.5	0.5	0.5	0.4	0.3	0.2	0.1
Dairy	0.1	0.1	0.1	0.2	0.2	0.2	0.1	0.1	0.1	0.0
Sugar refining	0.2	0.2	0.2	0.2	0.2	0.2	0.2	0.1	0.1	0.1
Vegetable oils	0.1	0.1	0.1	0.1	0.1	0.1	0.1	0.1	0.0	0.0
Other food	1.0	1.0	1.2	1.2	1.4	1.5	1.0	0.7	0.5	0.4
Miscellaneous industries	0.7	0.3	0.5	0.3	0.5	0.4	0.3	0.3	0.3	0.2
Public utilities	0.5	3.2	2.8	3.0	2.0	2.1	2.4	3.0	2.5	2.6
Construction	2.7	3.3	6.1	4.8	4.9	4.3	5.0	3.2	1.6	0.8
Trade	13.5	11.2	14.8	12.6	13.3	12.5	12.0	8.7	7.5	6.6
Transport	2.6	2.3	4.1	3.0	3.8	4.4	6.2	7.0	5.6	3.6
Communications	0.2	0.4	0.6	0.8	1.0	1.5	1.6	1.6	1.4	1.6
Financial institutions	1.0	2.3	2.4	4.4	6.9	5.3	6.7	10.5	14.6	22.3
Farm services	21.0	15.1	15.8	12.1	11.2	9.8	9.0	6.5	5.1	3.9
Enterprise services	1.6	2.6	4.0	3.6	4.1	4.0	4.2	3.8	4.8	8.5

Table 7.3.   *(Continued)*

Sector	Occupations (wage class)									
	1	2	3	4	5	6	7	8	9	10
Building rentals	0.1	0.2	0.3	0.3	0.6	0.4	0.6	0.4	0.6	0.9
Public administration	6.4	29.4	23.3	31.2	26.7	29.3	29.2	36.3	40.8	33.7
Other private Services	2.2	2.8	2.9	3.0	2.4	3.5	2.3	1.8	1.8	1.1
Total	100.0	100.0	100.0	100.0	100.0	100.0	100.0	100.0	100.0	100.0

Source: Authors' computations.

Model Closure

In choosing a model closure, the analysis in this chapter aims to mimic the GTAP model that generated the foreign price scenario. On the supply side, total national employment was fixed by occupation, with jobs moving freely among sectors and regions.[14] The model allows substitution between occupations, driven by relative wages. Similarly, capital is fixed nationally but is mobile between sectors and regions. The land stock (used just in the agriculture activity) is fixed.[15] Because agriculture is an activity that produces 11 products, land is allocated to these competing products through relative prices, allowing the crop mix to change. On the demand side, government and investment spending are fixed in real terms, and a fixed trade balance enforces the national budget balance, which is accommodated by changes in real consumption. The trade balance, then, drives the level of absorption. As noted previously, the numeraire is the Brazilian consumer price index, so all prices reported here are relative to the CPI.

Finally, tax revenue losses because tariff cuts are replaced: real aggregate revenue from all indirect taxes is kept fixed via a uniform endogenous change in the power of indirect taxes on sales to households. This mechanism is equivalent to a lump-sum tax of value proportional to each household's spending.[16] It also mimics the traditional method of raising tax revenues in Brazil, through indirect tax collection.

Table 7.4.   Wage Bill Distribution According to Occupational Wages and Household Income Classes (1996 Brazilian reais, millions)

Household income classes	Occupational wages classes (personal)										Total
	OCC1	OCC2	OCC3	OCC4	OCC5	OCC6	OCC7	OCC8	OCC9	OCC10	
POF[1]	1,531	1,637	0	0	0	0	0	0	0	0	3,168
POF[2]	538	2,409	1,632	783	0	0	0	0	0	0	5,362
POF[3]	1,804	3,996	1,201	2,460	4,327	3,728	342	0	0	0	17,859
POF[4]	766	1,513	861	1,380	1,077	616	5,020	0	0	0	11,233
POF[5]	932	2,787	1,147	1,649	2,746	2,254	5,945	3,526	0	0	2,0985
POF[6]	537	1,811	795	1,410	2,133	2,127	4,305	5,517	405	0	19,039
POF[7]	576	2,315	1,178	2,012	3,038	3,102	8,717	7,654	12,773	0	41,365
POF[8]	201	1,137	524	1,045	1,819	1,969	4,896	5,585	13,211	1,427	31,814
POF[9]	123	695	401	762	1,312	1,449	4,571	5,218	15,864	16,994	47,388
POF[10]	83	527	301	576	1,135	1,185	3,939	5,086	18,480	134,499	165,811
Total	7,091	18,827	8,040	12,077	17,586	16,430	37,734	32,586	60,732	152,920	364,024

Source: Authors' computations.

Results

The CGE Model Results

The Brazilian economy has a limited exposure to external trade. The shares of exports and imports in total GDP were 7.0 percent and 8.9 percent, respectively, in the 1996 base year. These shares have increased recently, but not by enough to significantly change this picture.[17] Table 7.5 shows more information about the structure of Brazilian external trade as well as of related parameters and production structure; table 7.6 shows the nature and size of the shocks applied to the model.

As stated before, the shocks applied to the model were generated by a previous run of the GTAP model in which the Doha scenarios were implemented. The GTAP effects on the Brazilian economy were then transmitted to the Brazil CGE model through changes in tariffs and import prices changes and shifts in the demand schedules for the Brazilian exports.[18]

An inspection of tables 7.5 and 7.6 can give an idea of the importance of these shocks combined with the importance of each commodity in Brazilian external trade. Brazilian exports are spread among many different commodities, with no specialized trend. Raw agricultural products have a very small share in total exports, composed almost entirely of soybeans. Processed food and agriculturally based exports (including wood and furniture, rubber, paper, textiles, and apparel), however, account for a significant 0.369 share of total exports in the base year, highlighting the importance of agriculture in the Brazilian economy.

Imports as a share of each domestic production are concentrated in wheat, oil, machinery, electric materials, electronic equipment, and chemical products. In terms of total import shares, however, oil products (raw and refined), machinery, electric materials, electronic equipment, and chemical products are the most important products.

Table 7.5 also shows some relevant parameters and other production characteristics of the model. The Armington elasticities are borrowed from the GTAP database. The same is true for the export demand elasticities (not shown in the table), which are made equal to the GTAP region-generic elasticity of substitution among imports in the Armington structure.

The agriculture sector is modeled as a multiproduction sector, producing 11 commodities. Thus, the capital to labor ratio (a ratio of values) in table 7.5 is the same for every agricultural product. The value of land is not included in the value of capital here. If land were included, the value of the capital to labor ratio in agriculture would rise to 0.99. The value added and value of production column, however, includes the returns to land for agriculture.

The presentation of Brazilian impacts due to multilateral trade reform begins with some macro results to establish a benchmark for the regional and

Table 7.5. Brazilian External Trade Structure

Commodity	Armington elasticities	External trade				Production	
		Share in total Brazilian exports	Exported share of total output	Import share in local markets	Share in total imports	Capital to labor ratio	Value added and value of production
Coffee	2.38	0	0	0	0	0.64	0.61
Sugar cane	2.2	0	0	0	0	0.64	0.61
Paddy rice	2.2	0	0	0.02	0.001	0.64	0.61
Wheat	2.2	0	0	0.68	0.020	0.64	0.61
Soybeans	2.2	0.019	0.170	0.06	0.004	0.64	0.61
Cotton	2.2	0	0	0.02	0	0.64	0.61
Corn	2.2	0.001	0.015	0.01	0.001	0.64	0.61
Livestock	2.8	0	0	0.01	0.001	0.64	0.61
Raw milk	2.2	0	0	0	0	0.64	0.61
Poultry	2.8	0	0	0.01	0	0.64	0.61
Other agriculture	2.38	0.022	0.002	0.02	0.015	0.64	0.61
Mineral extraction	2.8	0.059	0.019	0.09	0.006	0.44	0.28
Petroleum and gas extraction	2.8	0	0.398	0.41	0.063	4.19	0.51
Non-metallic minerals	2.8	0.014	0.002	0.04	0.009	1.58	0.38
Iron production	2.8	0.073	0.033	0.03	0.009	2.99	0.18
Non-ferrous metals	2.8	0.041	0.154	0.1	0.014	2.99	0.23
Other metals	2.8	0.018	0.196	0.06	0.018	0.32	0.36
Machinery and tractors	5.2	0.038	0.037	0.22	0.088	1.53	0.56
Electric materials	2.8	0.027	0.077	0.19	0.040	0.86	0.27

Table 7.5. *(Continued)*

Commodity	Armington elasticities	External trade				Production	
		Share in total Brazilian exports	Exported share of total output	Import share in local markets	Share in total imports	Capital to labor ratio	Value added and value of production
Electronic equipment	2.8	0.018	0.047	0.36	0.123	3.04	0.38
Automobiles	5.2	0.029	0.057	0.1	0.034	2.60	0.25
Other vehicles and spare parts	5.2	0.068	0.144	0.2	0.057	0.69	0.30
Wood and furniture	2.8	0.026	0.078	0.02	0.004	0.66	0.40
Paper	1.8	0.032	0.067	0.06	0.018	0.45	0.28
Rubber industry	1.9	0.012	0.071	0.1	0.010	2.41	0.32
Chemicals	1.9	0.016	0.066	0.15	0.032	3.61	0.35
Petrol refining	1.9	0.031	0.034	0.11	0.083	6.08	0.31
Miscellaneious chemicals	1.9	0.015	0.039	0.1	0.028	1.11	0.28
Pharmaceuticals	1.9	0.007	0.021	0.15	0.028	1.84	0.46
Plastics	1.9	0.004	0.021	0.07	0.010	1.46	0.43
Textiles	2.2	0.020	0.052	0.11	0.031	1.98	0.26
Apparel	4.4	0.003	0.011	0.03	0.005	0.37	0.38
Footwear	4.4	0.043	0.294	0.10	0.006	0.71	0.35
Coffee processing	3.1	0.033	0.237	0	0	2.64	0.21
Vegetable processing	2.2	0.058	0.105	0.04	0.012	1.69	0.22
Slaughtering	2.2	0.025	0.055	0.02	0.004	1.45	0.19
Dairy	2.2	0.001	0.003	0.05	0.007	2.99	0.22

Table 7.5. Brazilian External Trade Structure (Continued)

Commodity	Armington elasticities	External trade				Production	
		Share in total Brazilian exports	Exported share of total output	Import share in local markets	Share in total imports	Capital to labor ratio	Value added and value of production
Sugar refining	2.2	0.029	0.217	0	0	0.32	0.16
Vegetable oils	2.2	0.065	0.229	0.04	0.006	2.72	0.11
Other food	2.2	0.022	0.029	0.05	0.020	1.03	0.27
Miscellaneous industries	2.8	0.010	0.049	0.22	0.028	1.22	0.43
Public utilities	1.9	0	0	0.03	0.014	0.91	0.59
Construction	1.9	0	0	0	0	4.06	0.66
Trade	1.9	0.009	0.016	0.01	0.011	0.18	0.53
Transport	1.9	0.053	0.084	0.04	0.022	0.19	0.49
Communications	1.9	0.005	0.014	0.01	0.003	1.97	0.78
Financial institutions	1.9	0.007	0.006	0.01	0.006	0.23	0.64
Farm services	1.9	0.016	0.010	0.05	0.067	0.36	0.67
Enterprise services	2.1	0.019	0.027	0.05	0.029	0.52	0.72
Building rentals	1.9	0	0	0	0	51.56	0.95
Public administration	1.9	0.010	0.003	0.01	0.012	0.00	0.73
Other services	2.1	0	0	0	0	0.01	0.93

Source: Authors' computations

Table 7.6.   Shocks to the CGE Model

Commodity	Import tariffs		Import CIF prices		Implied export price shift[a]	
	Doha	Full liberalization	Doha	Full liberalization	Doha	Full liberalization
Coffee	-0.04	-6.43	0.74	1.92	-0.74	-0.73
Sugar cane	0	-4.99	1.02	1.80	7.73	9.65
Paddy rice	0	-0.17	2.8	6.47	7.58	38.41
Wheat	0	-0.12	1.95	8.49	0.94	-1.80
Soybeans	0	-0.09	2.54	5.92	3.90	15.49
Cotton	0	-5.55	2.45	4.26	5.37	18.13
Corn	0	-0.55	2.41	7.56	6.32	25.24
Livestock	0	-0.37	1.05	2.40	0.24	-4.50
Raw milk	0	0	0.73	-0.26	-1.11	-9.08
Poultry	0	-4.53	0.45	1.9	0.47	0.39
Other agriculture	-0.04	-6.43	0.74	1.92	-0.74	-0.73
Mineral extraction	0	-2.95	0.16	0.12	0.48	1.40
Petroleum and gas extraction	0	0	0.14	0.6	0.20	1.70
Non-metallic minerals	-0.01	-9.82	0.13	0.26	0.78	2.76
Iron production	-0.07	-10.72	0.04	0.19	0.25	0.88
Non-ferrous metals	-0.23	-7.57	0.03	-0.27	0.80	1.70
Other metals	-0.04	-14.25	-0.01	0.13	0.45	1.76
Machinery and tractors	-0.02	-2.59	-0.17	-0.27	-0.09	-0.45
Electric materials	-0.1	-10.92	-0.02	0.05	0.19	0.36
Electronic equipment	-0.01	-10.84	0	0.05	0.28	0.67
Automobiles	-2.14	-16.91	0.24	-0.16	0.53	5.13
Other vehicles and spare parts	-0.02	-2.59	-0.17	-0.27	-0.09	-0.45
Wood and furniture	-0.84	-11.81	0.06	0.24	0.49	1.54
Paper	0	-8.54	0	-0.04	0.21	0.28
Rubber industry	-0.28	-7.98	0	-0.25	0.35	0.30

Table 7.6.   Shocks to the CGE Model *(Continued)*

| Commodity | Import tariffs | | Import CIF prices | | Implied export price shift[a] | |
	Doha	Full liberali- zation	Doha	Full liberali- zation	Doha	Full liberali- zation
Chemicals	-0.28	-7.98	0	-0.25	0.35	0.30
Petrol refining	0	-0.41	0.14	-0.31	0.45	2.65
Miscellaneous chemicals	-0.28	-7.98	0	-0.25	0.35	0.30
Pharmaceu- ticals	-0.28	-7.98	0	-0.25	0.35	0.30
Plastics	-0.28	-7.98	0	-0.25	0.35	0.30
Textiles	0	-13.6	0.65	0.33	1.34	0.79
Apparel	0	-17.18	1.00	0.25	1.46	-0.67
Footwear	-0.14	-11.64	0.43	0.21	0.26	-0.32
Coffee processing	-0.05	-16.54	0.25	0.2	1.50	1.66
Vegetable processing	-0.21	-7.66	0.74	0.46	2.20	10.32
Slaughtering	0	-4.02	2.17	2.91	18.02	38.79
Dairy	-0.02	-6.39	4.43	6.74	7.56	15.41
Sugar refining	0	-13.18	5.22	5.93	4.30	14.73
Vegetable oils	0	-7.18	0.88	3.39	3.50	-0.70
Other food	-0.21	-7.66	0.74	0.46	2.20	10.32
Miscellaneous industries	-0.05	-15.39	0.05	0.1	0.11	-0.15
Public utilities	0	0	-0.05	0.07	-0.08	-0.32
Construction	0	0	0.03	0.15	-0.03	0.02
Trade	0	0	0.05	0.89	0.01	0.52
Transport	0	0	-0.01	0.3	0.03	0.51
Communica- tions	0	0	-0.03	0.4	-0.06	0.03
Financial institutions	0	0	-0.07	0.38	-0.10	-0.01
Farm services	0	0	-0.10	0.21	-0.11	-0.01
Enterprise services	0	0	-0.06	0.29	-0.04	0.16
Building rentals	0	0	2.53	7.76	2.69	8.29

Table 7.6. (Continued)

Commodity	Import tariffs		Import CIF prices		Implied export price shift[a]	
	Doha	Full liberali-zation	Doha	Full liberali-zation	Doha	Full liberali-zation
Public admin-istration	0	0	-0.05	0.07	-0.08	-0.32
Other services	0	0	-0.10	0.21	-0.11	-0.01

Source: Based on results from chapter 3.

a. Vertical shift in export demand schedule calculated from GTAP results.

poverty analysis. When interpreting these results, one should bear in mind that the model has a top-down inter-regional specification, meaning that regional results depend on national results, but not vice versa. National macro results can be seen in table 7.7.

Because the closure fixes total supply of all primary factors (land, the 10 categories of labor, and capital), the GDP shows only a slight increase in the simulations. The real exchange rate rises (revaluation) as a result of the shocks, with corresponding gains in the external terms of trade.

For factor market results, recall that land is used only by agriculture, and capital and the 10 types of labor are fixed nationally but mobile between sectors. The average (aggregated) capital rental increases in all scenarios. With capital stocks and labor fixed in total, the expanding industries would attract capital and labor from the contracting ones. In these industries, those with falling capital to labor ratios increase the marginal productivity of capital, and hence capital returns, determining an increase in aggregated results. The price of land also shows a strong increase, reflecting the increase in production of activities using this factor (agriculture). National changes in industry output are shown in table 7.8.

As can be seen in table 7.8, agriculture and agriculture-related industries (the food industry in general) are expanding industries in all scenarios. The only exception is the vegetable oils industry, which contracts under full liberalization. Model results show a general fall in activity in the Brazilian manufacturing sectors after trade liberalization. This suggests that regions specializing in manufacturing would fare worse. The Doha results are similar, just differing in size (but not sign) when compared with the full-liberalization scenario, with a few exceptions.

Table 7.7.   Selected Macroeconomic Results

Macros	Scenarios (percentage changes)	
	Doha	Full liberalization
Real household consumption	0.22	0.61
Real investment	0.00	0.00
Real government expenditure	0.00	0.00
Exports volume	0.91	13.21
Imports volume	1.98	12.39
Real GDP	0.04	0.26
Aggregated employment	0.00	0.00
Real wage	0.02	-0.22
Aggregated capital stock	0.00	0.00
Average rate of return	0.24	1.36
CPI (numeraire)	0	0
GDP price index	0.05	-0.33
Export price index	0.11	-0.38
Imports (CIF) price index	-1.10	-1.65
Imports (domestic prices) price index	-1.23	-7.63
Real devaluation	-1.15	-1.32
TOT	1.22	1.28
Nominal exchange rate	-1.26	-1.99
Balance of trade as a GDP share	0.00	0.00
Price of agricultural land	7.7	20.97

Source: Authors' simulation results.

Table 7.9 shows regional results. In this table, states are grouped according to their macroregions inside Brazil. For each of the 10 labor types, total employment is fixed, thus labor demand (and unemployment) will be redistributed among regions according to changes in regional industry output. Employment falls in São Paulo and Rio de Janeiro in the southeast (the most populous and industrialized states) and also in Amazonas, Distrito Federal (Brasília), and Amapá.

The states of São Paulo and Rio de Janeiro are industrial states, hosting the bulk of Brazil's manufacturing. As seen before, manufacturing is contracting in general in all three scenarios. The same effect drives the result for Amazonas, where there is a free exporting zone, and reduced mining activity drives the results for Amapá.

Table 7.8. Activity Level Variation by Industry: Percentage Change

Activity level	Doha	Full liberalization
Agriculture	1.35	3.60
Mineral extraction	-1.00	-1.21
Petroleum and gas extraction	-1.45	-0.99
Non-metallic minerals	-0.36	-1.13
Iron production	-2.13	-3.75
Non-ferrous metals	-1.55	-0.50
Other metals	-1.19	-4.11
Machinery and tractors	-2.25	-4.95
Electric materials	-1.27	-5.22
Electronic equipment	-0.60	-3.36
Automobiles	-1.06	-6.35
Other vehicles and spare parts	-3.32	-6.55
Wood and furniture	-0.33	0.01
Paper	-0.58	-1.14
Rubber manufactures	-1.60	-4.76
Chemicals	-0.86	-3.81
Petrol refining	-0.39	-0.48
Miscellaneous chemicals	-0.23	-1.23
Pharmaceutical products	-0.05	-0.01
Plastics	-0.49	-2.16
Textiles	0.27	-3.06
Apparel	0.20	-1.52
Footwear	-4.94	-10.86
Coffee processing	0.39	0.72
Vegetable processing	0.79	4.52
Slaughtering	7.78	18.81
Dairy	0.71	0.86
Sugar refining	4.52	19.08
Vegetable oils	1.95	-5.61
Other food	0.34	1.36
Miscellaneous industries	-1.08	-7.75
Public utilities	-0.07	-0.15
Construction	0.00	0.00
Trade	0.09	0.41
Transport	-0.10	0.52
Communications	-0.01	0.01
Financial institutions	-0.07	-0.28
Farm services	-0.05	-0.14

**Table 7.8.   Activity Level Variation by Industry:
             Percentage Change (Continued)**

Activity level	Doha	Full liberalization
Enterprise services	-0.30	-0.35
Building rentals	0.14	0.23
Public administration	-0.03	-0.03
Other private Services	0.14	-0.01

Source: Authors' simulation results.

The trade liberalization scenarios seem to redistribute economic activity toward poorer regions. This occurs because higher-value-added sectors (manufacturing) shrink, and relatively lower-value-added sectors (agriculture) grow.

Poverty and Income Distribution Results

In the previous section, it was seen that model results are differentiated among regions and industries. The outcome of these changes on income and income inequality measures, as well as over income group–specific consumer price indexes (CPIs) are presented in table 7.10. In this table, the POF groups are groups of household income, with POF[1] the lowest and POF[10] the highest. The Gini index fell by 0.21 percent in the Doha scenario and 0.52 percent in the full liberalization.

These results confirm the general understanding that the Gini index usually changes very little with policy measures in the short run and accord with observed facts in Brazil in the last 15 years. Even though the country faced a strong trade liberalization process in the 1990s, it was observed that the Gini index changed very little in the period.

The CPI column in each scenario is the particular CPI change for each household income class, because the consumption bundle of each class is different. It is interesting to notice that the bulk of the real income effect comes from the income generation side and not from the fall in prices. Actually, there is a strong increase in some food products, such as meats, in all scenarios, driven mainly by the liberalization in the rest of the world. This is in contrast to what was expected by Rocha (1998), who predicted that opening the Brazilian economy to the external market would help reduce inequality in Brazil through reductions in prices in the poorest regions. The results in this chapter suggest that the CPI

Table 7.9. Regional Results in 27 Regions (percentage change)

State	Aggregate employment		Gross regional product	
	Doha	Full liberalization	Doha	Full liberalization
Rondônia	0.75	1.92	0.99	2.53
Acre	0.40	1.02	0.54	1.42
Amazonas	-0.14	-0.35	-0.19	-0.58
Roraima	0.48	1.33	0.74	2.09
Pará	0.32	0.89	0.44	1.25
Amapá	-0.03	0.00	-0.02	0.06
Tocantins	2.04	5.34	2.33	6.14
Maranhão	0.86	2.35	1.14	3.12
Piauí	0.86	2.15	1.24	3.16
Ceará	0.33	0.77	0.50	1.18
Rio Grande do Norte	0.17	0.45	0.24	0.64
Paraíba	0.23	0.56	0.35	0.85
Pernambuco	0.14	0.34	0.19	0.47
Alagoas	0.43	1.56	0.51	1.80
Sergipe	0.15	0.34	0.21	0.50
Bahia	0.24	0.62	0.22	0.64
Minas Gerais	0.07	0.24	0.07	0.24
Espírito Santo	0.07	0.25	0.10	0.37
Rio de Janeiro	-0.15	-0.26	-0.11	-0.13
São Paulo	-0.21	-0.60	-0.25	-0.75
Paraná	0.27	0.70	0.34	0.86
Santa Catarina	0.21	0.50	0.21	0.54
Rio Grande do Sul	0.01	0.09	0.02	0.21
Mato Grosso do Sul	1.49	3.82	1.74	4.41
Mato Grosso	1.06	2.76	1.24	3.11
Goiás	0.71	1.80	0.85	2.14
Distrito Federal	-0.04	-0.09	0.01	0.05

Source: Authors' simulation results.

would actually go up more in the lowest income classes but these increases are more than compensated by the income elevation.

It is important to notice that the highest positive changes in household income are concentrated on the lowest-income households, decreasing monotonically as household income increases. As can be seen in table 7.11, the reduction in the number of poor households is concentrated in the poorest groups. High positive

Table 7.10.   **Average Household Income, CPI by Household Income Class and Gini Index Percentage Change**

	Doha		Full liberalization	
	Income	CPI	Income	CPI
POF[1]	6.45	0.16	16.54	0.44
POF[2]	1.23	0.14	2.82	0.41
POF[3]	0.69	0.11	1.39	0.33
POF[4]	0.29	0.08	0.46	0.22
POF[5]	0.19	0.08	0.01	0.23
POF[6]	-0.02	0.06	-0.35	0.18
POF[7]	-0.10	0.04	-0.60	0.12
POF[8]	-0.26	0.00	-0.93	0.04
POF[9]	-0.27	-0.01	-0.91	-0.03
POF[10]	-0.33	-0.08	-1.09	-0.27
Gini	-0.21		-0.52	

Source: Authors' simulation results.

figures in POF groups 7 and 8 are percentage changes over very low numbers, because there are very few poor households in these income classes.[19]

The headcount ratio index (FGT0 in table 7.11) captures the extension of poverty but is insensitive to its intensity (Hoffmann 1998). The change in the intensity of poverty can be seen through the FGT1 index, poverty gap, or insufficiency of income ratio. A reduction in FTG1 means a reduction in the severity of poverty in each household income class. As seen in table 7.11, the FGT1 index decreases more than the headcount ratio in all scenarios. This means that there was actually an income distribution improvement, but not enough to drive a large number of persons (or households) out of poverty. This is due to the high value of those indexes in the base year.

In addition, the effects on Brazil of its own liberalization (assuming other countries did not liberalize) were computed (but are not tabulated here due to space constraints). The Brazilian own-tariff reduction contributes very little to the Doha scenario and is dominated by the other countries' actions even in the full-liberalization scenario.

Finally, table 7.12 shows model results relating to the regional breakdown inside Brazil. These results summarize at regional level the outcome of the simulated scenarios, as a net effect of the regional industries. They reflect, then, the pattern of regional specialization in production.

Table 7.11.   Percentage Changes in the Proportion of Poor Households (FGT0) and in the Poverty Gap Ratio (FGT1) by Household Income Groups

Household income class	Original value		Doha		Full liberalization	
	FGT0	FGT1	FGT0	FGT1	FGT0	FGT1
POF[1]	0.9617	0.7334	-0.52	-1.45	-1.55	-3.74
POF[2]	0.7657	0.3047	-0.48	-1.31	-1.26	-2.91
POF[3]	0.5355	0.1496	0.00	-0.89	-0.91	-1.39
POF[4]	0.2837	0.0539	-1.72	0.39	-2.28	2.67
POF[5]	0.1143	0.0189	-1.03	2.71	1.55	9.85
POF[6]	0.0390	0.0054	1.78	11.22	9.44	33.32
POF[7]	0.0082	0.0009	10.96	57.55	32.24	156.86
POF[8]	0.0008	0.0001	92.35	417.68	247.52	1107.21
POF[9]	0.0000	0.0000	0.00	0.00	0.00	0.00
POF[10]	0.0000	0.0000	0.00	0.00	0.00	0.00
Brazil	0.308	0.145	-0.37	-1.08	-0.78	-2.43

Source: Authors' simulation results.

Note: FGT0: Foster-Greer-Torbecke proportion of poor households index (headcount ratio). FGT1: poverty gap ratio.

Table 7.12 shows that the states of Amazonas, Amapá, São Paulo, and Rio de Janeiro would be the only ones where the number of households below the poverty line would increase in both simulations, although only slightly. Amazonas and Amapá have small populations, but São Paulo and Rio de Janeiro are the most densely populated and industrialized states in Brazil. As noted before, the result is related to the high concentration of contracting (high-value-added) industries in the regions of São Paulo, Rio de Janeiro, and Amazonas, mainly automobiles, machinery and tractors, electric materials, electronic equipment, and other vehicles and spare parts; the result for Amapá is driven by the mining industries.

Concluding Remarks

One of the main objections raised by some opponents to multilateral trade reform in agriculture is that the bulk of the benefits will go to rich landowners in farm export–oriented economies such as Brazil, thereby worsening an already skewed income distribution. The findings in this chapter refute this hypothesis. In fact, multilateral trade reform under the Doha Development Agenda is found to

Table 7.12.   Percentage Changes in Number of Poor Households by Region and Total Number Change

State	Scenario	
	Doha	Full liberalization
Rondônia	-0.73	-1.58
Acre	-0.36	-0.47
Amazonas	0.42	0.80
Roraima	-0.60	-1.74
Pará	-0.24	-0.82
Amapá	2.41	2.06
Tocantins	-1.34	-3.94
Maranhão	-0.87	-2.04
Piauí	-0.34	-1.32
Ceará	-0.32	-0.88
Rio Grande do Norte	-0.53	-0.83
Paraíba	-0.82	-1.56
Pernambuco	-0.35	-1.09
Alagoas	-0.38	-1.35
Sergipe	-0.41	-0.61
Bahia	-0.45	-1.04
Minas Gerais	-0.48	-1.08
Espírito Santo	-0.71	-1.29
Rio de Janeiro	0.77	0.99
São Paulo	0.72	1.97
Paraná	-1.19	-2.47
Santa Catarina	-1.79	-2.08
Rio Grande do Sul	-0.54	-2.12
Mato Grosso do Sul	-2.77	-6.44
Mato Grosso	-2.32	-6.06
Goiás	-1.06	-2.80
Distrito Federal	0.11	0.18
Change in total number of households	-55,908	-139,874
Change in total number of persons	-235,886	-481,989

Source: Authors' simulation results.

reduce inequality as well as poverty in Brazil. Although wealthy farmers may indeed gain, largely through higher returns to their land, the poor gain proportionately more. Their gains are derived through the labor market. Because 40 percent of the lowest-skill group work in agriculture, an expansion of that sector benefits the poorest households, which rely heavily on earnings from low-skill work.

More generally, the model results show that even important trade policy shocks do not generate dramatic changes in the structure of Brazilian poverty and income distribution. The simulated effects on poverty and income distribution are positive, but very small. This is partly due to the fact that the Brazilian economy is not very oriented toward external trade. The domestic market is far bigger and more important for the general economy than the external market, as researchers have long understood. This makes Brazil naturally less sensitive to tariff structure changes, as well as to changes in export demands.

There are modest impacts of trade reform on poverty because poverty is approached here through the household dimension, tracking the changes in the labor market from individual workers to households. This tends to blunt the impacts that trade may have on the employment of any individual and on poverty at the household level. In the PNAD 2001 data used in this chapter, the head of the family's income accounts for about 65 percent of aggregated household income in Brazil. Therefore, using head-of-household income as a proxy for household income may poorly predict the effect of policy changes, as convincingly argued by Bourguignon, Robilliard, and Robinson (2003). If spending (and welfare) is in any sense a household phenomenon, this is the appropriate method. Even though there may be a somewhat higher computational cost associated with this procedure, it seems worthwhile.

The role played by the agriculture sector in the analysis should also be stressed. As seen before, agriculture still accounts for a large share of employment for the poorest in Brazil. Despite the steady decline over time of agricultural employment as a share of total employment, the importance of agricultural policies for poverty alleviation in Brazil should not be overlooked.

Finally, it should be noted that this study assesses only the static impact of trade liberalization scenarios. The research methodology used here fails to capture many other effects generally associated with external trade liberalization, such as endogenous technology improvements and other dynamic effects. Indeed, the results of this study suggest that if any strong impact on poverty is supposed to arise from trade liberalization, it must be expected to arise from these other aspects.

Notes

1. For the simulations reported here, the export demand elasticities were set to values derived from the GTAP model to increase consistency between results for the world and Brazil models.

2. To fit with the assumptions of the GTAP model, the constant elasticity of transformation between domestic and exportable goods was set to infinity for the simulations reported in this chapter.

3. One of the activities (agriculture) produces 11 commodities; a CET function determines output mix.

4. As in the GTAP, labor supplies were fixed. Further, each household in the micro dataset used here had 1 of the 270 expenditure patterns identified in the main CGE model. There is very little scope for the MS to disagree with the CGE model.

5. The methodology is described in more detail in the appendix to the World Bank Policy Research Working Paper version of this chapter (Ferreira-Filho and Horridge, 2005). Only the main ideas are presented here.

6. Mark Horridge developed this method for this project.

7. POF[1] ranges from 0 to 2 minimum wages, POF[2] from 2+ to 3, POF[3] from 3+ to 5, POF[4] from 5+ to 6, POF[5] from 6+ to 8, POF[6] from 8+ to 10, POF[7] from 10+ to 15, POF[8] from 15+ to 20, POF[9] from 20+ to 30, and POF[10] is above 30 minimum wages. The minimum wage in Brazil in 2001 was around US$76 per month.

8. The equivalent household concept measures the subsistence needs of a household by attributing weights to its members: 1 to the head, 0.75 to the other adults, and 0.5 to the children (for example, to feed 2 persons does not cost double). Because poverty is defined here on an equivalent basis, a few (very large) families in middle-income groups fall below the poverty line.

9. This poverty line was equivalent to US$48 per month in 2001.

10. Barros, Henriques and Mendonça (2001), working with a poverty line that takes into account nutritional needs, find that 34 percent of Brazilian households were poor in 1999.

11. The proportion of households below the poverty line in the other income groups are 0.284 percent for the fourth, 0.14 percent for the fifth, 0.04 percent for the sixth, 0.008 percent for the seventh, and 0.001 percent for the eighth. There are no households below the poverty line for the two highest income classes.

12. The poverty gap and poverty line values are constructed with "adult equivalent" per capita household income.

13. See the World Bank Policy Research Working Paper version of this chapter for more details on the breakdown of poverty by region (Ferreira-Filho and Horridge, 2005).

14. There is a tension between the GTAP-like closure in this chapter and Brazilian reality. The microdata show substantial unemployment of less skilled groups in all regions. For the MS, it was assumed that jobs created (or lost) in a region were allotted to (or taken from) households in that region. An alternate scenario, in which fixed real wages replaced national labor constraints, yielded results similar to those reported here.

15. The factor market closure causes the model to generate changes in prices for 10 labor types, capital, and land—that is, price changes are uniform across regions. Changes in demand for each of the 12 factors also vary by sector and region. Each adult in the PNAD microdata is identified by region and labor type; those employed are also identified by sector. Changes in microdata poverty levels are driven by wage changes and by the redistribution of jobs between sectors and regions (and hence between households).

16. That is, neither the distribution of spending nor relative prices facing households is altered. With fixed labor supplies, distortion of any labor-leisure choice does not arise.

17. The share of imports plus exports in Brazilian GDP in 2001 and 2002 were, respectively, 22.3 percent and 23.4 percent.

18. The shifts in the demand schedules for Brazilian exports were calculated using export price and quantity results from the GTAP with export demand elasticities drawn from GTAP data.
19. Some middle-income households have many family members. With low per capita income, they fall below the poverty line.

References

Barros, R. P., and R. Mendonça. 1997. "O Impacto do crescimento econômico e de reduções no grau de desigualdade sobre a pobreza." Texto para discussão 528, Instituto de Pesquisa Econômica Aplicada (IPEA), Rio de Janeiro.

Barros, R. P., C. H. Corseuil, and S. Cury. 2001. "Salário mínimo e pobreza no Brasil: Estimativas que consideram efeitos de equilíbrio geral." Texto para Discussão 779, IPEA, Rio de Janeiro.

Barros, R. P., R. Henriques, and R. Mendonça. 2001. "A Estabilidade inaceitável: desigualdade e pobreza no Brasil." Texto para Discussão 800, IPEA, Rio de Janeiro.

Bourguignon, F., A. S. Robilliard, and S. Robinson. 2003. "Representative versus Real Households in the Macro-Economic Modeling of Inequality." Working Paper 2003-05. Département et Laboratoire d'Économie Théorique et Appliquée, Centre National de la Recherche Scientifique, École des Hautes Études en Sciences Sociales, Paris.

Dixon, P., B. Parmenter, J. Sutton, D. Vincent. 1982. *ORANI: A Multisectoral Model of the Australian Economy*. Amsterdam: North-Holland.

Ferreira-Filho, J.B. and M. Horridge. 2005. "The Doha Round, Poverty and Regional Inequality in Brazil." Policy Research Working Paper 3701, World Bank, Washington, DC.

Foster, James, Joel Greer, and Erik Thorbecke. 1984. "A Class of Decomposable Poverty Measures." *Econometrica* 52: 761–65.

Green, F., A. Dickerson, and J. S. Arbache. 2001. "A Picture of Wage Inequality and the Allocation of Labor through a Period of Trade Liberalization: The Case of Brazil." *World Development* 29 (11): 1923–39.

Gurgel, A., G. W. Harrison, T. F. Rutherford, and D. G. Tarr. 2003. "Regional, Multilateral, and Unilateral Trade Policies of MERCOSUR for Growth and Poverty Reduction in Brazil." Research Working Paper 3051, World Bank, Washington, DC.

Hoffmann, R. 1998. *Distribuição de renda: Medidas de desigualdade e pobreza*. São Paulo: Editora da Universidade de São Paulo.

Horridge, J. M. 2000. "ORANI-G: A General Equilibrium Model of the Australian Economy." Working Paper OP-93, Centre of Policy Studies, Monash University, Melbourne.

IBGE (Instituto Brasileiro de Geografia e Estatística). 1996a. *Censo agropecuário do Brasil*. Rio de Janeiro.

———. 1996b. *Pesquisa de orçamentos familiares*. Rio de Janeiro..

———. 2001. *Pesquisa Nacional por Amostra de Domicílios*. Rio de Janeiro.

Rocha, S. 1998. "Desigualdade regional e pobreza no Brasil: a evolução—1985/95." Texto para Discussão 567, IPEA, Rio de Janeiro.

Savard, L. 2003. "Poverty and Income Distribution in a CGE-Household Sequential Model." International Development Research Centre, University of Laval, Quebec.

8

GROWING TOGETHER OR GROWING APART? A VILLAGE-LEVEL STUDY OF THE IMPACT OF THE DOHA ROUND ON RURAL CHINA

Marijke Kuiper and Frank van Tongeren

Summary

Most studies of the opening of the Chinese economy focus on the national level. The few existing disaggregated analyses are limited to analyzing changes in agricultural production. This chapter uses an innovative village equilibrium model that accounts for nonseparability of household production and consumption decisions. This allows analysis of the impact of trade liberalization on household production, consumption, and off-farm employment; the interactions among these three aspects of household decisions; and the interactions among households in a village economy. The village model is used to analyze the impact of price changes and labor demand, the two major pathways through which international trade affects households. Analysis of the impact of trade liberalization for one village in the Jiangxi province of China reveals that changes in relative prices and outside-village employment have opposite impacts on household decisions. At the household level, the impact of price changes dominates the employment impacts. When full trade liberalization and the more limited Doha scenario are compared, reactions are more modest in the latter case for most households, but the response is nonlinear to increasing depth of trade reforms. This is explained by household-specific transaction (shadow) prices in combination with endogenous choices to participate in the output markets.

219

Rising income inequalities are a growing concern in China. Whether trade liberalization allows incomes to grow together or to grow apart depends on whether one accounts for the reduction in aggregate consumption demand when household members migrate. Assessment of the net effect on the within-village income distribution shows that even poorer households are able to catch up. Poorer households that own draft power gain most from trade liberalization. The households that have to rely on the use of own-labor for farm activities, and are endowed with neither traction power nor a link to employment opportunities in the prospering coastal regions, have fewer opportunities for adjustment.

Introduction

A gradual integration into the global economy, combined with far-reaching domestic reforms, has made China a showcase of attaining rapid economic growth through market-based reforms. The rapid economic growth during the past decades, however, has been accompanied by an increasing disparity between coastal and interior regions and between rural and urban areas. The coastal cities benefited most from the increasing export opportunities because of a combination of geographic factors and deliberate policies (Démurger and others 2002).

The extent of reforms in combination with the sheer size of the Chinese economy has resulted in a body of literature with a growth rate rivaling China's GDP growth. Most studies of the opening of the Chinese economy to the rest of the world focus on the national-level impacts. One exception is a study by Diao, Fan, and Zhang (2003) of the regional impact of China's recent WTO accession. As in other national-level studies, they find a positive aggregate effect for China as a whole. This aggregate effect obscures differences across regions. Reflecting past trends of diverging growth between coastal and inland provinces (see, for example, Démurger and others [2002] and Jones, Li, and Owen [2003]), income gaps among provinces are found to widen following WTO accession. They also find that rural-urban migration provides an important mechanism for transmitting urban growth to the rural areas. Central provinces bordering the booming coastal provinces (Anhui, Jiangxi, Hubei, and Hunan) especially benefit from an increase in rural-urban migration.

A second exception to the common use of a national-level analysis is a study by Huang, Li, and Rozelle (2003) analyzing the impact of WTO accession on farm households. They find that despite a small positive aggregate impact of the WTO, the distribution of benefits gives cause for concern. Households in richer coastal areas benefit most, having higher-yielding lands and cultivating internationally competitive crops. Another interesting finding of their household-level analysis is an increase in aggregate agricultural production, despite a decrease in the agricultural price index. Farmers respond to the changes in relative prices induced by the WTO by shifting to more competitive activities (livestock, fish, vegetables, and rice), resulting in a net increase in agricultural production. These two studies show that a disaggregated analysis of the impact of trade reform yields insights that diverge from insights gained at the national level. The objective of this chapter is to contribute a village-level perspective on trade reform in China. Adjustment responses of different household types and within-village interactions are central to this analysis. This study complements earlier studies by concentrating on the differential impact of trade liberalization on households within a village. A new methodology that accounts for family-farm production specifics in a village-economy setting provides a unique perspective on the impact of trade reform. Going beyond the household-level study of Huang, Li, and Rozelle (2003), the analysis in this chapter also takes account of the impact of farm income on rural household consumption, as well as the impact of rural-urban migration, thereby extending the household analysis beyond developments in the agricultural sector.

This study combines a macro-level analysis of trade reform with a village-level general equilibrium model of a rice-producing village in Jiangxi province. To be able to combine the macro- and village-level analyses of trade reform, it is necessary to ascertain how trade reform affects households. Prices and labor demand form the key transmission mechanisms through which macro-level trade reform affects rural households (Winters 2002). Thus, the focus is on changes in prices for consumed goods, agricultural inputs and outputs, and the increased demand for labor by labor-intensive sectors in which China has a comparative advantage.

This analysis of further trade reform builds on a baseline that encompasses China's recent WTO accession, phasing out of the export quota for textiles under the Agreement on Textiles and Clothing. This chapter draws on the global results from chapter 3 for an assessment of the macro-level impacts of further reform under the Doha Round and feed these into the village-level model. Specifically, the impacts of the standard Doha scenario described in chapter 2, as well as of the full-liberalization scenario, are simulated. In both cases, the effects of changing prices for inputs and outputs from the effects of increases in off-farm employment and wages are disentangled.

The full-liberalization scenario provides a useful benchmark against which the less ambitious Doha scenario can be compared. Analysis of consumption reveals that the poorer households face a stronger rise in expenditures. This is due to a larger share of agricultural goods in their consumption and a shift from being net sellers to self-sufficiency in the case of some households.

Analysis of the impact of changes in agricultural input and output prices (with unchanging employment and wages) shows an increased village supply of rice and other livestock, which corresponds to the findings of national-level studies and the results of the farm household analysis in Huang, Li, and Rozelle (2003). This increased supply of rice, however, is the net result of three household groups increasing rice production and one group reducing rice production.

The net impact of more off-farm employment (at constant prices) after global trade reform is a decrease in rice supply caused by an increasing scarcity of labor. Again, there are divergent household responses, with some households increasing rice production because of lower costs of animal traction rented within the village. Because this is opposite in sign to the impact of higher prices, it is interesting to ask which dominates. The analysis presented here shows that the impact of price changes thus dominates the impact of increased employment.

A more modest liberalization within the context of the Doha Round has a similar, but less pronounced, impact to that observed under full trade liberalization. The notable exception is the village rice economy. Under the full-liberalization scenario used in this chapter, rice production becomes more intensive in land and labor, and village-marketed surplus increases.

A Household Perspective on General Equilibrium Modeling

A disaggregated perspective can lead to new insights in the impact of trade reform. Separating farm production decisions from household consumption decisions is standard practice in general equilibrium models, both macro as well as existing village general equilibrium models. Ignoring the interdependency of household production and consumption decisions, however, can be misleading when market imperfections render these two aspects of household decisions nonseparable.

Nonseparability of household production and consumption decisions occurs when the effective price of a commodity used in both production and consumption is not exogenous to the household but determined endogenously by household demand and supply. In this case, production decisions will affect supply of the commodity, which affects its shadow price and hence consumption decisions, and vice versa. Such nonseparability occurs if households are not price takers in a market, if markets are missing, or if there is a gap between buying and selling prices (Löfgren and Robinson 1999). The seminal work of de Janvry, Fafchamps, and Sadoulet (1991) shows how rational behavior of farmers in combination with market failures may give rise to sluggish or counterintuitive household responses.

A number of points are essential to farm household modeling. First, standard economic rules for production and consumption remain valid. Differences with a separate analysis of production and consumption decisions occur because of endogenous prices, not because of different behavior by the household. Consequently, standard approaches to modeling production and consumption decisions can be followed. But endogenous household prices complicate empirical work. The endogenous household shadow prices are an analytical construct and thus cannot be directly observed. This complicates the estimation of demand and supply functions for nonseparable household models.

Second, household models tend to generate ambiguous results and quickly become analytically intractable. Ambiguous results may already occur with perfect markets. Assume that prices for food increase. This will increase food production and thus household income. The higher income prompts an increase in consumption, which may outweigh the increase in food production, depending on the preferences of the household. The food price increase then does not lead to an unequivocal increase in marketed surplus. In fact, if the income effect is strong enough, sales by the household will actually fall. Thus, in those cases where an analytical solution of the household model can be obtained, it will generally be difficult to sign the effects because of counteracting effects on the production and consumption sides of the household. Models with multiple missing markets complicate things even more.

A third point about household modeling is the importance of accounting for different levels of market integration of households from a policy perspective, as can be illustrated with a price band model (figure 8.1). Starting from an exogenous market price, transaction costs increase the effective purchase price and decrease the effective sales price faced by the household. Household demand and supply then determine the household-specific shadow price of the commodity, with effective purchase and sales prices forming upper and lower boundaries. Figure 8.1 shows the supply curve for three different types of households. Depending on the intersection of the demand and supply curve, a household is (a) a net buyer, (b) self-sufficient, or (c) a net seller of the commodity. If the household is a net buyer or seller, the household shadow price equals the effective purchase or sales price. If the household is self-sufficient (case b), the household shadow price is endogenously determined within the price band and decisions become nonseparable. A missing market can be conceptualized in this model as a wide price band (in the most extreme case, a sales price of zero and an infinite purchase price) such that all households always operate within it.

Household response then consists of two decisions a discrete decision on market position, determining their position as net buyer, net seller, or not participating, and a continuous decision on production and consumption levels, determining supply response. The position of the household in the market determines the effective decision-making prices for the second decision. Net buyers will respond

Figure 8.1.   Household Supply Response with Price Bands

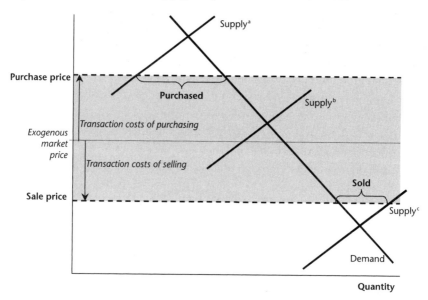

Source: Adapted from Sadoulet and de Janvry (1995).
a. Supply of a net buyer.
b. Supply of a self-sufficient household.
c. Supply of a net seller.

differently to a price increase from net sellers, and households operating within their price band will not show any response to the price change. The position of the household in the market thus has an important impact on the household response to price incentives.

Nonseparability has become an important feature of household models, but it is absent from AGE models. A study by Löfgren and Robinson (1999) provides a stylized application of including farm-household models in a general equilibrium model, but this approach has not previously been implemented in an empirical analysis.

Given the recent transformations in China, markets are still developing and imperfections can be expected to abound. Studies of factors influencing migration decisions (Hare 1999; Murphy 2000; Rozelle and others 1999; Rozelle, Taylor, and de Brauw 1999) and of patterns in inequality (Benjamin and Brandt 1999) refer to imperfect land, labor, and credit markets as being relevant in the Chinese context. Such a partial integration in markets may give rise to nonseparability of household decisions or may create (thin) local markets through which household decisions affect each other.

If households interact with each other in local village markets, and these markets are not integrated with markets outside the village, local general equilibrium effects occur. Studies of market integration in China find villages to be integrated in markets for major outputs (Huang, Li, and Rozelle 2003) and for fertilizer (Qiao and others 2003). Although villages may thus be assumed to be integrated into agricultural input and output markets, integration of factor markets is still limited. Labor markets are highly segmented (Gilbert and Wahl 2003), resulting in a rural labor surplus (Cook 1999), which is only partly absorbed in township-village enterprises. The local village labor markets are limited in rural areas, including the labor market in this chapter's case study village in Jiangxi province. A prime reason for limited development of a rural labor market is the collective ownership of land, which grants all households access to land. Consequently, there are no landless households that would specialize in wage-earning activities and hence little scope for local labor markets.

In spite of land tenure reforms that have granted household user rights for 30 years (and which were recently changed to permit inheritance), land rights remain ambiguous (Huang and Rozelle 2004). Land is allocated on the basis of demographic criteria, and readjustments occur to adjust for changes in household size, despite formal household user rights. The result is an ambiguous land tenure situation (Ho 2001) in which households have an incentive to keep their land cultivated to avoid losing it during the next readjustment. Households that migrate to urban areas rent their land to other local households, seeking to maintain their claim to the land in case they are unable to secure a living in the urban areas. Given the ambiguity of land tenure, land rental markets are inherently local in nature.

Village interactions may also arise through informal credit markets. Government intervention in the formal banking sector remains strong. Regulated interest rates are well below market clearing levels, and soft loans to state enterprises seize a large share of available funds. Rural households are thus rationed out of credit markets. In the late 1980s, rural cooperative funds developed, targeted at rural households. These funds proved to be too successful competitors with existing rural credit cooperatives, and they were dissolved in 1999 (Park, Brandt, and Giles 2003). As a result of the lack of formal credit options, households have to rely on local, informal credit markets. This study therefore uses a village-level general equilibrium model to account for the interactions among households in the local markets for land and capital, while paying due attention to nonseparability of household decisions flowing from the presence of significant transaction costs.

Taylor and Adelman (1996; 2003) pioneered the use of general equilibrium models at the village level. Their model closely follows the structure of macro-level models—for example, by modeling production at the sector level, which misses the impact of nonseparability of household decisions. This chapter takes a different approach to village modeling, placing differences in household response due to nonseparability at the center of the model. This household perspective on general equilibrium modeling results in a model structure different from that used in macro-level general equilibrium models and existing village-level models. In this chapter, production activities are modeled as being household specific. This allows for idiosyncratic household responses consistent with nonseparability of production and consumption decisions. A second major difference is the nesting structure used for modeling production decisions. For each activity, the production structure is calibrated based on the household survey data.[1] As a result, there are household-specific production functions capturing differences in household access to inputs.[2]

By placing households at the center of the model, the village model used in this study is able to capture differences in production decisions reflecting differences in access to inputs, interactions between household production and consumption decisions, and interactions among different households within a village economy.

Models and Data

Linking Macro Results to the Village Model

This chapter analyzes the village-level impact of the two liberalization scenarios discussed in part 1 of this book: full trade liberalization and a Doha Round scenario. Because the Chinese economy is not modeled at the national level, the Global Trade Analysis Project (GTAP) results used in this chapter are those that include China's tariff cuts as well as liberalization in the rest of the world (recall chapter 3).

To link the macro shocks for China to the village model, this chapter follows the conceptual framework of Winters (2002) and focus on prices and labor demand. Studies of market integration of three main staple crops and fertilizer (Huang, Li, and Rozelle, 2003; Qiao and others 2003) show integrated regional and national markets, with village-level prices responding to changes at the national level. These integrated commodity markets allow direct translation of relative price changes derived from the macro-level analysis to the village level.

In addition to the transmission of price changes, this chapter analyzes the impact of changes in employment opportunities. Studies of trade liberalization find an expansion of labor-intensive sectors in which China has a comparative advantage. Thus there is a need to link aggregate expansion of employment to village-level changes in temporary migration to urban areas. Lacking data to quantify the link between national-level changes in employment and household decisions, percentage changes in aggregate labor demand are assumed to be completely transmitted to the village. Percentage changes in outside village employment are thus set equal to changes in aggregate labor demand. Such a one-on-one relation between national-level employment and off-farm activities of the households in the case study village seems justified, given the findings in Diao, Fan, and Zhang (2003). Comparing the change in rural-urban migration across regions after WTO accession, they find the fastest increase in rural-urban migration in the central provinces. The case study village is located in Jiangxi, one of these central provinces, and migration outside the province plays an important role in the village economy, justifying the assumption of a complete transmission of the demand for labor to the village level. (The case study village is more thoroughly described below.)

Similarly, changes in outside-village wages and changes in nonagricultural wages are taken from the GTAP simulations. As will be seen below, the rural-urban wage differential is endogenously determined through modeling of household-specific shadow wages. Mapping macro-level changes computed with the GTAP model to the village level results in the shocks summarized in table 8.1.

The Case Study Village

The case study village has been selected to be representative of rice-producing villages in the plains area of Jiangxi province, one of the poorer provinces in China. Data on production and consumption of 168 households were collected for 2000, using standard household questionnaires with questions on source and destination of commodities added to allow construction of a village social accounting matrix (SAM). These surveyed households account for about a quarter of the village population, totaling 729 households.

Differences among households are at the center of the village equilibrium model. Four groups of households are distinguished, using ownership of draft power (cattle or tractor) and access to extraprovince employment as grouping criteria. The resulting groups represent households with differential capacity for earning a living from agriculture and from (transitory) migration to coastal cities.

The upper part of table 8.2 presents the activities of each household type in terms of contribution to value added. In the first column for the unlinked households with no draft power, it can be seen that crops are the dominant source of farm value added. One-season rice contributes 9.4 percent to value added, and the more intensive two-season rice contributes as much as 28.5 percent. Other crops, such as vegetables, contribute another 21.2 percent to household value added. The share of livestock is rather limited, with pigs and other livestock each contributing 0.1 percent. For this household group, the total contribution of agricultural activities to value added is 59.2 percent, and the remainder is coming

Table 8.1. Shocks Administered to Village Model (% change with respect to base)

	Full liberalization		Doha Scenario	
	Prices (scenario A)	Employment (scenario B)	Prices (scenario A)	Employment (scenario B)
Agricultural outputs				
One-season rice	7.4	n.a.	1.3	n.a.
Two-season rice	7.4	n.a.	1.3	n.a.
Other crops	4.1	n.a.	1.1	n.a.
Pigs	5.0	n.a.	1.3	n.a.
Other livestock	5.0	n.a.	1.3	n.a.
Agricultural inputs				
Fertilizer	0.6	n.a.	0.2	n.a.
Herbicides	0.6	n.a.	0.2	n.a.
Pesticides	0.6	n.a.	0.2	n.a.
Seed	5.1	n.a.	1.3	n.a.
Purchased feed	5.1	n.a.	1.3	n.a.
Other inputs	0.9	n.a.	0.3	n.a.
Consumption goods				
Food	3.3	n.a.	0.9	n.a.
Processed food	3.3	n.a.	0.9	n.a.
Nonfood	1.8	n.a.	0.6	n.a.
Durables	0.0	n.a.	0.0	n.a.
Other expenditures	1.8	n.a.	0.6	n.a.
Wages				
Nonagricultural employment	n.a.	2.2	n.a.	0.7
Migration, inside province	n.a.	2.2	n.a.	0.7
Migration, outside province	n.a.	0.6	n.a.	0.3
Outside-village employment				
Nonagricultural employment	n.a.	1.8	n.a.	1.5
Migration, inside province	n.a.	1.8	n.a.	1.5
Migration, outside province	n.a.	2.2	n.a.	1.9

Source: Authors' simulations

Note: n.a. = not applicable under this scenario. Each of the complete liberalization experiments applies a combined shock of prices and employment (that is, scenario A + scenario B = complete liberalization – either Full Liberalization or Doha).

from engaging in off-farm activities. Hiring out its labor to other villagers contributes 1.3 percent to value added, and working in local businesses earns 19.4 percent of value added. Outside-village employment is a significant income source for this household group, with a share of 18.1 percent. For this unlinked household, migration opportunities are restricted to moving inside the province, which contributes 1.8 percent of value added.

For all household types, off-farm employment contributes a significant share of income, but there are important differences in the nature of nonagricultural income sources. Comparison of the two household groups that have no link outside the province shows that households lacking draft power are oriented more toward local off-farm employment. The households with draft power obtain 71.4 percent of value added from agriculture, which is similar to the importance of agriculture for the other household group owning draft power. The household group with access to migration but lacking draft power derives about 40 percent of value added from outside-province migration and derives only about 45 percent of value added from agricultural activities. Differential access to agricultural and migration opportunities is thus reflected in the composition of household value added.

Differences in activities result in differences in income patterns across the four household groups. The bottom part of table 8.2 presents income per adult consumer equivalent[3] to allow a direct comparison across households. As a crude poverty assessment for each household group, available income is computed in terms of U.S. dollars per day. Three of the household groups fall in between the one dollar and two dollars per day poverty lines. The notable exception is the household group with an outside link and lacking draft power, with just over two dollars per day. This is in line with the rural-urban income differences because this household group specializes in outside-province migration.

To get a clear view of differences in household endowments that affect household response, the middle part of table 8.2 details income sources. Specific features of the village social accounting matrix (SAM) and equilibrium model arise in this table. For example, income from labor and irrigated land is split between shadow income[4] and above shadow income. The household survey data reveal imperfect labor and land markets. Households are involved in a variety of off-farm activities with different wages. These wages are well above the estimated shadow wage, indicating restricted access to off-farm employment and suggesting a situation of labor surplus at the local level. This is not unexpected, given the high population density in rural China and similar findings in a study by Bowlus and Sicular (2003).

Table 8.2.   Activities and Income by Household Group

Link outside province:	No link		Link		
Owning draft power:	No	Yes	No	Yes	Village
N =	78	100	256	295	729
Composition of activities (% value added)					
Agriculture					
One-season rice	9.4	10.8	8.2	10.5	9.5
Two-season rice	28.5	28.2	18.6	27.1	23.9
Other crops	21.2	24.7	18.4	22.4	20.9
Cattle	n.a.	7.5	n.a.	8.1	4.1
Pigs	0.1	0.1	0.2	0.4	0.3
Other livestock	0.1	0.1	0.0	0.0	0.0
Village employment					
Agricultural labor	1.3	2.2	n.a.	0.1	0.4
Local business	19.4	13.5	2.4	2.7	5.2
Outside village					
Outside employment	18.0	12.9	9.1	5.4	8.9
Migration					
Inside province	2.1	n.a.	4.2	0.9	2.3
Outside province	n.a.	n.a.	38.8	22.3	24.6
	100	100	100	100	100
Sources of household income (% total income)					
Labor					
Shadow wage income	57.4	52.8	52.6	62.1	57.4
Above shadow wage income	17.5	12.3	23.3	6.0	13.5
Land					
Irrigated land shadow income	12.4	13.3	12.8	11.4	12.1
Irrigated land, above shadow income	4.8	6.5	1.4	4.5	3.7
Nonirrigated land	7.3	7.9	7.7	6.6	7.2
Capital					
Cattle	n.a.	3.3	n.a.	3.1	1.8
Tractor	n.a.	1.6	n.a.	0.8	0.6
Transfer					
Within-village transfers	0.6	0.3	0.01	0.5	0.3
Receipts from outside the village	0.0	1.9	2.2	5.0	3.3
	100	100	100	100	100
Income per adult consumer equivalent					
Annual income in 1,000 yuan (Y)	2.2	2.3	3.0	2.7	2.7
Income in U.S. dollars per day	1.5	1.6	2.1	1.9	1.8

Source: Authors' simulations.

Note: n.a. = not applicable. The household is not involved in this activity.

In the SAM and village equilibrium model, the demand-constrained labor market is accounted for by valuing labor against household-specific shadow wages, estimated using the household survey data. In the case of off-farm activities, labor then earns revenue above the shadow wage, which is tracked in a separate account of the SAM. For example, for the unlinked households with no draft power, labor is the most important endowment, contributing 74.9 percent to its income, broken down into 57.4 percent coming from shadow wages and 17.5 percent from above shadow wages.

Although there is a rental market of sorts for irrigated land (paddy fields), the village model does not include a land market. Analysis of the village trade in land showed that all four household groups are net renters of land. This is due to a bias in the surveyed sample of households, which excludes households that have migrated from the village. These households are renting out land for a price below its productive value. This difference can be interpreted as an insurance premium the households are willing to pay to maintain access to their land, which is collectively owned, in case they need to return to the village. The households remaining in the village thus get an indirect transfer of money from the migration of entire households, through having to pay less than the productive value for land rented. Analysis of the migration of entire households is beyond the scope of this chapter's model. Therefore the supply of land is fixed at the level observed in the SAM, effectively removing the land market from the model. Taking again the example of the unlinked households with no draft power, the return earned on irrigated land endowment contributes 17.2 percent to its income, broken down into a shadow rent component of 12.4 percent and the above shadow rent component of 4.8 percent. This above shadow rental income results from renting in land at a price below its marginal production value from migrant households. Nonirrigated land contributes another 7.3 percent to the household income.

A last remark on the village SAM pertains to the lack of data for modeling capital flows in the village. The SAM shows that the household group most involved in migration is a net supplier of capital to the other three groups of households. Although the survey contains some data on the conditions in which such funds are loaned, insufficient information is available to model a village-level capital market. It is therefore assumed that the household group lacking draft power but having an outside link spends a fixed share of its income on within-village transfers. These transfers are allocated to the three household groups based on their share of transfers in the SAM. The model thus includes a rather simple mechanism through which the income from migration is transmitted through village linkages.

To summarize: this chapter analyzes the response of four different types of households, distinguished on the basis of their access to agricultural income and income from outside-province migration. Analyzing sources of income pointed to imperfect labor and land markets. These are accommodated by estimating household-specific shadow prices, introducing profits earned from off-farm employment and renting of land, and modeling household production and consumption decisions as nonseparable.

The Village Equilibrium Model

Despite introducing nonseparability of household production and consumption decisions, the mathematical structure of the model closely resembles macro-level general equilibrium models. Consumption decisions are modeled through a linear expenditure system, and production is modeled by nested constant elasticity of substitution (CES) functions. Table 8.3 summarizes the key substitution elasticities for each activity. The estimation procedure for obtaining these substitution elasticities exploits the interhousehold variation in the survey data. The nesting structure differs across activities and is determined by statistical testing based on pairwise comparisons. Kuiper (2005) provides full details of this method.

The village model does not attempt to treat two-way flows of commodity trade with the outside world. Households consume farm output but do not purchase these goods from outside the village or other households in the village. Household sales to outside-village markets are thus equal to total production minus household consumption.

Village markets exist for traction by draft animals or tractors and locally produced consumption goods. Of these village markets, only animal traction has an endogenous village price in the model. The SAM indicates that only limited use is made of the tractors. This underuse of available tractors is therefore modeled through fixed prices for tractor services, the volume of which adjusts endogenously to demand.

Off-farm employment options were found to be restricted, resulting in wages exceeding the shadow price of labor. This is handled in the village equilibrium model by fixing the levels of outside-village employment and having households earn a profit above labor costs from off-farm activities. Levels of village employment (agricultural and nonagricultural) cannot be fixed, although for these activities, wages also exceed shadow wages. Agricultural employment is therefore assumed to be demand driven, with prices being exogenously fixed.[5] Demand for nonagricultural labor in the village economy is linked to local business activities, to which the chapter now turns.

Because of lack of data on other inputs, local business activities use only labor (village nonagricultural labor), yielding a return that exceeds the shadow wage. All households are involved in local business activities, and all of them purchase locally produced goods. This reflects a heterogeneity in goods not captured by the

**Table 8.3. Substitution Elasticities for Cropping Activities
(Village Average)**

	Land	Labor	Animal traction	Tractor	Other inputs
One-season rice					
Labor	0.39				
Animal traction	0.39	1.87			
Tractor	0.39	1.87	79.21		
Other inputs	1.72	2.09	2.09	2.09	1.84
Two-season rice					
Labor	0.66				
Animal traction	0.66	0.66			
Tractor	0.66	0.66	53.65		
Other inputs	0.98	0.98	0.98	0.98	1.35
Other crops					
Labor	0.33				
Animal traction	0.33	2.88			
Tractor	n.a.	n.a.	n.a.		
Other inputs	0.57	1.41	1.41	n.a.	1.06

	Labor	Crop residues	Purchased feed
Pigs			
Crop residues	1.53		
Purchased feed	1.53	1.53	
Other inputs	1.53	1.53	1.49
Other livestock			
Crop residues	0.87		
Purchased feed	0.87	0.87	
Other inputs	0.87	0.87	0.87

Source: Kuiper (2005).

Note: n.a. = not applicable. Elasticities as well as the structure of the production functions are calibrated with the survey data. For details, see Kuiper (2005). Because of differences in cost shares, substitution elasticities vary slightly by household group.

aggregates used in the SAM and village model. Because of a lack of data, village prices of local goods are fixed to deal with the gap between product prices and costs of labor. Assuming fixed prices seems justified, because prices of village-produced goods are common knowledge, and shadow wages cannot be observed. Given the unobservable character of shadow wages, it seems unlikely that a change in labor costs will be reflected by a change in the village price. A second reason for fixing prices of local business activities is the absence of a peak season. Production can therefore be shifted to times when little labor is needed in agriculture, limiting the need to increase the price when shadow wages increase.

For all demand-driven activities (local consumption goods, hired agricultural labor, tractor services), market equilibrium is established by allocating demand to suppliers based on the initial market shares recorded in the SAM.

Finally, all surveyed households are net sellers of agricultural production—that is, they begin in regime 3 of figure 8.1. The simulations may result in a regime change for households, possibly turning some household groups into net buyers. Lacking observations from the survey, this study uses an estimate of transaction costs for rice from Park and others (2002) to set the width of the price band at 25 percent of the selling price. Thus, households will become net buyers if their shadow price rises 25 percent above the initial selling price.

Thus, to summarize, the village equilibrium model resembles macro-level general equilibrium models (of the sort used throughout this book) in the way in which consumption and production are modeled. A major difference with macro- and existing village-level models is household-specific production, which is affected by household consumption decisions through endogenous household shadow prices. Lack of data resulted in most village markets being modeled as fixed-price, demand-driven equilibria. The only exception is the village market for animal traction, which is balanced through an endogenous village price. Household production and consumption decisions are calibrated on the household survey data, resulting in household-specific demand and supply functions.

Full Liberalization Impacts

There are two major pathways through which trade liberalization affects households: changes in prices of consumed goods, agricultural inputs and outputs, and changes in off-farm employment and wages. This section first analyzes each of these two pathways separately before looking at the combined impact of the full-liberalization scenario.

The Impact of Price Changes with Full Liberalization

The discussion of price changes focuses on the changes in production. Prices of consumption goods increase as the overseas demand for China's products increases strongly and the country experiences a real appreciation (recall chapter 3). The price increases in agricultural output, however, outstrip the increased cost of consumption. More important, whereas households have limited opportunities to change their consumption patterns, they have much more flexibility in changing their mix of production.

With full liberalization, all household groups increase other livestock production, and three of four intensify rice production and shift toward two-season rice (table 8.4). Two forces account for these shifts in production. First, livestock production is cash constrained because of the absence of a credit market. The rise in output prices increases the availability of cash for all households, resulting in an expansion of previously constrained livestock production. The switch to other livestock instead of pigs is due to differences in input use. Pig production uses purchased feed, which experiences a strong price increase of 4.1 percent; external inputs used in other livestock production increase by only 0.4 percent, which is well below the rise in output prices.

The second driving force behind the shift in production patterns is the increase in rice prices, making more intensive rice production attractive. Rice production can be intensified by switching from one-season to two-season rice, thus doubling the use of the available irrigated land. Having two cropping

Table 8.4. Household Production and Marketed Surplus with Full-Liberalization Scenario A (exogenous increase in prices for outputs, inputs and consumption) (percentage change)

Link outside province:	No link		Link		
Owning draft power:	No	Yes	No	Yes	Village
Production					
Crops					
One-season rice	-18.8	90.3	-46.6	-67.4	-31.8
Two-season rice	8.5	-32.5	23.6	32.7	17.3
Other crops	-1.1	-1.9	0.0	-1.7	-1.1
Livestock					
Pig production	-31.1	-83.8	-5.2	-24.6	-22.9
Other livestock	432.1	3093.4	56.5	367.6	650.0
Marketed surplus					
Crops					
One-season rice	-39.5	125.6	-90.6	-100.0	-52.4
Two-season rice	19.4	-100.0	68.0	91.7	45.4
Other crops	-72.7	-36.4	0.4	-23.0	-16.1
Livestock					
Pig production	-32.9	-100.0	-5.8	-38.6	-27.9
Other livestock	946.4	6539.5	207.1	1187.0	1923.5

Source: Authors' simulations.

seasons strongly increases the demand for labor, which explains the opposite production response of the household group with draft power but lacking an outside link. This household starts to rent out draft power and invests the proceeds in intensive (other) livestock production, and it reallocates labor from two-season rice production toward intensive livestock production. It ceases to be a seller of two-season rice and pigs, moving into regime 2 in figure 8.1. It almost becomes a buyer of pigs, with its household-specific price for pigs rising by 21 percent, but this price rise falls just within the 25 percent price band, and hence it does not yet become a buyer. Similarly, the fourth household in table 8.4 ceases to sell one-season rice.

To summarize, changes in agricultural input and output prices increase the availability of cash, allowing an expansion of previously constrained livestock production. It further leads to an intensification of rice production for those household groups that have sufficient labor resources.

The Household as a Supplier of Labor: The Impact of Increasing Off-Farm Employment

Off-farm employment is an important source of income. For the village as a whole, 41 percent of income is generated from off-farm sources, both inside the village in local business activities and outside the village and even from employment outside the province. For the household lacking draft power but having an outside link, for example, migration accounts for close to 40 percent of value added. An increase in off-farm employment opportunities is simulated in full-liberalization scenario B through rising wages and increased employment demand. To clarify the impact of this second pathway through which trade liberalization affects households, the analysis next abstracts from the price changes of inputs and outputs associated with full liberalization.

Of course, per capita consumption is increased by the additional income. This holds especially for the households involved in migration, because the number of household members present in the village decreases. This also leaves more income for the remaining household members.

Increased off-farm employment decreases the available agricultural labor force, which leads to less labor-intensive agricultural production for three of the household groups, resulting in a slight decrease of two-season rice and a marked increase of other livestock production (table 8.5). The driving force behind this response is the village market for animal draft services. With "linked" households moving to one-season rice, demand for animal traction is reduced and its price falls. This means that the renting in of draft power becomes cheaper for the household group with no animal traction and no outside employment.

Table 8.5. Household Production and Marketed Surplus with Full-Liberalization Scenario B (exogenous increase in off-farm employment) (percentage change)

Link outside province:	No link		Link		
Owning draft power:	No	Yes	No	Yes	Village
Production					
Crops					
One-season rice	-1.4	-0.3	1.2	37.2	17.3
Two-season rice	0.3	0.2	-0.4	-16.2	-7.7
Other crops	-0.1	-0.1	-0.3	-0.1	-0.1
Livestock					
Pig production	1.0	1.9	1.3	-1.6	0.5
Other livestock	-15.4	-47.0	-9.4	52.4	4.0
Marketed surplus					
Crops					
One-season rice	-3.7	-0.6	2.4	54.6	27.9
Two-season rice	-0.3	-0.1	-1.2	-47.9	-22.1
Other crops	-17.6	-1.8	-1.1	-0.8	-1.3
Livestock					
Pig production	1.0	2.2	1.4	-2.5	0.6
Other livestock	-34.7	-100.0	-34.4	169.9	11.6

Source: Authors' simulations.

The third household receives about 40 percent of its income from migrant labor. It responds to the employment opportunities generated by full liberalization by shifting resources out of agriculture and concentrating more on off-farm employment. It does, however, keep some rice production and pigs. Pig production uses less labor than other livestock and is thus a more attractive option with increasing shadow wages resulting from a rise in off-farm employment.

The driving forces behind the diverging response of the fourth household group, those owning draft power and having a link outside the province, are endowments of labor and access to migration. The access to migration outside the province provides an important source of cash, just as it does for the other household group with an outside link. The fourth household, however, has the largest labor endowment of all households, and this tempers the rise in its shadow wages. As a result, the labor and cash-intensive other livestock production is more attractive than pig production for this one household group.

It is interesting that the second household, with no outside link but with ownership of draft power, chooses to stop selling other livestock. Its shadow price of other livestock rises just above the market price, and it becomes more attractive to use the output for own-consumption.

To summarize the results in this section, an increase in off-farm employment reduces the agricultural labor force. Although the wage hike encourages a switch toward less labor-intensive pig production on the part of some households, the village as a whole shows little change in pig production, but a large increase in other livestock production.

Combining Price and Employment Effects

The above discussion shows that price effects of liberalization may move opposite to the effects of improved off-farm employment opportunities, depending on the initial household endowments and their links with the economy outside the village. The combined effect is summarized in table 8.6.

At the village level, price and employment changes have an opposite impact on rice and pigs exported from the village. Where rising output prices promote rice

Table 8.6. Household Production and Marketed Surplus with the Full-Liberalization Scenario[a]

| Link outside province: | No link | | Link | | Village |
Owning draft power:	No	Yes	No	Yes	average
Production					
Crops					
One-season rice	-22.8	90.7	-42.0	-45.0	-20.4
Two-season rice	9.7	-32.1	21.5	23.0	12.3
Other crops	-1.2	-2.1	-0.2	-1.5	-1.1
Livestock					
Pig production	-30.5	-83.7	-4.2	-22.8	-21.8
Other livestock	419.8	3088.5	48.0	360.3	642.0
Marketed surplus					
Crops					
One-season rice	-48.5	125.9	-81.6	-67.5	-34.1
Two-season rice	21.2	-100.0	62.0	61.9	30.5
Other crops	-91.3	-40.1	-0.6	-23.8	-17.7
Livestock					
Pig production	-32.3	-100.0	-4.7	-36.2	-26.7
Other livestock	918.6	6528.3	175.9	1162.1	1898.9

Source: Authors' simulations.

a. Full-liberalization scenario = exogenous changes in prices (A) and exogenous increase in off-farm employment (B).

and other livestock production, increasing off-farm employment opportunities tend to reduce the marketed surplus of labor-intensive agricultural output. When these two elements of the full-liberalization scenario are combined, the price effects dominate and the result is a more labor-intensive package of outputs. The net effect is a marked 37 percent rise in village-marketed surplus, mainly driven by expansion of other livestock production. To put this huge increase in perspective, it is important to be aware that the contribution of this commodity to the village's marketed surplus is just 2 percent in the base, whereas it becomes 29 percent in the wake of full liberalization. The other important surplus commodity is two-season rice, which contributes 62 percent of the village-marketed surplus in the base and still accounts for 50 percent in the full-liberalization scenario.

Doha Impacts

Having established the maximum potential impacts of trade reform on this village economy, the analysis now turns to the Doha scenario as outlined in chapters 2 and 3. The second set of bars in figure 8.2 summarizes production responses at the village level. For pig production and other livestock, the Doha scenario produces a less pronounced response than the full-liberalization scenario. This is to be

Figure 8.2. Village Production Response under Alternative Liberalization Scenarios

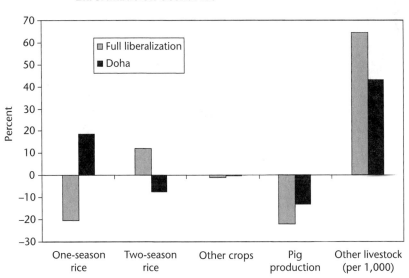

Source: Authors' simulations.

expected, because the exogenous price shocks are smaller under Doha. But in both cases, pig production decreases and other livestock production increases remarkably (note that changes in other livestock production are expressed as per 1,000 instead of per 100 for expositional clarity).

For rice production, a more interesting aggregate response emerges. Under the full-liberalization scenario, rice production becomes more labor- and land-intensive, with an increase in two-season rice and a decrease in one-season rice. This is due to the combined effect of households three and four moving into more intensive rice production in response to rising prices (table 8.6) while household two specializes in renting out traction power and consequently has to switch to less intensive own–rice production.

Under the Doha scenario, however, there is a de-intensification of rice production in the village and a drop in aggregate rice output. Rice prices do not increase enough and shadow wages do not rise enough to induce the "linked" households to specialize in more labor-intensive forms of farming. For these linked households, economic developments outside the village are paramount. Those linked households without draft power are the most engaged in outside-province migration and are already able to realize substantial gains from the more modest Doha scenario by seizing the improved employment opportunities.

Impacts on Inequality

Growing income inequalities are now at the top of the policy agenda in China. The rural-urban income inequalities are transmitted to the village by asymmetric access to migration. The household group with the strongest involvement in migration also has the highest income per adult equivalent (see table 8.2). The increase in employment after trade liberalization may therefore be expected to increase within-village income inequality. The impact of an increase in agricultural output prices, however, may be expected to benefit the households owning draft power but lacking an outside link, because the activities of this household group are concentrated in agriculture.

Table 8.7 summarizes income effects in terms of equivalent variation per adult equivalent. The simulated income gains are substantial, with an average increase of income over base levels as high as 21 percent under the full-liberalization experiment. Under the Doha scenario, the income gains are reduced to about 5 percent as a result of the smaller price changes facing the village economy.

In both cases, above-average gains from price effects are observed for the household without an outside link but owning draft power. Under full liberalization, this household group gains Y 725 per adult equivalent—33 percent of its

Table 8.7. Equivalent Variation per Adult Equivalent by Household Group (in yuan) and as Percentage of Base Adult Equivalent Income

Link outside province:	No link		Link		Village
Owning draft power:	No	Yes	No	Yes	average
Full trade liberalization					
Prices	378	752	199	601	465
	17%	33%	7%	22%	17%
Employment	59	29	123	47	71
	3%	1%	4%	2%	3%
Prices and employment	441	806	321	702	563
	20%	35%	11%	26%	21%
Doha					
Prices	80	166	42	105	90
	4%	7%	1%	4%	3%
Employment	33	16	90	34	50
	1%	1%	3%	1%	2%
Prices and employment	121	168	131	133	136
	5%	7%	4%	5%	5%

Source: Authors' simulations.

Note: Y 1 ≈ US$0.25; adult equivalents are corrected for the absence of migrants.

base-level income per adult equivalent. Ownership of capital in the form of draft power is decisive for the relative size of the gains.

Most gains from increased employment opportunities fall on the households engaged in outside employment and not owning draft power. Under full liberalization, this amounts to Y 123, 4 percent of its base household income. Employment contributes 38 percent of the total gains under this scenario, and price changes contribute 62 percent (table 8.8). Under the more modest Doha scenarios, with limited price changes, the employment component contributes as much as 70 percent of the gains for this household group. In general terms, outside-village employment effects after trade liberalization indeed increase income inequality within the village, but the welfare gains from employment are substantially smaller than the gains from prices changes. Combining both effects, it can be noted that the rising income inequality may be compensated by gains from specialization for those who stay behind. The net effect on the within-village income distribution is determined by the interplay of initial endowments, village markets for inputs and outputs, and market imperfections. As a result, it appears that even poorer households begin to catch up. The households that have to rely on the use of own-labor on the household farm and are not endowed with traction power or a link to employment opportunities in the prospering coastal regions have fewer opportunities for adjustment. In fact, the only option for them is to farm rice more intensively and shift into labor-intensive other livestock production.

Conclusions

This study used an innovative village equilibrium model, which fully accounts for nonseparability of household production and consumption response. This allowed analysis of the impact of trade liberalization on agricultural supply response and off-farm employment, simultaneously accounting for household consumption decisions. The village model is used to analyze the impact of trade liberalization, which was quantified through macro-level shocks to the Chinese economy obtained from GTAP model simulations. The impact of price changes and labor demand, the two major pathways through which international trade affects households, were analyzed.

The full-liberalization benchmark shows results that are well in line with the findings of national-level studies and the results of the household analysis in Huang, Li, and Rozelle (2003). Analysis of the impact of changes in agricultural input and output prices shows an increased village supply of rice and livestock

Table 8.8.   Contribution of Price Changes and Employment to Income Gains

Link outside province:	No link		Link		Village
Owning draft power:	No (%)	Yes (%)	No (%)	Yes (%)	average (%)
Full trade liberalization					
Prices	86	93	62	86	83
Employment	13	4	38	7	13
Interaction effects	1	3	0	8	5
Total	100	100	100	100	100
Doha					
Prices	66	99	32	79	66
Employment	27	10	69	26	37
Interaction effects	7	-8	-1	-5	-3
Total	100	100	100	100	100

Source: Authors' simulations.

other than pigs. As the cash constraint is lifted in the wake of rising incomes after liberalization, the households invest the proceeds in the capital-intensive activity of livestock production. The increased supply of rice is the result of more complex interactions, however, because some household groups increase rice production and others reduce rice production.

Apart from influencing agricultural input and output prices, trade liberalization increases off-farm employment opportunities. The net impact of more off-farm employment is a decrease in rice supply, caused by an increasing scarcity of labor. Again, there is diverging household response, with some households increasing rice production as a result of lower costs of animal traction rented within the village.

Employment and migration leads to less intensive rice production and a drop in village-marketed surplus. Combined with the price effects from full liberalization, increases in rice surplus can be observed. This is interesting because one household specializes in renting out traction services to the households engaged in migrant employment and decreases its own rice production. In terms of the village supply response, the impact of the change in prices thus dominates the impact of increased employment.

The two pathways through which trade affects households thus have an opposite impact on household production response. Assessing the combined effect at the household level shows that the dominant aspect of trade liberalization depends on household endowments and production activities. Changes in intravillage specialization were observed, depending on the households' endowments and the strength of their linkages with the outside economy. It was also found that a strong involvement in off-farm employment does not necessarily imply that the employment aspect of trade liberalization dominates household response, thereby hampering ex ante judgments about the most relevant aspect of trade liberalization for a specific household type.

A more modest liberalization within the context of the Doha Round has a different impact on the village rice economy from that of full trade liberalization. The reason for this nonlinear response to increasing depth of trade reforms lies in the household-specific transaction (shadow) prices in combination with endogenous choices to participate in the output markets. Taking transaction costs into account, some households choose to withdraw from the market if their own shadow price is greater than the market price. Clearly, a partial reform scenario, such as Doha, leads to less pronounced output price changes than full liberalization.

Under the Doha scenario, average income gains amount to about 5 percent, but under full liberalization, the gains are four times as high. However, the impacts vary by household type, and the question arises whether such changes will reduce or exacerbate existing inequalities in China. Whether trade liberalization allows incomes to grow together or grow apart depends on whether one accounts for the reduction in consumption demand when household members migrate. Assessing the net effect on the within-village income distribution shows that even poorer households are able to catch up. The households that have to rely on the use of own-labor on the household farm and are not endowed with traction power or a link to employment opportunities in the prospering coastal regions have fewer opportunities for gains. Thus, although rural-urban migration can transfer benefits from economic growth in the coastal provinces to inland provinces, asymmetric access to migration implies that the rising rural-urban income differences are transferred as well.

Notes

1. The estimation in this chapter also rejected the commonly assumed separability of factors and intermediate inputs, and this assumption was therefore dropped in the village equilibrium model.

2. Detailed description of the village equilibrium model and calibration procedures can be obtained from the authors: Marijke.Kuiper@wur.nl.

3. Adult equivalent instead of per capita consumption is used to account for differences in consumption between males and females and between age groups. Lacking survey data, conversion factors were taken from detailed consumption data of a study in Bangladesh (Zeller and others 2001). In addition to differences in age and gender, consumer equivalents were corrected for the length of absence of household members due to temporary migration.

4. Nonseparability results in household-specific shadow prices that balance households' unobservable demand and supply. Therefore, an agricultural production function was estimated, explaining the total value of household output in terms of labor, land, manure, feed, and external inputs. The shadow prices are derived from this estimated production function as the marginal value product of each input. Specifically, for each household in the sample, the household-specific shadow prices for household nontradables are derived as the marginal value product of each input. Averaging over the households within a household group yields a shadow price for each household nontradable and each household group. These shadow prices are used in constructing the SAM and in calibrating the village equilibrium model.

5. Agricultural wages are in excess of shadow wages. Households are therefore always willing to supply additional agricultural labor when it is demanded.

References

Benjamin, D., and L. Brandt. 1999. "Markets and Inequality in Rural China: Parallels with the Past." *The American Economic Review* 89 (2): 292–95.

Bowlus, A. J., and T. Sicular. 2003. "Moving towards Markets? Labor Allocation in Rural China." *Journal of Development Economics* 71: 561–83.

Cook, S. 1999. "Surplus Labour and Productivity in Chinese Agriculture: Evidence from Household Survey Data." *The Journal of Development Studies* 35 (3): 16–44.

de Janvry, A., M. Fafchamps, and E. Sadoulet. 1991. "Peasant Household Behavior with Missing Markets: Some Paradoxes Explained." *Economic Journal* 101: 1400–17.

Démurger, S., J. D. Sachs, W. T. Woo, S. Bao, and G. Chang. 2002. "The Relative Contributions of Location and Preferential Policies in China's Regional Development: Being in the Right Place and Having the Right Incentives." *China Economic Review* 13: 444–65.

Diao, X., S. Fan, and X. Zhang. 2003. "China's WTO Accession: Impacts on Regional Agricultural Income—a Multi-Region, General Equilibrium Analysis." *Journal of Comparative Economics* 31: 332–51.

Gilbert, J., and T. Wahl. 2003. "Labor Market Distortions and China's WTO Accession Package: An Applied General Equilibrium Assessment." *Journal of Comparative Economics* 31: 774–94.

Hare, D. 1999. "'Push' versus 'Pull' Factors in Migration Outflows and Returns: Determinants of Migration Status and Spell Duration among China's Rural Population." *The Journal of Development Studies* 35 (3): 45–72.

Ho, P. 2001. "Who Owns China's Land? Policies, Property Rights, and Deliberate Institutional Ambiguity." *The China Quarterly* 166: 394–420.

Huang, J., N. Li, and S. Rozelle. 2003. "Trade Reform, Household Effects, and Poverty in Rural China." *American Journal of Agricultural Economics* 85 (5): 1292–98.

Huang, J., and S. Rozelle. 2004. "Agricultural Development and Policies in China." In *China's Food Economy in the Early 21st Century; Development of China's Food Economy and Its Impact on Global Trade and on the EU*, ed. F. W. van Tongeren and J. Huang, pp. 26–78. The Hague: Agricultural Economics Research Institute (LEI).

Jones, D. C., C. Li, and A. L. Owen. 2003. "Growth and Regional Inequality in China during the Reform Era." *China Economic Review* 14: 186–200. Jones *et al.*, 2003

Kuiper, M. 2005. "Village Modeling—a Chinese Recipe for Blending General Equilibrium and Household Modeling." Ph.D. diss., Wageningen University.

Löfgren, H., and S. Robinson. 1999. "Nonseparable Farm Household Decisions in a Computable General Equilibrium Model." *American Journal of Agricultural Economics* 81 (3): 663–70.

Murphy, R. 2000. "Migration and Inter-Household Inequality: Observations from Wanzai County, Jiangxi." *China Quarterly* 164: 965–82.

Park, A., L. Brandt, and J. Giles. 2003. "Competition under Credit Rationing: Theory and Evidence from Rural China." *Journal of Development Economics* 71 (2): 463–95.

Park, A., H. Jin, S. Rozelle, and J. Huang. 2002. "Market Emergence and Transition: Arbitrage, Transaction Costs, and Autarky in China's Grain Markets." *American Journal of Agricultural Economics* 84 (1): 67–82.

Qiao, F., B. Lohmar, J. Huang, S. Rozelle, and L. Zhang. 2003. "Producer Benefits from Input Market and Trade Liberalization: The Case of Fertilizer in China." *American Journal of Agricultural Economics* 85 (5): 1223–27.

Rozelle, S., L. Guo, M. Shen, A. Hughart, and J. Giles. 1999. "Leaving China's Farms: Survey Results of New Paths and Remaining Hurdles to Rural Migration." *China Quarterly* 158: 367–93.

Rozelle, S., J. E. Taylor, and A. de Brauw. 1999. "Migration, Remittances, and Agricultural Productivity in China." *The American Economic Review* 89 (2): 287–91.

Sadoulet, E., and A. de Janvry. 1995. *Quantitative Development Policy Analysis*. Baltimore and London: Johns Hopkins University Press.

Taylor, J. E., and I. Adelman. 1996. *Village Economies: The Design Estimation and Use of Villagewide Economic Models*. Cambridge: Cambridge University Press.

———. 2003. "Agricultural Household Models: Genesis, Evolution, and Extensions." *Review of Economics of the Household* 1: 33–58.

Winters, L. A. 2002. "Trade, Trade Policy and Poverty: What Are the Links?" *The World Economy* 25: 1339–67.

Zeller, M., M. Sharma, A. U. Ahmed, and S. Rashid. 2001. "Group Based Financial Institutions for the Rural Poor in Bangladesh. An Institutional and Household Level Analysis." Research Report 120, International Food Policy Research Institute, Washington, DC.

PART IV

A FOCUS ON
LABOR MARKETS

9

STRUCTURAL CHANGE AND POVERTY REDUCTION IN BRAZIL: THE IMPACT OF THE DOHA ROUND

*Maurizio Bussolo, Jann Lay, and
Dominique van der Mensbrugghe*

Summary

Over the medium time horizon, skill upgrading, intersectoral technological progress differentials, and migration of labor out of farming are some of the major structural adjustment factors shaping the evolution of an economy and its connected poverty trends. Our main focus is understanding, for the case of Brazil, how a trade shock interacts with these structural forces, and ascertaining whether it enhances or hinders medium term poverty reduction. A recursive-dynamic computable general equilibrium model simulates Doha scenarios and compares them against a Business as Usual scenario. The poverty effects are estimated using a microsimulation model that primarily takes into account individuals' labor supply decisions. Our analysis shows that trade liberalization does indeed contribute to *structural* poverty reduction. However, unless increased productivity and stronger growth rates are attributed to trade reform, its contribution to medium term poverty reduction is rather small.

Introduction

In their review of the relationship between trade liberalization and poverty, Winters, McCulloch, and McKay (2004) conclude that trade liberalization "may be

249

one of the most cost-effective anti-poverty policies available to governments" although they go on to note that it may not be the most powerful policy and its effectiveness is likely to vary substantially from case to case. In the medium- to long-run time horizon, economies adjust not only to trade policy reforms but also to many other changes, including technological progress, changes in the skill composition of the population, and varying consumption patterns. This chapter's main objective is to assess the role of trade liberalization in poverty reduction over a time horizon during which these other structural trends are operating. In particular, this chapter assesses the poverty impact of a Doha Round (and a full-liberalization) scenario on Brazil against a baseline scenario that incorporates some of the main features of medium-run structural change but no changes in trade policies.

Recent research has demonstrated that growth can differ tremendously in its potential to reduce poverty both across countries and over time.[1] In high-inequality countries such as Brazil, even a slight worsening of the income distribution can imply that growth has very little impact on poverty. Ascertaining how trade liberalization affects the pattern of income growth is therefore a core part of the analysis of the nexus of trade and poverty in the longer run. The labor market is a key factor determining such impacts. Both changes in relative factor prices and changes in endowments play an important role in the medium to long run.

Changes in sectoral employment can also contribute significantly to poverty reduction, because they may enable people to escape low-wage poverty traps. There is considerable evidence of the existence of such poverty traps that can arise in the presence of discrete occupational and technology choices and fixed costs (Barrett 2004). Moving out of agriculture—where poverty rates are often much higher than in other sectors—is one example of this type of occupational choice, and one of particular interest in the Brazilian context, where there has been a massive reduction in agricultural employment in recent years. This reduction in agricultural employment may have contributed to poverty reduction, because poverty rates among agricultural households are considerably higher than among nonagricultural households.

Trade liberalization is expected to favor agriculture in Brazil. By retaining workers in agriculture, it may thus work against the "natural" forces of structural change with an adverse impact on poverty reduction. However, trade liberalization may also relieve some of the pressure on nonagricultural incomes resulting from out-migration from agriculture as incomes in that sector rise. This ambiguity in the poverty impacts of trade reform illustrates the necessity of quantifying each of these transmission channels to evaluate the overall poverty and distributional impact of trade reform. The methodology used here combines a dynamic computable general equilibrium (CGE) model with a microsimulation (MS) model for Brazil. Using a time horizon of 15 years, a business-as-usual (BaU) scenario and two counterfactual trade reform scenarios are developed in the CGE model, and aggregate results on relative factor prices and resource movements from agricultural to nonagricultural sectors are linked to an MS. This macro-micro modeling framework enables analysis of the medium- to long-term poverty and distributional impact of different growth patterns.

The chapter is structured as follows. It begins by providing some background information on the Brazilian case and motivation for the chapter's approach. Then, the macro and micro modules of the model are described. The results of the simulations are reported and commented on in the following section. The last section summarizes and concludes.

Background and Motivation

The main objective of this chapter is to assess whether trade reform favors the Brazilian poor. It is therefore important to know who the poor are, where they live, and especially how they earn their living. In addition, it should prove helpful to identify economic trends that have been particularly important for the poor. Brazil's per capita income has remained stagnant for much of the past 25 years, and the very unequal distribution of income has remained more or less unchanged. Accordingly, poverty in Brazil has remained fairly constant over the past 25 years (Bourguignon, Ferreira, and Lustig 2005; Verner 2004). In light of the substantial structural changes that have occurred over this period, especially increasing urbanization, a massive decline in agricultural employment, increasing unemployment, educational expansion, and demographic changes, this outcome appears "paradoxical" in the words of Bourguignon, Ferreira, and Lustig (2005). Ferreira and Paes de Barros (2005) explore this apparent paradox using an MS approach and show that these various features of structural change have tended to offset one another when it comes to poverty and inequality impacts between the years 1976 and 1996.

Poverty in Brazil varies considerably among regions, rural and urban areas, and city sizes, with poverty rates being particularly high in rural areas, small and medium-size towns and the metropolitan peripheries of the north and northeast (Ferreira, Lanjouw, and Neri 2001). In 1996, the north and northeast accounted for 55 percent of the poor and 34 percent of the Brazilian population. At the national level, about 20 percent of the population lived in rural areas, contributing 35 percent of total poverty.[2] The high poverty rates in rural areas, particularly in the north and northeast, are related to the predominance of agricultural employment in these regions. The northeast had the highest share of agriculture in aggregate employment in 2001, with 34 percent compared to only 11.5 percent in the southeast.[3] According to Ferreira, Lanjouw, and Neri (2001), 20 percent of all households had a household head employed in agriculture, and these households contributed 34 percent to overall poverty in 1996.

Changes in poverty also differ widely across regions and activities. Verner's (2004) figures based on the Pesquisa Nacional por Amostragem de Domicílios (National Household Survey; PNAD)[4] suggest that the poverty headcount in the northeast declined from almost 60 percent in 1990 to 42.3 percent in 2001, whereas poverty in Brazil's most populous state, São Paulo, rose slightly, from 8.6 to 9.4 percent during the same period. For urban areas, Ferreira and Paes de Barros (2005) show that extreme poverty increased between 1976 and 1996. In contrast, Paes de Barros (2004) reports that the poverty incidence among both rural households and those households engaged in agricultural activities declined from levels of about 60 percent to about 50 percent between 1992 and 2001.

One important factor for understanding these developments is the structural change in Brazilian agriculture in the 1980s and 1990s. This has had a profound impact on both rural livelihoods and poverty in Brazil and living conditions in the urban areas through the migration of rural labor to the cities. With the exception of Paes de Barros (2004), research efforts in this direction, however, have focused on agricultural performance rather than on how this performance affects people's livelihoods.

In their assessment of the impact of sector-specific as well as economywide reforms on Brazilian agriculture, Helfand and Rezende (2004) conclude that agriculture became one of the most dynamic sectors in the Brazilian economy. Between 1980 and 1998, real GDP grew by about 40 percent and real agricultural output by about 70 percent. In many subsectors, agricultural yields increased significantly and the area devoted to export crops, in particular soybeans and sugarcane, was expanded. Agriculture benefited from a favorable macroeconomic environment and trade reforms that led to less industrial protection coupled with elimination of taxes and quantitative restrictions on agricultural exports. In addition, specific agricultural reforms—the reform of agricultural credit and price support policies, an agrarian reform program that included land reform, and the deregulation of domestic markets for agricultural goods—were important drivers of the observed agricultural performance.[5]

However, the increase in agricultural productivity was accompanied by a massive layoff of hired labor and important changes in the size distribution of farms. According to the agricultural census from 1996, the number of small farms declined dramatically, and agricultural employment shrank by 23 percent between 1986 and 1996, although these figures should be taken with some caution (Helfand and Rezende 2004).

Nonagricultural activities appear to have compensated for the loss in agricultural employment in rural areas, but unemployment rates in urban areas have risen in that period (Dias and Amaral 2002). The analysis in this chapter based on the 1997 and 2001 PNADs suggests that this decline in agricultural employment has continued after 1996. In 2001, agriculture accounted for 20.6 percent of employment in Brazil, down from 24.2 percent in 1997. Unemployment in rural areas has stayed constant at about 2.5 percent during this period, whereas urban unemployment has risen from 9.44 to 10.6 percent, an increase that may be related to the decline in agricultural employment.[6]

Fewer agricultural employment opportunities may also be one of the reasons for further urbanization in Brazil, although it is difficult to establish this link empirically, as explained in more detail elsewhere in this chapter. The rural population declined sharply in the past decade, falling from 24.41 percent in 1991 to 21.64 percent in 1996 (IBGE 1997) and 16 percent in 2001 (PNAD 2001). The trends in rural poverty mentioned above suggest that the described developments have improved rural livelihoods. Nevertheless, poverty rates in rural areas remain well above urban poverty rates.

Future developments in agriculture are a subject of some debate, but it is likely that many of the recent trends, in particular the decline in agricultural employment and the modest increase in incomes from agriculture, will continue. They are therefore incorporated in the BaU scenario in this chapter, against which the trade reform scenarios are to be judged.

The analysis here addresses the poverty and distributional impact of some of the structural changes that are particularly relevant for Brazil. The focus is particularly on structural change in agriculture, and how this interacts with trade policies. Of course, the reader should bear in mind that more than two-thirds of the Brazilian poor either live in urban areas or derive their income from nonagricultural activities, and this model devotes relatively less attention to how structural change might affect them.

The Modeling Framework

The analytical framework consists of a sequentially dynamic CGE model linked to an MS. The MS takes the changes in factor and goods prices as given; hence, there is no feedback between these two parts of the model. This framework is particularly well suited for the questions at hand, because the CGE model captures some of the main features of structural change and the relative price changes accompanying them. The MS, in turn, then allows for a detailed empirical assessment of the household responses to these changes.

The Macro Model

A 1997 social accounting matrix (SAM) has been used as the initial benchmark equilibrium for the CGE model. This SAM has been assembled from various sources, including the 1997 input-output table, the earlier SAM assembled by Harrison and others (2003), and the 2001 PNAD. For purposes of this model, the full SAM—which includes 41 sectors, 41 commodities, 12 factors (skilled and unskilled labor by gender and by farm and nonfarm occupation, agricultural and nonagricultural capital, and land and natural resources), an aggregate household account, and other accounts (government, savings and investment, and rest of the world)—has been aggregated to a smaller size of 17 sectors and commodities and 7 factors (skilled and unskilled labor by farm and nonfarm occupation, capital, and land and natural resources).

The CGE model is a standard neoclassical, recursive-dynamic general equilibrium model, and the next subsections describe its main features. Given this chapter's focus on labor markets and dynamic structural trends, the following discussion emphasizes the modeling of factor markets and growth.[7]

Production
Output is produced using nested constant elasticity of substitution (CES) functions that, at the top level, combine intermediate and value added aggregates. At the second level, intermediate inputs are obtained by combining all products in fixed proportions (Leontief structure), and value added is produced by aggregating the primary factors. At this level, primary factors are a capital-labor bundle and an aggregate land input. Lower levels of the production function disaggregate capital and labor, and then labor, into different categories.

Income Distribution and Absorption
Labor income and capital earnings are allocated to households according to a fixed coefficient distribution matrix derived from the original SAM. As will be shown below, one of the main advantages of using the micromodule is the enrichment of this rather crude macro distribution mechanism. Private consumption demand is obtained through maximization of household-specific utility functions following the linear expenditure system (LES). Private savings are a fixed proportion of income. Once the total value of private consumption is determined, government and investment demands[8] are disaggregated into sector demands according to fixed coefficient functions.

International Trade

The model assumes imperfect substitution among goods originating in different geographic areas.[9] Import demand results from a CES aggregation function of domestic and imported goods. Export supply is symmetrically modeled as a constant elasticity of transformation (CET) function. Producers decide to allocate their output to domestic or foreign markets responding to relative prices. The assumptions of imperfect substitution and imperfect transformability grant a certain degree of autonomy of domestic prices with respect to foreign prices and prevent the model from generating corner solutions.

To facilitate the incorporation of shocks from the global CGE model (recall chapter 3), export demand functions were added so that the increased market access accompanying multilateral trade liberalization scenarios can be simulated more precisely.[10] No international import supply functions have been added; Brazil is treated as a price taker for its imports. The balance of payments equilibrium is determined by the equality of foreign savings (which are exogenous) to the value of the current account.

Factor Markets

Two types of labor are distinguished, skilled and unskilled. These categories are considered imperfectly substitutable inputs in the production process. Moreover, some degree of factor market segmentation is assumed: capital and land are perfectly mobile across sectors, natural resources are sector specific, and labor markets for the unskilled are segmented between agriculture and nonagriculture, whereas skilled workers are fully mobile.

The labor market specification is a key element of the model and an important driver of poverty and distributional results. Therefore, its specification calls for some clarification and justification. The segmentation of the labor market by skill has become a standard assumption in CGE modeling, and it is easily justifiable for the case of Brazil. The inequalities of Brazilian society in terms of educational endowments and, more important, access to education and on-the-job training certainly support this assumption, even over a longer time horizon.

The assumption that the market for unskilled labor is further segmented into agricultural and nonagricultural activities is more controversial, particularly in light of its importance for the poverty and distributional results. To test the validity of this assumption, the authors check whether incomes in agriculture are still below incomes in other sectors once the following wage determinants are controlled for: education, experience, gender, racial dummies, and employment status variables such as self-employment, seasonal employment, and employment in the informal sector. Additionally, to take into account price differentials across space, geographic variables capturing differences among Brazilian regions as well as a rural-urban dummy variable are included in the wage estimation.

The largest nonagricultural sector (in terms of employment), "other services," is taken as the reference group. Regression analysis shows that, relative to this reference group, agricultural labor incomes are significantly lower for individuals in similar circumstances.[11] Underreporting of income, externalities linked to working in agriculture, and other factors may partially explain this negative bias in agricultural incomes; however, the authors believe this earnings gap is also due to barriers to mobility between agricultural and nonagricultural employment that prevent individuals from moving out of the agricultural sector. The econometric analysis (see also section "Who Moves Out of Agriculture") identifies two such barriers that are relevant over a medium-run time horizon: land ownership and the specificity of human capital acquired in agricultural occupations.

With this empirical support for the hypothesis that the Brazilian labor market for unskilled labor is segmented into agricultural and nonagricultural employment, the dual labor market for unskilled workers is modeled following the standard Harris-Todaro specification, whereby the decision to migrate is a function of the expected income in the nonagricultural (urban) segment relative to the expected income in the agricultural (rural) segment.

Model Closure

The equilibrium condition on the balance of payments is combined with the other closure conditions so that the model can be solved for each period. The government budget surplus is fixed, and the household income tax schedule shifts, to achieve this predetermined net fiscal position for the government. Second, investment must equal savings, which originate from households, corporations, government, and the rest of the world. Aggregate investment is set equal to aggregate savings, and aggregate government expenditures are exogenously fixed.

Growth Equations

Sectoral shifts among agriculture and nonagriculture and human capital upgrading are two of the main features that have characterized recent growth processes in Brazil and in most developing nations. To capture these features in a transparent and simple dynamic framework, productivity growth rates are calibrated separately for the agriculture and nonagriculture sectors. Brazilian agriculture has historically recorded high productivity growth, and this exogenous historical growth rate for productivity in agriculture is imposed uniformly across all factors in that sector. In contrast, the growth rate of productivity for the nonagriculture sector is calibrated by imposing an exogenous growth path for real GDP. This dynamic calibration results in the observed labor savings in agriculture production trends of the past decade continuing in the forecasting period.[12] Other elements of simple dynamics include exogenous growth of labor supply, with skilled labor growing faster than unskilled labor, and investment-driven capital accumulation.

The MS Model

The micro model is linked to the macro model through changes in the following set of endogenous variables: (a) changes in agricultural and nonagricultural labor income of unskilled labor (two variables), (b) changes in labor income of skilled labor (one variable), and (c) changes in the sectoral (agriculture versus nonagriculture) composition of the unskilled workforce (one variable). In addition, the fact that unskilled and skilled labor supplies grow at different rates is taken into account. The MS does not produce a series of cross-sections through time, but only simulates one cross-section that reflects the cumulative changes in the aforementioned exogenous and endogenous variables over the entire period from 2001 to 2015. In accordance with the structure of the CGE model, the micro model simulates the decision to move from agriculture into nonagriculture sectors only for unskilled workers.

The MS module consists of a set of equations that describe the income generation process of the household. It includes logit equations for moving out of agriculture, estimated separately for household heads and nonheads. The wage-profit equations are estimated separately for unskilled agricultural, unskilled nonagricultural, and skilled labor using ordinary least squares. Together, the mover-stayer model and the wage-profit equations provide the basis for the MS of household-level outcomes. The left-hand-side variable of the mover-stayer model is a dichotomous variable that assumes a value of 1 if an individual has moved out of agriculture during the past 12 months and 0 otherwise. The model is estimated on a sample that includes stayers in agriculture along with last year's movers. An overview of key estimation results is provided below. The wage-profit equations explain between 30 and 50 percent of variability of log wages-profits using a relatively short list of explanatory variables, including education, work experience, gender, racial, and regional dummies. The estimation of agricultural wages and profits also controls for the number of nonremunerated household members.

The 2001–15 MS involves three steps. First, households are reweighted to reflect the change in the skilled to unskilled labor ratio, as predicted by the CGE model over this period. In the second step, unskilled labor moves out of agriculture until the new share of unskilled labor in agriculture given by the CGE is reproduced. Third, wages and profits are adjusted according to the CGE results, taking into account the changes in the skill composition of the workforce as well as the sectoral movements of unskilled labor from agriculture into nonagricultural sectors. In sum, by using the estimated equations, the MS is "forced" to reproduce the aggregate results for employment and wage changes generated by the CGE model. Technically, this requires changing the constants in each of the equations.[13]

To account for total household income in addition to labor income, transfer and capital income as reported in the PNAD are considered. Transfer income is scaled up or down according to the GDP per capita growth rate, and capital income is adjusted according to the change in the rental rate on capital as reported in the CGE model. The sum of all household members' individual incomes is divided by the number of household members to give the household income per capita. Regional poverty lines are developed by taking the R$80 per capita poverty line (in current 2001 prices) for urban Rio de Janeiro as a basis and adjusting it for regional price differences following Paes de Barros (2004).

Who Moves Out of Agriculture?

The "employment history" section of the PNAD is key to the analysis of the decision to move out of agriculture. This data, which is nonexistent in most other countries' household surveys, offers the information needed for estimating the intersectoral migration choice model. In this section, the PNAD provides additional data that allows identification of the movers out of agriculture and, very important for this undertaking, the characteristics of these individuals at the time of moving. For example, the PNAD reports which type of land right they had and whether they were self-employed before they moved out of agriculture. This information has not been previously exploited by researchers, and it is key to the findings here.

Estimation of the mover-stayer model using these data allows highlighting of the main factors affecting the propensity to move out of agriculture. For both heads and nonheads of households, a higher level of educational attainment positively influences this propensity, whereas age is one of the most significant factors that negatively affects the choice of moving. As one would expect, older individuals are less likely to move out of agriculture. Owning land or other agricultural production factors, such as livestock, also appears to act as an important barrier to intersectoral movements. Finally, household heads from the north are more likely to move out of agriculture than those elsewhere in Brazil. Household heads appear to respond to intersectoral wage differentials to a lesser degree than other family members, thus showing a tendency to be "trapped" in agricultural activities, possibly as a result of factor market imperfections. However, their decision to stay or move is of great importance for the choice of other household members. For these individuals, the strongest determinant of moving out of agriculture is a dummy indicating whether the household head is employed in a nonagricultural sector. Furthermore, the decision on the part of the household head to leave agriculture also strongly influences the choice of the nonheads. Nonremunerated nonheads of households are less likely to move out of agriculture, a finding that points toward the importance of positive externalities associated with this type of agricultural employment.

Brazil in the Next Decade: A Baseline Scenario

A central question of this chapter involves assessing the poverty effects of trade policy reforms over the longer run when the forces of structural adjustment shape the income generation process. The starting point is the CGE model used to build a BaU scenario depicting the evolution of the Brazilian economy over the next decade. This baseline scenario should not be considered as a statistical forecast, but rather as a consistent "projection" of the economy into a future where intersectoral productivity growth differentials, skill upgrading, and migration of labor out of farming activities play major roles. This BaU scenario sets the backdrop against which the alternative scenarios involving trade policy reforms can be evaluated. The next subsections describe in detail the macro and micro results for the BaU and trade scenarios.

Macroeconomic Characteristics of the Baseline

In the BaU scenario, real GDP for Brazil is projected to grow (from 2005 onward) at the annual rate of 3.3 percent; this is optimistic when compared to the 1980–2000 rate of 2 percent. The projected GDP growth performance is supported by strong factor productivity growth rates. As explained above, productivity in the agriculture sector is assumed to be factor neutral, and its growth rate is exogenously set at 2.9 percent per year; in the nonfarm sectors, growth of labor productivity is calibrated at 1.02 percent per year and growth of capital productivity at 0.82 percent per year.

The changes in the structure of labor markets, shown in table 9.1, are of particular relevance for poverty and income distribution trends. As can be seen, the differences in productivity growth rates across sectors, combined with faster growth in the supply of skilled versus unskilled labor (education increases the supply of skilled workers, which is growing at a 2.0 percent annual rate versus a yearly 1.6 percent growth rate for the unskilled labor supply), generate structural adjustments in line with those observed for the last decade. This includes continued out-migration of unskilled workers from agriculture. The declining labor demand in agriculture is driven by three factors: the relatively higher rate of labor productivity growth in agriculture relative to the rest of the economy, an income elasticity of private consumption for agricultural commodities that is less than one, and international prices for traded agricultural products decreased through time in the BaU scenario.

These trends in the supply and demand for labor are equilibrated by movements in relative wages. Over the next decade, real wages of skilled labor are projected to increase at 1.3 percent annually. In nonagricultural sectors, wages for unskilled workers increase at the annual rate of 0.9 percent; however, their upward trend is dampened by migration of unskilled workers from agriculture. The latter contributes to a five-percentage-point reduction in agricultural labor supply, leading to higher agricultural wages, which are growing at an annual rate of 1.7 percent over the baseline period, thereby narrowing the agriculture-nonagriculture wage gap.

The BaU macroeconomic market trends are linked to developments at the sectoral level (shown in table 9.2). Output growth rates are slightly lower for the agricultural sectors than for the nonagricultural ones. Agriculture exports grow at a slightly slower pace than nonagriculture exports because of falling primary commodity international prices in the BaU scenario. In addition, productivity gains dictate that fewer workers are needed to achieve the same output. Meanwhile, rising wages, in particular for unskilled workers, induce producers to substitute skilled workers for unskilled ones. The rightmost panel of the table shows the relative skill intensities and employment sizes of each sector. Services are the largest employers of both skilled and unskilled workers, but, on average, they use skilled labor more intensively. Agriculture employs almost one-third of unskilled workers and uses this factor quite intensively, whereas manufacturing labor intensities fall in between agriculture and services.

Distributional and Poverty Results for the BaU Scenario

MS of these structural trends using the linking variables described above and Brazilian household data results in a moderate decrease in poverty between 2001 and 2015. Considering the full sample of households, the headcount poverty ratio (P0) declines by about 6 percentage points under the BaU scenario (see table 9.3). The reductions in the average normalized poverty gap (P1) and the poverty severity index (P2) indicate that those who remain poor also become better off, thereby reducing the gap to the poverty line.[14] Inequality changes very little, as indicated by the 0.1 decrease in the Gini coefficient. These indexes all indicate that some progress in reducing aggregate poverty and inequality would be achieved in a BaU scenario, but these aggregate measures may conceal relevant distributional changes at a more disaggregated level.

Table 9.1. Medium-Term Labor Market Structural Adjustments

Sector	Productivity of labor	Income elasticity of demand	Employment		Wages		Unskilled labor migration as % of:		Cumulative migration 2001–15
	Yearly growth rate	Constant	Skilled	Unskilled	Skilled	Unskilled	Sending population	Receiving population	2001–15
			Yearly growth rate		Yearly growth rate		Yearly %		Millions
Agriculture	2.9	.54	n.a.	0.0	n.a.	1.7	1.7	n.a.	-4.0
Nonagriculture	1.0	1.05	n.a.	2.2	n.a.	0.9	n.a.	0.5	4.0
Economywide	—	—	2.0	1.7	1.3	n.a.	n.a.	n.a	n.a.

Source: Author's calculations.

Note: — = not available; n.a. = not applicable.

Table 9.2. The BaU Scenario's Output and Trade Sectoral Growth Rates and Employment Intensities

Sector	Annual average growth rates			Labor demand		Employment percentages			
						By sector		By skill	
	Output	Imports	Exports	Skilled	Unskilled	Skilled	Unskilled	Skilled	Unskilled
Cereal and grains	3.2	2.5	2.3	0.3	0.1	0	5	2	98
Oilseeds	3.1	2.2	2.4	0.1	-0.1	0	1	6	94
Raw sugar	3.2	n.a.	n.a.	0.2	0.1	0	1	4	96
Other crops	2.9	1.3	2.5	0.0	-0.1	1	12	3	97
Livestock	3.2	1.5	n.a.	0.3	0.1	2	4	10	90
Raw animal products	3.3	2.5	1.6	0.4	0.3	0	3	1	99
Oil and minerals	3.3	3.0	2.9	1.5	1.7	0	0	15	85
Light manufacturing	3.3	0.8	3.7	1.0	1.2	1	2	16	84
Food industries	3.2	0.5	3.4	1.0	1.2	2	3	16	84
Wood products and paper	3.3	0.9	3.5	1.0	1.2	2	2	15	85
Chemicals and petroleum products	3.3	1.8	2.9	1.1	1.3	2	1	30	70
Metals and mineral products	3.5	1.8	3.3	1.2	1.4	2	2	17	83
Machinery and equipment	3.6	1.9	3.5	1.4	1.6	3	2	28	72
Other services	3.0	2.6	1.7	2.1	2.3	58	30	33	67
Construction	3.2	n.a.	n.a.	2.3	2.5	2	8	6	94
Trade and communications	3.1	2.4	1.8	2.2	2.4	15	18	17	83
Public services	3.1	2.7	1.7	2.2	2.4	9	4	41	59
Agriculture	3.0	1.9	2.4	n.a.	0.0	4	27	6	94
Nonagriculture	3.2	2.0	3.1	n.a.	2.2	96	73	26	74
Economywide	3.2	2.0	3.1	2.0	n.a.	100	100	24	76

Source: Authors' calculations.

Note: n.a. = not applicable.

Table 9.3. Poverty and Inequality in the BaU Scenario, by Sectors

Variable	All households		Nonagricultural households		Agricultural households	
	2001 level	2001–15 change	2001 level	2001–15 change	2001 level	2001–15 change
per capita income	314.9	1.5	351.9	1.2	148.3	2.3
Gini	58.6	-0.1	57.1	0.6	56.6	-0.7
P0	23.6	-5.6	18.6	-3.1	46.2	-13.8
P1	9.6	-3.0	7.1	-1.6	21.0	-8.0
P2	5.3	-1.8	3.7	-0.9	12.3	-5.2
Population (%)	100	n.a.	81.8	3.3	18.2	-3.3
Contribution to P0	n.a.	n.a.	64.4	8.8	35.6	-8.8

Source: Authors' calculations.

Note: n.a. = not applicable. Per capita income is 2001 reals, and the change is given as annual growth rate. All levels are in percent and changes in percentage points.

Perhaps the most obvious way to gather more detailed information is to analyze the poverty and inequality impacts separately for the agricultural and nonagricultural households. A household is classified as "agricultural" when its head or at least two of its members are employed in agriculture. According to this classification, in 2001, agricultural households accounted for 18.2 percent of the Brazilian population, poverty incidence among them reached nearly 50 percent, and their contribution to total poverty was about 36 percent (see table 9.3). Between 2001 and 2015, the share of agricultural households in the population is projected to shrink by 3.3 percentage points after the decline in agricultural employment of more than 5 percentage points. Poverty among agricultural households falls by more than 13 percentage points (of agricultural population), whereas poverty among nonagricultural households decreases by only 3.1 percent. Accordingly, the contribution of agricultural households to the headcount falls by almost 9 percentage points.

A more detailed analysis also shows that the lack of progress in aggregate inequality is due to the fact that the agricultural and nonagricultural groups' individual inequality indicators move in opposite directions. Among nonagricultural households, inequality rises because skilled labor earnings, a major source of income for these households, grow faster than earnings from unskilled labor. Conversely, inequality among agricultural households falls, mainly because richer agricultural households earn a higher share of their income from nonagricultural labor.

Another way of analyzing detailed distributional effects is to consider growth incidence curves. These curves plot per capita income growth at income percentiles (Ravallion and Chen 2003) and are shown in figure 9.1 for all households as well as for the agricultural and nonagricultural subgroups.[15] Per capita income growth is much higher for agricultural households, reflecting the increase in unskilled agricultural wages from the CGE model's results. In addition, the agricultural growth incidence curve illustrates a strong pro-poor distributional shift. The agricultural households' distributional shifts also explain the pro-poor changes in the national income distribution, because only minor distributional changes are registered in the nonagricultural distribution. However, richer nonagricultural households experience somewhat higher gains than poorer households. Incomes for the poor nonagricultural households increase by a meager 1–1.5 percent annually.

These more detailed analyses of the long-term evolution of the Brazilian income distribution highlight the different roles played by changes in inequality and shifts in the growth rates of the average incomes. The following two questions then arise: if the current (2001) distribution of income were to remain unchanged, to what extent would the additional growth under the BaU scenario

**Figure 9.1.   Growth Incidence Curves, BaU Scenario:
All, Agricultural, and Nonagricultural Households**

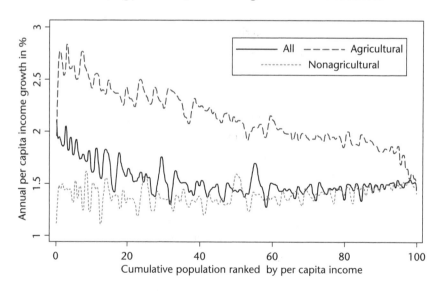

Source: Authors' calculations.

contribute to reducing poverty? And what is the role of the BaU sectoral differential in growth rates for agriculture and nonagriculture in reducing poverty?

Answering these questions requires performing two additional MSs. The first simulation generates a counterfactual distribution under the assumption that all incomes of all sources grow by 1.5 percent annually. This implies shifting the entire income distribution "to the right," leaving its shape unchanged. Individuals do not change employment sectors, and hence households retain their initial nonagricultural or agricultural classification. Results from this simulation are presented in table 9.4 and changes are given as a percentage share of the BaU change (BAU change I). In addition, a second set of counterfactual distributions was simulated for agricultural and nonagricultural households separately with per capita incomes of the respective household types growing with the BaU rates, that is, by 1.3 percent annually for nonagricultural and 2.4 percent annually for the agricultural households (BAU change II).

Comparison of the counterfactual simulations of the "completely" distributionally neutral (BAU change I) and the "separately" neutral (BAU change II) scenarios shows that the growth bias in favor of agricultural households is poverty reducing. Yet, the difference between the BaU and the completely neutral scenario does not seem pronounced. This is due to the fact that in the latter, poverty among nonagricultural households is reduced much more than in the BaU, where the income distribution among these households worsens. This "slight" worsening of the income distribution significantly hampers the potential of growth to reduce poverty among nonagricultural households. In addition, the differences between the two neutral scenarios for nonagricultural households illustrate that a 0.2 percentage point difference in annual growth rates for 14 years can make a substantial difference in terms of poverty reduction.

The last two columns of table 9.4 illustrate the importance of growth for reducing poverty among agricultural households as well. A 0.9 percentage point difference in annual income growth rates for 14 years implies a reduction of about 5 percentage points in the headcount over this period. In contrast to what is seen for nonagricultural households, the impact of the pro-poor distributional shift for agricultural households observed in the BaU is relatively small. In other words, had the income distribution among agricultural households not improved, growth would have reduced poverty by only a little less.

The poverty reductions recorded in the BaU scenario are due to a combination of factors, including: the change in skill endowments, the increase in real factor prices, and the intersectoral movement of workers. A main advantage of MS is the ability to decompose the total effect in different partial effects that can be attributed to single causes. A slight complication arises because of the interaction effect among these three factors because incomes increase at different rates

Table 9.4. Poverty and Inequality in a Distributionally Neutral Scenario

	All households			Agricultural households			Nonagricultural households		
	2001 level	BaU change I (%)	BaU change II (%)	2001 level	BaU change I (%)	BaU change II (%)	2001 level	BaU change I (%)	BaU change II (%)
per capita income	314.9	100.0	100.0	351.9	117.7	98.6	148.3	65.7	102.9
P0	23.6	91.7	102.4	18.6	139.8	133.3	45.9	56.5	90.5
P1	9.6	90.9	97.7	7.1	132.5	119.7	20.8	61.9	93.2
P2	5.3	86.8	97.9	3.7	125.6	114.3	12.1	62.6	93.4

Source: Authors' calculations.

Note: This table shows results for two MSs. The first simulation generates a counterfactual distribution under the assumption that all incomes of all sources grow by 1.5 percent annually. This implies shifting the entire income distribution "to the right" leaving its shape unchanged. Individuals do not change employment sectors, and hence households retain their initial nonagricultural or agricultural classification. Results are presented in the columns with heading "change I" as percentage share of the BaU change (where, in fact, households change occupations and experience different gains according to the structure of their income sources). In the second counterfactual, distribution for agricultural and nonagricultural households is shifted separately, using per capita income growth rates of the respective household types (1.3 percent annually for nonagricultural and 2.4 percent annually for the agricultural households), and results are denoted by the heading "change II."

in agricultural and nonagricultural sectors. By simulating counterfactual distributions with only one or two of these changes included, it is possible to decompose the total effect into individual or joint (interactive) contributions. This is the subject of the next investigation.

Figure 9.2 displays the results of the poverty decomposition for the BaU scenario. Factor price changes account for the largest share of total poverty reduction. The change in the composition of the workforce (skill upgrading) does not contribute much to poverty reduction, whereas the sectoral shifts in the workforce are quite important, in particular for the poorest of the poor, as the higher contribution of the sectoral change component with regard to P2 indicates. This is because households with members moving out of the agricultural sector tend to escape poverty. The interaction component hampers poverty reduction (negative contribution in figure 9.2) because people moving out of agriculture experience a lesser rate of increase in their incomes over the BaU time frame.

Figure 9.2. Decomposition of Poverty Changes, BaU Scenario, All Households

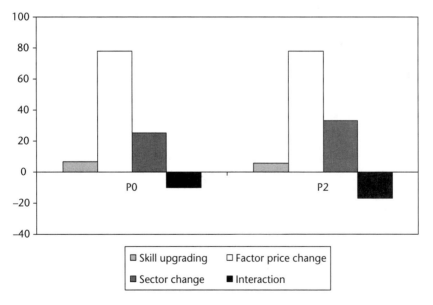

Source: Authors' calculations.

Note: The figure displays the contribution of the component to the total change in P0 and P2, respectively, in percent. The contributions add to 100. Contributions refer to reductions in the respective poverty indexes.

In sum, the distributional and poverty analysis suggests that the BaU scenario leads to modest poverty reduction. Agricultural households fare relatively well, and the poverty incidence and intensity among them are substantially reduced. Decomposition analyses show that sectoral change contributes significantly to poverty reduction, although factor income growth is the most important source of poverty reduction. Microaccounting exercises underline the importance of growth for poverty reduction, but they also illustrate that small increases in inequality can considerably reduce the poverty reduction potential of growth in the context of a high-inequality country, such as Brazil. With this background, the chapter now turns to the central question of this book: Can this rate of poverty reduction be enhanced by global trade reforms?

Macroeconomic Impacts of Trade Reforms

The trade shocks simulated in the dynamic CGE model consist of changes in Brazilian tariff protection against imports from the rest of the world and of exogenous changes of international prices of traded goods and export quantities demanded by foreigners.[16] The shocks are assumed to take place progressively through a gradual phasing in starting in 2005 and lasting 6 years. Table 9.5 displays these shocks as percentage changes of the final year (2015) between the BaU and the trade reform scenarios. In keeping with the other chapters in this volume, the government fiscal balance remains unchanged, thus tariff revenue losses are compensated by an equiproportional direct tax paid by households. This tax is the least distortionary instrument that can be readily used in this model; however, in practice, the Brazilian government may choose other forms of compensatory taxes, which may alter relative prices and have significant income distribution effects, as explored in other chapters in this volume.

The full liberalization scenario has the largest impacts: tariffs are completely eliminated, and Brazil enjoys strong terms of trade gains. The Doha shocks generate almost no tariff cuts in Brazil because of the extensive binding overhang (recall chapter 2), and they are accompanied by fairly muted global price effects. To fully anticipate their final effects, these shocks need to be mapped to the economic structure of Brazil.

Table 9.6 presents this structure. For instance, in the full-liberalization scenario, export-oriented sectors (those displaying high shares of export to domestic output), such as oilseeds, other crops, and the food industries, record considerable increases of their export prices. Conversely, import-competing sectors, such as chemicals and oil-derived products and capital goods, do not face high increases in their international prices. These combined export and import price movements result in strongly favorable terms of trade (TOT) gains, inducing significant

Table 9.5. Trade Shock: Tariff Reductions and International Price Changes

Commodity	Own tariff reductions		Change in import prices		Change in export prices	
	Full liberalization	Doha	Full liberalization	Doha	Full liberalization	Doha
Cereals and grains	-100	n.a.	8	2.1	16	6.0
Oilseeds	-100	n.a.	6	2.5	14	4.9
Raw sugar	n.a.	n.a.	2	1.0	14	5.4
Other crops	-100	0	2	0.9	13	4.8
Livestock	-100	n.a.	2	1.1	25	9.8
Raw animal products	-100	n.a.	2	0.4	18	6.7
Oil and minerals	-100	n.a.	0	0.1	2	1.3
Light manufacturing	-100	0	1	1.2	9	4.0
Food industries	-100	-1	0	0.6	7	3.2
Wood products and paper	-100	-2	0	0.0	4	2.0
Chemicals and petroleum products	-100	-3	-1	0.0	3	1.7
Metals and mineral products	-100	-1	0	0.0	3	1.7
Machinery and equipment	-100	-2	0	0.0	2	1.7
Other services	n.a.	n.a.	0	0.0	5	2.2
Construction	n.a.	n.a.	0	0.0	4	1.9
Trade and communications	n.a.	n.a.	0	-0.1	5	2.1
Public services	n.a.	n.a.	0	-0.1	5	2.3
Agriculture	-100	0	5	1.5	14	4.9
Nonagriculture	-100	-2	0	0.1	4	2.1
Economywide	-100	-2	0	0.1	5	2.4

Source: Authors' calculations.
Note: n.a. = not applicable.

reallocation of resources toward export-oriented sectors. Additional push for this reallocation comes from Brazil's own liberalization, which entails a reduction of the antiexport bias implicit in the higher protection rates for manufacturing of the initial tariff structure. The sectoral effects projected in the wake of trade reforms detailed in the complete elimination of tariffs in the full-liberalization case explain the large increase of imports (measured in volume), which, in the final year of this scenario, is 21 percent above the value in the same year of the BaU. Increases in imports of agricultural goods are much weaker: an aggregate 6 percent increase versus the 21 percent surge of the nonagriculture bundle. The combination of lower initial tariffs and stronger international price increases for agriculture, relative to nonagriculture, explains the difference in import response of these two broad sectors of the Brazilian economy. Given the very limited scope of tariff reductions under the Doha scenario, import changes are much smaller.

With a relatively high elasticity of substitution in demand (set uniformly at 4), cheaper imports have the potential to displace domestic production, especially for those goods whose demand is fulfilled by a large share of foreign supply. For Brazil, this is the case for the chemicals and capital goods sectors. In the full-liberalization scenario, domestic production experiences significant output reductions in these sectors; however, this does not happen in the Doha scenario, where Brazilian tariffs are hardly reduced. The competition from cheaper imports is also reflected—again, only for the full-liberalization case—in the decline of prices of domestic output.

These import-demand side effects are linked to the supply response, to which the analysis now turns. For producers of exportable goods, the reduction of prices in local markets combined with unchanged or rising export prices creates incentives to increase the share of sales to foreign markets. This export response (shown in the columns "Export volumes" in table 9.7) varies across sectors and is linked to the pattern of Brazil's comparative advantage and the increase in international prices. Brazil's comparative advantage can be ascertained by considering the export orientation ("Exports to domestic output") column in table 9.6, which highlights three sectors in particular: oilseeds, other crops, and the agricultural transformation industry. These sectors, which also enjoy large jumps in their international price, experience export surges. As a result of the generally positive export price shocks, other sectors join in an overall expansion of supply to foreign markets. Rising export sales more than offset, or at least compensate, reductions of domestic sales and lead to changes observed in the columns labeled "Domestic output" in table 9.7. Given the foreign closure rule for the Brazilian model, economywide increases of import volumes are balanced by a comparable increase in exports.[17]

Table 9.6.   Initial (Year 2001) Structure of the Brazilian Economy

Commodity	Tariff rates	Sectoral imports	Imports to domestic demand of composite	Sectoral ouput	Sectoral exports	Exports to domestic output
Cereals and grains	7	1	15	1	0	1
Oilseeds	6	0	8	0	4	29
Raw sugar	0	0	0	0	0	0
Other crops	9	2	3	4	8	7
Livestock	3	0	1	1	0	0
Raw animal products	8	0	1	1	0	1
Oil and minerals	4	7	33	1	7	25
Light manufacturing	17	4	5	5	3	2
Food industries	18	3	3	7	19	11
Wood products and paper	9	2	5	3	7	10
Chemicals and petroleum products	9	15	10	9	8	3
Metals and mineral products	12	5	6	5	13	11
Machinery and equipment	19	37	27	8	20	11
Other services	0	11	3	23	5	1
Construction	0	0	0	8	0	0
Trade and communications	0	10	5	13	5	2
Public services	0	2	1	11	1	0
Agriculture	8	4	4	7	12	6
Nonagriculture	11	96	6	93	88	4
Economywide	11	100	6	100	100	4

Source: Authors' calculations.

Table 9.7.   Brazil's Structural Adjustment, Percent Changes in the Final Year between BaU Scenario and Trade Shocks

Commodity	Import volumes		Domestic demand of domestic products		Price of domestic output in domestic markets		Export volumes		Domestic output		Price of domestic output	
	Full liberalization	Doha	Full liberalization	Doha	Full liberalization	Doha	Full liberalization	Doha	Full liberalization	Doha	Full liberalization	Doha
Cereal and grains	-6	-3	4	1	-2	1	68	13	5	1	-2	1
Oilseeds	-18	-7	5	1	-6	0	60	8	20	3	-3	1
Raw sugar	23	2	0	0	-2	1	n.a.	n.a.	0	0	-2	1
Other crops	-4	1	1	0	-1	1	6	-3	1	0	-1	1
Livestock	22	5	3	1	-2	1	n.a.	n.a.	3	1	-2	1
Raw animal products	-6	1	2	1	-2	1	5	-1	2	1	-2	1
Oil and minerals	48	-3	1	-1	-5	1	26	1	7	0	-4	1
Light manufacturing	59	1	0	1	-5	0	159	61	5	3	-4	1
Food industries	23	4	0	0	-4	1	30	4	3	1	-4	1
Wood products and paper			-1	0	-4	1	11	-1	0	0	-4	1
Chemicals and petroleum products	18	3	-2	0	-4	1	9	-1	-2	0	-4	1
Metals and mineral products	24	2	-4	-1	-5	1	15	-1	-2	-1	-4	1
Machinery and equipment	42	3	-12	-1	-6	1	11	-2	-10	-1	-5	1
Other services	n.a.	n.a.	1	0	-4	1	n.a.	n.a.	1	0	-4	1
Construction	-14	3	0	0	-3	1	8	-1	0	0	-3	1
Trade and communications	-12	3	0	0	-3	1	6	-2	0	0	-3	1
Public services	-13	3	0	0	-3	1	7	-2	0	0	-3	1
Agriculture	6	-1	2	1	-2	1	22	0	3	1	-2	1
Nonagriculture	21	3	-1	0	-4	1	21	2	0	0	-4	1
Economywide	21	3	-1	0	-4	1	21	2	0	0	-4	1

Source: Authors' calculations.

Note: n.a. = not applicable.

In summary, trade reforms promote a production structure specialized toward exportables, which in Brazil translates into a specialization toward primary or agricultural transformation sectors. This agriculture export-led boom is fully achieved only in the full-liberalization scenario, where domestic tariffs are fully eliminated and there are strong international price changes.[18] From the point of view of poverty and income distribution, changes in factor markets are the most important aspect of the structural adjustment caused by trade reform. Changes in wages and sectoral employment are linked to changes of goods prices through the production technology and the functioning of the factor markets. A key aspect of the different production technologies is the difference in factor intensity across sectors shown in table 9.2. Recall that this chapter seeks to mimic realistic adjustment possibilities in the labor market by assuming that skilled workers can freely move across all sectors, whereas unskilled workers face two segmented markets and can just imperfectly migrate from the agriculture to the nonagriculture segment. As a result of the boom in agriculture, which is very intensive in unskilled labor, the full trade liberalization induces a significant increase in the wage rate for unskilled workers, as reported in table 9.8. When compared with the BaU scenario, the yearly rate of growth of wages of unskilled workers in agriculture is 0.4 percentage point higher, and this results in a cumulative 14 year growth of 34 percent—much higher than the cumulative growth of 26 percent under the BaU scenario. Migration decreases with higher agricultural wages. About 340,000 workers who moved out of agriculture in the BaU scenario no longer do so in the full-liberalization case. This has some effect on the aggregate distribution of unskilled workers between agriculture and nonagriculture, as shown in the last column of table 9.8. The Doha effects are much weaker.

Distributional and Poverty Impacts of Trade Reform

Two fundamental results emerge from analyzing the micro impacts of the trade scenarios. First, the initial hypothesis that trade liberalization, by working against the "natural" forces of structural change, might weaken long-term poverty reduction, has been soundly rejected. Although fewer people migrate toward more highly paid nonagricultural jobs, poverty is further reduced in the trade liberalization scenarios, largely through increased agricultural incomes. However (and this is the second fundamental result), trade reform as envisaged in the core Doha scenario for this book—and even in the hypothetical full-liberalization scenario— pales in importance in the fight against poverty in the face of the overall assumptions about productivity and economic growth that govern the BaU scenario. The full-liberalization scenario leads to a further reduction in the headcount poverty index of 0.5 percentage point, whereas for the Doha scenario the effects are almost

Table 9.8.   Factor Market Effects

Scenario / Sector	Employment		Wages		Unskilled labor migration as % of:		Cumulative migration	Unskilled employment
	Skilled	Unskilled	Skilled	Unskilled	Sending population	Receiving population	2001–15	2015
	Yearly growth rates				Yearly %		Millions	%
BaU								
Agriculture	—	0.02	—	1.68	1.66	n.a.	-4.04	21.51
Nonagriculture	—	2.20	—	0.91	n.a.	0.53	4.04	78.49
Economywide	2.0	1.7	1.26	—	n.a.	n.a.	0	100.0
Full liberalization								
Agriculture	—	0.18	—	2.10	1.51	n.a.	-3.71	21.99
Nonagriculture	—	2.15	—	1.07	n.a.	0.49	3.71	78.01
Economywide	2.0	1.7	1.32	—	n.a.	n.a.	0	100.0
Doha								
Agriculture	—	0.06	—	1.78	1.62	n.a.	-3.96	21.64
Nonagriculture	—	2.19	—	0.93	n.a.	0.52	3.96	78.36
Economywide	2.0	1.7	1.27	—	n.a.	n.a.	0	100.0

Source: Authors' calculations.

Note: — = not available; n.a. = not applicable.

negligible. Of course, such trade reforms may well affect the rate of productivity growth, and hence the fundamental determinants of the BaU outcome, but this linkage is not explored here.

As for the BaU scenario, a thorough assessment of the trade scenarios needs to go beyond these aggregate indicators and should rely on more disaggregate poverty and distributional analyses. In search of trade-induced poverty effects, the remaining part of this section considers an array of indicators, from growth incidence curves to poverty statistics estimated on specific subsamples of the survey data. In particular, poverty and distributional impacts are separately measured for the agricultural and nonagricultural groups and the movers and stayers.[19]

Figure 9.3 shows the growth incidence curves for the poorest 30 percent of all households under the three scenarios. The curve for the Doha scenario lies slightly above the BaU curve. The full-liberalization reform also shifts the whole curve upward, but this shift is larger than that of the Doha case, and it seems to favor the poorest among the poor; in other words, full liberalization appears to induce an

Figure 9.3. Growth Incidence Curves for the BaU and Trade Scenarios, Poorest 30 Percent of All Households

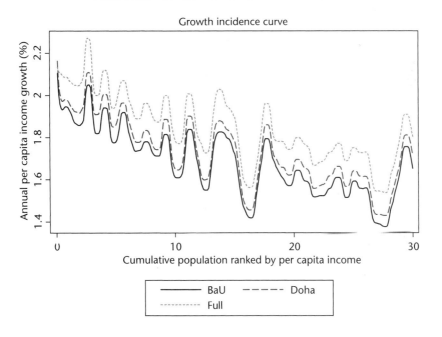

Source: Authors' calculations.

additional pro-poor distributional shift, resulting from Brazil's own-liberalization in the full-liberalization package of reforms.

Table 9.9a-b shows the results for agriculture and nonagriculture groups of households. Compared to the BaU scenario, inequality for all households falls as a result of decreased inequality among agricultural households and lower inequality increase among nonagricultural households, although inequality between these two groups may have risen somewhat. Despite declining inequality and slightly higher per capita income growth, the rate of poverty reduction for agricultural households barely changes. This is due to the lower migration levels induced by the trade shocks (see table 9.10c below). Indeed, in the Doha scenario, the reduction in the population share of agricultural households is only very slightly below that achieved in the BaU scenario. More remarkable is the additional poverty reduction for nonagricultural households, which can largely be explained by a decrease in inequality because per capita income growth is only marginally higher under trade reform.

Given its larger price and quantities shocks, the full-liberalization scenario yields more significant poverty changes, as shown in table 9.9b. In contrast to the Doha scenario, agricultural households gain considerably from full liberalization, and their headcount index is reduced by almost 1.5 percentage points. These sector-specific income gains more than compensate the further (albeit small) reduction of agricultural out-migration.

For nonagricultural households, the full-liberalization scenario improves the income distribution, and the Gini increases by only 72 percent of the increase recorded in the BaU scenario. Growth is only slightly higher for this group of households but, as shown above, minor distributional shifts accompanied by slightly higher growth can result in significant poverty reduction.

Trade shocks simultaneously increase agricultural incomes and reduce intersectoral migration; how these two contrasting forces affect poverty outcome depends on the income levels (and therefore on the socioeconomic characteristics) of those who decide to stay instead of moving. Table 9.10 sheds some light on this issue. It shows the poverty levels and changes under the BaU and trade scenarios for agricultural households according to their migration decision. Table 9.10a shows those who *remained* in agriculture, the "stayers." First, consider the BaU case. With those households that will not move identified, it is possible to calculate the headcount for this group in the initial year (2001): their poverty headcount is equal to 44.1 percent, more than 2 percentage points below the 46.2 percent level[20] calculated for all 2001 agricultural households (that is, the combination of stayers and potential movers). This lower level of poverty implies that moving households are on average poorer than those who remain in agriculture. Accordingly, the changes in P0 are 12.1 instead of 13.7 percentage points. In

Table 9.9a. Poverty and Inequality in the Doha Scenario, by Sector

Variable	All households			Nonagricultural households			Agricultural households		
	2001 levels	2001–15 changes	BaU change (%)	2001 levels	2001–15 changes	BaU change (%)	2001 levels	2001-15 changes	BaU change (%)
Per capita income	314.9	1.5	101.5	351.9	1.3	102.1	148.3	2.4	101.3
Gini	58.6	-0.2	194.4	57.1	0.5	81.8	56.6	-0.8	111.5
P0	23.6	-5.8	103.4	18.6	-3.3	106.5	46.2	-14.0	101.5
P1	9.6	-3.1	102.7	7.1	-1.6	104.6	21.0	-8.2	102.1
P2	5.3	-1.9	102.5	3.7	-0.9	104.3	12.3	-5.3	102.0
Population (%)	100.0	n.a.	n.a.	81.8	3.2	98.3	18.2	-3.2	98.3
Contribution to P0	n.a.	n.a.	n.a.	64.4	8.6	96.0	35.6	-8.6	96.0

Source: Authors' calculations.

Note: n.a. = not applicable.

Table 9.9b.   Poverty and Inequality in the Full Liberalization, by Sector

Variable	All households			Nonagricultural households			Agricultural households		
	2001 levels	2001–15 changes	BaU change (%)	2001 levels	2001–15 changes	BaU change (%)	2001 levels	2001–15 changes	BaU change (%)
Per capita income	314.9	1.6	106.4	351.9	1.3	106.8	148.3	2.6	109.8
Gini	58.6	-0.3	312.2	57.1	0.5	72.0	56.6	-0.9	117.0
P0	23.6	-6.1	109.2	18.6	-3.6	116.3	46.2	-14.9	108.0
P1	9.6	-3.2	108.2	7.1	-1.8	113.7	21.0	-8.6	107.4
P2	5.3	-1.9	107.8	3.7	-1.0	113.0	12.3	-5.6	107.2
Population (%)	100.0	n.a.	n.a.	81.8	3.1	93.0	18.2	-3.1	98.0
Contribution to P0	n.a.	n.a.	n.a.	64.4	8.4	96.0	35.6	-7.6	96.0

Source: Authors' calculations.
Note: n.a. = not applicable.

Table 9.10a. Poverty Impact of Trade, by Migration Choices

Variable	Households remaining in agriculture			
	2001 level of variable	BaU 2001–15 baseline change in variable	Doha % of BaU change	Full % of BaU change
P0	44.1	-11.7	101.7	109.5
P1	20.0	-7.0	102.4	108.5
P2	11.7	-4.6	102.3	108.2
Population (%)	n.a.	14.9	100.4	101.5

Source: Authors' calculations.
Note: n.a. = not applicable.

Table 9.10b. Poverty Impact of Trade, Nonagricultural Stayers

Variable	Nonagricultural households, before and after			
	2001 level of variable	BaU 2001–15 baseline change in variable	Doha % of BaU change	Full % of BaU change
P0	18.6	-3.8	104.0	110.7
P1	7.1	-1.8	103.3	109.8
P2	3.7	-1.0	103.2	109.5
Population (%)	82.4	n.a.	n.a.	n.a.

Source: Authors' calculations.
Note: n.a. = not applicable.

Table 9.10c. Poverty Impact of Trade, Sectoral Movers

Variable	Agricultural households that have become nonagricultural			
	2001 level of variable	BaU 2001–15 baseline change in variable	Doha % of BaU change	Full % of BaU change
P0	56.6	-22.4	105.1	108.2
P1	26.0	-14.0	102.0	105.4
P2	15.2	-9.4	101.7	105.1
Population (%)	n.a.	3.1	98.0	92.5

Source: Authors' calculations.
Note: n.a. = not applicable.

2015, about 15 percent of the population still resides in agricultural households under the BaU scenario.[21] The agricultural expansion after trade liberalization has only a minor effect on agricultural employment and not nearly enough to offset the reduction in agricultural employment under the BaU scenario. Accordingly, the change in the share of agricultural households due to trade liberalization is only minor, particularly for the Doha scenario. Yet, when translated into actual migrating individuals, this small share change means that almost 400,000 individuals (those who would have become members of nonagricultural households in the BaU scenario) remain in agricultural households under the full-liberalization scenario. Although these "potential mover households" are on average poorer than the typical "stayer household," as illustrated below, poverty among agricultural households decreases compared to the BaU scenario. Hence, it can be inferred that the relatively poor stayers gain under both trade scenarios, although this gain is very small for the Doha scenario.

As indirectly inferred by the analysis of the stayers, the group of movers is expected to experience the largest welfare gains. As shown in table 9.10c, under the BaU scenario, agricultural households who become nonagricultural households record a 22.4 percentage points reduction in their headcount index, down from a considerably higher initial level of 53.4 percent. This is a critical insight uniquely available through the use of the MS approach. The predicted additional poverty reduction for this group of mover households under the trade scenarios is modest and attributable to the income increases trade reforms induce in the nonagriculture sectors as well as due to the fact that the households that still move out of agriculture under the trade scenarios are actually poorer, on average.

One final category needs to be examined: the nonagricultural stayers. This is a large group, representing 80 percent of the population; however, given the negligible migration out of the nonagricultural sector observed in the data, this group is explicitly excluded from the migration choice. For these households, full liberalization brings about an additional reduction in the poverty headcount of 0.4 percentage point,[22] and the Doha scenario, through its favorable impact on nonagricultural unskilled wages, also makes a small but positive contribution.

Conclusions

The analysis in this chapter suggests that the economic effects of the Doha Round are rather limited for Brazil, in part as a result of the lack of tariff cuts in Brazil itself. Yet, through a slight improvement in the urban income distribution, the Doha scenario has some positive effect on poverty. In contrast, by adding domestic trade reforms and deepening reforms elsewhere, the full-liberalization scenario implies substantial welfare gains that are concentrated among some of the poorest groups in the country, particularly those in agriculture. Consequently, the rural poor in Brazil benefit more than the average. This result is driven by the export boom in agriculture and agricultural processing industries, growing labor demand, and associated higher wages. After full liberalization, a smaller number of workers remain in agriculture compared to the BaU scenario. Given that intersectoral migration substantially improves the income situation of many households under the baseline, one might conjecture that full liberalization would weaken poverty reduction. However, this is not the case, because the gain in agricultural incomes more than compensates for the reduced benefits from lower migration flows.

The positive impact of full liberalization is not limited to rural areas and nonagricultural activities. The urban poor gain from higher unskilled wages, even in nonagricultural sectors. This is reflected in the pro-poor shift in the urban income distribution. In addition, the urban poor benefit indirectly from the gains in agriculture because the pressure on nonagricultural unskilled workers is relieved somewhat. Trade reform, and particularly domestic trade reforms, may particularly help the poor Brazilian farmers, but only broad-based high growth will eradicate urban poverty.

An important limitation of the analysis in this chapter is that the potential interactions between trade liberalization and the rate of productivity growth in Brazil are not considered. The latter is assumed to be exogenous and fixed at its BaU level for all scenarios. This growth rate fuels the strong poverty reduction in the baseline scenario. Given the growing evidence of a beneficial impact of trade liberalization on productivity (see Winters, McCulloch, and McKay [2004]; see also chapter 17 in this book), it must be noted that this chapter's assessment of the potential for additional poverty reduction in the wake of a Doha Round is likely to be on the conservative side. Nonetheless, significant reductions in poverty beyond that achieved in the BaU scenario will likely require additional, complementary reforms. Based on the mover-stayer analysis in this chapter, policies aimed at facilitating the movement of the poorest rural households out of agriculture could be particularly beneficial.

Notes

1. See Bourguignon (2003), Ravallion (2001), Ravallion and Datt (1999), and Kappel, Lay, and Steiner (2005).

2. Poverty is measured by the headcount ratio. The poverty figures in this paragraph are taken from Ferreira, Lanjouw, and Neri (2001).

3. The figures on agricultural employment are own calculations based on the PNAD 1997 and the PNAD 2001.

4. The PNAD is a regularly conducted representative household survey. The sample had a size of about 380,000 individuals in 2001.

5. See Helfand and Rezende (2004) and Dias and Amaral (2002) for details.

6. Data from employment histories in the PNAD reveal that in both 1997 and 2001, about 6 percent of those who became unemployed in the last year were employed in agricultural sectors before. Taking into account the fact that approximately 20 percent of the workforce are employed in agriculture, this figure is rather low and may be taken as a sign that the rise in urban unemployment is not causally linked to the decline in agricultural employment.

7. An even more detailed documentation for the macro model is found in Bussolo, Lay and van der Mensbrugghe (2005).

8. Aggregate investment is set equal to aggregate savings, and aggregate government expenditures are exogenously fixed.

9. See Armington (1969) for details.

10. This chapter follows the Horridge and Zhai approach to shifting export demand. For more details, see the appendix to chapter 3.

11. Regression results are reported in Bussolo, Lay and van der Mensbrugghe (2005).

12. Additional support for this treatment of productivity comes from a recent panel study of sectoral productivity growth in OECD and developing countries (Martin and Mitra 1999). In this study, depending on the estimation method, the average growth rate for total factor productivity in agriculture in middle-income developing countries ranges from 1.78 percent to 2.91 percent per year.

13. A complete description of the MS model, including the estimation of the wage-profit equations and the migration choice equations, as well as the reweighing procedure and the other steps, is found in Bussolo, Lay and van der Mensbrugghe (2005).

14. The income gap ratio (average income shortfall of the poor divided by the poverty line) can be calculated as P1/P0. This ratio is 0.4 for all households in this case—that is, the perfectly targeted cash transfer needed to lift every poor person out of poverty is 40 percent of the poverty line. Thus, 0.4 times the percentage point change in P0 (here 2.4) provides a percentage point change benchmark for evaluating the change in P1 as an indicator of the depth of poverty, because this would be the change in P1 that would be observed had the average income of the poor stayed constant while the headcount declined.

15. The household category (agricultural or nonagricultural household) is the category the household belonged to in the base year 2001.

16. To mimic the global model results for increased demand for Brazilian exports and changes in international prices, a downward-sloping export demand function is introduced, as discussed in the appendix to chapter 3. During a shock, for obvious reasons, both prices and quantities cannot be targeted, and the shock is implemented by modifying both the international price index (the price shock) and the intercept (the quantity shock). The Brazil (single-country) model will then endogenously determine the quantity supplied.

17. Because of the closure rule of the external account (the fixing of foreign savings) and the full employment assumption, the slightly lower expansion of the volumes of exports with respect to import volumes is compensated with a real exchange rate appreciation that originates from rising domestic resource costs.

18. When they simulate analogous trade reforms, Harrison and others (2003) generate comparable sectoral reallocation results, as well as factor market outcomes similar to those shown in table 9.8. This consistency should not be surprising, given that the model in this chapter does not significantly differ from theirs and the initial sectoral bias in the Brazilian tariff structure as well as intersectoral factor intensities are very close in the two approaches.

It should be stressed that in the model in this chapter, trade opening produces only allocative efficiency gains and not other, potentially stronger dynamic productivity gains, which are explored in chapter 17 in this volume.

19. In Bussolo, Lay and van der Mensbrugghe (2005), detailed poverty impacts of trade reform are analyzed for a number of additional groupings, for example by educational attainments, occupational status, or region of residence.

20. Shown in Table 9.3.

21. The initial poverty levels among those who stay in agriculture under the trade scenarios are almost identical to the initial levels among the BaU stayers, so they are not reported here. The same holds for the movers, for whom results are reported later.

22. The 0.4 percentage point is calculated using table 9.9 figures: 0.4 = -3.8 - (-3.8/100 x 110.7/100) x 100.

References

Armington, P. S. 1969. "A Theory of Demand for Products Distinguished by Place of Production." *IMF Staff Papers* 16: 159–78.

Barrett, C. B. 2004. *Rural Poverty Dynamics: Development Policy Implications.* Paper prepared for invited presentation at the 25th International Conference of Agricultural Economists, Durban, South Africa, August 17–23, 2003.

Bourguignon, F. 2003. "The Growth Elasticity of Poverty Reduction: Explaining Heterogeneity across Countries and Time Periods," in *Inequality and Growth*, ed. T. S. Eicher and S. J. Turnovsky. Cambridge, MA: MIT Press.

Bourguignon, F., F. H. G. Ferreira, and N. Lustig. 2005. "A Synthesis of the Results." In *The Microeconomics of Income Distribution Dynamics in East Asia and Latin America*, ed. F. Bourguignon, F. H. G. Ferreira, and N. Lustig, 357–406. New York: Oxford University Press; Washington, DC: World Bank.

Bussolo, M., J. Lay, and D. van der Mensbrugghe. 2005. "Structural Change and Poverty Reduction in Brazil: The Impact of the Doha Round." Policy Research Working Paper, World Bank, Washington, DC.

Dias, G. L. S., and C. M. Amaral. 2002. "Structural Change in Brazilian Agriculture, 1980–98." In *Brazil in the 1990s—an Economy in Transition*, ed. R. Baumann, 204–232. New York: Palgrave.

Ferreira, H. G., P. Lanjouw, and M. Neri. 2001. "A Robust Poverty Profile for Brazil Using Multiple Data Sources." Paper presented at the Latin American and Caribbean Economic Association meeting, Montevideo, October 18–20 2001.

Ferreira, F. H. G., and R. Paes de Barros. 2005. "The Slippery Slope: Explaining the Increase in Extreme Poverty in Urban Brazil, 1976–96." In *The Microeconomics of Income Distribution Dynamics in East Asia and Latin America*, ed. F. Bourguignon, F. H. G. Ferreira, and N. Lustig, 83–124. New York: Oxford University Press; Washington, DC: World Bank.

Harrison, G. W., T. F. Rutherford, D. Tarr, and A. Gurgel. 2003. "Regional, Multilateral, and Unilateral Trade Policies of MERCOSUR for Growth and Poverty Reduction in Brazil." Policy Research Working Paper 3051, World Bank, Washington, DC.

Helfand, S. M., and G. C. de Rezende. 2004. "The Impact of Sector-Specific and Economy-Wide Reforms on the Agricultural Sector in Brazil: 1980–98." *Contemporary Economic Policy* 22 (2): 19–212.

IBGE. 1997. *Anuário estatístico do Brasil 57.* São Paulo.

Kappel, R., J. Lay, and S. Steiner. 2005. "Uganda: No More Pro-Poor Growth?" *Development Policy Review*, 23 (1): 27–53.

Martin, W., and D. Mitra. 1999. "Productivity Growth and Convergence in Agriculture and Manufacturing." Policy Research Working Paper 2171, World Bank, Washington, DC.

Paes de Barros, R. 2004. *Pobreza rural e trabalho agrícola no Brasil ao longo da década de noventa.* Unpublished paper.

Ravallion, M., and S. Chen. 2003. "Measuring Pro-Poor Growth." *Economics Letters* 78 (1): 93–99.

Ravallion, M. 2001. "Growth, Inequality, and Poverty: Looking beyond Averages." *World Development* 29 (11): 1803–15.

Ravallion, M., and G. Datt. 1999. "When is Growth Pro-Poor? Evidence from the Diverse Experiences of India's States." Policy Research Working Paper 2263, World Bank, Washington, DC.

Verner, D. 2004. "Making the Poor Count Takes More than Counting the Poor—a Quick Poverty Assessment of the State of Bahia, Brazil." Policy Research Working Paper 3216, World Bank, Washington, DC.

Winters, L. A., N. McCulloch, and A. McKay. 2004. "Trade Liberalization and Poverty: The Evidence So Far." *Journal of Economic Literature* 152: 72–115.

10

IMPACTS OF THE DDA ON CHINA: THE ROLE OF LABOR MARKETS AND COMPLEMENTARY EDUCATION REFORMS

Fan Zhai and Thomas W. Hertel

Summary

This chapter offers an assessment of the implications of multilateral trade reforms for poverty in China by combining global results from chapter 3 with a national computable general equilibrium (CGE) model that features disaggregated households in both the rural and urban sectors. Using the World Bank's $2/day poverty line, the findings indicate that multilateral trade reforms do in fact reduce poverty in China. The biggest reductions occur in the rural areas—largely as a result of higher prices for farm products.

Urban poverty falls in two of the three household groups considered in this analysis, since the increased demand for China's products in world markets boosts factor earnings sufficiently to offset the impact of higher food prices. For the remaining group—which is heavily dependent on transfer payments—it is assumed that indexation of these payments will largely offset the adverse consequences of higher prices. However, a decline in other income sources is sufficient to cause a small increase in poverty, and this increase is large enough to boost the overall urban poverty headcount very modestly. But since the urban poor only represent 5 percent of the total poor in China and the national poverty headcount falls.

This chapter also explores the implications of complementary reforms in China—in particular the impact of increased investments in rural education. These are aimed at increasing labor productivity, as well as enhancing the mobility of the rural labor force, thereby putting these workers in a better position to benefit from trade reforms. The specific scenario considered is one in which rural enrollment rises by 16 percent. The analysis takes account of the cost of funding these additional students, as well as the reduction in the workforce that results from having more pupils in school. Nevertheless, these reforms generate very substantial gains for China's economy. They also serve to boost rural incomes and reduce the incidence of rural poverty. Indeed, when combined with global trade liberalization, poverty in China is estimated to drop by about 55 million people.

Introduction

With its rapid economic growth and integration into the world economy over the last two decades, China has emerged as a global economic force. Now it is the fourth largest trader and the largest FDI recipient in the world. China's foreign trade and investment are expected to be further boosted by WTO accession, including the recent elimination of textile and apparel quotas, as well as prospective multilateral trade liberalization in the context of the Doha Development Agenda (DDA). However, against the background of rapid economic growth and openness, the income distribution has deteriorated sharply in China. The ratio of urban to rural incomes increased from 2.2 in 1990 to 3.1 in 2002, which is extremely high by international standards. In the meantime, income inequality within rural areas, as measured by the Gini coefficient, rose from 0.31 in 1990 to 0.36 in 2001, and it increased from 0.23 to 0.32 in urban areas over the same period (Li and Yue 2004).

This widening income disparity is the result of profound structural changes in the Chinese economy. The experience of the last decade suggests that trade liberalization might contribute to the increased inequality (Kanbur and Zhang 2001). China's WTO accession has further heightened the concern about the increasing rural-urban disparity, because most analyses suggest that accession will exacerbate inequality by lowering barriers to grain imports and increasing opportunities for manufacturing exports as well as foreign investment in urban-based services (Bhattasali, Li, and Martin, 2004). Hertel, Zhai, and Wang (2004) find that the poorest rural, agriculture-specialized households that have limited labor mobility out of farming might lose from WTO accession. How will these outcomes be affected by a potential Doha reform package? Do complementary reforms exist that might lessen adverse impacts on the poor? This chapter focuses on the potential for rural education reforms to enhance the poverty outcomes under a potential DDA.

It has been widely recognized that education plays a critical role in creating human capital and subsequently prompting economic development and reducing poverty. However, investment in education is often inadequate relative to other investments, because of the presence of associated externalities, labor market distortions that depress private returns to education, and the generally low level of public support for education (Heckman 2002). Moreover, disparities in funding for education have resulted in nonuniform access to education across regions and between urban and rural areas. In China, education spending has been disproportionately directed toward urban areas at the cost of rural areas. In 2001, per capita spending on compulsory education in urban areas was a 16 percent higher than in rural areas (Wang 2003).

This chapter uses a household-disaggregated applied general equilibrium (AGE) model to assess the differential household effects of multilateral trade liberalization under the DDA of the WTO, as well as the additional impacts of increasing spending on rural education. The framework used here explicitly models the linkages between education and labor productivity improvement as well as off-farm labor mobility, which is a critical vehicle for poverty reduction in rural China.

This chapter is organized as follows: section 1 describes the specification of the CGE model used in this study. Section 2 elaborates on how the educational expenditures and output are modeled in terms of the supply of labor force by skill and associated efficiency. Section 3 assesses the impact of Doha Round trade liberalization, as well as increasing rural educational expenditures, on rural-urban inequality. The final section offers conclusions.

The CGE Model

The CGE model of China used in this study is the latest in a long line of model developments based at the Development Research Center of the State Council in Beijing. The model has its intellectual roots in the group of single-country, AGE models used over the past two decades to analyze the impact of trade policy reform (Dervis, de Melo, and Robinson 1982; Shoven and Whalley 1992). Here, the focus is on the main features of the model.

Household Behavior

To come to grips with the poverty question, it is critical to disaggregate households to the maximum extent possible, subject to the limitations posed by survey sampling, computational constraints, and human capacity for analysis. Following previous work (Hertel, Zhai, and Wang 2004; Hertel and Zhai 2004), rural and urban households are disaggregated into 40 rural and 60 urban representative households according to their primary source of income and relative income level. Recent analysis of trade and poverty by Hertel and others (2004) suggests the merit of distinguishing those households that are specialized (95 percent or more of their income from one source) in transfer payments, labor wages and salaries, or self-employment income. According to the available survey data, the rural households are stratified by agriculture-specialized and diversified (all other) and the urban households by three strata: transfer-specialized, labor-specialized, and diversified. Within each stratum, households are ordered from poorest to richest, based on per capita income, and then grouped into 20 vingtiles, each containing 5 percent of the stratum population.

Household income derives from labor income, profits from family-owned agriculture and nonagriculture enterprises, property income, and transfers. Households consume goods and services according to a preference structure determined by the extended linear expenditure system. Through specification of a subsistence quantity of each good or service, this expenditure function generates nonhomothetic demands whereby the larger the relative importance of subsistence consumption (for example, it would be high for rice and low for automobiles), the more income-inelastic the household's demand for that good.

The other important dimension of household behavior is the supply of labor to off-farm activities. In China, the off-farm labor supply decision is complicated by institutional factors that have been built into the system keep the agricultural population in place (Zhao 1999b). During earlier years, the Chinese government sought to make it costly for individuals to leave the rural areas by tying incomes to daily participation in collective work. More recently, the absence of well-defined land tenure has raised the opportunity cost of leaving the farm (Yang 1997). Households that cease to farm the land may lose the rights to it, so they have a strong incentive to continue some level of agricultural activity, even when profitability is quite low (Zhao 1999a). With only modest growth in rural, nonfarm activities, this seriously limits the ability of households to obtain off-farm work (Zhao 1999b).[1]

A constant elasticity of transformation (CET) function is used to model the off-farm labor supply of rural households. The labor allocation between farm and off-farm jobs is determined by the ratio of the shadow value of labor in agriculture, relative to the off-farm wage rate, and the elasticity of transformation,[2] which reflects imperfect labor mobility. There are many reasons for this imperfect mobility of labor, including education, experience, and simple geography that can serve to isolate farm households from the nonfarm labor market. Owing to the absence of an effectively functioning land market, the shadow value of labor in agriculture in this function takes into account the potential impact that reducing agricultural employment will have on the household's claim to farmland. This incremental factor is calculated as the marginal value product of land, multiplied by the rate at which decreased on-farm labor reduces the household's land endowment.[3]

Rural-Urban Migration

Despite the large income and poverty differential between rural and urban households, permanent migration in China has been limited. This is due to a combination of both direct and indirect measures. First, households must have an appropriate registration (*hukou*) to legally reside in an urban area. Without this registration, access to many of the urban amenities, including housing and education, is limited and quite expensive. In light of these barriers to moving the entire household to an urban area, rural-urban migration is largely a transitory phenomenon.

For the modeling exercise, it is important to obtain an estimate of the wage gap motivating the temporary migration of workers from the rural to the urban sector in China. Zhao (1999a) documents an average annual wage gap between rural and urban work of 2,387.6 yuan for unskilled rural workers of comparable background and ability in Sichuan province in 1995. The majority of the wage gap is due to social costs associated with migration, including the disutility of being away from family, poor quality of housing, limited social services for migrants, and the general uncertainty associated with being an unregistered worker in an urban area (Zhao 1999a, 1999b). Although these transactions costs are unobservable, they clearly represent a very significant burden on the migrants and their families.

If there were no barriers to the movement of labor between rural and urban areas, real wages would be expected to be equalized for an individual worker with given characteristics. Shi, Sicular, and Zhao (2002) explore the question of rural-urban inequality in greater detail for nine provinces using the China Health and Nutrition Survey (CHNS). The authors conclude that the apparent labor market distortion is about 42 percent of the rural-urban labor income differential and 48 percent of the hourly earnings differential.[4] When applied to the average wage differential, this amounts to an ad valorem rate of apparent transaction "tax" on rural wages of 81 percent.[5]

These transaction costs are modeled as real costs assumed by the temporary migrants. Of course, these migrants are heterogeneous, and the extent of the burden varies widely. Those individuals who are single and live close to the urban area in which they are working are likely to experience minor inconvenience as a result of this temporary migration. They can be expected to be the first to migrate (all things being equal) in response to higher urban wages. However, some migrants have large families and come from a great distance. Their urban living conditions are often very poor, and it is not uncommon for them to be robbed on the train when they are returning home after their work. For such individuals, the decision to migrate temporarily is likely to be a marginal one—and one that they may not choose to repeat. With this heterogeneous population in mind, a transactions cost function is postulated. This function is increasing in the proportion of the rural population engaged in temporary work. It has a simple, constant-elasticity functional form, which begins at the origin and reaches the observed wage gap (adjusted for transport and living costs) at the current level of temporary migration (about 70 million workers). Further increases in temporary migration are assumed to have only a modest impact on these transaction costs.[6]

Production, Exports, and Imports

Since the 1990s, processing exports have grown rapidly as a result of their preferential treatment, which includes duty-free imports. This sector now accounts for more than half of China's total exports. This is explicitly captured in the CGE model by incorporating two separate foreign-trading regimes. One is the export processing regime, which receives duty-free imports and is therefore extremely open, with considerable foreign investment. Under this regime, firms process and assemble the imported goods, turning them into finished goods for export; these imported intermediate goods are exempted from tariffs and VATs. Therefore, export-processing firms are more intensive in their use of imported intermediate inputs, and all of their output is exported. The other sector is the ordinary trade regime, which is carried out under traditional taxes and regulations. The firms under the ordinary trade regime sell products on the domestic market or export to the rest of the world, according to a CET function. Therefore, the ordinary exports are treated as differentiated products from those sold on the domestic market. It is also assumed that the buyers of the rest of the world choose a mix of the ordinary exports and the processing exports to minimize their costs.

There are two types of imports in the model. The imports of duty-free processing goods are used by export-processing firms as their intermediate inputs. Ordinary imports are modeled using the Armington assumption, that is, they are assumed to be differentiated from Chinese products produced by ordinary firms. The small country assumption is assumed for imports, thus world import prices are exogenous in terms of foreign currency. Exports are demanded according to constant-elasticity demand curves. Therefore, the terms of trade (TOT) for China are endogenous in the simulation in this chapter. The values of export demand and Armington elasticities, which are reported in table 10.1, are based on the estimation by Hertel and others (2003). Table 10.1 also lists a variety of useful information on production and trade patterns of the Chinese economy, based on the 1997 Chinese social accounting matrix (SAM).

Table 10.1. Elasticity Parameters for Trade and Sectoral Structure of Production and Trade

Sector	Trade elasticity			Sectoral structure				
	Armington	CET	Export demand	Output share (%)	Value added share of output (%)	Capital-labor ratio	Exports, outputs (%)	Imports, domestic use (%)
Rice	5.1	3.6	10.1	1.2	63.0	0.1	0.9	0.9
Wheat	4.5	3.6	8.9	0.7	62.9	0.1	0.0	7.9
Corn	1.3	3.6	2.6	0.4	63.0	0.1	7.9	1.1
Cotton	2.5	3.6	5.0	0.3	62.7	0.1	0.0	10.7
Other nongrain crops	2.5	3.6	4.9	3.8	62.9	0.1	2.3	0.8
Forestry	2.5	3.6	5.0	0.4	70.6	0.1	3.6	6.7
Wool	6.5	3.6	12.9	0.0	47.3	0.1	8.9	55.5
Other livestock	1.5	3.6	3.1	3.8	48.2	0.1	0.9	0.1
Fishing	1.3	3.6	2.5	1.1	59.0	0.2	1.2	0.2
Other agriculture	2.5	3.6	5.0	0.6	54.9	0.2	1.2	0.0
Coal mining	3.1	4.6	6.1	1.1	49.3	0.4	3.1	0.4
Crude oil and natural gas	7.4	4.6	14.9	0.8	64.6	3.8	14.4	23.9
Ferrous ore mining	3.0	4.6	5.9	0.2	27.2	0.7	0.0	29.6
Nonferrous ore mining	4.2	4.6	8.4	0.4	31.7	0.7	1.1	6.5
Other mining	0.9	4.6	1.8	0.9	36.5	0.5	4.3	5.5
Vegetable oil	3.3	4.5	6.6	0.6	15.4	2.4	4.3	12.1
Grain mill and forage	2.6	4.5	5.2	1.6	15.7	2.4	1.6	4.0
Sugar	2.7	4.7	5.4	0.2	10.1	0.3	3.3	6.0
Processed food	2.8	4.5	5.6	2.6	21.9	1.1	9.7	2.5

Table 10.1. *(Continued)*

Sector	Trade elasticity			Output share (%)	Sectoral structure			
	Armington	CET	Export demand		Value added share of output (%)	Capital-labor ratio	Exports, outputs (%)	Imports, domestic use (%)
Beverage	1.2	4.7	2.3	1.3	19.7	1.1	3.1	0.5
Tobacco	1.2	4.7	2.3	0.7	12.1	1.7	3.2	1.3
Textile	3.8	5.4	7.5	4.6	22.8	1.0	18.4	10.1
Apparel	3.7	5.8	7.4	1.9	31.8	0.6	37.0	3.6
Leather	4.1	4.6	8.1	1.1	18.9	0.5	32.6	13.2
Sawmills and furniture	3.4	4.6	6.8	1.1	23.2	0.7	13.1	5.6
Paper and printing	3.0	4.6	5.9	1.7	27.4	0.6	2.0	9.9
Social articles	3.8	5.6	7.5	1.1	25.9	0.9	40.0	8.9
Petroleum refining	2.1	3.8	4.2	1.6	12.5	1.7	5.7	11.6
Chemicals	3.3	3.8	6.6	4.1	20.1	1.0	8.3	16.5
Medicine	3.3	3.8	6.6	0.9	28.1	1.8	5.9	1.7
Chemical fibers	3.3	3.8	6.6	0.6	17.1	1.4	6.6	18.2
Rubber and plastics	3.3	3.8	6.6	2.1	19.2	0.9	15.7	6.9
Building materials	2.9	3.8	5.8	4.4	26.2	0.7	3.4	1.2
Primary iron and steel	3.0	4.6	5.9	2.7	16.3	0.6	5.5	8.6
Nonferrous metals	4.2	4.6	8.4	1.2	13.4	0.7	8.0	13.0
Metal products	3.8	4.6	7.5	2.5	19.3	0.7	13.1	7.0
Machinery	2.8	4.6	5.6	2.5	31.0	1.1	5.9	13.2
Special equipment	2.8	4.6	5.6	1.8	24.3	0.8	5.6	23.3
Automobile	2.8	4.6	5.6	1.7	21.2	1.0	1.9	4.1

Table 10.1. *(Continued)*

Sector	Trade elasticity			Sectoral structure				
	Armington	CET	Export demand	Output share (%)	Value added share of output (%)	Capital-labor ratio	Exports, outputs (%)	Imports, domestic use (%)
Other transport equipment	4.3	4.6	8.6	1.3	24.2	0.8	9.7	12.1
Electric machinery	4.1	4.6	8.1	2.8	18.1	0.9	15.9	9.5
Electronics	4.4	4.6	8.8	2.5	21.2	1.1	36.3	34.1
Instruments	4.1	4.6	8.1	0.4	27.3	0.9	49.5	43.2
Other manufacturing	3.8	3.8	7.5	0.8	53.3	1.0	8.1	3.1
Utilities	2.8	3.8	5.6	2.2	36.1	2.0	0.9	0.0
Construction	1.9	3.8	3.8	8.7	26.4	0.3	0.1	0.3
Transportation	1.9	2.8	3.8	2.5	50.4	1.0	9.4	1.8
Post and communications	1.9	2.8	3.8	1.0	53.5	3.5	5.7	1.3
Commerce	1.9	2.8	3.8	6.5	37.2	0.5	0.9	1.3
Finance	1.9	2.8	3.8	1.8	37.9	1.1	0.5	1.2
Social services	1.9	2.8	3.8	3.7	45.0	1.2	10.1	5.3
Education and health	1.9	2.8	3.8	3.3	46.4	0.3	0.7	0.5
Public administration	1.9	2.8	3.8	2.2	45.0	0.2	0.1	0.6

Source: Hertel and others (2003); 1997 Chinese SAM.

Production in each of the sectors of the economy is modeled using nested constant elasticity of substitution (CES) functions, and constant returns to scale are assumed. In the top level of the nest, value added and a composite of intermediate inputs produce outputs. Then a further CES function disaggregates the value added into a capital-labor composite and agricultural land. The capital-labor composite is further split into the capital–skilled labor composite and the aggregated less skilled labor (which is composed of semiskilled labor and unskilled labor.) The values of substitution elasticities in production functions are listed in table 10.2. A low substitution elasticity of 0.3 between capital and skilled labor is assumed here to introduce capital-skill complementarity. The elasticity of substitution between semiskilled labor and unskilled labor is set to 1.5, based on estimates for the United States by Katz and Murphy (1992) and Heckman and Lochner (1998).

Within each labor category (unskilled, semiskilled, and skilled), rural and urban workers are distinguished. These two categories of workers substitute imperfectly in production. This is an indirect means of building into the model a geographic flavor because some sectors will be located largely in urban areas, and others will be predominantly in rural areas. By limiting the substitutability of rural and urban labor in each sector, the model proxies the economic effect of geographically distributed activity. This is particularly important in China, where significant barriers to rural and urban mobility remain (see section 1.2 above). Ideally, the geographic distribution of industrial activity would be modeled, but unfortunately the data do not exist to support this split.

All commodity and nonlabor factor markets are assumed to clear through prices. With the exception of the farm or nonfarm labor supply decision, labor is

Table 10.2.   Substitution Elasticities in Production

Type of elasticity	Agriculture	Nonagriculture
Value added-aggregated intermediate input	0.10	0.10
Capital-labor composite-land	0.30	n.a.
Capital-skilled labor composite- aggregate less skilled labor		
Old vintage	0.45	0.65
New vintage	0.95	1.10
Capital-skilled labor	0.30	0.30
Unskilled labor-semiskilled labor	1.50	1.50
Urban labor-rural labor	2.20	2.20

Source: DRC CGE model.

assumed to be perfectly mobile across sectors. Capital is assumed to be partially mobile, reflecting differences in the marketability of capital goods across sectors.

Recursive-Dynamic and Steady-State, Comparative Static Closures

The CGE model is benchmarked to China's 1997 SAM, and it incorporates dynamics in two alternative ways. The recursive-dynamic version of the model is used to update the SAM to 2005 and assess the impact of intervening events on China's patterns of trade, production, and consumption. In this version of the model, the classical savings-investment mechanism determines the capital stock in the medium and long term. Dynamics originate from the accumulation of productive factors and productivity changes. The steady-state, comparative static version is used to assess the impact of trade and educational reforms, starting from the 2005 base. Here, the longer-term accumulation effects are taken into account by introducing a different capital market closure following Harrison, Rutherford, and Tarr (1997) and Francois and McDonald (1996). The aggregate capital stock is allowed to adjust to its long-term equilibrium based on an exogenous capital rental rate (fixed at the benchmark level). The theoretical underpinnings of this closure are based on the concept of an invariant capital stock equilibrium as proposed by Hansen and Koopmans (1972).

Modeling Education

Education affects the economy in several important ways. It improves the skills of workers, thereby enhancing their productivity and garnering them a higher wage. In the context of rural China, education is also a key determinant of an individual's potential suitability for off-farm work (Yang 2004; Zhang, Huang, and Rozelle 2002). Because the farm–off-farm labor market linkage has proven key to the transmission of trade reform benefits to the rural poor (Hertel, Zhai, and Wang 2004), this mechanism receives special attention here. This section describes the framework through which education expenditure affects the production of human capital and its distribution among different household groups, as well as the linkage between schooling attainment and off-farm mobility of labor in rural areas.

The Role of Education in the Model

In the CGE model, each household is endowed with 17 groups of workers, distinguished by their total years of schooling, ranging from 0 to 16. Based on this level of educational attainment, the skill level of household members in the workforce can be inferred. Unskilled labor refers to workers with 0 to 6 years of educational attainment. Semiskilled workers have 7 to 12 years of educational attainment, and skilled workers have an educational attainment from 12 to 16 years. For each household, the labor endowment by skill is determined by its age-specific school participation rates and labor force participation rates.

The age-specific school participation rates are determined by the education costs per pupil-year and the total educational expenditure. It is assumed that a change in total education expenditure induces a proportional change in school participation rates across all ages. The education expenditure comprises private expenditure and government expenditure, which are assumed to be fully fungible. Government and private education expenditures enter the budget constraints of government and households, respectively. However, private decisions are not the result of household investment choices. Rather, throughout the analysis, private and public expenditures are assumed to be made in equal proportions.

In the model, education enhances labor productivity through two channels. First, more education improves the skill composition of the labor force, resulting in a greater supply of skilled labor and lesser supply of unskilled labor. Second, for each skill level, more education yields a higher level of average schooling attainment, thereby improving its average labor productivity. The second channel is captured by linear increasing functions between labor efficiency and the average years of schooling for the three types of labor.

As noted above, the off-farm labor supply decision of rural households is modeled as a CET function of the ratio of the shadow value of labor in agriculture, relative to the off-farm wage rate. It is assumed that the elasticity of transformation is a linear, increasing function of average years of schooling within the labor skill groups. This specification, which implies that rural households with higher educational attainment respond more effectively to farm-nonfarm wage gaps, is based on recent empirical evidence (Zhang, Huang, and Rozelle 2002).

Model Calibration and Choice of Parameters

Detailed data on the population and labor force are necessary to calibrate the education block of the model. The age distribution of the rural and urban populations, respectively, is calculated according to their mortality tables from the 2000 national population census, under the assumption of a stationary population, that is, no change in the age structure. The age distribution of each of the 40 rural household groups is assumed to be the same, and similarly with the 60 urban household groups. Age-specific labor participation rates by urban and rural classifications are also obtained from the 2000 national population census. They were scaled up or down to the aggregated labor force participation rate of each representative household to obtain the age-specific labor participation rates by household.

National average school participation rates by age are calculated from official enrollment and dropout rates for primary school, middle school, high school, and university or college. Then the age-specific school participation rates of each household are estimated by solving a quadratic program, which minimizes the difference between the school participation rates of each household and the national average school participation rates, subject to the constraints implied by the base year skill composition of each household's labor endowment.

The productivity increments associated with educational attainment enhancement are derived from the study by Shi, Sicular, and Zhao (2002). These authors estimate wage (or shadow wage) equations for agricultural and rural, nonfarm workers. These equations include educational attainment as an explanatory variable. Their estimates suggest that additional education has the greatest impact on rural nonfarm wages, with one additional year of schooling boosting hourly wages (and presumably productivity) by 15 percent. Additional schooling also has an impact on agricultural productivity, with an additional year of schooling boosting total factor productivity on the farm by 2 percent. When adjusted for the share of labor in agricultural output, this is equivalent to a 2.5 percent increase in labor productivity. Specification of the values of the off-farm labor supply elasticity draws on the econometric work of Sicular and Zhao (2004) and Zhang, Huang, and Rozelle (2002). Sicular and Zhao report results from a household labor supply model estimated using labor survey data from the 1997 CHNS dataset for nine central provinces. From their labor supply equations for self-employed agricultural labor and self-employed nonagricultural labor, it is possible to calculate elasticities of labor transfer from farm to nonfarm activities. They report a variety of elasticities in their paper.[7] This chapter adopts their estimate of 2.67 for use in this work as the overall farm–off-farm transformation elasticity for the total rural labor force.

To obtain separate estimates of the farm–off-farm transformation elasticity for three skill levels of labor, the rate at which increased schooling attainment enhances the transformation elasticity is used, based on the study by Zhang, Huang, and Rozelle (2002). These authors explore the labor supply behavior of a panel of 310 individuals in 109 families observed in four villages of Jiangsu province in 1988, 1992, and 1996. They find that for every additional year of education, farmers had a 14 percent greater chance of finding an off-farm job in 1996, all things being equal. Using the base year ratio of the shadow value of labor in agriculture relative to the off-farm wage rate, as well as the total farm and off-farm labor supplies, this increasing opportunity for access to off-farm jobs associated with higher educational attainment translates into an increment of 0.58 in transformation elasticity for each additional year of schooling. This is used to calculate the farm–off-farm transformation elasticities by skill level according to the average years of schooling for each skill level of the rural labor force. The resulting values for this elasticity are 0.68 for unskilled labor, 4.01 for semiskilled labor, and 7.49 for skilled labor.

Simulations

Simulation Design

The baseline scenario from 1998–2005 is constructed by using the recursive-dynamic version of the model. The baseline scenario establishes a plausible growth trajectory for the Chinese economy, which takes into account events such as China's WTO accession and its recent dramatic surge in exports, which have doubled in the last four years. The updated 2005 database is then used as the new benchmark equilibrium from which the comparative steady-state model is used to conduct the policy simulations. A series of trade reform scenarios is then considered, followed by a final scenario that is designed to capture the added impact of rural education reform.

The first trade reform scenario (*ROW-Lib*) considers the impacts of global trade liberalization excluding China. In particular, this entails elimination of all import tariffs in the rest of the world. In addition, agricultural export subsidies are eliminated, as are subsidies for domestic agricultural production in the OECD. The second scenario (*Uni-Lib*) focuses on China's unilateral liberalization. All import tariffs and nontariff barriers of China are eliminated in this scenario. The third scenario (*Full-Lib*) considers the impact of global free trade by combining the first and the second scenarios. The fourth scenario is the standard Doha scenario.

To reflect the impacts of multilateral trade liberalization in the single-country model, external market impacts are incorporated into the Chinese CGE model through exogenous shifts in import prices and export demand schedules. The sizes of these exogenous trade shocks are obtained from global simulations. The tariff reduction in China is excluded in this Global Trade Analysis Project (GTAP) simulation but is included in the simulation of the single-country model.

Table 10.3 reports the results provided by the global analysis, detailed in chapter 3, for the *Full-Lib* and *Doha* scenario impacts on China (with China's own reforms excluded). In the case of *Full-Lib*, there are some enormous percentage increases in China's export volumes generated by the elimination of very high rates of protection elsewhere in Asia. Rice, corn, grain milling, and other food

Table 10.3.   Inputs from the Global Model[a] (percent change)

Sector	Export volume Full-Lib	Export volume Doha	Export price Full-Lib	Export price Doha	Import price Full-Lib	Import price Doha	Tariff Full-Lib	Tariff Doha
Rice	7,574.5	454.4	12.2	2.1	12.2	1.3	-100	0
Wheat	43.2	7.6	5.4	1.4	5.4	1.3	-100	0
Corn	88.8	21.3	7.6	1.9	7.6	5.5	-100	-28
Cotton	71.9	28.5	5.7	1.7	5.7	5.0	-100	-20
Other crops	37.9	14.9	6.7	1.6	6.1	3.6	-100	-21
Forestry	0.9	-1.4	2.5	0.7	2.5	0.1	-100	-24
Wool	3.0	-6.3	7.7	2.2	7.7	2.4	-100	-2
Other livestock	-3.1	-1.3	7.1	1.8	7.1	0.7	-100	-23
Fishing	9.8	2.8	5.0	1.2	5.0	0.2	-100	-29
Other agriculture	71.9	28.5	5.7	1.7	5.7	5.0	-100	-20
Coal mining	1.9	0.5	2.0	0.5	2.0	0.3	-100	-30
Crude oil and gas	-1.9	-0.3	1.0	0.1	0.7	0.1	-100	n.a.
Ferrous ore mining	-2.4	-1.4	2.4	0.7	2.4	0.2	-100	-30
Nonferrous ore mining	-3.6	-1.8	2.3	0.7	2.3	0.2	-100	-31
Other mining	0.8	0.2	1.9	0.5	1.9	0.5	-100	-29
Vegetable oil	-18.8	-9.2	5.7	1.7	5.7	0.4	-100	-22
Grain mill and forage	525.3	53.2	6.9	1.4	6.9	2.6	-100	0
Sugar	83.4	25.0	5.0	1.4	5.0	1.5	-100	-1
Processed food	36.6	-0.5	5.9	1.4	5.5	0.9	-100	-25
Beverage	19.9	2.2	4.5	1.2	4.5	0.2	-100	-22
Tobacco	19.9	2.2	4.5	1.2	4.5	0.2	-100	-22
Textile	13.7	5.5	3.3	1.0	3.3	0.2	-100	-33

Table 10.3. *(Continued)*

Sector	Export volume Full-Lib	Doha	Export price Full-Lib	Doha	Import price Full-Lib	Doha	Tariff Full-Lib	Doha
Apparel	17.0	9.0	2.9	0.9	2.9	0.4	-100	-32
Leather	15.2	7.0	3.7	1.1	3.7	-0.3	-100	-32
Sawmills and furniture	-4.7	-2.8	2.8	0.8	2.8	0.2	-100	-32
Paper and printing	-5.1	-3.1	3.0	0.9	3.0	0.3	-100	-33
Social articles	-4.3	-2.0	2.9	0.9	2.9	0.0	-100	-28
Petroleum refining	3.8	-0.5	1.2	0.3	1.2	0.1	-100	-30
Chemicals	0.6	-0.7	2.5	0.7	2.5	0.1	-100	-28
Medicine	0.6	-0.7	2.5	0.7	2.5	0.1	-100	-28
Chemical fibers	0.6	-0.7	2.5	0.7	2.5	0.1	-100	-28
Rubber and plastics	0.6	-0.7	2.5	0.7	2.5	0.1	-100	-28
Building materials	8.8	2.1	2.6	0.8	2.6	0.2	-100	-32
Primary iron and steel	-2.4	-1.4	2.4	0.7	2.4	0.2	-100	-30
Nonferrous metals	-3.6	-1.8	2.3	0.7	2.3	0.2	-100	-31
Metal products	4.4	0.9	2.5	0.7	2.5	0.1	-100	-33
Machinery	-18.3	-5.6	2.3	0.7	2.3	0.0	-100	-33
Special equipment	-18.3	-5.6	2.3	0.7	2.3	0.0	-100	-33
Automobile	-18.3	-5.6	2.3	0.7	2.3	0.0	-100	-33
Other transport equipment	15.7	-1.3	2.4	0.7	2.4	0.0	-100	-32
Electric machinery	-4.1	-2.3	2.4	0.7	2.4	0.0	-100	-33
Electronics	-4.8	-2.8	1.8	0.5	1.8	0.1	-100	-33
Instruments	-4.1	-2.3	2.4	0.7	2.4	0.0	-100	-33
Other manufacturing	-4.3	-2.0	2.9	0.9	2.9	0.0	-100	-28

Table 10.3. *(Continued)*

Sector	Export volume		Export price		Import price		Tariff	
	Full-Lib	Doha	Full-Lib	Doha	Full-Lib	Doha	Full-Lib	Doha
Utilities	-2.4	-1.3	2.4	0.7	2.4	0.0	0	0
Construction	-6.3	-2.6	2.7	0.8	2.7	-0.1	0	0
Transportation	-5.5	-2.3	3.0	0.9	2.9	0.2	0	0
Post and communications	-5.4	-2.2	2.6	0.8	2.6	0.0	0	0
Commerce	-5.6	-2.5	3.1	0.9	3.1	0.3	0	0
Finance	-5.6	-2.3	2.7	0.8	2.7	-0.1	0	0
Social services	-6.2	-2.4	2.8	0.8	2.8	-0.1	0	0
Education and health	-6.5	-2.3	2.8	0.8	2.8	0.0	0	0
Public administration	-6.5	-2.3	2.8	0.8	2.8	0.0	0	0

Source: GTAP simulations.

Note: n.a. = not applicable.

a. These results are obtained by solving the global model with China's shocks omitted. The export price and volume changes are used, along with the export demand elasticity, to compute the shift in the export demand schedule.

products all show very large proportionate increases. Of course, the associated volume changes are often quite modest, because China is not a large exporter of most of these products. Moreover, after the China CGE model is solved with implied shifts in export demands and import prices, the resulting equilibrium change in export volumes predicted by the national model is much smaller than that suggested by the GTAP simulations. (See the appendix to Chapter 3 for a detailed comparison.)

World food and agricultural prices facing China rise relative to nonfood prices, based on the global modeling exercise, with the increases ranging from 4 percent to 12 percent in the case of full liberalization, but considerably smaller for the *Doha* scenario. These are reported in the second and third sets of columns in table 10.3. The final set of columns in table 10.3 reports the percentage cut in the tariff rates in China under each scenario. In the case of *Doha*, they are in the range of one-quarter to one-third of *Full-Lib* (-100 percent).

The final scenario of this chapter explores the potential poverty impacts of investing in rural education. This scenario equalizes the urban-rural imbalance in per capita government spending on education by increasing government spending on rural education by 16 percent to bring per capita rural spending in line with that in urban areas.[8] Since the emphasis here is on the impact of this reform in the context of multilateral trade liberalization, it is treated as a combined scenario, with the rural educational reforms added to the global liberalization scenario (*Full-Lib*). The shorthand for this combined scenario is *Edu-Lib*.

Economywide Impacts of Multilateral Trade Liberalization

The macroeconomic results from the trade reform scenarios are reported in the first four columns of table 10.4. The reported values are deviations from the baseline in 2005. The reduction in global trade barriers gives a substantial boost to trade in China, with both exports and imports rising by about 2–3 percent in the Doha Round trade liberalization and 5–6 percent in the scenario of global free trade (*Full-Lib*). Aggregate welfare, which is measured by the summation of individual household equivalent variation (EV) and reported as a percentage of GDP, would increase by about 0.4 percent under the Doha trade reforms and 0.8 percent in the scenario of global free trade, because of improved TOT and reduced distortions between world prices and domestic prices. China's welfare gain from global trade liberalization comes entirely from the liberalization of other countries. Actually, in the scenario of unilateral trade liberalization, China experiences a welfare loss of 0.3 percent of its GDP as a result of a deterioration in its TOT, which are endogenous in this model. This reflects China's relatively low-level import protection after its WTO accession and its growing influence in world export markets, which in turn tends to reduce its export demand elasticities.

Table 10.4. Aggregated Results (percent change)

					Edu-Lib	
	ROW-Lib	Uni-Lib	Full-Lib	Doha	Incre-mental	Cumu-lative
Macroeconomic variables						
Welfare (EV)	1.0	-0.3	0.8	0.4	1.2	2.0
GDP	0.1	-0.1	0.1	0.0	1.2	1.2
Exports	0.2	4.4	4.8	2.2	1.0	5.8
Imports	1.9	3.8	5.9	2.9	0.8	6.7
TOT	1.4	-0.8	0.5	0.5	-0.3	0.3
CPI	4.6	-2.1	2.4	0.7	0.9	3.3
Capital stock	1.7	-0.6	1.1	0.3	1.1	2.2
Factor prices						
Returns to agricultural land	23.2	-7.2	15.5	5.2	7.0	23.5
Unskilled wages						
Urban	5.2	-1.9	3.3	1.0	14.8	18.6
Rural, nonagricultural	5.3	-1.9	3.3	1.0	16.7	20.6
Agricultural	6.1	-2.3	3.9	1.3	28.3	33.3
Semiskilled wages						
Urban	5.4	-1.9	3.4	1.1	-4.0	-0.7
Rural, nonagricultural	5.8	-2.0	3.7	1.2	-4.9	-1.4
Agricultural	5.2	-1.9	3.3	1.0	-4.2	-1.0
Skilled wages						
Urban	5.6	-1.7	3.8	1.2	-0.5	3.3
Rural, nonagricultural	5.6	-1.7	3.8	1.2	-0.5	3.3
Agricultural	5.9	-1.8	4.0	1.2	-3.9	-0.1
Labor migration (million)						
Off-farm labor	-3.3	1.2	-2.2	-0.8	4.9	2.8
Unskilled	-0.5	0.2	-0.4	-0.1	-10.2	-10.6
Semiskilled	-2.6	1.0	-1.7	-0.6	13.3	11.6
Skilled	-0.2	0.1	-0.1	0.0	1.9	1.8
Rural-urban	-2.4	0.9	-1.5	-0.6	2.0	0.4
Unskilled	-0.3	0.1	-0.2	-0.1	-10.4	-10.6
Semiskilled	-1.9	0.7	-1.2	-0.5	10.5	9.2
Skilled	-0.2	0.1	-0.1	0.0	1.9	1.8
Labor migration (%)						
Off-farm labor	-2.5	0.9	1.6	-0.6	3.8	2.1
Unskilled	-0.9	0.3	-0.6	-0.2	-18.4	-18.9
Semiskilled	-3.8	1.4	-2.5	-0.9	19.7	16.7
Skilled	-2.3	1.0	-1.4	-0.5	27.9	26.1
Rural-urban	-3.7	1.4	-2.3	-0.9	3.1	0.7
Unskilled	-1.0	0.4	-0.7	-0.2	-38.2	-38.6
Semiskilled	-6.1	2.4	-3.9	-1.4	34.2	29.0
Skilled	-3.0	1.2	-1.8	-0.7	35.9	33.5

Source: Simulation results.

With fixed labor endowments, full employment, and no productivity changes, China's GDP is little changed under trade reform. The small increase under *Full-Lib* is driven by the effects on labor reallocation and capital accumulation. In the case of Doha Round trade liberalization as well as global free trade, stronger export demand in agricultural products and larger cuts in tariff rates for manufactured goods divert the labor force from high productivity, manufacturing sectors to lower productivity, agricultural sectors, when compared to the baseline outcome.[9] Although capital stock rises slightly, spurred by the trade liberalization, the increased capital stock is largely offset by the productivity loss associated with more labor employed in agriculture and the rural sector, resulting in minimal gains in real GDP. However, in the scenario of China's unilateral liberalization, the deterioration in terms of trade reduces the profits of exports, which consequently discourages the capital accumulation, resulting in a lower level of steady-state capital stock. Although some of the agricultural labor force is diverted to nonagricultural activities, this does not offset the adverse effect of less capital stock. As a consequence, GDP slightly declines in the scenario of China's unilateral liberalization.

Turning to the changes in factor prices, it can be seen that the effects of global free trade and Doha Round trade liberalization on wages are largely neutral across skill levels and between rural and urban sectors. The increase in agricultural profitability, which is reflected in the rise of returns to agricultural land, increases the on-farm demand for labor and therefore reduces off-farm labor supply by about 0.8 million in the Doha Round trade liberalization and 2.2 million in the scenario of global free trade, relative to baseline. Urban and rural nonfarm wages are linked through the temporary migration of individuals to urban areas. In the multilateral trade liberalization scenarios, temporary migration from the rural to the urban sector is slowed, with about 1.5 million fewer migrants under *Full-Lib* than would be the case in the baseline.

Because poverty and income distribution are central to this chapter, it provides several such measures for China as a whole in table 10.5. The urban-rural income ratio declines in all three global trade liberalization scenarios, although the magnitude of this change is very small—0.01 point in the case of global free trade. This is also reflected in a small improvement in urban-rural inequality, as measured by the Gini coefficient. However, there are no discernible changes in inequality within the urban and rural areas.

Using the US$2 per day poverty line, Chen and Ravallion (2004) estimate that 45.2 percent of the rural population in China and 4.1 percent of the urban population are in poverty. Applying these figures to the benchmark data for 2005 provides the poverty line of Y4,730 (1997 prices) for urban households and Y3,580 (1997 prices) for rural households. By assuming a uniform distribution of the population within each of the vingtiles, it is possible to estimate how the poverty headcount changes in the wake of these reforms. This information is also reported

Table 10.5.   Effects on Inequality and Poverty

				Edu-Lib	
	Base	Full-lib	Doha	Incremental	Cumulative
Inequality					
Urban-rural income	3.213	0.012	0.005	-0.230	-0.242
Ratio					
Gini	0.438	0.001	0.001	-0.015	-0.016
Urban	0.291	0.000	0.000	0.003	0.003
Rural	0.298	0.000	0.000	0.001	0.001
Poverty headcount	ratio (%)	Changes (percentage point)			
Total	31.3	-0.8	-0.4	-3.3	-4.2
Urban	4.1	-0.1	0.0	0.3	0.2
Transfer specialized	24.7	0.0	0.0	0.1	0.1
Labor specialized	3.8	-0.1	-0.1	0.3	0.2
Diversified	2.5	-0.1	0.0	0.3	0.2
Rural	45.2	-1.2	-0.6	-5.2	-6.4
Agriculture-specialized	54.3	-1.2	-0.5	-4.7	-5.8
Diversified	44.1	-1.2	-0.6	-5.3	-6.5
	(millions of persons)	(% change)			
Total	413.7	-2.7	-1.3	-11.0	-13.4
Urban	18.2	-2.1	-1.2	7.3	5.0
Transfer-specialized	5.3	-0.1	-0.1	0.5	0.4
Labor-specialized	6.7	-2.5	-1.4	8.5	5.8
Diversified	6.1	-3.5	-2.0	12.0	8.1
Rural	395.5	-2.7	-1.3	-11.8	-14.2
Agriculture-specialized	49.8	-2.1	-1.0	-8.8	-10.7
Diversified	345.7	-2.8	-1.3	-12.3	-14.7

Source: Simulation results.

in table 10.5. In the *Full-Lib* scenario, the monetary poverty line increases by 2.4 percent following the change in the CPI (table 10.4). Nevertheless, higher factor earnings mean that the poverty headcount ratio declines for all household groups.

Because transfer incomes are assumed to be constant in real terms and are indexed by the CPI, the urban transfer-specialized household group experiences only a modest decline in its poverty headcount, reflecting a decline in nontransfer income, which makes up less than 5 percent of this group's total income. The aggregate urban poverty headcount decreases by about 2.1 percent. Rural households enjoy a 2.7 percent reduction in poverty headcount, which amounts to a 1.2 *percentage point* reduction in rural poverty (that is, the proportion of the entire

Figure 10.1. Change in Sector Output, Full-Lib

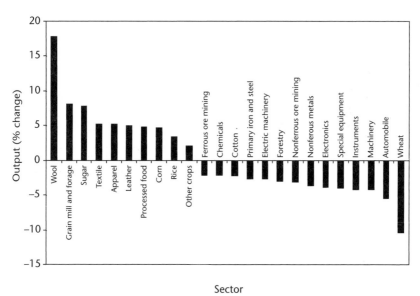

Source: Authors' simulations.

rural population in poverty falls by 1.2 percent). Given the large population base in rural China, this translates into a rural poverty reduction of 10.6 million people. The *Doha* scenario shows a similar pattern of poverty reduction across households, but with lesser absolute reductions. Overall, the impoverished share of the national population falls from 31.3 percent of total population to 30.5 percent in the scenario of global free trade, and to 30.9 percent under the Doha Round scenarios.

Sector Impacts

Figure 10.1 and figure 10.2 report a subset of the changes in sector output, in descending order, omitting the changes that are less than 2 percent for global free trade and less than 0.7 percent in absolute value for the Doha Round trade liberalization, respectively. In both scenarios, the largest increases in output are due to the expansion of textiles and apparel exports, with these products, as well as the production of synthetic fibers, increasing by substantial amounts in the wake of tariff cuts in overseas markets. Some agricultural sectors, such as wool, corn and grain milling, and feedstuffs, also enjoy a boost in output, particularly under the

Figure 10.2. Change in Sector Output, Doha

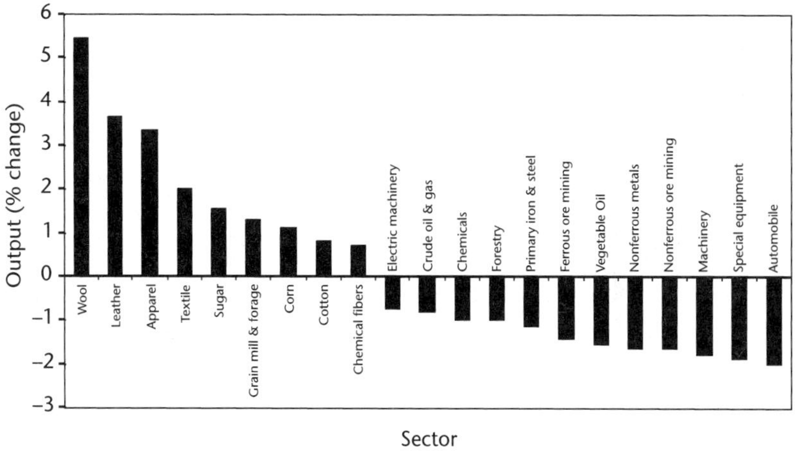

Source: Authors' simulations.

Full-Lib scenario (figure 10.1). On the other end of the spectrum, the most heavily protected sectors, with sizable trade exposure, experience declining output—automobiles, machinery, special equipment, nonferrous metal products, and vegetable oil. In the case of global free trade, wheat production shows the largest reduction in output, because of the very large reduction in China's tariff under that scenario.

Trade volume changes associated with each of the trade reform experiments are reported in table 10.6. With the exception of a few mining products and transport services for which there is no cut in protection, import volumes increase for all sectors in the economy in the scenarios of Doha Round trade liberalization. The largest increases are for automobiles, as well as textiles, apparel, and leather products, where the demand for intermediate inputs increases strongly. Export volumes for most products also increase—especially for rice, corn, grain milling and feedstuffs, textiles, and apparel—fueled by increased demand in the global market. Those sectors with slight or negative increments in exogenous export demand, such as vegetable oil, nonferrous metals, some mining products, machinery, special equipment, and automobiles, experience reductions in export volumes under the *Doha* scenario.

In the case of global free trade, the changes in both imports and exports are much more significant. Despite relatively large increases in the world price of

**Table 10.6. Sector Volume Impacts of Trade Liberalization:
Percentage Deviation from Baseline**

Sector	Full-Lib		Doha	
	Import	Export	Import	Export
Rice	-29.3	290.5	-0.6	60.7
Wheat	83.7	n.a.	0.6	n.a.
Corn	55.2	54.4	6.6	13.4
Cotton	54.5	28.8	5.6	12.3
Other nongrain crops	33.6	22.1	2.9	7.0
Forestry	16.9	-2.5	5.2	-1.7
Wool	2.7	27.9	2.9	5.8
Other livestock	2.2	4.3	3.1	0.3
Fishing	5.8	9.7	1.5	2.2
Other agriculture	17.3	34.9	2.5	13.5
Coal mining	15.2	-0.9	4.9	-0.6
Crude oil and natural gas	1.0	-1.8	0.1	-0.8
Ferrous ore mining	-2.5	-1.0	0.1	-1.0
Nonferrous ore mining	-3.6	-3.1	0.0	-1.4
Other mining	1.6	0.1	0.6	0.0
Vegetable oil	29.0	20.1	5.2	-4.8
Grain mill and forage	-2.2	247.4	-3.2	29.5
Sugar	38.1	162.7	0.9	22.7
Processed food	18.1	32.8	7.7	1.7
Beverage	17.1	18.4	3.4	2.3
Tobacco	7.3	17.3	2.8	2.3
Textile	12.9	15.6	7.4	5.6
Apparel	15.2	13.0	7.1	8.5
Leather	13.1	12.9	9.8	9.5
Sawmills and furniture	4.5	-1.6	3.0	-0.5
Paper and printing	4.0	-1.7	2.6	-0.7
Social articles	0.7	-1.6	2.7	1.1
Petroleum refining	7.9	1.8	2.5	-0.2
Chemicals	6.6	0.8	3.2	0.1
Medicine	12.3	1.4	5.1	0.2
Chemical fibers	10.5	1.9	5.6	2.0
Rubber and plastics	6.1	0.2	3.4	1.5
Building materials	11.7	5.0	4.9	1.6
Primary iron and steel	3.2	-1.7	2.0	0.6
Nonferrous metals	1.2	-3.4	1.6	-0.4
Metal products	8.2	2.6	4.2	1.6
Machinery	7.1	-12.1	3.4	-3.0

Table 10.6. *(Continued)*

Sector	Full-Lib		Doha	
	Import	Export	Import	Export
Machinery	7.1	-12.1	3.4	-3.0
Special equipment	4.5	-12.0	2.4	-3.0
Automobile	26.8	-11.1	9.4	-2.6
Other transport equipment	6.9	11.5	3.8	1.9
Electric machinery	9.7	-3.3	4.9	0.8
Electronics	-1.6	-5.8	0.9	-0.2
Instruments	3.0	-3.7	1.9	0.6
Other manufacturing	5.9	-2.2	3.6	0.3
Utilities	-1.4	-0.2	1.1	-0.3
Construction	-0.8	-2.4	1.4	-1.0
Transportation	-1.2	-1.1	0.7	-0.7
Post and communications	-1.7	-0.7	0.8	-0.3
Commerce	-0.5	-1.5	1.0	-0.8
Finance	-0.5	-1.8	1.4	-0.7
Social services	-0.5	-1.6	1.4	-0.7
Education and health	0.2	-2.7	1.7	-0.9
Public administration	0.0	-2.8	1.6	-1.0

Source: Simulation results.

Note: n.a. = not applicable (no trade flow).

imports into China, import volumes grow by 20–50 percent in most crops and food sectors, because of their large reduction in import protection. One exception is imports of rice, which would decline as a result of the low initial protection and large increment in the import price. Similar to the cases of Doha Round trade liberalization, the rise of imports in automobiles and textiles and apparel are also large. The agricultural and food sectors, textiles and apparel, and the other transportation equipment sector are the major gainers in terms of export volume. However, there are also manufacturing sectors that would experience reductions in export volume.

The large expansion in China's agricultural exports under the global free trade scenario can be better understood against the backdrop of the significant cuts in agricultural protection in the Republic of Korea and Japan. Given its close geographic proximity to (and strong trade linkage with) these countries, China would benefit from the strong agricultural import growth in these markets after global trade liberalization. However, because of its small export volumes in most agricultural products, China is still a small agricultural exporter in the world market. In the case of grains, this chapter's baseline scenario predicts that China's exports of rice and corn will be Y 2.0 billion and Y 4.8 billion (1997 prices), respectively, in 2005. Even under the scenario of global free trade, its exports of rice and corn are only Y 7.9 billion and Y 7.5 billion (1997 prices). These changes are no larger than recent annual fluctuations in exports of these commodities.[10]

Household Impacts

The analysis now turns to figures 10.3a and 10.3b, which report the household impacts of trade liberalization, by stratum, across the income spectrum. The first point to note from figure 10.3a is that global trade liberalization benefits all households, except those reliant on transfers. Because the transfers are held constant in real terms, and transfers make up most of their income, the transfer group is little affected by the trade liberalization.

Among the other urban households, the smallest welfare increases in figure 10.3a are associated with urban, diversified households. This contrasts with the relatively larger gains made by the urban, labor-specialized households. The difference occurs because the urban diversified households have significant income from capital earnings, particularly the wealthiest households. The increases in rates of return to other factors are larger than the increases in capital stock, thus the highest-income, diversified households benefit proportionately less than the other, labor-specialized urban household groups. The largest increases in welfare after global trade liberalization accrue to the rural households, especially the wealthier, agriculture-specialized households. They benefit because returns to agricultural land increase relative to other factor prices. Real income rises less for rural, diversified households because of the dominance of nonfarm wage earnings. Similar patterns of household incidence emerge from the *Doha* scenario.

Impact of Investing in Rural Education

As noted previously, one of the keys to enhancing the welfare of the rural poor—particularly those reliant on agriculture for their income—is to enhance their off-farm employment opportunities. Econometric evidence suggests that education has proven to be one of the key determinants of off-farm employment. Therefore, this chapter turns next to a comparison of the impact of improved access to education for the rural households with the global free trade experiment implemented previously. The incremental aggregate effects of rural education reform are reported in the sixth column of table 10.4. Real GDP and welfare rise by 1.3 percent

Figure 10.3a.   Impacts on Households, Full-Lib

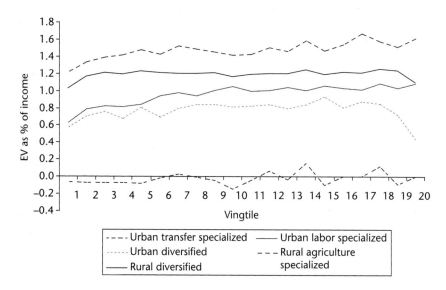

Figure 10.3b.   Impacts on Households, Doha

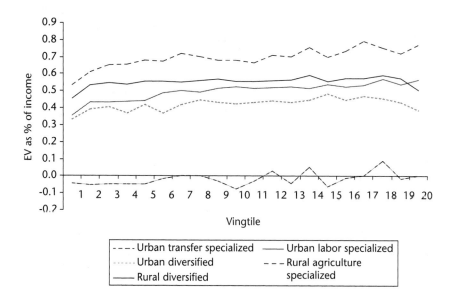

Source: Authors' simulations.

and 1.2 percent, respectively, as a result of increasing the rural education spending by 16 percent. Clearly, from an economywide point of view, rural education is a favorable investment, given the assumptions about productivity differentials, education costs, and financing mechanisms (a mix of public and private funding).

Three factors contribute to the observed GDP growth after investment in rural education: (1) As a result of improved access to education, average schooling attainment of unskilled rural labor increases by 1.7 years.[11] It results in higher productivity, which largely offsets the decline in the amount of unskilled labor supply. (2) Improved rural education increases the supply of rural semiskilled and skilled labor 16 percent, and unskilled labor declines by 23 percent. This favorable change in skill composition induces an economywide productivity gain. However, the forgone working hours from higher school participation rates are quite modest: the supply of aggregate rural labor declines by only 0.29 percent.[12] (3) Higher educational attainment also improves off-farm labor mobility. As a result of improved rural education, 4.9 million additional workers leave agriculture and an additional 2.0 million temporal migrants move to urban areas. This movement of labor from relatively low-productivity sectors (agriculture and rural nonfarm employment) into higher-productivity activities (rural nonfarm work and urban employment, respectively) also boosts overall productivity.

With an increase in the pool of semiskilled rural workers of 42.4 million, migration among this group out of agriculture increases by 13.3 million workers. Temporary migration of semiskilled workers to urban areas also rises by 10.5 million workers, contributing to a decline in urban semiskilled wage rates. Because this work abstracts from any transaction costs associated with the temporary rural-urban migration of skilled labor, the bulk of the increased supply of rural skilled workers (about 1.9 million, or 82 percent of the supply increment) migrates to urban areas. However, its impact on the urban skilled wage is very limited, given the small size of temporary skilled migration compared to the stock of urban skilled workers. Also, with the combination of a diminished supply and an enhanced schooling attainment of unskilled workers in the rural areas, wages for this group rise sharply. As a consequence, both off-farm employment and temporary migration of unskilled labor to urban areas actually decline.

The distributional impacts of improved rural education can be seen in figure 10.4a, which reports the *incremental* welfare change of disaggregated household groups in urban and rural China. Most urban households lose under this scenario because they face more intense competition from increasingly well-educated and mobile rural workers. Furthermore, given the closure rules used in this chapter's model, the additional government expenditure on rural education is financed via a direct tax on household income. Therefore, urban households pay part of the costs of increased rural education.[13] Lower-income households in the urban areas experience bigger losses because they rely more heavily on semiskilled labor income. As a consequence, the urban Gini index rises by 0.003 (table 10.5). However, household welfare rises for all rural households. The largest proportional increase in welfare is for the agriculture-specialized rural households, which benefit from the strong increase in rural unskilled wages. Overall, the benefits from rural educational reform are spread relatively evenly across income levels, and the rural Gini index is hardly changed. The educational reform induces a 0.23 point decline in the urban-rural income ratio and a 0.015 decline in national Gini coefficient, indicating an improvement in urban-rural income distribution in China. Returning to table 10.5, it can be seen that the rural poverty headcount falls significantly, by 11.8 percent, after the investment in rural education. The largest fall is ascribed to diversified rural households. The poverty headcounts of urban labor-specialized and diversified urban household groups increase by 8.5 percent and 12.0 percent, respectively. However, given the share of urban poverty in the overall population, the deterioration of urban poverty is more than offset by the alleviation of rural poverty, and national poverty headcount falls by 44.3 million.

The combined aggregate impact of both global free trade and improvement in rural education is reported in the final columns of tables 10.4 and 10.5. The results show that these reforms are potentially significant for the Chinese economy. As a major indicator of overall efficiency, GDP increases by 1.2 percent, and aggregate welfare rises by 2.0 percent.

Figure 10.4b shows the cumulative effect of global free trade and educational reform on disaggregate urban and rural household welfare. Here, the potential urban-rural redistribution of welfare is striking. The equivalent variation for agriculture-specialized rural households is about 7–9 percent of initial income. Other rural households also benefit from these reforms. In contrast, urban household welfare falls by as much as 2 percent of initial income for the poorest urban households. Clearly, the reforms aiming at global free trade and promoting rural education would boost rural household welfare, but this does come at the expense of urban households, particularly the lower-income groups. However, when viewed in a historical context, this redistribution is quite modest. It does little more than undo the worsening of the urban-rural income disparity that has arisen since 1998.

The combined education and trade reforms also contribute significantly to rural poverty reduction. The rural poverty headcount ratio declines by 14.2 percent, or 6.4 percentage points—from 45.2 percent in the base case to 38.8 percent in the *Edu-Lib* scenario—and the urban headcount ratio rises slightly, from 4.07 percent to 4.27 percent. Overall, the number of people in poverty nationwide declines by 55 million when rural education reforms are combined with global trade liberalization.

Figure 10.4a. Incremental Impacts on Households, Edu-Lib

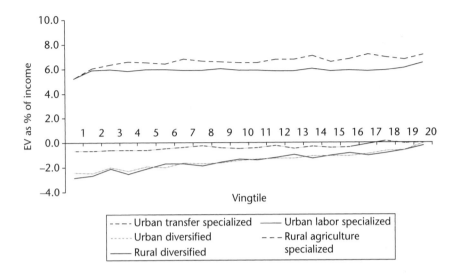

Figure 10.4b. Cumulative Impacts on Households, Edu-Lib

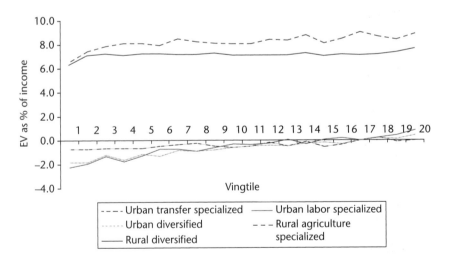

Source: Authors' simulations.

Of course, an important question remains: How much interaction is there between the rural education reforms and multilateral trade liberalization? To isolate this interaction, the *Full-Lib* scenario was repeated using the database and parameters that result from implementation of the education reforms. The results of the *Full-Lib* experiment in the wake of the education reform were nearly identical, suggesting that there is little interaction between the two policies. In other words, the cumulative impact of undertaking both sets of reforms is essentially the sum of the two individual impacts.

Conclusions and Policy Implications

The goal of this chapter has been to assess the implications of multilateral trade reforms for poverty in China, which is done by combining results from a global modeling exercise with a national CGE model that features disaggregated households in both the rural and urban sectors. Three different scenarios are examined: one involving global trade liberalization and two involving possible DDA reforms. Using the World Bank's US$2 per day poverty line, the results show that multilateral trade reforms do in fact reduce poverty in China. The biggest reductions occur in the rural areas, largely as a result of higher prices for farm products. Because this is where the bulk of the poor in China reside, an overall reduction in poverty follows.

Urban poverty falls in two of the three household groups considered in this analysis, because the increased demand for China's products in world markets boosts factor earnings sufficiently to offset the impact of higher food prices. For the remaining group, which is heavily dependent on transfer payments, it is assumed that indexation of these payments will largely offset the adverse consequences of higher prices. However, a decline in other income sources is sufficient to cause an increase in poverty, and this increase is large enough to boost the overall urban poverty headcount. However, the urban poor represent only 5 percent of the total poor in China, and thus the national poverty headcount falls.

The implications of complementary reforms in China are also explored—in particular, increased investments in rural education aimed at equalizing per capita spending between rural and urban areas. This boosts rural enrollments by 16 percent, which has the twin benefits of increasing labor productivity as well as enhancing the mobility of the rural labor force, thereby putting these workers in a better position to benefit from trade reforms. The analysis in this chapter takes account of the cost of funding these additional students, as well as the reduction in the workforce that results from having more pupils in school. Nevertheless, these reforms generate very substantial gains for China's economy. They also serve to boost rural incomes and reduce the incidence of rural poverty. Indeed, when combined with global trade liberalization, poverty in China is estimated to drop by about 55 million people.

Notes

1. However, as noted by Parish, Zhe, and Li (1995), the rural labor market is looking more like a market all the time.

2. See Hertel and Zhai (2004) for the details of the off-farm labor supply behavior in the model.

3. In this model, it is assumed that the elasticity of land with respect to on-farm labor is unitary.

4. There are likely other, unobserved factors inducing this rural-urban wage differential, in which case estimation of the labor market distortion via subtraction of known factors is biased in the direction of overstating the *hukou*-related distortion. Therefore, it is useful to also estimate the direct impact of household registration status on the observed wage difference among households. Shi (2002) takes this approach to the problem, using the same CHNS dataset. He finds that only 28 percent of the rural-urban wage difference can be explained directly via the coefficient on the *hukou* registration variable. This is quite a bit less than the 48 percent left unexplained via the subtraction approach of Shi, Sicular, and Zhao (2002).

5. See Hertel and Zhai (2004) for a detailed description of how this ad valorem distortion is obtained.

6. It is assumed that a doubling of temporary migration would increase the marginal cost of migration by only 10 percent.

7. Because of the variety of labor supply elasticities in response to the three different wages in their model, the authors obtain a variety of labor transfer elasticities, depending on the "thought experiment" being conducted. These are asymmetric, with the response to a change in shadow wages differing from the response of labor supply to a change in the market wage. However, this response is treated as symmetric in the model in this chapter. This makes it difficult to choose the correct parameter for the analysis. The focus is on the transfer of labor from agriculture to market wage employment in response to a change in returns to agriculture, because this transfer accounts for the bulk of the labor flow in this analysis.

8. A caveat should been mentioned here. The scenario of education reform assumes that the private education spending of rural households increases proportionally to the public spending. It implies that the education demand in rural areas is constrained by the supply-side factors. This seems reasonable, given the low level of rural education in China, the potential benefits from education investment, and the long-term nature of the simulation.

9. In this model, there are exogenous differences in labor productivity across sectors, inferred from observed wage rates.

10. In the case of rice exports, this increase is comparable in size to that observed between 1997 and 1998, when rice exports increased from about Y 2 billion to nearly Y 9 billion, after which it steadily declined, returning to about Y 2 billion by 2004. In the case of maize, the projected change is smaller than recent annual export fluctuations.

11. The model predicts that only the unskilled labor force will experience an increment in schooling attainment because it is assumed that the same proportional increase in the school participation rates occurs across grades. Thus, the increase in semiskilled labor at the low end is offset by a reduction at the high end as more semiskilled workers become skilled. However, at the low end, the increase in unskilled labor is fueled by a decline in the share of illiterate people in the unskilled labor force.

12. The relatively small reduction in the rural labor force is perhaps somewhat surprising. However, this is the consequence of several factors. First, the 1.7 increment to schooling years applies only to the unskilled rural labor force. Second, the ages of the labor force in this model are from 15 to 70. The ages of pupils are from 7 to 25, thus increasing enrollment rates of primary school (0–6 schooling

years for pupils at 7–12 years old) and middle school (7–9 schooling years for pupils at 13–15 years old) has no direct impact on total labor supply.

13. Because it is assumed that the income tax is levied on the nontransfer incomes, urban transfer-specialized households do not bear the costs of additional rural education.

References

Bhattasali, Deepak, Shantong Li, and Will Martin, eds. 2004. *China and the WTO: Accession, Policy Reform, and Poverty Strategies.* New York: Oxford University Press; Washington, DC: World Bank.

Chen, Shaohua, and Martin Ravallion. 2004. "Welfare Impacts of China's Accession to the WTO." In *China and the WTO: Accession, Policy Reform, and Poverty Strategies,* ed. Deepak Bhattasali, Shantong Li, and Will Martin, 283–304.New York: Oxford University Press; Washington, DC: World Bank.

Dervis, K., J. de Melo, and Sherman Robinson. 1982. *General Equilibrium Models for Development Policy.* Cambridge, U.K.: Cambridge University Press.

Francois, Joseph and Bradley McDonald. 1996. "Liberalization and Capital Accumulation in the GTAP Model." GTAP Technical Paper 7, Purdue University, West Lafayette, IN. www.gtap.org.

Hansen, Terje, and Tjalling Koopmans. 1972. "On the Definition and Computation of a Capital Stock Invariant under Optimization." *Journal of Economic Theory* 5: 487–523.

Harrison, Glenn, Thomas Rutherford, and David Tarr. 1997. "Quantifying the Uruguay Round." *Economic Journal* 107 (444): 1405–30.

Heckman, James J. 2002. "China's Investment in Human Capital." NBER Working Paper 9296. National Bureau of Economic Research, Cambridge, MA.

Heckman, James J., and Lance Lochner. 1998. "Explaining Rising Wage Inequality: Explorations with a Dynamic General Equilibrium Model of Labor Earnings with Heterogeneous Agents." *Review of Economic Dynamics* 1 (1): 1–58.

Hertel, Thomas W., ed. 1997. *Global Trade Analysis: Modeling and Applications.* Cambridge: Cambridge University Press.

Hertel, Thomas, David Hummels, Maros Ivanic, and Roman Keeney. 2003. "How Confident Can We Be in CGE-Based Assessments of Free Trade Agreements?" GTAP Working Paper 26, Purdue University, West Lafayette, IN.

Hertel, Thomas W., Paul V. Preckel, John Cranfield, and Maros Ivanic. 2004. "Poverty Impacts of Multilateral Trade Liberalization." *World Bank Economic Review* 18 (2): 205–36.

Hertel, Thomas, and Fan Zhai. 2004. "Labor Market Distortions, Rural-Urban Inequality, and the Opening of China's Economy." Policy Research Working Paper 3455. World Bank, Washington, DC.

Hertel, Thomas, Fan Zhai, and Zhi Wang. 2004. "Implications of WTO Accession for Poverty in China." In *China and the WTO: Accession, Policy Reform, and Poverty Strategies,* ed. Deepak Bhattasali, Shantong Li, and Will Martin, 283–304.New York: Oxford University Press; Washington DC: World Bank.

Kanbur, R., and Xiaobo Zhang. 2001. "Fifty Years of Regional Inequality in China: A Journey through Revolution, Reform and Openness." CEPR Discussion Paper 2887. Centre for Economic Policy Research, London.

Katz, L., and K. Murphy. 1992. "Changes in Relative Wages, 1963–1987: Supply and Demand Factors." *Quarterly Journal of Economics* 107 (1): 35–78.

Li, Shi, and Ximin Yue. 2004. "Latest Changes in Individual Income Inequality in China." Working Paper, Economic Research Institute, China Academy of Social Science, Beijing.

Parish, William L., Xiaoye Zhe, and Fang Li. 1995. "Nonfarm Work and Marketization of the Chinese Countryside." *China Quarterly* 143: 697–730.

Shi, Xinzheng, 2002. "Empirical Research on Urban-rural Income Differentials: The Case of China." Unpublished manuscript, CCER, Beijing University.

Shi, Xinzheng, Terry Sicular, and Yaohui Zhao. 2002. "Analyzing Urban-Rural Income Inequality in China." Paper presented at the International Symposium on Equity and Social Justice in Transitional China, Beijing, July 11–12.

Shoven, J. B., and J. Whalley. 1992. *Applied General Equilibrium Analysis.* Cambridge, U.K.: Cambridge University Press.

Sicular, Terry, and Yaohui Zhao. 2004. "Earnings and Labor Mobility in Rural China: Implications for China's Accession to the WTO." In *China and the WTO: Accession, Policy Reform, and Poverty Strategies,* ed. Deepak Bhattasali, Shantong Li, and Will Martin, 239–260. New York: Oxford University Press; Washington, DC: World Bank.

Wang, Dewen. 2003. "China's Rural Compulsory Education: Current Situation, Problems and Policy Alternatives." Working Paper Series 36, Institute of Population and Labor Economics, Chinese Academy of Social Sciences, Beijing.

Yang, Dennis T. 1997. "China's Land Arrangements and Rural Labor Mobility." *China Economic Review* 8 (2): 101–16.

———. 2004. "Education and Allocative Efficiency: Household Income Growth during Rural Reforms in China." *Journal of Development Economics* 74 (1): 137–62.

Zhang, Linxiu, Jikun Huang, and Scott Rozelle. 2002. "Employment, Recessions, and the Role of Education in China." *China Economic Review* 13 (2, 3): 313–28.

Zhao, Yaohui. 1999a. "Labor Migration and Earnings Differences: The Case of Rural China." *Economic Development and Cultural Change* 47 (4): 767–82.

———. 1999b. "Leaving the Countryside: Rural-to-Urban Migration Decisions in China." *American Economic Review* 89 (2): 281–86.

11

THE SOCIAL IMPACT
OF A WTO AGREEMENT
IN INDONESIA

Anne-Sophie Robilliard and Sherman Robinson

Summary

Indonesia has experienced rapid growth and the expansion of the formal financial sector during the last quarter of the 20th century. Although this tendency was reversed by the shock of the financial crisis that spread throughout Asia in 1997 and 1998, macroeconomic stability has since been restored, and poverty has been reduced to precrisis levels. Poverty reduction nevertheless remains a critical challenge for Indonesia, with more than 110 million people (53 percent of the population) living on less than US$2 per day.

The objective of this study is to help identify ways in which the Doha Development Agenda (DDA) might contribute to further poverty reduction in Indonesia. To provide a good technical basis for answering this question, this chapter uses an approach that combines a computable general equilibrium (CGE) with a microsimulation (MS) model. This framework is designed to capture important channels through which macroeconomic shocks affect household incomes. It will allow recommendations to be made on specific trade reform options as well as on complementary development policy reforms.

The framework presented in this study generates detailed poverty outcomes of trade shocks. Given the magnitude of the shocks examined here and the structural features of the Indonesian economy, only the full-liberalization scenario generates significant poverty changes. Their impact is examined under alternative specifications of the functioning of labor markets. These alternative assumptions generate different results, and all of them agree that the impact of full liberalization on poverty would be beneficial, with wage and employment gains dominating the adverse food price changes that could hurt the poorest households. Two alternative tax replacement schemes are examined. Although the direct tax replacement appears to be more desirable in terms of efficiency gains and translates into higher poverty reduction, political and practical considerations could lead the government of Indonesia to choose a replacement scheme through the adjustment of VAT rates across nonexempt sectors.

Although the poverty reduction in terms of the number of people lifted out of poverty might appear impressive, the overall impact of trade liberalization is quite modest. One should also keep in mind that these results do not capture two opposing channels through which trade liberalization could affect poverty and income distribution. On the one hand, the results in this chapter are likely to underestimate the cost of temporary unemployment endured by displaced workers in some sectors. The reallocation could be all the more harmful because unemployment benefits are not available for most Indonesian workers. On the other hand, because it is static in nature, this model ignores positive dynamic gains from liberalization.

Introduction

Over the last 30 years, decreasing tariffs in both developed and developing countries, as well as declining transport costs and economic growth, have led to a sustained increase in the exports and imports of goods and services by developing countries. This might have benefited many developing countries, contributing to enhanced productivity growth and the development of the financial sector, but it is not obvious whether the poorest households have gained from increased trade liberalization. Such doubts are reinforced because this liberalization has so far been relatively asymmetric, with rich country protection still high in labor-intensive sectors such as wearing apparel and agriculture. This asymmetry is further exacerbated by the subsidies provided to OECD farmers by their governments.

Indonesia has experienced rapid growth and the expansion of the formal financial sector during the last quarter of the 20th century. After a period of economic slowdown following the financial crisis, macroeconomic stability has been restored and growth has picked up, reaching 5.1 percent in 2004. Poverty reduction nevertheless remains a critical challenge for Indonesia, with more than 110 million people (53 percent of the population) living on less than US$2 per day.

The objective of this study is to help identify ways in which the DDA might contribute to further poverty reduction in Indonesia. To provide a good technical basis for answering this question, an approach is used that combines a CGE with an MS model. This framework is designed to capture important channels through which macroeconomic shocks affect household incomes. It will allow recommendations to be made on specific trade reform options as well as on complementary development policy reforms.

This chapter is organized as follows. First, some features of the Indonesian economy are presented, in particular with regard to trade. Second, the analytical framework developed to analyze the impact of further trade liberalization on poverty and income distribution is presented. Third, simulation results are described and commented on. In the fourth section, some of the key assumptions made in the reference scenario are examined, and the impact of trade reform on poverty when these are relaxed is explored. The last section concludes.

Economic and Policy Environment

Table 11.1 shows that Indonesia's overall openness to foreign trade is relatively high, with exports (imports) amounting to more than 37 percent (28 percent) of GDP. Not surprisingly, table 11.1 also shows that trade exposure is heterogeneous across sectors. Indonesia's trade appears to be concentrated in petroleum and manufactured products. However, agricultural sectors appear to be weakly exposed to trade, contributing very little to total exports and imports, a result of Indonesia's export diversification toward manufacturing products. The textile and wearing apparel industry's contribution to exports is significant (12.7 percent), and that sector's exposure to trade is important, with an export ratio of 41.4 percent and an import ratio of 20.0 percent. Overall, the most exposed nonoil sectors appear to be the wood and wood products industry; the paper printing, transport equipment, and metal products industries, and the chemical fertilization, clay products, cement, and basic metal manufacturing industries.

Official data from the WTO Secretariat indicate that average applied most-favored-nation (MFN) tariffs have declined between 1998 and 2002, reflecting mainly unilateral cuts over this period (WTO 2003). Although more than 90 percent of Indonesia's tariffs are bound, a large gap remains between bound and applied rates (35 percentage points, on average). Almost all applied rates are ad valorem, and there are no tariff quotas. Nevertheless, the scope of import restrictions and licensing appears to have increased through new special import licensing from 2002. These affect sensitive products, such as rice and sugar, and are granted based on domestic needs. It should be noted that the new government is looking into removing or reducing these licenses. Import duties across commodities in the base year appear to be relatively low, with values ranging from 1.5 percent for nonfood crops to 6.6 percent for textile and wearing apparel

Table 11.1. Trade Structure of Indonesia

	Exports		Imports		Parameters	
	Shares of total exports	Exports as a percent of sector output	Shares of total imports	Imports as a percent of composite good supply	Armington elasticities	Import tariff rates
Farm food crops	0.1	0.2	2.4	7.7	4.7	2.2
Farm nonfood crops	0.6	6.2	0.0	0.3	5.9	1.5
Livestock products	0.0	0.1	0.5	2.7	7.1	3.1
Forestry and hunting	0.1	2.0	n.a.	n.a.	5.0	0.0
Fishery, drying, and salting of fish	0.3	3.1	0.0	0.1	2.5	6.2
Total agriculture	**1.1**		**2.9**			
Coal, metal ore, petroleum, and natural gas	17.9	63.0	2.2	16.2	10.1	1.8
Other mining and quarrying	0.1	3.1	0.4	6.6	1.8	1.5
Food, beverages, and tobacco manufacturing	7.3	11.2	3.7	4.9	4.3	6.2
Spinning, textile, leather, and wearing apparel manufacturing products	12.7	41.4	5.2	20.0	7.6	6.6
Wood and wood products	8.4	58.9	0.2	2.8	6.8	4.9
Paper printing, transport equipment, metal products, and other manufacturing products	15.7	37.9	42.7	57.2	7.6	3.0
Chemical fertilization, clay products, cement, and basic metal manufacturing products	21.3	36.1	27.1	37.0	6.8	2.9

The Social Impact of a WTO Agreement in Indonesia **323**

Table 11.1. *(Continued)*

	Exports		Imports		Parameters	
	Shares of total exports	Exports as a percent of sector output	Shares of total imports	Imports as a percent of composite good supply	Armington elasticities	Import tariff rates
Total industry	83.5		81.4			
Wholesale and retail trade, transport, storage, and warehousing	1.0	2.2	0.8	1.6	3.8	0.0
Restaurants	1.4	7.5	0.6	3.1	3.8	0.0
Hotels and lodging places	4.0	44.0	1.1	17.1	3.8	0.0
Road transport and railways	1.6	8.5	1.0	5.7	3.8	0.0
Air and water transport and communications	5.3	28.8	4.7	25.6	3.8	0.0
Banking and insurance	0.6	5.5	1.9	14.5	3.8	0.0
Real estate and business services	0.1	0.4	2.5	10.6	3.8	0.0
Public administration, defense, and social, recreational, and cultural services	1.2	3.0	2.0	5.1	3.8	0.0
Personal household and other services	0.2	1.7	1.2	8.4	3.8	0.0
Total services	**15.4**		**15.7**			

Source: Updated SAM 2002, GTAP Version 6, and authors' calculations.
Note: n.a. = not applicable.

products. These low values hide somewhat higher values for very specific products that cannot be captured, given the level of aggregation of commodities in the database used here. Despite these higher tariffs, Indonesia has overall low tariffs, including in agriculture.

The contribution of tariffs to Indonesia's tax revenue is also an important question. Tariffs accounted for 6.0 percent of government revenue, and corresponded to 0.8 percent of GDP in 2002, the base year chosen as the starting point of the model in this chapter. Indonesia's budget does not appear to be highly dependent on imports duties, but the tax replacement scheme could potentially alter the impact of trade liberalization, depending on the choice of replacement tax used.

Despite Indonesia's economic recovery since the 1998 crisis, more than 110 million people (53 percent of the population) are still living on less than US$2 per day. According to Indonesia's official poverty lines, poverty incidence was 18.2 percent in 2002 at the national level, with higher levels in the rural sector (21.2 percent) than in the urban sector (14.5 percent). As a consequence, two-thirds of the poor in Indonesia live in the rural sector. Full liberalization in the rest of the world, particularly the removal of domestic agricultural support in OECD countries, is expected to lead to an increase in the prices of agricultural products. The impact on agricultural households should be positive, but the impact on poverty depends on whether poor agricultural households are net buyers or net sellers of food products. Of course, the size of the domestic market and the resulting low exposure of agricultural sectors to foreign trade mentioned above are likely to dampen the impact of world price changes on the domestic market. In the urban areas, poor households could suffer from an increase in the price of food. The resulting overall poverty impact is thus difficult to predict and depends on the relative size of the efficiency and hence income gains generated by the removal of the import duties and of the changes in the relative price of food.

Analytical Framework: A Macro-Micro Model for Indonesia

This section describes the specification of the Indonesia macro-micro model used to analyze the social impact of various trade liberalization scenarios. A more detailed discussion of the specification and econometric estimates of the various equations of the household income generation model and simulation methodology may be found in Bourguignon, Robilliard, and Robinson (2003).

This chapter's approach combines an MS model with a CGE model in a sequential fashion. The term "microsimulation" spans a number of different approaches used in social sciences. Their common denominator is to focus primarily on the economic behavior of agents and investigate the impact of public policy and shocks at the microeconomic level. These models typically take representative samples of micro agents (households or firms) and measure the effect of government policy on these samples. Various MS techniques are described in more detail in the annex to the associated working paper (Robilliard and Robinson 2005; see also Cogneau, Grimm, and Robilliard 2003).

Specifications of the Indonesia CGE model

The CGE model is based on a standard social accounting matrix (SAM) and is designed to capture structural features of the economy as well as the general equilibrium effects of the macro constraints arising from macroeconomic shocks. The model was developed from the neoclassical-structuralist modeling tradition originally presented in Dervis, de Melo, and Robinson (1982). It is formulated as a set of simultaneous linear and nonlinear equations, which define the behavior of economic agents, as well as the economic environment in which these agents operate.

Indonesia's economy is dualistic, which the model captures by distinguishing between formal and informal activities in each sector. The two subsectors differ in the type of factors they use. This distinction allows treating formal and informal factor markets differently. For all activities, the production technology is represented by a set of nested CES (constant elasticity of substitution) value added functions and fixed coefficient (Leontief) intermediate input relationships. On the demand side, consumers purchase a composite good, and imperfect substitutability is assumed between formal and informal products of the same commodity. Domestic prices of commodities are flexible, allowing markets to clear in a competitive setting where individual suppliers and demanders are price takers.

Following Armington (1969), the model assumes imperfect substitutability, for each good, between imports and the corresponding composite domestic commodity. For export commodities, the allocation of domestic output between exports and domestic sales is determined on the assumption that domestic producers maximize profits subject to imperfect transformability between these two alternatives. The composite production good is a constant elasticity of transformation (CET) aggregation of sectoral exports and domestically consumed products. The trade elasticities used to calibrate the functions used in the CGE model were taken from Version 6 of the Global Trade Analysis Project (GTAP) database. These have recently been econometrically estimated for at the disaggregated GTAP commodity level (Hertel and others 2004).

There are eight labor categories in the Indonesia CGE model: urban male unskilled, urban male skilled, urban female unskilled, urban female skilled, rural male unskilled, rural male skilled, rural female unskilled, and rural female skilled. The distinction between rural and urban labor implies that workers are not allowed to shift between rural and urban production sectors. Male and female, as well as skilled and unskilled labor, are assumed to be imperfect substitutes in the production activity of urban or rural sectors. Alternative specifications of the functioning of the labor markets can be implemented in the model. In the reference simulations, wages are assumed to adjust so as to clear all labor markets. This is consistent with the full employment assumption used in the global model. Two alternative specifications are also examined.

Land appears as a factor of production in the agricultural sectors. Only one type of land is considered in the model, but capital markets are segmented into six categories: owner-occupied housing, other unincorporated rural capital, other unincorporated urban capital, domestic private incorporated capital, public capital, and foreign capital. Given the medium-term perspective of the model, it is assumed that land is activity specific and other types of capital are competitively allocated among the different sectors so that its marginal value product is equalized across activities.

Equilibrium in a CGE model is defined by a set of constraints that need to be satisfied by the economic system but are not considered directly in the decisions of micro agents. Aside from the supply-demand balances in product and factor markets, three macroeconomic balances are specified in the Indonesia CGE model: (1) the fiscal balance, with government savings equal to the difference between government revenue and spending; (2) the external trade balance (in goods and nonfactor services), which implicitly equates the supply and demand for foreign exchange; and (3) savings-investment balance. We assume that savings are investment driven and adjust through flexible saving rates for firms, that foreign savings are in fixed supply with the demand for foreign exchange equated through an endogenous exchange rate, and that government income is also fixed, with lost tariff revenue replaced through a variable tax rate on households. This closure is expected to be relatively neutral in terms of the distributive impact of the shocks implemented. An alternative tax replacement scheme is also examined.

The original CGE model was constructed to reflect Indonesia's economic precrisis situation and is based on a 1995 SAM. To capture the postcrisis structural features of the Indonesian economy, the 1995 Indonesia SAM was updated using cross-entropy methods (see Robinson, Cattaneo, and El-Said 2001). The updating procedure imposes the following pieces of information from 2002: value added by activity; the structure of imports and exports by commodity; and the data contained in a macro SAM. Table 11.2 summarizes the aggregate values of the resulting 2002 SAM.[1]

Table 11.2. A Macroeconomic SAM for Indonesia (2002 rupiah, billions)

	Activity	Commodity	Household	Government	World	Investment	Total
Activity		1,610,012					1,610,012
Commodity	1,538,826		1,042,148	132,219	569,962	325,334	2,069,663
Household	71,186		110,845		19,246		1,558,072
Government		12,005					194,036
World		447,626	405,079	61,817	-141,562		447,626
Investment			1,558,072		447,646	325,334	325,334
Total	1,610,012	2,069,663	1,558,072			325,334	

Source: Live Database on Line (World Bank); Essama-Nssah (2004).

Specification of the Indonesia microsimulation model

The microsimulation model is based on household and individual level data from the Special Survey on Saving and Household Investment (SKTIR) for the year 1996 and simulates income generation mechanisms for 9,800 households corresponding to 42,400 individuals.[2] Four occupational choices are distinguished at the individual level: (1) inactivity, (2) wage work, (3) self-employment, and (4) multiactivity (wage work *and* self-employment). All individuals aged 15 years and older are assumed to participate in the occupational choice. Following McFadden's approach to discrete choice behavior (1974), it is assumed that an individual chooses the outcome that maximizes the utility gained from that choice. It is also assumed that the occupational choice behavior of household heads is different from that of spouses or other members of the household. More specifically, for purposes of this analysis, it is posited that the decision process is sequential and that occupational choices for spouses and other members depend on characteristics of the household head and his or her occupational choice.

The microeconomic database of the original Indonesia model is the 1996 SUSENAS SKTIR. All individuals aged 10 years and older were interviewed on their sources of income. The sample is updated using a cross-entropy approach (Robilliard and Robinson 2003). This method generates new sets of household statistical weights that are consistent with projected population and structure of the labor force for 2002. Changes in the labor force structure are based on observed changes in the 1996 and 1999 SAKERNAS national labor force surveys for Indonesia.

The two models are solved separately. The macro or CGE model communicates with the MS model by generating a vector of prices, wages, and aggregate employment variables corresponding to a given shock or policy. Then the MS model is used to generate changes in individual wages, self-employment incomes, and employment status in a way that is consistent with the set of macro variables fed by the macro model. When this is done, the full distribution of real household income corresponding to the simulated shock or policy may be evaluated. Consistency of the MS model with the equilibrium of aggregate markets in the CGE model requires that three conditions hold. First, changes in average earnings with respect to the benchmark in the MS module must be equal to changes in wage rates provided by the CGE model for each labor market category. Second, changes in agricultural and nonagricultural self-employment income in the MS module must be equal to changes in the corresponding income per worker provided by the CGE model. Finally, changes in the number of wage workers and self-employed workers by labor market category in the MS model must match those same changes generated by the CGE model.

Implementation and Analysis of Trade Policy Shocks

Various scenarios are examined to inform the DDA negotiations. These scenarios are built upon the work laid out in chapters 2 and 3 of this volume and entail shocks to Indonesia's import prices, export prices, and tariffs.[3] In the case of Indonesia, the pre-experiment outlined in chapter 3 was also quite important. Recall that it was designed to take into account China's accession to the WTO, the completion of the Uruguay Round Agreement on Textiles and Clothing commitment to abolish textiles and apparel quotas, and the EU's enlargement to 25 countries. This presimulation scenario (*PRESIM*) is given explicit attention in this chapter, because it generates a new base from which all subsequent liberalization simulations will start.

The employment and earnings impacts generated by the CGE model are fed into the MS model.[4] As described above, the MS is used to generate a new distribution of income that can then be compared to the base distribution. Both poverty and inequality indicators are presented, and poverty indicators are computed using official poverty lines.[5] The macroeconomic and social impacts of the first set of scenarios are presented in tables 11.3 and 11.4.

First, the impact of the *PRESIM* is examined. The aggregate real impact is small and negative. Private consumption decreases by 0.2 percent. Imports and exports also decrease by 1.4 and 1.0 percent, respectively. These results stem from a slight deterioration of the terms of trade (TOT) facing Indonesia as the demand for its exports fall in the wake of quota elimination and are driven by the fact that the estimated quota rents in the initial database are much larger for exports from China than for other textile exporting countries like Indonesia (Francois and Spinanger 2004). At a more disaggregated level, the shock leads to some reallocation of factors across sectors. Not surprisingly, the textile and wearing apparel sectors face the worst TOT shock, with export prices falling by 3.8 percent and import prices increasing very slightly. As a result, value added from the textile and wearing apparel sectors decreases by more than 30 percent, and factors of production are reallocated toward other manufacturing sectors.

At the household level, the poverty and inequality impacts are relatively small. However, these results likely underestimate the cost of reallocation suffered by workers in the textile and wearing apparel sectors. Although these costs are not captured by the model, some displaced workers could suffer, at least temporarily, from unemployment, particularly because they are likely to come from informal sectors that do not provide unemployment benefits.

Starting from the updated base year generated with the *PRESIM* scenario, the full trade liberalization impact is examined through a set of three simulations. The first examines the impact of unilateral liberalization of Indonesia (*ULIB*); the second considers the impact of full liberalization excluding Indonesia (*FLIBX*);

Table 11.3. Macroeconomic Results of Trade Liberalization Reference Scenarios

	Base	PRESIM	New base	ULIB	FLIBX	Full-lib	Doha
Private consumption	1,042.1	-0.2	1,040.3	0.0	0.7	0.7	0.1
Investment demand	325.3		324.7				
Government consumption	132.2		132.2				
Total absorption	1,499.7	-0.1	1,497.3	0.0	0.5	0.5	0.1
Exports value	569.9	-1.0	566.0	4.6	2.1	5.9	0.4
Imports value	447.6	-1.4	443.1	5.9	4.3	9.1	0.8
Real GDP at factor costs	1,538.8	-0.1	1,537.8	0.0	0.0	0.0	0.1
Nominal GDP at factor costs	1,538.8	-0.1	1,537.8	0.8	0.4	1.2	0.0
Urban agricultural income	112.3	0.7	113.1	0.0	2.5	3.3	0.1
Rural agricultural income	208.7	0.6	210.0	-0.2	2.5	3.0	0.5
Urban nonagricultural income	182.5	0.3	183.0	1.4	0.4	1.8	0.6
Rural nonagricultural income	112.3	-0.5	111.7	0.9	0.7	1.5	0.0
Urban unskilled wage income	223.3	-0.3	222.5	1.0	0.1	0.9	0.1
Rural unskilled wage income	43.6	-0.1	43.6	0.8	0.1	1.0	0.0
Urban skilled wage income	77.2	-0.2	77.0	1.0	0.3	1.3	0.0
Rural skilled wage income	67.0	-0.1	67.0	0.6	0.6	1.2	0.0
Nonlabor income	603.1	-0.2	601.8	1.0	-0.4	0.4	0.1

Source: Author's simulations.

Note: Base and new base values in trillions of rupiah; percent changes for the nonbase columns. *PRESIM*=presimulation scenarios entailing China's WTO accession, the completion of the UR-ATC commitment to abolish textiles and apparel quotas, and the EU's enlargement to 25 members; *ULIB*=unilateral liberalization; *FLIBX*=full liberalization excluding Indonesia; *Full-Lib*=full liberalization including Indonesia; *Doha*=Doha Scenario.

Table 11.4. Social Impact of Trade Liberalization Reference Scenarios

	Base	PRESIM	New base	ULIB	FLIBX	Full-Lib	Doha
National level							
Per capita income	7,188.2	0.0	7,188.2	0.6	0.5	1.2	0.1
General entropy index (0)	35.7	-0.1	35.7	0.3	-0.1	-0.3	0.0
General entropy index (1)	48.4	-0.1	48.4	0.2	-0.1	-0.6	0.0
Gini index	45.7	-0.1	45.7	0.1	-0.1	-0.2	0.0
Poverty headcount	18.3	-0.2	18.3	-1.0	-2.0	-3.5	-0.1
Poverty gap	4.8	-0.2	4.8	-0.8	-1.6	-3.4	-0.1
Squared poverty gap	1.9	-0.2	1.9	-0.8	-1.3	-3.3	-0.1
Number of poor	39,253,480	-78,507	39,174,973	-374,680	-798,764	-1,384,164	-48,152
Urban areas							
Per capita income	9,775.9	0.0	9,775.9	0.8	0.3	1.1	0.0
General entropy index (0)	38.5	-0.1	38.5	0.1	0.3	-0.4	0.1
General entropy index (1)	52.9	-0.1	52.8	0.0	0.3	-0.6	0.1
Gini index	47.3	0.0	47.3	0.0	0.1	-0.2	0.0
Poverty headcount	14.5	-0.2	14.5	-2.2	-0.8	-3.4	0.0
Poverty gap	4.1	-0.1	4.1	-1.5	-0.1	-2.8	0.1
Squared poverty gap	1.8	-0.1	1.8	-1.4	0.1	-2.9	0.1
Number of poor	13,322,340	-26,645	13,295,695	-287,148	-109,962	-454,021	0
Rural areas							
Per capita income	5,235.6	0.1	5,240.8	0.2	0.9	1.4	0.1
General entropy index (0)	25.0	-0.1	25.0	0.0	0.0	0.0	0.0
General entropy index (1)	30.3	-0.2	30.2	-0.2	0.1	-0.2	0.0
Gini index	38.4	-0.1	38.4	0.0	0.0	0.0	0.0
Poverty headcount	21.2	-0.2	21.2	-0.3	-2.7	-3.6	-0.2
Poverty gap	5.3	-0.3	5.3	-0.4	-2.4	-3.8	-0.2
Squared poverty gap	2.1	-0.3	2.1	-0.4	-2.1	-3.6	-0.2
Number of poor	25,931,138	-51,862	25,879,276	-87,530	-688,798	-930,140	-48,150

Source: Authors' simulations.

Note: Base values percent changes for columns. Poverty indicators are computed using national poverty lines (World Bank 2003). *PRESIM* = presimulation scenarios entailing China's WTO accession, the completion of the UR-ATC commitment to abolish textiles and apparel quotas, and the EU's enlargement to 25 members; *ULIB* = unilateral liberalization; *FLIBX* = full liberalization excluding Indonesia; *Full-Lib* = full liberalization including Indonesia; *Doha* = Doha scenario.

and the third analyzes the combined impact of full liberalization including Indonesia (*Full-Lib*).

Unilateral liberalization, whereby Indonesia cuts all the duties facing imports from the rest of the world, has some impact on nominal GDP[6] and generates an increase in both exports and imports. At the sector level, there is some reallocation of factors out of textiles and wearing apparel and toward the paper printing, transport equipment, and metal products industries. Although the removal of the imports tariff hurts the sectors that benefited from higher relative protection levels, the total impact on household income is positive: as can be seen in table 11.4, per capita income increases by 0.6 percent at the national level, a number that is consistent with the increase in nominal GDP.

Results suggest that unilateral liberalization would generate an increase in the average per capita household income of 0.6 percent, and the impact on the distribution of income would be negative but small. As a result of the average per capita income increase, poverty decreases modestly. The poverty headcount decreases by 1.0 percent at the national level (falling from 18.3 percent to 18.1 percent of the entire population), and the impact appears higher in the urban areas. Higher-order poverty indicators vary by the same magnitude, a result that indicates that the poorest of the poor also benefit from the unilateral liberalization, despite the slight worsening in the distribution of income. Overall, these changes translate into a total of 375,000 people escaping poverty.

As a result of full trade liberalization in the rest of the world, the Indonesian economy faces decreasing import and export prices but an improvement in overall TOT: the export price index decreases by 0.6 percent, and the import price index decreases by 2.3 percent. Despite this average decrease, import prices for agricultural goods increase. The impact on nominal GDP at factor cost is positive, and both imports and exports increase by 4.3 and 2.1 percent, respectively. In terms of absorption components, both government consumption and investment are assumed to be fixed, and private consumption increases by 0.7 percent. At the sector level, changes are driven by the differential exposure to foreign trade and the TOT shocks, and some reallocation of factors occurs, mainly between manufacturing activities. These shocks translate into a 0.5 percent increase in per capita income at the household level. The increase is much smaller in the urban sector and is accompanied by a worsening in the income distribution. As a result, the poverty impact is small in terms of incidence, and both the poverty gap and squared poverty gap increase, suggesting that some of the poorest households fare badly.[7] This result stems from the adverse impact on urban households of rising food prices. Results in the rural sector are quite different, with a 0.9 percent increase in the average per capita income and almost no change in inequality indicators. As a result, nearly 690,000 people are lifted out of poverty in the rural areas when the rest of the world liberalizes trade.

The full liberalization scenario (*Full-Lib*) combines reforms in the rest of the world and Indonesia and generates more favorable aggregate results, with exports and imports increasing by 5.9 percent and 9.1 percent, respectively. Total employment is assumed to fixed, but the full liberalization entails some reallocation of labor toward self-employment for each labor category, namely a reallocation of labor out of formal sectors and toward agricultural sectors. This stems from the fact that import prices for nonagricultural goods decrease more than for agricultural products as a result of the full liberalization. As a consequence, there is an improvement in the distribution of income overall, as well as within urban and rural areas: Poverty falls, with nearly 1.4 million people escaping poverty, a number resulting from the drop in the incidence of poverty from 18.3 percent to 17.7 percent.

The final scenario explored in tables 11.3 and 11.4 is the core *Doha* scenario. In the case of Indonesia, the impacts are very small—just a 0.1 percent impact on per capita consumption—and less than a 1 percent rise in aggregate imports and exports. There is a negligible impact on inequality, but, according to the model predictions, rising incomes boost about 50,000 people out of poverty.

Examining Alternative Scenarios

A number of alternative scenarios are examined in this section. They are aimed a exploring the importance of some of the assumptions regarding labor markets that are made in the reference simulations, as well as the choice of tax instrument for the replacement of tariff revenue.

Tax Replacement Scheme

In the reference simulation, direct taxes on household income are adjusted in an equiproportionate manner to compensate for the revenue loss due to the cut in import duties. This was done to permit comparability with other studies in this volume. This type of tax replacement scheme would be very efficient, but it would entail a major fiscal reform, which is unlikely to occur in the current political and practical context in Indonesia.[8] Therefore, the analysis now turns to the impact of trade reform under an alternative tax replacement scheme whereby value added rates adjust to make up for the revenue loss.[9]

As mentioned above, import tariffs accounted for 6.0 percent of government income and 0.8 percent of GDP in 2002. The contribution of the VAT government revenue was six times higher, representing 36.5 percent of government income and 4.6 percent of GDP. The compensation for lost revenue through the adjustment of VAT results in a 17 percent increase in rates across nonexempt sectors.

Tables 11.5 and 11.6 show that the increase in trade volume is comparable under the VAT replacement tax. However, the outcome in terms of efficiency gains is much smaller. In the urban sector, the lower per capita income gain is accompanied by a slight worsening of the distribution of income. The resulting poverty reduction amounts to 2.3 percent, with lesser rates of poverty reduction for the higher-order poverty indicators. Overall, 900,000 people are lifted out of poverty instead of the 1,400,000 with the direct tax replacement scheme.

Table 11.5. Macroeconomic Results of Alternative Scenarios

Variable	Base	FLIBVAT	FLIB_2	FLIB_3
Private consumption	1,040.3	0.7	1.7	0.7
Investment demand	324.7			
Government consumption	132.2			
Total absorption	1,497.3	0.5	1.2	0.5
Exports value	566.0	5.8	6.5	6.0
Imports value	443.1	9.0	9.9	9.2
Real GDP at factor costs	1,537.8	0.0	0.7	0.0
Nominal GDP at factor costs	1,537.8	0.4	1.9	1.0
Urban agricultural income	113.1	3.3	5.0	1.8
Rural agricultural income	210.0	3.0	3.9	1.9
Urban nonagricultural income	183.0	1.4	2.1	2.3
Rural nonagricultural income	111.7	1.2	1.8	1.7
Urban unskilled wage income	222.5	0.0	1.3	0.8
Rural unskilled wage income	43.6	0.6	1.5	0.6
Urban skilled wage income	77.0	0.5	1.3	0.9
Rural skilled wage income	67.0	0.5	1.0	0.4
Nonlabor income	601.8	-0.9	1.6	0.4
Urban unskilled employment	15.0		1.5	
Urban skilled employment	17.5		1.0	
Rural unskilled employment	34.2		1.7	
Rural skilled employment	9.8		1.1	
Total employment	76.5		1.4	

Source: Author's simulations.

Note: Base values in trillions of rupiah, except employment outcomes in millions of workers; percent changes for the nonbase columns. *FLIB_2* = full liberalization including Indonesia, with flexible unemployment; *FLIB_3* = full liberalization including Indonesia, with sector-specific labor; *FLIBVAT* = full liberalization including Indonesia, with VAT rates adjustment as the tax replacement scheme.

Labor Markets

The results of the simulations examined thus far in the paper have rested on the assumption of fixed employment in all labor markets. That assumption led to modest changes in growth and welfare at the household level. In this section, the impact of the full liberalization scenario is examined with two alternative

Table 11.6. Social Impact of Alternative Scenarios

	Base	FLIBVAT	FLIB_2	FLIB_3
National level				
Per capita income	7,188.2	0.8	1.7	1.0
General entropy index (0)	35.7	-0.1	0.1	0.3
General entropy index (1)	48.4	-0.1	-0.3	0.4
Gini index	45.7	-0.1	0.1	0.2
Poverty headcount	18.3	-2.3	-3.2	-2.4
Poverty gap	4.8	-2.3	-3.4	-2.1
Squared poverty gap	1.9	-2.0	-3.7	-2.2
Number of poor	39,174,973	-902,032	-1,236,696	-961,328
Urban areas				
Per capita income	9,775.9	0.6	1.4	1.1
General entropy index (0)	38.5	0.3	0.4	0.3
General entropy index (1)	52.8	0.3	0.0	0.4
Gini index	47.3	0.1	0.2	0.2
Poverty headcount	14.5	-1.3	-1.2	-2.5
Poverty gap	4.1	-0.5	-2.0	-2.1
Squared poverty gap	1.8	-0.5	-2.5	-2.2
Number of poor	13,295,695	-169,782	-164,989	-328,554
Rural areas				
Per capita income	5,240.8	1.2	2.0	0.8
General entropy index (0)	25.0	0.0	0.5	0.2
General entropy index (1)	30.2	0.0	0.0	0.1
Gini index	38.4	-0.1	0.3	0.1
Poverty headcount	21.2	-2.8	-4.1	-2.4
Poverty gap	5.3	-3.3	-4.3	-2.1
Squared poverty gap	2.1	-3.0	-4.4	-2.2
Number of poor	25,879,276	-732,250	-1,071,706	-632,774

Source: Author's simulations.

Note: Base values in the first column and percent changes in the following columns. Poverty indicators are computed using national poverty lines (World Bank 2003). *FLIB_2* = full liberalization including Indonesia, with flexible unemployment; *FLIB_3* = full liberalization including Indonesia, with sector-specific labor; *FLIB_VAT* = full liberalization including Indonesia, with VAT rates adjustment as the tax replacement scheme.

specifications of labor market functioning. In the first alternative closure, hourly wages are assumed to be fixed, with labor markets clearing through the adjustment of total employment (*FLIB_2*). This specification is expected to generate higher aggregate welfare effects as previously idle resources are brought into play. In a second specification, employment is assumed to be fixed—not only in the aggregate, but also by sector (*FLIB_3*). With less flexibility, this sector-specific labor scenario is expected to generate lower aggregate welfare gains.

In the case of flexible unemployment, the growth impact is higher than under the full employment assumption. It is driven by an increase in employment of approximately 1.4 percent, ranging from 1.0 percent to 1.8 percent across labor categories. As a result, the employment changes fed into the MS model are bigger. This generates higher per capita income changes, but although the overall impact on distribution remains positive, it deteriorates in the urban areas. This leads to smaller changes in poverty in the urban areas, where the poverty headcount decreases by only 1.2 percent despite the higher per capita increase. As a consequence, the aggregate poverty reduction is somewhat smaller under this unemployment closure (-1,260,000) than under the reference scenario.

How can it be that a scenario in which unemployment falls generates a smaller poverty reduction than one in which unemployment is fixed? The answer is that it all depends on who gets the jobs. If the jobs go to second or third earners in nonpoor households, then the income distribution can worsen, because the pool of unemployed keeps wages from rising and therefore mitigates the benefits to households for which the number of wage earners is fixed. Of course, the issue of who gets the new jobs is subject to considerable uncertainty, and this is reflected in the random draws for the error term associated with the occupational choice model. Therefore, there is clearly a need for Monte Carlo analysis, which will be discussed in the next section.

Under the sector-specific labor assumption, there is no reallocation of labor across sectors and efficiency gains are smaller. The resulting poverty outcomes are also smaller and overall income distribution worsens as a result of a smaller improvement in per capita income in rural areas relative to urban areas.

Monte Carlo Analysis

Given the stochastic nature of the occupational choice model in the MS model, it makes sense to perform Monte Carlo experiments to examine the sensitivity of poverty and income distribution outcomes.[10] Is it possible that the poverty outcome discussed above in the case of the unemployment closure is not robust? Monte Carlo experiments are performed on the full-liberalization scenario under the three alternative labor market closure specifications: the fixed employment closure (*Full-Lib*), the flexible employment closure (*FLIB_2*), and the sector-specific labor closure (*FLIB_3*).

The Monte Carlo results presented in table 11.7 provide a much better idea of the robustness of the findings presented in tables 11.4 and 11.6. First, note that the magnitude of the standard deviation on the inequality indicators suggests that the changes in income distribution are not significantly different from zero in any simulation. Moreover, when the full range of possible outcomes in the occupational choice model is considered, the sign of difference in the poverty outcome between the fixed employment specification and the flexible employment closure is reversed. Under the flexible employment closure, the trade liberalization scenario generates higher poverty reductions. However, the size of the standard deviation on the poverty outcomes suggests that the difference in poverty outcomes under the reference scenario and the flexible unemployment closure may not be significant. Also, it is clear that the third case—that of fixed labor—does generate significantly smaller poverty reduction.

Of course, any model is an abstraction of reality, and labor markets in Indonesia probably don't function precisely in the manner described under any of the three alternative specifications; rather, they are likely to reflect of combination of these polar views of the world. Therefore, these results should be viewed as providing a range of plausible poverty outcomes subject to the other assumptions embedded in the model.

Summary and Conclusions

The framework presented in this study has permitted us to generate detailed poverty outcomes resulting from international trade shocks. Given the magnitude of the shocks examined here and the structural features of the Indonesian economy, only the full liberalization scenarios generate significant poverty changes. Their impacts are examined under alternative specifications of the functioning of labor markets. These assumptions generate quite different results, but all conclude that full liberalization's impact on poverty would be positive, with efficiency and income gains dominating the adverse food price changes that could hurt the poorest households. Results also suggest that poverty reduction would be higher in the rural than in the urban sector. Two alternative tax replacement schemes are examined. Although the direct tax replacement appears to be more desirable in terms of efficiency gains and translates into higher poverty reduction, political and practical considerations could lead the government of Indonesia to choose a replacement scheme through the adjustment of VAT rates across nonexempt sectors. Such a move would dampen down the poverty-reducing potential of trade reform.

Table 11.7.   Monte Carlo Simulations on the Social Impact of Alternative Labor Market Closures

	Base	Full-Lib	Standard deviation	FLIB_2	Standard deviation	FLIB_3	Standard deviation
National level							
Per capita income	7,188.2	1.2	0.0	1.7	0.0	1.0	0.0
General entropy index (0)	35.7	-0.3	0.6	-0.3	0.7	0.2	0.3
General entropy index (1)	48.4	-0.9	1.8	-1.4	2.0	0.1	1.0
Gini index	45.7	-0.1	0.2	-0.1	0.3	0.1	0.1
Poverty headcount	18.3	-3.2	0.3	-4.0	0.5	-2.5	0.1
Poverty gap	4.8	-3.4	0.4	-3.9	0.6	-2.2	0.1
Squared poverty gap	1.9	-3.3	0.5	-3.8	0.9	-2.2	0.2
Urban areas							
Per capita income	9,775.9	1.1	0.1	1.4	0.1	1.1	0.0
General entropy index (0)	38.5	-0.4	1.2	-0.6	1.4	0.1	0.7
General entropy index (1)	52.8	-1.2	2.8	-1.8	3.2	-0.1	1.6
Gini index	47.3	-0.2	0.5	-0.3	0.6	0.1	0.3
Poverty headcount	14.5	-2.5	0.9	-2.9	1.1	-2.6	0.3
Poverty gap	4.1	-2.6	0.7	-3.1	1.2	-2.2	0.3
Squared poverty gap	1.8	-2.6	0.9	-3.3	1.7	-2.3	0.4
Rural areas							
Per capita income	5,240.8	1.4	0.0	2.0	0.1	0.8	0.0
General entropy index (0)	25.0	0.1	0.2	0.5	0.4	0.2	0.0
General entropy index (1)	30.2	0.1	0.2	0.2	0.7	0.3	0.0
Gini index	38.4	0.0	0.1	0.2	0.2	0.1	0.0
Poverty headcount	21.2	-3.5	0.2	-4.5	0.6	-2.4	0.1
Poverty gap	5.3	-3.9	0.3	-4.4	0.7	-2.1	0.1
Squared poverty gap	2.1	-3.8	0.5	-4.1	1.1	-2.1	0.1
Number of experiments		98		98		99	

Source: Authors' simulations.

Note: Full-Lib = full liberalization including Indonesia, with fixed unemployment; *FLIB_2* = full liberalization including Indonesia, with flexible unemployment; *FLIB_3* = full liberalization including Indonesia, with sector-specific labor.

As with any such study, there are a number of important limitations to this work. First of all, one should keep in mind that the results are likely to underestimate the cost of temporary unemployment endured by displaced workers in some sectors, particularly because unemployment benefits are not available for most Indonesian workers. Of course, these costs could be mitigated by gradually phasing in the trade reforms. And they would be further diminished if these trade reforms raised the overall growth rate of the Indonesian economy. Such dynamic growth gains—fueled by increased productivity and investment— have been ignored here but are addressed in the final three chapters of this volume.

Notes

1. The fully disaggregated SAM used has 39 activity accounts and 22 commodity accounts. Full detail is presented in the Policy Research Working Paper accompanying this chapter (Robilliard and Robinson, 2005).

2. The Special Survey on Saving and Household Investment (SKTIR) was integrated as a part of a module (submodule) of the SUSENAS survey. It was administered to only a subsample of the SUSE-NAS sample.

3. More details of the shocks fed into the CGE model are given in annex B of the World Bank Policy Research Working Paper version of this chapter (Robilliard and Robinson 2005). Because the Indonesia model assumes export prices are exogenous and fixed, the approach used here diverge from the approach outlined in chapter 3 and simply shock export prices. This specification gives this model a zero optimal tariff, unlike that implicit in the GTAP simulations.

4. A total of 32 variables generated by the CGE model are fed into the microsimulation module.

5. The use of official poverty lines gives a much lower incidence of poverty than the US$2 per day mark and less scope for change.

6. Nominal GDP is computed with respect to the consumer price index (CPI). Because the CPI is the appropriate numeraire for the analysis conducted at the household level, nominal GDP is the macro aggregate that is consistent with the changes in per capita income at the household level. Note that poverty and inequality indicators in the MS module are based on total per capita earned income, with no deduction of direct taxes. The issue of tax replacement will be debated in subsequent simulations.

7. The poverty gap measures the distance between the average poor household income per capita and the poverty line; the squared poverty gap gives a measure of the distribution of income among poor households.

8. Personal tax rates range from 5 percent for the lowest bracket to 35 percent for the highest. All rates except the highest were lowered in 2001.

9. VAT rates are relatively homogeneous across nonexempt sectors. It is assumed that informal sectors are not subjected to VAT because of the difficulty of collecting these taxes at the level of informal production units.

10. The term "Monte Carlo experiments" refers here to the replication of MS results using different draws of the residuals for the occupational choice model as well as for the wage equation model. One hundred draws were performed for each simulation. The draws that did not generate a feasible solution where dropped, which explains why the number of observations is smaller than 100 in table 11.7.

References

Armington, P. S. 1969. "A Theory of Demand for Products Distinguished by Place of Production." *IMF Staff Papers* 16 (2): 179–201.

Bourguignon, F., A. S. Robilliard, and S. Robinson. 2003. "Representative versus Real Households in the Macro-Economic Modeling of Inequality." In *Frontiers in Applied General Equilibrium Modeling: Essays in Honor of Herbert Scarf*, ed. T. Kehoe, T. N. Srinivasan, and J. Whalley, 219–254. Cambridge, U.K.: Cambridge University Press.

Cogneau, D., M. Grimm, and A. S. Robilliard. 2003. "Evaluating Poverty Reduction Policies: The Contribution of Microsimulation Techniques." In *The New International Strategies for Poverty Reduction*, ed. J.P. Cling, M. Razafindrakoto, and F. Roubaud, 340–393. London: Routledge.

Dervis, K., J. de Melo, and S. Robinson. 1982. *General Equilibrium Models for Development Policy*. New York: Cambridge University Press.

Essama-Nssah, B. 2004. "Building and Running General Equilibrium Models in EViews." Policy Research Working Paper 3197. World Bank, Washington, DC.

Francois, J., and D. Spinanger. 2004. "ATC Export Tax Equivalents." GTAP Version 6. https://www.gtap.agecon.purdue.edu/databases/v6/v6_doco.asp.

Hertel, T., D. Hummels, M. Ivanic, and R. Keeney. 2004. "How Confident Can We Be in CGE-Based Assessments of Free Trade Agreements?" GTAP Working Paper 26. Purdue University, W. Lafayette, IN.

McFadden, D. 1974. "Conditional Logit Analysis of Qualitative Choice Behavior." In *Frontiers in Econometrics*, ed. P. Zarembka, 105–42. New York: Academic Press.

Robilliard, A. S., and S. Robinson. 2003. "Reconciling Household Surveys and National Accounts Data Using a Cross Entropy Estimation Method." *Review of Income and Wealth* 49 (3): 395–406.

Robilliard, A. S., and S. Robinson. 2005. "The Social Impact of a WTO Agreement on Indonesia." Forthcoming Policy Research Working Paper, World Bank, Washington, DC.

Robinson, S., A. Cattaneo, and M. El-Said. 2001. "Updating and Estimating a Social Accounting Matrix Using Cross Entropy Methods." *Economic Systems Research* 13 (1): 47–64.

WTO (World Trade Organization). 2003. *Trade Policy Review—Indonesia 2003*. Geneva.

World Bank. 2003. *Indonesia Development Policy Report: Beyond Macroeconomic Stability*. Report 27374-IND. Washington, DC.

PART V

FISCAL REPLACEMENT OF LOST TARIFF REVENUE

12

THE POVERTY IMPACTS OF THE DOHA ROUND IN CAMEROON: THE ROLE OF TAX POLICY

Christian Arnault Emini, John Cockburn,
and Bernard Decaluwé[*]

Summary

This chapter assesses the possible impacts of the Doha Round on poverty in Cameroon. During the recent period of economic recovery, Cameroon has enjoyed a sharp decline in poverty, with the headcount index falling from 53.3 percent of inhabitants in 1996 to 40.2 percent in 2001, mostly thanks to economic growth rather than redistribution. Will the current trade negotiations under the Doha Round reinforce or curb this trend? The chapter applies a computable general equilibrium (CGE) microsimulation (MS) model that involves 10,992 households to address this question.

* The authors are grateful to Véronique Robichaud for her technical assistance, and to Nabil Annabi, Thomas Hertel, Alan Winters, Patrick Osakwe, and the participants at the conference, "Putting Development Back into the Doha Agenda," held in The Hague, December 2–4, 2004, for their valuable comments. The authors remain, of course, responsible for all possible errors and omissions. This work was carried out with financial assistance from the World Bank–Netherlands Partnership Program, as well as the Poverty and Economic Policy Research Network, which is financed by the International Development Research Centre.

The Doha Round is found to be poverty reducing for Cameroon. For the whole country, the estimate of net number of people who are lifted out of poverty is 22,000, according to this scenario. Further investigations indicate that more ambitious world trade liberalization leads to greater poverty alleviation at the national level, and Cameroon's domestic trade liberalization has adverse poverty and inequality impacts, despite giving rise to higher aggregate welfare. Under the Doha scenario, the cuts in Cameroon's tariffs are very small (the average tariff rate moves from 11.79 percent in the base run to merely 11.66 percent), so that liberalization effects in the rest of the world (ROW) on world prices more than offset the adverse own-liberalization effects in this scenario. If full trade liberalizations in ROW and Cameroon are combined, the adverse impacts of own-liberalization outweigh the favorable outcomes of the ROW liberalization.

The results in this chapter suggest furthermore that the choice of tax replacement instrument can have an important bias in poverty impacts: poverty gets worse in this country case study when an imperfect VAT is used instead of a neutral replacement tax to compensate lost tariff revenue, and it gets even worse when a consumption tax is used. Key reasons here are the supplementary distortions, which are nil in the case of a neutral tax and greatest in the case of a consumption tax. Finally, beyond the Doha scenarios that are the focus of this study, the poverty-worsening impacts of own-liberalization depicted here raise concerns for Cameroon. In particular, they suggest that accompanying measures should be considered to avoid poverty increases in the framework of Economic Partnership Agreements (EPAs) currently in negotiation between the African, Caribbean, and Pacific Group of States (ACP) and the EU, which propose a drastic dismantlement of ACP tariffs over the next few years.

Introduction

From 1965 to 1985, Cameroon recorded tremendous economic growth. The yearly average growth rate of per capita GDP amounted to 4 percent during the period 1965–76, 13 percent from 1977 to 1981, and 8 percent from 1982 to 1985. By 1985, Cameroon was ranked among middle-income countries, according to World Bank taxonomy (De Monchy and Roubaud 1991). After this 20-year golden age, Cameroon faced a deep-seated crisis from 1986 to 1994. GDP declined by more than 6 percent per year between 1986 and 1993, producing a 50 percent fall in per capita income (World Bank 1996). Cameroon recovered from 1995 onward, regaining a steady growth path and an annual real GDP growth rate of roughly 4.5 percent. This new expansion phase has been characterized by a sharp decline in poverty. For instance, the headcount index (share of poor population) fell from 53.3 percent to 40.2 percent between 1996 and 2001 (Republic of Cameroon 2003; Cameroon National Institute of Statistics [CNIS] 2002b).

In spite of this remarkable improvement, the prevalence of poverty still remains high and widespread in Cameroon. Indicators of human development considerably deteriorated during the crisis years, and recent economic improvements have not yet been sufficient and sustained enough to fully remedy the situation. Consequently, the country still carries the label of a heavily indebted poor country (HIPC).[1] It is thus understandable that Cameroon continues to agonize about whether it can meet the Millennium Development Goal of halving its 1990s level of extreme poverty by 2015.

Economic perspectives, as well as the design and outcomes of economic policies, are now more than ever constrained by international commitments because of ongoing globalization. Doha trade negotiations, undertaken under the aegis of the WTO, constitute a major crucible within this process. The objective of this chapter is to assess the possible poverty impacts in Cameroon of the Doha Round of trade negotiations as well as more ambitious world and domestic trade liberalization.

Trade liberalization can affect income opportunities of the poor in a number of ways. In general, the final poverty incidence depends on the relationship among trade liberalization, growth, and income distribution.[2] This new round has been heralded since the beginning as the Doha Development Round, with promises that the Doha Round should provide major opportunities for developing countries to derive more benefits from trade. However, exposure to increased international competition can be a double-edged sword for developing countries. The contribution of the Doha Round to achieving Cameroon's target on poverty alleviation will depend on the specific details of the new trade agreement.

The remainder of this chapter includes seven sections. Section 1 presents some background on trade and poverty in Cameroon. Section 2 is devoted to modeling specificities and data. Then, in section 3, the poverty impacts of the successful conclusion of the Doha Round of negotiations are analyzed. Section 4 is devoted to the analysis of various trade liberalization scenarios by use of a neutral tax as the replacement mechanism to offset losses in tariff revenues. In section 5, the poverty implications of fixed versus endogenous terms of trade when Cameroon liberalizes unilaterally are assessed. Section 6 compares the differential impacts of trade liberalization using three alternative replacement taxes. Concluding remarks are in section 7.

Poverty and Trade Background

Poverty Trends during 1996–2001

Cameroon undertook two household surveys during the last decade, in 1996 and 2001. Between these two years, the country recorded a drastic fall in poverty prevalence. Using a poverty line of 232,547 CFA francs (approximately 87 percent of the conventional US$1 per day in 2001), the headcount index (the proportion of people who are counted as poor) decreased by 13.1 percentage points; from 53.3 percent in 1996 to 40.2 percent in 2001. The poverty gap, which measures the degree to which the poor fall below the poverty line on average, also declined from 19.1 percent to 14.1 percent during this period. The squared poverty gap, which evaluates the extent of severe poverty among the poor, also declined from 9 percent to 7 percent.

A breakdown of poverty indicators shows that this sharp poverty alleviation is largely attributable to economic growth, rather than redistribution (Republic of Cameroon 2003). Economic growth contributed about 90 percent of the reduction in the headcount index, supporting the view that "growth is good for the poor," as underlined in studies such as Dollar and Kraay (2000). Indeed, changes in the income distribution are found to have actually increased the poverty gap and squared poverty gap, suggesting that some emphasis on redistribution is required to better alleviate poverty.

The decrease in all three poverty measures was more substantial in urban areas than in rural Cameroon, further increasing the rural-urban poverty divergence. The difference between the percentage of poor in rural and in urban areas has risen from 18.2 points in 1996 to 27.8 points in 2001. With regard to the poverty gap, this rural-urban differential has gone from 6.8 to 12 points. Similarly, the squared poverty gap has gone from being 3.2 points higher in rural areas in 1996 to 6.6 points higher in 2001.

Poverty does not affect people and regions evenly throughout the country. In 2001, the more one moves from the Atlantic coast and southern Cameroon toward the interior and the north, the larger the share of people living below the poverty line.

Trends in Cameroon's Trade

Cameroon's trade has grown considerably during the three last decades. In domestic currency, imports and exports have increased at average annual rates of 4.06 percent and 3.76 percent, respectively, between 1982 and 2002 in real terms (World Bank 2004). This expansion was greatest after 1994, in the postdevaluation[3] and new economic recovery era. In fact, Cameroon's external trade declined during the 1986–93 economic crisis, with imports and exports falling in real terms by an average of 3.59 percent and 3.79 percent per year, respectively. But the economic recovery beginning in 1994 has been characterized by a significant resurgence of external trade, beyond the devaluation's immediate mechanical effect.

Imports have grown faster than exports during this postdevaluation period. From 1994 to 2002, the value of imports has increased by a factor of 2.23 in real terms, with a 10.56 percent annual average growth rate; the value of exports has increased by a factor of only 1.58 in real terms, with an average growth rate of 5.85 percent per year during the same period. This has resulted in a continuous fall in the rate of coverage of imports by exports,[4] from 124.29 percent in 1995 to 85.70 percent in 2002. Indeed, 2001 and 2002 are the only years for which Cameroon has recorded a trade deficit since 1988.

However, the net-of-oil trade balance has been in deficit continuously since 1997, reflecting the country's dependence on oil exports. Cameroon has produced crude oil since 1977, and, from 1980 on, crude oil has generally accounted for 40 percent to 60 percent of Cameroon's export revenues. The rapid decline in oil prices in 1985 and 1986 is generally identified as the source of Cameroon's economic crisis.

Cameroon's lack of export diversification is illustrated by the fact that its five principal exports accounted for 74–81 percent of total export revenue over the last five years. All these products are either agricultural or based on natural resources. Using the three-digit Standard International Trade Classification (SITC) categorization,[5] these products in 2003 were broad-bean cocoa (product code 072), raw cotton (263), crude oil (333), wood processing (635), and refined petroleum (334).[6] The top five imports, classified using two-digit SITC categories, in 2003 were hydrocarbons (33), road vehicles (78), cereals and cereal preparations (04), general industrial machinery and equipment (74), and electrical machinery, apparatus, and appliances (77). During the last five years, these five product clusters have accounted for 50–53 percent of the total value of imports (CNIS 2004).

The EU is by far the most important trading partner of Cameroon. In 2003, 64.5 percent of Cameroon's exports and 54.6 percent of its imports were exchanged with the EU.[7] The EU is followed by Africa (13.6 percent of exports and 22.5 percent of imports), Asia (10.3 percent of exports and 15.6 percent of imports), North America (7.6 percent of exports and 5.5 percent of imports), and Latin America (1.4 percent of exports and 2.1 percent of imports).

Modeling Features and Data

The CGE MS model in this chapter involves 10,992 households compiled from the Household Living Standards Survey (ECAM II), undertaken in Cameroon in 2001 (CNIS 2002a, 2002b, 2003). Other data were processed from Cameroon's 2001 Supply and Use Tables and the underlying Integrated Economic Account Tables. The general architecture of the CGE is based on the *EXTER* archetype model

(Decaluwé, Martens, and Savard 2001). MSs are carried out according to the methods of Cockburn (2001) and Cloutier and Cockburn (2002). VAT modeling is based on Emini (2000a, 2000b).

The model includes 10 production sectors, each using a nested production technology. Primary factors of production are combined according to a constant elasticity of substitution (CES) function to constitute value added, which in turn combines with intermediate consumptions through Leontief functions. There are two agricultural sectors: foodstuff and cash-crop agriculture. Both use four primary factors of production: agricultural unskilled labor, agricultural skilled labor, agricultural capital, and land. The eight other sectors are nonagricultural and use three kinds of primary factors: nonagricultural unskilled labor, nonagricultural skilled labor, and nonagricultural capital. Capital is sector specific and fixed. Agricultural labor, skilled and unskilled, is mobile between agricultural sectors, just as nonagricultural labor is mobile between nonagricultural sectors (excluding the oil and public sectors, where all factors are fixed).

A summary of key parameters and shares for the model in the baseline year of 2001 is provided in table 12.1. Services, industry, and agriculture represent 47.5, 31.9, and 20.6 percent, respectively, of national value added. But the greatest share of gross production goes to industry (44.5 percent), followed closely by services (40.0 percent) and, far behind, agriculture (15.5 percent).

The impacts of trade liberalization crucially depend on sectoral import and export shares and ratios. Foodstuffs (18.2 percent of national value added and 13.2 percent of overall production) are almost entirely nontradeable (0.8 percent of exports and 1.1 percent of imports). Exports are 79.5 percent industrial, 12.7 percent services, and 7.9 percent agricultural goods, with the main products being crude oil (43.6 percent of total exports), wood products (11.9 percent), cash crops (7.1 percent), and refined petroleum (5.8 percent). These sectors are substantially export oriented, with export orientation ratios (exports as a share of output) of 98.5, 37.1, 43.0, and 28.0 percent, respectively. Cameroon's imports are predominantly composed of industrial goods (84.7 percent of imports). The highest import-penetration ratio (imports as a share of total domestic demand of a good) is recorded for crude oil (95.0 percent), followed by other manufactured goods (29.1 percent), processed food (12.3 percent), and refined petroleum (10.7 percent).

In the next sections, this model is used first to examine the likely impacts of a successful conclusion to the Doha Round and then to analyze the outcomes from more ambitious world and Cameroon free trade scenarios. The latter is then decomposed to isolate the poverty implications of the terms of trade (TOT) and finally compare the impacts of alternative tax mechanisms that the government might adopt to compensate for losses in tariff revenues.

Table 12.1. Key Elasticities and Parameter Values in the Model

Production sectors	VA[a] share (%)	X[a] share (%)	VA/X[a] (%)	Capital-labor ratio	Share (%)	Export intensity[b] (%)	CET elasticities[c] (%)	Export demand elasticities	Export tax rates (%)	Share (%)	Import intensity (%)	Armington elasticities[c] (%)	Import tariff rates[d] (%)
		Production				Exports[a] (%)			Trade		Imports[a] (%)		
Foodstuff agriculture	18.2	13.2	73.0	0.26	0.8	0.9	4.3	6.0	0.22	1.1	0.9	4.3	12.2
Cash-crop agriculture	2.3	2.3	53.1	1.13	7.1	43.0	6.5	6.0	0.00	0.0	0.1	6.5	8.0
Agriculture	**20.6**	**15.5**	**70.0**		**7.9**	**7.2**				**1.1**	**0.9**		
Forestry	1.1	2.7	22.8	0.94	1.1	6.0	5.0	6.0	8.67	0.1	0.5	5.0	7.4
Crude oil	9.6	6.3	80.9	51.87	43.6	98.5	14.2	6.0	0.25	17.2	95.0	14.2	3.2
Food processing	7.8	11.6	35.5	1.74	5.7	6.9	5.0	6.0	0.23	13.0	12.3	5.0	23.8
Wood processing	2.2	4.5	25.7	2.81	11.9	37.1	6.8	6.0	0.31	0.0	0.2	6.8	28.1
Refined petroleum	0.5	2.9	9.9	9.57	5.8	28.5	4.2	6.0	0.03	2.1	10.7	4.2	18.3
Miscellaneous industries	10.6	16.5	33.9	1.08	11.3	9.7	7.3	6.0	0.29	52.1	29.1	7.3	14.6
Industry	**31.9**	**44.5**	**37.9**		**79.5**	**25.2**				**84.7**	**22.9**		
Tradeable services	42.9	36.2	62.6	0.90	12.7	4.9	3.8	6.0	0.00	14.3	4.6	3.8	0.0
Public services	4.6	3.8	64.4	0.47	0.0	0.0	1.5	6.0	0.00	0.0	0.0	1.5	0.0
Services	**47.5**	**40.0**	**62.8**		**12.7**	**4.5**				**14.3**	**4.2**		
All sectors	**100.0**	**100.0**	**52.8**		**100.0**	**14.1**				**100.0**	**12.0**		

Source: Authors' construction.

a. Based on the 2001 SAM; *VA* = value added; *X* = production.
b. Export intensity = exports as a share of output.
c. Armington elasticities calculated from the GTAP for commodity aggregations. These values are used symmetrically for constant elasticity of transformation (CET) elasticities.
d. Import intensity = import as a share of domestic demand.

Impacts of the Doha Scenario

As set out in box 1.1, and elaborated in chapter 2, the Doha scenario involves a reduction in world and domestic tariffs, export subsidies, and domestic agricultural support. Tables 12.2–12.5 report the impacts of the Doha scenario on Cameroon along with those for several subsequent experiments. These tables cover changes in macroeconomic variables (12.2), changes in household income and poverty (12.3 and 12.4), and the sectoral impacts (12.5). For Cameroon, changes in tariff rates under the Doha scenario are minimal (table 12.5, second group of columns), with the average tariff level falling from 11.79 percent to 11.66 percent. Results from global simulations using the Global Trade Analysis Project (GTAP) model indicate that implementing the expected Doha agreement would lead to a small increase in average world import prices for Cameroon (0.47 percent) and practically no change in its world export prices (0.04 percent). Variations in export prices do not exceed 0.2 percent in any sector. The food processing and foodstuff sectors are the only sectors where the increase in world import prices exceeds 1 percent: 3.2 percent and 2.2 percent, respectively. The largest tariff cuts are also observed in these two sectors (8.7 and 2.7 percent, respectively).

Macro and Sectoral Effects

At the aggregate level, the Doha scenario has practically no impact on Cameroon. The real exchange rate appreciates by one 10th of 1 percent, and wage rates stay practically constant with a small increase (0.5 percent) in agricultural labor markets (table 12.2, first column).

At the sectoral level (table 12.5), impacts are also weak. In the food-processing industry, for which the increase in world import prices is greatest (3.2 percent), effects are mitigated by the counteracting fall in domestic tariffs (a reduction from 23.8 percent to 21.7 percent). The combined effect leads nevertheless to a 1.57 percent increase in the domestic import price and a 4.42 percent fall in import volumes. The resulting increase in local demand for domestic production leads to a small expansion of output and producer prices in the food-processing industry (0.50 percent), despite a small reduction in its exports. Indeed, as the world export price for food processing rises by only 0.1 percent, the increase in producer prices further reduces the sector's export competitiveness.

In the agriculture sectors, the cash-crop industry faces a fall in both world import prices (0.28 percent) and world export prices (0.18 percent), although the variations are very small. This leads to a drop in both exports and domestic

Table 12.2.   Changes in Selected Macro Variables (percent)

Scenarios Variables	Doha	ROW	Cam–1	Cam–2	Full	Full–VAT	Full–Con
Aggregate features of scenarios							
Index of world prices of exports	0.04	0.77	0.00	0.00	0.77	0.77	0.77
Index of world prices of imports	0.47	0.76	0.00	0.00	0.76	0.76	0.76
Overall tariff rate in Cameroon	–1.10	0.00	–100.00	–100.00	–100.00	–100.00	–100.00
Price effects							
Real exchange rate[a]	–0.17	–0.42	9.23	6.29	8.76	5.70	8.85
TOT	0.04	–0.02	–2.43	0.00	–2.40	–1.60	–2.41
Producer price index	0.21	1.19	–8.45	–5.92	–7.35	–4.66	–7.42
Producer price index of exports	0.08	0.75	–2.43	0.00	–1.64	–0.84	–1.65
Producer price index of locally sold production	0.23	1.26	–9.55	–7.01	–8.38	–5.33	–8.47
Market price index of locally sold production	0.27	1.26	–7.84	–5.54	–6.70	–4.23	–8.49
Market price index of imports	0.36	0.67	–9.83	–10.18	–9.06	–5.55	–10.89
Total absorption price index	0.29	1.18	–8.11	–6.26	–7.05	–4.39	–8.85
CPI	0.41	1.37	–8.53	–6.05	–7.23	–1.91	–7.36
Volume effects							
Output	0.02	0.01	–0.10	–0.10	–0.09	0.08	–0.05
Exports	–0.25	0.07	15.14	20.68	15.11	9.96	15.16
Locally sold output	0.09	0.01	–2.59	–3.52	–2.57	–0.77	–2.53
Imports	–0.64	0.31	14.76	24.72	14.85	9.82	14.92
Total demand of composite goods	0.00	0.04	–0.52	–0.14	–0.49	0.50	–0.45
Household consumption	–0.20	–0.05	0.10	0.21	0.02	–2.61	–4.69

output and an increase in cash-crop imports. The GTAP simulation of the Doha scenario predicts a relatively large increase in the world import price for food-stuffs (2.23 percent), which is partially offset by a reduction in the tariff rate from 12.2 percent to 11.9 percent. This leads to a significant drop in food-

Table 12.2.   (Continued)

Scenarios Variables	Doha	ROW	Cam–1	Cam–2	Full	Full–VAT	Full–Con
Remuneration of factors							
Wage rate of agricultural labor	0.50	3.60	–11.70	–7.67	–8.50	–5.40	–8.00
Wage rate of skilled agricultural labor	0.50	3.60	–11.70	–7.60	–8.50	–5.40	–8.00
Wage rate of unskilled agricultural labor	0.50	3.60	–11.70	–7.70	–8.50	–5.40	–8.00
Wage rate of nonagricultural labor	0.13	0.74	–9.98	–7.14	–9.24	–5.53	–9.52
Wage rate of skilled nonagricultural labor	0.14	0.78	–9.95	–7.09	–9.18	–5.44	–9.45
Wage rate of unskilled nonagricultural labor	0.10	0.61	–10.08	–7.29	–9.47	–5.84	–9.77
Average wage rate of composite labor	0.24	1.60	–10.49	–7.30	–9.02	–5.49	–9.06
Wage rate of agricultural labor	0.50	3.60	–11.70	–7.67	–8.50	–5.40	–8.00
Wage rate of nonagricultural labor	0.13	0.74	–9.98	–7.14	–9.24	–5.53	–9.52
Rate of return to capital	0.21	1.29	–7.75	–5.36	–6.69	–4.43	–6.80
Rate of return to agricultural capital	0.44	3.56	–9.58	–4.99	–6.43	–3.97	–5.81
Rate of return to nonagricultural capital	0.19	1.04	–7.55	–5.40	–6.72	–4.48	–6.90
Rate of return to land	0.40	3.50	–8.00	–3.00	–4.90	–3.00	–3.00
Household budget and welfare							
Household gross income	0.21	1.30	–8.32	–5.77	–7.12	–4.41	–7.18
Household consumption budget	0.21	1.32	–8.43	–5.85	–7.22	–4.47	–11.71
EV[b] as percentage of initial consumption	–0.20	–0.05	0.06	0.19	0.00	–2.69	–4.72

Source: Authors' construction based on simulation results. Aggregate features of scenarios are compiled from the GTAP global model results.

Note: Doha = Doha scenario; *ROW* = ROW liberalization; *Cam-1* = Cameroon liberalization with neutral replacement tax and endogenous TOT; *Cam-2* = Cameroon liberalization with neutral replacement tax and fixed TOT; *Full* = combined ROW and Cameroon full liberalization with neutral replacement tax; *Full-VAT* = combined ROW and Cameroon full liberalization with VAT as replacement tax; *Full-Con* = combined ROW and Cameroon full liberalization with consumption replacement tax.

a. Real exchange rate = ratio of the nominal exchange rate multiplied by the index of world export prices, divided by the domestic output price index.
b. EV = Hicksian equivalent variation. A positive value implies a welfare improvement and a negative value indicates a welfare worsening.

Table 12.3.   Sources of Household Factor Incomes

Shares in the base run (in percent)	Urban house-holds	Rural house-holds	Male-led house-holds	Female-led house-holds	Poor in base run	Nonpoor in base run
Wages earned on skilled agricultural labor	1.86	13.41	7.20	5.46	13.30	5.95
Wages earned on unskilled agricultural labor	2.54	33.12	14.71	20.00	35.34	13.02
Wages earned on skilled nonagricultural labor	56.24	20.99	42.29	35.82	21.94	43.67
Wages earned on unskilled nonagricultural labor	12.21	10.78	11.65	11.39	15.37	11.06
Returns to agricultural capital	4.99	12.39	5.73	7.51	5.58	6.15
Returns to nonagricultural capital	22.01	7.51	17.58	18.91	6.56	19.43
Returns to land	0.15	1.80	0.85	0.92	1.91	0.72
Total	100.00	100.00	100.00	100.00	100.00	100.00

Source: Authors' calculations.

stuff imports (6.34 percent) in favor of locally produced substitutes (increase of 0.09 percent).

On the whole, the Doha scenario involves a rise in world import prices (0.47 percent) and a resulting substitution of local demand toward domestically produced substitutes: imports and exports decline (by 0.64 percent and 0.25 percent, respectively) and locally sold production expands (by 0.06 percent). The food-processing and foodstuff sectors are the most affected and strongly influence the overall impacts on the economy.

In terms of impacts on factor markets, begin by noting that agricultural labor moves from cash crops to foodstuff, and food processing draws nonagricultural labor from most of the other nonagricultural sectors. All factor remuneration rates increase, although the changes are very small (see table 12.2). Wage rates rise more for unskilled labor (0.33 percent) than for skilled labor (0.19 percent). Average returns to capital and land increase respectively by 0.21 percent and 0.40 percent. On average, changes in remuneration rates are more favorable to agricultural factors (+0.50 percent for agricultural labor, +0.44 percent for agricultural capital, and +0.40 percent for land) than to nonagricultural factors (+0.13 percent for nonagricultural labor and +0.19 percent for nonagricultural capital).

Table 12.4. Poverty and Inequality Indexes before and after Simulations

Scenarios Household groups	Poverty (%) and inequality indexes	Baseline	Doha	ROW	Cam-1	Cam-2	Full	Full-VAT	Full-Con
Cameroon	Poverty headcount	40.22	40.08	39.28	41.52	40.64	40.78	42.14	43.44
	Poverty gap	13.76	13.75	13.28	14.79	14.28	14.33	14.85	15.58
	Poverty severity	6.38	6.37	6.08	7.18	6.81	6.82	7.07	7.54
	Gini index	0.4575	0.4570	0.4542	0.4670	0.4631	0.4630	0.4609	0.4624
	Number of former poor escaping from poverty		23,000	161,000	110,000	107,000	106,000	24,000	42,000
	Number of former nonpoor becoming poor		1,000	16,000	311,000	172,000	193,000	327,000	540,000
	Net change in the number of poor people		−22,000	−145,000	+201,000	+65,000	+87,000	+303,000	+498,000
Urban areas	Poverty headcount	17.97	17.90	17.86	18.59	18.47	18.90	19.78	21.33
	Poverty gap	4.56	4.59	4.56	4.97	4.84	4.93	5.15	5.70
	Poverty severity	1.75	1.77	1.75	2.08	1.98	1.98	2.05	2.33
	Gini index	0.4538	0.4537	0.4533	0.4612	0.4595	0.4602	0.4573	0.4606
Rural areas	Poverty headcount	52.17	52.00	50.79	53.85	52.56	52.54	54.16	55.32
	Poverty gap	18.70	18.68	17.97	20.07	19.36	19.39	20.06	20.89
	Poverty severity	8.86	8.84	8.41	9.92	9.40	9.43	9.77	10.34
	Gini index	0.3906	0.3904	0.3885	0.3974	0.3946	0.3944	0.3930	0.3941

Table 12.4. (Continued)

Household groups	Scenarios Poverty (%) and inequality indexes	Baseline	Doha	ROW	Cam-1	Cam-2	Full	Full-VAT	Full-Con
Male-led households	Poverty headcount	40.54	40.37	39.65	42.00	41.10	41.28	42.60	44.08
	Poverty gap	14.01	14.00	13.50	15.23	14.66	14.73	15.18	15.98
	Poverty severity	6.51	6.49	6.19	7.45	7.03	7.05	7.27	7.78
	Gini index	0.4615	0.4610	0.4581	0.4711	0.4672	0.4670	0.4648	0.4664
Female-led households	Poverty headcount	39.18	39.16	38.10	39.99	39.19	39.18	40.68	41.38
	Poverty gap	12.95	12.96	12.58	13.39	13.09	13.06	13.77	14.29
	Poverty severity	5.97	5.97	5.75	6.33	6.11	6.09	6.45	6.76
	Gini index	0.4443	0.4438	0.4412	0.4535	0.4498	0.4499	0.4478	0.4494
Poor people in base run	Poverty headcount	100.00	99.64	97.41	98.23	98.28	98.30	99.62	99.33
	Poverty gap	34.20	34.19	33.02	36.50	35.36	35.49	36.76	38.30
	Poverty severity	15.86	15.84	15.12	17.80	16.90	16.94	17.57	18.69
	Gini index	0.1777	0.1775	0.1764	0.1918	0.1866	.1865	0.1828	0.1866
Nonpoor people in base run	Poverty headcount	0.00	0.02	0.18	3.37	1.87	2.09	3.48	5.84
	Poverty gap	0.00	0.00	0.00	0.19	0.11	0.10	0.10	0.30
	Poverty severity	0.00	0.00	0.00	0.04	0.02	0.01	0.01	0.04
	Gini index	0.3709	0.3705	0.3684	0.3791	0.3759	.3760	0.3737	0.3756

Source: Authors' construction based on simulation results and the 2001 Cameroon household survey.

Note: Doha = Doha scenario; ROW = ROW liberalization; Cam-1 = Cameroon liberalization with neutral replacement tax and endogenous TOT; Cam-2 = Cameroon liberalization with neutral replacement tax and fixed TOT; Full = combined ROW and Cameroon full liberalization with neutral replacement tax; Full-VAT = combined ROW and Cameroon full liberalization with neutral replacement tax; Full-Con = combined ROW and Cameroon full liberalization with consumption replacement tax.
ROW and Cameroon full liberalization with VAT as replacement tax; Full-Con = combined ROW and Cameroon full liberalization with consumption replacement tax.

Table 12.5. Doha Scenario with VAT as the Replacement Tax: Sectoral Effects

Production sectors	Percent changes in world prices from GTAP simulations		Tariffs (in percent)		Percent changes in domestic market prices							Percent changes in volumes					
	World export prices	World import prices	Original tariffs	New tariffs	Producer prices	Export prices	Import prices	Prices of locally sold output[a]	Prices of locally sold output[b]	Prices of composite goods[b]	Consumer prices[b]	Output	Exports	Imports	Locally sold domestic output	Total demand of composite goods	Household consumption
Foodstuff agriculture	0.015	2.233	12.2	11.9	0.46	0.19	2.02	0.46	0.46	0.48	0.48	0.06	-1.07	-6.34	0.09	0.03	-0.10
Cash-crop agriculture	-0.177	-0.284	8.0	8.0	0.18	0.04	-0.32	0.27	0.28	0.27	0.28	-0.45	-1.28	4.23	0.25	0.26	-0.03
Forestry	-0.122	-0.108	7.4	7.3	0.07	-0.01	0.18	0.08	0.08	0.08	0.08	-0.23	-0.64	-0.69	-0.19	-0.19	-0.04
Crude oil	0.111	0.114	3.2	3.2	0.11	0.11	0.11	0.11	0.11	0.11	0.00	0.00	0.00	-0.06	-0.01	-0.05	0.00
Food processing	0.115	3.234	23.8	21.7	0.50	0.24	1.57	0.52	0.53	0.68	0.89	0.58	-0.74	-4.42	0.70	0.07	-0.44
Wood processing	-0.061	-0.064	28.1	27.9	0.00	-0.02	0.18	0.01	0.16	0.16	0.42	-0.18	-0.27	-0.17	-0.07	-0.07	-0.23
Refined petroleum	0.105	0.073	18.3	18.3	0.07	0.10	0.17	0.06	0.16	0.16	0.23	-0.06	0.04	-0.14	-0.11	-0.11	-0.13
Miscellaneous industries	0.103	0.017	14.6	14.5	0.14	0.12	0.24	0.14	0.20	0.21	0.38	0.07	-0.08	-0.16	0.11	0.03	-0.20
Tradeable services	-0.064	-0.024	0.0	0.0	0.11	0.01	-0.02	0.12	0.17	0.16	0.18	-0.11	-0.46	0.67	-0.06	-0.03	-0.13
Public services	0.000	0.000	0.0	0.0	0.39	0.00	0.00	0.39	0.39	0.39	0.00	0.00	0.00	0.00	0.00	0.00	0.00
All sectors	0.044	0.471	11.79	11.66	0.21	0.08	0.36	0.23	0.27	0.29	0.41	0.02	-0.25	-0.64	0.09	0.00	-0.20

Source: Authors' construction based on simulation results (for changes in domestic prices and volumes) and on GTAP results (for changes in world prices and tariffs).

a. Exclusive of taxes.

b. Inclusive of all taxes on goods.

Household Income Effects

These small increases in factor remunerations result in a slight rise (0.21 percent) in household gross income at the national level (table 12.2). On the basis of the initial factor endowments of household groups and changes in the remuneration rates of various factors, total factor income for urban households increases by 0.16 percent, and rural households enjoy a relatively substantial 0.40 percent increase due to a greater rise in skilled and unskilled agricultural wage rates, as well as rates of return to agricultural and nonagricultural capital, which account altogether for about 66 percent of rural household factor income (table 12.3). Factor incomes in male-led households grow very slightly more (0.27 percent) than in female-led households (0.24 percent), given their larger shares of labor and agricultural capital income. Factor incomes of households that were initially poor rise more (0.37 percent) than for the initially nonpoor (0.25 percent) as a result of much higher shares of labor income. In general, households enjoying greater improvement in income are those more endowed with skilled or unskilled agricultural labor or both, or with agricultural capital. Those experiencing smaller improvement are households mainly endowed with nonagricultural labor.

Poverty Effects

The implementation of the Doha agreement appears likely to slightly reduce poverty and inequality (table 12.4). The national headcount index (the percentage of poor) falls from 40.22 percent to 40.08 percent, the poverty gap from 13.76 to 13.75, poverty severity from 6.38 to 6.37, and the Gini index from 0.458 to 0.457. Even though a small improvement, this implies a nonnegligible net reduction in the number of poor (22,000 people). Rural households benefit more than urban households, notably in terms of the poverty gaps and severity and the Gini index, as a result of stronger income gains. In the same way, male-led households benefit slightly more than female-led households, and those who are initially poor benefit more than the initially nonpoor.

Indeed, the headcount index of the initially nonpoor household group increases from 0.00 to 0.02 percent, implying that 1,000 individuals become poor. At the same time, the headcount index of the initially poor household group shifts from 100.00 to 99.64 percent, indicating that 23,000 formerly poor people have escaped from poverty. People who escape poverty belong to households whose head is involved in agriculture, fishing, hunting, or the food industry or is in public service. Households entering poverty have a head who is involved in transport or miscellaneous services. Headcount indexes of all other household groups (according to the main activity of the head) remain unchanged.

World and Domestic Free-Trade Simulations

The three scenarios performed in this section involve the complete elimination of import tariffs: first, in ROW, then in Cameroon, and then in both regions. The macroeconomic closure of the model for these scenarios follows the one used in the other country studies in this book: employment, real investment, real public expenses, and the trade balance are fixed. To compensate for lost tariff revenue, a neutral production tax, evenly levied on locally sold production and imports, is introduced. Endogenous terms of trade, with free on board (FOB) export prices potentially differing from their corresponding world export prices, are assumed.

Table 12.6 compares the impacts of full liberalization in ROW with that of domestic trade reform in Cameroon, focusing on prices and volumes of goods and services flows. According to results from the GTAP world model, a complete liberalization in ROW would lead to a nonnegligible increase in world import prices, especially for foodstuff agriculture (7.08 percent) and food processing (4.76 percent), as well as an increase in export prices of foodstuff agriculture (3.20 percent), cash crops (1.86 percent), and food processing (1.75 percent).[8] However, unilateral liberalization by Cameroon means a 100 percent reduction in domestic tariffs from an average tariff rate of 11.79 percent and a maximum rate of 28 percent and 23 percent, respectively, for the wood-processing and food-processing industries. Finally, the full-liberalization scenario, in which ROW and Cameroon both eliminate their respective barriers to trade, simultaneously involves an increase in world import and export prices and a complete removal of domestic tariffs. Depending on the sector and the initial level of tariffs, this tariff removal can completely offset the increase in world import prices in the determination of the local prices of imports.

Macro Effects

In table 12.2 dramatically opposing price effects in the ROW free-trade scenario compared to Cameroon's own-liberalization (*Cam-1*) can be observed. Prices uniformly increase under ROW free trade as a result of increases in world import and export prices, but they fall substantially with domestic liberalization. The movement in domestic prices for imports and exports is also substantially different. In the ROW liberalization scenario, the increase in import prices (0.67 percent) is less important than the increase in export prices (0.75 percent). When Cameroon liberalizes alone, import prices drop substantially (-9.83 percent), and export prices drop much less (-2.43 percent). When the two scenarios are combined, impacts of Cameroon's own-liberalization dominate ROW impacts. Indeed, the real exchange rate depreciation (8.76 percent) is nearly equal to the own-liberal-

Table 12.6. ROW versus Domestic Liberalization: Sectoral Effects on Prices and Volumes of Goods and Services

Production sectors	Percent changes in world prices from GTAP simulations		Tariffs (in percent)			Percent changes in domestic market prices							Percent changes in volumes					
	World export prices	World import prices	Original tariffs	Cut in original tariffs	New tariffs	Producer prices	Export prices	Import prices	Locally sold output prices[a]	Prices of locally sold output[b]	Prices of composite goods[b]	Consumer prices[b]	Output	Exports	Imports	Locally sold domestic output	Total demand of composite goods	Household consumption
ROW liberalization only																		
Cash-crop agriculture	1.73	0.51	8.0	0.00	8.0	1.94	1.86	0.51	2.01	2.01	2.00	2.00	−0.20	−0.72	10.30	0.23	0.24	0.16
Forestry	0.80	0.54	7.4	0.00	7.4	0.62	0.73	0.57	0.61	0.61	0.61	0.61	−0.11	0.43	0.04	−0.14	−0.14	0.16
Crude oil	0.49	0.44	3.2	0.00	3.2	0.49	0.49	0.44	0.47	0.47	0.44	0.00	0.00	0.01	−0.02	−0.39	−0.04	0.00
Food processing	1.49	4.79	23.8	0.00	23.8	2.30	1.75	4.76	2.34	2.33	2.68	2.60	1.15	−1.53	−9.94	1.35	−0.04	−0.54
Wood processing	0.70	0.24	28.1	0.00	28.1	0.67	0.68	0.23	0.67	0.66	0.66	0.67	0.03	0.10	0.34	−0.01	−0.01	−0.06
Refined petroleum	0.53	0.33	18.3	0.00	18.3	0.41	0.49	0.34	0.38	0.39	0.39	0.38	−0.06	0.24	0.02	−0.19	−0.16	0.18
Miscellaneous industries	0.95	−0.15	14.6	0.00	14.6	0.39	0.69	−0.15	0.36	0.36	0.18	0.35	−0.52	1.64	3.05	−0.74	0.36	0.36
Tradeable services	0.67	0.36	0.0	0.00	0.0	0.70	0.69	0.36	0.70	0.71	0.69	0.69	−0.08	−0.12	1.24	−0.08	−0.01	0.04
Public services	0.00	0.00	0.0	0.00	0.0	2.10	0.00	0.00	2.10	2.10	2.10	0.00	0.00	0.00	0.00	0.00	0.00	0.00
All sectors	0.77	0.76	11.79	0.00	11.79	1.19	0.75	0.67	1.26	1.26	1.18	1.37	0.01	0.07	0.31	0.01	0.04	−0.05

Table 12.6. (Continued)

Production sectors	Percent changes in world prices from GTAP simulations		Tariffs (in percent)			Percent changes in domestic market prices							Percent changes in volumes					
	World export prices	World import prices	Original tariffs	Cut in original tariffs	New tariffs	Producer prices	Export prices	Import prices	Locally sold output prices[a]	Prices of locally sold output[a]	Prices of composite goods[a]	Consumer prices[b]	Output	Exports	Imports	Locally sold domestic output	Total demand of composite goods	Household consumption
Cam-1: Domestic liberalization only with neutral replacement tax																		
Foodstuff agriculture	0.00	0.00	12.2	-100	0.00	-11.02	-4.64	-9.80	-11.08	-9.30	-9.30	-10.98	-1.32	33.02	0.81	-1.60	-1.58	0.42
Cash-crop agriculture	0.00	0.00	8.0	-100	0.00	-6.53	-4.19	-5.97	-8.51	-6.67	-6.67	-8.50	10.00	29.31	-8.65	-4.15	-4.15	-0.06
Forestry	0.00	0.00	7.4	-100	0.00	-8.13	-4.20	-6.14	-8.39	-6.58	-6.58	-8.35	4.96	29.40	1.09	3.52	3.50	-0.15
Crude oil	0.00	0.00	3.2	-100	0.00	-0.08	-0.06	-1.15	-1.60	0.38	-1.08	0.00	0.00	0.34	0.04	-19.49	-0.94	0.00
Food processing	0.00	0.00	23.8	-100	0.00	-10.75	-4.77	-17.77	-11.28	-9.55	-11.06	-9.07	-3.32	34.11	51.65	-6.16	0.97	0.15
Wood processing	0.00	0.00	28.1	-100	0.00	-5.24	-3.39	-20.28	-6.42	-4.50	-4.56	-6.31	7.87	23.02	238.41	-0.92	-0.53	-0.75
Refined petroleum	0.00	0.00	18.3	-100	0.00	-3.31	-1.20	-13.84	-4.20	-2.70	-4.14	-3.55	-1.77	7.52	57.44	-5.52	1.22	-1.90
Miscellaneous industries	0.00	0.00	14.6	-100	0.00	-9.24	-4.98	-11.34	-9.79	-8.04	-9.27	-5.85	-2.95	35.89	21.39	-7.15	1.14	-1.21
Tradeable services	0.00	0.00	0.0	-100	0.00	-8.89	-3.63	2.01	-9.20	-7.36	-7.00	-8.87	0.76	24.80	-30.99	-0.47	-1.88	0.74
Public services	0.00	0.00	0.0	-100	0.00	-8.46	0.00	0.00	-8.46	-8.46	-8.46	0.00	0.00	0.00	0.00	0.00	0.00	0.00
All sectors	0.00	0.00	11.79	-100	0.00	-8.45	-2.43	-9.83	-9.55	-7.84	-8.11	-8.51	-0.10	15.14	14.76	-2.59	-0.52	0.10

Source: Authors' construction based on simulation results (for changes in domestic prices and volumes) and on GTAP results (for changes in world prices and tariffs).

a. Exclusive of taxes.

b. Inclusive of all taxes on goods.

ization scenario (9.23 percent). In contrast, increases in both import and export prices under ROW free trade lead to a small real appreciation of the exchange rate (0.42 percent).

Concerning effects on trade and production, Cameroon and ROW liberalization also have opposing impacts. Under ROW liberalization, changes in world prices have nearly no impact on aggregate imports, exports, and locally sold production. On the contrary, Cameroon's unilateral liberalization creates a substantial increase in imports (14.76 percent) and exports (15.14 percent) and consequently a reduction in local production exchanged on the domestic market (-2.59 percent). In the combined scenario, once more, the expansion of trade is nearly identical to the situation under Cameroon's own-liberalization (14.85 percent for imports and 15.11 percent for exports).

Sectoral Effects, the Labor Market, and Reallocation of Resources

To understand the transmission mechanisms, it is important to look carefully at the sectoral factor reallocation processes in each scenario.

ROW liberalization scenario

Even with very low import penetration and export intensity ratios in foodstuff agriculture (table 12.1), a strong increase in world prices leads to a fall in foodstuff imports (-15.60 percent) and an increase in their exports (1.09 percent) and producer prices (2.95 percent), because domestic and foreign foodstuffs are considered to be good substitutes.[9] Foodstuff production is very intensive in labor[10] and particularly in unskilled agricultural workers (69 percent of labor; see table 12.1). Indeed, markets for skilled and unskilled agricultural workers are dominated by the foodstuff sector, which absorbs nearly 93 percent of agricultural workers. Thus, the increase in domestic foodstuff prices pushes up unskilled and skilled agricultural wages (3.60 percent each), as well as the returns to land.

In turn, the increase in the cost of agricultural labor and land drives costs and, consequently, producer prices (1.94 percent) in the cash-crop sector. The increase in the world export price of cash crops (1.86 percent) is not sufficient to cover the extra costs,[11] thus cash-crop exports fall (-0.72 percent). Because the cash-crop market is export oriented, a reduction in exports (combined with an increase in import competition) negatively affects this sector, reducing domestic production by 0.20 percent and moderating the domestic price increase (2.01 percent). As a result, land and agricultural labor move toward the foodstuff sector, whereas the returns to immobile capital increase more in this sector.

In the nonagricultural sectors, the GTAP model predicts an increase in the world import price of (agriculturally based) food processing (4.79 percent) and a much less important increase on the export side (1.49 percent). In the other sectors, the changes in prices are less than 1 percent. The food-processing sector represents 11 percent of total output and 25 percent of the industrial sector, and it is linked to the international market with an export intensity ratio of 7 percent and an import penetration ratio of 12 percent (table 12.1). Domestic and imported processed foods are considered to be close substitutes (elasticity of 6.49).

Under these conditions, the increase in world prices creates upward pressure on producer and consumer prices in the food-processing sector (2.30 percent and 2.60 percent, respectively) and contributes to a rise in domestic production (1.15 percent). The cost-based, contractive impact on the other nonagricultural sectors is small but widespread, from almost 0 in the wood-processing industries to a maximum fall of 0.52 percent in miscellaneous industries. As a result, there is a reallocation of labor toward the food-processing sector. Given the lower than average share of unskilled (versus skilled) labor in food processing, there is a bigger increase in nonagricultural skilled wage rates (0.78 percent) relative to unskilled wage rates (0.61 percent).

In terms of international trade, the increase in world import prices for processed food reduces import demand (-9.94 percent) and increases domestic demand for local production (1.35 percent). On the export side, the food-processing industry is unable to increase its export performance (-1.53 percent) because the increase in world export prices for food processing (1.75 percent) is not high enough to compensate for the increase in production costs (2.30 percent). In the other nonagricultural sectors, imports and exports generally increase moderately, with the strongest impacts in miscellaneous industries, for which world export prices increase by almost 1 percent.

Cameroon Unilateral Liberalization Scenario

The industrial sector is the most protected sector in Cameroon. Initial tariffs in the wood-processing, food-processing, refined petroleum, and miscellaneous industries are, respectively, 28.1, 23.8, 18.3, and 14.6 percent. A complete removal of customs barriers results in a reduction in the domestic prices of these imports and an increase in their volume.[12] The food-processing and miscellaneous industries are most affected by this increased import competition, given their high initial import penetration ratios and degree of substitution with respect to imports (table 12.1). Consequently, domestic demand, consumer prices, and producer prices for these industries all decline more than in the other industrial sectors. Industrial producers respond to falling domestic prices by expanding exports, especially in the food-processing and miscellaneous industries. However, this export expansion is insufficient to offset the loss in local sales, such that output declines in all but the export-intensive wood-processing industry and its main source of inputs, the forestry industry.

On the agriculture side, initial tariffs are higher in the foodstuff sector (12.2 percent) than in the cash-crop sector (8.0 percent), and, consequently, trade liberalization leads to a greater reduction in foodstuff import prices. These price variations are passed on to domestic producer and consumer prices in these two sectors, leading local producers to substitute massively toward export markets. In the export-intensive cash-crop sector, output consequently expands, whereas it contracts in the inward-oriented foodstuffs industry. Output in refined petroleum and miscellaneous industries also contracts.

As a result of these output variations, labor moves toward the expanding export-intensive sectors: cash crops, forestry, and wood processing. Agricultural wages fall slightly more (-11.70 percent) than industrial wages (-10.07), reflecting greater reductions in agricultural producer prices. Because the expanding sectors have roughly the same shares of unskilled labor in composite labor as other sectors, skilled and unskilled wages fall in the same proportion. Returns to land fall less than agricultural wages, because producer prices fall more in the labor-intensive foodstuffs sector than in the land-intensive cash-crop sector. The returns to (immobile) capital rise for cash crops (0.40 percent), given that producer prices fall less than wages and returns to land, whereas the contrary is observed for returns to capital in the foodstuffs sector.

Combined Full Liberalization of ROW and Cameroon

The results from the combined ROW and Cameroon liberalization are very similar to those for Cameroon liberalization alone (*Cam-1*), because the increase in world prices due to free world trade is dwarfed by the reduction in prices resulting from the elimination of Cameroonian tariffs. At the macro level, for example, the real exchange rate depreciates by 8.76 percent compared to a 9.23 percent depreciation in the case of the Cameroon unilateral liberalization. (It appreciates by 0.42 percent in the case of the ROW liberalization.). The consumer price index is down 7.23 percent compared to 8.53 percent, imports are up 14.85 percent compared to 14.76 percent, exports are nearly at the same level, and wage rates in the agriculture sector decline less.[13]

Household Income Effects

Initial income shares and changes in household factor incomes for all scenarios are summarized in table 12.3. Variations in factor remunerations affect the income of household groups according to their respective factor endowments in the base run. Urban households derive most of their income from skilled wages and returns to nonagricultural capital (80 percent). Rural households derive a large proportion of income from agricultural factors, even if a nonnegligible proportion comes from other income sources. They consequently have more diversified income sources compared to urban households.

ROW free trade increases rural incomes (2.46 percent) more than urban incomes (1.02 percent), given the larger increase in the returns to agricultural factors. Incomes in male-headed households rise slightly less than in female-led households, given the greater dependence on income from agricultural factors in female-headed households. The base-year poor also experience a larger increase in income (2.41 percent versus 1.53 percent for the base-year nonpoor), once again due to a larger share of agricultural factor income.

As expected, there are opposite effects under the Cameroon unilateral liberalization. Incomes fall as a result of the import price–led reduction in domestic output and factor prices, especially for agricultural wages. Rural and base-year poor households suffer more because of their higher shares of agricultural wage income.

In the combined ROW and Cameroon scenario, household incomes fall, although less than under unilateral Cameroonian liberalization. The impacts offset each other in such a way that rural and base-year poor households have only slightly larger falls in their incomes than their urban and base-year nonpoor counterparts. The impacts of ROW liberalization imply that incomes fall slightly more for urban and base-run nonpoor households than in rural and base-run poor households in the case of the combined scenario.

Poverty Effects

In the analysis of variations in the Foster, Greer, and Thorbecke (FGT) poverty indicators, impacts derive from two sources: (1) the change in household income and (2) the change in consumer prices. These, in turn, affect the poverty line. Overall, it is clear that free world trade slightly reduces poverty, whereas domestic liberalization substantially increases poverty (table 12.4).

As a consequence of ROW liberalization, the poverty headcount index decreases from 40.22 percent to 39.28 percent for the entire country, the poverty gap falls from 13.76 to 13.28, poverty severity declines from 6.38 to 6.08, and the Gini index goes from 0.458 to 0.454. ROW free trade reduces poverty in rural areas, where income gains are greatest, but leaves the situation of the urban poor practically unchanged, precisely for the poverty gap and poverty severity (table 12.4). One of the explanations for this stagnation in urban areas is the fact that the sharp poverty alleviation in households linked to the food processing industry (poverty headcount shifts here from 20.54 percent to 14.15 percent) is strongly mitigated by the poverty worsening among households operating in the textile industry (poverty headcount rises from 29.20 percent to 31.28 percent), which represent a greater proportion of the total population. Overall, ROW liberalization benefits both male- and female-led households, but, as expected, the fall in poverty is more significant in female-led households as a result of the greater increase in their incomes. ROW free trade allows 2.59 percent of the poor, or roughly 161,000 individuals (table 12.4), to escape poverty. However, 0.17 percent of the nonpoor (about 16,000 individuals) fall into poverty. In net terms, the total number of poor declines by 145,000 individuals. Those household groups that would most profit from ROW liberalization are those whose head is principally involved in agriculture activities, fishing, hunting, breeding, the food processing industry, the wood products industry, or food trade. The greatest losers from ROW liberalization would be households whose head works in the textile industry or transport.

Under Cameroon's unilateral liberalization with neutral replacement tax (*Cam-1*), aggregate consumption and household welfare improve, by 0.10 percent and 0.06 percent of initial consumption, respectively. This indicates an overall increase in efficiency in the wake of tariff reform. The welfare gain would have been more substantial if some rigidities were not introduced into the labor market.[14] But, notwithstanding this aggregate welfare gain, Cameroon's own-liberalization induces a strong increase in poverty. The national poverty headcount index jumps from 40.22 percent to 41.52 percent. The poverty gap and poverty severity indexes also deteriorate considerably, increasing respectively from 13.76 percent to 14.79 percent and from 6.38 percent to 7.18 percent, and, not surprisingly, inequality increases, with a shift in the Gini coefficient from 0.458 to 0.467.

Given that the reduction in rural income is larger than the reduction in urban income, poverty increases more among rural households than among urban households. Unilateral liberalization enables fewer individuals to escape poverty (110,000 compared to 161,000 with ROW liberalization), while dramatically increasing the number of base-year nonpoor who fall into poverty (311,000 versus 16,000). In net terms, assuming a neutral replacement tax, Cameroon's unilateral liberalization is predicted to raise the number of poor individuals by 201,000. This poverty worsening would be experienced by all household groups except those whose head works in mining, the wood products industry, metals, energy, gas, and water, or transport. Particularly strong increases in poverty are noted among households whose head is involved in the food, textile, or chemical industry.

Considering the combined Cameroon and ROW liberalization, the poverty-increasing effects of Cameroon's own-liberalization dominate. Indeed, the differential poverty impacts of this combined scenario are nearly the same between household groups as those following unilateral Cameroonian liberalization.

Decomposing Impacts of Own-Liberalization

Given the importance of the impact of own-liberalization on poverty in Cameroon, this issue bears further investigation. In the analysis above, this result may be driven, in part, by the worsening of TOT for Cameroon as exports increase in the face of a finite elasticity of world demand. If, instead, it is assumed that Cameroon is not required to cut prices to expand its exports—in technical terms, the price elasticities of world demand for Cameroon's exports are infinite (the small country assumption)—there would be no such TOT effect. It is more realistic to assume that Cameroon would need to reduce prices to expand exports, but it is not clear by how much. Therefore, the earlier results (*Cam-1*) are compared to the case of infinitely elastic world demand (*Cam-2*) to get an idea of the magnitude of these TOT effects.

The Contribution of TOT Effects to Overall Impacts at the Macro and Sectoral Levels

In the earlier case with TOT effects, the level of Cameroon's FOB export prices decreases by an average of 2.43 percent compared to world export prices, implying a significant worsening of TOT (table 12.2). When it is assumed that Cameroon FOB export prices remain equal to world export prices (fixed TOT), producer and consumer prices fall less than before (table 12.2), respectively, by 5.92 percent (versus 8.45 percent before) and 6.05 percent (versus 8.53 percent) on average. Household total income and consumption budget also drop, by 5.77 percent (versus 8.32 percent) and 5.85 percent (versus 8.43 percent), respectively, leading to a higher welfare gain amounting to 0.19 percent (versus 0.06 percent) of the base-run consumption budget. Thus, it can be concluded that the effects of TOT deterioration significantly reduce the revealed potentiality of own free trade to improve welfare in a context of a neutral replacement tax. Moreover, the scenario with fixed TOT shows greater increases in export and import volumes—20.68 percent (versus 15.14 percent) and 24.72 percent (versus 14.76 percent), respectively—mainly through rises in exports of industrial goods and imports of processed foods.

As in the endogenous TOT case, the expanding sectors are mainly export-oriented sectors with low initial import penetration ratios—namely, the cash-crop and wood-processing sectors, as well as the forestry sector, which is the main source of inputs for the expanding wood-processing sector. Tradeable services also expand slightly because their initial tariff rates are nil. The contracting sectors are chiefly those with high import penetration ratios, high initial tariff rates, or both. It is worth noting that the crude oil sector, which is the most export oriented sector and has the highest import penetration ratio, registers no change in output by assumption because output is believed to be determined exogenously.

Factor remuneration rates fall in both fixed TOT and endogenous TOT scenarios, but the drop is less important when assuming fixed TOT. The deterioration of TOT contributes 32 percent of the fall in the remuneration of agricultural unskilled and skilled labor, 48 percent of that for agricultural capital, 63 percent for land, 28 percent for nonagricultural unskilled labor, and 29 percent for nonagricultural skilled labor and nonagricultural capital.

Contribution of TOT Deterioration to Overall Poverty Impacts of Unilateral Liberalization

Even with fixed TOT, unilateral liberalization in Cameroon worsens the initial poverty situation, although the increases in poverty are smaller (table 12.4). From this, it may be concluded that the earlier deterioration of TOT contributes 67.66 percent of the total increase in the percentage of poor, 49.51 percent of the increase in the poverty gap, 46.25 percent of the rise in poverty severity, and 41.05 percent of the increase in income inequalities as measured by the Gini index.

The role of the deterioration of TOT is thus clearly important in understanding the predicted increase in poverty after Cameroon's own-liberalization. However, it is also clear that the adverse influence of other factors remains high. The expansion of some export-oriented sectors is not enough to offset the contraction of other sectors in the determination of factor remunerations relevant to the poor. This implies that, even with constant TOT, own-liberalization may have adverse poverty impacts in a commodity-exporting economy, even if average welfare increases. The key factors in this outcome are the degree of distortion in the initial tariff structure, the relative labor intensity of the export-oriented sectors, and the choice of the replacement tax mechanism.

Evaluating the Replacement Tax Alternatives

Impacts of trade liberalization will ultimately depend on the replacement tax used to offset cuts in import tariffs. To capture the possible bias induced by the choice of the replacement tax, the effects of combined ROW and Cameroon liberalization using the previous neutral replacement tax (*Full* scenario) are compared to the effects of two other scenarios of combined full liberalization where replacement taxes are alternatively a VAT (*Full-VAT*) and a uniform consumption tax (*Full-Con*). Uniform consumption tax is proportional to consumption budget by definition, whereas the VAT implemented in Cameroon is progressive. Both the neutral tax and the consumption tax are used here only as analytical devices, because their implementation in Cameroon would not be feasible in the current institutional environment.

An Overview of the VAT in Cameroon

The VAT is the most likely candidate for the replacement tax in Cameroon, because the community rules adopted within the framework of Central African Customs and Economic Union (CACEU) dictate that member states rely on the VAT as the principal domestic indirect tax instrument. Since the 1994 fiscal and customs reform, the VAT has increasingly become the main goods and services tax in Cameroon. In 2001, VAT revenues accounted for 53 percent of total tax revenues levied on goods and services; while imports tariffs contributed 27 percent; excises and miscellaneous taxes, 19 percent; and export duties, 1 percent.

Notwithstanding its dominant status, the Cameroon VAT remains very "imperfect" compared to a "pure" VAT,[15] mainly because of the narrowness of the VAT base and the partial and delayed deductibility of VAT paid upstream on inputs. Indeed, refunds of VAT credits are statutorily delayed in Cameroon because of the "one-month latency rule," according to which companies must wait one month before finally recovering their refundable VAT. Two VAT regimes coexist: a normal regime and a simplified regime. Companies that belong to the simplified regime cannot claim any VAT credits on their input purchases. Moreover, VAT applied to products subject to the simplified regime is not refundable, even for the companies belonging to the normal regime.

The VAT base is narrow because many activities are exempted, either because their sales revenue is below the minimal threshold or, more generally, because they operate in the informal sector. In 2001, the informal sector represented 77 percent of total employment and 50.6 percent of total value added in Cameroon. The narrowness of the VAT base has led to low effective VAT rates. The official nominal VAT rate was 18.7 percent in 2001, but the average effective VAT rates were 1.64 percent for nondeductible products sold on the domestic market, 7.29 percent for nondeductible imports, and 2.38 percent for all nondeductible products.

These three VAT effective rates are somewhat theoretical, because the VAT bases used for their computation include input purchases, which are in principle exempted. The real VAT base is composed of purchases by households, government, and firms not involved in the VAT system. This base (63.47 percent of total demand) yields an average effective VAT rate of 3.74 percent for 2001. This implies that only 20 percent of purchases made by final VAT taxpayers supported the 18.7 percent VAT nominal rate.

VAT revenues and effective rates are inversely linked to the share of informal activities for a given sector or product. This share is greatest in the agricultural sector (96 percent) and services, and it is smaller in the industrial sector. Thus, it is hardly surprising that industrial products, representing 40.46 percent of purchases made by final VAT taxpayers, generate 74.93 percent of VAT revenues, and agricultural products, representing 14.42 percent of purchases made by final VAT taxpayers, contribute only 0.43 percent of total VAT revenues.

In 2001, rural households devoted 61 percent of their household expenditures to agricultural goods, versus only 29 percent for industrial goods. Consequently, rural households are much less subject to the VAT than urban households. Given that more than 80 percent of the poor are located in rural areas, the VAT system is therefore progressive, on average. Indeed, although the poor represent 40.22 percent of total population, consuming 11.36 percent of total household consumption, they contributed only 9.43 percent of VAT revenues on household consumption, with an effective VAT rate equal to 2.89 percent. In contrast, the nonpoor paid an effective VAT rate of 3.58 percent.

Comparative Macro and Sectoral Effects

On the whole, the three tax replacement scenarios shift macro variables in the same direction (table 12.2), but the magnitude of changes is generally smaller in the VAT case and greater in the case of a consumption tax. The rise in VAT rates partly offsets the fall in market prices, especially where initial real effective VAT rates are high. Consequently, consumer prices fall less following the *Full-VAT* scenario (by 1.91 percent on average) than in the cases of consumption tax and neutral tax (on average by 7.36 and 7.23 percent, respectively). In fact, all consumer prices fall in the cases of *Full-Con* and *Full* scenarios, but in the VAT case, there is an increase in consumer price in all sectors for which the real effective rate of the VAT is higher than the mean (3.74 percent) in the base run—that is, in the wood-processing, refined petroleum, and miscellaneous industries. As expected, in the scenario with the VAT, the reduction in household demand is smaller for goods with lower initial real effective VAT rates and larger for goods with high initial effective VAT rates.[16] In addition, the VAT is less biased against sectors with high household consumption shares. The replacement of tariffs with the neutral tax does not induce additional distortions (household consumption and welfare remain practically unchanged), contrary to the replacement by the VAT or by the consumption tax. Additional distortions are smaller when replacing tariffs with the VAT than with the consumption tax (the decline in household welfare represents 2.69 percent and 4.72 percent of the baseline consumption budget, respectively).

Comparative Household Income Effects

In accordance with the differential falls in factor returns, the average reduction in household incomes is smaller with the VAT: -4.41 percent compared to a 7.12 percent fall with the neutral tax and a 7.18 percent fall with the consumption tax (table 12.2). Regardless of the household group considered in table 12.3 (urban versus rural households, male-led versus female-led households, base-year poor versus nonpoor), the losses in household factor incomes are roughly 40 percent smaller with the VAT compared to the two other scenarios. In the three scenarios, the loss in nominal income remains slightly larger in urban and in base-run nonpoor households than in their respective counterparts. Taking into account changes in CPIs as reflected through changes in consumption, the household real income remains almost unchanged with the neutral replacement tax (+0.02 percent), whereas it falls with the VAT (-2.61 percent) and the consumption replacement tax (-4.69 percent).

Comparative Poverty Effects

Full liberalization with a neutral replacement tax clearly increases poverty less than with the VAT or the household consumption tax. This is due to the overall efficiency improvement following replacement of the tariffs with a nondistorting tax. When the neutral replacement tax is used, the poverty headcount index rises from 40.22 percent to 40.78 percent at the national level; it climbs to 42.14 percent with the VAT and to 43.44 percent with a consumption tax. The VAT's outcome is more favorable than the consumption tax because of the progressive nature of the VAT. Although a smaller number of base-year nonpoor people fall into poverty with the neutral replacement tax (193,000 versus 327,000 with the VAT and 540,000 with the consumption tax), the number of base-year poor people who escape from poverty with this neutral tax is on the contrary greater (106,000 versus 24,000 with the VAT and 42,000 with the consumption tax). The extrapolated increase in the net number of poor individuals is equal to 87,000 in the neutral tax case compared to 303,000 and 498,000, respectively, if the VAT and consumption tax are used.

The magnitude of the changes in the poverty gap and severity is also always smaller with the neutral tax than with the VAT, and even smaller than with the consumption tax, whether considering urban, rural, male-led, or female-led households. However, the smallest increase in inequality as measured by Gini index is noted in the case with the VAT as the replacement tax, thanks to the progressive nature of the Cameroonian VAT. The base-run poor who escape poverty in the three scenarios are mostly those belonging to households where the head is employed in wood products industry.

Concluding Remarks

The general conclusion that emerges from this study is that the Doha Round is likely to alleviate poverty mildly in Cameroon, with falls in both overall poverty and income inequality, allowing 22,000 people to escape from poverty in net terms. Of course, poverty alleviation within the entire nation does not exclude the possibility that some initially nonpoor people become poor, and this does appear to be the case here.

Further experiments on trade liberalization show that free trade in ROW strongly alleviates poverty, at least at the national level, whereas Cameroon's own liberalization worsens poverty and inequality. When ROW and own-liberalization are combined, the adverse impacts of own-liberalization proves to strongly outweigh the favorable outcomes of the ROW liberalization. This result, which arises from the different factor intensities of the import-competing and export sectors, is very worrisome because, besides the Doha scenario, the EPAs currently negotiated between ACP countries and the EU propose a sharp reduction in domestic tariffs in ACP countries. Moreover, although the main results of this study assume finite elasticities of demand for exports, the study also shows that own-liberalization can have adverse poverty impacts, even when the analysis abstracts from potential deterioration in the TOT.

The results in this chapter also underscore the importance of the choice of tax replacement instrument for the overall and the poverty impacts of trade liberalization: poverty worsens in this country case study when an imperfect VAT is used and becomes yet worse when a consumption tax is used instead of a neutral replacement tax. Essentially, the more distorted the replacement tax, the more the adverse poverty effects of own-liberalization are strengthened.

In the end, it appears from this analysis that the Doha Development Agenda could indeed contribute to further poverty alleviation in Cameroon. However, policymakers should be aware of the importance of choosing appropriate replacement taxes and the potentially adverse impacts of the elimination of domestic tariffs. They should also be aware that some households will lose out and possibly fall into poverty, even if national poverty rates fall. This underscores the need for targeted safety net programs to accompany any significant trade reforms in Cameroon.

Notes

1. Within the framework of the Enhanced HIPC Initiative, Cameroon reached the Decision Point in October 2000 and is now making efforts to reach the Completion Point.

2. For a discussion of poverty impacts of trade, see Hertel and Reimer (2004).

3. Cameroon and other CFA franc countries experienced a 50 percent devaluation in January 1994.

4. The coverage rate—that is the ratio of exports over imports—may be seen as the ability of a country to pay its imports using its export revenues.

5. The SITC is a statistical classification of commodities in world trade developed by the United Nations to facilitate international comparison of commodity trade data.

6. Other products that have been among the top five exports for at least one year during the last decade are forest products, aluminum, coffee, and bananas.

7. The EU is considered here as the 15 member countries of 2003, before its enlargement to 25 members in 2004.

8. These price changes are reported relative to the numeraire of constant world factor prices (see chapter 3). In general equilibrium, only *relative* price changes matter. The price changes used for Cameroon also, of course, reflect the composition of the country's trade flows in terms of the 57 GTAP commodities used in chapter 3.

9. Elasticity of substitution is equal to 4.3 for this product on both the export and import sides (table 12.1).

10. Given a value added rate of 73 percent and a capital-labor ratio as low as 0.26 (table 12.1).

11. Export prices of Cameroonian cash crops increase more than world prices: 1.85 versus 1.73 percent.

12. The increase in imports of wood products is impressive (310.08 percent), but it is important to remember that the initial import penetration ratio is very low (0.2 percent).

13. More detailed results are available in the World Bank Policy Research Working Paper version of this chapter (Emini, Cockburn and Decaluwé, 2005).

14. It is assumed that both skilled and unskilled labor in the crude oil sector and public services are exogenous and consequently not mobile across other sectors. The real wage rate of these sectors is also fixed.

15. VAT systems vary from "embryonic" to asymptotic "pure" types. All nonpure VAT systems are qualified as imperfect VATs. Shoup (1990) counts 576 VAT types. For more information on VAT modalities and types, see Shoup (1990) and Cnossen (1991).

16. More detailed results are available in the World Bank Policy Research Working Paper and the MPIA Working Paper versions of this chapter (Emini, Cockburn, and Decaluwé (2005a, 2005b).

References

Cloutier, Marie-Hélène, and John Cockburn. 2002. "How to Build an Integrated CGE Micro-Simulation Model: Step-by-Step Instructions with An Illustrative Exercise." Centre Interuniversitaire sur le Risque, les Politiques Economiques et l'Emploi, Université Laval, Québec, Canada.

CNIS (Cameroon National Institute of Statistics). 2002a. *Conditions de vie des populations et profil de pauvreté au Cameroun en 2001: Rapport principal de l'ECAM II.* Yaoundé.

———. 2002b. *Evolution de la pauvreté au Cameroun entre 1996 et 2001.* Yaoundé.

———. 2003. *Deuxième enquête camerounaise auprès des ménages. Présentation des bases de données de l'enquête.* Yaoundé.

———. 2004. *Cameroon Statistics Yearbook 2004.* Yaoundé.

Cnossen, Sijbren. 1991. "Design of the Value Added Tax: Lessons from Experience." In *Tax Policy in Developing Countries, a World Bank Symposium,* ed. Javad Khalilzadeh-Shirazi, and Anwar Shah, 72–85. Washington, DC: World Bank.

Cockburn, John. 2001. "Trade Liberalization and Poverty in Nepal: A Computable General Equilibrium Micro-Simulation Analysis." Working Paper 01-18. Centre de Recherche en Economie et Finance Appliquées, Université Laval, Québec, Canada.

De Monchy, G., and F. Roubaud. 1991."Cameroun : Evolution économique rétrospective et perspectives macro-économiques à l'horizon 1995." Institut de Recherche pour le Developpement, Paris.

Decaluwé, Bernard, André Martens, and Luc Savard. 2001. *La politique économique du développement et les modèles d'équilibre général calculable.* Montréal: Les Presses de l'Université de Montréal.

Dollar, D., and A. Kraay. 2000. "Growth Is Good for the Poor." Development Research Group, World Bank, Washington, DC.

Emini, C. A. 2000a. "Analyse de l'incidence d'une TVA imparfaite à l'aide d'un modèle calculable d'équilibre général. Application au cas camerounais." Cahier de recherche 00-06. Centre de Recherche en Economie et Finance Appliquées, Université Laval, Québec, Canada.

———. 2000b. "Long Run versus Short Run Effects of a Value Added Tax. A Computable General Equilibrium Assessment for Cameroon." Cahier de recherche 00-12. Centre de Recherche en Economie et Finance Appliquées, Université Laval, Québec, Canada.

Emini, C. A., J. Cockburn and B. Decaluwé. 2005a. "The Poverty Impacts of the Doha Round in Cameroon: The Role of Tax Policy."

Emini, C. A., J. Cockburn, and B. Decaluwé. 2005b. "The Poverty Impacts of the Doha Round in Cameroon: The Role of Tax Policy." Policy Research Working Paper 3746, October, World Bank, Washington, DC.

Hertel, T., and J. J. Reimer. 2004. "Predicting the Poverty Impacts of Trade Liberalization: A Survey." Policy Research Working Paper 2790. World Bank, Washington, DC.

Republic of Cameroon. 2003. "Poverty Reduction Strategy Paper." Prime Ministry, Yaoundé.

Shoup, Carl S. 1990. "Choosing among Types of VATs." In *Value Added Taxation in Developing Countries. A World Bank Symposium*, ed. Malcolm Gillis, C. S. Shoup, and G. P. Sicat, 3–16. Washington, DC: World Bank.

World Bank. 1996. "Cameroon: Country Assistance Strategy." Report 12275-CM. Washington, DC.

———. 2004. "2004 World Bank Africa Database CD-ROM." Operational Quality and Knowledge Services, World Bank Africa Region, Washington DC.

13

DOHA SCENARIOS, TRADE REFORMS, AND POVERTY IN THE PHILIPPINES: A CGE ANALYSIS

Caesar B. Cororaton,
John Cockburn, and Erwin Corong

Summary

Since the early 1980s, the Philippines has undertaken substantial trade reform. The current Doha Round of WTO negotiations is now likely to bring further reform and shocks to world import prices and export demand. The impact of all these developments on the poor is not very clear and is the subject of very intense debate.

A detailed, economy-wide computable general equilibrium (CGE) model is used to run a series of policy experiments. Poverty is found to increase slightly with the implementation of the Doha scenario. These effects are focused primarily on rural households in the wake of falling world prices and demand for Philippine agricultural exports.

The impacts of full liberalization, involving worldwide free trade and complete domestic liberalization, are found to depend strongly on the mechanism the government adopts to offset forgone tariff revenue. If an indirect tax is used, the incidence of poverty falls marginally, but the depth (poverty gap) and severity (squared poverty gap) increase substantially. If, instead, an income tax is used, all measures of poverty increase. In both cases, full liberalization favors urban households as exports, which are primarily nonagricultural, expand.

Separate simulations indicate that worldwide free trade is poverty reducing and favors rural households, whereas domestic liberalization is poverty increasing and favors urban households. Under worldwide free trade, rural households benefit from increasing world agricultural demand. The antirural bias of domestic liberalization stems from the fact that import prices fall more for agricultural goods than for industrial goods, because initial, import-weighted average tariff rates are higher for the former.

The current Doha agreement appears likely to slightly increase poverty, especially in rural areas and among the unemployed, self-employed, and rural low-educated. The Philippines is found to have an interest in pushing for more ambitious world trade liberalization, because worldwide free trade holds out promise for reducing poverty.

Introduction

Since the early 1980s, the Philippines has undertaken substantial trade reform: Tariff rates have been reduced, tariff structures simplified, and quantitative restrictions converted to tariffs. The current Doha Round of WTO negotiations is now likely to bring major changes for the Philippines, particularly its agriculture sector, as well as pressure for further liberalization of its trade policies. The impact of all these developments on the poor is the subject of very intense debate. Will the outcome of the Doha Round, together with further Philippine trade liberalization, be favorable or harmful for the poor? Will the effects differ between different types of poor? What alternative or accompanying policies may be used to ensure a more equitable distribution of the gains from freer trade? What are the channels through which these changes are most likely to affect the poor? To answer these challenging questions, a 35-sector CGE model with an emphasis on the agricultural sector is used. This is consistent with the agricultural focus of the Doha Round and the strong concerns about the potential impacts of Doha on Philippine agricultural products of special interest to the poor.

There have been numerous attempts to adapt CGE models to the analysis of income distribution and poverty issues. Many authors impose strong assumptions concerning the distribution of income among households in each category. A popular approach is to assume a lognormal distribution of income within each category, where the variance is estimated with the base-year data (De Janvry, Sadoulet, and Fargeix 1991). In the spirit of this same approach, Decaluwé and others (2000) argue that a beta distribution is preferable to other distributions because it can be skewed left or right and thus may better represent the types of intracategory income distributions commonly observed. Regardless of the assumed distribution, the CGE model is used to estimate the change in the average income for each household category, and the variance of this income is assumed to be fixed.

Instead, this chapter uses the actual distribution of income within 12 household categories, based on the 1994 Family Income and Expenditure Survey (FIES) of 24,797 Philippine households, without imposing a fixed functional form. The 12 household categories are obtained by grouping households by region (urban or rural), the education of the household head, and this individual's occupation. Changes in average household income are derived for each household category from the CGE model and then applied to all corresponding households in the FIES to compute changes in household welfare and poverty.

Background

Agricultural Stagnation

The agricultural sector employs about 35 percent of the Philippine labor force and accounts for roughly 20 percent of GDP. If linkages with agriculture-related sectors, including food processing and the farm supply industry, are added to this total, the farm- and food-related industry contributes 40 percent of GDP and employs two-thirds of the labor force (David 1997). This sector has been characterized by low rates of productivity increase and correspondingly low growth rates in the last two decades. Growth decelerated from an annual average of 6.7 percent in the 1970s to 1.1 percent in the first half of the 1980s. Although the second half of the 1980s saw some recovery, agriculture again lost steam in the 1990s, with an annual growth rate of just 2 percent.

The Green Revolution was the main driving force behind the high growth in the 1970s. However, because of an inherent policy bias against agriculture, coupled with the collapse in world commodity prices, this momentum was not sustained. David (2003) concludes that the negative impact of the government's anti-agriculture policy bias was even greater than that of declining world commodity prices. The policy bias toward import substitution and against agriculture and exports led to market distortions, which promoted rent-seeking activities and distorted economic incentives against investments in agriculture up to the 1970s. Moreover, the policy of maintaining an overvalued exchange in support of industrial policy greatly penalized and reduced the rates of return to agriculture during this period (Intal and Power 1990).

Agriculture exports were a major source of foreign exchange in the country in the 1970s. The sector as a whole was a net exporter, contributing two-thirds of total exports and representing only 20 percent of total imports, thereby providing the foreign exchange needed to support the import-dependent manufacturing sector (Intal and Power 1990). However, the 1990s saw a clear change in agricultural trade patterns as farm exports stagnated and imports increased dramatically to the point that the Philippines became a net importer of agricultural goods. David (2003) attributes this evolution to the country's fading comparative advantage and low productivity levels in agriculture.

Post–World War II Trade Policies

The balance of payments (BOP) crisis that transpired barely four years after World War II shaped the Philippine industrial and agricultural policy landscape. High import demand for the purposes of economic reconstruction, coupled with distressed local production, led to a decline in international reserves and the 1949 BOP crisis. This spurred a policy response centered on import and foreign exchange controls through the identification of essential imports, the imposition of import quotas, and the government allocation of scarce foreign exchange. Though initially intended to be a temporary measure, these policy responses soon became a prominent fixture that resulted in a development strategy geared toward industrial import substitution with lesser emphasis on the agricultural and export sectors.

Import Substitution

The enactment of the highly protective 1957 tariff code reinforced the government's import substitution policy by providing incentives to domestic producers of final consumer goods. High tariff rates were imposed on nonessential consumer goods, and low rates were applied to essential producer inputs. This created a strong bias against agriculture and exports. An analysis of effective protection rates (EPRs) by sector and commodity (Power and Sicat 1971; Tan 1979) revealed that the highest EPRs from the 1950s to the 1970s were granted to import-substituting consumer industries; in contrast, agriculture and primary (mining) products, which accounted for two-thirds of exports during the period, were characterized by the lowest EPRs. The weighted average EPR provided to the manufacturing sector was 44 percent in 1974, compared to a much lower 9 percent protection for agriculture and mining. In spite of the passage of the revised 1973 tariff code, which was primarily aimed at decreasing tariff dispersion, a large disparity in tariff levels persisted, especially by Southeast Asian standards.

Export Taxes on Agriculture

Agricultural export taxes ranging from 4 to 10 percent were introduced after the 1970 devaluation to stabilize the BOP position. Initially intended to be temporary, the agricultural export tax ended up being incorporated into the 1973 tariff and customs code as a major source of government revenue. The world commodity prices boom in 1974 prompted the imposition of an additional export tax to enhance government revenue. Not surprisingly, this worsened the bias against agriculture, resulting in additional resource reallocation from agriculture to other sectors of the economy, particularly toward the import-substituting consumer goods sector (Intal and Power 1990). Furthermore, the dispersion in tariff rates openly encouraged assembly operations that focused mainly on the production of import-dependent, low value added products. Overall, these policies not only prevented the growth of the agricultural and primary sectors, they also discouraged the development desirable backward integration (Bautista and Tecson 2003).

Overvaluation of Exchange Rate

The overvalued exchange rate arising from the highly protective trade policy regime also contributed to the bias against agriculture. This occurred despite the removal of exchange rate controls in 1960 and the de facto devaluations of 1962 and 1970. The overvaluation of the peso varied significantly, from 14 percent over the 1962–66 period, to as high as 32 percent from 1975 to 1979 (Intal and Power 1990). The overvaluation of the exchange rate resulted in negative protection rates for rice, sugar, and coconut range from 13 percent to 33 percent. This, too, significantly reduced the returns to agricultural production (Intal and Power 1990).

Government Intervention

Government interventions in the input markets further exacerbated the antiagriculture bias. The input prices of fertilizers, hand tractors, and irrigation pumps were higher than their corresponding world prices by 10, 33, and 30 percent, respectively (David 1983). Government pricing and marketing interventions in agriculture, purportedly aimed at protecting the domestic economy from instability in world commodity prices, led to the establishment of government marketing agencies that had monopoly power for imports and monopsony power for exports. In reality, they siphoned off the gains from trade by diverting proceeds from agricultural producers and creating rent-seeking activities (Bautista and Tecson 2003). In particular, heavy restrictions on trading of food grains (rice, corn, and wheat), coconut, and sugar reduced domestic prices. For instance, the government controlled the allocation between exports and domestic sales of sugar, with domestic sales forced to sell below world prices. The establishment of a de facto government-funded coconut parastatal with substantial monopsony power took advantage of the favorable international market at the expense of domestic coconut producers. Similarly, a government food grain marketing agency reduced the returns to domestic producers because the agency controlled the domestic price of food grains.

Philippine Trade Reform

This pattern of intervention in the Philippine economy was unsustainable and it is hardly surprising that reforms became necessary. The first phase of the trade reform program (TRP) started in the early 1980s with three major components: the 1981–85 tariff reduction, the import liberalization program, and the complementary realignment of the indirect taxes. During this period, maximum tariff rates were reduced from 100 percent to 50 percent and sales taxes on imports and locally produced goods were equalized. The markup applied on the value of imports (for sales tax valuation) was also reduced and eventually eliminated.

Implementation of the TRP was suspended in the mid-1980s because of a BOP crisis. In fact, some of the items that were deregulated earlier were re-regulated during the period. When the Aquino government took over in 1986, the TRP of the early 1980s was resumed, resulting in the reduction of the number of regulated items from 1,802 in 1985 to 609 in 1988. Export taxes on all products except logs were also abolished.

In 1991, the government launched TRP-II, which sought to realign tariff rates over a five-year period. The realignment involved the narrowing of the tariff rates through a reduction of tariff peaks, with the goal of clustering tariffs within the 10–30 percent range by 1995. This resulted in a near equalization of protection for agriculture and manufacturing by the start of the 1990s, reinforced by the introduction of protection for "sensitive" agricultural products.

In 1992, a program of converting quantitative restrictions (QRs) into tariff equivalents was initiated. In the first stage, QRs of 153 commodities were converted into tariffs. In a number of cases, these tariff rates exceeded 100 percent, especially during the initial years of the conversion. However, a built-in program for reducing tariff rates over a five-year period was also put into effect. QRs were removed for a further 286 commodities in the succeeding stage. At the end of 1992, only 164 commodities were subjected to QRs. However, there were some policy reversals along the way. For example, in 1993, QRs were reintroduced for 93 items, largely as a result of the Magna Carta for Small Farmers in 1991.

In 1994, the government started implementing TRP-III at the same time that the Philippines was admitted to the WTO. Tariff rates were successively reduced on capital equipment and machinery (January 1, 1994); textiles, garments, and chemical inputs (September 30, 1994); 4,142 manufacturing goods (July 22, 1995); and "nonsensitive" components of the agricultural sector (January 1, 1996). Through these programs, the number of tariff tiers was reduced, as were the maximum tariff rates. In particular, the overall program was aimed at establishing a four-tier tariff schedule: 3 percent for raw materials and capital equipment that are not available locally, 10 percent for raw materials and capital equipment that are available from local sources, 20 percent for intermediate goods, and 30 percent for finished goods. This further reduced the antiagriculture tariff bias, which by 1995 had turned into effective protection for agriculture. Indeed, EPRs in agriculture and industry went from 9 percent and 44 percent, respectively, in 1979 to 25 percent and 20 percent in 1999, and to 24 percent and 15 percent by 2000 (Bautista, Power, and Associates 1979; Manasan and Pineda 1999; Habito 2002).

Between 1994 and 2000, the overall weighted nominal tariff declined by 66.9 percent, the declines ranging from 88.9 percent in mining to 64.0 percent for non-food manufacturing, 57.6 percent for livestock, 45.6 percent for crops, to 19.9 percent for other agriculture. In 2000, the average sectoral tariff rate was highest in food manufacturing (16.6 percent) and lowest in other agriculture (0.2 percent).

Revenue from import tariffs remains one of the major sources of government funds. In 1990, the share of revenue from import duties and taxes in total revenue was 26.4 percent. It increased marginally to 27.7 percent in 1995, but then dropped sharply to 19.3 percent in 2000, largely as a result of the tariff reduction program. The reduction in tariff revenue was largely replaced by an increase in income and profit taxes from 27.3 percent in 1990 to 30.7 percent in 1995 and 38.6 percent in 2000, with the excise and sales tax share fluctuating between 23 and 28 percent.

Poverty Profile in the Philippines

Figure 13.1 presents the evolution of the poverty headcount index and the Gini coefficient from 1985 to 2000. The poverty headcount index dropped continuously from 49.2 percent in 1985 to 36.9 percent in 1997, but then rebounded to 39.5 percent in 2000 as a result of the 1998 El Nino and the Asian crisis. El Nino resulted in a 30 percent contraction in agriculture, the greatest drop in more than 30 years. However, income inequality has steadily increased over this period as the Gini coefficient climbed from 0.42 in 1985 to 0.51 in 2000.

In 1994, the base year of the household survey underlying this analysis, about 41 percent of the population of 67 million was below the poverty threshold. Generally, rural households, which represent roughly half the population, are substantially poorer than urban households. Whether in urban or rural areas, households with low-educated heads are by far the poorest. These four household categories (low-educated salaried and self-employed households in rural and urban areas)

Figure 13.1.   Income Distribution and Poverty: The Philippines (1985–2000)

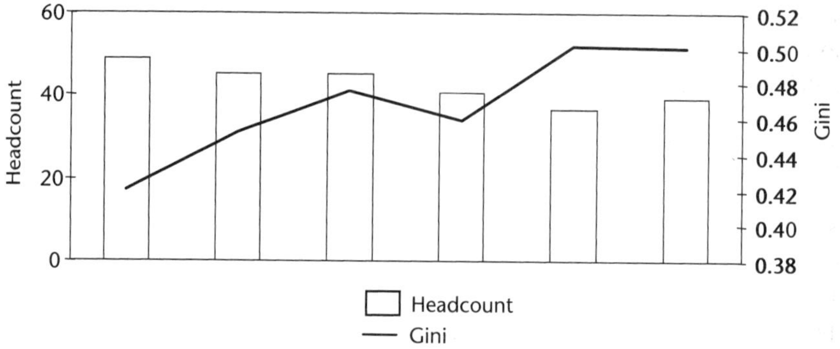

Source: FIES (1985, 1988, 1991, 1994, 1997, 2000).

combine to encompass more than 60 percent of the total population of the Philippines and the bulk of the poor.[1]

Model Specification

Basic Structure

The model of the Philippine economy used in this study has 35 production sectors, with 13 sectors for agriculture, fishing, and forestry; 19 for industry; and 3 for service sectors, including government service. In the agricultural sector, the model distinguishes capital, land, and four types of labor inputs: skilled (high education = high-school diploma) and unskilled (low education) agricultural labor, and skilled and unskilled production workers.[2] Agricultural workers are employed only in agriculture, and the small number of production workers employed in agriculture are mobile between the farm and nonfarm sectors. Nonagricultural sectors, except government service, use capital as well as skilled and unskilled production worker inputs. Capital is sector specific in this short-run closure. The demand for intermediate inputs and value added represents fixed proportions of total output, whereas the components of value added are aggregated using a Cobb-Douglas function.

A constant elasticity of transformation (CET) function transforms local products into exports. Indirect taxes are added to the local price to determine domestic prices, which, together with the import price, will determine the composite price of domestically consumed goods via a constant elasticity of substitution (CES) price aggregator. All prices adjust to clear the factor and product markets. Consumer demand is derived from Cobb-Douglas utility functions for each household in the model. A downward-sloping export demand curve is assumed to match up with the global model.

Model Closure

Nominal government consumption is equal to exogenous real government consumption multiplied by its (endogenous) price. Fixing real government spending neutralizes any possible welfare or poverty effects of variations in government spending. Total government income is held fixed. Any reduction in government income from tariff cuts is compensated endogenously by the introduction of an additional uniform sales tax. The government's budget balance (public savings) is endogenously determined, although the only variations are due to changes in the nominal price of government consumption.

Total nominal investment is equal to exogenous total real investment multiplied by its price. Total real investment is held fixed to abstract from intertemporal welfare or poverty effects. The price of total real investment is endogenous. The current account balance (foreign savings) is held fixed, and the nominal exchange rate is the model's numeraire. The foreign trade sector is effectively cleared by changes in the real exchange rate, which is the ratio of the nominal exchange rate multiplied by the world export prices, divided by the domestic price index. The propensities to save of the various household groups in the model adjust proportionately to accommodate the fixed total real investment assumption. This is done through a factor in the household saving function that adjusts endogenously.

Economic Structure

Table 13.1 presents the basic structure and parameters of the model. The sectoral export demand curve elasticities used in the model are equal to the import-import Armington elasticities of substitution estimated for the Global Trade Analysis Project (GTAP) model (Hertel and others 2004). The sectoral CES and CET elasticities in the model are in turn assumed to be the same as the import-domestic Armington elasticities in the GTAP model. Total exports in 1994 were composed of 6.1 percent agriculture exports, 63.1 percent industrial exports, and 30.8 percent service sector exports. The principal industrial exports are semiconductors and textiles and garments. The semiconductor industry is highly export

Table 13.1.   Elasticities and Key Parameters, 1994

Sector	GTAP elasti-cities	Foreign trade Exports (%)[a] Share	Exports (%)[a] Intensity	Imports (%)[a] Share	Imports (%)[a] Intensity	Production VA share (%) (VA/X)	VA share (%) (VA/VA)	Labor-capital ratio
Irrigated Palay rice	10.1	n.a.	n.a.	0.00	0.03	73.88	1.95	0.94
Nonirrigated Palay rice	n.a.	n.a.	n.a.	n.a.	n.a.	92.98	0.83	2.07
Corn	2.6	0.01	0.24	0.16	3.86	79.73	1.09	2.15
Bananas	3.7	1.25	58.96	n.a.	n.a.	62.94	0.49	3.28
Fruit	3.7	0.73	13.57	0.40	7.25	75.86	1.52	1.63
Coconut	3.7	0.36	10.74	n.a.	n.a.	86.53	1.07	3.02
Sugarcane	n.a.	n.a.	n.a.	n.a.	n.a.	71.87	0.56	1.14
Other agricultural crops	6.5	0.67	7.08	0.17	1.70	78.36	2.81	1.46
Hogs	4.0	n.a.	n.a.	0.57	6.46	56.05	1.59	1.09
Poultry products	4.0	0.00	0.05	0.04	0.43	55.57	1.83	0.96
Other livestock	3.1	0.02	0.40	0.03	0.61	74.04	1.39	0.50
Fishing	2.5	3.09	21.62	0.03	0.23	71.74	3.80	0.58
Other agriculture	6.8	n.a.	n.a.	0.12	2.93	77.00	0.99	2.30
Agriculture		**6.13**		**1.51**			**19.9**	
Mining	12.7	2.51	50.23	8.22	75.28	54.96	1.02	0.88
Meat processing	8.3	0.09	0.66	0.97	6.37	28.46	1.43	0.30
Fruit and vegetable canning	4.0	1.36	30.80	0.18	5.34	36.90	0.60	0.87
Fish processing	8.8	2.03	41.93	0.03	1.04	24.51	0.42	0.75
Coconut processing	4.0	2.93	65.57	0.43	21.01	22.33	0.36	0.90
Rice and corn milling	5.2	0.03	0.17	0.19	0.89	32.32	2.44	0.29
Sugar milling and refining	5.4	0.38	9.80	0.26	6.56	30.11	0.43	0.85
Beverages, sugar, and so on	2.8	0.20	4.03	0.20	3.89	45.73	0.83	0.53
Other food processing	4.8	1.31	6.24	4.81	19.09	29.25	2.22	0.80
Textile and garments	7.6	12.08	57.00	8.56	46.13	36.32	2.81	0.81
Wood and paper products	6.3	3.72	32.81	5.28	39.54	34.76	1.43	0.61
Fertilizer	6.6	0.49	42.25	1.24	64.00	33.47	0.14	0.48
Other chemicals	6.6	1.87	14.36	10.24	46.33	40.75	1.95	0.35
Petroleum products	4.2	1.09	5.96	3.48	16.75	20.19	1.32	0.48
Metal products	7.3	6.06	49.54	8.44	56.44	23.73	1.05	0.47
Semiconductors	8.8	14.09	76.17	12.53	72.96	24.85	1.66	0.73
Machinery (including cars)	7.4	6.56	39.53	24.76	70.94	19.79	1.15	0.80
Other manufacturing	6.8	5.85	39.38	8.66	46.66	37.61	2.03	0.79
Construction and utilities	4.7	0.45	1.06	n.a.	n.a.	52.86	8.24	0.58
Industry		**63.10**		**98.49**			**31.5**	
Wholesale trade	3.8	12.99	21.74	n.a.	n.a.	64.06	14.24	0.51
Other service	3.8	17.78	15.20	n.a.	n.a.	61.44	26.64	0.37
Government services	n.a.	n.a.	n.a.	n.a.	n.a.	69.02	7.67	n.a.
Services		**30.77**					**48.54**	
Total		**100.0**		**100.0**			**100.0**	

Source: Authors' calculations.

Note: n.a. = not applicable (due to absence of trade flow). VA = value added; X = output. Subscript *i* refers to sectoral output or value-added.

intensive, followed by coconut processing, bananas, and the textiles and garment sector. Industrial imports account for 98.5 percent of total imports. The sectors that are the most import intensive are mining (75.3 percent, mainly due to crude oil imports), semiconductors, machinery, and fertilizer.[3] Although agriculture generally has a higher value added ratio compared to industry, its contribution to domestic value added is smaller, 19.9 percent compared to industry's 31.5 percent and services' 48.5 percent. Labor intensity is uniformly higher in the agricultural sectors, with the exception of fishing and other livestock.

Definition of the Scenarios

In all Philippine simulation experiments, the calibrated tariff rates in the model, which are initially set at 1994 levels, are recalibrated to the 2001 tariff rates used in the GTAP model for the Philippines. The solution of the model using the recalibrated tariff rates serves as the base model to which all subsequent policy simulations are compared. For all but the last scenario, the GTAP world model is run separately to generate estimates of the resulting changes in world prices for Philippine exports and imports, demand for Philippine exports, and, in the case of the Doha scenarios, new Philippine tariff rates.[4] The following experiments are conducted and analyzed:

1. The core Doha scenario outlined in chapter 2, with the indirect tax for revenue replacement
2. Rest of the world (ROW) free trade, full domestic liberalization,[5] and indirect tax as replacement tax
3. ROW free trade, full domestic liberalization, and income tax as replacement tax
4. ROW free trade, no domestic liberalization, and indirect tax as replacement tax
5. Full domestic liberalization, no ROW trade reform, and indirect tax as replacement tax

Experiment 1 involves Doha-specified reductions in world and domestic tariff rates, export subsidies, and domestic support. An indirect tax is introduced to compensate lost domestic tariff revenue. Scenarios 2 and 3 are the full (ROW and domestic) liberalization scenarios, involving the elimination of all world and domestic import tariffs, under two alternative replacement tax schemes: indirect tax and income tax, respectively. Finally, scenarios 4 and 5 isolate the respective impacts of ROW and full domestic liberalization from scenario 2.

Table 13.2 summarizes the 2001 tariff rates for the Philippines, as well as the variations in world import and export prices, world export demand, and Philippine import tariff rates as estimated by the GTAP world model. As noted in

Table 13.2. GTAP-Simulated World Prices and Demand Variations

Sector	2001 GTAP tariffs	Doha World export Price	Doha World export Demand	Doha World import Price	Doha New tariff	Full liberalization World export Price	Full liberalization World export Demand	Full liberalization World import price
Agriculture								
Irrigated Palay rice	20.9	n.a.	n.a.	3.6	20.9	n.a.	n.a.	8.3
Nonirrigated Palay rice	n.a.	n.a.	n.a.	n.a.	n.a.	n.a.	n.a.	n.a.
Corn	25.7	0.2	3.8	1.9	22.6	−1.6	35.4	8.4
Bananas	n.a.	−0.2	−6.3	n.a.	n.a.	−1.9	−6.3	n.a.
Fruit	8.8	−0.2	−6.3	0.9	7.6	−1.9	−6.3	2.2
Coconut	n.a.	−0.2	−6.3	n.a.	n.a.	−1.9	−6.3	n.a.
Sugarcane	n.a.	n.a.	n.a.	n.a.	n.a.	n.a.	n.a.	n.a.
Other agricultural crops	4.7	0.3	−0.7	2.0	4.7	1.9	49.9	8.2
Hogs	3.0	n.a.	n.a.	2.3	3.0	n.a.	n.a.	6.6
Poultry products	3.0	0.5	−7.9	2.3	3.0	−0.7	39.4	6.6
Other livestock	5.9	0.1	−0.4	1.4	5.0	−1.5	10.8	4.4
Fishing	4.1	0.4	0.3	0.5	4.1	1.4	2.5	2.1
Other agriculture	0.1	n.a.	n.a.	0.6	0.1	n.a.	n.a.	1.8
Industry								
Mining	3.0	0.7	0.0	0.1	3.0	0.9	2.0	0.6
Meat processing	17.8	0.2	41.3	0.7	14.3	−0.4	172.3	0.0
Fruit and vegetable canning	6.2	0.4	3.7	0.5	6.1	0.5	16.9	0.6
Fish processing	30.2	0.1	36.4	0.0	20.6	−0.4	170.8	−2.2
Coconut processing	6.2	0.4	3.7	0.5	6.1	0.5	16.9	0.6
Rice and corn milling	49.9	0.1	−36.0	0.1	49.9	−2.1	−24.6	6.8
Sugar milling and refining	46.7	0.5	56.7	4.8	39.2	0.3	188.4	6.7
Beverages, sugar, and so on	11.1	0.3	22.7	1.0	10.4	0.5	108.8	2.6
Other food processing	5.2	0.4	2.4	1.9	5.1	1.1	12.3	3.0
Textile and garments	6.5	0.5	11.0	0.4	6.5	−0.7	44.9	0.7
Wood and paper products	4.7	0.3	−1.9	0.3	4.7	0.6	3.8	1.1
Fertilizer	4.5	0.2	3.4	0.1	4.5	−0.6	28.6	0.4
Other chemicals	4.5	0.2	3.4	0.1	4.5	−0.6	28.6	0.4
Petroleum products	2.7	0.1	0.9	0.1	2.7	−2.0	13.3	−0.2
Metal products	3.9	0.3	−2.1	0.2	3.9	1.0	−3.7	0.6
Semiconductors	0.1	0.2	−1.3	0.1	0.1	0.5	−3.4	0.4
Machinery (including cars)	3.9	0.2	−1.2	0.2	3.9	−0.3	9.0	0.5
Other manufacturing	5.1	0.4	−4.0	0.2	5.1	0.6	−2.0	0.9
Construction and utilities	0.0	0.3	−1.4	n.a.	n.a.	1.2	−3.6	n.a.
Services								
Wholesale trade	0.0	0.3	−0.9	n.a.	n.a.	1.1	−1.6	n.a.
Other service	0.0	0.3	−1.2	n.a.	n.a.	1.7	−4.5	n.a.
Government services	n.a.	n.a.	n.a.	n.a.	n.a.	n.a.	n.a.	n.a.

Source: Authors' calculations.

Note: n.a. = not applicable.

chapter 3, the export price and volume changes can be combined with a knowl-edge of the slope of the export demand schedule to compute the vertical shift in export demand that is used in the national model.

Given the agricultural focus of the Doha negotiations, it is important to recall that almost all Philippine trade is industrial in nature, although food processing represents roughly 10 percent of exports (table 13.1). With the exception of fruit, world export prices increase slightly (by less than 1 percent) under the Doha sce-nario, whereas variations are greater and more often negative in the case of full liberalization. Much more substantial impacts are noted in terms of world demand for Philippine exports, particularly under full liberalization.[6] These impacts are strongly positive for Palay rice,[7] textiles and garments, and a number of food-processing industries (meat and fish processing, sugar and beverages). However, they are moderately negative for several agricultural products (fruit, sugarcane, and, in the case of the Doha scenario, livestock) and certain manufac-turing and service sectors.

On the import side, world prices increase for almost all imports, with the strongest increases among agricultural goods and under full liberalization. The changes in Philippine tariff rates are minimal under the Doha scenario, because these reductions apply to bound tariff rates, which are much higher than the applied tariff rates presented in table 13.2. Under the full-liberalization scenario, all Philippine import tariffs are eliminated.

The net impacts of these changes on the agricultural sector, which is the source of income for most of the poor, are difficult to anticipate a priori. Although world prices and demand fall for a number of agricultural exports, reduced import com-petition (higher world import prices) and increased world prices and demand for agro-industrial exports are likely to have positive effects on domestic demand for agricultural goods. The chapter now turns to the simulation results from the CGE model to try to sort these (and other) different effects out and determine the net poverty impacts.

Doha Results

Macro and Sectoral Effects

The macro effects of the Doha simulation are reported in the first column of table 13.3. On average, export prices (0.41 percent) increase more than import prices (0.21 percent). Domestic producers increase their export volumes in response and reduce their local sales. The combination of reduced local sales and increased import and export prices raises domestic consumer and output prices. As local prices increase relative to imports prices, Philippine consumers substitute toward imports.

At a sectoral level, the Doha results suggest a reallocation of exports and production from the inward-oriented agricultural and service sectors toward the export-oriented industrial sectors. Table 13.2 presents the world import price, export price, and export demand effects of the Doha scenario according to the 35 sectors of the CGE model used in this chapter. World export prices and demand increase overall, but they decline in the agricultural sector, driven by declines in export demands for fruits and vegetables, fats and oils, and rice. In the wake of the Doha reforms, Philippine exports of these products become relatively less competitive in several key markets, including Japan, the EU-15, the Republic of Korea and Taiwan, China. For example, in the case of processed rice, the Philippines has tariff-free access into the EU already, so that when tariffs on competitors are cut, the price of Philippine rice in the EU relative to the average import price for rice rises by 28 percent. Consequently, there is little surprise that the Philippines loses export share in these markets.

Table 13.3.   Macro Effects
(percent change from base)

Variable	Doha 1	Full liberalization		ROW and domestic liberalization (DL)	
		Indirect tax 2	Income tax 3	ROW 4	DL 5
Change in overall nominal tariff rate	0.00	−100.00	−100.00	0.00	−100.00
Domestic prices					
Imports	0.21	−2.41	−3.23	0.56	−2.94
Exports	0.41	0.91	0.90	1.55	−0.63
Domestically sold output[a]	0.37	−0.01	−0.83	1.63	−1.61
Household CPI[a]	0.39	−0.33	−1.16	1.71	−2.00
Domestic output	0.41	−0.46	−0.42	1.79	−2.21
Real exchange rate change[b]	−0.01	1.68	1.68	−0.03	1.70
Domestic volumes					
Imports	0.15	4.37	4.35	0.74	3.61
Exports	0.13	3.88	4.05	0.24	3.63
Domestically sold output	−0.01	−0.96	−0.93	0.00	−0.96
Total domestic consumption	0.03	0.16	0.17	0.15	0.01
Domestic output	0.02	0.04	0.10	0.05	−0.02

Source: Authors' calculations.

a. Including indirect taxes.

b. World export price/domestic output price.

In response to these shocks, Philippine agricultural producers reorient their sales toward the domestic market, and industrial producers turn increasingly to the export market. This development is reinforced by the greater increase in the world prices of agricultural imports relative to industrial imports (table 13.4), which lead domestic consumers to substitute away from agricultural imports toward domestically produced agricultural products. This also explains why consumer prices rise relatively in the agricultural sector. For output prices, however, the increase is greater in the industrial sector than in the agricultural or service sectors, and when one also accounts for the larger input cost savings for industrial sectors, industrial sector value added prices are seen to increase more (0.69 percent) than for the agricultural (0.42) or service sectors (0.38) (table 13.4). Producers respond by reallocating agricultural and service output toward the industrial sector. Within the industrial sector, the food-processing and textile and garments sectors emerge as the main "winners" from the Doha accord, given strong growth in world demand for these products.

Incomes and Poverty

All factor prices increase relative to the numeraire (the nominal exchange rate) as a result of rising world export demand under the Doha scenario (table 13.5). However, these increases are somewhat smaller for factors used intensively in the agriculture and service sectors, given the general reallocation of production toward the industrial sector and rising relative output prices for industrial goods.

These variations in factor remunerations affect the income of different household groups according to their respective income shares (table 13.6). There is a stronger distinction between households headed by salaried workers (including civil servants) and those headed by the self-employed and unemployed than there is between urban and rural households. Whereas households with salaried heads derive most of their income from wages, households with self-employed and unemployed heads are more dependent on capital and foreign income. Nonetheless, rural households do derive a somewhat larger share of income from agricultural factors (labor and agricultural capital) compared to urban households. This is particularly true for rural households with low-educated heads, who represent nearly three-quarters of the rural population.

Household income changes for the various scenarios are summarized in table 13.7. Rising factor remunerations under the Doha scenario translate into increases in income for all household groups. Rural and urban households have approximately equal gains on average, although the sources—agriculture versus nonagricultural income—of these gains are quite different. Urban and rural households headed by salaried workers, including civil servants, gain most, given

Table 13.4. Effects on Prices and Volumes by Major Sector (percent change from base year)

Scenario / Sector	Prices						Volumes						
	Import	Export	Dom.	Cons.	Output	VA	Import	Export	Dom.	Cons.	Output	VA	Labor
1. Doha													
Agriculture	1.04	−0.34	0.45	0.46	0.42	0.42	−1.60	−2.12	0.16	0.12	−0.03	−0.02	−0.05
Industry	0.20	0.62	0.34	0.29	0.44	0.69	0.18	0.68	−0.08	0.02	0.12	0.11	0.33
Service	n.c.	0.14	0.36	0.36	0.35	0.38	n.c.	−0.48	−0.08	−0.08	−0.08	−0.08	−0.17
Total	0.21	0.41	0.37	0.34	0.41	n.c.	0.15	0.13	−0.01	0.03	0.02	n.c.	n.c.
2. Full liberalization, ROW, and domestic liberalization with replacement indirect tax													
Agriculture	−0.43	−0.80	−0.07	−0.09	−0.91	−1.13	−1.21	−1.72	−0.02	−0.04	−0.17	−0.12	−0.21
Industry	−2.44	1.38	−0.40	−1.20	−0.55	−0.06	4.45	6.02	−1.77	0.48	0.24	0.16	0.65
Service	n.c.	0.33	0.53	0.53	−0.20	−0.21	n.c.	0.85	−1.77	−0.14	−0.14	−0.14	−0.29
Total	−2.41	0.91	−0.01	−0.53	−0.46	n.c.	4.37	3.88	−0.96	0.16	0.04	n.c.	n.c.
3. Full liberalization, ROW, and domestic liberalization with replacement income tax													
Agriculture	−1.27	−0.71	−0.72	−0.74	−0.72	−0.54	−0.85	−1.97	−0.02	−0.04	−0.19	−0.14	−0.26
Industry	−3.26	1.33	−1.36	−2.10	−0.64	1.06	4.43	6.37	−1.65	0.55	0.43	0.29	1.02
Service	n.c.	0.38	−0.21	−0.21	−0.10	0.43	n.c.	0.65	−1.65	−0.24	−0.24	−0.24	−0.50
Total	−3.23	0.9	−0.83	−1.35	−0.42	n.c.	4.35	4.05	−0.93	0.17	0.1	n.c.	n.c.
4. ROW liberalization													
Agriculture	5.11	0.28	2.33	2.39	2.35	2.67	−5.56	−5.32	0.48	0.34	0.00	0.01	0.02
Industry	0.50	1.98	1.40	1.10	1.71	2.51	0.83	1.71	−0.26	0.13	0.25	0.21	0.65
Service	n.c.	0.95	1.61	1.61	1.65	1.84	n.c.	−1.49	−0.26	−0.19	−0.19	−0.19	−0.39
Total	0.56	1.55	1.63	1.43	1.79	n.c.	0.74	0.24	0.00	0.15	0.05	n.c.	n.c.
5. Domestic liberalization													
Agriculture	−5.23	−1.09	−2.34	−2.42	−3.17	−3.68	4.62	3.90	−0.53	−0.42	−0.16	−0.12	−0.22
Industry	−2.91	−0.59	−1.77	−2.26	−2.23	−2.56	3.60	4.25	−1.50	0.36	−0.03	−0.07	−0.04
Service	n.c.	−0.62	−1.05	−1.05	−1.82	−2.01	n.c.	2.38	−1.50	0.06	0.06	0.06	0.13
Total	−2.94	−0.63	−1.61	−1.93	−2.21	n.c.	3.61	3.63	−0.96	0.01	−0.02	n.c.	n.c.

Source: Authors' simulations.

Note: n.c. = not computed; Dom. = domestic sales of local production; Cons. = consumption (domestic); VA = value added.

Table 13.5. Effects on Factor Remunerations (percent change from base year)

Scenarios	Wage rates				Land rent	Return to capital			
	Agriculture[a]		Nonagriculture			Agriculture	Industry	Service	All
	Skilled	Unskilled	Skilled	Unskilled					
1. Doha	0.31	0.31	0.56	0.61	0.30	0.53	0.74	0.30	0.49
2. Full liberalization (indirect tax)	–1.49	–1.49	–0.01	0.30	–2.08	–0.87	–0.18	–0.34	–0.37
3. Full liberalization (income. tax)	–0.91	–0.91	0.87	1.21	–1.48	–0.33	1.06	0.20	0.42
4. ROW liberalization	2.45	2.45	2.25	2.34	2.46	2.98	2.66	1.65	2.20
5. Domestic liberalization	–3.80	–3.80	–2.23	–2.02	–4.41	–3.74	–2.83	–1.95	–2.53

Source: Authors' simulations.

a. The returns to skilled and unskilled labor in agriculture move in lockstep as a result of the assumption of equal factor intensities across agricultural subsectors (owing to a lack of information).

Table 13.6. Sources of Household Income at the Base (percent)

Sources	Urban						Rural					
	Salaried		Civil servants	Self-employed		Family business	Salaried		Civil servants	Self-employed		Family business
	Low-ed	High-ed		Low-ed	High-ed		Low-ed	High-ed		Low-ed	High-ed	
Skilled agricultural labor	0.0	0.0	0.0	0.0	0.0	0.0	0.0	29.5	6.4	0.0	7.4	6.0
Unskilled agricultural labor	0.0	0.0	0.0	0.0	0.0	0.0	61.9	0.0	0.8	18.9	0.0	7.5
Skilled production labor	0.0	66.3	62.2	0.0	26.1	8.6	0.0	51.1	59.8	0.0	20.2	4.9
Unskilled production labor	66.5	0.0	3.7	22.1	0.0	2.8	19.3	0.0	5.2	10.2	0.0	4.4
Capital in agriculture	1.2	0.5	0.9	10.8	2.0	5.3	2.7	1.4	3.9	30.1	17.5	29.8
Capital in industry	0.8	0.8	0.4	2.9	1.9	12.0	0.6	0.4	0.4	2.1	1.8	5.6
Capital in service	17.7	15.2	18.5	38.2	34.9	54.0	7.0	8.8	9.5	16.7	22.3	22.9
Land rent	0.6	0.4	1.3	1.8	1.4	1.1	0.9	0.9	3.0	3.1	3.1	2.9
Dividends	4.0	10.1	4.1	3.8	13.9	8.7	0.6	2.2	3.1	2.1	7.3	6.1
Government transfers	5.1	3.2	3.7	9.9	7.0	3.3	3.3	3.2	3.6	7.8	8.3	3.9
Foreign income	4.1	3.5	5.3	10.4	12.8	4.2	3.6	2.5	4.3	9.2	12.1	5.8
Total	100.0	100.0	100.0	100.0	100.0	100.0	100.0	100.0	100.0	100.0	100.0	100.0

Source: Authors' computations.

Note: low-ed = zero education to third year of high school; high-ed = high school graduate and up.

Table 13.7.   Changes in Household Income and Sources (percent change from base)

Household type	Doha	Full liberalization (indirect tax)	Full liberalization (income tax)		ROW liberali-zation	Domestic liberali-zation
	Total	Total	Total	After tax	Total	Total
Urban	0.37	−0.11	0.48	−1.35	1.64	−1.73
Low-ed salaried	0.47	0.12	0.84	−0.94	1.92	−1.78
High-ed salaried	0.43	−0.07	0.61	−1.29	1.79	−1.83
Civil servants	0.44	−0.09	0.61	−1.25	1.86	−1.93
Low-ed self-employed or unemployed	0.33	−0.19	0.33	−1.44	1.60	−1.75
High-ed self-employed or unemployed	0.28	−0.17	0.30	−1.50	1.31	−1.45
Family business	0.35	−0.24	0.35	−1.46	1.66	−1.86
Rural	0.37	−0.60	−0.04	−1.79	2.01	−2.55
Low-ed salaried	0.35	−0.93	−0.33	−2.04	2.21	−3.04
High-ed salaried	0.42	−0.50	0.19	−1.58	2.09	−2.54
Civil servants	0.45	−0.22	0.49	−1.32	2.00	−2.18
Low-ed self-employed or unemployed	0.36	−0.61	−0.11	−1.84	2.01	−2.55
High-ed self-employed or unemployed	0.32	−0.39	0.09	−1.67	1.65	−2.00
Family business	0.38	−0.56	−0.02	−1.82	2.04	−2.54
Total	0.37	−0.28	0.31	−1.50	1.77	−2.00

Source: Authors' computations.

Note: low-ed = zero education to third year of high school; high-ed = high school graduate and up.

the high share of (nonagricultural) production wages in their income. The sole exceptions are households headed by low-educated, rural salaried workers, the second poorest household category, who rely heavily on unskilled agricultural wages. The incomes of urban and rural households headed by the self-employed or unemployed also have smaller nominal income gains, given the smaller share of production wages and high shares of agricultural and service capital remuneration in their income.

In the Foster, Greer, and Thorbecke (FGT) calculations, poverty effects come from two sources: the change in household income and the change in consumer prices, which affects the nominal value of the poverty line. The results of the calculations for the three poverty indexes—headcount, gap, and severity—are presented in table 13.8, along with data on initial values. The latter show that poverty

Table 13.8. Poverty Indexes: Initial Value and Percent Change from Base under Alternative Scenarios

Household type	Share of pop- ulation	Base 1994	Doha	Full liberalization		ROW liberali- zation	Domestic liberali- zation
				Indirect tax	Income tax		
			Change (%)	Change (%)	Change (%)	Change (%)	Change (%)
	1	2	3	4	5	6	7
Headcount index							
Urban	49.7	28.0	0.02	−0.46	0.26	0.10	−0.49
Low-ed salaried	9.6	41.7	0.00	−0.85	−0.33	0.00	−0.47
High-ed salaried	9.4	15.5	−0.22	−0.48	0.30	−0.43	−0.22
Civil servants	4.7	10.2	0.00	0.00	0.00	0.00	0.00
Low-ed self-employed or unemployed	14.0	42.3	0.10	−0.27	0.50	0.15	−0.52
High-ed self-employed or unemployed	9.2	16.9	0.00	−0.43	0.76	0.76	−0.97
Family business	2.8	18.2	0.00	0.00	0.80	0.00	0.00
Rural	50.3	53.2	0.05	0.20	0.65	−0.29	0.58
Low-ed salaried	9.7	58.7	0.00	0.30	0.83	−0.68	1.32
High-ed salaried	2.8	31.3	0.00	1.02	1.55	−0.98	1.55
Civil servants	2.4	22.4	0.00	−0.81	0.00	−1.36	0.00
Low-ed self-employed or unemployed	26.8	61.0	0.04	0.20	0.61	−0.17	0.40
High-ed self-employed or unemployed	5.0	37.5	0.32	0.00	0.73	0.32	0.00
Family business	3.6	39.9	0.00	0.00	0.00	−0.19	0.00
Total	100.0	40.7	0.04	−0.02	0.52	−0.16	0.21
Poverty gap							
Urban	49.7	8.9	0.02	−0.55	0.26	0.07	−0.60
Low-ed salaried	9.6	12.9	−0.15	−1.10	−0.62	−0.32	−0.74
High-ed salaried	9.4	3.7	−0.16	−0.67	0.62	−0.38	−0.27
Civil servants	4.7	2.5	−0.16	−0.56	0.52	−0.60	0.08
Low-ed self-employed or unemployed	14.0	14.9	0.10	−0.32	0.47	0.24	−0.57
High-ed self-employed or unemployed	9.2	4.8	0.23	−0.31	1.02	0.87	−1.16
Family business	2.8	6.0	0.05	0.07	0.93	−0.08	0.15
Rural	50.3	18.4	0.09	0.47	1.17	−0.48	0.91
Low-ed salaried	9.7	19.7	0.12	1.01	1.56	−0.78	1.75
High-ed salaried	2.8	9.7	−0.05	0.29	0.86	−0.79	1.10
Civil servants	2.4	6.8	−0.15	−0.24	0.40	−0.71	0.50
Low-ed self-employed or unemployed	26.8	21.9	0.08	0.36	1.07	−0.40	0.72
High-ed self-employed or unemployed	5.0	12.0	0.15	0.05	1.03	0.12	−0.09
Family business	3.6	12.0	0.05	0.45	1.45	−0.70	1.12
Total	100.0	13.7	0.07	0.14	0.88	−0.30	0.4

Table 13.8. *(Continued)*

Household type	Share of pop-ulation	Base 1994	Doha	Full liberalization		ROW liberali-zation	Domestic liberali-zation
				Indirect tax	Income tax		
			Change (%)	Change (%)	Change (%)	Change (%)	Change (%)
	1	2	3	4	5	6	7
Poverty severity							
Urban	49.7	3.9	0.00	−0.66	0.28	0.08	−0.74
Low-ed salaried	9.6	5.6	−0.18	−1.28	−0.71	−0.37	−0.87
High-ed salaried	9.4	1.3	−0.15	−0.74	0.67	−0.45	−0.30
Civil servants	4.7	0.9	−0.22	−0.65	0.54	−0.65	0.11
Low-ed self-employed or unemployed	14.0	6.9	0.13	−0.41	0.58	0.29	−0.71
High-ed self-employed or unemployed	9.2	2.1	0.24	−0.34	1.06	0.92	−1.26
Family business	2.8	2.8	0.04	0.07	1.04	−0.11	0.18
Rural	50.3	8.4	0.11	0.58	1.47	−0.61	1.14
Low-ed salaried	9.7	8.8	0.15	1.27	1.96	−0.97	2.19
High-ed salaried	2.8	4.3	−0.05	0.35	0.99	−0.92	1.27
Civil servants	2.4	2.9	−0.17	−0.28	0.49	−0.84	0.59
Low-ed self-employed or unemployed	26.8	10.3	0.11	0.46	1.37	−0.51	0.94
High-ed self-employed or unemployed	5.0	5.0	0.20	0.08	1.36	0.16	−0.12
Family business	3.6	5.2	0.06	0.50	1.64	−0.79	1.27
Total	100.0	6.2	0.08	0.19	1.10	−0.39	0.55

Source: 1994 FIES and authors' simulations.

Note: low-ed = zero education to third year of high school; high-ed = high school graduate and up.

in both rural and urban areas is highest for the low-educated households, which represent more than 60 percent of the total population.

Overall, poverty increases slightly under the Doha scenario, regardless of the indicator used. This deterioration is due to the fact that consumption prices rise more on average than household nominal incomes, primarily because of the small deterioration in terms of trade.[8] In general, rural households are somewhat more affected than urban households, because their nominal incomes increase by a lesser amount and their consumer price indexes (not shown) increase slightly more. There is a strong contrast between households headed by the self-employed or unemployed and rural households, for whom poverty increases, and those headed by salaried workers (including civil servants but excluding rural low-educated workers), for whom poverty declines. This is due to strong increases in production worker wages. The sole exceptions are households headed by low-educated rural wage workers, for whom poverty increases as a result of their reliance on unskilled agricultural wages. Indeed, the greater increase in rural poverty can be primarily traced to the contrasting impacts on low-educated workers in rural and urban areas (table 13.6).

In summary, these scenarios suggest that the Doha scenario will increase poverty slightly for all household categories, because consumer prices rise more than household incomes. Poverty increases most among rural households and the urban self-employed or unemployed. These results can be traced back to the finding from the GTAP world model that the Doha accord is likely to increase world prices and demand for Philippine industrial exports while reducing world prices and demand for Philippine agricultural exports. As a result, the inward-oriented agricultural and service sectors contract while the export-oriented industrial sector expands. Rural households suffer from the resulting fall in relative returns to agricultural factors, and the urban self-employed or unemployed suffer from declining returns to service sector capital.

Full-Liberalization Simulations

These simulations involve the complete elimination of import tariffs in the Philippines and ROW. According to the GTAP world model, this would lead to increased world import prices and export demand, along with reduced world export prices (table 13.2). The analysis now turns to the macro, sectoral, household, and poverty effects.

Macro and Sectoral Effects

The macro impacts of the full-liberalization scenarios are substantially larger than those of the Doha scenario, regardless of the choice of replacement tax (table 13.3). The elimination of domestic tariffs reduces domestic import prices by 2.41 percent to 3.23 percent despite increasing world import prices. At the same time, increased world demand for Philippine exports offsets falling world export prices such that domestic export prices rise by nearly 1 percent. In response, local producers reorient their production from the domestic market toward the export market at the same time as local consumers substitute toward cheaper imports. As local demand falls faster than local supply, local producer and consumer prices fall. The drop in local prices results in a depreciation in the real exchange rate of 1.68 percent, which reinforces the rise in exports and imports. When the two replacement taxes are compared, import and consumer prices fall more when lost tariff revenue is replaced by the introduction of a uniform income tax, but volume responses are roughly the same.

To compare sectoral results with those of the Doha simulations, table 13.4 breaks down the price and volume effects by major sector for all scenarios. Full liberalization leads to a smaller contraction in agricultural exports, but a much larger increase in industrial exports due to greatly increased world demand for Philippine industrial exports. This is the main force driving the larger reallocation of domestic output, value added, and labor from the agricultural and service sectors toward the industrial sector. Output and, more starkly, value added prices also fall more in the agricultural sector as a result of declining export prices. At the same time, full liberalization leads to substantial reductions in import prices, particularly for industrial imports. This leads to an increase in industrial imports and a strong reduction in consumer prices for industrial goods. In a more disaggregate analysis, industrial output expansion is traced primarily to the textile and garments sector and several food-processing sectors (fish processing, coconut processing, and fruit and vegetable canning).

When a compensatory income tax is substituted for the consumption tax, import, domestic sales, and consumer prices all fall more, given the absence of a price-increasing indirect tax. However, because producers no longer need to absorb part of the indirect tax, output and value added prices fall less and indeed increase in the case of industrial and service value added prices. Domestic production is consequently reoriented more markedly from the service sector in favor of the industrial sector.

Incomes and Poverty

In the full-liberalization scenario with a replacement indirect tax, all but unskilled wages drop, with the greatest reductions among agricultural factors (table 13.5). This result can be traced primarily to the fall in domestic prices resulting from the removal of import tariffs. Agricultural factors lose most as output is reoriented from the agricultural and service sectors toward the export-expanding industrial sector. Nominal factor remunerations fall less, and indeed increase in some cases, with the introduction of a compensatory income tax, although the pro-industrial nature of the results remains intact. This can be explained by smaller domestic price reductions in the absence of a new indirect tax.

Under full liberalization with a compensatory indirect tax, all households suffer from declining nominal income with the exception of urban households headed by low-educated salaried workers (table 13.7). The drop in income is more than five times greater for rural households than for urban households, because they rely on agricultural wages, agricultural capital, or both, for which the rates of remuneration decline dramatically. Among rural households, it is precisely the poorest and most populous household categories—those with low-educated heads—who suffer most. Nominal income losses are even stronger when a compensatory income tax is used, despite the fact that nominal factor remuneration rates decline less and, in several cases, increase. This is because income tax is paid solely by households, whereas the indirect tax is shared among all domestic consumers. Contrast the changes in total and after-tax incomes in these cases. Although the difference between urban and rural households is smaller, the pattern of impacts among urban and rural households remains the same.

The poverty effects with full (ROW and domestic) trade liberalization and a compensatory indirect tax (scenario 2) are complex (table 13.8). Although the headcount index declines marginally by -0.02 percent, both the poverty gap and the severity indexes increase. The urban-rural contrast is dramatic, with urban poverty declining and rural poverty increasing in roughly the same proportions as a result of the adverse agricultural impacts of full liberalization. Indeed, poverty declines for most urban household groups, which are less tied to declining agricultural incomes, bur it increases for most rural household groups. When a compensatory income tax is introduced instead, poverty increases for both urban and rural households, although more so among rural households.

In conclusion, full liberalization generally increases poverty more than the Doha agreement. However, poverty actually falls among urban households. This is primarily due to the adverse rural impacts as Philippine agricultural producers are confronted with lower-priced imports, in the wake of full liberalization. The introduction of an income tax instead of an indirect tax to compensate for lost tariff revenue results in greater poverty increases, because households bear the full weight of this tax.

Disaggregating the Full Liberalization Scenario

Simulations 4 and 5 break down the effects of eliminating all tariffs in the rest of the world (worldwide free trade) and in the Philippines (domestic liberalization) from simulation 2.

Macro and Sectoral Effects

There are dramatically opposing price effects in these two scenarios (table 13.3). Although prices uniformly increase under worldwide free trade, primarily as a result of increased export demand and prices, they fall under the domestic liberalization scenario as a result of falling import prices. However, both simulations result in increased trade, due to increased export demand under worldwide free trade and increased import competition and real exchange rate devaluation under domestic liberalization. Whereas ROW free trade boosts trade through increased world export prices and demand, domestic liberalization does so through reduced domestic import prices. These contrasting price effects generally offset each other when ROW and domestic liberalization are combined in simulation 2, whereas the export, import, and consumption volume effects reinforce each other.

Contrasting results are also found in the sector analysis (table 13.4). ROW liberalization leads to a reallocation of production from services to industry, with agricultural output practically unchanged, whereas domestic liberalization pushes production from agriculture—and, to a lesser extent, industry—toward services. These contrasting effects can be linked to the strong increase in industrial export prices under ROW liberalization and increased competition from cheaper agricultural and industrial imports under domestic trade liberalization. Rising agricultural import prices lead to a greater increase in agricultural prices under ROW liberalization. In contrast, greater reductions in agricultural import and export prices bring down agricultural prices more than industrial and service prices with domestic liberalization.

Incomes and Poverty

The most dramatic contrast is observed in comparing the nominal factor remuneration effects of ROW and domestic liberalization (table 13.5). ROW liberalization leads to strong increases in nominal factor remunerations, particularly for agricultural factors, as a result of increased import prices and export demand. In contrast, falling output and value added prices, particularly in the agricultural sector, under domestic liberalization lead to strong reductions in nominal factor remunerations for agricultural factors in particular.

ROW trade liberalization has strong positive effects on the nominal income of all household categories, particularly in rural areas, because agricultural factors are the biggest gainers (table 13.7). In contrast, domestic liberalization reduces nominal income for all household categories, especially rural households. Once again, these results can be traced to the fall in factor remunerations, particularly among agricultural factors.

An attempt to disentangle the impacts of ROW liberalization under scenario 4 and full domestic liberalization under 5 makes it clear that the former is poverty reducing and domestic liberalization is poverty increasing. This occurs because the increases in nominal income (table 13.7) outstrip the increase in the household consumer price index (CPI) (table 13.3) under ROW liberalization, but nominal income and the household CPI fall equally with domestic liberalization. ROW and domestic liberalization also have contrasting urban-rural effects. The former reduces rural poverty and increases urban poverty, but the contrary is true of the domestic liberalization scenario. These results can be traced to the antiagricultural impacts of domestic liberalization and the pro-agricultural effects of trade reforms in ROW.

Conclusion

This analysis of the poverty impacts of trade reform under the Doha Development Agenda, as well as more comprehensive trade reforms, reveals mixed effects. Poverty increases slightly with the implementation of the expected Doha agreement, especially among rural households and the agricultural self-employed or unemployed. These household categories include the poorest and most populous households in the Philippines. These results can be traced to the Doha-generated reduction in world prices and demand for Philippine agricultural exports and the resulting increase in industrial output and, consequently, production worker wage rates.

Full liberalization (involving ROW and domestic liberalization) with a compensatory indirect tax (to offset lost tariff revenue) reduces the incidence of poverty marginally but substantially increases the poverty gap and poverty severity. Poverty increases in rural areas and falls in urban areas, because full liberalization favors nonagricultural sectors over agricultural sectors. When an income tax is used instead of an indirect tax, poverty increases more in both rural and urban areas, although the increase is larger in rural areas.

To understand the full-liberalization results, separate simulations are run for ROW trade and domestic liberalization, respectively. This shows that ROW reforms favor rural households and are poverty reducing, whereas domestic liberalization favors urban households and is poverty increasing. Under ROW trade reform, income gains outstrip consumer price increases, particularly for rural households, who derive most of their income from agricultural factors. Agricultural factor remuneration increases as consumers turn away from increasingly expensive agricultural imports and bid up the price of locally produced agricultural goods. In contrast, domestic liberalization leads to increased poverty as household income falls by more than consumer prices. Here, the antirural bias stems from the fact that import prices fall more for agricultural goods than for industrial goods.

In conclusion, the current Doha agreement appears likely to slightly increase poverty in the Philippines, especially in rural areas and among the unemployed, self-employed, and rural low-educated. Based on these findings, it appears that the Philippines has an interest in pushing for more ambitious trade liberalization in the rest of the world, because this holds out the promise of reducing poverty.[9] On the contrary, domestic liberalization is found to potentially increase poverty because of its adverse impact on the rural sector. This suggests that combining domestic reforms with reforms in ROW is an attractive proposition. Whereas ROW liberalization favors rural households and actually increases urban poverty, the opposite is true of domestic liberalization. This suggests that some regional compensatory policies might also be considered.

Notes

1. Additional background information and data on trade and poverty in the Philippines is available in the World Bank Policy Research Working Paper version of this chapter (Cororaton, Cockburn, and Corong, 2005).

2. This work retains the sectoral labor disaggregation in the Labor Force Survey, where some production workers are also employed in agriculture. One restrictive assumption imposed was that only those production workers employed in agriculture can move to the other sectors, given a change in the relative factor price.

3. The Philippines does not produce all items in the semiconductor sector, but instead imports these items. For example, it does not have the facilities to produce wafers (motherboards) and monitors, which are major parts of computers. Domestic production focuses on hard disks, disk drives, processors, and some chips. Thus, although there are substantial domestic production and exports in the semiconductor sector, there are also substantial imports.

4. Tariff rate changes are derived from GTAP-estimated variations in the power of tariffs under Doha scenarios. If x is the tariff rate, the power of tariff is $p\_tm = (1 + x/100)$. The GTAP generates results for p_tm, which in turn is used to compute the new tariff rate in the Philippine model.

5. All domestic tariffs are set to zero.

6. These price changes are reported relative to the numeraire of average world factor prices (see chapter 3). In general equilibrium, only *relative* price changes matter, the "average" price level effects being absorbed by the exchange rate. The price changes used for Cameroon also, of course, reflect the composition of Cameroon's trade flows in terms of the 57 GTAP commodities used in chapter 3. The Philippines experiences falling agricultural export prices despite the increases in world prices because it loses preferences in both East Asia and the EU.

7. Because Palay rice exports were practically nil in the base year, these large percentage increases have no actual impact on the results.

8. No major differences in consumption patterns are noted among household groups because all groups devote roughly 10 percent of their consumption to agricultural goods, 50–60 percent to industrial goods, and 30–40 percent to services. Thus, the differential consumption price effects for each household group are not explored.

9. It might also indicate the Philippines' interest in extending serious liberalization to the movement of service providers (people), which is shown to be poverty reducing in Bangladesh in chapter 15 of this volume. The Philippines is a major supplier of migrant labor.

References

Bautista, R., and G. Tecson. 2003. "International Dimensions." In *The Philippine Economy: Development, Policies and Challenges*, ed. A. Balisacan and H. Hill, 136–171. Quezon City: Ateneo de Manila Press.

Bautista, R., J. Power, and Associates. 1979. "Industrial Promotion Policies in the Philippines." Philippine Institute for Development Studies, Makati City, Philippines.

Cororaton, C., J. Cockburn and E. Corong. 2005. "Doha Scenarios, Trade Reforms, and Poverty in the Philippines." Policy Research Working Paper 3738, World Bank, Washington, DC.

David, C. 1983. "Economic Policies and Agricultural Incentives." *Philippine Economic Journal* 11: 154–82.

———. 1997. "Agricultural Policy and the WTO Agreement: The Philippine Case." Discussion Paper 97-13. Philippine Institute for Development Studies, Makati City, Philippines.

———. 2003. "Agriculture." In *The Philippine Economy: Development, Policies and Challenges*, ed. A. Balisacan and H. Hill: 175–218. Quezon City: Ateneo de Manila Press.

De Janvry, A., E. Sadoulet, and A. Fargeix. 1991 "Politically Feasible and Equitable Adjustment: Some Alternatives for Ecuador." *World Development* 19 (11): 1577–94.

Decaluwé, B., A. Patry, L. Savard, and E. Thorbecke. 2000. "Poverty Analysis within a General Equilibrium Framework." Working Paper 9909. Department of Economics, Laval University, Québec, Canada.

Habito, C. 2002. "Impact of International Market Forces, Trade Policies, and Sectoral Liberalization Policies on the Philippines Hogs and Poultry Sector." In *Livestock Industrialization, Trade and Social-Health-Environment Impacts in Developing Countries*, ed. Costales, C. and C. Delgado: Annex IV. Food and Agricultural Organization of the United Nations, Rome, Italy.

Hertel, T., D. Hummels, M. Ivanic, and R. Keeney. 2004. "How Confident Can We Be in CGE-Based Assessments of Free Trade Agreements?" GTAP Working Paper 26. Center for Global Trade Analysis, Purdue University, W. Lafayette, IN.

Intal, P., and J. Power. 1990. "Trade, Exchange Rate, and Agricultural Pricing Policy in the Philippines, Comparative Studies on Political Economy of Agricultural Pricing Policy." World Bank, Washington DC.

Manasan, R., and V. S. Pineda. 1999. "Assessment of Philippine Tariff Reform: 1998 Update." Accelerating Growth, Investment and Liberalization with Equity (AGILE) Program Study Report, Makati City, Philippines.

Power, J. H., and G. P. Sicat. 1971. *The Philippines Industrialization and Trade Policies*. London: Oxford University Press.

Tan, E. 1979. "The Structure of Protection and Resource Flows in the Philippines." In *Industrial Promotion Policies in the Philippines*, ed. R. Bautista, J. Power, and Associates, 126–171. Makati City: Philippine Institute for Development Studies.

PART VI

CROSS-COUNTRY ANALYSIS

14

THE EFFECTS
OF A PROSPECTIVE
MULTILATERAL TRADE
REFORM ON POVERTY
IN DEVELOPING
COUNTRIES

Maros Ivanic

Summary

The goal of this chapter is to evaluate the impact of three prospective trade reforms on poverty in 15 developing regions and identify the most significant components of these reforms from a poverty perspective. To that end, the chapter uses the latest Global Trade Analysis Project (GTAP) data, household survey data, and a modified version of the GTAP model that includes an implicitly, directly additive demand system (AIDADS) representation of consumer preferences. Poverty impacts are assessed using postsimulation techniques based on the household survey data.

Results suggest that the near-term effects of the core Doha scenario on poverty in the 15 countries in this sample would be mixed, with substantial reductions in some cases, some countries unaffected, and others show small poverty increases. Introducing reciprocal (that is, deeper) cuts in bound tariffs in the developing countries improves the poverty outcome overall. Indeed, the core Doha scenario is less poverty friendly than the reforms that are not undertaken in this scenario. The reason for this is the heavy emphasis of Doha on cuts to export subsidies and domestic support, both of which tend to raise poverty in this sample of countries. However, the most poverty-friendly reform measure, cuts in developing country tariffs, is nearly absent from the core Doha scenario. These limited cuts in developing countries' applied tariffs are caused by extensive binding overhang and nonreciprocal tariff cuts in the developing countries.

Introduction

Measuring poverty impacts is an important issue in the current debate of trade liberalization that has been labeled "a development round." To assess the poverty effects of multiregional trade liberalization, this chapter performs a simulation exercise in which a trade reform is implemented in a global computable general equilibrium (CGE) model and, subsequently, in a household model that includes income information for a large number of household groups in 15 developing countries. The two models permit an assessment of the change in the households' real income and the resulting poverty effects after the trade reform.

To make predictions, this chapter uses the latest version of the GTAP database as well as the recent household survey data from 15 developing countries (section 1) to run a global CGE model (section 2) and simulate the medium-run impacts of three considered trade reforms (section 3) on the consumer prices and household income and estimate the impact of these reforms on poverty in the 15 developing countries (section 4). The results are summarized with additional concluding remarks (section 5).

Data

GTAP Version 6 data (prerelease 6.5) documented by Dimaranan and McDougall (2002) were used in the form of a regional aggregation that captures 15 developing (focus) countries for which household survey data were available. In addition, the most important world trading blocks are disaggregated (table 14.1.) The commodity aggregation on the production side distinguishes the most important traded commodities. On the consumer side, the aggregation is far more limited because the estimated consumer demand system is available only for six broad commodity goods. Table 14.2 shows the two commodity aggregations and the relationship between them—that is, which producer goods map to each of the six consumer good categories.

The available survey data were reconciled with the GTAP data to ensure consistency in their information according to the method of Ivanic (2004). The reconciliation followed a few simple principles: the value of GDP and its two main components (agricultural and nonagricultural production) was compared with the survey data. In each case, the survey showed less value added in either sector than the national accounts data; therefore, each survey total was increased and

Table 14.1. Regional Aggregation Used in the Model

Regions included in the model	
ANZ	Australia, New Zealand
DEVASIA	Developed Asian countries
SEA	Southeast Asian developing countries
SA	South Asian developing countries
USA	the United States
Canada	Canada
LAC	Latin America and the Caribbean
EU15	Old EU countries
EU10	New EU countries
RestEFTA	Rest of the European Free Trade Area (Norway, Iceland, and Switzerland)
OEEFSU	Other Europe, former Soviet Union
MENA	Middle East and North Africa
SSA	Sub-Saharan Africa
Focus regions	
BAN	Bangladesh
BRA	Brazil
CHI	Chile
COL	Colombia
IND	Indonesia
MAL	Malawi
MEX	Mexico
MOZ	Mozambique
PER	Peru
PHI	Philippines
THA	Thailand
UGA	Uganda
VEN	Venezuela
VIE	Vietnam
ZAM	Zambia

Source: Author.

Table 14.2.   Producer and Consumer Commodity Aggregation Used in the Model

Consumption	Production	Consumption	Production
Staple grains	Rice Wheat Feed grains Processed rice	Nondurables	Forestry Beverages and tobacco Textiles Wearing apparel Wood and paper
Livestock	Meat and livestock Raw milk Fishing Processed meat Processed diary		Petrochemicals Other manufactures
		Durables	Mining Metals Automobiles
Other food products	Other agricultural Oilseeds Raw sugar Fats and oils Processed sugar Other processed food	Electronics
		Services	House utilities Trade and transportation Construction Business finance Government service

Source: Author.

brought into accord with the GTAP data. Because the most underreported category of household income appeared to be capital, the survey was changed by scaling the reported household capital income to match the level suggested by the GTAP data. In the second stage of the reconciliation process, survey information on the amounts of skilled and unskilled labor was imposed on the GTAP data. Because the survey data permitted an explicit estimation of imputed labor, this information was also used to create a specific version of the GTAP database where capital explicitly excluded self-employed labor, a definition more suitable under the medium-run closure of the model.

Stratification of Households According to Main Source of Income

In addition to being reconciled with the household survey data, the GTAP data were also split to represent the endowments of 140 household groups—20 vicensile (equal groups from poorest to richest) within each of seven strata. The strata were defined to contain those households that obtain more than 95 percent of their total income from agricultural profits, nonagricultural profits, labor, and transfers. Based on their location, the labor stratum was split into rural and urban. The remaining households that were not specialized in any specific income source were allocated to the two last strata, urban and rural diversified households.

The importance of income specialization among households in developing countries has been highlighted in the work of Hertel and others (2004); Hertel, and others (2003); and Ivanic (2002). According to these findings, a significant portion of households specialize in a single income source, and the extent of specialization is greatest among the poor. The phenomenon of income specialization of households is particularly important in light of the differential changes in factor returns that frequently result from trade liberalization. Moreover, specialization is also nonrandomly associated with poverty. In many countries, specialization in an agricultural stratum is associated with higher poverty incidence. Thus, separating households by their income source improves the understanding of the structure of poverty in a given country as well as the potential for significant changes in the wake of trade reform.

Model and Method

The model used in this work is a modified version of the standard GTAP model (Hertel 1997). The key change is that the constant difference of elasticities (CDE) demand system has been replaced with the AIDADS demand system (Rimmer and Powell 1992) following the approach of Yu and others (2004). The demand parameters have been obtained from the work of Cranfield and others (2004, 2003, 2002). The parameters of the AIDADS demand structure were available for only six aggregate goods. They were estimated globally using consumption data from the 1996 International Comparison Project as well as survey-based data on the distribution of income within countries. After estimation, the parameters were calibrated to fit the aggregate per capita consumption in each region. Because the commodity aggregation in the GTAP database was far more extensive than the six commodities included in the AIDADS demand structure, the 31 production commodities were mapped to the six consumption goods. Table 14.2 shows the mapping between the 31 GTAP producer goods and the six estimated consumer goods.

Estimation of the poverty level of income in the benchmark equilibrium is based on the poverty rate in each country as reported by the World Bank in conjunction with the income distribution from the available surveys. The poverty level of income is that level of income that yields the reported poverty rate. This in turn determines a level of utility for the observed set of prices in each country.

This poverty level of utility is kept constant between the simulations. After the simulation, the new poverty level of income is calculated as the level of income that achieves the original poverty level of utility under the new consumer prices.

Because the household surveys suggest that transfers make up an important part of household earnings in many countries, especially the poorest households, it was necessary to model transfers in the household model. These transfers are indexed by the cost of the household consumption basket (CPI).

The final special feature of the model is the tax replacement closure. It ensures that the lost or gained tax revenue is replaced by a uniform ad valorem tax on primary factor endowments, making each scenario fiscally neutral.

The method of this chapter is outlined in figure 14.1, which shows not only all the data used in the analysis, but also the relationship among, and sequence of, all the steps taken to establish the link between trade reform and poverty.

Scenarios and Experimental Design

Trade Reform Scenarios

In this section, two specific scenarios of trade reform are considered and compared to full trade liberalization. The first is the core Doha scenario explained in detail in chapter 2, and the second is the Doha-All scenario discussed briefly in that chapter. In the latter case, developing countries and least developed countries (LDCs) engage in reciprocal tariff cuts so that their bound tariff rates fall by the same percentage as in the developed countries. Because this analysis is conducted with a revised version of the global GTAP model—designed to work in concert with the microsimulation (MS) analyses for each of the 15 focus countries—the global results outlined in chapter 3 are not drawn upon. Rather, the global impacts of these scenarios are simulated within the analytical framework laid out above.

In addition to these two Doha scenarios, this chapter follows the lead of the earlier country case studies and also considers a full trade liberalization scenario. Representing the maximum extent of the trade reform, full trade liberalization involves the full reduction of all import tariffs, export subsidies, and domestic support. Its inclusion, along with the prospective trade reforms—Doha and Doha-All—provides a meaningful reference point. Understanding the effects of a full reform indicates whether the chosen step is in the right direction and whether its size is significant.

All scenarios were simulated under a single run using the decomposition feature (described in detail below) of the GEMPACK software. Under this procedure, only the full-liberalization reform was actually computed, and the Doha–Special and Differential Treatment (SDT) and Doha-All scenarios were extracted from

Figure 14.1. Description of the Method

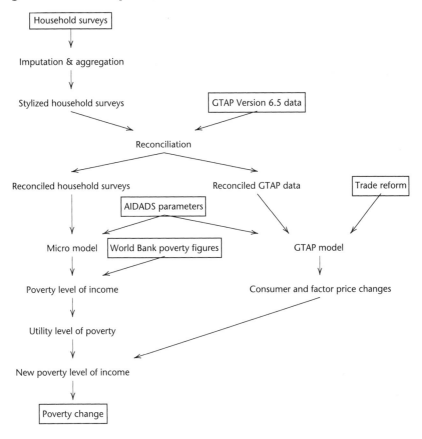

Source: Author.

the results based on a decomposition of the individual elements of reform. To ensure that this method of decomposition and extraction provides accurate results, we performed separate runs of the Doha scenarios and compared them to the results extracted from the full-liberalization run by the decomposition method. The two sets of results were found to be almost indistinguishable, thereby ensuring the accuracy of the method.

Decomposing Differences between Doha and Full Liberalization

The Doha and full-liberalization scenarios are significantly different in three aspects: the level of tariff reduction among the developed countries, the size of their domestic support cuts, and the level of participation in tariff reduction by the developing countries. Both scenarios involve the abolition of export subsidies. Because each of these differences can by itself in either way significantly contribute to poverty change, it is important to understand the individual impact of each of the components. To that end, the poverty effects of a series of 12 partial reforms are evaluated, wherein the first 5 combine to replicate the Doha scenario, 3 more incremental reforms represent the difference between the Doha and Doha-All scenarios, and the last 4 complement Doha-All to obtain full trade liberalization.

The first set of the components—the Doha scenario—includes removal of export subsidies on food products, the reduction in the tariffs and domestic support of developed countries, and reductions in the tariffs of the developing countries. The second set of components—Doha-All—includes further reductions in tariffs by the developing countries as dictated under the fully reciprocal tariff-cutting formula. The last step—completing full trade liberalization—includes the complete removal of remaining developed countries' tariffs and domestic support, as well as the removal of tariffs remaining in the developing countries following the Doha-All scenario.

Decomposition of the endogenous outcomes in the model (for example, prices and poverty) with respect to these exogenous policy shocks was performed using the standard decomposition feature of the GEMPACK software (Harrison, Horridge, and Pearson 1999).

Factor Mobility Assumptions

Assumptions on factor mobility play a vital role in the general equilibrium analysis of poverty model because they determine both the employment of the factors and their returns. Although a short-run closure, with most factors only imperfectly substitutable across sectors, is well suited for capturing the initial impact of economic shocks, it abstracts from the impact of trade reform on economywide, unskilled wage rates, which are often considered an important avenue for poverty reduction in the medium run (recall the findings for Brazil in chapters 7 and 9, for example). Because of this, it appears sensible to incorporate a different closure that reflects the ability of some factors—especially labor and capital—to move among sectors in search of the highest return. This medium-run closure corresponds to the assumption that capital of most small businesses, as well as the labor employed by them, is flexible in changing the nature of their business over the model's time horizon. The only sluggish factor is agricultural land, which can be assumed to be reallocated among sectors in a limited way only as a result of geographic and agronomic considerations.

Results

Price Results

The price results of the three simulations are presented in tables 14.3–14.5. Each table lists the consumer price changes, factor return changes, and change in national income (in percent), all deflated by the change in the price index of consumption at the poverty level of utility.

The results suggest that the effects of the two Doha trade reforms are rather small (tables 14.3 and 14.4): all national real income changes fall in the range of −1.1, 0.7 percent, which reflects a rather modest impact on the focus countries. The effects of these reforms on primary factors are also relatively small, with the exception of the factor that is sector specific (agricultural land) and is therefore expected to exhibit the greatest variation in the changes to its return because of its inelastic supply.

In contrast to the Doha trade reforms, the effect of full liberalization is more significant (table 14.5). The most strongly affected country is Vietnam, where reform induces a positive 5.8 percent change in national income deflated by the CPI at the poverty level.

Poverty Results

The general equilibrium model is used to simulate the impacts of the described trade reform on countries' consumer and factor prices and households' incomes and utility levels. Using the initial poverty level of utility benchmarked for each region, the number of households that fell into or were removed from poverty are then determined. The poverty percentage changes for each scenario on each stratum within each country are shown in table 14.6. The final row of each section in this table also shows the share of the strata in the total poverty in each country, which determines the weight of each stratum's poverty change toward the nation-wide poverty change (shown in the total column). Table 14.7 reports the estimated poverty headcount change (in thousands) for all strata in each of the 15 countries after all three simulations.

The poverty changes in both tables show a close relationship with the factor price changes (deflated by the CPI at the poverty level of consumption). For example, looking at the deflated factor return changes under full trade liberalization in the Philippines (table 14.5), it can be seen that the most important primary factors (labor and capital) experience an increase in their returns, but the return to land falls. Because these returns are deflated by the cost of consumption at the poverty level of income, it must be that poverty will increase among those

Table 14.3. Price and Income Changes (in percent) under Doha-SDT Deflated by the Domestic CPI at the Poverty Level of Consumption

Country	Consumption goods						Factors						Income	Real income[a]
	Staple grains	Livestock	Other food	Nondurables	Durables	Services	Land	Unskilled labor	Skilled labor	Capital	Natural resources	Transfers		
Bangladesh	0	0.1	0.2	-0.1	0	0	0.9	0	-0.1	0	-0.7	-0.5	0	0
Brazil	-0.1	2.2	0.8	-0.8	-2.3	-0.2	128.4	0.4	0.7	-0.7	-17.1	-4.1	0.4	0.7
Chile	-0.2	1.5	0.6	-0.7	-0.7	-0.6	15.8	-0.1	-0.5	-0.5	-5.7	-1.3	-0.3	0.1
Colombia	-0.3	0.6	0.9	-0.4	-0.6	-0.5	10.7	-0.5	-0.5	0	-1.4	-0.2	-0.1	0
Indonesia	0	0.3	0.2	-0.4	-0.3	-0.1	0.3	0.4	0.3	0.5	-3.2	-0.8	0	0.1
Malawi	0	0.2	-0.3	-0.1	0	0.2	-3.5	0.1	0.3	-0.2	-1.3	-0.9	0.1	0.1
Mexico	-0.1	0.1	0.2	-0.2	0	-0.1	3.5	-0.2	-0.3	-0.5	0.8	0.5	-0.2	-0.1
Mozambique	-0.2	-0.1	0.5	0.2	-0.2	-0.2	0.1	-0.4	-0.4	-0.1	-1.4	0.1	-0.4	-0.4
Peru	0.1	0.1	0.2	-0.2	-0.2	-0.1	3.8	0	-0.2	-0.1	-2.1	-0.4	-0.1	0
Philippines	-0.1	0.1	0.2	-0.1	-0.1	0	-0.2	0.3	0.7	-0.3	-0.9	-0.8	0.1	0.1
Thailand	1.1	0.6	0	-1.3	-0.4	0.1	16.7	0.4	-0.1	-0.1	-1.8	-1.3	0.3	0.4
Uganda	0.1	0	-0.2	0.1	0.1	0	-0.4	-0.2	-0.2	-0.3	-0.4	0.5	-0.2	-0.1
Venezuela R. B. de	0.2	0.3	-0.3	-0.1	-0.3	0.2	1	-0.4	-0.6	-0.3	2.1	0.7	-0.2	-0.2
Vietnam	-0.8	-0.1	0.3	1	0.9	-0.3	-5.5	-0.9	-0.1	-0.7	0.9	1.5	-0.9	-1
Zambia	0.2	-0.1	0.3	0.1	-0.3	-0.3	2	-0.1	-0.4	-0.5	-0.9	-0.3	-0.2	-0.2

Source: Author's calculations.

a. Deflated by the CPI.

Table 14.4. Price and Income Changes (in percent) under Doha-All Deflated by the Domestic CPI at the Poverty Level of Consumption

Country	Consumption goods						Factors						Income	Real income[a]
	Staple grains	Livestock	Other food	Nondurables	Durables	Services	Land	Unskilled labor	Skilled labor	Capital	Natural resources	Transfers		
Bangladesh	0	-0.1	0.2	-0.1	0	0	0.5	0	-0.1	0	-0.8	-0.4	0	0
Brazil	0	2.4	0.8	-0.8	-2.9	-0.1	130.8	0.3	0.6	-0.1	-16.9	-4	0.4	0.7
Chile	-0.2	1.6	0.6	-0.8	-0.8	-0.6	16.6	-0.1	-0.5	-0.6	-6.8	-1.4	-0.3	0.1
Colombia	-0.2	0.7	1	-0.4	-0.7	-0.5	10.9	-0.6	-0.5	-0.6	-0.7	0.1	-0.1	-0.1
Indonesia	0.1	0.3	0.2	-0.6	-0.4	-0.1	0.9	0.5	0.3	0	-4.2	-0.9	0	0.1
Malawi	0.1	0.3	-0.4	-0.3	-0.1	0.3	-4.2	0.3	0.5	0.8	-1.4	-1.2	0.3	0.3
Mexico	0	0	0	-0.3	0.2	0.1	2	-0.1	-0.2	-0.1	0.7	0.7	-0.1	-0.1
Mozambique	-0.1	-0.1	0.5	0.1	-0.2	-0.2	0.3	-0.3	-0.4	-0.4	-1.8	0.1	-0.3	-0.3
Peru	0.1	0	0.1	-0.2	-0.1	-0.1	3.4	0	-0.1	-0.1	-1.8	-0.2	0	0
Philippines	-0.3	0.1	0.1	0.1	0.1	0.2	-0.7	0.5	1	0.1	-0.8	-0.4	0.3	0.2
Thailand	2	0.9	0	-2.2	-0.6	0.4	24.8	0.5	-0.4	-0.4	-3.6	-1.7	0.3	0.5
Uganda	0.1	-0.1	-0.3	0.1	0.1	0.1	-0.5	-0.2	-0.2	0	-0.4	0.7	-0.2	-0.2
Venezuela R. B. de	0.4	0.3	-0.7	-0.1	-0.4	0.4	0.8	-0.6	-0.8	-0.4	3.2	1.1	-0.2	-0.3
Vietnam	-0.9	-0.2	0.3	1.2	1.1	-0.3	-7	-1	-0.1	-0.8	0.9	1.8	-1	-1.1
Zambia	0.3	-0.1	0.3	0	-0.3	-0.3	2.3	0	-0.3	-0.5	-1.1	-0.3	-0.2	-0.1

Source: Author's calculations.

a. Deflated by the CPI.

Table 14.5. Price and Income Changes (in percent) under Full Liberalization Deflated by the Domestic CPI at the Poverty Level of Consumption

Country	Consumption goods						Land	Factors					Income	Real income[a]
	Staple grains	Livestock	Other food	Nondurables	Durables	Services		Unskilled labor	Skilled labor	Capital	Natural resources	Transfers		
Bangladesh	1.9	-0.1	-0.4	-4.8	2	2.5	-9.4	-0.4	-1	-0.3	-18	-0.6	-0.7	-0.5
Brazil	0.7	4.7	1.7	-1.7	-7.9	0.4	237.2	-0.5	-0.1	-0.5	-23.4	-6.1	0.3	0.8
Chile	0.5	3.4	1.4	-3	-2	-0.1	33.5	-0.5	-1.8	-1.5	-11.4	-3.4	-0.8	-0.1
Colombia	0.2	1.1	1.7	-1.9	-0.8	-0.1	17.7	-1.6	-1.4	-1.7	5.6	1.9	-0.7	-0.6
Indonesia	0.7	0.8	0.7	-2.8	-2.4	0.9	-2.7	1.3	0.5	0.7	-17.8	-3.9	-0.1	0.1
Malawi	3.6	2.1	-0.7	-6.8	-1.3	2.3	13.9	1.2	-0.7	-0.4	-4.1	-2.4	0.7	0.8
Mexico	0.6	0	0.3	-1.5	-0.6	0.7	2.6	-0.3	-0.6	-0.3	-0.3	0.5	-0.3	-0.4
Mozambique	2.8	0.7	-4.4	-3.5	2.1	2.8	1.2	0.3	0.2	0.9	-6.5	1.6	0.5	0.4
Peru	0.3	0.7	0.4	-1.6	-0.7	0.8	13.1	0.9	-0.1	-0.1	4	0.5	0.2	0.1
Philippines	-1	0.4	0.4	-0.3	0.6	1.4	-2.8	1.5	3	0.8	-5.9	-2.4	0.8	0.6
Thailand	6.6	3.5	0	-6.7	-5.8	3.1	48.4	0.7	-2.2	-1.2	-17.1	-7.1	-0.1	0.2
Uganda	0.5	0.1	-0.4	-0.8	0.3	0.4	-1.2	-0.9	-1	-0.2	-0.6	2.4	-0.6	-0.6
Venezuela R. B. de	0.8	0.7	-1.4	-0.2	-0.8	0.8	1.8	-1.3	-1.5	-0.9	10.6	2.9	-0.3	-0.4
Vietnam	8	6	-0.8	-15.7	-18.1	8.3	-5.2	11.1	4.9	5.1	-18.5	-8.3	5.8	5.8
Zambia	0.5	1.5	-1.3	-3.1	0	1.9	-3	-0.6	-0.2	0.2	-9.8	-0.6	-0.4	-0.5

Source: Author's calculations.

a. Deflated by the CPI.

Table 14.6.   Percent Change in Poverty under Three Scenarios

Country	Reform	Agriculture	Nonagriculture	Urban labor	Rural labor	Transfer	Urban diverse	Rural diverse	Total
Bangladesh	Doha-SDT	0.00	0.00	0.00	0.00	0.00	−0.10	0.00	0.00
	Doha-All	−0.10	−0.10	−0.10	0.00	0.00	−0.10	−0.10	−0.10
	Full-Lib	0.60	1.10	0.80	0.70	0.20	1.40	0.80	0.80
	Share[a]	0.15	0.12	0.03	0.23	0.03	0.06	0.38	1.00
Brazil	Doha-SDT	−3.40	−1.00	−1.80	−2.30	0.00	−3.10	−2.30	−2.10
	Doha-All	−3.30	−0.80	−1.40	−1.90	0.00	−3.00	−2.20	−1.80
	Full-Lib	−3.90	1.00	1.70	2.20	0.00	−2.90	−1.90	−0.20
	Share	0.26	0.13	0.25	0.19	0.11	0.03	0.03	1.00
Chile	Doha-SDT	−4.60	0.40	0.20	0.20	0.10	−1.80	−1.30	−1.60
	Doha-All	−4.90	0.30	0.10	0.10	0.10	−2.00	−1.50	−1.70
	Full-Lib	−9.80	1.40	1.00	0.80	0.30	−3.40	−2.20	−3.10
	Share	0.24	0.01	0.09	0.08	0.25	0.17	0.15	1.00
Colombia	Doha-SDT	0.20	0.30	1.00	1.00	0.00	0.40	0.50	0.30
	Doha-All	0.20	0.30	1.10	1.20	0.10	0.50	0.60	0.40
	Full-Lib	0.80	0.90	3.30	3.40	0.30	1.60	1.80	1.20
	Share	0.27	0.40	0.06	0.06	0.10	0.06	0.05	1.00
Indonesia	Doha-SDT	−0.70	−0.70	−0.90	−1.00	0.00	−0.80	−0.70	−0.70
	Doha-All	−0.80	−0.80	−1.00	−1.10	0.00	−0.90	−0.90	−0.80
	Full-Lib	−2.00	−2.20	−2.80	−3.00	0.30	−2.00	−2.00	−2.00
	Share	0.39	0.12	0.02	0.07	0.03	0.07	0.30	1.00
Malawi	Doha-SDT	0.10	−0.10	−0.30	−0.10	0.00	0.10	0.00	0.00
	Doha-All	0.00	−0.10	−0.60	−0.30	−0.10	−0.10	−0.10	0.00
	Full-Lib	−0.50	−0.10	−1.10	−0.80	−0.10	−2.10	−0.80	−0.60
	Share	0.48	0.08	0.00	0.06	0.06	0.02	0.30	1.00
Mexico	Doha-SDT	0.10	0.40	0.70	0.40	0.20	0.30	0.30	0.30
	Doha-All	0.00	0.20	0.30	0.20	0.00	0.10	0.10	0.10
	Full-Lib	0.10	0.50	0.90	0.60	0.30	0.50	0.40	0.40
	Share	0.05	0.07	0.08	0.15	0.22	0.16	0.27	1.00
Mozambique	Doha-SDT	0.00	0.10	0.40	0.00	0.10	0.30	0.10	0.10
	Doha-All	0.00	0.10	0.40	0.00	0.10	0.30	0.10	0.10
	Full-Lib	0.00	−0.10	−0.30	0.00	−0.10	−0.30	−0.10	−0.10
	Share	0.30	0.15	0.05	0.07	0.12	0.12	0.20	1.00

Table 14.6. *(Continued)*

Country	Reform	Agriculture	Nonagriculture	Urban labor	Rural labor	Transfer	Urban diverse	Rural diverse	Total
Peru	Doha-SDT	−0.10	0.00	0.00	0.00	0.00	0.00	0.00	0.00
	Doha-All	−0.10	0.00	0.00	0.00	0.00	0.00	0.00	0.00
	Full-Lib	−1.60	−0.40	−1.90	−1.40	−0.10	−0.70	−0.70	−0.50
	Share	0.06	0.34	0.00	0.02	0.24	0.11	0.23	1.00
Philippines	Doha-SDT	0.40	−0.30	−0.90	−0.60	−0.10	−0.20	−0.20	−0.20
	Doha-All	1.00	−0.60	−1.40	−1.10	−0.50	−0.40	−0.30	−0.20
	Full-Lib	3.80	−1.90	−4.30	−3.20	−1.30	−1.00	−0.60	−0.50
	Share	0.11	0.06	0.02	0.05	0.03	0.23	0.50	1.00
Thailand	Doha-SDT	−3.50	−0.90	−1.30	−1.10	−0.50	−1.40	−2.20	−2.00
	Doha-All	−5.00	−1.10	−1.60	−1.30	−0.50	−1.80	−3.10	−2.70
	Full-Lib	−8.80	−1.20	−2.20	−1.70	1.10	−2.20	−4.50	−3.70
	Share	0.06	0.02	0.00	0.06	0.11	0.07	0.68	1.00
Uganda	Doha-SDT	0.10	0.20	0.20	0.30	0.00	0.10	0.20	0.20
	Doha-All	0.20	0.20	0.20	0.40	0.00	0.20	0.20	0.20
	Full-Lib	0.60	0.90	1.00	1.60	0.10	0.60	0.70	0.70
	Share	0.10	0.03	0.00	0.03	0.03	0.05	0.76	1.00
Venezuela R.B. de	Doha-SDT	0.30	0.50	0.70	0.40	0.00	1.00	0.60	0.50
	Doha-All	0.40	0.60	1.00	0.60	0.00	1.40	0.80	0.60
	Full-Lib	0.80	1.30	2.00	1.20	0.10	2.80	1.70	1.30
	Share	0.06	0.22	0.24	0.13	0.20	0.09	0.05	1.00
Vietnam	Doha-SDT	0.80	0.70	0.70	1.20	0.20	0.90	0.60	0.70
	Doha-All	1.00	0.70	0.80	1.30	0.20	1.00	0.70	0.80
	Full-Lib	−1.90	−6.50	−6.90	−14.60	−1.10	−7.90	−5.50	−5.80
	Share	0.05	0.14	0.00	0.02	0.02	0.09	0.67	1.00
Zambia	Doha-SDT	0.00	0.10	0.10	0.00	0.00	0.20	0.00	0.10
	Doha-All	0.00	0.10	0.00	0.00	0.00	0.10	0.00	0.00
	Full-Lib	0.00	0.20	0.30	0.10	0.00	0.40	0.10	0.10
	Share	0.29	0.23	0.11	0.07	0.06	0.11	0.11	1.00

Source: Author's calculations.
a. Share of total poverty in the given stratum.

Table 14.7.   Change in Poverty Headcount (thousands) under Three Scenarios

Country	Reform	Agriculture	Nonagriculture	Urban labor	Rural labor	Transfer	Urban diverse	Rural diverse	Total
Bangladesh	Doha-SDT	–2	–2	0	–2	0	–1	–5	–13
	Doha-All	–3	–4	–1	–5	0	–2	–8	–23
	Full-Lib	37	51	10	65	2	35	122	323
Brazil	Doha-SDT	–83	–13	–42	–40	0	–10	–7	–195
	Doha-All	–80	–10	–34	–32	0	–10	–6	–173
	Full-Lib	–94	12	40	39	0	–9	–6	–17
Chile	Doha-SDT	–8	0	0	0	0	–2	–1	–10
	Doha-All	–8	0	0	0	0	–2	–1	–11
	Full-Lib	–16	0	1	0	1	–4	–2	–20
Colombia	Doha-SDT	4	9	4	5	0	2	2	27
	Doha-All	5	10	5	6	1	3	3	33
	Full-Lib	18	30	15	16	3	8	8	98
Indonesia	Doha-SDT	–94	–30	–5	–26	0	–18	–80	–254
	Doha-All	–111	–34	–6	–29	0	–22	–96	–300
	Full-Lib	–282	–98	–17	–80	3	–49	–219	–742
Malawi	Doha-SDT	2	0	0	0	0	0	0	1
	Doha-All	1	–1	0	–1	0	0	–2	–3
	Full-Lib	–19	–1	0	–4	–1	–3	–18	–45
Mexico	Doha-SDT	1	5	9	11	6	9	12	53
	Doha-All	0	2	4	4	2	3	4	19
	Full-Lib	1	6	12	14	11	14	17	75
Mozambique	Doha-SDT	1	2	3	0	1	6	3	15
	Doha-All	1	2	2	0	1	5	3	13
	Full-Lib	–1	–2	–2	0	–2	–5	–3	–14

Table 14.7. *(Continued)*

Country	Reform	Agriculture	Nonagriculture	Urban labor	Rural labor	Transfer	Urban diverse	Rural diverse	Total
Peru	Doha-SDT	0	0	0	0	0	0	0	0
	Doha-All	0	0	0	0	0	0	0	-1
	Full-Lib	-3	-5	0	-1	-1	-3	-5	-18
Philippines	Doha-SDT	5	-2	-2	-3	0	-6	-9	-18
	Doha-All	12	-4	-4	-6	-1	-9	-15	-26
	Full-Lib	46	-12	-11	-17	-4	-24	-34	-56
Thailand	Doha-SDT	-3	0	0	-1	-1	-1	-20	-26
	Doha-All	-4	0	0	-1	-1	-2	-27	-35
	Full-Lib	-7	0	0	-1	2	-2	-39	-49
Uganda	Doha-SDT	1	1	0	1	0	1	12	16
	Doha-All	2	1	0	1	0	1	14	18
	Full-Lib	6	3	0	5	0	3	52	69
Venezuela	Doha-SDT	1	6	10	3	0	6	2	28
	Doha-All	1	8	13	4	1	7	3	36
	Full-Lib	3	17	28	9	1	15	5	77
Vietnam	Doha-SDT	13	28	1	9	1	24	130	207
	Doha-All	16	31	1	10	2	28	146	234
	Full-Lib	-29	-277	-8	-110	-8	-227	-1,136	-1,795
Zambia	Doha-SDT	0	2	1	0	0	2	0	6
	Doha-All	0	2	0	0	0	1	0	4
	Full-Lib	0	3	3	1	0	4	1	10

Source: Author's calculations.

households whose income derives mainly from land (agricultural households) and will fall for the others, as table 14.6 confirms. In the case of Brazil, the results are reversed—the real returns to all factors except land fall. This results in an increase in poverty for all strata except those relying on earnings from agricultural land (agricultural and diversified households). The same relationship between poverty-deflated factor prices and poverty is present for all other countries under all simulations.

The poverty effects of the reforms across all 15 countries are summarized in table 14.8, which lists the expected poverty effects by stratum and type of reform. These effects are summarized in a single number that reports the difference in probability for poverty reduction and poverty growth. A value of negative one means that a particular reform is found to increase poverty in each case (probability for poverty reduction is zero); a value of one means that in each country, the reform resulted in lower poverty (probability of poverty rise equal to zero). A value of zero means that the probability of experiencing poverty reduction and poverty growth were equal, based on the particular set of countries considered. The table is constructed using the new decomposition technique referred to above, so that each row shows the incremental effect of a particular instrument or reform. The summary rows for Doha, Doha-All and full liberalization capture the combined effect of those complete reform packages—that is, the sum of all preceding rows.

Focusing initially on the complete reform impacts, it can be seen that Doha and Doha-All yield numbers in the neighborhood of zero for most stratum impacts and for the national impacts. That is, poverty increases in about as many countries as it falls. Doha-All is shown to be a bit more poverty friendly, particularly with regard to the diversified households and also for the nation as a whole. The full-liberalization scenario yields a stronger result, with the probability of poverty reduction at 0.20, indicating that poverty falls in more cases than it rises. In order to understand these differences, we need to exploit the decomposition with respect to individual instruments.

Decomposition of the Differences in Poverty Effects of the Doha and Full-Liberalization Scenarios

To perform this decomposition, the full-liberalization shock was broken into 8 components of the Doha-SDT and Doha-All scenarios, and 4 additional reforms that complement the full trade liberalization were added, for a total of 12 scenarios in the following sequence: (1) complete removal of export subsidies by the developed countries, (2) cut (Doha-SDT level) in the tariffs of the developed countries, (3) cut (Doha level) of the domestic support of the developed countries, (4) cut (Doha-SDT level) in the developing countries' own tariffs, (5) cut

Table 14.8. Differences in the Probabilities of Poverty Growth and Poverty Reduction in a Sequential Application of the Reforms between Doha-SDT and Full Trade Liberalization

Reform (component)	Agriculture	Nonagriculture	Stratum Urban labor	Rural labor	Transfer	Urban diverse	Rural diverse	National	Magnitude[a]
Doha-SDT									
Export subsidies	-0.33	-0.87	-0.87	-0.87	-0.87	-0.73	-0.73	-0.73	0.040
DC tariff cuts	-0.33	-0.20	-0.20	-0.20	-0.20	-0.20	-0.20	-0.20	0.125
DC domestic support cut	0.20	-0.73	-0.60	-0.60	-0.73	-0.20	-0.20	-0.47	0.015
Own DGC tariff cuts	-0.60	-0.20	-0.07	-0.20	0.07	-0.20	-0.20	-0.20	0.020
Other DGC tariff cuts	0.60	0.20	0.47	0.47	-0.07	0.47	0.47	0.47	0.024
Doha SDT (complete reform)	-0.07	-0.20	-0.07	-0.07	-0.47	-0.07	-0.07	-0.07	
Doha-All									
DC tariff cuts	-0.20	-0.07	-0.07	-0.07	0.07	-0.07	-0.07	-0.07	0.005
Own DGC tariff cuts	-0.33	0.20	0.20	0.20	0.33	-0.07	-0.07	-0.07	0.021
Other DGC tariff cuts	0.47	0.33	0.33	0.33	0.07	0.47	0.47	0.47	0.025
Doha-All (complete reform)	-0.07	-0.20	-0.07	-0.07	-0.47	-0.07	-0.07	-0.07	
Full trade liberalization									
DC tariff removal	0.20	0.07	0.07	0.07	-0.07	0.20	0.20	0.20	0.176
DC domestic support removal	-0.33	-1.00	-1.00	-1.00	-0.87	-0.60	-0.73	-0.60	0.065
Own DGC tariff removal	-0.33	-0.33	-0.33	-0.33	-0.07	-0.47	-0.47	-0.47	0.314
Other DGC tariff removal	0.73	0.60	0.60	0.60	0.60	0.73	0.73	0.73	0.171
Full liberalization (complete reform)	0.07	-0.07	-0.07	-0.07	-0.33	0.20	0.20	0.20	

Source: Author's calculations.

Note: 1 = always poverty reduction; 0 = no poverty change; –1 = always poverty increase. DC = developed country; DGC = developing country.

a. Average absolute percentage change.

(Doha-SDT level) in the tariffs of other developing countries, (6) further cut (Doha-All level) in the tariffs of the developed countries, (7) further cut (Doha-All level) in the developing countries' own tariffs, (8) further cut (Doha-All level) in the tariffs of the rest of the developing countries, (9) complete removal of tariffs by the developed countries, (10) full reduction of domestic support in the developed countries, (11) full tariff removal by the focus countries, and (12) the full removal of tariffs by the rest of the countries.

The separate poverty effects of each of these reforms are reported in table 14.8, which shows the expected effect of each partial reform on overall poverty among the strata and on the national level. Note that the poverty estimates in this table were obtained by using income distributions that were homogeneous across households in the same stratum. This treatment was necessary to remove that part of the data heterogeneity on the level of the individual households that is responsible for a random change in poverty sign in the face of small shocks.

Table 14.8 provides important insights into the poverty impact of various components of the reforms and in this way aids understanding of why the overall effect of the Doha reform is poverty increasing and the effect of Doha-All and full trade liberalization is the opposite. The table lists individual components of both reforms: the first five represent Doha, the next three represent Doha-All, and the remaining four complete the full trade liberalization. The next seven columns—one for each stratum—show the expected poverty reduction (in the total of 15 countries) for each component of the reform. The last two columns show the same effects on the national level, as well as the weight of each reform in the total result.

The last two columns of the table show that the Doha reforms are dominated by the first two components—export subsidy removal and reductions in developed countries' tariffs—both of which have a negative effect on national poverty. Also negative, though less significantly, are the effects of preference-eroding reductions in developed countries' tariffs and the reduction in domestic support. The effect of these two components completely dominates the consistent poverty-reducing effect of the reduction of developing countries' tariffs that produces only small changes in poverty. The overall effect of the Doha reform is therefore marginally poverty increasing in this sample of countries. The effect of Doha-All is very similar to Doha on the national level, except that Doha-All creates more benefits for the poor through greater tariff reductions by the developing countries. The full-liberalization scenario adds more benefits of the reductions in the tariffs by both developing and developed countries, and these tend to offset the negative effects of further cuts in domestic support and developing countries' own tariff reductions, thereby leading to a slight poverty reduction, on average.

Figure 14.2 shows the decomposition of the poverty effects of the reforms in a visually intuitive way: each poverty effect is represented by a vertical bar, whose height represents the expected poverty reduction effect of the reform,[1] and its width represents the weight associated with the reform (this weight is taken from table 14.8). Thus, a tall, narrow bar means a very poverty-friendly reform with little total impact, and a wide, short bar means a significant impact on national poverty with an undecided effect on poverty across the entire sample. The definition of the construction of this chart provides a very useful interpretation of the area of each bar, which represents the weight of each reform in the total results— a sum of all the areas belonging to a given reform determines the total impact.

Considering the poverty effects of each Doha reform component on each stratum yields other interesting observations: The effect of the removal of export subsidies has an overall negative effect on poverty, but it has a far less negative effect on poverty among the agricultural households (see table 14.8). This is hardly surprising, as the removal of export subsidies—primarily in agriculture—raises agricultural prices, hence helping agricultural households. It can be observed that return to land increases in most cases under the Doha scenarios in tables 14.3 and

Figure 14.2. Decomposition of Poverty Effects of the Trade Reforms

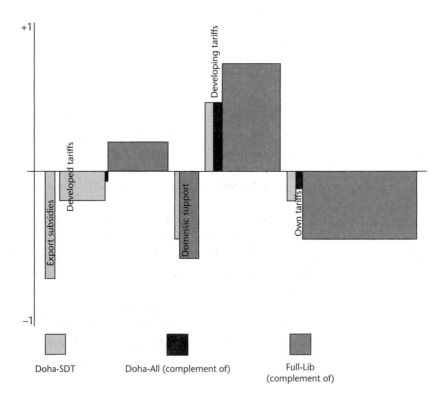

14.4. However, these high agricultural prices translate into higher food prices, thus hurting the poor in general. A similar pattern of favoring agricultural house- holds can be seen for other components of the reforms that make food prices rise, such as the cut in domestic support under both Doha scenarios, as well as its com- plete elimination under full trade liberalization.

In the bottom section of table 14.8, it can be seen that, unlike Doha and Doha- All, the full-liberalization scenario contains a significant stratum-wide positive effect of the removal of developing countries' tariffs on poverty. The same positive effect was present under the Doha reforms. However, as a result of the minimal tariff changes under the core Doha scenario, the poverty effects of that reform were rather small. The effects of other reform components are also magnified under the full trade reform: for example the effect of the domestic support cut, negligible under Doha, has a more significant poverty-increasing effect under full trade liberalization. With respect to each respective stratum, the full trade liberal- ization exhibits a much more uniform effect on poverty, despite somewhat poverty-increasing effects of developing countries' own tariff liberalization. The latter derives from the fact that each country in the global model has an optimal tariff, as a consequence of the Armington assumption (product differentiation by origin). Therefore, unilateral liberalization beyond the optimal tariff level results in a terms of trade (TOT) loss that outweighs the efficiency gain. However, when other countries also cut their tariffs, the adverse TOT effect is dampened, or even reversed, and the efficiency gains dominate.

Conclusion

The goal of this chapter is to describe the poverty effects of two possible trade reforms and contrast them to the limiting case of the full trade liberalization. It has been shown that differences in the patterns of the trade reform result in dif- ferent poverty results. In particular, by increasing the depth of cuts in bound tar- iffs under a Doha scenario, Doha-All improves the overall poverty outcome in this sample of 15 countries.

More complete trade liberalization—inclusive of trade and domestic reform— appears to be generally poverty reducing. This is explained by the overall poverty- reducing effect of the removal of tariffs by the developed countries beyond the Doha level and the reduction of developing countries' tariffs, a component that is missing in the Doha scenarios.

Based on the proposed trade reforms and the results shown in this chapter, a suggestion for a trade policy aimed at poverty reduction should probably include advice to developing countries to focus more attention on tariff reductions and less on the removal of domestic and export subsidies by industrialized countries.

Note

1. This shows the difference between the probability of poverty reduction and poverty growth: a value of one means that the probability of poverty reduction is one, and the value of negative one means that the probability of poverty growth is one.

References

Bangladesh Bureau of Statistics. 1996. *Household Expenditure Survey.* Dhaka.

BID-BIRD-CEPAL Colombia. 1998. *Encuesta nacional de hogares—fuerza de trabajo.* Bogota.

BID-BIRD-CEPAL, Venezuela. 1998. *Encuesta de hogares por muestreo.*

Biro Pusat Statistik, Indonesia. 1993. *SUSENAS: Indonesia's Socio-Economic Survey.* Jakarta.

Central Statistical Office, Zambia. 1998. *Living Conditions Monitoring Survey II.*

Cranfield, J. A. L., P. V. Preckel, J. S. Eales, and T. W. Hertel. 2002. "Estimating Consumer Demand across the Development Spectrum: Maximum Likelihood Estimates of an Implicit Direct Additivity Model." *Journal of Development Economics* 68 (2): 289–307.

Cranfield, J. A. L., J. S. Eales, T. W. Hertel, and P. V. Preckel. 2003. "Model Selection when Estimating and Predicting Consumer Demands Using International, Cross Section Data." *Empirical Economics* 28 (2): 353–364.

Cranfield, J. A. L., P. V. Preckel, J. S. Eales, and T. W. Hertel. 2004. "Simultaneous Estimation of an Implicit Directly Additive Demand System and the Distribution of Expenditure—an Application of Maximum Entropy." *Economic Modelling* 21 (2): 361–85.

Dimaranan, B. V., and R. A. McDougall. 2002. "Global Trade, Assistance, and Production: The GTAP 5 Data Base." Purdue University, West Lafayette, IN.

General Statistics Office, Vietnam. 1998. *Household Living Standards Survey.*

Harrison, W. Jill, J. Mark Horridge, and K. R. Pearson. 1999. CoPS/IMPACT Working Paper Number IP-73, Monash University, Melbourne, Australia.

Hertel, T. W., ed. 1997. *Global Trade Analysis, Modeling and Applications.* Cambridge, U.K.: Cambridge University Press.

Hertel, T. W., M. Ivanic, P. V. Preckel, J. A. L. Cranfield, and W. Martin. 2003. "Short- versus Long-Run Implications of Trade Liberalization for Poverty in Three Developing Countries." *American Journal of Agricultural Economics* 85(5): 1299–1306.

Hertel, T. W., M. Ivanic, P. V. Preckel, and J. A. Cranfield. 2004. "The Earnings Effects of Multilateral Trade Liberalization: Implications for Poverty." *World Bank Economic Review* 18 (2): 205–36.

IBGE. 1998. *Pesquisa nacional por amostra de domicilios.*

Instituto Nacional de Estadística, Geografía e Informática, Mexico. 2000. *Encuesta nacional de ingresos y gastos de los hogares.*

Ivanic, M. 2002. "Assessment of Household Surveys and Their Contribution to Poverty Research: The Income Side of the Story." M.S. thesis, Purdue University, West Lafayette, IN.

MECOVI, Peru 1999. *Encuesta nacional de hogares.*

Ministerio de Planificación y Cooperación, Chile. 1998. *Encuesta de caracterización socioeconómica nacional.*

National Institute of Statistics, Mozambique. 2003. *IAF Household Survey.* Maputo.

National Statistical Office, Malawi. 1998. *Integrated Household Survey.* Zomba.

National Statistics Division, Thailand. 1996. *Thailand Socio-Economic Survey.* Bangkok.

National Statistics Office, the Philippines. 1999. *Annual Poverty Indicators Survey.* Manila.

———. 2004. "Reconciliation of the GTAP and Household Survey Data." Technical Report. Global Trade Analysis Project, Center for Global Trade Analysis, Purdue University, West Lafayette, IN.

Rimmer, M., and A. Powell. 1992. "An Implicitly Additive Demand System." *Applied Economics* 28: 1613–22.

Uganda Bureau of Statistics. 1999. *National Household Survey.* Entebbe.

Yu, W., T. W. Hertel, P. V. Preckel, and J. Eales. 2004. "Projecting World Food Demand Using Alternative Demand Systems." *Economic Modelling* 21 (1): 99–129.

PART VII

THE DOHA
DEVELOPMENT
AGENDA, GROWTH,
AND POVERTY

IMPLICATIONS OF WTO AGREEMENTS AND UNILATERAL TRADE POLICY REFORMS FOR POVERTY IN BANGLADESH: SHORT-VERSUS LONG-RUN IMPACTS

Nabil Annabi, Bazlul Khondker, Selim Raihan,
John Cockburn, and Bernard Decaluwé

Summary

This chapter examines the impacts of WTO agreements and domestic trade policy reforms on production, welfare, and poverty in Bangladesh. A sequential, dynamic computable general equilibrium (CGE) model, which takes into account accumulation effects, is used, allowing for long-run analysis. The study is based on the 2000 social accounting matrix (SAM) of Bangladesh, including 15 production sectors, four factors of production (skilled and unskilled labor and agricultural and nonagricultural capital), and nine household groups (five in rural areas and four in urban areas) based on the 2000 household survey. To examine the link between the macro effects and micro effects in terms of poverty, the representative household approach with actual intragroup income distributions is used.

The study presents five simulations for which the major findings are (1) the Doha scenario has negative implications for the overall macroeconomy, household welfare, and poverty in Bangladesh—terms of trade (TOT) deteriorate and consumer prices, particularly food prices, increase more than nominal incomes, especially among poor households; (2) worldwide free trade has similar, but larger, impacts; (3) domestic trade liberalization induces an expansion of agricultural and light manufacturing sectors and favorable changes in the domestic TOT; although the short-run welfare and poverty impacts are negative, these become positive in the long run, when capital has adjusted through new investments; rising unskilled wage rates make the poorest households the biggest winners in terms of welfare and poverty reduction; (4) domestic liberalization effects far outweigh those of worldwide free trade when these scenarios are combined; and (5) remittances constitute a powerful poverty-reducing tool because of their greater importance in the income of the poor.

Introduction

The current round of WTO negotiations, commonly referred to as the Doha Round, is likely to have profound and far-reaching impacts on developing countries such as Bangladesh. Furthermore, because these negotiations target especially the agricultural sector, it is the poorest members of these developing countries who will be most directly affected. This is because the poor, who are located overwhelmingly in rural areas, both consume proportionately more agricultural goods and derive a larger share of their income from the agricultural sector. It is unclear whether the net effects of Doha reforms will help or harm these most vulnerable populations, because the specific reforms and their channels of impacts are numerous and complex. Reforms in both developed and developing countries may encompass quota and tariff removal and reduction, the elimination of export taxes, the removal of domestic agricultural support, and accompanying domestic fiscal reforms to replace lost tariff revenues. The channels of influence are likely, in turn, to simultaneously influence household income (wage rates, returns to capital, remittances, and so on) and consumer prices in contrasting manners.

To address these important issues, this chapter examines the poverty effects of Doha agreements and domestic trade policy reforms in a sequential, dynamic CGE framework. The model takes into account accumulation effects and thus allows long-run poverty analysis. In addition, it enables tracking of the adjustment path in the economy, which may include substantial poverty effects.

The remainder of this chapter is a follows: First, the issues and the methodology are presented. Then the chapter provides analysis of the poverty and other implications of the Doha agreement, world and domestic trade liberalization, and increased remittances. Conclusions are provided in a final section.

An Overview of the Issues

Current Doha Round negotiations involve developed-country reforms that have at least three very important components from Bangladesh's perspective: agricultural trade liberalization, the further liberalization of textile and garment trade, and freer international movement of workers. Furthermore, the Doha Round will require reforms by Bangladesh, notably in the area of trade liberalization. Each of these issues is examined in the sections below.

Agricultural Trade Liberalization

It is generally suggested that the implementation of Doha agreements on agricultural trade is likely to increase the prices of food grains and commercial crops in the world market (Panagariya 2002; Beghin, Roland-Holst, and van der Mensbrugghe 2002). However, the implications for the developing countries of increased agricultural prices are unclear, and it is argued that the potential exporting countries could benefit and the net food importing countries may turn out to be the losers (Panagariya 2002). There are competing predictions of the impact of Doha Round agreements based on simulations results of various global trade models. Some studies foresee expansion of world trade, real output, wages, and incomes in developing countries (Beghin, Roland-Holst, and van der Mensbrugghe 2002; Conforti and Salvatici 2004). However, some studies raise concerns about the potential negative impacts for the net food importing countries (François, van Meijl, and van Tongeren 2003; Fabiosa and others 2003).

Liberalization of Textile and Garments Trade

Ready-made garment exports have been one of Bangladesh's dominant sources of foreign exchange earnings over the last decade. There is a considerable debate about the implications of the removal of quotas under the Uruguay Round Agreement on Textiles and Clothing (ATC) for developing countries (Hertel and others 1996; Hertel and Martin 2000; Yang, Martin, and Yanagishima 1997).[1] There are two concerns for Bangladesh: the first is the declining prices of textiles and garments in the international market after the ATC phase out (MacDonald and others 2001, Diao and Somwaru 2001); the second concern relates to the rising cost of material inputs for ready-made garment exports of Bangladesh after the removal of the ATC. It has been projected by some studies that, with the end of the ATC on January 1, 2005, Bangladesh is going to lose the export advantage it has enjoyed over other competitors (Lips and others 2003; Yang and Mlachila 2004). In addition, the Doha Round is likely to reduce tariffs on textiles and clothing and reduce or eliminate subsidies on cotton production. These will also impinge heavily on Bangladesh.

Free Movement of Natural Persons

It has been argued that liberalizing the movement of natural persons, even by a small relaxation of restrictions on labor mobility, would produce huge gains in terms of efficiency and poverty reduction in the world (Winters and Walmsley 2002; Rodrik 2004). However, regarding the liberalization of the movement of natural persons, little progress has been made in the WTO Rounds. This chapter argues that free movement of natural persons may substantially raise remittances into the Bangladesh economy. Among the very few studies of the welfare and poverty impact of remittances for developing countries, Rizwana and Kemal (2002) find that remittances, together with domestic trade liberalization, play a major role in poverty reduction in Pakistan.

Unilateral Trade Liberalization

The standard arguments in favor of trade liberalization are that it expands the small domestic market, provides access to FDI, facilitates technology transfer, creates marketing networks, and provides much-needed managerial and technical skills. It is also argued that these changes lead to higher economic growth and reduced poverty. In Bangladesh, trade liberalization programs and associated economic reforms during the 1980s and 1990s significantly liberalized its external trade and foreign exchange regimes. Specific measures included simplified import procedures and dramatic reduction of the number of tariff bands. In 1992, the highest customs duty rate was 350 percent. It was reduced to 37.5 percent in 2000. The unweighted average tariff rate declined from 114 percent in 1989 to 22 percent in 1999, and the import-weighted average tariff rate declined to 19 percent from 114 percent over the same period. There has also been a significant reduction of the number of commodities under quantitative restrictions (QRs). In 1987, the number of commodities under the four-digit code subject to QRs was 550, which declined to 124 under the import policy of 1997–2002. In addition, there have also been moves toward a more market-determined exchange rate regime. Finally, different export promotion measures were put in place with the aim of diversifying exports, improving quality, encouraging higher value added, and developing industries through backward linkages. However, there is considerable debate over whether these measures are consistent with other trade liberalization measures undertaken in the economy.

Methodology

In this chapter, a general equilibrium framework is used to assess the effects of trade policies on trade, production, factor markets, and poverty in Bangladesh. A dynamic CGE model is built and calibrated with a SAM for the year 2000. The representative household approach is followed, and the 2000 Bangladeshi Household Income and Expenditure Survey (HIES) is used to estimate poverty effects of different trade policy shocks. The next sections briefly describe the model and the data used.

Model Features

Much current debate focuses on the role of growth in alleviating poverty. However, the majority of CGE models used in poverty and inequality analysis are static in nature. The inability of this kind of model to account for growth effects makes it inadequate for long-run analysis of the poverty impacts of economic policies. It excludes accumulation effects and does not allow the study of the transition path of the economy where short-run policy impacts are likely to be different from those of the long run. To overcome this limitation, this chapter uses a sequential, dynamic CGE model. This kind of dynamics is not the result of intertemporal optimization by economic agents. Instead, these agents have myopic behavior. It is basically a series of static CGE models that are linked between periods by updating procedures for exogenous and endogenous variables. Capital stock is updated endogenously with a capital accumulation equation, and population (and total labor supply) is updated exogenously between periods. It is also possible to add updating mechanisms for other variables, such as public expenditure, transfers, technological change, or debt accumulation. A brief description of the static and dynamic aspects of the model is presented below. A complete list of equations and variables is presented in the annex to the working paper version of this chapter (Annabi and others 2005).

Static Module

In each sector, there is a representative firm, which earns capital income, pays dividends to households and foreigners, and pays direct income taxes to the government. A nested structure is adopted for production. Sectoral output is a Leontief function of value added and total intermediate consumption. Value added is in turn represented by a constant elasticity of substitution (CES) function of capital and composite labor. The latter is also represented by a CES function of two labor categories: skilled labor and unskilled labor. Both labor categories are assumed to be fully mobile in the model. In the different production activities, it is assumed that a representative firm remunerates factors of production and pays dividends to households.

Households earn their income from production factors: skilled and unskilled labor and agricultural and nonagricultural capital. They also receive dividends, intrahousehold transfers, government transfers, and remittances, and pay direct income tax to the government. Household savings are a fixed proportion of total disposable income. Household demand is represented by the linear expenditure system (LES). The model includes nine household categories according to characteristics of the household head, as identified in the HIES. Five of these categories correspond to rural households, and four are reserved for urban households. Minimal consumption levels are calibrated using guess-estimates of the income elasticity and the underlying Frisch parameters.

It is assumed that foreign and domestic goods are imperfect substitutes. This geographic differentiation is introduced by the standard Armington assumption used throughout this book with a CES function between imports and domestic goods. On the supply side, producers make an optimal distribution of their production between exports and local sales according to a constant elasticity of transformation (CET) function. Furthermore, a finite elasticity of export demand that expresses the limited power of the local producers on the world market is assumed. To increase their exports, local producers will, other things being equal, have to decrease their free on board (FOB) prices.

The government receives direct tax revenue from households and firms and indirect tax revenue on domestic and imported goods. Its expenditure is allocated between the consumption of goods and services (including public wages) and transfers. The model accounts for indirect or direct tax compensation in the case of a tariff cut. Furthermore, general equilibrium is defined by the equality (in each period) between supply and demand of goods and factors and the investment-saving identity. The nominal exchange rate is the numeraire in each period.

Dynamic Module

In every period, capital stock is updated with a capital accumulation equation. It is assumed that the stocks are measured at the beginning of the period and that the flows are measured at the end of the period. An investment demand function is used to determine how new investments will be distributed among the different sectors. This can also be done through a capital distribution function.[2] Note that investment here is not by origin (product) but rather by sector of destination. The investment demand function used here is similar to those proposed by Bourguignon, Branson, and de Melo (1989) and Jung and Thorbecke (2003). The capital accumulation rate (ratio of investment to capital stock) is increasing with respect to the ratio of the rate of return to capital and its user cost. The latter is equal to the dual price of investment times the sum of the depreciation rate and the exogenous real interest rate. The elasticity of the accumulation rate with respect to the ratio of return to capital and its user cost is assumed to be equal to two. Introducing investment by destination respects the equality condition with total investment by origin in the SAM. Besides, investment by destination is used to calibrate the sectoral capital stock in base run.

Total labor supply is an endogenous variable, although it is assumed to simply increase at the exogenous population growth rate. Note that the minimal level of consumption in the LES function also increases (as do other nominal variables, such as transfers) at the same rate. The exogenous dynamic updating of the model includes nominal variables (which are indexed), government savings, and the current account balance. The equilibrium between total savings and total investment is reached by means of an adjustment variable introduced in the investment demand function. The government budget equilibrium is met by a neutral tax adjustment.

The model is formulated as a static model that is solved sequentially over a 20-period time horizon.[3] It is homogeneous in prices and calibrated in a way to generate steady-state paths. In the baseline, all the variables are increasing in level at the same rate, and the prices remain constant. The homogeneity test—a shock on the numeraire, the nominal exchange rate, with the steady-state characteristics—generates the same shock on prices, and on unchanged real values, along the counterfactual path. This method is used to facilitate welfare and poverty analysis because all prices remain constant along the business as usual (BaU) path.

The Bangladesh SAM for 1999–2000

In this study, the model is calibrated numerically to a 2000 SAM of Bangladesh. The main sources of information for the SAM are (a) the 1999–2000 input-output table prepared by the Sustainable Human Development Project, Planning Commission, Government of Bangladesh; (b) the Household Income and Expenditure Survey (HIES) 1999–2000 by the Bangladesh Bureau of Statistics (2000a); (c) the Labour Force Survey 1999–2000 by the Bangladesh Bureau of Statistics (2000b); and (d) the National Income Estimates by the Bangladesh Bureau of Statistics (2002).

This research draws on an aggregate version of the SAM of Bangladesh that includes 15 sectors and four factors of production: skilled and unskilled labor and agricultural and nonagricultural capital. An important feature of the SAM is the decomposition of households into nine groups based on location (urban or rural) and assets (land or education). In the case of rural households, there are five groups: landless (no cultivable land), marginal farmers (up to 0.49 acre of land), small farmers (0.5 to 2.49 acres of land), large farmers (2.50 acres of land and more), and nonagricultural. There are four groups for urban households: illiterate (no education), low education (grades one to nine), medium education (grades 10 to 12), and high education (high school graduate and above).

Table 15.1 summarizes the basic structure of the 2000 Bangladesh SAM. Import duty rates range from as low as 1 percent (ready-made garments) to as high as 55.2 percent (petroleum). The sectoral import penetration ratio (ratio of imports to domestic demand) is highest for ready-made garments (44 percent), followed by petroleum (43 percent), and the highest shares in total imports are for machinery (32.8 percent), followed by petroleum (12 percent). The sectoral export orientation ratio (exports as a share of output) is highest for ready-made garments (92 percent), followed by leather (31 percent), and ready-made garments exports account for 67 percent of total exports. Together, the service and construction sectors account for 60 percent of total value added in the economy. The contributions of the agriculture and manufacturing sectors in total value added are 17 percent and 23 percent, respectively. The highest shares of intermediate consumption in output are for rice-ata[4] milling (85 percent), followed by other food (81 percent). The share of intermediate consumption in total demand is highest for the cereal crop sector (113 percent).[5]

Table 15.2 presents household income composition based on the SAM. It shows that factor income represents the largest source of income for all household categories. Unskilled labor income and nonagricultural capital income each represent 35 percent of total household income, and skilled labor income and agricultural capital income come next, with shares in households' income of 16.06 percent and 10.32 percent, respectively. Unskilled labor is the primary source of income for, in declining order of importance, landless, illiterate, marginal farmer, nonagriculture, and small farmer households. Low-, medium-, and high-education households receive most of their income from nonagricultural capital, although the latter two categories also receive a significant share of skilled labor income, whereas low-education households are heavily dependent on unskilled labor income. Large farmers have agricultural capital income as their principal source of income. Given these substantial differences in income sources, it can be expected that trade liberalization will have very different income effects depending on how factor remunerations are affected.

The 1999–2000 HIES

To examine the link between the macro effects and micro effects in terms of poverty, the representative household approach is used. For the nine household categories, the results of the model at the aggregate level are subsequently linked to the HIES, assuming that each household has the same variation in its income (or consumption) as the group or category to which it belongs. The HIES includes

Table 15.1. Base-Run Statistics

Sector	Tariff rates	Import penetration ratio	Import share	Export orientation ratio	Export Share	Value added share	Share of value added in production	Share of international demand in absorption	Export demand elasticity
Cereal crop	17.9	2.1	1.3	0.0	0.0	6.5	48.4	112.8	6.0
Commercial crop	7.1	15.4	8.5	3.5	2.7	5.0	45.0	50.0	4.9
Livestock and poultry	23.9	3.8	2.1	4.9	4.3	3.6	28.7	50.1	6.8
Forestry	22.5	0.1	0.0	0.0	0.0	1.5	52.5	63.9	6.7
Rice-ata milling	3.6	1.8	1.8	0.0	0.0	3.2	15.0	8.1	5.2
Other food	12.7	19.7	11.9	1.3	1.0	2.2	19.0	17.9	4.3
Leather	20.2	0.6	0.1	30.9	6.7	0.6	22.0	44.2	8.1
Textiles	10.6	8.1	3.4	5.5	3.5	2.8	29.8	54.6	7.5
Ready-made garments	1.0	44.1	2.9	91.9	67.0	3.4	32.8	4.8	7.4
Chemicals and fertilizer	20.8	29.4	9.9	4.2	1.6	1.7	28.4	77.9	6.6
Machinery	16.8	38.7	32.8	0.1	0.1	4.8	37.9	55.3	7.8
Petroleum	55.2	42.9	12.0	1.3	0.3	0.7	6.6	64.9	10.1
Other industries	27.3	20.5	10.4	4.0	2.5	3.3	30.7	69.7	6.4
Construction	0.0	0.0	0.0	0.0	0.0	9.3	56.1	11.4	3.8
Services	10.3	0.7	2.4	1.9	9.8	50.7	67.5	65.9	3.8

Source: SAM 2000 for Bangladesh.

Note: The last column of the table presents the export demand elasticity based on the GTAP model. Half of its value is used for the CES and CET. The capital-labor substitution elasticity is assumed to be equal to 1.2, and the skilled-unskilled labor substitution elasticity is assumed to be equal to 0.8. The capital stock depreciation rate is equal to 5 percent.

Table 15.2. Household Income Composition

Household type	Skilled labor	Unskilled labor	Nonagricultural capital	Agricultural capital	Dividends	Intra-household transfers	Public transfers	Remittances
Landless	3.19	90.63	0.00	0.00	n.a.	5.30	0.37	0.51
Marginal farmers	4.73	59.16	24.80	2.01	n.a.	8.38	0.35	0.57
Small farmers	17.07	37.67	24.57	15.67	n.a.	4.26	0.10	0.66
Large farmers	9.88	5.28	34.43	49.74	n.a.	0.41	0.01	0.24
Nonagriculture	23.01	40.45	27.79	4.79	n.a.	2.96	0.38	0.61
Illiterate	1.69	67.41	28.79	0.00	n.a.	1.66	0.05	0.40
Low education	7.31	41.07	41.27	6.69	n.a.	2.94	0.26	0.45
Medium education	30.82	1.20	58.75	7.88	0.06	0.37	0.74	0.18
High education	20.08	0.26	59.72	14.95	0.20	1.14	3.43	0.21
All	16.06	35.08	35.00	10.32	0.02	2.52	0.53	0.43

Source: SAM 2000 for Bangladesh.

Note: n.a. = not applicable (to this household type).

7,439 households, of which almost 80 percent live in rural areas. The base-run poverty profile is presented in the next section.

Simulation Design and Analysis

In this section, different simulations are performed, the macro and sectoral effects are discussed, and their implications for welfare and poverty in Bangladesh are analyzed. Note first that the presimulation, which adjusts the 2001 baseline for liberalizations that have occurred or will occur independently of the Doha Round (the abolition of ATC quotas, the admission of China into the WTO, and the expansion of the EU), shows negative impacts for the overall macroeconomy, household welfare, and poverty in Bangladesh. At the sectoral level, the export-oriented sectors, especially the ready-made garments sector, shrink. In both rural and urban areas, it is the poorest household categories that bear most of the burden of these negative shocks. Further experiments combining the ATC quota removal with domestic tariff cuts show that losses at the sectoral and household levels are reduced by the latter liberalization.

However, because the aim of this study is to isolate the effects of the Doha agreements, these elements are embedded in the BaU scenario (from the beginning of 2005) as well as in the rest of the scenarios described in this chapter. The following simulations are implemented from 2005 and onward:

- *Doha*—ROW reductions in tariffs, subsidies, and domestic support, with no domestic tariff cuts; special and differential treatment (SDT [see box 1.1])
- *Full-Lib-ROW*—ROW full trade liberalization with no domestic tariff cuts
- *Full-Lib-Own*—full domestic trade liberalization with no ROW trade liberalization
- *Full-Lib*—ROW and full domestic trade liberalization
- *Remit*—increase in remittances

Before discussion of the results, it is important to note that in static CGE models, counterfactual analysis is made with respect to the base run that is represented by the initial SAM. However, in dynamic models, the economy grows even in the absence of a shock, and the analysis should be done with respect to this growth path. Also, because this model is dynamic, it takes into account not only efficiency effects, present in static models, but also accumulation effects. The latter are linked to the ratio of capital rates of return to the cost of investment goods. Special attention is paid to these elements in the simulation analysis.

The results of all the simulations are described in tables 15.3–15.7: Table 15.3 presents macroeconomic effects; 15.4 and 15.5, the sectoral results for three key runs; 15.6, the income consequences; and 15.7, the poverty consequences for all five simulations.

The Doha Scenario

Overview of Shocks

As described in chapter 2, the Doha simulation involves the removal of all export subsidies, plus cuts in domestic support and tariffs in ROW. This scenario provides SDT for least developed countries (LDCs) such as Bangladesh, which are not required to cut tariffs at all. This simulation is performed by introducing the changes in world export prices, world import prices, and world demand for Bangladeshi exports as estimated from the Global Trade Analysis Project (GTAP) world model. Doha generally leads to increases in world prices for Bangladeshi imports and exports, as well as an increase in world demand for these exports.[6] These increases are particularly strong in the agricultural, food processing, and textile and garments sectors.

Macro Effects

At the aggregate level, real GDP is hardly affected in either the short or the long run (see table 15.3).[7] The results indicate a small decrease in aggregate welfare measured by equivalent variation (see figure 15.1) and a short-run increase in the poverty headcount, although these effects diminish in the long run. In addition, a decline in the domestic TOT (the ratio of export to import prices on the domestic market) is observed in both the short run and, to a lesser degree, the long run as world import prices increase more than world export prices for Bangladesh. The increases in world prices and demand lead to higher factor returns, particularly for agricultural capital and unskilled workers. Also note that the consumer price index (CPI) increases more in rural areas than in urban areas. Consumer prices—and thus the poverty line—increasing faster than wage rates is consistent with the decline in domestic TOT, the drop in welfare, and the rise in poverty. In sum, the aggregate results suggest that the Doha scenario is accompanied by small negative impacts that are likely to be dissipated in the long run.[8]

Sectoral Effects

Simulations run with the GTAP world model show that the Doha scenario implies strong relative increases in the world prices and demand for agricultural goods, particularly for the commercial crop, livestock and poultry, and the textile and ready-made garment sectors (see tables 15.4 and 15.5). Faced with rising import prices, import volumes decline in all agricultural sectors except forestry, for which

Table 15.3. Macro Results (percentage change from BaU path)

Variable	Doha		Full-Lib-ROW		Full-Lib-Own		Full-Lib		Remit	
	2005	2020	2005	2020	2005	2020	2005	2020	2005	2020
Real GDP	0.00	0.02	0.00	0.05	-0.19	1.39	-0.19	1.44	0.10	0.42
Welfare[a]	-0.06	-0.03	-0.16	-0.07	-0.39	0.89	-0.55	0.82	0.38	0.63
Headcount ratio	0.03	0.00	0.20	0.37	0.78	-4.81	1.07	-4.55	-0.79	-3.80
Domestic TOT[b]	-4.41	-3.70	-4.62	-3.88	11.29	9.45	10.77	8.95	-4.08	-3.33
Imports	-0.38	-0.33	-0.74	-0.88	12.05	26.61	11.40	25.62	1.45	1.50
Exports	-0.12	-0.00	-0.28	-0.51	19.18	43.29	18.91	42.48	-1.46	-1.51
Urban CPI	0.56	0.51	1.10	0.83	-9.61	-7.20	-8.61	-6.45	0.43	0.33
Rural CPI	0.61	0.53	1.21	0.88	-9.21	-6.96	-8.10	-6.16	0.42	0.31
Skilled wage rate	0.40	0.42	0.72	0.65	-11.06	-6.83	-10.43	-6.26	0.89	1.20
Unskilled wage rate	0.53	0.51	1.03	0.83	-9.33	-5.06	-8.39	-4.29	0.80	1.07
Agricultural capital rental rate	1.34	0.45	3.38	0.70	-9.08	-9.43	-5.84	-8.83	0.27	-0.33
Nonagricultural capital rental rate	0.30	0.44	0.38	0.67	-10.16	-9.51	-9.84	-8.93	0.23	-0.31
User cost of capital	0.34	0.38	0.53	0.51	-9.90	-7.71	-9.43	-7.28	0.44	0.21

Source: Authors' calculations, based on simulation results.

a. Welfare is measured as the sum of individual household equivalent variations.

b. Domestic TOT are represented by the ratio of the domestic export and import price indexes.

Figure 15.1.   Aggregate Welfare Effects

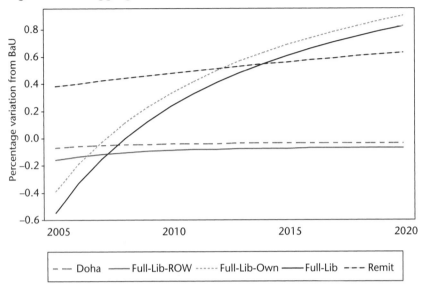

Source: Authors' simulations.

the increase in import prices is smallest. This leads to an increase in domestic demand for agricultural goods (except forestry) in both the short and long run. In the industrial sectors, import volumes tend to expand as import prices stagnate, leading to a decrease in local demand for competing domestic output. In both the short and long runs, rising world export prices and demand lead to export growth in the commercial crop and ready-made garment sectors and a contraction of exports in all other sectors, especially food and leather. As consumers substitute demand toward domestic goods and producers reorient production toward exports, prices on the domestic market increase, especially in the commercial crop sector (table 15.4).

As mentioned, the efficiency (reallocation) and long-run accumulation effects together determine the impacts on production and factor reallocation. As a result of rising export and domestic prices, output prices increase in all sectors in both the short and long run, with the short-run exception of leather (table 15.4). In the short run, value added prices increase most strongly for agricultural and light manufacturing (food processing and textile and garments) sectors, which are precisely the sectors with the largest increases in import prices, export prices, export demand, or all three as a result of the Doha agreement. These variations in value added prices influence the capital rental rate and labor wage rates and lead to a

Table 15.4. Sectoral Trade and Price Effects and Export Demand Shocks (percentage change from BaU path)

Variable	Year	CROP	COMC	LIVS	FORS	RATM	FOOD	LEAT	TEXT	GARM	CHEM	MACH	PETR	OIND	CNST	SERV
Doha scenario																
Import price[a]	2005	1.31	2.96	2.77	0.31	1.07	1.40	-0.17	0.59	0.10	0.08	0.07	0.09	0.17		0.04
World export demand[a]	2005	—	6.5	0.92	—	—	-4.04	-5.16	0.27	1.66	-0.77	-0.71	0.27	0.54		0.06
World export price[a]	2005	—	0.73	0.14	—	—	0.23	0.13	0.42	0.38	0.00	-0.01	0.04	-0.03		-0.03
FOB export price	2005	—	1.62	0.40	—	—	-0.24	-0.28	0.51	0.57	0.04	0.03	0.14	0.18		0.14
	2020	—	1.36	0.32	—	—	-0.33	0.01	0.47	0.51	0.10	0.11	0.23	0.22		0.15
Producer price	2005	0.52	1.11	0.71	0.40	0.48	0.78	-0.03	0.62	0.56	0.30	0.23	0.22	0.36	0.40	0.42
	2020	0.45	0.50	0.49	0.43	0.46	0.57	0.55	0.53	0.49	0.44	0.40	0.42	0.46	0.42	0.44
Value added price	2005	0.59	1.72	1.04	0.45	0.46	0.76	-1.45	0.43	0.74	0.03	0.10	-0.35	0.16	0.48	0.44
	2020	0.47	0.48	0.46	0.45	0.47	0.47	0.37	0.49	0.54	0.44	0.43	0.43	0.46	0.46	0.46
Rate of return to capital	2005	0.65	2.67	1.27	0.43	0.42	0.94	-2.54	0.38	0.95	-0.26	-0.15	-0.74	-0.08	0.45	0.39
	2020	0.45	0.47	0.44	0.44	0.45	0.45	0.31	0.49	0.58	0.44	0.40	0.42	0.44	0.44	0.44

Table 15.4. *(Continued)*

Variable	Year	CROP	COMC	LIVS	FORS	RATM	FOOD	LEAT	TEXT	GARM	CHEM	MACH	PETR	OIND	CNST	SERV
Full-Lib-ROW scenario																
Import price[a]	2005	2.78	7.84	4.20	1.37	4.54	2.89	-1.23	0.49	-0.09	-0.55	-0.34	0.35	0.22	—	0.61
World export demand[a]	2005	—	43.91	5.06	—	—	-8.94	-13.48	-1.57	0.79	1.88	0.45	1.63	15.78	—	2.16
World export price[a]	2005	—	2.03	0.43	—	—	0.36	0.20	0.74	0.58	-0.29	-0.26	0.08	-0.21	—	-0.22
FOB export price	2005	—	7.11	1.20	—	—	-0.70	-1.00	0.74	0.73	0.18	-0.03	0.35	1.68	—	0.50
	2020	—	6.25	0.97	—	—	-0.98	-0.36	0.68	0.74	0.32	0.17	0.41	1.66	—	0.47
Producer price	2005	0.99	2.77	1.36	0.75	0.93	1.59	-0.36	1.03	0.71	0.32	0.18	0.49	0.75	0.73	0.76
	2020	0.67	0.80	0.78	0.64	0.70	0.95	0.92	0.87	0.72	0.68	0.58	0.64	0.73	0.63	0.69
Value added price	2005	1.29	4.72	1.94	0.95	1.01	1.43	-3.71	0.10	0.48	-0.57	-0.24	-0.14	0.47	0.96	0.82
	2020	0.74	0.78	0.72	0.70	0.73	0.74	0.55	0.74	0.75	0.70	0.68	0.70	0.73	0.72	0.73
Rate of return to capital	2005	1.49	7.67	2.35	0.96	1.02	1.74	-6.26	-0.54	0.00	-1.51	-0.97	-0.61	0.12	0.94	0.70
	2020	0.68	0.74	0.68	0.68	0.68	0.70	0.44	0.70	0.69	0.69	0.60	0.70	0.69	0.67	0.68

Table 15.4. *(Continued)*

Variable	Year	CROP	COMC	LIVS	FORS	RATM	FOOD	LEAT	TEXT	GARM	CHEM	MACH	PETR	OIND	CNST	SERV
Full-Lib-Own scenario																
Import price[a]	2005	-15.24	-6.66	-19.33	18.37	-3.50	-11.31	-16.82	-9.64	-1.00	17.25	-14.42	-35.59	-21.45	—	-9.38
World export demand[a]	2005	0.00	0.00	0.00	—	—	0.00	0.00	0.00	0.00	0.00	0.00	0.00	0.00	—	0.00
World export price[a]	2005	—	0.00	0.00	—	—	0.00	0.00	0.00	0.00	0.00	0.00	0.00	0.00	—	0.00
FOB export price	2005	—	-3.25	-3.32	—	—	-3.21	-2.22	-2.59	-2.23	-3.96	-4.11	-5.57	-4.04	—	-3.71
	2020	—	-3.04	-2.56	—	—	-2.28	-4.07	-3.55	-5.91	-1.88	-2.07	2.02	-1.77	—	-2.74
Producer price	2005	-10.67	-8.73	-9.67	-10.70	-9.83	-9.66	-4.74	-6.39	-2.47	-12.39	-12.44	-22.53	-13.05	-10.52	-10.96
	2020	-7.84	-7.48	-7.36	-8.28	-7.06	-7.09	-7.74	-6.51	-6.43	-7.83	-8.38	-10.77	-7.82	-8.40	-7.77
Value added price	2005	-10.39	-7.04	-9.84	-10.33	-9.94	-11.41	6.57	-2.28	13.14	-16.25	-14.56	-64.68	-17.60	-9.08	-10.41
	2020	-7.62	-7.52	-8.26	-8.43	-7.78	-7.87	-8.15	-6.68	-4.78	-8.49	-8.84	-21.07	-8.09	-7.85	-7.20
Rate of return to capital	2005	-11.07	-5.12	-10.02	-10.50	10.16	-12.63	17.13	3.44	37.72	-20.03	-17.44	-79.40	-22.73	-8.71	-10.98
	2020	-9.37	-9.30	-9.60	-9.61	-9.39	-9.59	-9.46	-7.63	-4.38	-10.03	-10.92	-27.78	-9.92	-9.55	-9.37

Source: Authors' calculations.

Note: — = not available. CROP cereal crop; COMC commercial crop; LIVS livestock and poultry; FORS forestry; RATM rice-ata milling; FOOD other food; LEAT leather; TEXT textiles; GARM ready-made garments; CHEM chemicals and fertilizer; MACH machinery; PETR petroleum; OIND other industries; CNST construction; SERV services.

a. Results obtained from GTAP world model simulations.

Table 15.5. Sectoral Volume Effects (percentage change from BaU path)

Variable	Year	CROP	COMC	LIVS	FORS	RATM	FOOD	LEAT	TEXT	GARM	CHEM	MACH	PETR	OIND	CNST	SERV
Doha scenario																
Imports	2005	-2.29	-3.83	-6.39	0.29	-1.53	-1.15	0.71	0.09	0.58	0.57	0.44	0.38	0.47	—	0.70
	2020	-2.43	-4.98	-7.04	0.37	-1.56	-1.46	3.18	-0.05	0.37	0.97	0.78	1.01	0.75	—	0.75
Exports	2005	—	2.02	-0.85	—	—	-2.07	-1.93	-0.43	0.23	-1.06	-0.99	-0.74	-0.77	—	-0.58
	2020	—	3.30	-0.30	—	—	-1.68	-4.21	-0.11	0.68	-1.45	-1.63	-1.64	-1.04	—	-0.60
Production	2005	0.04	0.74	0.18	-0.01	-0.03	0.14	-0.88	-0.04	0.16	-0.23	-0.20	-0.31	-0.19	-0.02	-0.04
	2020	0.10	1.12	0.27	-0.03	0.01	0.28	-2.06	0.13	0.59	-0.34	-0.51	-0.69	-0.26	-0.04	-0.04
Capital stock	2005	0.03	0.31	0.12	0.00	0.00	0.07	-0.45	-0.01	0.05	-0.10	-0.08	-0.19	-0.07	0.00	-0.01
	2020	0.12	1.14	0.28	-0.02	0.03	0.30	-2.02	0.14	0.56	-0.33	-0.48	-0.68	-0.24	-0.03	-0.03
Skilled labor	2005	0.24	1.85	0.74	0.06	0.06	0.47	-2.32	0.02	0.48	-0.51	-0.39	-0.90	-0.34	0.08	0.02
	2020	0.17	1.21	0.33	0.03	0.08	0.35	-2.08	0.22	0.72	-0.31	-0.47	-0.67	-0.20	0.02	0.01
Unskilled labor	2005	0.09	1.69	0.59	-0.10	-0.09	0.32	-2.47	-0.13	0.33	-0.66	-0.54	-1.05	-0.49	-0.07	-0.13
	2020	0.07	1.10	0.23	-0.08	-0.02	0.25	-2.18	0.11	0.61	-0.41	-0.57	-0.78	-0.30	-0.08	-0.09

Table 15.5. *(Continued)*

Variable	Year	CROP	COMC	LIVS	FORS	RATM	FOOD	LEAT	TEXT	GARM	CHEM	MACH	PETR	OIND	CNST	SERV
Full-Lib-ROW scenario																
Imports	2005	-4.98	-10.13	-8.63	-2.04	-8.72	-2.37	3.96	1.64	1.25	2.16	1.45	0.34	1.15	—	0.21
	2020	-5.71	-13.65	-10.25	-2.39	-9.16	-3.35	9.71	1.10	1.31	3.18	2.24	0.88	1.13	—	0.10
Exports	2005	—	13.39	-0.22	—	—	-4.67	-4.65	-1.57	-0.31	-1.22	-1.37	-1.08	2.70	—	-0.59
	2020	—	17.99	1.27	—	—	-3.52	-9.45	-1.11	-0.39	-2.15	-2.88	-1.74	2.78	—	-0.47
Production	2005	0.17	2.25	0.32	0.01	0.01	0.25	-2.13	-0.51	-0.38	-0.76	-0.58	-0.37	-0.27	-0.01	-0.10
	2020	0.34	3.43	0.60	0.06	0.13	0.67	-4.60	-0.40	-0.45	-1.01	-1.35	-0.62	-0.22	-0.02	-0.06
Capital stock	2005	0.09	0.98	0.21	0.02	0.03	0.13	-1.04	-0.17	-0.08	-0.34	-0.26	-0.22	-0.10	0.02	-0.01
	2020	0.38	3.46	0.64	0.08	0.17	0.70	-4.51	-0.37	-0.41	-1.00	-1.29	-0.62	-0.18	0.02	-0.02
Skilled labor	2005	0.72	5.60	1.40	0.26	0.34	0.91	-5.52	-0.90	-0.47	-1.74	-1.24	-1.03	-0.38	0.27	0.05
	2020	0.48	3.61	0.73	0.15	0.26	0.80	-4.64	-0.27	-0.31	-0.95	-1.26	-0.56	-0.09	0.10	0.04
Unskilled labor	2005	0.36	5.22	1.04	-0.10	-0.02	0.55	-5.86	-1.26	-0.83	-2.09	-1.60	-1.39	-0.74	-0.09	-0.31
	2020	0.26	3.38	0.51	-0.07	0.04	0.58	-4.84	-0.49	-0.53	-1.16	-1.48	-0.78	-0.31	-0.12	-0.18

Table 15.5. *(Continued)*

Variable	Year	CROP	COMC	LIVS	FORS	RATM	FOOD	LEAT	TEXT	GARM	CHEM	MACH	PETR	OIND	CNST	SERV
Full-Lib-Own scenario																
Imports	2005	16.37	-5.12	42.61	35.48	-16.34	2.48	67.91	17.52	-9.36	12.43	6.31	58.03	27.07	—	-4.45
	2020	29.44	0.13	57.55	49.06	-8.18	9.03	50.28	30.69	-20.47	28.70	18.35	110.95	49.45	—	3.39
Exports	2005	—	17.60	25.78	—	—	15.08	19.99	21.76	18.13	30.53	38.68	78.34	30.20	—	15.45
	2020	—	16.30	19.32	—	—	10.40	40.04	31.14	56.93	13.37	17.69	-18.32	12.10	—	11.13
Production	2005	-0.61	1.65	-0.16	-0.15	-0.20	-1.11	7.85	4.66	17.04	-3.63	-2.71	-35.02	-5.01	0.33	-0.51
	2020	0.69	3.43	0.48	0.29	1.23	-1.21	19.38	16.48	53.77	-7.77	-9.25	-58.76	-8.53	1.27	0.46
Capital stock	2005	0.17	1.17	0.35	0.27	0.31	-0.07	6.02	2.45	7.51	-1.27	-0.86	-7.59	-1.62	0.55	0.19
	2020	2.24	5.05	1.66	1.34	2.66	0.29	20.77	17.44	53.24	-6.51	-7.55	-55.71	-7.05	2.79	2.38
Skilled labor	2005	0.71	6.06	1.67	1.01	1.47	-0.78	25.20	13.57	42.87	-7.90	-5.14	-68.90	-10.08	2.77	0.53
	2020	0.71	3.53	-0.05	-0.60	1.04	-1.49	18.54	17.36	57.52	-8.84	-10.23	-63.81	-8.97	1.02	0.58
Unskilled labor	2005	-1.60	3.64	-0.65	-1.30	-0.85	-3.05	22.33	10.97	39.60	-10.00	-7.31	-69.61	-12.13	0.42	-1.77
	2020	-1.54	1.22	-2.29	-2.82	-1.22	-3.69	15.89	14.74	54.00	-10.88	-12.24	-64.62	-11.00	-1.24	-1.66

Source: Authors' calculations.

Note: — = not available. CROP cereal crop; COMC commercial crop; LIVS livestock and poultry; FORS forestry; RATM rice-ata milling; FOOD other food; LEAT leather; TEXT textiles; GARM ready-made garments; CHEM chemicals and fertilizer; MACH machinery; PETR petroleum; OIND other industries; CNST construction; SERV services.

reallocation of resources, such that output expands in these sectors and contracts in heavy manufacturing sectors such as leather, petroleum, chemical products, machinery, and other industries (table 15.6), for which the Doha shocks to world prices and demand are relatively weaker.

To understand the impacts on factor remunerations, it is important to recall that labor is mobile across sectors in both the short run and long run, whereas capital is mobile only after the first year and through new investments. Therefore, much stronger short-term variations are seen in the returns to capital.[9] In the case of the *Doha* simulation, agricultural capital is the clear "winner," given the expansion of agricultural output, but the relative returns to nonagricultural capital decline (table 15.3). Because the expanding sectors are relatively more intensive in unskilled labor, unskilled wage rates increase more than skilled wage rates.

In the long run, resource allocation effects are similar, although the output effects, driven increasingly by the reallocation of capital investments rather than labor mobility, are much stronger (table 15.6). Initial increases in capital rental rates in the expanding sectors lead to a long-term reallocation of investment from the industrial sector to the agriculture sector. As a result, the long-term impacts on the returns to agricultural and nonagricultural capital are nearly equal.

In summary, through increases in export prices and demand and import prices, the *Doha* scenario benefits unskilled labor–intensive agriculture (particularly commercial crops) and light manufacturing (other food processing and textiles and ready-made garments). However, almost all other manufacturing and services sectors shrink, especially the leather sector. This leads to a particularly strong short-term increase in the returns to agricultural capital and, once investment responds, to long-term increases in unskilled wage rates.

Welfare Effects

To explore the welfare impacts of Doha as measured by equivalent variation (EV), the effects on household nominal incomes and the CPI are examined (see table 15.6). Nearly 80 percent of Bangladesh's population is rural, primarily composed of nonagricultural, small farmer, and landless households (see the first row of table 15.7). Factor remunerations represent the largest majority of household income in Bangladesh, and because the rates of remuneration of all factors increase (table 15.3), nominal income increases for all household groups. The accumulation of agricultural capital, which is owned primarily by small and, of course, large farmers, explains why these two household categories register the greatest increase in income. Landless households also emerge as relative winners, given the large share of their income that is derived from unskilled wages. In contrast, households with medium-educated heads are revealed to be the comparative losers in nominal income terms as a result of their reliance on nonagricul-

Table 15.6. Income and Welfare Effects (percentage change from BaU path)

Variable	Year	Rural households					Urban households			
		Landless	Marginal farmer	Small farmer	Large farmer	Nonagricultural	Illiterate	Low education	Medium education	High education
Doha scenario										
Income	2005	0.52	0.48	0.58	0.84	0.47	0.46	0.48	0.42	0.49
	2020	0.50	0.47	0.51	0.64	0.46	0.46	0.47	0.43	0.46
CPI	2005	0.62	0.62	0.61	0.60	0.60	0.59	0.57	0.54	0.52
	2020	0.54	0.54	0.53	0.53	0.53	0.52	0.51	0.50	0.49
Welfare (EV)	2005	−0.10	−0.14	−0.03	0.15	−0.11	−0.12	−0.08	−0.09	−0.01
	2020	−0.04	−0.06	−0.02	0.07	−0.06	−0.06	−0.04	−0.06	−0.01
Full-Lib-ROW scenario										
Income	2005	1.01	0.89	1.18	1.94	0.88	0.83	0.89	0.74	0.93
	2020	0.81	0.74	0.88	1.25	0.73	0.71	0.73	0.64	0.74
CPI	2005	1.25	1.24	1.23	1.19	1.19	1.17	1.11	1.04	1.01
	2020	0.90	0.89	0.89	0.87	0.87	0.86	0.84	0.81	0.79
Welfare (EV)	2005	−0.24	−0.34	−0.04	0.46	−0.28	−0.32	−0.20	−0.24	−0.03
	2020	−0.08	−0.15	−0.01	0.23	−0.13	−0.14	−0.10	−0.13	−0.02
Full-Lib-Own scenario										
Income	2005	−9.38	−9.62	−9.76	−9.64	−9.91	−9.57	−9.76	−10.32	−10.15
	2020	−5.23	−5.77	−6.13	−6.72	−6.06	−5.58	−6.04	−6.73	−6.77
CPI	2005	−9.16	−9.11	−9.12	−9.10	−9.30	−9.49	−9.58	−9.69	−9.88
	2020	−6.92	−6.87	−6.88	−6.86	−7.02	−7.13	−7.19	−7.24	−7.34
Welfare (EV)	2005	−0.22	−0.52	−0.59	−0.32	−0.59	−0.07	−0.17	−0.53	−0.11
	2020	1.83	1.15	0.71	0.13	0.98	1.60	1.13	0.46	0.26

Table 15.6. *(Continued)*

| Variable | Year | Rural households | | | | | Urban households | | | |
		Landless	Marginal farmer	Small farmer	Large farmer	Nonagri-cultural	Illiterate	Low education	Medium education	High education
Full-Lib scenario										
Income	2005	−8.45	−8.81	−8.67	−7.80	−9.11	−8.82	−8.95	−9.66	−9.30
	2020	−4.48	−5.10	−5.32	−5.54	−5.40	−4.93	−5.38	−6.16	−6.11
CPI	2005	−8.01	−7.96	−7.99	−8.00	−8.21	−8.42	−8.56	−8.74	−8.96
	2020	−6.11	−6.05	−6.07	−6.07	−6.23	−6.35	−6.43	−6.51	−6.63
Welfare (EV)	2005	−0.46	−0.87	−0.62	0.18	−0.88	−0.40	−0.37	−0.78	−0.14
	2020	1.75	1.00	0.71	0.37	0.85	1.46	1.03	0.32	0.23
Remit scenario										
Income	2005	0.95	0.94	0.99	0.77	0.96	0.86	0.86	0.70	0.71
	2020	1.20	1.14	1.17	0.86	1.17	1.08	1.04	0.86	0.84
CPI	2005	0.41	0.41	0.42	0.42	0.42	0.42	0.43	0.44	0.44
	2020	0.30	0.30	0.30	0.31	0.31	0.32	0.33	0.34	0.35
Welfare (EV)	2005	0.54	0.51	0.50	0.21	0.50	0.41	0.39	0.20	0.10
	2020	0.90	0.81	0.75	0.33	0.79	0.72	0.64	0.41	0.19

Source: Authors' calculations.

tural capital and skilled labor income. The long-run effects are somewhat smaller, especially for large farmer households, because investment in agricultural capital eats into their rents. Generally speaking, nominal income gains are greater for rural households.

Consumer prices increase more than nominal income for all but large farmer households, cutting real consumption. Consumer prices generally increase more for rural households under the *Doha* simulation, because they consume relatively more agricultural goods. This offsets the higher nominal income gains among rural households, such that real consumption and welfare vary in roughly the same proportion for urban and rural households, with the exception of large farmers. More importantly for poverty analysis, consumer prices tend to rise more for the poorer household groups as a result of their more intensive consumption of agricultural goods. Consequently, the reductions in real consumption and welfare are greatest for precisely the poorest household groups: landless and marginal farmers, nonagricultural rural households, and urban households where the head of household is illiterate (table 15.7). In the long run, real consumption and welfare changes are smaller with respect to the baseline scenario, although they follow the same pattern.[10]

Poverty Effects

FGT poverty indexes are used to evaluate the impacts of the simulation on the poverty profiles of the nine representative households (Foster, Greer, and Thorbecke 1984) (see table 15.7).[11] The variations in consumption for each household group from the dynamic model are applied to generate new consumption vectors for individual households from the Bangladeshi household survey.[12] Two different poverty lines for rural and urban households are used, which are endogenously determined by the model, taking into account the rural and urban CPIs. The first block of table 15.7 reports the base-case (year 2000) poverty profiles. It is evident that poverty is more acute in rural areas than in urban areas. Among rural households, poverty is most severe for the landless and marginal farmers. Among urban households, households with illiterate heads are the poorest. This table also presents the short-run (year 2005) and long-run (year 2020) poverty indexes measured along the BaU path. It suggests that accumulation effects captured by the model play a major role in alleviating poverty, because poverty falls dramatically in the long run. The large farmer category registers the greatest decrease in poverty, driven by their high agricultural capital income shares.

Changes in poverty indexes are determined by changes in the poverty line and changes in nominal consumption (or income). The poverty line represents the cost of a basic-needs basket of goods. If the change in poverty line is greater (smaller) than the change in nominal consumption, then poverty is likely to decrease (increase). Poverty effects are reported in the second block of table 15.7.

Table 15.7. BaU Poverty Levels and Poverty Effects

Scenario	Poverty index	Year	Rural households						Urban households				
			Landless	Marginal farmer	Small farmer	Large farmer	Nonagri-cultural	Total rural	Illiterate	Low education	Medium education	High education	Total urban
Proportion in 2000 survey			17.08	7.44	16.12	8.15	30.86	79.65	7.79	6.88	4.66	1.01	20.34
BaU simulation	P0	2000	73.6	64.2	47.9	23.0	45.5	51.5	70.7	30.5	7.7	0.0	39.1
		2005	69.3	55.3	41.8	18.2	41.1	46.3	65.5	26.6	6.0	0.0	35.5
		2020	39.8	28.6	15.8	6.0	19.0	22.4	38.7	11.3	1.4	0.0	19.0
	P1	2000	23.0	17.2	11.3	4.8	12.3	14.1	22.3	7.5	1.5	0.0	11.4
		2005	19.9	14.4	9.0	3.8	10.3	11.8	19.4	6.1	1.2	0.0	9.8
		2020	8.1	4.9	2.6	0.7	3.5	4.2	8.5	1.7	0.4	0.0	3.9
	P2	2000	9.2	6.3	3.7	1.4	4.5	5.2	9.3	2.5	0.5	0.0	4.5
		2005	7.5	5.0	2.9	1.0	3.6	4.2	7.7	1.9	0.4	0.0	3.7
		2020	2.5	1.3	0.7	0.1	1.0	1.2	2.8	0.4	0.1	0.0	1.3
Doha	P0	2005	0.00	0.31	0.09	-1.65	0.12	0.03	0.08	0.00	0.00	0.00	0.06
		2020	0.00	0.00	0.00	0.00	0.00	0.00	0.00	0.00	0.00	0.00	0.00
	P1	2005	0.21	0.36	0.11	-0.98	0.40	0.24	0.24	0.27	0.59	0.00	0.26
		2020	0.13	0.29	0.10	-0.93	0.30	0.18	0.16	0.24	0.23	0.00	0.18
	P2	2005	0.28	0.48	0.13	-1.40	0.50	0.31	0.30	0.35	0.59	0.00	0.32
		2020	0.15	0.33	0.10	-1.05	0.33	0.21	0.19	0.27	0.26	0.00	0.20

Table 15.7. *(continued)*

Scenario	Poverty index	Year	Rural households						Urban households				
			Landless	Marginal farmer	Small farmer	Large farmer	Nonagri-cultural	Total rural	Illiterate	Low education	Medium education	High education	Total urban
Proportion in 2000 survey			17.08	7.44	16.12	8.15	30.86	79.65	7.79	6.88	4.66	1.01	20.34
Full-Lib-ROW	P0	2005	0.30	0.61	0.09	-3.09	0.47	0.22	0.15	0.00	0.00	0.00	0.11
		2020	0.00	0.00	0.00	0.00	0.98	0.32	0.76	0.00	0.00	0.00	0.60
	P1	2005	0.49	0.91	0.11	-2.95	0.98	0.54	0.64	0.69	1.51	0.00	0.67
		2020	0.26	0.68	0.01	-3.22	0.65	0.35	0.42	0.56	0.54	0.00	0.44
	P2	2005	0.65	1.21	0.13	-4.23	1.23	0.71	0.81	0.90	1.52	0.00	0.84
		2020	0.30	0.77	0.01	-3.60	0.72	0.41	0.48	0.62	0.61	0.00	0.50
Full-Lib-Own	P0	2005	0.21	0.77	1.83	2.95	0.91	0.92	0.00	0.00	1.43	0.00	0.06
		2020	-6.30	-3.12	-3.88	0.00	-4.56	-4.83	-4.28	-6.75	0.00	0.00	-4.71
	P1	2005	0.43	1.25	2.17	1.74	2.31	1.47	-0.11	0.54	3.30	0.00	0.12
		2020	-7.02	-6.13	-4.45	-2.52	-4.30	-5.62	-6.06	-6.58	-1.51	0.00	-6.04
	P2	2005	0.57	1.67	2.59	2.46	2.90	1.80	-0.14	0.71	3.36	0.00	0.09

Table 15.7. (Continued)

Scenario	Poverty index	Year	Rural households						Urban households				
			Landless	Marginal farmer	Small farmer	Large farmer	Nonagri-cultural	Total rural	Illiterate	Low education	Medium education	High education	Total urban
Proportion in 2000 survey			17.08	7.44	16.12	8.15	30.86	79.65	7.79	6.88	4.66	1.01	20.34
Full-Lib	P0	2005	0.59	2.98	1.83	−1.65	1.30	1.24	0.15	0.26	1.43	0.00	0.23
		2020	−6.03	−2.65	−4.50	0.00	−3.99	−4.57	−4.10	−6.37	0.00	0.00	−4.49
	F1	2005	0.94	2.20	2.23	−1.57	3.33	2.01	0.56	1.26	4.89	0.00	0.82
		2020	−6.78	−5.45	−4.46	−5.98	−3.65	−5.29	−5.65	−6.04	−0.93	0.00	−5.61
	P2	2005	1.24	2.94	2.67	−2.25	4.18	2.53	0.70	1.64	5.00	0.00	0.97
		2020	−7.80	−6.02	−4.83	−6.59	−4.02	−6.00	−6.38	−6.87	−1.04	0.00	−6.30
Remit	P0	2005	−0.17	−0.76	−2.66	−1.65	−0.72	−0.94	−0.04	−0.04	0.00	0.00	−0.04
		2020	−4.18	−2.05	−3.88	0.00	−4.37	−3.83	−3.06	−6.37	0.00	0.00	−3.68
	P1	2005	−1.33	−1.49	−2.07	−1.38	−1.66	−1.58	−1.02	−1.44	−1.12	0.00	−1.11
		2020	−3.44	−4.00	−4.30	−4.64	−3.80	−3.75	−2.62	−3.74	−1.52	0.00	−2.76
	P2	2005	−1.74	−1.98	−2.46	−1.98	−2.06	−1.98	−1.28	−1.84	−1.11	0.00	−1.38
		2020	−3.97	−4.43	−4.66	−5.15	−4.18	−4.18	−2.97	−4.28	−1.70	0.00	−3.08

Source: HIES of 2000 and authors' calculations.

Note: P0 = poverty headcount ratio (percentage of poor); P1 = poverty gap (depth); P2 = squared poverty gap (severity). The BaU path takes into account the shocks of the ATC removal since 2005.

The results show that the average poverty headcount ratio increases by 0.03 percent in the short run, but it remains unchanged in the long run. The average poverty gap and squared poverty gap show an increase in the depth and severity of poverty in both the short and, to a slightly lesser extent, long run. In rural areas, poverty increases for all households except large farmers, who emerge as the winners from the *Doha* simulation. Regarding urban households, poverty increases for all but the households with highly educated heads. As mentioned, all poverty effects are similar, but smaller, in the long run. Generally speaking, it appears that the poorest household categories lose most from *Doha*, and large farmers are the biggest beneficiaries.

Conclusion

The *Doha* scenario is predicted to lead to increases in world demand for Bangladeshi agricultural and light manufacturing exports. As a result, the returns to and stock of agricultural capital increase proportionately more, along with unskilled wage rates. At the same time, rising import and export prices lead to increases in consumer prices, especially among rural and poor households, such that overall poverty increases. Indeed, poverty increases for all household categories except large farmers, for whom poverty declines through agricultural capital accumulation, and highly educated urban households, for whom initial poverty rates are nil. Landless farmers and illiterate urban households have relatively smaller poverty increases because of their reliance on unskilled wage income and the greater share of agricultural goods in their consumption. The biggest losers are marginal farmers and low- and medium-educated urban households, which are more dependent on skilled wages. There is no clear urban-rural difference in poverty effects, because rising agricultural prices simultaneously increase rural incomes and consumer price indexes.

ROW Free Trade

Overview of Shocks

When tariffs are eliminated in ROW (*Full-Lib-Row* simulation), world export and import prices, and world export demand, all increase strongly in the agricultural sectors (see table 15.4). World export demand also increases in the other industry sector, but declines for leather, food, and textiles. World prices for Bangladeshi imports also increase for the rice-milling and other food-processing sectors. Changes in all other sectors are minimal. Generally speaking, the shocks in world prices and demand are much greater than in the *Doha* simulations.

Macro Effects
The macro indicators suggest that the impacts of worldwide free trade are quite similar to those of the *Doha* scenarios, although much more pronounced (see table 15.3). In particular, welfare falls more and poverty increases more in both the short and long run, and domestic TOT, imports, and exports all decline more. Factor returns and consumer prices also increase more.

Sectoral Effects
At the sectoral level, increases in world prices and demand in the agricultural sector translate into an expansion of the Bangladeshi agriculture and food-processing sectors, similar to but stronger than in the *Doha* scenarios (see tables 15.4 and 15.5). The largest expansion, in terms of both output and exports, and the greatest reduction in imports are all observed in the commercial crop sector, where world prices and demand increase most. However, the greatest contraction is observed in the leather sector. As a result, short-term returns to agricultural capital increase strongly (3.38 percent), and capital investment is reoriented toward the agricultural sector, with a 14 percent increase in the commercial crop sector.

Welfare Effects
Regarding income and welfare effects, the patterns are quite similar, although generally much stronger (see table 15.6). Consumer price increases dominate nominal income increases. As a result, all households register greater welfare losses in both the short run and the long run, except large farmer households, which experience greater welfare gains, and small farmer households, for whom welfare losses are roughly equal to the *Doha* scenarios. Once again, these results are driven by agricultural capital accumulation in these two household categories. In relation to this, poverty generally increases more in this run than for the *Doha* simulation. The only exceptions are for small farmer households, where it increases by slightly less, and for large farmers, where it decreases more.

Conclusion
World free trade has similar, but stronger, effects than the Doha agreement. The agricultural and garment sectors expand, leading to higher returns to agricultural capital and unskilled labor and the accumulation of agricultural capital stock. Poverty increases as a result of increased consumer prices, although poverty declines among larger farmers and remains unchanged for small farmers, given their high agricultural capital endowments. Marginal farmers and low- and medium-educated urban households are the biggest losers as a consequence of their reliance on skilled wages and nonagricultural capital rents.

These losses from worldwide free trade may seem surprising at first, but they are easily comprehensible in terms of Bangladesh's heavy dependence on food and textile imports. The prices of both increase with worldwide free trade (see chapter 3), increasing both the cost of living and the price of inputs to Bangladesh's principal export industry.

Unilateral Trade Liberalization

Overview of Shocks

In this scenario, *Full-Lib-Own*, the focus is solely on the impact of domestic trade liberalization with world prices and demand held constant (see table 15.4). Note that the elimination of domestic tariffs leads to strong reductions in domestic import prices, particularly in the sectors with the highest initial tariff rates (see table 15.1): petroleum, other industry, livestock, forestry, chemicals and fertilizer, and leather. There is no clear agriculture-industry distinction in terms of initial tariff rates, because both sectors contain subsectors with high and low initial tariffs.

Macro Effects

The impacts on GDP and welfare illustrate the importance of analyzing trade liberalization in a dynamic framework; both measures decline in the short run and then strongly increase in the long run compared to the BaU simulation (see table 15.3 as well as figure 15.1). The short-run negative impact is explained by the fact that trade liberalization contracts the import-competing and highly protected sectors, and capital cannot be quickly reallocated to the expanding export-oriented sectors. Impacts are also much larger than under the previous scenarios. Positive growth is observed in the domestic TOT (the ratio of export to import prices on domestic markets) in both the short run and the long run, given the decline in domestic import prices. Imports and exports register strong positive growth, particularly in the long run. Reduced domestic import prices lead to a fall in consumer prices for both rural and, slightly more, for urban households. Skilled and unskilled wage rates decline, although less so in the long run when capital is reallocated toward the expanding sectors. The reduction in unskilled wage rates is somewhat smaller, given the expansion of unskilled labor–intensive textile and garment sectors. The user cost of capital also declines in both the short run and the long run.

Sectoral Effects

Tariff elimination leads to an immediate reduction in the domestic price of imports that is proportional to the initial sectoral tariff rates (see table 15.1). Domestic consumers respond by increasing import demand, once again in rough proportion to the fall in import prices, with the strongest increases in the leather, petroleum, livestock, other industry, and forestry sectors (see tables 15.4 and 15.5). The three sectors that had low initial tariff rates (commercial crops, rice-ata milling, and ready-made garments) register negative import growth in the short run as consumers substitute toward goods for which prices drop more dramatically. In the long run, import volumes grow more (or contract less) in all sectors except leather.

The current account balance is fixed in the short run and subsequently increases at a fixed rate. Thus, the increase in imports leads to a real devaluation and an increase in exports. The export response is generally smaller in the long run, with the dramatic exception of leather, textiles, and, especially, ready-made garments. In the long run, the ready-made garments sector flourishes, and its export volume increases by nearly 57 percent compared to the BaU scenario. With a negative sloping demand curve for exports, FOB export prices fall.

As consumers substitute toward cheaper imports and producers reorient production toward the export market, local sales of domestic goods contract in all but the commercial crop and textile and garment sectors—most dramatically in the petroleum and other industry sectors. In the long run, all the agricultural sectors have small positive growth in domestic sales, but this is true only for the textile and garments sector among the manufacturing sectors.

Output expands most in the three textile and garment sectors (ready-made garments, leather, and textiles). Export-intensive ready-made garments and leather benefit from export expansion, and all three sectors register input cost savings, as evidenced by the positive evolution in value added prices despite falling output prices. Greatly increased import competition for textiles is offset by increased input demand from the ready-made garments sector. In contrast, production contracts in the heavier manufacturing sectors for which export demand stagnates or declines. As a result, nonagricultural capital and labor migrate to the textile and garments sectors and away from the other manufacturing sectors, with relatively little movement in the agricultural sectors. In the long run, the nonagricultural capital stock response is much larger and tempers the reallocation of skilled and unskilled labor. There are also moderate capital stock increases in the agricultural and service sectors.

In the short run, nominal factor returns fall by roughly 10 percent as a result of declining domestic prices (see table 15.3). Overall investment falls in response to the average reduction in capital returns relative to the user cost of capital. This makes the long-term reduction in wage rates somewhat smaller, especially for unskilled wages. The average returns to capital fall slightly more in the nonagricultural sector, although these rates converge after long-term adjustment in sectoral investment rates (see table 15.5). Returns to capital fall relative to wage rates.

Welfare Effects

A fall in nominal income for all households is observed in both the short run and the long run (see table 15.6). This reduction is smallest among the poorest households—urban households with illiterate or low-educated heads and rural landless or marginal households—given their reliance on unskilled wages. Medium- and high-educated urban households, as well as nonagricultural rural households, are the biggest losers as a result of their high endowments in nonagricultural capital and skilled labor. In the short run, real consumption decreases for all households as nominal income falls more than consumer prices. However, the opposite is true in the long run. The figures of EVs are very much in line with real consumption growth, with the poorest household categories emerging as the biggest winners.

Poverty Effects

In the short run, poverty increases for all households, except those headed by highly educated heads, for which there is no change, and those headed by illiterate heads, for which poverty falls (see table 15.7). However, in the long run, poverty falls for all households, especially among the poorer households.

Conclusion

In conclusion, domestic liberalization leads to strong expansion of the agricultural and textile and garments sectors as a result of their lower initial tariffs (and thus smaller increases in import competition), substantial input cost savings, export growth, and, in the case of textiles, increased demand from the garments sector. As a result, unskilled wages fall less than skilled wages, and returns to agricultural capital fall relative to nonagricultural capital. In the short term, consumer prices fall less than nominal incomes, leading to welfare losses and poverty increases. However, when investment is reoriented toward the high-return sectors, nominal income losses become smaller than consumer price reductions, resulting in welfare gains and poverty reductions. The poorest rural and urban household categories emerge as the principal beneficiaries, whereas the wealthiest household categories benefit less. No clear urban-rural distinction is noted.

Full Liberalization of World and Domestic Trade

This simulation, *Full-Lib*, simply combines the shocks of the preceding two simulations involving simultaneous world and domestic free trade. At the macro level, the effects are quite similar to those under domestic liberalization. However, under the influence of simultaneous worldwide free trade, welfare and poverty effects are increased in the short run and the positive long-run gains are reduced. In addition, the positive impact on the domestic TOT, import, and exports are reduced. Furthermore, the reductions in both the urban and rural CPIs and in both the skilled and unskilled wage rates are less than those under domestic liberalization.

The sectoral effects also closely follow those of domestic liberalization. However, changes induced by worldwide free trade in import and export prices and export demand in favor of agricultural sectors do introduce some changes with respect to domestic liberalization alone. In particular, worldwide free trade accentuates the long-run expansion of agricultural sectors (particularly commercial crops), dampens the expansion of textile and garments sectors, and reinforces the contraction of the heavy industrial sectors.

The pattern of changes in welfare largely resembles those of the domestic liberalization scenario. However, short-term welfare losses tend to be greater and long-term welfare gains smaller, with the exception of large farmers, who experience welfare gains in the short and long terms. The similarity also carries over to the three poverty measures, although poverty increases more in the short run and less in the long run for most household categories. The principal exception is large farmers, who experience a reduction in poverty in the short run and larger poverty reductions in the long term.

Overall, this simulation illustrates the much more substantial and favorable impacts of domestic liberalization relative to worldwide free trade. Indeed, because worldwide free trade increases poverty for all but large farmers, it counteracts the positive effects of domestic liberalization, but only to a very limited degree. Large farmers emerge as the principal beneficiaries of global free trade. The difference between this result and the corresponding one for Cameroon (chapter 12) illustrates the importance of the country-specific approach of this book. It arises from the differences in production structure—Cameroon having large endowments of oil compared to Bangladesh's abundance of unskilled labor and lack of agricultural capacity.

Increase in Remittances

The *Remit* simulation takes a completely different view of trade liberalization and assumes increased international mobility of natural persons. A 50 percent increase in remittances is introduced (from 0.43 percent of GDP to 0.64 percent) and the current account balance is increased by the same amount. Based on data on the evolution of the number of workers abroad and remittances, the migration of workers required to support this increase in remittances is calculated. It amounts to only a small fraction of the total effective labor supply: a decrease in skilled and unskilled labor supply of 0.2 percent and 0.1 percent, respectively. It can be expected that these shocks will translate into an increase in imports and a decrease in exports. In addition, a higher level of transfers is likely to improve household welfare and contribute to poverty reduction.

The inflow of remittances increases real GDP and welfare while reducing poverty, especially in the long run. Remittances also provide additional foreign currency, which finances a small increase in imports and an equivalent reduction in exports. As a result, the domestic TOT effect is negative. The increase in domestic income raises domestic consumer prices, wage rates, and the user cost of capital. Although returns to capital increase in the short term, they fall in the long run.

Three main forces drive the sectoral effects. First, investment increases as a result of increased domestic consumer demand and resulting increases in returns to capital. This leads to an increase in construction and forestry output, because most forest products are sold as inputs to construction. Second, increased household income raises demand for the main household consumer goods: milled rice-ata, services, and food. Increased rice-ata milling output in turn increases demand for cereal crops. Finally, the reduction in exports falls primarily on the garment sector, which provides two-thirds of Bangladeshi exports. Because the construction sector employs 60 percent of workers and is very labor intensive, its expansion translates into a substantial increase in wage rates relative to capital returns.

Rural households, with the exception of large farmers, benefit most because of the higher share of remittances and wages in their total income (table 15.2). They are followed closely by the poorest urban households. In addition, CPIs increase slightly less for rural households because of their lower consumption of services, for which consumer prices increase strongly. As a result, welfare gains tend to be higher among rural households, with the exception of large farmers, who have a smaller share of remittance and wage income.

Poverty declines for all poverty measures and all household categories. However, it is the rural household categories that benefit most, because of the direct impact of remittance income and smaller increases in their CPIs.

Increased remittances directly raise household income and welfare while strongly reducing poverty. Rising domestic demand increases investment and, consequently, construction output, which raises wage rates relative to capital returns. Rural households benefit most, with the exception of large farmers, because they derive proportionately more income from remittances and wages and have smaller increases in their CPIs. More generally, an increase in remittances is shown to be a powerful tool to combat poverty, because poorer households are more dependent on this income source. It is probably too late for the Doha Round, but these results reinforce the view that liberalizing the mobility of labor should be a key objective for developing-country negotiators in future trade talks.

Conclusions

This study examines the impact of WTO agreements and unilateral trade policy reforms on production, welfare, and poverty in Bangladesh. The research applies a sequential, dynamic CGE model, which takes into account accumulation effects and allows long-run analysis.

The Doha agreement is found to have minor negative implications for the overall macroeconomy, household welfare, and poverty in Bangladesh, because the TOT deteriorate and consumer prices rise more than nominal incomes. Agricultural and light manufacturing sectors expand in response to rising world export prices and demand, increasing the relative returns to agricultural capital and unskilled labor. Nominal income consequently increases more for rural households, particularly landowners; consumer prices also increase more for rural households because of their high consumption of agricultural goods. More important, consumer prices increase more for the poorest household categories, for whom agricultural (food) consumption is proportionately higher. The net effect is greater welfare losses and poverty increases among the poorest households. The greatest beneficiaries of the Doha agreement appear to be rural large farmers who capitalize on rising returns to agricultural capital (primarily land). These results hold whether developing countries are provided SDT or not.

Global free trade's pattern of effects is almost identical to that of the Doha agreement, although the effects are much stronger. In particular, overall poverty increases by nearly 1 percent in the short term and 0.5 percent in the long term. Once again, large farmers are the big winners, and the poorest household categories emerge as the biggest losers. In contrast, domestic trade liberalization induces an expansion in agricultural and textile and garment sectors under the quadruple influence of low initial tariffs, input cost saving, export growth, and rising domestic demand. Unskilled wages rise relative to skilled wages, and the returns to agricultural capital increase relative to nonagricultural capital. Although the short-run welfare and poverty impacts are negative, once capital is able to adjust through investment in the long run, welfare increases and poverty declines. Contrary to the Doha agreement and global free trade scenarios, the poorest household categories are the biggest winners because of the increase in unskilled wage rates. Unilateral liberalization is found to far outweigh the effects of global free trade when these two scenarios are combined. Finally, an increase in remittances is shown to substantially reduce poverty, because poor households benefit proportionately more from this source of income.

Notes

1. The transitional WTO ATC replaced the Multifibre Arrangement in 1995.

2. Abbink, Braber, and Cohen (1995) use a sequential, dynamic CGE model for Indonesia in which total investment is distributed as a function of base year sectoral shares in total capital remuneration and sectoral profit rates.

3. The model is formulated as a system of nonlinear equations solved simultaneously as a constrained nonlinear system with GAMS/Conopt3 solver.

4 "Ata" is the coarse wheat flour.

5 This figure is greater than 100 because of the negative stock variation in this sector.

6. These price changes are reported relative to the numeraire of constant world factor prices (see chapter 3). In general equilibrium, only *relative* price changes matter; the "average" price level effects are absorbed by the exchange rate. The price changes used for Bangladesh also, of course, reflect the composition of Bangladesh's trade flows in terms of the 57 GTAP commodities used in chapter 3.

7. All results are interpreted with respect to the base-run simulation (BaU path).

8. Although real GDP remains unchanged in the short run, it increases slightly in the long run. The small positive impact in the long run is essentially due to capital accumulation. However, households are negatively affected because the increase in income is not sufficient to counterbalance the increase in prices in the Doha scenario. Thus, real consumption decreases and welfare change is negative.

9. Table 15.5 reports the results for this composite labor force factor. Therefore, although labor differentiated by skills is fully mobile across sectors and so earns a uniform wage, the labor composite is sector specific and reflects the composition of the labor force within each sector.

10. These results are consistent with Ravallion's analysis (1990) of rural Bangladesh, which showed how rice price rises translate only slowly into wage increases.

11. The FGT indexes allow comparison of three measures of poverty: headcount ratio; poverty gap index, and squared poverty gap index. To estimate these three indexes, a poverty line is first defined. The poverty line is the minimum income that is required to maintain a subsistence level of consumption. The first indicator, the headcount ratio, is the proportion of the population with a per capita income below the poverty line. This is the simplest measure of poverty. The second indicator, the poverty gap, measures the depth of poverty as the average distance separating the income of poor households from the poverty line. The final indicator, the squared poverty gap index, measures the severity of poverty, taking account of the inequality of income distribution among the poor.

12. Poverty analysis is performed with DAD (Distributive Analysis–Analyse Distributive) software, which is distributed at no charge at http://www.pep-net.org/.

References

Abbink, G. A., M. C. Braber, and S. I. Cohen. 1995. "A SAM-CGE Demonstration Model for Indonesia: Static and Dynamic Specifications and Experiments." *International Economic Journal* 9 (3): 15–33.

Annabi, N., B. Khondker, S. Raihan, J. Cockburn and B. Decaluwé. 2005. "Implications of WTO Agreements and Unilateral Trade Policy Reforms for Poverty in Bangladesh: Short- versus Long-Run Impacts." Forthcoming Policy Research Working Paper, World Bank, Washington, DC.

Bangladesh Bureau of Statistics. 2002. *Statistical Yearbook of Bangladesh 2002*. Dhaka: Ministry of Planning, Government of the People's Republic of Bangladesh.

———. 2000a. *Household Income and Expenditure Survey 1999–2000*. Dhaka: Ministry of Planning, Government of the People's Republic of Bangladesh.

———. 2000b. *Labour Force Survey 1999–2000*. Dhaka: Ministry of Planning, Government of the People's Republic of Bangladesh.

Beghin, J. C., D. Roland-Holst, and D. van der Mensbrugghe. 2002. "Global Agricultural Trade and the Doha Round: What Are the Stakes for North and South?" Paper presented at the OECD–World Bank Forum on Agricultural Trade Reform, Adjustment, and Poverty, Paris, May 23–24, and at the Fifth Conference on Global Economic Analysis, Taipei, June 5–7.

Bourguignon, F., W. H. Branson, and J. de Melo. 1989. "Macroeconomic Adjustment and Income Distribution: A Macro-Micro Simulation Model." OECD Technical Paper 1. Paris.

Conforti, P., and L. Salvatici. 2004. "Agricultural Trade Liberalisation in the Doha Round. Alternative Scenarios and Strategic Interactions between Developed and Developing Countries." FAO Commodity and Trade Policy Research Working Papers 10. Rome.

Diao, X., and A. Somwaru. 2001. "Impact of the MFA Phase-Out on the World Economy: An Intertemporal, Global General Equilibrium Analysis." TMD Discussion Paper 79. International Food Policy Research Institute, Washington, DC.

Fabiosa, J., J. Beghin, S. de Cara, C. Fang, M. Isik, and H. Matthey. 2003. "Agricultural Markets Liberalisation and the Doha Round." Paper presented at the 25th International Conference of Agricultural Economists (IAAE), Durban, South Africa, August 16–22.

Foster, J. E., J. Greer, and E. Thorbecke. 1984. "A Class of Decomposable Poverty Measures." *Econometrica* 52: 761–76.

François, J. H., H. van Meijl, and F. van Tongeren. 2003. "Trade Liberalisation and Developing Countries under the Doha Round." Tinbergen Institute Discussion Paper 2003-060/2, University of Rotterdam, Rotterdam, The Netherlands.

Hertel, T. W., and W. Martin. 2000. "Liberalising Agriculture and Manufacturers in a Millennium Round: Implications for Developing Countries." *World Economy* 23: 455–69.

Hertel, T. W., W. Martin, K. Yanagishima, and B. Dimaranan. 1996. "Liberalizing Manufactures Trade in a Changing World Economy." In *The Uruguay Round and the Developing Countries*, eds. W. Martin and A. Winters, 183–215. Cambridge, U.K.: Cambridge University Press.

Jung, H. S., and E. Thorbecke. 2003. "The Impact of Public Education Expenditure on Human Capital, Growth, and Poverty in Tanzania and Zambia: A General Equilibrium Approach." *Journal of Policy Modeling* 25: 701–25.

Lips, M., A. Tabeau, F. van Tongeren, N. Ahmed, and C. Herok. 2003. "Textile and Wearing Apparel Sector Liberalisation—Consequences for the Bangladesh Economy." Paper presented at the Sixth Conference on Global Economic Analysis, The Hague, The Netherlands, June 12–14.

MacDonald, S., A. Somwaru, L. Meyer, and X. Diao. 2001. "The Agreement on Textiles and Clothing: Impact on U.S. Cotton." *Cotton and Wool Situation and Outlook* (November): 26–29.

Panagariya, A. 2002. "Developing Countries at Doha: A Political Economy Analysis." Department of Economics, University of Maryland, College Park.

Rizwana, S., and A. R. Kemal. 2002. "Remittances, Trade Liberalisation and Poverty in Pakistan: The Role of Excluded Variables in Poverty Change Analysis." Pakistan Institute of Development Economics, Islamabad.

Ravallion, M. 1990. "Rural Welfare Effects of Food Price Changes under Induced Wage Responses: Theory and Evidence from Bangladesh." *Oxford Economic Papers* 44: 574–85.

Rodrik, D. 2004. "Globalization and Growth—Looking in the Wrong Places." *Journal of Policy Modeling* 26: 513–17.

Winters, A., and T. L. Walmsley. 2002. "Relaxing the Restrictions on the Temporary Movement of Natural Persons." Brighton, U.K.: University of Sussex.

Yang, Y., W. Martin, and K. Yanagishima. 1997. "Evaluating the Benefits of Abolishing the MFA in the Uruguay Round Package." In *Global Trade Analysis: Modelling and Applications*, ed. T. W. Hertel, 253–79. New York: Cambridge University Press.

Yang, Y., and M. Mlachila. 2004. "The End of Textile Quotas: A Case Study of the Impact on Bangladesh." Paper presented at the Seventh Annual Conference on Global Economic Analysis, Washington, DC, June 17–19.

THE IMPACT ON RUSSIA OF WTO ACCESSION AND THE DDA: THE IMPORTANCE OF LIBERALIZATION OF BARRIERS AGAINST FDI IN SERVICES FOR GROWTH AND POVERTY REDUCTION

*Thomas Rutherford, David Tarr,
and Oleksandr Shepotylo*

Summary

Taking price changes from the GTAP model of world trade, this chapter uses a small, open economy computable general equilibrium (CGE) comparative static model of the Russian economy to assess the impact of free trade in the rest of the world (ROW) and a successful completion of the Doha Development Agenda (DDA) on the Russian economy and especially on the poor. Those results are compared with the impact of Russian accession to the WTO on income distribution and the poor. The model incorporates all 55,000 households from the Russian *Household Budget Survey* (HBS) as "real" households in the model. Crucially, given the importance of FDI liberalization as part of Russian WTO accession, FDI and Dixit-Stiglitz endogenous productivity effects from liberalization of import barriers against goods and FDI in services are also included.

It is estimated that Russian WTO accession in the medium run will result in gains averaged over all Russian households equal to 7.3 percent of Russian consumption (with a standard deviation of 2.2 percent of consumption), with virtually all households gaining. The analysis finds that ROW free trade would result in a weighted average gain to households in Russia of 0.2 percent of consumption, with a standard deviation of 0.2 percent of consumption; a successful completion of the DDA would result in a weighted average loss to households of -0.3 percent of consumption (with a standard deviation of 0.2 percent of consumption). Russia, as a net food importer, loses from subsidy elimination, and the gains to Russia from tariff cuts in other countries are too small to offset these losses. These results strongly support the view that Russia's own liberalization is more important than improvements in market access as a result of reforms in tariffs or subsidies in ROW. Foremost among the Russian reforms is liberalization of barriers against FDI in business services.

These reasons for these results are (a) barriers to FDI in services are high relative to Russian barriers to imports of goods, so liberalization of services is crucial to the realization of large gains from WTO accession; (b) Russian exports are dominated by energy products, on which ROW tariffs are low, so there is little new market access provided to Russia from the ROW liberalization of these products; (c) Russia imports a lot of food products, which are subsidized on world markets and whose prices will rise in the DDA; and (d) FDI in services and endogenous productivity effects in imperfectly competitive goods and services sectors are crucial, because this chapter shows that a constant returns to scale (CRS) model would produce much smaller gains.

Introduction

There are two potentially quite important events on the horizon for Russia with respect to the WTO. First, Russia is negotiating accession to the WTO and, as of late 2004, had signed bilateral agreements on its accession with at least 12 WTO members, including the EU, China, and the Republic of Korea. At the same time, the members of the WTO are negotiating tariff and subsidy cuts under the DDA. As a result of WTO member countries' changes in tariffs and subsidies agreed under the DDA, Russia will face a new set of prices for its exports and imports on world markets. This chapter evaluates the impact of the likely changes in world prices as a result of a conclusion of the DDA (and of ROW free trade) on Russia and on poverty in Russia. These effects are also compared with the impact on Russia of Russian WTO accession.

Russian WTO accession is primarily a set of commitments by Russia to liberalize its own trade and, crucially, open up its FDI regime in business services. The comparison of Russian WTO accession with the impact of the DDA on Russia then devolves fundamentally to a question of whether Russia can gain more from trade and subsidy reform in ROW or from its own liberalization.

This chapter uses the model that the authors have developed through two earlier papers. Jensen, Rutherford, and Tarr (forthcoming) developed a small, open economy model of Russia that incorporated FDI in business services with Dixit-Stiglitz, love-of-variety, endogenous productivity effects from investment and trade liberalization in business services and imperfectly competitive goods sectors. Substantial gains for Russia were found from its WTO accession, deriving primarily from the liberalization of barriers against FDI in services. This chapter shows that a CRS model without FDI in business services (which the authors believe is an inappropriate model specification, given the importance of FDI commitments in Russian WTO negotiations) would produce estimated gains that are dramatically smaller. In Rutherford, Tarr, and Shepotylo (2004) (RT&S), the Jensen, Rutherford, and Tarr model is extended by incorporating all the 55,000 households of the Russian HBS as agents in the general equilibrium model. That is, the chapter utilizes a "real household" model of the Russian economy with endogenous productivity effects. RT&S show that WTO accession could be expected to benefit virtually all the poor, but an inappropriately specified CRS model, without liberalization of barriers against FDI in services, and endogenous productivity effects would produce much smaller average welfare gains and the wrong sign for about 7 percent of the Russian population.

This chapter uses the same model and dataset as that used in RT&S to examine the impact on poverty in Russia of the DDA and as a result of ROW free trade. Crucially, these impacts are compared with the impact on Russia of its own liberalization through the commitments it will make as part of its WTO accession. This process enables assessment of the relative benefits to Russia of liberalization of countries in ROW of their tariffs or subsidies with liberalization in Russia of its barriers against FDI and goods imports. The impacts on Russia overall are examined at the decile level, as well as on the entire distribution of Russian households through the real household model of Russia.

As with the other country case studies in this volume, the starting point for the analysis of the DDA and ROW free trade impacts is the vectors of percentage changes in the price of exports and imports for Russia as a result of the completion of the DDA or ROW free trade. These vectors are derived from simulations of the Global Trade Analysis Project (GTAP) model presented in chapter 3. These new price vectors are taken as exogenous shifts in the terms of trade (TOT) facing Russia.

The mean welfare gain to Russia from its WTO accession, averaged over all households, is 7.3 percent of Russian consumption (with a standard deviation of 2.2 percent of consumption) in the medium run. It is found that virtually all households obtain at least some increase in their income. Nearly all the household gains fall between 2.0 percent and 25 percent of consumption. Poor households do slightly better than rich households because the wage rate of unskilled labor rises more than the return on capital. If an inappropriately specified CRS model were used, the gains from WTO accession would be only about 1.2 percent of consumption, with about 7 percent of households expected to lose—that is, the WTO accession estimates are decisively affected by liberalization of barriers against FDI in business services sectors and endogenous productivity effects in business services and goods.

Regarding the impact on Russia of cuts in the tariffs and subsidies of other countries, it is found that ROW free trade (which encompasses free trade in goods outside Russia and the elimination of export subsidies, with domestic support for agriculture retained) would result in a weighted average gain to households in Russia of 0.2 percent of consumption, with a standard deviation of 0.2 percent of consumption. The analysis suggests that a successful completion of the DDA (which is modeled as the elimination of export subsidies, substantial cuts in tariffs outside Russia,[1] and reduction in domestic support for agriculture) would result in a weighted average loss to households of -0.3 percent of consumption. Russia, as a net food importer, loses from subsidy elimination, and the gains to Russia from tariff cuts in other countries are too small to offset these losses (in part because Russian exports are dominated by energy products, which face low tariffs in ROW). The impacts on Russia from these TOT changes tend to favor neither the rich nor the poor.

Thus, in the medium term, what other countries in the WTO do in terms of their tariff changes or changes in export subsidies or domestic support will have a very small effect on Russian households and poverty. However, it is estimated that virtually all households will gain from Russian WTO accession; these gains are substantial, and they are very slightly progressive.[2] The distribution of gains across the 55,000 households is decisively affected by the inclusion of liberalization of barriers against FDI in business services sectors and endogenous productivity effects in business services and goods. These results strongly support the view that Russia has by far the most to gain from its own liberalization, especially in business services, rather than from improvements in market access as a result of reforms in tariffs or subsidies in ROW. Foremost among the gains from its own liberalization is the gains from liberalization of barriers against FDI in business services. The broader implications here are that developing countries might experience larger gains in poverty reduction if the WTO could more effectively negotiate cuts in barriers against FDI in services.

Despite the significant gains estimated from WTO accession, during a transition period, it is likely that many households with displaced workers will lose as they are forced to seek new employment. This work suggests that there will be a decline in employment in light industry, the food industry, mechanical engineering and metal working, and construction materials. Workers in these sectors will suffer losses from transitional unemployment and will likely incur expenses related to retraining or relocation. Some of the poorest members of the population are ill equipped to handle these transition costs. Thus, despite a likely substantial improvement in the standard of living for almost all Russians after adjustment to the WTO, government safety nets are very important to help with the transition—especially for the poorest members of society.

The model and data are briefly described in the next section. The focus in this chapter is on the evidence for endogenous productivity effects from liberalization of barriers against imports and FDI in services. Results are presented in section 2. Brief conclusions are in the final section.

The Model

A small, open economy CGE model of the Russian economy with 55,000 households is used. As noted, this chapter builds on two earlier papers where the model and data are documented. Jensen, Rutherford, and Tarr (forthcoming) describe the structure of the single representative agent model, disaggregation of the official Russian input-output table, and calculation of the Russian tariff and export tax rates. RT&S extend the model to incorporate the entire 55,098 households of the Russian HBS.[3] The reader is referred to those papers for more detailed documentation of the model. Given its importance to this chapter, it is worthwhile to briefly summarize some of the important evidence on the liberalization of barriers against FDI in services, productivity impacts of greater variety of imported goods, and the approach to estimating barriers to FDI in Russian business services sectors.

The key modeling features that distinguish this chapter from previous applied general equilibrium (AGE) modeling exercises linking trade and poverty is that FDI in business services and additional varieties of business services are permitted to endogenously increase the productivity of sectors using that service through the Dixit-Stiglitz variety effect (see Markusen, Rutherford, and Tarr [forthcoming] for elaboration). The approach also allows for Dixit-Stiglitz productivity effects in goods, for both final consumers and intermediate use, as explained in Ethier (1982). These features have a fundamental effect on the results for the estimated impact of WTO accession on poverty in Russia.

Competitive Sectors

There are 35 sectors in the model listed in table 16.1. These sectors fall into three categories: competitive sectors producing goods and services, imperfectly competitive goods sectors, and imperfectly competitive services sectors. The structure of production is depicted in figure 16.1. In competitive sectors, price equals marginal costs and imports and domestic goods are differentiated (the Armington assumption). See de Melo and Tarr (1992) for a description of the details of how these sectors are modeled. Protection rates are reported in table 16.2 and will be further discussed below.

Table 16.1. Structure of Value Added, Factor Shares, Imports, and Exports in Russia [a]

Sectors	Imports[a]		Exports[b]		Value Added (%)	Factor shares as percent of value added[c]		
	Share	Intensity	Share	Intensity		Unskilled Labor (%)	Skilled Labor (%)	Capital (%)
Sectors					100.0	21	63	16
Business services								
Railway transportation	0	1	0	1	3.3	11	85	5
Truck transportation	1	4	0	1	1.5	8	88	4
Pipelines transportation	1	2	0	0	3.6	11	58	31
Maritime transportation	2	52	1	56	0.3	14	81	5
Air transportation	0	8	2	39	0.6	14	84	2
Other transportation	0	2	0	3	1.1	9	85	6
Telecommunications	1	11	0	5	1.2	16	79	5
Financial services	0	3	0	2	1.5	10	86	4
Science and science servicing	0	5	0	6	0.8	35	61	4
Subtotal	5		3		13.9			
Differentiated Goods								
Ferrous metallurgy	4	18	10	37	1.9	9	85	7
Nonferrous metallurgy	2	16	17	55	2.3	12	81	7
Chemical and oil-chemical industry	7	29	8	33	1.8	20	74	7
Mechanical engineering and metal working	27	36	9	17	5.2	30	66	4
Timber and woodworking and pulp and paper industry	2	17	5	31	1.4	17	79	5
Construction materials industry	1	8	0	2	1.6	19	75	5
Light industry	17	69	1	13	0.7	63	32	5
Food industry	21	30	3	6	3.3	17	76	7
Other industries	1	13	0	5	0.6	22	76	3
Subtotal	82		53		18.8			

Table 16.1. (Continued)

	Imports[a]		Exports[b]		Value Added (%)	Factor Shares as Percent of value added[c]		
	Share	Intensity	Share	Intensity		Unskilled Labor (%)	Skilled Labor (%)	Capital (%)
Extractive industries								
Oil extraction	1	8	18	70	2.9	1	12	87
Gas	0	1	15	26	0.9	1	10	89
Coal mining	0	5	1	10	1.1	2	52	47
Subtotal	1		34		4.9			
Constant returns industries								
Electric industry	0	0	0	1	3.6	9	84	6
Oil processing	1	7	6	18	0.8	3	89	8
Other fuel industries	0	0	0	3	0.0	49	33	18
Construction	2	3	0	0	8.6	10	86	4
Agriculture and forestry	3	4	0	1	7.6	47	31	22
Post	0	4	1	9	0.3	15	78	7
Trade	2	2	0	1	22.9	20	53	27
Public catering	0	1	0	2	0.1	19	81	1
Other goods-producing sectors	1	16	0	0	0.8	23	76	1
Communal and consumer services	0	0	0	0	5.6	19	72	9
Public health, sports, and social security	0	0	0	0	3.1	44	52	4
Education, culture, and art	0	1	0	0	4.0	56	40	4
Geology and hydrometeorology	0	0	0	0	0.2	45	52	3
Administration and public associations	0	0	0	0	4.8	22	76	1
Subtotal	9		7		62.3			

Source: Author's calculations.

Note: Because of rounding, the sum of shares as a percentage does not always equal 100.

a. Share is sector imports as a percentage of economywide imports. Intensity is sector imports as a percentage of sector consumption.

b. Share is defined analogous to imports. Intensity is sector exports as a percentage of sector output.

c. After reconciliation with the HBS.

Table 16.2.   Tariff Rates, Export Tax Rates, Estimated Ad Valorem Equivalence of Barriers to FDI in Services Sectors and Estimated Improved Market Access from WTO Accession (ad valorem in percent by sector)

Sectors		Tariff rates	Export tax rates	Estimated change in export prices from WTO accession	Equivalent % barriers to FDI	
					Base year	Post-WTO accession
ELE	Electric industry	4.5	0.0	0.0		
OLE	Oil Extraction	0.0	7.9	0.0		
OLP	Oil processing	3.8	4.6	0.0		
GAS	Gas	0.5	18.8	0.0		
COA	Coal mining	0.0	0.0	0.0		
OFU	Other fuel industries	2.6	2.6	0.0		
FME	Ferrous metallurgy	2.9	0.4	1.5		
NFM	Nonferrous metallurgy	7.4	5.3	1.5		
CHM	Chemical and oil-chemical industry	7.1	1.6	1.5		
MWO	Mechanical engineering and metalworking	7.2	0.0	0.0		
TPP	Timber and woodworking and pulp and paper industry	9.9	6.9	0.0		
CNM	Construction materials industry	10.6	1.6	0.0		
CLO	Light industry	11.8	4.1	0.5		
FOO	Food industry	11.3	3.1	0.5		
OTH	Other industries	6.4	0.0	0.5		
AGF	Agriculture and forestry	8.2	0.6	0.0		
OIN	Other goods-producing sectors	0.0	0.0	0.5		
TMS	Telecommunications				33	0
SCS	Science and engineering servicing				33	0
FIN	Financial services				36	0
RLW	Railway transportation				33	0
TRK	Truck transportation				33	0
PIP	Pipelines transportation				33	0
MAR	Maritime transportation				95	80
AIR	Air transportation				90	75
TRO	Other transportation				33	0

Source: Authors' estimates.

Figure 16.1.   Production and Allocation of Output

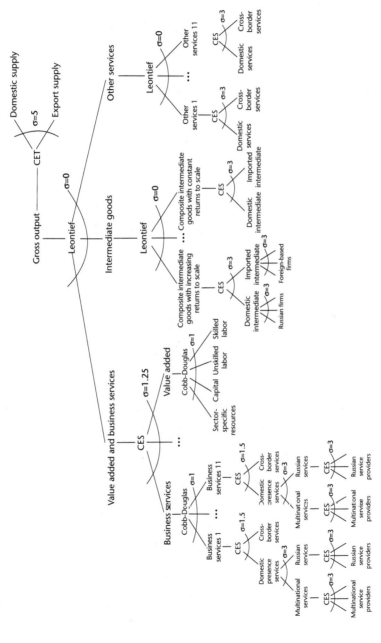

Source: Authors.

Imperfectly Competitive Sectors

In imperfectly competitive goods sectors, goods are produced with a fixed cost and constant marginal costs. Foreign firms supply the Russian market with production facilities abroad. Symmetry is assumed among domestic firms as well as among foreign firms, but costs differ between domestic and foreign firms. This model has firm-level competition with pricing decisions based on large-group monopolistic competition. The ratio of marginal costs to average costs is assumed fixed, which with the pricing assumption implies that output per firm is fixed. Both final and intermediate users of the output of imperfectly competitive sectors obtain a variety-adjusted unit more cheaply when there are additional varieties on offer via the Dixit-Stiglitz effect. Entry and exit are determined by a zero profit condition.

Business Services Sectors

Business services are supplied both by competitive firms on a cross-border basis and, because many services are more effectively supplied with a domestic presence, by imperfectly competitive firms (both multinational and Russian) that have a domestic presence in Russia. For imperfectly competitive firms, the cost and pricing structure is similar to that of imperfectly competitive goods producers, except that production of services by multinational service providers is done in Russia. Multinational service providers will import some of their technology or management expertise when they decide to establish a domestic presence in Russia. Thus, their cost structure differs from that of Russian service providers. They incur costs related to both imported inputs and Russian primary factors, in addition to intermediate factor inputs. These services are characterized by firm-level product differentiation. Restrictions on FDI, right of establishment, the movement of business personnel, lack of intellectual property protection, and contract enforcement have major, direct impacts on multinational firms providing services to the market.

The number of multinational and Russian firms that are present in the Russian market depends on profitability in that market. For multinational firms, the barriers to FDI affect profitability. Reduction in the constraints on FDI will typically lead to productivity gains from the Dixit-Stiglitz variety effect because when more varieties of services are available, buyers can obtain varieties that more closely fit their needs.

Primary Factors

Primary factors of production are capital and skilled and unskilled labor. There are five types of capital in the model: (1) mobile capital that can be used in any sector without adjustment costs (46 percent of the total capital stock); (2) sector-specific capital in the energy sectors, namely ownership of the mineral resources in oil extraction, gas, and coal mining (representing 15 percent of total capital); (3) sector-specific capital required for expansion of output in imperfectly competitive domestic firms producing either goods or services (representing 32 percent of the capital in the benchmark); (4) sector-specific capital required for expansion of output in imperfectly competitive foreign firms producing either goods or services (representing 5 percent of the capital in the benchmark); and (5) ownership of licenses for monopoly rents in services sectors (representing 2 percent of capital in the benchmark). There are no data that would allow association of specific capital holdings in given sectors with particular households. Thus, it is assumed that all households that hold capital also hold the different types of capital in the same proportions.

Household Consumer Demand

It is assumed that each household maximizes a Cobb-Douglas utility function of the aggregate 35 goods in the model subject to its budget constraint (which is factor income net of transfers). Factor income shares, aggregated to the decile level, are reported in table 16.3.[4] Each of the 35 aggregate commodities is a CES (Armington) aggregate of imported goods or services and goods or services produced in Russia. In imperfectly competitive goods sectors, imported and Russian produced goods are Dixit-Stiglitz aggregates of the outputs of foreign or Russian firms. The structure of consumer demand in imperfectly competitive services sectors (equivalent to business services in this model) is depicted on the left side of figure 16.1 under "Business services." Competitively supplied cross-border services and imperfectly competitive services produced in Russia are a constant elasticity of substitution (CES) (Armington) aggregate as well. Services produced in Russia are a Dixit-Stiglitz aggregate of services provided by multinational service providers and Russian service providers. Given the elasticity assumptions in this chapter, there is pure firm-level product differentiation (no preference biases for varieties according to country of origin) for all Dixit-Stiglitz goods and services.

Consumer demand, as well as firm-level demand, exhibits love of variety in imperfectly competitive goods. Given that there are weak separability and homothetic functions at all levels of consumer demand, the conditions for two-stage (or multistage) budgeting are satisfied. Given the initial data on each of the households and the assumptions on the structure of demand, the approach involves solving for the parameter values in each of the 55,000 household utility functions that are consistent with optimization by the households. Thus, the demand functions of all households are dependent on their initial choices and, in general, differ from one another.[5]

Table 16.3. Factor Income Shares and Their Standard Deviations by Consumption Decile

	All households			Rural households			Urban households		
	Unskilled labor (%)	Skilled labor (%)	Capital %	Unskilled labor (%)	Skilled labor (%)	Capital (%)	Unskilled labor (%)	Skilled labor (%)	Capital (%)
Decile 1 (0–10%)	40.9 (39.5)	56.8 (39.8)	2.3 (5.3)	45.8 (39.5)	50.8 (39.6)	3.4 (6.2)	35.6 (38.6)	63.2 (38.8)	1.2 (3.8)
Decile 2 (11–20%)	37.6 (37.6)	58.5 (38.0)	3.9 (8.8)	42.8 (38.2)	51.5 (38.2)	5.8 (11.3)	34.1 (36.7)	63.4 (37.0)	2.6 (6.1)
Decile 3 (21–30%)	32.2 (37.1)	62.3 (37.6)	5.4 (10.1)	40.0 (37.9)	52.5 (38.2)	7.5 (12.8)	28.5 (36.2)	67.0 (36.5)	4.5 (8.4)
Decile 4 (31–40%)	30.1 (36.2)	62.9 (36.5)	7.0 (10.8)	36.8 (39.3)	54.2 (38.6)	9.1 (13.3)	27.3 (34.5)	66.5 (34.9)	6.2 (9.4)
Decile 5 (41–50%)	27.5 (35.4)	62.5 (35.2)	10.0 (12.3)	34.7 (38.3)	53.7 (36.0)	11.6 (13.9)	25.0 (34.0)	65.5 (34.4)	9.5 (11.7)
Decile 6 (51–60%)	25.3 (34.7)	60.9 (34.1)	13.8 (14.6)	35.4 (40.0)	49.3 (36.8)	15.3 (16.4)	22.1 (32.1)	64.5 (32.3)	13.3 (13.9)
Decile 7 (61–70%)	20.7 (30.9)	61.4 (31.9)	17.9 (16.0)	33.2 (38.3)	50.4 (35.9)	16.4 (16.9)	17.6 (27.8)	64.1 (30.1)	18.3 (15.7)
Decile 8 (71–80%)	16.8 (28.5)	62.1 (29.7)	21.1 (16.2)	31.2 (36.8)	48.0 (34.6)	20.8 (19.1)	13.9 (25.4)	65.0 (27.6)	21.1 (15.5)
Decile 9 (81–90%)	16.1 (27.2)	55.2 (28.4)	28.7 (17.3)	28.0 (37.3)	46.6 (32.9)	25.4 (19.3)	14.4 (24.7)	56.5 (27.4)	29.2 (16.9)
Decile 10 (91–100%)	11.2 (24.9)	47.2 (27.0)	41.7 (22.1)	23.3 (33.9)	39.9 (27.7)	36.8 (21.1)	10.5 (23.9)	47.6 (26.9)	41.9 (22.2)

Source: Authors' calculations.

Note: Numbers in parentheses are the standard deviations of the decile factor share.

Evidence on the Productivity Impact of Services Liberalization

A growing body of evidence and economic theory suggests that the close availability of a diverse set of business services is important for economic growth. The key idea is that a diverse set (or higher-quality set) of business services allows users to purchase a quality-adjusted unit of business services at lower cost. As early as the 1960s, the urban and regional economics literature argued that nontradeable intermediate goods (primarily producer services produced under conditions of increasing returns to scale) are an important source of agglomeration externalities that account for the formation of cities and industrial complexes, as well as differences in economic performance across regions. The more recent economic geography literature (for example, Fujita, Krugman, and Venables [1999]) has also focused on the fact that related economic activity is economically concentrated as a result of agglomeration externalities (for example, computer businesses in Silicon Valley, ceramic tiles in Sassuolo, Italy).

Evidence comes from a variety of sources. Ciccone and Hall (1996) show that firms operating in economically dense areas are more productive than firms operating in relative isolation. Hummels (1995) shows that most of the richest countries in the world are clustered in relatively small regions of Europe, North America, and East Asia, and the poor countries are spread around the rest of the world. He argues this is partly explained by transportation costs for inputs, because it is more expensive to buy specialized inputs in countries that are far away than it is for the countries where a large variety of such inputs are located. Marshall (1988) shows that in three regions in the United Kingdom (Birmingham, Leeds, and Manchester) almost 80 percent of the services purchased by manufacturers were bought from suppliers within the same region. He cites studies that show that firm performance is enhanced by the local availability of producer services. In developing countries, McKee (1988) argues that the local availability of producer services is very important for the development of leading industrial sectors.

As Romer (1994) has argued, product variety is a crucial and often overlooked source of gains to the economy from trade liberalization. In this chapter's model, greater availability of varieties is the engine of productivity growth, but it appears that there are also other mechanisms through which trade may increase productivity.[6] Consequently, variety is taken as a metaphor for the various ways increased trade can increase productivity. Winters, McCulloch, and McKay (2004) summarize the empirical literature by concluding that "the recent empirical evidence seems to suggest that openness and trade liberalization have a strong influence on productivity and its rate of change." There are several key articles regarding product variety. Broda and Weinstein (2004) find that increased product variety contributes to a fall of 1.2 percent per year in the "true" import price index. Hummels and Klenow (2002) and Schott (forthcoming) have shown that product variety and quality are important in explaining trade between nations. Feenstra and others (1999) show that increased variety of *exports* in a sector increase total factor productivity in most manufacturing sectors in Taiwan, China, and the Republic of Korea, and they have some evidence that increased input variety also increases total factor productivity. Finally, Feenstra and Kee (2004) show that the export variety and productivity of a country are positively correlated.

Barriers to FDI in Services Sectors

In Russia, it is relatively easy to find a number of prominent examples of barriers in the services sectors. For example, in telecommunications, Rostelekom has a monopoly on long-distance, fixed-line telephone service. In its bilateral agreement on WTO accession with the EU, Russia has agreed to end the Rostelekom monopoly. In banking, although Russia allows multinationals to invest in new banks in Russia, there is a prohibition on multinationals opening branches in Russia. This distinction has been a significant point of contention in the accession negotiations. There are also limits on how much of the insurance market can be controlled by foreign banks. Also, maritime transportation *within* Russia is limited to Russian ships. Commitments within the context of WTO accession should provide significantly greater access to multinational service providers in these key sectors.[7]

To estimate the ad valorem equivalence of barriers to FDI, this work began by commissioning surveys in telecommunications; banking, insurance, and securities; and maritime and air transportation services by Russian research institutes that specialize in these sectors. Using these surveys as well as supplementary data, Kimura, Ando, and Fujii (2004a, 2004b, 2004c) used the methodology explained in the volume by Findlay and Warren (2000) to estimate the barriers to FDI in the Russian services sector.

For each of these service sectors, authors in the Findlay and Warren volume evaluated the regulatory environment across many countries; the same regulatory criteria were assessed for all countries in a particular service sector. The price of services was then regressed against the regulatory barriers to determine the impact of any of the regulatory barriers on the price of services. Assuming that the international regression is valid for Russia and using their survey-based assessment of the regulatory environment, Kimura, Ando, and Fujii estimated the ad valorem equivalent impact of a reduction in barriers to FDI in these services sectors. The results are reported in table 16.2.

Estimated Impacts of Russian WTO Accession

Specification of the Counterfactuals

This chapter examines and compares the potential impact on Russia of the DDA as well as the impact on Russia of the changes it will make as a result of commitments it will take on as part of its WTO accession. First, results are produced for Russian WTO accession. These results are based on the integrated "real" 55,000-household model explained in RT&S (2004). In the WTO scenario, it is assumed that (1) barriers against FDI in business services are reduced as indicated in table 16.2; (2) seven sectors subject to antidumping actions in export markets receive slightly improved prices in their market access (this is implemented as an exogenous increase in their export price as shown in table 16.2); and (3) the tariff rates of all sectors are reduced by 50 percent. In all scenarios, unless otherwise stated, it is assumed that the government taxes households in equal percentages of household income so that government revenue remains unchanged. The macroeconomic impacts of this scenario are presented in column 1 of table 16.5. In Jensen, Rutherford and Tarr (forthcoming), it is shown that the most important impact of WTO accession on Russia is the liberalization of barriers against FDI in business services.[8] Column 2 presents results where only these barriers are liberalized (by the amount shown in table 16.2). In column 3, the barriers against FDI in services are reduced by 50 percent of the cuts shown in table 16.2. Column 4 presents results of a scenario in which tariff barriers are reduced by cutting them by 50 percent across the board.

Columns 5 and 6 present results of the impact of changes in world prices deriving from reforms undertaken at the global level. The changes in world prices derived from the GTAP model are taken as exogenous changes in the export and import prices facing Russia and are reported in detail in table 16.4. Then the 55,000-household model is run to examine the impact of these price changes on sector output, exports, imports, household welfare, and other economic variables. Column 5 considers full elimination of tariffs outside Russia and full elimination of export subsidies outside Russia, with cuts in domestic agricultural support. Column 6 evaluates the impact on Russia of the likely impact of the DDA without Russian participation in the cuts in tariffs and subsidies beyond its WTO accession commitments. This is defined as full elimination of export subsidies and cuts in domestic agricultural support and tariffs in industrial countries, with developing countries making lesser cuts, as detailed in chapter 2.

Table 16.4. Changes in Export and Import Prices Facing Russia on World Markets as a Result of the Doha Round or Rest of the World Free Trade[a] (ad valorem in percent by sector)

Sectors		Doha SDT[a]		ROW Free Trade	
		Export prices	Import prices	Export prices	Import prices
ELE	Electric industry	0.2	-0.1	0.7	0.0
OLE	Oil Extraction	0.2	0.1	1.0	0.3
OLP	Oil processing	0.2	0.1	1.0	0.3
GAS	Gas	0.1	-0.1	0.5	0.2
COA	Coal mining	0.2	0.9	0.9	1.1
OFU	Other fuel industries	0.2	0.1	0.9	0.3
FME	Ferrous metallurgy	0.2	-0.1	0.8	-0.3
NFM	Nonferrous metallurgy	0.2	-0.1	0.7	-0.7
CHM	Chemical and oil-chemical industry	0.2	-0.2	0.7	-0.3
MWO	Mechanical engineering and metal working	0.2	-0.2	0.7	-0.2
TPP	Timber and woodworking and pulp and paper industry	0.2	-0.2	0.8	-0.2
CNM	Construction materials industry	0.2	0.0	0.8	0.2
CLO	Light industry	0.3	0.1	1.5	-0.3
FOO	Food industry	0.5	2.3	1.5	2.7
OTH	Other industries	0.2	-0.1	0.8	-0.3
AGF	Agriculture forestry	0.1	0.4	0.7	0.9
OIN	Other goods-producing sectors	0.3	0.0	0.9	-0.2

Source: GTAP model estimates.
a. Doha SDT assumes expected Doha Round reductions in tariffs and domestic support subsidized with smaller cuts for developing countries and no cuts for the LDCs, without participation of Russia.

Aggregate Results in the Full, 55,000-Household Model

Aggregate results are summarized in table 16.5. Welfare results in this table are obtained by aggregating the equivalent variation (EV) gains (as a percent of consumption) of the 55,000 consumers.[9]

WTO Accession Scenarios

For the general WTO scenario (column 1 in table 16.5), rather substantial aggregate gains are obtained for a comparative state trade model, equal to 7.3 percent of aggregate consumption, with a standard deviation in the welfare gains among

Table 16.5. Impact of Russian WTO Accession and the DDA on Economywide Variables in Russia[a]

Commodity	WTO accession (1)	Reform of FDI barriers only (2)	WTO accession w/partial reform of FDI barriers (3)	50% Reduction of tariff barriers in Russia only (4)	Rest of the world free trade full removal of domestic support (5)	Doha (6)
Aggregate welfare						
Welfare (EV as % of consumption)	7.3	5.3	4.1	1.3	0.2	-0.3
	(2.2)[a]	(1.5)	(1.3)	(0.8)	(0.2)	(0.2)
Welfare (EV as % of GDP)	3.4	2.4	1.9	0.6	0.1	-0.1
Government budget						
Tariff revenue (% of GDP)	0.9	1.4	0.8	0.8	1.3	1.3
Tariff revenue (% of change)	-33.2	10.9	-35.2	-38.3	3.9	2.6
Aggregate trade						
Real exchange rate (% of change)	2.6	1.1	1.8	2.0	-0.9	-0.5
Aggregate exports (% of change)	14.4	3.7	11.9	8.1	0.5	-0.6
Returns to mobile factors						
Unskilled labor (% of change)	3.7	2.9	1.7	0.6	0.2	-0.1
Skilled labor (% of change)	5.3	2.8	3.2	1.7	0.0	-0.3
Capital (% of change)	1.8	1.4	2.2	1.0	-0.2	-0.3
Percent of factors that must adjust						
Unskilled labor	1.2	0.4	1.3	1.2	0.3	0.4
Skilled labor	1.4	0.7	1.0	0.6	0.2	0.3
Capital	0.5	0.1	0.4	0.3	0.3	0.4

Source: Authors' estimates.

Note: Results are percentage of change from initial equilibrium.

a. Numbers in parentheses are the standard deviations.

households of 2.2 percent of consumption.[10] Column 2 shows that the main driving force for this result is the reduction of Russian barriers against FDI in the services sectors. Liberalization of barriers to FDI is responsible for an estimated welfare gain of 5.3 percent of consumption (with a standard deviation in the welfare results among households of 1.5 percent of consumption), more than 70 percent of the total welfare gain from Russian WTO accession. Given that these estimates indicate that barriers against FDI in services are much higher than tariff barriers, and that there will be only small gains in market access, the relative importance of liberalization of barriers to FDI is not surprising. Column 3 also shows the results of estimates of the impact of only a 50 percent reduction in the barriers to FDI, along with the same improved market access and tariff reduction that would be implemented in the WTO scenario. The gains are reduced to 4.1 percent of consumption, with a standard deviation in the welfare gain of 1.3 percent of consumption; the gains remain substantial, but significantly reduced as a result of a less significant reduction in FDI barriers. A 50 percent reduction in tariff barriers yields a welfare gain of 1.3 percent of consumption (with a standard deviation of 0.8 percent). Although the gains are significantly less than the gains from services liberalization, this is a large gain for a country whose tariffs are not very high. The significant size of the gain is due to the endogenous productivity effects of goods liberalization.[11]

The intuition for these results is the following: Reduction of barriers against multinational service providers or foreign goods producers increases the (tariff-ridden) demand curve for multinational services or foreign goods. In imperfectly competitive sectors, this induces entry of new multinational service providers or new varieties of foreign goods until zero profit is restored. Despite the reduction in domestic varieties, there is a net increase in varieties overall. This serves to lower the quality-adjusted cost of purchasing the services or goods in downstream industries, and this acts like an externality that increases total factor productivity in the downstream using sectors.[12]

Because households cannot change their factor endowments among unskilled labor, skilled labor, and capital, but they can substitute among commodities consumed, impacts on factor incomes through changes in factor prices tend to dominate the welfare impacts in this type of model.[13] In the WTO scenario, the wage rate of skilled labor increases by 5.3 percent, the wage rate of unskilled labor increases by 3.7 percent, and the return on capital increases by 1.8 percent. Although the return to capital rises relative to a basket of consumption goods, it does not rise as much as wages. The return to capital increases less than wages because owners of "specific capital" in imperfectly competitive sectors that are subject to increased competition from imports or from FDI will see a reduction in the value of their returns. Returns to mobile capital increase by more than

6 percent, even faster than returns to skilled labor, because the economy shifts resources into the more capital-intensive sectors and away from more unskilled labor-intensive sectors, such as light industry and mechanical engineering and metal working. But the return on sector-specific capital in the imperfectly competitive sectors falls so that the total return on capital rises less than wages. The ratio of skilled to unskilled labor in the expanding sectors is greater than that in the contracting sectors. As a result, the wage rate of skilled labor rises faster than the wage rate of unskilled labor.[14]

Changes in the World Trading Environment: Impacts on Russia

Columns 5 and 6 of table 16.5 examine the impact on Russia as a result of changes in the world trading environment. Column 5 examines the impact of ROW free trade (without Russian participation),[15] the removal of all export subsidies in agriculture, and the removal of domestic support in agriculture. Russia's estimated welfare gain will be 0.2 percent of consumption, with a standard deviation among households of 0.2 percent of consumption.

Although the impact on Russia of ROW free trade outside Russia and the removal of export subsidies alone are positive, the most noticeable aspect of these estimates is how small they are in relation to the 7.3 percent estimated gain that Russia will obtain from its commitments as part of its WTO accession. This result follows a common strand in the literature, suggesting that the largest gains from trade liberalization come from own-liberalization and not from the actions of other countries. In this case, the liberalization of Russian barriers against FDI with endogenous productivity effects from liberalization of trade and FDI barriers are also incorporated as part of the WTO accession scenario.[16]

Column 6 examines possible outcomes of the DDA without any reforms in Russia. It is estimated that, on average, Russia will lose about -0.3 percent of consumption, with a standard deviation across households of 0.2 percent of consumption. These losses are due to the TOT loss to Russia from paying higher prices for food imports as a result of export subsidy removal. Without very substantial tariff cuts in ROW to offset the losses from removal of export subsidies in agriculture, Russia loses from the adverse TOT effects of higher prices for food imports.

To verify this intuition, the impact of the elimination of export subsidies, without any change in tariffs or domestic support, is evaluated separately. It is estimated that Russia will lose -0.4 percent of consumption from the removal of export subsidies. These results are explained by the fact that Russia is a net food importer. Elimination of export subsidies in agriculture results in higher prices for food and agricultural products on world markets. Thus, the TOT shift against Russia as a result of the elimination of these subsidies.

Results Aggregated to the Decile Level

To ascertain the impact of the DDA and WTO accession on the poor, the 55,000 households are separated into ten deciles, with 10 percent of the households in each. Households are ranked according to per capita income, with decile 1 made up of the poorest 10 percent of the households, decile 10 made up of the richest 10 percent, and so on. The model is run with all 55,000 households. The results of the aggregated EV gains (as a percent of consumption) of the households in each decile are presented in table 16.6. The aggregated results for rural and urban households in each decile are also presented in this table. In addition, the standard deviation of the disaggregated EV results within each decile is shown.

WTO Accession and FDI Liberalization
Columns 1 and 2 of table 16.6 present the results for Russian WTO accession and Russian reduction of barriers against FDI in services where the gains of the households within each decile are weighted to obtain weighted average mean gains for the households. All 10 representative households gain significantly, but the richest households gain slightly less in percentage terms than the poorest. This is because the return on capital increases less than the wage rate of unskilled labor. Table 16.4 shows that the rich depend more on earnings from capital than the rest of the population, so the impact on their income is affected more by the relatively lower increase in the returns to capital.[17] Skilled labor is more evenly distributed across income deciles, reflecting the fact that government employees, such as researchers and teachers, often receive very low wages and retirees living on a pension were often skilled workers.[18]

Rural households typically gain less than urban households. This occurs because rural households have less education and are therefore classified as less skilled than urban workers in the same income group, and unskilled wages do not increase as much as skilled worker wages.

ROW Free Trade and the DDA Scenarios
The results in column 4 of table 16.6 show that the impact of ROW free trade, removal of export subsidies, and reduction in domestic support yields very little difference in the results across deciles. Household welfare in all deciles increases by an amount between 0.1 percent and 0.3 percent of consumption. That is, the results for all deciles fall within 0.1 percent of the weighted average for the entire population (also shown in table 16.5) of 0.2 percent welfare increase as a percent of consumption. Similar results apply to the Doha scenario shown in column 5—the weighted average estimated welfare gains for virtually all deciles is within 0.1 percent of the estimated weighted average for the entire population in the respective

Table 16.6 The Mean and Standard Deviation of the Welfare Impacts of WTO Accession on Russian Households, from Poorest to Richest (welfare change as a percent of consumption)

Household type[a]		WTO accession (1)		Reform of FDI barriers (2)		50% tariff reduction (3)		Rest of the world free trade / Full removal of domestic support (4)		Doha (5)	
		Mean	SD[b]	Mean	SD	Mean	SD	Mean	SD	Mean	SD
Decile 1 (0–10%)	Rural	7.0	(4.0)	5.3	(3.0)	0.8	(1.2)	0.3	(0.3)	-0.2	(0.3)
	Urban	8.3	(2.0)	5.8	(1.3)	1.4	(0.9)	0.2	(0.2)	-0.4	(0.2)
	Combined	7.6	(3.4)	5.5	(2.4)	1.1	(1.1)	0.2	(0.3)	-0.3	(0.2)
Decile 2 (11–20%)	Rural	6.7	(2.2)	5.1	(1.6)	0.8	(0.9)	0.3	(0.2)	-0.2	(0.2)
	Urban	8.2	(1.7)	5.6	(1.1)	1.4	(0.8)	0.1	(0.2)	-0.4	(0.2)
	Combined	7.6	(2.0)	5.4	(1.3)	1.1	(0.9)	0.2	(0.2)	-0.3	(0.2)
Decile 3 (21–30%)	Rural	6.6	(2.4)	5.0	(1.6)	0.8	(0.9)	0.2	(0.2)	-0.2	(0.2)
	Urban	8.3	(1.8)	5.6	(1.1)	1.4	(0.8)	0.1	(0.2)	-0.4	(0.2)
	Combined	7.7	(2.1)	5.4	(1.3)	1.2	(0.9)	0.2	(0.2)	-0.3	(0.2)

Table 16.6 (*Continued*)

Household type[a]	WTO accession (1)		Reform of FDI barriers (2)		50% tariff reduction (3)		Rest of the world free trade — Full removal of domestic support (4)		Doha (5)	
	Mean	SD[b]	Mean	SD	Mean	SD	Mean	SD	Mean	SD
Decile 4 (31–40%) Rural	6.6	(2.1)	5.0	(1.6)	0.8	(0.9)	0.2	(0.2)	-0.2	(0.2)
Urban	8.2	(1.6)	5.6	(1.1)	1.4	(0.7)	0.1	(0.2)	-0.4	(0.2)
Combined	7.7	(1.9)	5.4	(1.3)	1.3	(0.8)	0.2	(0.2)	-0.3	(0.2)
Decile 5 (41–50%) Rural	6.4	(2.0)	4.8	(1.4)	0.8	(0.8)	0.2	(0.2)	-0.2	(0.2)
Urban	8.1	(1.7)	5.6	(1.2)	1.4	(0.7)	0.1	(0.2)	-0.4	(0.2)
Combined	7.7	(2.0)	5.4	(1.3)	1.3	(0.8)	0.2	(0.2)	-0.3	(0.2)
Decile 6 (51–60%) Rural	6.2	(1.9)	4.7	(1.3)	0.8	(0.8)	0.2	(0.2)	-0.2	(0.2)
Urban	8.0	(1.6)	5.5	(1.1)	1.5	(0.7)	0.1	(0.2)	-0.4	(0.2)
Combined	7.5	(1.9)	5.3	(1.2)	1.3	(0.8)	0.1	(0.2)	-0.3	(0.2)
Decile 7 (61–70%) Rural	6.2	(2.2)	4.8	(1.6)	0.8	(0.9)	0.2	(0.2)	-0.2	(0.2)
Urban	7.8	(1.7)	5.5	(1.3)	1.5	(0.6)	0.1	(0.2)	-0.4	(0.2)
Combined	7.5	(2.0)	5.3	(1.4)	1.3	(0.7)	0.2	(0.2)	-0.3	(0.2)

Table 16.6 (Continued)

Household type[a]	WTO accession (1)		Reform of FDI barriers (2)		50% tariff reduction (3)		Rest of the world free trade — Full removal of domestic support (4)		Doha (5)	
	Mean	SD[b]	Mean	SD	Mean	SD	Mean	SD	Mean	SD
Decile 8 (71–80%) Rural	6.0	(1.9)	4.6	(1.3)	0.8	(0.8)	0.2	(0.2)	-0.2	(0.2)
Urban	7.8	(1.7)	5.4	(1.2)	1.5	(0.6)	0.1	(0.2)	-0.4	(0.2)
Combined	7.5	(1.9)	5.3	(1.2)	1.4	(0.7)	0.2	(0.2)	-0.3	(0.2)
Decile 9 (81–90%) Rural	6.1	(2.4)	4.8	(2.1)	0.8	(0.8)	0.2	(0.2)	-0.2	(0.2)
Urban	7.3	(1.6)	5.3	(1.3)	1.4	(0.6)	0.2	(0.2)	-0.3	(0.2)
Combined	7.2	(1.8)	5.2	(1.5)	1.3	(0.7)	0.2	(0.2)	-0.3	(0.2)
Decile 10 (91–100%) Rural	5.6	(2.3)	4.4	(2.0)	0.8	(0.8)	0.3	(0.2)	-0.2	(0.2)
Urban	6.8	(1.9)	5.2	(1.6)	1.3	(0.6)	0.2	(0.2)	-0.3	(0.2)
Combined	6.8	(2.0)	5.1	(1.7)	1.3	(0.6)	0.2	(0.2)	-0.3	(0.2)

Source: Author's calculations.

a. The model is executed with 55,000. Decile 1 is the poorest percent of all households on a per capita consumption basis. Results for decile 1 (combined, rural, and urban) are a weighted average of the ev as a percentage of consumption of the households (combined, rural, and urban) in the decile. Other deciles are calculated analogously.

b. Numbers in the parentheses are the standard deviations of the welfare impacts scenario. The standard deviation for households within the deciles is 0.2 percent of consumption for all but one group.

The similarity of results across deciles for these three scenarios occurs because, in each scenario, the wage rate of unskilled labor is estimated to increase by the same percentage as the return to capital. This means that the disparate shares of capital and unskilled labor in income between the rich and poor don't come into play. Therefore, the welfare gains across the income spectrum can be expected to be comparable.

Analyzing the Distributional Impacts for Individual Households

The distribution of gains from Russian WTO accession across all 55,000 households is summarized in figure 16.2, along with the distribution of gains for the poorest 10 percent and richest 10 percent of all households. The distribution in figure 16.2 is centered on a mean gain of income of 7.3 percent, with a standard deviation equal to 2.2 percent of consumption. It is evident from figure 16.2 that virtually all households will gain in the new equilibrium, relative to the status quo. The results indicate that 98 percent of the population will gain between 3.2 percent and 13 percent of consumption; 99.9 percent of the households will gain

Figure 16.2. Distributions of Estimated Welfare Gains from Russian WTO Accession for the Entire Sample, the Poorest Decile, and the Richest Decile

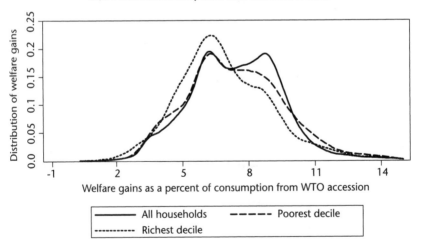

Source: Authors' calculations.

Note: Observations in a range from 0 percent to 15 percent are shown. Deciles are constructed to be representative of 10 percent of Russian population based on the weights of the HBS.

between 2 percent and 25 percent of consumption.[19] The distribution of gains for the poorest decile of the population is close to the distribution for the entire population, although the mean of the gains is slightly larger, and the richest decile gains slightly less than the average of the population—that is, WTO accession produces slightly progressive effects for the reasons already mentioned.[20]

Figures 16.3 and 16.4 plot the comparable distributions across the 55,000 households based on ROW free trade and the Doha scenario. For ROW free trade, it is estimated that 98 percent of the households will experience a change in welfare of between -0.3 percent and 0.7 percent of consumption. For the Doha scenario, it is estimated that 98 percent of the households will experience a change in welfare of between -0.8 percent and 0.2 percent of consumption. As was evident in the results at the decile level, the impact on the rich and the poor does not differ significantly: the impacts of ROW free trade or Doha on Russian households are neither progressive nor regressive.

Figure 16.5 compares the distributions of gains for all Russian households from the WTO accession, ROW free trade, and Doha scenarios. The figure makes it evident that WTO accession results in dramatically larger gains for Russian

Figure 16.3. Distributions of Estimated Welfare Gains for Russian Households from ROW Free Trade for the Entire Sample, the Poorest Decide, and the Richest Decile

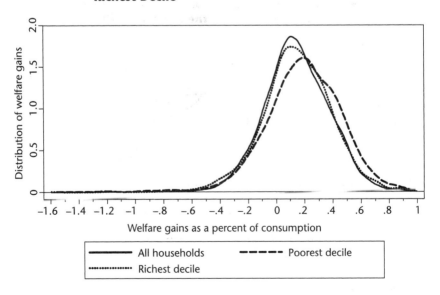

Source: Authors' calculations.

Note: Graph is truncated in a range from -1.6 to 1.

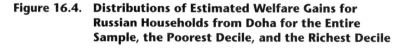

Figure 16.4. Distributions of Estimated Welfare Gains for Russian Households from Doha for the Entire Sample, the Poorest Decile, and the Richest Decile

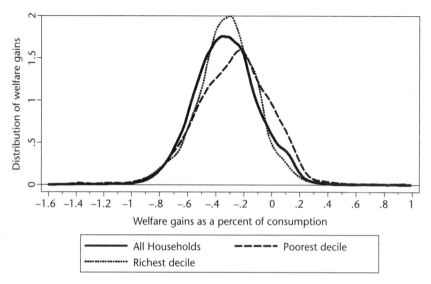

Source: Author's calculations.
Note: Graph is truncated in a range from -1.6 to 1.

households than the impact on Russia of either ROW free trade or Doha. ROW free trade is more beneficial than Doha for Russian households. However, the distributions of gains from ROW free trade and the Doha scenario significantly overlap with each other, so that a large part of the distribution from Doha is obscured by the ROW free trade distribution. The difference in impact on Russia between ROW free trade and Doha is rather small compared with the estimated gains that Russia could reap from its own reforms as embodied in its WTO accession commitments.

Policy Implications

Although this analysis has not accounted for the transition costs associated with such trade reforms, it is clear that the process of adjustment to this new trade and investment climate is likely to result in losses for many households. As discussed at length in Jensen, Rutherford, and Tarr (forthcoming), a decline in employment in light industry, the food industry, mechanical engineering and metal working, and construction materials is expected. These displaced workers will have to find new

Figure 16.5. Distributions of Estimated Welfare Gains: WTO Accession, Doha, and ROW Free Trade Model Results Compared (55,098 households sampled)

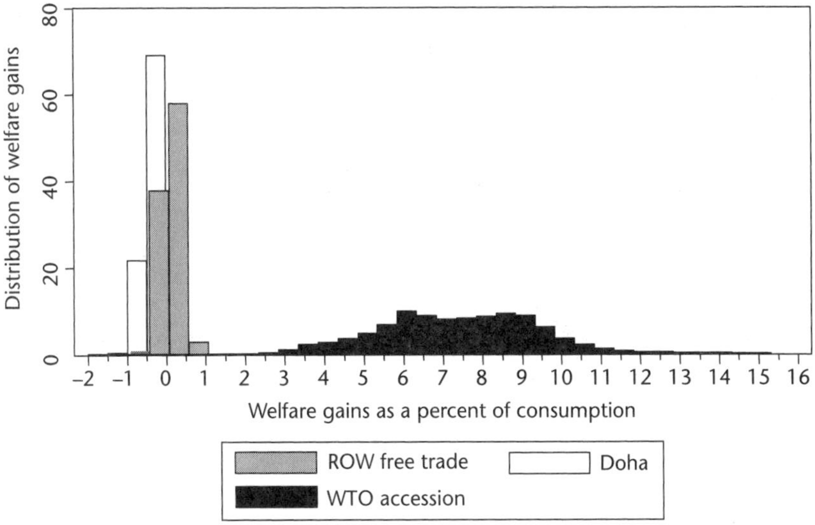

Welfare gains as a percent of consumption

- ROW free trade
- WTO accession
- Doha

Source: Authors' calculations.

employment. They will suffer losses from transitional unemployment and will likely incur expenses related to retraining or relocation. Thus, despite a likely substantial improvement in the standard of living for almost all Russians after adjustment to a new equilibrium after accession to the WTO, government safety nets are very important to help with the transition—especially for the poorest members of society, who can ill afford a harsh transition.

The central finding in this chapter is that Russia will gain more from WTO accession commitments than from a prospective Doha scenario, and this is primarily due to its own services liberalization. The findings suggest that, in the medium term, what other countries in the WTO do in terms of their tariff changes or changes in export subsidies or domestic support will have a very small effect on Russian households and poverty. However, virtually all households will gain from Russian WTO accession in the medium term: these gains are substantial and they are very slightly progressive. These findings suggest that the gains to other developing countries from participation in the WTO might be considerably enhanced if reductions in barriers against FDI in services were included in the negotiations. By deepening reforms to include the services sector, the prospects for enhanced economic growth and sustained poverty reduction are much improved.

Notes

1. This analysis does not assume any Russian tariff cuts as part of the DDA to sharply contrast own liberalization versus ROW liberalization regarding impacts on Russia.

2. A small, open economy model of Russia is used. In a small, open economy model, there are no adverse TOT effects. That is, the optimal tariff for Russia in this model is zero. Unilateral tariff cuts increase welfare in this model all the way to a zero tariff. However, the GTAP model is a multiregion model with an Armington structure that implies that all countries, as unique suppliers of their differentiated goods, have market power on their exports and an optimal tariff. Given the elasticities assumed in the GTAP model, the optimal tariff is about 15 percent, so unilateral tariff cuts below 15 percent are typically welfare reducing.

3. The development of a new algorithm was key to solving a CGE model with such a large number of household-agents in the model. In RT&S we explain the intuition for that algorithm and provide a graphical interpretation. With the Internet version of this chapter, the General Algebraic Modeling System (GAMS) code for that algorithm is provided.

4. Households are modeled endogenously based on the 55,000 households of the Russian HBS. The HBS, which is representative at the regional level, has very detailed information on household consumption expenditures and information about age, gender, education, and occupation of each member of the household. It also has information about expenditures and savings and, by implication, household income. The major shortcoming of the HBS for the purposes here is that it does not contain information on the sources of income of the households. For sources of household income, a different source of information is required. Here the authors turn to the Russian Longitudinal Monitoring Survey, which has less than 5,000 observations and is not representative of the population on the regional level. However, it has extensive information on individual and household sources of income: wages and profits from first, second, and third jobs; pensions and unemployment benefits; and profits and dividends from accumulated assets.

Both small area estimation and matching techniques are used to generate sources of income data for all 55,000-plus households in the HBS. The procedures are described in RT&S. Results from both techniques yield similar results.

5. The model is solved using GAMS–MPSGE (Rutherford 1999) and the algorithm developed for this problem to solve general equilibrium models with a large number of agents.

6. Trade liberalization may induce firms to move down their average cost curves, import higher-quality products, or shift production to more efficient firms within an industry. Tybout and Westbrook (1995) find evidence of this latter type of rationalization for Mexican manufacturing firms.

7. Estimates of barriers in air and maritime transportation are higher than in other sectors because of strong barriers to operation within Russia in these sectors. But because there is less international pressure in these sectors for cuts in these barriers, the authors believe that WTO accession will not have as significant an effect in these sectors.

8. Barriers against business services are liberalized only in the WTO accession scenario. Given that business services represent only 14 percent of value added, this is a strong result. The intuition is explained in section 4.2 below.

9. The EV of each household is weighted by its share of base-year expenditures.

10. CGE evaluations of trade policy changes typically estimate gains of less than 1 percent of GDP. See Rutherford and Tarr (2002) for a discussion and several examples.

11. The large gains are achieved although the Russian capital stock is held constant in this model.

12. It has been shown (RT&S 2004) that if constant returns to scale are assumed in all sectors of the economy, the estimated welfare gains from Russian WTO accession are reduced to 1.2 percent of consumption. These results show that incorporating liberalization of barriers to FDI in the analysis as well as the Dixit-Stiglitz-Ethier formulation for endogenous productivity effects are both crucial in explaining the rather substantial estimated gains from Russian WTO accession.

13. See, for example, Harrison, Rutherford, and Tarr (2003).

14. The data do not allow us to distinguish capital holdings at the household level among the various types of capital. Thus, all households are assumed to hold the five kinds of capital in the model in equal proportions. Households that depend disproportionately on specific capital that falls in return would be expected to lose from WTO accession.

15. It is assumed that any commitments for tariff reduction as part of the DDA will not apply to Russia, because Russia is not yet a member of the WTO and the terms of its accession agreement will define its tariff regime within the time frame of the DDA. Thus, it is assumed that Russia does not participate in these global liberalization scenarios. However, Russia is assumed to benefit from improved market access as a result of liberalization in other countries—presuming that WTO membership will be in place by the time the Doha scenario is implemented.

16. To put these numbers in perspective, Rutherford and Tarr (2002) have analytically derived the relationship between a permanent increase in the steady-state growth rate and EV. A welfare gain of 10 percent of consumption corresponds to a permanent increase in the growth rate of about 0.4 percent. Although cross-country assessments of the impact of trade liberalization on growth have been criticized, several authors have estimated that trade liberalization could increase the growth rate by between 1 percent and 2.5 percent. One criticism of these regressions is that trade liberalization is often accompanied by macro stabilization, institutional reforms, and other market reforms, and the trade liberalization variable in the cross-country regressions may be picking up these other effects. But WTO accession involves a range of reforms, including institutional reforms necessary to accompany FDI liberalization, and trade liberalization may be a sine qua non of the overall reform process, because other interventions such as state subsidies often are unsustainable in an open economy.

17. Household income in Russia exceeds household consumption for almost all households because Russia has a large current account surplus. Consistency between the macro balances and the household data in construction of the SAM implies that household factor income must be larger than household consumption for most households to allow for the transfer of capital to foreigners as well as to pay for investment. It follows that the change in factor income as a percent of consumption will be larger than the change in factor income as a percent of household income.

18. An individual is classified as skilled if he or she has any education post–high school. In this study, skills are defined at the individual level. Labor and capital shares are defined individually, as are aggregated factor shares within the household.

19. For the scenario in which barriers to FDI are cut by only 50 percent of the cuts in the WTO accession scenario, 98 percent of the households experience a gain of between 0.9 percent and 6.3 percent of consumption.

20. Although households that are heavily endowed with specific capital in declining sectors will lose on average from WTO accession, those who can form joint ventures with foreign investors will likely see the value of their specific capital holdings increase.

References

Broda, Christian, and David Weinstein. 2004. "Globalization and the Gains from Variety." NBER Working Paper 10314. National Bureau of Economic Research, Cambridge, MA. http://www.nber.org/papers/w10314

Ciccone, A., and R. Hall. 1996. "Productivity and the Density of Economic Activity." *American Economic Review* 86 (1): 54–70.

de Melo, Jaime, and David G. Tarr. 1992. *A General Equilibrium Analysis of US Foreign Trade Policy.* Cambridge, MA: MIT Press.

Ethier, W. J. 1982. "National and International Returns to Scale in the Modern Theory of International Trade." *American Economic Review* 72 (2): 389–405.

Feenstra, R., D. Madani, T. H. Yang, and C. Y. Liang. 1999. "Testing Endogenous Growth in South Korea and Taiwan." *Journal of Development Economics* 60: 317–41.

Feenstra, Robert C., and Hiau Looi Kee. 2004. "On the Measurement of Product Variety in Trade." *American Economic Review* 94 (2): 145–49.

Findlay, Christopher, and Tony Warren, eds. 2000. *Impediments to Trade in Services: Measurement and Policy Implications.* London: Routledge.

Fujita, Masahisa, Paul Krugman, and Anthony J. Venables, 1999. *The Spatial Economy: Cities, Regions, and International Trade.* Cambridge, MA: MIT Press.

Harrison, Glenn W., Thomas F. Rutherford, and David G. Tarr. 2003. "Trade Liberalization, Poverty and Efficient Equity." *Journal of Development Economics* 71 (June): 97–128.

Hummels, David. 1995. "Global Income Clustering and Trade in Intermediate Goods." Ph.D. dissertation, University of Michigan.

Hummels, David, and Peter Klenow. 2002. "The Variety and Quality of a Nation's Trade." NBER Working Paper 8712. National Bureau of Economic Research, Cambridge, MA.

Jensen, Jesper, Thomas F. Rutherford, and David G. Tarr. Forthcoming. "The Impact of Liberalizing Barriers to Foreign Direct Investment in Services: The Case of Russian Accession to the World Trade Organization." *Review of Development Economics.* http://www.worldbank.org/trade/russia-wto

Kimura, Fukunari, Mitsuyo Ando and Takamune Fujii. 2004a. "Estimating the Ad Valorem Equivalent of Barriers to Foreign Direct Investment in the Telecommunications Services Sectors in Russia.?" http://www.worldbank.org/trade/russia-wto.

Kimura, Fukunari, Mitsuyo Ando and Takamune Fujii. 2004b. "Estimating the Ad Valorem Equivalent of Barriers to Foreign Direct Investment in the Maritime and Air Transportation Service Sectors in Russia." http://www.worldbank.org/trade/russia-wto.

Kimura, Fukunari, Mitsuyo Ando and Takamune Fujii. 2004c. "Estimating the Ad Valorem Equivalent of Barriers to Foreign Direct Investment in Financial Services Sectors in Russia," http://www.worldbank.org/trade/russia-wto.

Markusen, James, Thomas Rutherford, and David Tarr. Forthcoming. "Foreign Direct Investment in Services and the Domestic Market for Expertise." *Canadian Journal of Economics.* Available as Policy Research Working Paper 2143, World Bank. http://www.worldbank.org/trade.

Marshall, J. N. 1988. *Services and Uneven Development.* London: Oxford University Press.

McKee, D. L. 1988. *Growth, Development, and the Service Economy in the Third World.* New York: Praeger.

Romer, Paul. 1994. "New Goods, Old Theory and the Welfare Costs of Trade Restrictions." *Journal of Development Economics* 43 (1): 5–38.

Rutherford, Thomas F. 1999. "Applied General Equilibrium Modeling with MPSGE as a GAMS Subsystem: An Overview of the Modeling Framework and Syntax." *Computational Economics* 14 (1/2): 1–46.

Rutherford, Thomas F., and David G. Tarr. 2002. "Trade Liberalization, Product Variety and Growth in a Small Open Economy: A Quantitative Assessment." *Journal of International Economics* 56 (2): 247–72.

Rutherford, Thomas F., David G. Tarr, and Oleksandr Shepotylo. 2004. "Poverty Effects of Russia's WTO Accession: Modeling "Real" Households and Endogenous Productivity Effects." http://www.worldbank.org/trade/russia-wto

Schott, Peter. Forthcoming. "Across-Product versus Within-Product Specialization in International Trade" *Quarterly Journal of Economics.*

Tybout, James, and Daniel Westbrook. 1995. "Trade Liberalization and the Dimensions of Efficiency Change in Mexican Manufacturing Industries." *Journal of International Economics* 39 (1): 53–78.

Winters, L. Alan, Neil McCulloch, and Andrew McKay. 2004. "Trade Liberalization and Poverty: The Evidence So Far." *Journal of Economic Literature* 42 (March): 72–115.

GLOBAL IMPACTS OF
THE DOHA SCENARIOS
ON POVERTY

Kym Anderson, Will Martin,
and Dominique van der Mensbrugghe

Summary

This paper illustrates some of the potential consequences of the WTO's Doha round of multilateral trade negotiations on incomes and poverty globally. Using the global LINKAGE model to generate changes in domestic and international prices that have a direct impact on factor incomes and consumer prices, we estimate the change in real income at the poverty line that would accompany various reform scenarios. When accompanied by additional information about the elasticity of poverty with respect to income, this provides an estimate of the change in poverty by country. Under most liberalization scenarios considered, unskilled wages rise more than average incomes, but the estimated impact on global poverty is modest, especially if developing countries are unwilling to undertake much reform.

Introduction

This chapter illustrates some of the potential consequences of a Doha agreement and alternative reform scenarios on incomes and poverty globally. Use of global models can set the overall stage for the impacts of multilateral trade reforms, even though by design they are not particularly well suited for looking at poverty impacts because few global models contain systematic information at the household level. Global models can nonetheless provide some useful information for assessing potential poverty impacts of multilateral trade reform. In particular, they generate changes in domestic and international prices that have a direct impact on factor incomes and consumer prices. These may be used to construct an estimate of the change in real income at the poverty line. When accompanied by additional information about the elasticity of poverty with respect to income, this can provide an estimate of the change in poverty by country.

An overall benchmark for assessing the gains from partial trade reform that are likely to arise from a successful conclusion to the current multilateral trade negotiations is full merchandise trade reform. Using the World Bank's LINKAGE model (see van der Mensbrugghe [2004b]), it is estimated that the global gains from full merchandise trade reform would amount to about US$290 billion in 2015. This is below the previous estimate (using the same model) of about US$400 billion.[1] These differences can be explained by noting three facts. First, a new Global Trade Analysis Project (GTAP) dataset is used here, with a 2001 base year instead of the earlier 1997 benchmark. The tariff data reflect reforms between 1997 and 2001 and the incorporation of nonreciprocal tariff preferences, which were largely ignored in the previous version. Second, the new dataset reflects the changing structure of the global economy, particularly the rising prominence of Asia's economies.[2] Third, the baseline developed in this chapter takes account of recent reform commitments, such as China's WTO accession agreement, final implementation of the Uruguay Round (including elimination of quotas on textile and clothing imports), and the EU's eastward expansion in 2004. These changes alone are estimated to be worth more than US$70 billion to the global economy (evaluated in 2015). When incorporated into the baseline, they are no longer permitted to contribute to the estimated global welfare gains from trade liberalization.

A successful Doha Round could generate between US$95 billion and $126 billion per year by 2015 in real global income gains. This assumes that there are no exemptions for sensitive and special agricultural products. Most of the gains would be garnered by the rich countries that have agreed to undertake a more aggressive reform, particularly in agriculture. The significant binding overhang in most developing countries suggests that only modest reforms are likely to emerge there. Under such a scenario, rich countries would achieve between 40 percent and 45 percent of what they could gain from full merchandise trade reform, and developing countries would achieve about 20 percent. In aggregate, this would provide the world about one-third of the potential welfare gains from freeing global merchandise trade.

Trade reform promotes growth, but it is also likely to reduce poverty in developing countries because, under most liberalization scenarios, unskilled wages rise more than average incomes. Nonetheless, the impact of global trade reform on global poverty, as measured by the model in this chapter, is modest. By 2015, as currently projected in the baseline, the majority of the poor will be concentrated in Sub-Saharan Africa and to a lesser extent in South Asia. Despite the rather high increase in unskilled wages in the former emanating from trade reform, the region has a relatively low elasticity of poverty reduction relative to economic growth. Overall, the number of poor (those living on less than US$1 per day) would decline by 32 million by 2015, a reduction of some 5 percent compared to the projected baseline level of 622 million, of which 21 million would be in Sub-Saharan Africa. The modest extent of reform by developing countries explains the smallness of the poverty impact from the Doha Round.

The remainder of the chapter is organized as follows. Section 1 provides a brief overview of the model, which is followed by a brief section describing the base-year patterns of protection. The third section discusses some baseline issues. The fourth and fifth sections discuss results of the simulations, the sixth discusses poverty impacts, and the final section provides some concluding remarks.

Model Overview

The model used for this analysis is the World Bank's global dynamic computable general equilibrium (CGE) model, LINKAGE (van der Mensbrugghe 2004b). The model is a relatively standard GE model with a few distinguishing characteristics. First, it is recursive dynamic, with a 2001 base year, and typically solved through to 2015. The dynamics are driven by exogenous population and labor supply growth, savings-driven capital accumulation, and labor-augmenting technological progress. In any given year, factor stocks are largely fixed. Producers minimize costs subject to constant returns to scale (CRS), consumers maximize utility, and all markets clear with flexible prices. There are three types of production structures. Crop sectors reflect the substitution possibility between extensive and intensive farming. Livestock sectors reflect the substitution possibilities between ranch- and range-fed production. All other sectors reflect the standard capital-labor substitution (with two types of labor—skilled and unskilled).[3] There is a single representative household for each country or region. It allocates income to consumption using the extended linear expenditure system (LES). Trade is modeled using a nested Armington structure. First, aggregate import demand is the outcome of allocating domestic absorption between domestic goods and aggregate imports. At the next level, aggregate import demand is allocated across source countries to determine the bilateral trade flows.

There are six sources of protection in the model. The most important is bilateral tariffs. There are also bilateral export subsidies.[4] Domestic protection includes subsidies on intermediate demand, output, and payments to capital and land in agriculture.

The model has three closure rules. First, government fiscal balances are fixed in any given year.[5] The fiscal objective is met by changing the level of lump-sum taxes on households. This implies that changes in revenues—for example, the loss of tariff revenues—are replaced by higher direct taxes on households. Second, the current account balance is fixed. Given that other external financial flows are fixed, this implies that ex ante changes to the trade balance are reflected in ex post changes to the real exchange rate. For example, if import tariffs are reduced, the propensity to import increases. Additional imports are financed by increasing export revenues, and this is typically achieved via a real exchange rate depreciation. Finally, investment is savings driven. With fixed public and foreign saving, investment will be driven by two factors—changes in the savings behavior of households and changes in the unit cost of investment. The latter can play an important role in a dynamic model to the extent imported capital goods are taxed. Because the capital account is exogenous, rates of return across countries can differ over time and across simulations. The model solves only for relative prices. The numeraire, or price anchor, in the model is given by the export price index of manufactured exports from high-income countries. This price is fixed at unit value in the base year and throughout time.

The new version of the LINKAGE model, Version 6, is based on the latest release of the GTAP dataset, Release 6.0.[6] Compared with Version 5 of the GTAP dataset, Version 6 has a 2001 base year instead of 1997, updated national and trade data, and, importantly, a new source of the protection data. The new protection data come from a joint Centre d'Etudes Prospectives et d'Informations Internationales (CEPII) (Paris)–International Trade Centre (ITC) (Geneva) project. The product of this joint effort, known as MAcMap, is an HS-6 detailed database on bilateral protection that integrates trade preference, specific tariffs, and tariff rate quotas (TRQs).[7] In summary, the new GTAP database has lower tariffs than the previous database because of the reform efforts between 1997 and 2001—for example, China's progress toward WTO accession and continued implementation of the Uruguay Round Agreement—and the inclusion of bilateral trade preferences.

The version of LINKAGE used for this study comprises a 27-region, 25-sector aggregation of the GTAP dataset.[8] There is a heavy emphasis on agriculture and food, which make up 13 of the 25 sectors, and a focus on the largest commodity exporters and importers.

Overview of Protection

An overview of protection in the LINKAGE model is offered in tables 2.7 and 2.8 of chapter 2 of this book, so it will not be repeated here. However, it is important to bear in mind the main features of global protection gleaned from this earlier chapter as impacts of its removal are analyzed. Recall that the main source of protection resides in tariffs or border barriers, with many countries having significant domestic distortions in agriculture. As noted in chapter 2, the world average tariff on agriculture and food is 16.7 percent, with little difference between high-income and developing countries,[9] 16.0 percent and 17.7 percent, respectively. Of course, the averages obscure large variations across countries and commodities. Not surprisingly, the highest agricultural tariffs are in the high-income Asian economies, but several low-income countries also have high tariffs—for example India, Vietnam, the rest of Sub-Saharan Africa, and the rest of South Asia. These same developing countries tend to have high tariffs in other sectors as well—for example, India's tariff on textile and clothing is more than 26 percent, and on other goods, it is nearly 25 percent. In summary, the patterns of protection are relatively clear, agriculture and food have the highest level of protection, followed by textile and apparel and then other goods. Developed-country protection is largely concentrated in agriculture and food, and developing-country protection is by and large more uniform across broad sectors.

Recall that precommitments (handled via a pre-experiment) represent those tariff changes that have been agreed to in 2001, but not yet fully implemented. These are implemented as part of the baseline scenario. As can be seen from table 2.7 in chapter 2, these precommitments are small except for the case of China. Under WTO accession, its average tariff declines by more than one-half—from 13.6 percent to 6.1 percent, subsequent to the 2001 starting point. Other significant changes include agriculture and food in the case of the Republic of Korea and Taiwan, China, and Thailand.[10] There is not much discernable impact from the final phases of the Uruguay Round. These would mostly be reflected in developing countries that had a longer phase-in period. However, the impact would be slight because the tariff bindings are well above applied tariffs in most cases.

Table 2.8 in chapter 2 shows the average tariffs faced by exporters in these broad sectors. Taking all goods together, exporters from Argentina face the highest average tariffs, along with Brazil. This is due to their propensity to export agricultural products to high-tariff regions. However, Canada and Mexico face the lowest tariffs in their export markets. This reflects the impacts of NAFTA, because intraregional trade dominates export market share for these two countries. The United States, a more diversified exporter, faces an average tariff considerably higher than its two partners in NAFTA. Unlike import protection levels, the patterns of barriers faced by exporters is less distinctive, although existing preferential trade agreements have some impact, as does the resource intensiveness of exports. Neither Russia, nor the Middle East and North Africa (both big energy exporters) face particularly high average tariffs. The final baseline tariffs—that is, those after incorporation of existing commitments—are lower than the initial tariffs. Argentina in particular benefits from greater market access into China, with the average tariff faced by its exporters declining from 14.1 percent to 9.4 percent (and from 23.0 percent to 13.7 percent in the case of agriculture and food).

Scenarios

Base-Data and Base-Year Adjustments

The starting point for the model simulations is the GTAP dataset, Version 6.0, which is aggregated to 27 regions and 25 sectors (see annex A). The aggregated dataset is then adjusted to incorporate additional information on protection. In particular, an output subsidy of 36 percent is imposed on U.S. cotton (the plant-based fiber [pfb] sector),[11] and bilateral tariffs are lined up with the scenario file prepared by CEPII.[12] A process based on the GTAP *Altertax*[13] procedure is used to impose these changes while minimizing the distortions to the original GTAP dataset.

Baseline Scenario

The starting point for the baseline scenario is the adjusted 2001 GTAP database. The model is solved in recursive dynamic fashion through to 2015, lining up with the World Bank's most recent medium- and long-term forecast for the global economy.[14] The baseline scenario includes two changes to the base-year level of protection. First, the export tax equivalents on textiles and clothing are removed, emulating the removal of quotas. Second, tariffs are adjusted to match existing commitments—completion of Uruguay Round commitments, Chinese WTO accession, EU expansion, and so forth (recall the pre-experiment column in table 2.7). Both of these changes are phased in between 2002 and 2004. From 2005 forward, there are no changes in the levels of protection.

Reform Scenarios

For purposes of comparison with the Doha scenarios, two benchmark simulations are developed. The first is the baseline or reference scenario, described above; the second is a scenario of complete merchandise trade reform that provides the maximum potential gain from eliminating import protection (and export subsidies and domestic support in agriculture). To provide a more complete picture of the impacts of multilateral trade reform, the global reform scenario is decomposed into partial shocks. The decompositions look at the sources of gain by broad sector—agriculture and food, textile and clothing, and other manufacturing—and by broad income classification—high-income countries versus developing countries.[15]

The remaining scenarios all pertain to some version of a possible Doha accord. The central Doha scenario is the same one explored throughout this book and outlined in detail in chapter 2. Some attention is also devoted to an alternative scenario, Doha-All, in which developing countries and least developed countries (LDCs) cut their bound tariffs at the same rate as for industrial countries. (Readers will recall that this scenario of fully reciprocal tariff cuts was also explored in chapter 15.) This is of particular interest, because it represents a concrete instance of deeper developing-country commitments in the Doha Round.

These two Doha scenarios entail relatively modest reform, as can be seen by the average cut in protection in table 2.7 in chapter 2 (columns 3 and 4). For high-income countries, the average cut for both Doha scenarios is 1.3 percentage points (from 2.9 percent to 1.6 percent). This is largely driven by the relatively small tariffs in other manufacturing and the large weight this sector represents in total trade for high-income countries. The cuts in agricultural and food tariffs are more substantial, being nearly halved on average (15.9 percent to 8.2 percent), as are those for textiles and clothing (from 7.3 percent to 4.1 percent).

The implied tariff reductions for developing countries are similarly modest, but for different reasons. The average tariff drops from 8.4 percent to 7.5 percent in the case of the central Doha scenario, and further to 6.8 percent when developing-country cuts (including those of LDCs) are fully reciprocal (Doha-All). The principal reason for the modest reductions lies in the huge gap between applied tariffs and tariff bindings. Recall from chapter 2 that average bound tariffs in agriculture are 2.4 times as high as applied tariffs, and this ratio is 5 in the case of the LDCs.[16] Thus, when bound tariffs are reduced, there is often no real liberalization because they remain above the currently applied tariffs.[17]

Global Merchandise Trade Reform

Welfare Impact

Table 17.1 presents the standard welfare impact, or change in real income.[18] Global merchandise trade reform that includes elimination of domestic support would generate US$287 billion in additional income in 2015 at the global level compared with the baseline scenario. Almost 70 percent of the global gains would accrue to the high-income countries. However, as a share of income, developing countries do somewhat better, with an average increase of 0.8 percent compared to 0.6 percent for high-income countries. The results vary widely across developing countries, ranging from little impact in the case of Bangladesh and China to upward of 5 percent increases in parts of East Asia.

Table 17.1 Gains from Global Merchandise Trade Reform

Region	Real income	TOT impact	Real income	TOT impact
	US$ billions		Percent of baseline income in 2015	
Australia and New Zealand (ANZ)	6.1	3.5	1.0	0.6
EU-25 plus EFTA	65.2	0.5	0.6	0.0
United States	16.2	10.7	0.1	0.1
Canada	3.8	-0.3	0.4	0.0
Japan	54.6	7.5	1.1	0.2
Korea, Rep. of, and Taiwan, China	44.6	0.4	3.5	0.0
Hong Kong, China, and Singapore	11.2	7.9	2.6	1.8
Argentina	4.9	1.2	1.2	0.3
Bangladesh	0.1	-1.1	0.2	-1.4
Brazil	9.9	4.6	1.5	0.7
China	5.6	-8.3	0.2	-0.3
India	3.4	-9.4	0.4	-1.1
Indonesia	1.9	0.2	0.7	0.1
Thailand	7.7	0.7	3.8	0.4
Vietnam	3.0	-0.2	5.2	-0.4
Russia	2.7	-2.7	0.6	-0.6
Mexico	3.6	-3.6	0.4	-0.4
South Africa	1.3	0.0	0.9	0.0
Turkey	3.3	0.2	1.3	0.1
Rest of South Asia	1.0	-0.8	0.5	-0.4
Rest of East Asia	5.3	-0.9	1.9	-0.3
Rest of Latin America and the Caribbean (LAC)	10.3	0.0	1.2	0.0
Rest of Europe and Central Asia (ECA)	1.0	-1.6	0.3	-0.6
Middle East and North Africa	14.0	-6.4	1.2	-0.5
Selected Sub-Saharan Africa (SSA) countries	1.0	0.5	1.5	0.7
Rest of SSA	2.5	-2.3	1.1	-1.0
ROW	3.4	0.1	1.5	0.1
High-income countries	201.6	30.3	0.6	0.1
Quad (Canada, EU, Japan, and United States) plus Australia and New Zealand	145.8	22.0	0.5	0.1
Other high-income countries	55.8	8.3	3.3	0.5
Developing countries (WTO definition)	141.5	-21.4	1.2	-0.2
Low- and middle-income countries	85.7	-29.7	0.8	-0.3
Middle-income countries	69.5	-16.7	0.8	-0.2
Low-income countries	16.2	12.9	0.8	-0.7

Table 17.1 (*Continued*)

Region	Real income	TOT impact	Real income	TOT impact
	US$ billions		Percent of baseline income in 2015	
Low- and middle-income countries, excluding China and India	80.1	-21.3	1.1	-0.3
Low-income, excluding India	12.7	-3.6	1.2	-0.3
Middle-income, excluding China	63.9	-8.4	1.1	-0.2
East Asia and the Pacific	23.5	-8.5	0.7	-0.2
South Asia	4.5	-11.2	0.4	-0.1
ECA	7.0	-4.0	0.7	-0.4
Middle East and North Africa	14.0	-6.4	1.2	-0.5
SSA	4.8	-1.8	1.1	-0.4
LAC	28.7	2.2	1.0	-0.1
World total	287.3	0.6	0.7	0.0

Source: Authors' World Bank LINKAGE model simulations

Table 17.1 also provides an indication of the terms of trade (TOT) impact from the full reform scenario. South Asia is the region most affected by the terms of trade impacts (a loss of US$11 billion, or about 1 percent of income), although this loss is more than offset by the efficiency gains. Across Sub-Saharan Africa, the picture is mixed. The group of countries included in the southern and eastern subregion sees a TOT gain. However, the rest of Sub-Saharan Africa faces a relatively significant loss—a total of US$2.3 billion relative to a net gain of US$2.5 billion. Although this region is too aggregated to accurately gauge the nature of the TOT loss, it does include major oil exporters that are unlikely to benefit much from better market access because, by and large, oil imports face low tariffs.[19] Moreover, the oil exporters, and some of the other major mineral- or tropical product (for example, cocoa)–dependent countries are typically net food importers and are therefore likely to lose from the increase in international food prices.

Decomposition by Region and Sector

There are a number of ways to decompose the global trade reform scenario to better understand the sources of the gains. One common decomposition is to assess the impacts of developing-country liberalization versus industrial-country liberalization and further decompose these shocks across broad economic sectors—agriculture and food, textiles and apparel, manufacturing, and total. This decomposition is provided in table 17.2. First, as noted before, the entries on the bottom right-hand corner of the table show that developing countries receive about 30 percent (US$86 billion of $287 billion) of the global gains. Second, global liberalization of agriculture and food yields 63 percent of the total gains (top of last block of numbers, final column). This is consistent with the high tariffs in agriculture and food (16.6 percent global average) versus other sectors but is nonetheless remarkable, given the relatively low share of agriculture in GDP—even in developing countries as an aggregate. For developing countries, the gains from global agricultural liberalization are about 63 percent of total gains, with textiles and clothing bringing in an additional 27 percent so that the contribution of other manufacturing is only 10 percent. The gains in agriculture for developing countries are roughly equally divided between south-south agricultural liberalization (US$28 billion) and increased market access in developed countries (US$26 billion). Improved market access in high-income countries for textiles and clothing yields somewhat better returns for developing countries than their own reform (US$13 billion versus $9 billion), but the reverse is true in other manufacturing—though in both cases, the gains are small.

This symmetry exists also for industrial countries, but to a greater extent. Industrial-country reform in agriculture yields most of the gain for industrial countries (US$109 billion), whereas greater market access in the south yields them only US$19 billion. However, developing-country manufacturing reform yields large payoffs for high-income countries (US$14 billion in textiles and clothing and US$52 billion in other manufacturing). Similar to developing countries, own-manufacturing reform yields negligible benefits.

Productivity Impacts of Global Trade Reforms

Though the LINKAGE model is dynamic, the growth impacts of reform captured by this model are relatively modest. For example, if one compares the dynamic results of 2015—scaled back to 2001 levels of income—with comparative static results, the difference in the gains is estimated to be about 24 percent.[20] This result is not so surprising when one considers the assumptions made in the model. The labor force is exogenous across simulations, as is productivity. Thus, the only channel for growth effects to be felt comes from changes in the level of investment. Savings behavior is largely fixed, but the unit cost of investment can change as tariffs on imported capital goods decline. For the same amount of savings, this implies a greater volume of investment.[21]

There is an increasing literature on the linkage between openness in trade and investment, on the one hand, and productivity growth on the other. There are at least four channels widely cited. First, a rise in the level of imports can lead to

Table 17.2. Regional and Sectoral Source of Gains from Global Trade Reform

Region	Gains by region in US$ billion			Percent of global gain		
	Developing	High income	World	Developing	High income	World
Developing countries liberalize:						
Agriculture and food	28	19	47	33	9	17
Textiles and clothing	9	14	23	10	7	8
Other manufacturing	6	52	58	7	26	20
All sectors	43	85	128	50	42	45
High-income countries liberalize:						
Agriculture and food	26	109	135	30	54	46
Textiles and clothing	13	2	15	17	1	6
Other manufacturing	4	5	9	3	3	3
All sectors	43	116	159	50	58	55
All countries liberalize:						
Agriculture and food	54	128	182	63	63	63
Textiles and clothing	22	16	38	27	8	14
Other manufacturing	10	57	67	10	28	23
All sectors	86	201	287	100	100	100

Source: Authors' World Bank Linkage model simulations

pro-competitive effects and force domestic producers to improve their products and reduce their costs—similar to the pro-productivity arguments regarding export growth. There is now a wide body of literature exploring this channel, dating back to at least Harris's seminal paper of 1984 and with a broad overview provided in Francois and Roland-Holst (1997). Most of the studies show that the role of scale economies and pro-competitive effects can be important, but there is less consensus on the exact specification of market behavior—free entry and exit, Cournot versus Bertrand behavior, and so forth. Nor is there much empirical evidence on the cost disadvantage ratio or on price markups, particularly in developing countries. In an effort to circumvent some of these issues, it is possible to posit a reduced form relation that links sectoral productivity to changes in the price of imports relative to the price of domestic goods. This is an approach used by Itakura, Hertel, and Reimer (2003), for example.

A second channel relies on the technology embedded in imports—either in improved intermediate goods or in capital good imports. Access to greater varieties of inputs can increase productive efficiency,[22] and consumers can also benefit from a greater choice of varieties. This is the avenue for growth emphasized in chapter 16, with a particular emphasis on services sector reforms in Russia.

A third channel is offered by the linkage between trade reform and increased FDI inflows, the latter bringing in new capital, knowledge, and management skills. This channel may be hard to separate out from either the import or export channel because FDI is typically associated with increased imports of technology-laden inputs or capital or both and with a high share of exported output.

Finally, there is the linkage between increased exports and productivity growth. Here, the evidence is mixed. Empirical estimates are problematic because of the direction of causality. Looking at firm level data for Indonesia, Sjöholm (1999) finds evidence supporting the export-productivity linkage, with weaker evidence supporting an import-productivity linkage. Bernard and Jensen (2004) report a similar finding using firm data for the United States.

In an effort to capture some of these effects, an alternative dynamic specification is introduced in which sector-specific labor productivity is allowed to respond to changes in sectoral openness. The latter is measured by the export to output ratio. This relation is modeled as follows:

$$(17.1) \quad \pi_i = \alpha_i + \chi_i + \gamma$$

$$(17.2) \quad \chi_i = \pi_i = \beta_i \left(\frac{E_i}{X_i}\right)^{\varepsilon_i}$$

Equation 17.1 defines sector-specific productivity, π. It is composed of three components—two of which are sector specific, α and χ, and the third is economywide, γ. The first sector-specific parameter is a sectoral shifter that allows baseline productivity differentials across sectors. For example, it is typically assumed that productivity in manufacturing is higher than in services. The second sector-specific parameter is linked to the export-output ratio. It is calibrated (through the β parameters) in the baseline simulation so that it represents some fixed percentage of total productivity. It is assumed for the purposes of this simulation that it represents 40 percent of total productivity growth. The economywide parameter is calibrated in the baseline simulation as a residual to achieve a prespecified target for GDP growth. In most reform scenarios, all three factors are exogenously fixed. In the alternative scenario, where productivity is permitted to be influenced by openness, the χ-factor will evolve depending on the elasticity, ε, which is here assumed to be equal to 1 for manufactures and 0.5 for agriculture.[23] Assume, for example, that the total sectoral productivity growth rate is 5 percent and the χ-factor in the baseline is 2 percent. If the reform scenario leads to a 10 percent increase in the export-output ratio, the χ-factor will increase to 2.2 percent. Therefore, total (labor-augmenting) productivity in the sector will increase to 5.2 percent, or an increase of 4 percent over the baseline level.[24]

Key results pertaining to the trade-productivity linkages are summarized in table 17.3. The main dynamic gains occur for developing countries. Whereas high-income countries see an increase in their gains from 0.6 percent of baseline income to 0.8 percent, developing countries see a more significant gain, from 0.8 percent to 2.0 percent. At the global level, the gains would increase by 61 percent—amounting to US$461 billion in 2015. These gains are substantially lower

Table 17.3 Impacts of Global Merchandise Trade Reform with and without Productivity Changes

Region	Productivity fixed		Productivity linked to export-output ratio	
	US$ billion	%	US$ billion	%
High-income countries	201.6	0.6	261.1	0.8
Quad countries plus ANZ	145.8	0.5	202.5	0.7
Other high-income countries	55.8	3.3	58.6	3.5
Developing countries (WTO definition)	141.5	1.2	258.7	2.2
Low- and middle-income countries	85.7	0.8	200.1	2.0
Middle-income countries	69.5	0.8	145.1	1.8
Low-income countries	16.2	0.8	55.0	2.8
World total	287.3	0.7	461.2	1.1

Source: Authors' World Bank LINKAGE model simulations.

than previous estimates (World Bank 2002, 2004). For example, in World Bank (2002), the gains for developing countries increased by a multiple of 3.2 rather than the more modest multiple of 2.3 reported in this chapter. There are essentially two main reasons for this result. The first lies in the fact that the trade barriers are substantially lower compared with the earlier work—incorporating trade reforms between 1997 and 2001, preferences, and, significantly in the case of China, baseline policy changes. The second reason is the lower assumed elasticity between openness and productivity in the agricultural sectors, which has been reduced from 0.75 to 0.5.[25]

Table 17.4 reports the average change in the growth of productivity in manufacturing relative to the baseline labor productivity growth rate for selected countries and regions in 2015.[26] The largest impacts are in the regions that have a relative comparative advantage in manufacturing—for example, South Asia. The predominant agricultural exporters—Argentina, Brazil, and the rest of Latin America, for example—see relatively negligible productivity impacts from

Table 17.4 Impact of Labor Productivity from Full Merchandise Trade Reform

Region	Labor productivity growth in baseline in 2015	Difference in labor productivity growth with reform in 2015
Argentina	4.2	0.2
Bangladesh	4.5	1.2
Brazil	4.2	0.2
China	6.8	0.5
India	5.0	1.7
Indonesia	2.2	0.1
Thailand	3.0	0.4
Russia	3.7	0.6
Mexico	4.4	0.4
South Africa	3.9	0.3
Turkey	3.9	0.5
Rest of East Asia	1.2	0.0
Rest of South Asia	4.0	0.9
Rest of LAC	3.0	0.2
Rest of ECA	4.1	0.4
Middle East and North Africa	3.8	0.5
Selected SSA countries	3.5	1.2
SSA	2.8	0.5

Source: Authors' World Bank LINKAGE model simulations.

reform. Because productivity is assumed to be labor augmenting, the macro impacts will be reflected by changes in the share of labor employed in manufacturing relative to aggregate value added.

The pro-growth scenario is essentially meant to be illustrative, but the assumptions and their impacts are consistent with other empirical work in this area. For example, Dessus, Fukasaku, and Safadi at the OECD (1999) estimate a macro relationship between openness—as measured by the export plus import to GDP ratio—and per capita GDP, and they derive an elasticity of 0.09. This is only about one-fourth of the elasticity implied by this work (0.4). However, once one adjusts for the share of agriculture and manufacturing in GDP and the share of labor in value added (because the measure of productivity does not apply to services and is only labor augmenting), the skill- and sector-specific elasticity of 0.4 implies a macro trade to GDP elasticity[27] below 0.1, which is about the same as that of the OECD work.

In a similar vein, Itakura, Hertel, and Reimer (2003) develop a formula that links gains in efficiency to export performance, on the assumption that firms are heterogeneous and that exporters are more efficient than other firms:

$$(17.3) \quad Efficiency = \frac{(\delta - 1)s_E s_D (\hat{E} - \hat{D})}{s_D + \delta \, s_E}$$

In this formula, δ represents the ratio of the technology index between export-oriented firms relative to domestic-oriented firms, s_E is the share of exports in production, s_D is the share of output supplied to the domestic market, and E and D represent exports and domestic supply (with hats used for percentage changes). Based on estimates from Bernard and Jensen (2004) for U.S. firms, they assume that the ratio of the technology indexes is 1.08—that is, exporting firms are on average 8 percent more efficient than firms oriented exclusively toward the domestic market. Here, formula (3) is inverted to derive the implied δ generated by the results reported in this chapter. In other words, the results from the model provide the change in export and domestic supply (and the initial shares), plus the change in *labor* productivity. The latter is adjusted by the labor share to estimate the average sectoral change in total factor productivity. The implied average productivity differential over all developing countries and all manufacturing sectors is a ratio of 1.05, though with wide variations across manufacturing sectors and regions. This is surprisingly close to the original estimates of Bernard and Jensen.

In summary, although this is clearly an area that needs more research, there is accumulating evidence that increased openness affects productivity. Thus, it makes sense to factor this into this chapter's analysis. This has been done, and the parametric specification used in this chapter is broadly consistent with empirical evidence, both at the macro- and the micro-level. Overall, adding this factor boosts global welfare gains by about 60 percent.

Doha Scenarios

The real income impacts of the various Doha scenarios are summarized in tables 17.5 and 17.6, respectively, shown in level terms (US$ billion) and as a percent of baseline income. Results for the core Doha scenario, as well as for the Doha-All scenario, are reported here. In the case of the former, the impacts of allowing for agricultural and manufacturing productivity to respond to increases in the export to output ratio are also assessed. Relative to the global merchandise trade reform benchmark, the core Doha scenario would yield, respectively, 42 percent of the potential gains for rich countries and only 18 percent for developing countries (and 34 percent for the world total). Among developing regions, Doha's share of potential gains is greatest for South Asia (47 percent) and for Latin America and the Caribbean (26 percent), with negative gains for the Middle East and North Africa and a relatively paltry 7 percent for Sub-Saharan Africa. Adding the productivity boost provides nearly a doubling of the gains from the static simulation, but this is still relatively small compared to what could be achieved with greater reform—particularly relative to the full reform scenario with dynamic gains. The Doha-All scenario, in which developing countries reform use the same tariff-cutting formulas as developed countries, has an additional, but modest, impact for developing countries. The largest benefits arise for the agricultural exporters. Many benefit from improved market access in other developing countries that otherwise are able to maintain higher tariff barriers in the core Doha scenario.

Based on current discussions of Doha modalities in Geneva, these scenarios appear to be the most optimistic outcome one might expect in terms of improving agricultural and manufacturing access. The consideration of additional modalities (for example, the exclusion of some sensitive products) could significantly weaken the gains depicted in this chapter. Also, these scenarios ignore other potentially beneficial reforms that could emanate from a successful conclusion to the ongoing negotiations, such as trade facilitation and further opening of the services sectors.

Impacts on Poverty

Assessing reform impacts on poverty with a global model could be seen as somewhat heroic, given the aggregate nature of these models. They nonetheless contain quite a bit of information from which it is possible to make some judgment at least on the nature of changes in poverty if not a precise quantitative estimate. The simplest approach is to take the growth in real income, apply an estimated income to poverty elasticity and assess the impacts on the headcount index. This approach assumes distribution neutrality: the poor receive the same increase in real income as the average household in the economy. A more appropriate approach is to link key model variables to the possible change in the average per capita consumption of the poor, that is, to capture from model results some of the distributional aspects of the changes in real income and not simply the average gain. This has been done by calculating the change in the average wage of unskilled workers deflated by a food and clothing CPI—presumably the most relevant one for the poor. Table 17.7 summarizes the key results from the global reform scenario and some of the Doha alternatives, including two that were not discussed in this chapter.

Under the full merchandise trade reform scenario, extreme poverty in developing countries would drop by 31.9 million in 2015 relative to the baseline level of 622 million, a reduction of 5 percent. With real incomes climbing by only 0.8 percent, this would seem to imply a relatively high poverty to income elasticity. However, recall that in this chapter, poverty calculations are based on the change in the real wage of unskilled workers deflated by the food and clothing CPI. The average change in the real unskilled wage over all developing countries is 3.6 percent—more than four times greater than the average income increase. Critically, it is assumed that the change in unskilled wages is fully passed through to households. Also, although the model closure has the loss in tariff revenues replaced by a change in direct household taxation, the poverty calculation assumes that these tax increases affect only skilled workers and high-income households—a realistic assumption in many developing countries.[28] Under the broader definition of poverty—the number of poor living on US$2 per day or less—the number of poor would fall by 65.6 million under the full reform scenario compared to an aggregate baseline level in 2015 of 1.95 billion. This represents a less significant proportionate reduction, only 3.6 percent, because the US$2 per day poverty-income elasticity is significantly lower than the US$1 per day poverty-income elasticity.

These poverty impacts from full merchandise trade reform are significantly lower than past estimates. For example in the 2002 *Global Economic Prospects* (GEP), the number of poor people living on a US$1 per day was estimated to fall by 110 million, and the number living on US$2 per day to fall by 320 million (World Bank 2002). The new numbers reflect three changes in increasing significance. The first is the change in the baseline poverty forecast. The baseline US$1 per day poverty forecast is currently 622 million, compared to 734 million in the 2004 GEP (World Bank 2004). Using the 2004 GEP forecast would raise those lifted out of poverty to 38 million and 80 million, respectively, for US$1 per day and US$2 per day poverty lines from the current estimate of 32 million and 66 million. The second change is the new estimate of the change in the food wage.

Table 17.5 Real Income Gains from Doha Scenarios, 2015

Region	Real income gains (US$ billion)			TOT impact (US$ billion)		
	Doha	Doha + productivity	Doha-All	Doha	Doha + productivity	Doha-All
ANZ	2.4	0.8	2.8	1.5	1.5	1.7
EU-25 plus EFTA	31.4	38.2	35.7	-4.6	-4.7	-2.0
United States	4.9	15.0	6.6	0.6	0.9	1.9
Canada	0.9	1.3	1.0	-0.5	-0.6	-0.5
Japan	23.7	23.9	25.4	1.5	1.8	2.8
Korea, Rep. of, and Taiwan, China	15.0	14.9	22.6	1.5	1.6	1.2
Hong Kong, China, and Singapore	1.5	1.6	2.2	1.1	1.3	1.7
Argentina	1.3	0.0	1.6	0.6	0.6	0.6
Bangladesh	-0.1	-0.1	-0.1	-0.1	-0.1	-0.1
Brazil	3.6	0.2	3.9	2.1	2.1	2.0
China	1.7	14.6	1.6	-2.6	-3.0	-4.9
India	2.2	5.1	3.5	-0.9	-0.9	-1.9
Indonesia	1.0	2.3	1.2	0.3	0.3	0.4
Thailand	2.0	1.9	2.7	0.6	0.6	0.7
Vietnam	-0.5	-0.4	-0.6	-0.3	-0.3	-0.3
Russia	0.8	1.7	1.5	-1.1	-1.0	-1.5
Mexico	-0.9	-0.4	-0.2	-0.7	-0.6	-1.0
South Africa	0.4	0.4	0.7	0.1	0.1	0.2
Turkey	0.7	0.9	1.4	0.0	0.0	0.0
Rest of South Asia	0.3	0.4	0.7	0.1	0.1	0.1
Rest of East Asia	0.3	0.8	0.6	-0.1	-0.1	-0.2
Rest of LAC	3.9	3.5	4.0	1.2	1.1	0.9
Rest of ECA	-0.6	-0.4	-0.7	-0.4	-0.4	-0.6

Table 17.5 (Continued)

Region	Real income gains (US$ billion)			TOT impact (US$ billion)		
	Doha	Doha + productivity	Doha-All	Doha	Doha + productivity	Doha-All
Middle East and North Africa	-0.6	-0.8	0.1	-1.1	-1.1	-1.6
Selected SSA countries	0.1	0.1	0.2	0.1	0.1	0.1
Rest of SSA	-0.1	0.0	0.3	-0.1	-0.1	-0.3
ROW	0.6	0.2	0.6	0.3	0.3	0.2
High-income countries	79.9	95.8	96.4	1.1	1.7	6.8
Quad (Canada, EU, Japan, and United States) plus Australia and New Zealand	63.4	79.2	71.6	-1.5	-1.1	3.9
Other high-income countries	16.5	16.6	24.8	2.6	2.9	2.9
Developing countries (WTO definition)	32.6	46.4	47.7	0.7	0.4	-4.3
Low- and middle-income countries	16.1	29.9	22.9	-1.9	-2.5	-7.2
Middle-income countries	12.5	22.3	17.1	-1.3	-1.7	-5.4
Low-income countries	3.6	7.6	5.9	-0.6	-0.8	-1.9
Low- and middle-income countries, excluding China and India	12.2	10.2	17.8	1.6	1.4	-0.5
Low-income, excluding India	1.4	2.5	2.3	0.2	0.2	0.1
Middle-income, excluding China	10.8	7.7	15.5	1.3	1.3	-0.5
East Asia and the Pacific	4.5	19.2	5.5	-2.2	-2.6	-4.4
South Asia	2.5	5.4	4.2	-0.8	-0.9	-1.9
ECA	0.8	2.2	2.1	-1.4	-1.3	-2.1
Middle East and North Africa	-0.6	-0.8	0.1	-1.1	-1.1	-1.6
SSA	0.4	0.6	1.2	0.1	0.1	0.0
LAC	7.9	3.2	9.2	3.3	3.1	2.6
World total	96.1	125.7	119.3	-0.8	-0.7	-0.4

Source: Authors' World Bank Linkage model simulations.

Table 17.6 Real Income Gains from Doha Scenarios as Percent Change from Baseline, 2015

Region	Real income gains (US$ billion)			TOT impact (US$ billion)		
	Doha	Doha + productivity	Doha-All	Doha	Doha + productivity	Doha-All
ANZ	0.42	0.14	0.48	0.27	0.26	0.30
EU-25 plus EFTA	0.31	0.38	0.36	-0.05	-0.05	-0.02
United States	0.03	0.11	0.05	0.00	0.01	0.01
Canada	0.10	0.14	0.11	-0.06	-0.06	-0.05
Japan	0.48	0.48	0.51	0.03	0.04	0.06
Korea, Rep. of, and Taiwan, China	1.19	1.18	1.79	0.12	0.12	0.10
Hong Kong, China, and Singapore	0.35	0.38	0.52	0.25	0.31	0.39
Argentina	0.34	0.00	0.39	0.14	0.14	0.15
Bangladesh	-0.10	-0.08	-0.09	-0.08	-0.09	-0.09
Brazil	0.55	0.03	0.59	0.33	0.33	0.31
China	0.07	0.56	0.06	-0.10	-0.11	-0.19
India	0.25	0.57	0.40	-0.10	-0.11	-0.22
Indonesia	0.37	0.88	0.44	0.11	0.10	0.14
Thailand	0.99	0.92	1.33	0.30	0.27	0.33
Vietnam	-0.83	-0.76	-0.97	-0.53	-0.60	-0.61
Russia	0.16	0.36	0.31	-0.22	-0.21	-0.32
Mexico	-0.11	-0.05	-0.02	-0.08	-0.07	-0.11
South Africa	0.25	0.30	0.49	0.10	0.10	0.10
Turkey	0.26	0.35	0.55	0.01	0.02	0.02
Rest of South Asia	0.17	0.21	0.39	0.05	0.03	0.05
Rest of East Asia	0.09	0.29	0.22	-0.05	-0.05	-0.08
Rest of LAC	0.46	0.41	0.47	0.15	0.13	0.11
Rest of ECA	-0.22	-0.15	-0.26	-0.13	-0.14	-0.21
Middle East and North Africa	-0.05	-0.07	0.01	-0.09	-0.09	-0.14

Table 17.6 *(Continued)*

Region	Real income gains (US$ billion)			TOT impact (US$ billion)		
	Doha	Doha + productivity	Doha-All	Doha	Doha + productivity	Doha-All
Selected SSA countries	0.19	0.23	0.26	0.13	0.14	0.15
Rest of SSA	-0.02	-0.01	0.13	-0.05	-0.07	-0.13
ROW	0.26	0.07	0.28	0.13	0.15	0.10
High-income countries	0.25	0.30	0.30	0.00	0.01	0.02
Quad (Canada, EU, Japan, and United States) plus Australia and New Zealand	0.21	0.26	0.23	0.00	0.00	0.01
Other high-income countries	0.97	0.98	1.46	0.15	0.17	0.17
Developing countries (WTO definition)	0.27	0.39	0.40	0.01	0.00	-0.04
Low- and middle-income countries	0.16	0.29	0.22	-0.02	-0.02	-0.07
Middle-income countries	0.15	0.27	0.21	-0.02	-0.02	-0.07
Low-income countries	0.18	0.38	0.30	-0.03	-0.04	-0.09
Low- and middle-income countries, excluding China and India	0.18	0.15	0.27	0.02	0.02	-0.01
Low-income, excluding India	0.13	0.23	0.21	0.02	0.02	0.01
Middle-income, excluding China	0.19	0.14	0.28	0.02	0.02	-0.01
East Asia and the Pacific	0.13	0.56	0.16	-0.06	-0.08	-0.13
South Asia	0.21	0.47	0.36	-0.07	-0.08	-0.17
ECA	0.08	0.22	0.21	-0.14	-0.13	-0.20
Middle East and North Africa	-0.05	-0.07	0.01	-0.09	-0.09	-0.14
SSA	0.10	0.13	0.27	0.03	0.02	-0.01
LAC	0.29	0.12	0.33	0.12	0.11	0.09
World total	0.23	0.30	0.28	0.00	0.00	0.00

Source: Authors' World Bank LINKAGE model simulations.

Table 17.7a Macro Poverty Impacts from Global Reform and Alternative Doha Scenarios, US$1 per Day

		Full merchandise trade			Doha alternatives					
	Baseline	Comparative static	Dynamic	Dynamic with productivity effects	Agriculture only	Agriculture with sensitive products	Full Doha	Full Doha with productivity effects	Doha-all: includes reciprocal cuts	Full Doha comparative static
2015 Headcount (%)										
East Asia and the Pacific	0.9	0.8	0.8	0.7	0.9	0.9	0.9	0.9	0.9	0.9
China	1.2	1.1	1.1	1.0	1.2	1.2	1.2	1.1	1.1	1.2
East Asia, excluding China	0.4	0.2	0.2	0.1	0.3	0.3	0.3	0.3	0.3	0.3
ECA	0.4	0.3	0.3	0.3	0.3	0.4	0.3	0.3	0.3	0.3
LAC	6.9	6.7	6.6	6.5	6.9	6.9	6.9	6.9	6.8	6.9
Middle East and North Africa	0.9	0.8	0.7	0.7	0.9	0.9	0.9	0.9	0.9	0.9
South Asia	12.8	12.6	12.5	12.1	12.8	12.8	12.7	12.7	12.6	12.8
SSA	38.4	36.6	36.0	35.7	38.4	38.4	38.3	38.3	38.1	38.3
Developing Countries	10.2	9.8	9.7	9.5	10.2	10.2	10.2	10.1	10.1	10.2
	2015 level	Decrease from baseline, millions					Decrease from baseline, millions			
2015 headcount (%)										
East Asia and the Pacific	18.6	2.0	2.2	4.1	0.1	0.0	0.3	0.9	0.5	0.3
China	16.3	0.9	1.0	2.6	0.0	0.0	0.2	0.6	0.3	0.2
East Asia, excluding China	2.3	1.0	1.2	1.5	0.0	0.0	0.1	0.2	0.2	0.1
ECA	1.7	0.2	0.2	0.3	0.0	0.0	0.0	0.0	0.1	0.0
LAC	42.9	1.3	2.1	2.3	0.3	0.1	0.4	0.4	0.5	0.2
Middle East and North Africa	3.5	0.5	0.7	0.8	0.0	0.0	0.0	0.0	0.0	0.0
South Asia	215.9	3.8	5.6	12.5	0.2	0.1	1.4	2.6	3.0	1.0
SSA	339.5	16.0	21.1	23.5	-0.1	-0.2	0.5	0.5	2.2	0.3
Developing Countries	622.0	23.8	31.9	43.5	0.5	-0.1	2.5	4.3	6.3	1.7

Table 17.7b Macro Poverty Impacts from Global Reform and Alternative Doha Scenarios, US$2 per Day

	Full merchandise trade			Doha alternatives					
Baseline	Comparative static	Dynamic	Dynamic with productivity effects	Agriculture only	Agriculture with sensitive products	Full Doha	Full Doha with productivity effects	Doha-all: includes reciprocal cuts	Full Doha comparative static
2015 Headcount (%)									
East Asia and the Pacific 11.3	10.2	10.1	9.5	11.2	11.3	11.1	11.0	11.1	11.2
China 9.7	9.3	9.3	8.7	9.7	9.7	9.6	9.4	9.5	9.6
East Asia, excluding China 14.7	12.2	11.9	11.1	14.6	14.7	14.5	14.2	14.3	14.6
ECA 5.2	4.8	4.8	4.6	5.1	5.2	5.1	5.1	5.1	5.1
LAC 19.6	19.2	19.0	18.9	19.6	19.6	19.5	19.5	19.5	19.6
Middle East and North Africa 11.9	10.6	10.4	10.1	12.0	12.0	11.9	11.9	11.8	11.9
South Asia 54.2	53.8	53.6	52.9	54.2	54.2	54.0	53.9	53.9	54.1
SSA 69.2	67.4	66.9	66.6	69.2	69.2	69.1	69.1	68.9	69.2
Developing Countries 32.0	31.1	30.9	30.4	31.9	32.0	31.9	31.8	31.7	31.9
	2015 level	Decrease from baseline, millions					Decrease from baseline, millions		
2015 headcount (%)									
East Asia and the Pacific 229.8	21.1	23.6	36.6	0.5	0.0	2.5	6.3	4.3	1.7
China 134.4	4.7	5.2	13.4	0.1	-0.2	1.1	3.3	1.7	1.1
East Asia, excluding China 95.4	16.4	18.4	23.2	0.4	0.1	1.4	3.0	2.5	0.6
ECA 24.7	1.7	1.8	2.5	0.1	0.0	0.2	0.3	0.5	0.2
LAC 121.8	2.6	4.1	4.6	0.6	0.1	0.7	0.7	1.0	0.3
Middle East and North Africa 45.7	4.9	6.0	6.8	-0.1	-0.2	0.0	-0.1	0.3	0.0
South Asia 912.2	6.5	9.6	21.4	0.4	0.1	2.3	4.4	5.1	1.6
SSA 612.2	15.5	20.4	22.8	-0.1	-0.2	0.5	0.4	2.1	0.2
Developing Countries 1,946.3	52.3	65.6	94.7	1.3	-0.3	6.2	12.1	13.3	4.1

Source: Authors' World Bank LINKAGE model simulations and World Bank (2005).

Both the unweighted and population-weighted estimates of the food wage impacts from global reform are reduced by 50 percent compared to the previous results.[29] This is largely due to the role of the new tariff database (particularly preferences and the policy reforms that are now subsumed in the baseline). If the previous estimates of the change in the food wage are used, the reductions in poverty would rise to 63 million and 190 million, respectively. The third change reflects the use of region- and indicator-specific income poverty elasticities.[30] Using the old uniform elasticities (with a value of 2.0) in place of the survey-based estimates currently used, the poverty estimate impact rises to 100 million and 280 million, respectively—close to the old poverty impact estimates.[31]

Table 17.7 also provides the poverty impacts of two additional full-reform simulations. One is the comparative static simulation, excluding dynamic effects. The effects on global poverty are somewhat smaller than when dynamics are taken into account—a reduction of the number of poor of 23.8 million as opposed to a reduction of 31.9 million. The table also shows the impacts on poverty from full reform in the dynamic simulation with productivity changes. The aggregate impact on poverty remains quite modest—a decline of 43.5 million in the number of poor, compared to 31.9 million without the productivity effects. Although the increase in unskilled productivity tends to raise wages, the lower ex ante demand for labor dampens the effect, given that labor supply is assumed to be exogenously determined.

Under the Doha scenarios reported in table 17.7, the poverty impacts are more modest. The number of poor living on US$1 per day or less would fall by 2.5 million in the case of the core Doha scenario (of which 0.5 million are in Sub-Saharan Africa) and by 6.3 million in the case of Doha-All (of which 2.2 million are in Sub-Saharan Africa). This corresponds to the relatively modest ambitions of the merchandise trade reforms as captured in these Doha scenarios. Allowing for the productivity effect, the decrease in the number of poor would rise modestly to 4.3 million (from 2.5 million without productivity impacts).

Table 17.7 also reports impacts from three additional Doha scenarios not discussed earlier. One reflects a Doha agreement in agriculture only (Doha-Ag). This scenario shows the importance for poverty implications of including manufactured products in the negotiations because the poverty impacts are just 0.5 million in an agriculture-only scenario. The second scenario, Doha-Ag-Sp, shows the impacts of allowing all countries to exempt 2 percent of their tariff lines as sensitive products (plus another 2 percent in developing countries for special products). As shown in chapter 2, this greatly dilutes the gains from a potential agricultural deal. Indeed, according to the estimates in table 17.7, there could even be a poverty *increase*. A final scenario assesses the impacts of the core Doha scenario in a comparative static framework. This would slightly diminish the poverty reduction to 1.7 million individuals lifted out of poverty (from 2.5 million in the corresponding dynamic scenario).

These simple calculations are not a substitute for the more detailed analysis that has been generated by the individual country case studies in chapters 3–16 through use of detailed household surveys. However, it is useful to have a global assessment, and one that provides a sense of the possible range of poverty impacts. Moreover, the elasticity approach[32] may be somewhat conservative because these are derived elasticity estimates from the baseline scenario.[33]

Conclusions

The global economy of 2015 is likely to look quite different from the world economy of 2001 or 2005—particularly if the growth assumptions underlying this chapter's baseline scenario obtain. The changing structure of production, demand, trade, and comparative advantage will engender different impacts from trade reform compared to a static analysis, even if the current patterns of protection that hold today are carried forward into the next 10 years. One inevitable proposition is that agriculture will continue to lose prominence as a share of global output, and services will gain. Despite this, the role of agricultural protection will continue to have a major impact on the overall gains from merchandise trade reform—it alone being responsible for more than 60 percent of the total gains. The world will also witness an increasing share of output from today's developing countries, because growth on average in developing countries exceeds that of rich countries.[34] Nonetheless, rich countries will gain more from global merchandise trade reform than developing countries in dollar terms—US$201 billion versus $86 billion (in 2015). As a percent of baseline income, however, developing countries have more to gain from full elimination of trade barriers and domestic support in agriculture. To the extent that trade reform generates positive externalities in the form of improved productivity, the gains to developing countries could increase up to US$200 billion, an increase of 2.0 percent in baseline income in 2015.

The current shape of the ongoing Doha discussions suggests that reforms in agriculture and manufacturing will be relatively modest, but hopefully there will be significant improvements in agricultural market access in industrial countries. In the central Doha scenario, the overall gains from a WTO accord could amount to US$96 billion, of which US$80 billion would be reaped by rich countries. This scenario assumes no exemption of sensitive and special farm products and only modest reductions in developing-country tariffs (because of their large binding overhang). If developing countries—including LDCs—participate more fully, the global gains would rise to US$120 billion.

The global impacts from trade reform on poverty are positive to the extent that the existing patterns of trade protection favor skilled labor and capital relative to unskilled workers, so that their removal lifts unskilled wages, the primary source of income for many of the world's poor. On average in developing countries, the real wage of unskilled workers—deflated by a food and clothing CPI—rises four times as much as average real income (3.6 percent versus 0.8 percent). Assuming import tariff revenues are replaced by taxes on the nonpoor, the number of poor at the US$1 per day level would decline by some 32 million globally under a full trade reform scenario. The impacts from a Doha scenario are much less, corresponding to only a modest increase in real wages of the unskilled.

These results are likely to be seen by some as too pessimistic, and others might view them as overly optimistic, with solid arguments on both sides. The specific modalities assumed in the central Doha scenario involve much deeper cuts in bound tariffs than in previous WTO rounds. However, it should be borne in mind that the analysis reported in this chapter only touches on some of the issues being discussed in the context of the Doha Development Agenda (DDA)—perhaps the thorniest in agriculture—while ignoring other aspects that potentially have significant development impacts, most notably services and trade facilitation. In the end, it will be the final overall package that will determine the long-term impacts for the world's poor.

Chapter 17 Annex A:
Model Details

Table 17A.1. Sectoral Concordance for the LINKAGE Model

Modeled regions[a]
1 ANZ Australia and New Zealand and Canada (anz, nzl)
2 EUR EU-25 with EFTA (aut, bel, dnk, fin, fra, deu, gbr, grc, irl, ita, lux, nld, prt, esp, swe, cyp, cze, hun, mlt, pol, svk, svn, est, lva, ltu, che, xef, xer)
3 CAN Canada (can)
4 USA United States (usa)
5 JPN Japan (jpn)
6 HYA Republic of Korea and Taiwan, China (kor, twn)
7 HYC Hong Kong, China, and Singapore (hkg, sgp)
8 ARG Argentina (arg)
9 BGD Bangladesh (bgd)
10 BRA Brazil (bra)
11 CHN China (chn)
12 IND India (ind)
13 IDN Indonesia (idn)
14 MEX Mexico (mex)
15 RUS Russia (rus)
16 ZAF South Africa (zaf)
17 THA Thailand (tha)
18 TUR Turkey (tur)
19 VNM Vietnam (vnm)
20 XSA Rest of South Asia (lka, xsa)
21 XEA Rest of East Asia and the Pacific (mys, phl)
22 RLC Rest of Latin America and the Caribbean (col, per, ven, xap, chl, ury, xsm, xca, xfa, xcb)
23 XEC Rest of Europe and Central Asia (alb, bgr, hrv, rom, xsu)
24 MNA Middle East and North Africa (xme, mar, tun, xnf)
25 SSS Selected Sub-Saharan African countries (bwa, mwi, moz, tza, zmb, zwe, xsd, mdg, uga, xss)
26 XSS Rest of Sub-Saharan Africa (xsc, xsd, xss)
27 ROW Rest of the world (xoc, xea, xse, xna)

Postsimulation aggregate regions by income classification[b]
1 HIY High-income (anz, eur, can, usa, jpn, hya, hyc)
2 HYO Quad countries plus ANZ (anz, eur, can, usa, jpn)
3 OHY Other high-income (hya, hyc)
4 LMY Developing (arg, bgd, bra, chn, ind, idn, mex, rus, tha, tur, vnm, zaf, xsa, xea, rlc, xec, mna, sss, xss, row)
5 LMW Developing, using WTO classification (hya, hyc + LMY)
6 MIY Middle-income (arg, bra, chn, mex, rus, tha, tur, zaf, xea, rlc, xec, mna)
7 LIY Low-income (bgd, ind, idn, vnm, xsa, sss, xss, row)
8 LMX Developing, excluding China and India (LMY - chn, ind)
9 MIX Middle-income, excluding China (MIY - chn)
10 LIX Low-income, excluding India (LIY - ind)
11 WLT World total (HIY + LMY)

Table 17A.1. *(Continued)*

Postsimulation aggregate regions by regional classification[c]
1 EAP East Asia and the Pacific (chn, idn, tha, vnm, xea)
2 SAS South Asia (bgd, ind, xsa)
3 ECA Europe and Central Asia (rus, tur, xec)
4 MNA Middle East and North Africa (mna)
5 SSA Sub-Saharan Africa (zaf, sss, xss)
6 LAC Latin America and the Caribbean (arg, bra, mex, rlc)

a. The modeled regions are an aggregate of the 87 GTAP regions. The GTAP acronyms are in parentheses. For details on the countries included in the GTAP aggregate regions, see either the GTAP Web site or van der Mensbrugghe (2004a).

b. Regional aggregations containing Europe have a counterpart that excludes intra-European trade. These are, respectively, EUX, HIX, HYX, and WLX.

c. ROW is not included in a regional aggregate, which therefore will not sum to the LMY total. Note that most of the EU-accession countries are still classified as developing countries by World Bank definitions, but not included in the ECA definition above.

Table 17A.2. Sectoral Concordance for the LINKAGE Model

Modeled sectors		
1	RIC	Rice (pdr, pcr)
2	WHT	Wheat (wht)
3	GRO	Other cereals (gro)
4	OSD	Oil seeds (osd)
5	SUG	Sugar (c_b, sgr)
6	V_F	Vegetables and fruits (v_f)
7	PFB	Plant-based fibers (pfb)
8	OCR	Other crops (ocr)
9	LVS	Livestock (ctl, oap, rmk, wol)
10	FFL	Fossil fuels (coa, oil, gas, p_c)
11	ONR	Other natural resources (frs, omn)
12	PMT	Processed meats (cmt, omt)
13	MIL	Dairy products (mil)
14	VOL	Vegetable oils and fats (vol)
15	OFD	Other food, beverages, and tobacco (fsh, ofd, b_t)
16	TEX	Textiles (tex)
17	WAP	Wearing apparel (wap)
18	LEA	Leather (lea)
19	CRP	Chemicals, rubber, and plastics (crp)
20	I_S	Iron and steel (i_s)
21	MVH	Motor vehicles and parts (mvh)
22	CGD	Capital goods (otn, ele, ome)
23	OMF	Other manufacturing (lum, ppp, nmm, nfm, fmp, omf)
24	CNS	Construction (cns)
25	SVC	Utilities and services (ely, gdt, wtr, trd, otp, wtp, atp, cmn, ofi, isr, obs, ros, osg, dwe)
Postsimulation aggregate sectors		
1	AGR	Agriculture (ric, wht, gro, osd, sug, v_f, pfb, ocr, lvs)
2	PFD	Processed food (pmt, mil, vol, ofd)
3	AGF	Agriculture and food (ric, wht, gro, osd, sug, v_f, pfb, ocr, lvs, pmt, mil, vol, ofd)
4	TWP	Textiles and wearing apparel (tex, wap, lea)
5	OMX	Other manufacturing (ffl, onr, crp, i_s, mvh, cgd, omf)
6	NTR	Nontradeables (cns, svc)
7	MRT	Merchandise trade (All sectors except nontradeables)
8	IND	Industrial sectors (merchandise trade excluding agriculture)
9	INX	Industrial sectors excl processed foods (merchandise trade excluding agriculture and food)
10	MNF	Manufacturing (industrial sectors, excluding natural resources—ffl and onr)
11	MNX	Manufacturing, excluding processed foods
12	TOT	All goods and nonfactor services (all sectors)

Notes

1. See, for example, World Bank (2002, 2004).

2. The new dataset also reflects changes in the dollar evaluation of the global economy—with a relatively strong dollar in 2001 compared to 1997. It is unclear in which direction this would affect the estimated impacts of trade reform.

3. Both are aggregated into a single labor bundle substitutable with capital. The model allows for skilled labor to be combined with capital and this capital–skilled labor bundle to be substitutable with unskilled labor.

4. The textile and apparel quotas are modeled as export tax equivalents, implying that the quota rents accrue to the exporting country. The LINKAGE model is also designed to implement TRQs, though none are used in the simulations described in this chapter.

5. For the sake of simplicity, they are fixed at their base-year level, minimizing potential sustainability problems.

6. GTAP is an international consortium of trade researchers from universities, research institutions, and national and international agencies. It is based at Purdue University. The GTAP Center provides four key resources to the trade community. First is an integrated and consistent international database for trade policy analysis. The current version is composed of 87 country and region groupings and 57 economic sectors. The second is a publicly available global trade model, also known as the GTAP model. (Note that the LINKAGE model is distinct from the GTAP model, though it uses the same underlying database.) The third is an annual course in applied trade modeling. Finally, GTAP organizes and cohosts the annual Conference on Global Economic Analysis. More information on the GTAP Center and project can be found at http://www.gtap.agecon.purdue.edu.

7. More information on the MAcMap database is available at http://www.cepii.fr/anglaisgraph/bdd/macmap.htm and from Bouët and others (2004).

8. Details on the aggregation are available in annex A of this chapter.

9. This chapter uses the World Bank definitions for developing countries, unless otherwise stated. This means that East Asia's newly industrialized economies are classified with the high-income countries.

10. EU expansion is not depicted in these tables because intra-EU trade is excluded. It would be modest at any rate, because tariffs between the EU and the candidate countries had been converging.

11. This is an approximation of the effect of the various programs supporting cotton production in the U.S., see Sumner (2006).

12. The CEPII scenario file contains 10 Doha scenarios, the base tariffs, and the preshock tariffs. The base tariffs are consistent with the GTAP tariffs at the 87-region, 57-sector level, that is, they correspond exactly to the GTAP Version 6.0 tariffs. However, when aggregated to the level of aggregation used in the model, they could differ from the CEPII aggregation if the CEPII trade weights are used because the aggregate tariffs can be quite sensitive to the trade weights. In all aggregations, the GTAP cost, insurance, and freight (CIF)-based trade weights are used to aggregate the tariffs. In the adjustment process, the GTAP weighted CEPII base tariffs are imposed over the GTAP tariffs.

13. See Malcolm (1998).

14. See World Bank (2005).

15. For most purposes, this chapter uses the World Bank's definition of developing countries. One exception is the EU-accession countries that are incorporated into the EU aggregate. Another is that this chapter also reports the WTO-accepted definition of developing countries that includes the newly industrialized economies of East Asia.

16. The scenarios, though assessed at an aggregate level, are based on formula cuts at the six-digit level thanks to the MAcMap database that also incorporates the existing tariff bindings.

17. Francois and Martin (2004) have explored potential gains from setting bindings at applied levels even in the absence of actual liberalization. It could encourage imports by reducing the risk of reversal in tariff policies.

18. Technically, it is a measure of Hicksian equivalent variation.

19. Taxes on energy may be high, but these are typically not reflected in tariffs.

20. See Anderson, Martin, and van der Mensbrugghe. (2006), table 12.2.

21. There are also dynamic changes in the structure of output and trade that can lead to changing comparative advantage and net export positions.

22. See, for example, Coe, Helpman, and Hoffmaister (1997) and Grossman and Helpman (1991).

23. The agricultural elasticity is set to one-half of the manufacturing elasticity for several reasons. One is that most of the econometric evidence has been linked to manufacturing only, with little or no empirical support in agriculture. As well, agriculture in many developing countries is still dominated by subsistence farming, with weak linkages even to the domestic market. Many of the more developed agricultural exporters—for example, Chile and Brazil—are already closely integrated with world markets. Enhancing productivity in the short and medium terms will be driven more by changes in land tenure policies, as well as improvements in local infrastructure and extension services. Finally, based on estimates from Martin and Mitra (1999), a relatively high level of agricultural productivity in the baseline is assumed.

24. See *Global Economic Prospects* ([GEP] World Bank 2002) for further discussions on these assumptions and how they compare with other studies. For more details on the specification, see van der Mensbrugghe (2004a).

25. See van der Mensbrugghe (2005) for further details.

26. It should be noted that baseline productivity is calibrated to line up with exogenous assumptions regarding per capita GDP growth. The openness shifter is calibrated so that in the baseline it represents 40 percent of total sectoral productivity, and the uniform shifter is calibrated to achieve the overall GDP growth target. Productivity in this version of the model is labor augmenting only.

27. For example, if manufacturing is 33 percent of output and labor has a 50 percent share, the macro elasticity would be 0.066.

28. Even if the fiscal closure affects a domestic sales or value added tax instead of direct taxes on households, in many countries, food, at least, is typically exempt from taxation, or the tax is difficult to collect in practice because of the informal nature of many food markets.

29. Earlier studies with the LINKAGE model found an estimated impact of roughly an 8 percent increase in the food wage (averaged over all developing countries). The new impact is roughly a 4 percent increase. The largest changes occur in China and the Middle East and North Africa, the regions with the most significant revision in tariffs. For China, the revision is largely due to the baseline changes, that is, WTO accession commitments. In the case of the Middle East and North Africa, it reflects a significant revision of the base-year tariffs, in part influenced by preferences.

30. Earlier studies with the LINKAGE model assumed a uniform poverty elasticity of 2.0 across regions and for both the US\$1 per day and US\$2 per day poverty lines. The assumption of the uniform poverty elasticity was maintained mainly to keep results comparable across studies despite newer estimates showing the relative variation across regions. For the US\$1 per day index, the range over regions is 0.9 to 3.0. For the US\$2 per day index, the range is 0.5 to 2.0. The average over regions is declining over time because those regions with high elasticities also tend to have high growth; therefore poverty becomes more and more concentrated in regions with relative low poverty elasticities with respect to income growth.

31. See van der Mensbrugghe (2005) for additional details.

32. The World Bank's headcount index forecast is derived from an estimated Lorenz curve based on the most recently available household survey and not from an elasticity approach. A forecast of the growth of per capita consumption is plugged into the Lorenz curve–based functional form for the headcount index, assuming distribution neutrality. See Datt (1998) for a derivation of this methodology.

33. Elasticities at the low end of the income spectrum should be rising over time as mean incomes rise; therefore the marginal elasticity in 2015 should normally be higher than the average implied elasticity between 2001 and 2015.

34. Overall, the level of convergence will be modest because many developing countries' per capita growth rates are projected to lag behind rich countries' growth rates in the baseline, with the key exception of East Asia.

References

Anderson, Kym, Will Martin, and Dominique van der Mensbrugghe. 2006. "Market and Welfare Implications of Doha Reform Scenarios." In *Agricultural Trade Reform and the Doha Development Agenda*, ed. K. Anderson and W. Martin. Basingstoke, U.K.: Palgrave Macmillan; Washington, DC: World Bank.

Bernard, Andrew B., and J. Bradford Jensen. 2004. "Exporting and Productivity in the USA." *Oxford Review of Economic Policy* 20 (3): 343–57.

Bouët, Antoine, Yvan Decreux, Lionel Fontagné, Sébastien Jean, and David Laborde. 2004. "A Consistent, ad valorem Equivalent Measure of Applied Protection across the World: The MAcMap-HS6 Database." CEPII, Paris.

Coe, David, Elhanan Helpman, and Alexander Hoffmaister. 1997. "North-South R&D Spillovers." IMF Working Paper WP/94/144. International Monetary Fund, Washington, DC.

Datt, Gaurav. 1998. "Computational Tools for Poverty Measurement and Analysis." FCND Discussion Paper 50. Food Consumption and Nutrition Division, International Food Policy Research Institute, Washington, DC.

Dessus, Sébastien, Kiichiro Fukasaku, and Raed Safadi. 1999. "Multilateral Tariff Liberalization and the Developing Countries." OECD Development Centre Policy Brief 18. OECD, Paris.

Francois, Joseph, and Will Martin. 2004. "Commercial Policy Variability, Bindings, and Market Access." *European Economic Review* 48 (3): 665–79.

Francois, Joseph, and David W. Roland-Holst. 1997. "Scale Economies and Imperfect Competition." In *Applied Methods for Trade Policy Analysis: A Handbook*, eds. Joseph Francois and Kenneth Reinert, 331–363. Cambridge, U.K.: Cambridge University Press.

Grossman, Gene M., and Elhanan Helpman. 1991. "Trade, Innovation and Growth." *American Economic Review* 80: 86–91.

Harris, Richard. 1984. "Applied General Equilibrium Analysis of Small Open Economies with Scale Economies and Imperfect Competition." *American Economic Review* 74: 1016–33.

Itakura, Ken, Thomas W. Hertel, and Jeffrey J. Reimer. 2003. "The Contribution of Productivity Linkages to the General Equilibrium Analysis of Free Trade Agreements." Center for Global Trade Analysis, Purdue University, West Lafayette, IN.

Malcolm, Gerard. 1998. "Adjusting Tax Rate in the GTAP Data Base." GTAP Technical Paper 12. Center for Global Trade Analysis, Purdue University, West Lafayette, IN.

Martin, William, and Devashish Mitra. 1999. "Productivity Growth and Convergence in Agriculture and Manufacturing." Country Economics Department Working Paper 2171. World Bank, Washington, DC.

Sjöholm, Fredrik. 1999. "Exports, Imports and Productivity: Results from Indonesian Establishment Data." *World Development* 27 (4): 705–15.

Sumner, Daniel A. 2006. "Reducing Cotton Subsidies: The DDA Cotton Initiative." In *Agricultural Trade Reform and the Doha Development Agenda*, ed. K Anderson and W. Martin. Basingstoke, U.K.: Palgrave Macmillan; Washington, DC: World Bank.

van der Mensbrugghe, Dominique. 2004a. "Comparison of GTAP Release 5.4 and GTAP Release 6.05." World Bank, Washington, DC.

———. 2004b. "LINKAGE Technical Reference Document: Version 6.0." World Bank, Washington, DC. http://siteresources.worldbank.org/INTPROSPECTS/Resources/334934-1100792545130/LinkageTechNote.pdf.

———. 2005. "Estimating the Benefits: Why Numbers Change." In *Trade, Doha, and Development: A Window into the Issues*, ed. Richard Newfarmer. Washington, DC: World Bank.

World Bank. 2002. *Global Economic Prospects and the Developing Countries: Making Trade Work for the World's Poor*. Washington, DC: World Bank.

———. 2004. *Global Economic Prospects: Realizing the Development Promise of the Doha Agenda*. Washington, DC: World Bank.

———. 2005. *Global Economic Prospects: Trade, Regionalism, and Development*. Washington, DC: World Bank.

INDEX